PHILADELPHI

**Work, Space, Family, and Group Experience
in the Nineteenth Century**

Essays Toward an Interdisciplinary History of the City

Edited by
THEODORE HERSHBERG

OXFORD UNIVERSITY PRESS
Oxford   New York   Toronto   Melbourne
1981

OXFORD UNIVERSITY PRESS

Oxford   London   Glasgow
New York   Toronto   Melbourne   Wellington
Nairobi   Dar es Salaam   Cape Town
Kuala Lumpur   Singapore   Jakarta   Hong Kong   Tokyo
Delhi   Bombay   Calcutta   Madras   Karachi

Library of Congress Cataloging in Publication Data
Main entry under title:
Philadelphia: work, space, family, and group experience in the nineteenth century.
Essays based on data compiled by the Philadelphia
Social History Project.
Bibliography: p.
1. Philadelphia—Social conditions—Addresses, essays, lectures.
2. Philadelphia—Economic conditions—Addresses, essays, lectures.
3. Philadelphia—Population—History—19th century—Addresses, essays, lectures.
I. Hershberg, Theodore. II. Philadelphia Social History Project.
HN80.P5P48   974.8'11041   80–10843
ISBN 0-19-502752-3   ISBN 0-19-502753-1 pbk.

Essay 1 is reprinted from the *Journal of Urban History* vol. 5, no. 1 (Nov. 1978), pp. 3–40, by permission of the Publisher, Sage Publications, Inc.

Essay 9 is reprinted from *Journal of Family History,* Autumn 1976, pp. 7–32. Copyright 1976 by the National Council on Family Relations. Reprinted by permission.

Essay 10 is reprinted from the *Journal of Urban History* vol. 3, no. 4 (Aug. 1977), pp. 391–408, by permission of the Publisher, Sage Publications, Inc.

Essay 13 is reprinted from *The Journal of Interdisciplinary History,* VI (1975), 211–33, by permission of *The Journal of Interdisciplinary History* and The M.I.T. Press, Cambridge, Mass. Copyright © 1975, by the Massachusetts Institute of Technology and the editors of *The Journal of Interdisciplinary History.*

Essay 14 is reprinted from "A Tale of Three Cities: Blacks and Immigrants in Philadelphia: 1850–1880, 1930 and 1970" by Theodore Hershberg et al. in volume 441 of *The Annals of the American Academy of Political and Social Science.* © 1979, by The American Academy of Political and Social Science, all rights reserved.

First published by Oxford University Press, New York, 1981
First issued as an Oxford University Press paperback, 1981
Printed in the United States of America

For my mother and father
Manya and Abraham

Prologue

This volume has two purposes. The first is to present selected results from research under way at the Philadelphia Social History Project, an experiment in collaborative, multidisciplinary, and interdisciplinary research. The second is to make readers more aware of the critical relationship that exists between how research is organized and the nature of the resulting knowledge.

We set out to conduct historical research into life in an industrializing metropolis. Our sense of the importance of the structure and process of research emerged gradually as a by-product of the substantive effort. The difficulties that we encountered in carrying out research across disciplinary lines appeared initially to result entirely from disciplinary jargon and from the unfamiliarity of different theories, methods, and techniques brought to the larger effort by the respective researchers. We anticipated these difficulties and, though they were problematic, welcomed the opportunity to grapple effectively with them. Later it became painfully clear that far more was complicating the research than the not insignificant clash of personalities, politics, and methodologies of individual researchers and the distinctiveness of their disciplinary backgrounds.

The problem, we came to realize, is lodged deep within the structure of the American research university. Seen from a sociology of knowledge perspective, the discipline-dominated world of higher education has an enormous impact on research in the humanities and social sciences. Current university reward structures, and the disciplinary constituencies they represent and protect, affect far more powerfully than most people appreciate the kinds of questions that may be successfully addressed in research. They exert such influence precisely because they weigh so heavily in determining how research is organized. These structures inhibit collaborative, multidisciplinary, and interdisciplinary research both by posing genuine career risks through hiring and tenure decisions to those considering such research and by constraining the nature of the intellectual interaction for participants by limiting the degree to which they are willing to cross disciplinary lines in their research activities.

It is certainly our hope that these essays, the first fruits of this new model of research process, will be well received. Yet it must be understood that the process itself exists independently of the particular product represented by this volume. Whatever the contribution made by this collection to the knowledge base of urban-industrial development, in other words, its second purpose deserves to be considered on its own. The fragmentation of knowledge which characterizes modern society must be overcome. If this effort moves us however modestly in that direction, it will have succeeded.

It is appropriate, therefore, to begin our discussion with the vehicle that organized the substantive research results presented in this volume. The central concern of the Philadelphia Social History Project (PSHP) is with how the processes of urbanization and industrialization shaped both the development of the nineteenth-century metropolis and the experience of its diverse population groups—what was the dynamic and what were its effects. Our earliest goals were far less broad, and their evolution was inextricably tied to the sequence of questions asked, the different types of evidence required to answer them, and the involvement of scholars from disciplines other than history.

Research began in April 1969, when funds were provided by the Center for Studies of Metropolitan Problems, National Institute of Mental Health, to undertake a comparative study of blacks and Irish and German immigrants in order to determine whether the burdens and disabilities faced by black Americans were peculiar to their historical experience or simply obstacles which every immigrant group entering society had to overcome. Like other studies that emerged at this time under the rubric of the "new urban history," the initial data collected from the manuscript schedules of the federal census of population described only the personal attributes of the ordinary people being studied. As a result, despite the richness of the information made machine-readable and the power of computer technology to manipulate and assist in studying history from the bottom up, the limitations of these data for understanding the linkages between the experience of common people and the urban-industrial context in which they lived became obvious.

To learn how micro-level behavior and the urban-industrial environment systematically interacted and how group experience was differentially affected, we expanded our data base to include information describing Philadelphia's industrial base and spatial arrangements, its commercial, transportation, and municipal facilities, its public and private institutions, and its vital statistics (see Appendix II for a detailed discussion). While only social historians were interested in the initial research, the gradual addition of this new data attracted pre- and post-doctoral scholars from a variety of social science backgrounds. Today, over thirty persons, representing economics, sociology, demography, geography, and city planning as well as history are affiliated with the PSHP. They bring with them invaluable expertise for the study of the city—different theories, concepts, methods, and techniques—developed in their respective disciplines.

The PSHP's history can be usefully divided in three phases. The first involved both the creation of the data base, which serves as the foundation for our research efforts, and the development of the requisite methodologies and computer techniques, which makes it possible to exploit this rich resource. The data base used in the writing of this volume's substantive essays required six years to build. New information is always being added, and the addition of each new data set confirms the wisdom of the axiom that the whole is greater than the sum of its parts.

Working with a new technology initially designed and subsequently supported largely to serve the business community meant that these early years were devoted to overcoming a myriad of technical and methodological problems that were severely compounded in the study of a city with the sheer size and complexity of Philadelphia. A variety of computer programs—"software"—were written to process and verify the data, to manipulate and link them across disparate files, and to develop the appropriate intellectual categories to facilitate the study of occupation, industry, family and urban space. The PSHP's first round of publications reflected these concerns (see Appendix I for a full bibliography of PSHP writings).

The data base and the collaborations of scholars from different disciplines constitute an unprecedentedly supportive environment in which to undertake historical urban research. The data base is more than a machine-readable library. Precisely because it is *machine-readable,* it is better understood as a new type of research laboratory. It permits those concerned with historical development and the complexities of social change to test hypotheses—a capability absent from most previous research. What is more, it liberates this process from the enormously time-consuming, expensive, and painstaking task of collecting the data—a barrier which has dissuaded many scholars, especially social scientists accustomed to working with already machine-readable contemporary data, from undertaking historical research. Thus the comprehensive data base approach to historical research might be thought of as an instrument with the potential to serve scholars in the humanities and the social sciences as the microscope served researchers in the biological sciences.

A common machine-readable data base can support *multidisciplinary* and *interdisciplinary* research. These are distinct but not mutually exclusive research forms. It is important to appreciate, however, that neither the existence of a common data base nor the participation of social scientists and historians guarantees the emergence of interdisciplinary research. These features, on the other hand, are sufficient for multidisciplinary research which proceeds when scholars from a variety of disciplines draw separately on the same data base to examine discrete subjects of their own choosing.

The multidisciplinary approach characterized the PSHP's second phase in which focus shifted from the methodological to the substantive. In the years following the creation of the data base, we undertook a series of separate studies across a broad analytic spectrum. Four substantive areas emerged naturally in the development of the research. They represented a division of labor based upon the professional competencies and specific interests of our research associates and provided the basis for the sections in which this volume is divided: the nature of work; the uses of urban space; the family, its economy, and the organization of the life course; and the experience of subgroups within the larger population. The distinguishing characteristic of this phase of research was the discrete nature of the studies undertaken. We wanted to establish the material parameters of life in nineteenth-century Philadelphia—to get a sense of the lay of the land—and the broad range of basic studies in the initial round of substantive research provided this basic understanding.

This second phase was marked by the voluntary association with the PSHP of researchers from the social sciences who possessed the requisite skills to undertake systematic analysis of the city's basic demographic processes, spatial arrangements, and economic activities. Their involvement in a historical research project is by no means usual. Many social scientists view traditional historical research methodology as essentially unscientific and impressionistic, but they saw in the data base a kind of research laboratory where information existed in a form that met their disciplinary standards for systematic analysis. Thus their participation was a response to the creation of a hospitable research environment. Such an approach has the potential to be a working model of interdisciplinary structure and, even more, a collaborative and interdisciplinary research culture.

The multidisciplinary approach preserves the paradigmatic concerns of each discipline. For example, consider the study of urban space across the different disciplines. An economist might look at location in terms of cost minimization and use equilibrium theory to balance the competing tugs of transportation costs among raw materials, production, and market sites; a sociologist might consider location in terms of social distance, of social control, and of symbolic land use; a geographer might deal with location in terms of central place theory and use diffusion or space-time convergence models, or might stress environmental over economic factors; a historian might focus on antecedent and adjacent land-use patterns. Each of these efforts emerges from a different discipline, but they share only a common focus on urban space.

In making clear that such an approach does not constitute interdisciplinary research, we are in no sense disparaging it. Indeed, most of the essays in this volume are the fruits of such activity. If the participation of individual social scientists were the only benefit of the common data base approach to historical urban research, this would in substantial respects be a significant improvement over the individual scholar working alone. Having a variety of perspectives, as in the above example, is better than one. Especially in areas where disciplinary training leaves one ill-equipped to undertake certain kinds of research, the results of mutlidisciplinary research are a valuable contribution to our base of knowledge about urban-industrial development.

In the current third phase of PSHP research which began in 1977–1978, new analytic goals were set which emphasize integrative over discrete studies. Instead of the four substantive areas that characterized our earlier research, focus shifted to the formation of the urban environment, a wide range of behavior, and the experience of diverse population groups—and the interrelationships within and between each of these areas. These new goals require two types of accompanying changes—involving both the analytic and the organizational—and *interdisciplinary* rather than purely multidisciplinary research. While the latter will continue as part-time or unsalaried affiliated research associates draw on the PSHP data base, full-time professionals from social science disciplines are being hired to work as part of our research team.

Interdisciplinary research is a problematic undertaking, and our tentativeness about it is reflected in our subtitle: *Essays Toward an Interdisciplinary History of the City*. On the level of theory, neither multidisciplinary nor interdisciplinary research at the PSHP proceeds from a central framework. There is a continuing consensus that while such a framework might be considered an ultimate goal, it is neither required nor attainable in the foreseeable future. The research underway is considered too diverse and the workings of the city as a whole too complex to be forced into a single theoretical model. Unlike the "extremely simple model of the world" used by economists to deal with relationships which "are so much more specifiable and certain and logical," the nature of the questions we face, as Eric Lampard noted, "is more difficult, complex and obscure. The work will be more empirical."[1] Whether the consequences at the micro-level of urbanization and industrialization can be adequately captured in grand theory remains a debatable question. We continue to seek a "middle ground," characterized by Michael Katz, as lying between "the particularistic specificity of traditional history and the generalizations of social theory."[2] That is, theory, at one level or another and with greater or lesser degrees of disciplinary purity, guides all components of our research, but it does not explain its overall configuration.

Interdisciplinary research can be said to emerge when the explanatory frameworks of individual disciplines are expanded to include variables normally found outside their standing paradigm. Interdisciplinary research, according to this definition, for example, occurs when the economist—in addition to variables describing capital, wages, and technology —considers the cultural and social characteristics of the labor-force; and when the demographer—in addition to variables describing the personal attributes of the movers and stayers—considers the economic, ecological, and institutional characteristics of communities at both ends of the migration stream. As PSHP researchers exchange their respective analytic world views, they become aware of the extent to which the assumptions of their respective disciplines narrow their research designs. Thus they are more open to consider new categories of explanation. Some of the essays which follow reflect this intellectual expansion.

The existence of a common data base makes this kind of analytic integration possible, and, because the data are machine-readable, the integration of these new variables can be systematic. "Knowledge that is diffused among different minds," as Stuart Hampshire observed, is in a sense "sterile," because ". . . it cannot be put together, in a single act of mind, to generate further thought."[3] But with a comprehensive data base facilitating interdisciplinary research, the fragmentation of our knowledge about cities can be overcome and the relationships among the disparate components found in the urban-industrial system can begin to be systematically explored.

Philadelphia: Work, Space, Family, and Group Experience in the Nineteenth Century is divided into three parts: an Introduction; thirteen empirical essays representing the substantive results of our early research; and an Epilogue. The *Introduction* has two purposes. First, to discuss the conceptual confusion that confounds research in what has been called the "new urban history." Second, to demonstrate that this grows not from the failings of individual scholars, but from the compartmentalized manner in which research on the city is organized, and to elaborate the data base mechanism capable of facilitating the integration of knowledge across disciplinary lines. The *Epilogue,* "Sustaining Interdisciplinary Research," explores the reasons why so little interdisciplinary research is now underway and offers to universities and funding agencies some concrete suggestions which should be implemented if interdisciplinary research efforts are to survive, especially in this protracted period of financial retrenchment in higher education.

Though some readers will be concerned only with the results of our research, we hope to demonstrate that the ends and means are integrally related, that the findings are themselves very much dependent upon the way in which research is organized. As we noted in the opening paragraphs, it is important to recognize that the departmental structure of our colleges and universities inhibits the integration of specialized knowledge. Despite an enormous amount of lip service paid over the years to the importance of and need for interdisciplinary research, the state of research organization in higher education poses a serious barrier that will not be surmounted without fundamental changes in existing structures. Significant changes can come about, however—and only—if researchers, the schools in which they work, and the agencies that support their efforts will cooperate in the development of appropriate new research forms.

While the experience of the PSHP can be offered now as a successful model for emulation where the collection and processing of data and collaboration of scholars from different disciplinary backgrounds are concerned, it is still too early in our analytic integration phase to claim that we have also mastered the many aspects of interdisciplinary research. It is not clear that we have even exhaustively identified, let alone resolved, the problems of organization and interpretation associated with such an approach to knowledge. Nevertheless, we have learned enough about interdisciplinary research to offer our experience as an encouraging though tentative beginning whose progress should help others avoid mistakes and move in fruitful intellectual and organizational directions. Thus far, collaboration and cooperation across interdisciplinary and institutional lines, the concentration of resources, and a common data base have been identified as the essential components of our collective experiment in research.

The main body of this volume consists of fourteen essays selected from among the first fifty completed at the PSHP. It will soon be apparent to the reader that our collection of essays differs from those in conventional anthologies: all draw upon a common data base and all discuss some aspect of life in Philadelphia in the years between 1850 and 1880. Half the essays have been published in scholarly journals; the remaining seven appear in print here for the first time. All but six are co-authored; a total of seventeen scholars from ten institutions and five disciplines participated in their writing (see *Contributors*).

Neither the essays nor other sections of this volume are burdened by discussion of methodology. While a subject of central importance to efforts in the new history, it has been elaborated at length in "The Philadelphia Social History Project: A Methodological History" and in "A Special Issue: The Philadelphia Social History Project," of *Historical Methods,* the only journal within the discipline of history devoted to methodological concerns.[4]

The substantive essays represent a kind of initial rough sweep across the salient features of the landscape that was nineteenth-century Philadelphia. Viewed against the background of all the information collected, they barely scratch the surface of the data base. The essays are not presented in the chronological sequences in which they were written, though such an ordering would no doubt prove useful to readers concerned with how our research actually proceeded; that is, how knowledge gained early in the research affected subsequent efforts. Instead, the essays are organized into four sections—Work, Space, Family, and Group Experience—to provide the reader with an intellectually sound introduction to life in the nineteenth-century industrializing city. Each section is introduced by a brief discussion which summarizes major themes and relates them to a larger body of literature and issues.

Determining the audience to whom this volume was to be addressed was not a simple task. The very notion of an interdisciplinary history of the city means that there are many constituencies—economists, sociologists, demographers, geographers, as well as historians—each with their own special set of distinguishing characteristics and interests. These range from footnotes and bibliographic conventions, through stylistic considerations (in writing does one follow the lead of a Hofstadter or a Merton?), to content itself—the questions posed and the nature of evidence and proof. At the same time that we considered the interests of scholars in separate disciplines, we wanted students from a variety of undergraduate majors to be able to read this volume and take from it a richer comprehension of urban life in the last century. The result, of course, must in some ways be a compromise, but we are not aware that we have diluted important meanings. Perhaps some specialists will be disappointed, but we hope that the breadth of the material presented here will compensate for the absence of depth in any given area of the research. As our research proceeds, it may be possible to satisfy the appetite of even the most devoted specialist.

With an audience composed to a considerable extent of non-historians, it is appropriate to say a few words about the new urban history of which the PSHP is decidedly a part. Although several dates could be identified as a beginning, most writers would agree that the new history emerged in the early 1960s. Its goals, as distinct from its actual accomplishments which to be sure are far more limited, were to emphasize the analytic over the narrative, to be more self-consciously involved in theory building and hypothesis testing. It was to be interdisciplinary in design, especially influenced by research underway in the social sciences. The new history included a shift in focus from particular events and institutions to general patterns and large-scale social forces. Perhaps its most essential feature was its concern with writing history from the bottom up. It would deal not with the movers and shakers of society—the powerful and the mighty —but with the ordinary and unexceptional people whose life experiences had long been ignored by historians.

This focus meant that different sources of historical information had to be consulted. The common people of previous centuries were not literate. Thus they were not able to record their experiences in the diaries, memoirs, and manuscript collections that normally provide historians with contemporary evidence. As a result, historians turned to routinely generated sources of information that described large numbers of ordinary persons. These documents are called indirect records, because they were collected by third parties, most frequently by agencies of local, state, and national governments. Thus manuscript censuses, city directories, tax assessors' lists, birth, marriage and death certificates, parish registers, and the like comprise the information base from which the new history is written. Because the genealogical approach could not suffice where thousands rather than merely several individuals were involved, the use of these sources required the development of techniques to handle masses of information. The advent of electronic data processing equipment, more familiar to us as computer technology, made the new research possible.

The focus of the essays in this volume and of much of the research currently under way is on the "material" aspects of the urban-industrial experience. To illustrate but not exhaust what is meant by material, our focus is on the demographic, the economic, the ecological, the technological, their inter-relationships, and the simple behaviors and complex processes associated with these. Contemporary survey researchers understand the shortcomings of attitudinal data: people rarely *do* what they *say*. Thus we emphasize what economists call "revealed preferences": we focus not on where people said they wanted to live, but on where they did live; not on the kind of jobs they wanted to work at, but on the jobs they held; not on the family type which they may have considered ideal, but on the actual familial settings in which their lives unfolded.

This is not to suggest that we are uninterested or unaware of the importance of the attitudinal, or that we do not intend to deal thoroughly with such factors in subsequent research. Nor is it our intention to maintain an artificial separation between the material and the attitudinal. New PSHP research embraces the latter and recognizes them as necessary to a complete understanding of the human experience. It is not that we believe that the material components are necessarily going to prove the most important—that of course will depend on the nature of the specific questions posed—but that by beginning with the material we will be able to learn the extent of their explanatory power and thus narrow considerably the range of acceptable interpretation for observed behavior. Although not all PSHP associates would agree, there is a general consensus that research should begin with an examination of the material environment that provided the context for and underlay the organization of life in the urban-industrial city of the last century.

To build and maintain a data base with the size and scope of the PSHP's and to provide salaries for the professional and support staff requires a substantial level of funding. The PSHP could not exist without external support, and we wish to express our appreciation to those federal agencies who funded our research: the Center for Studies of Metropolitan Problems, National Institute of Mental Health, for four successive grants beginning in 1969 (MH 16621) and 1979 (MH 33510); the Division of Research Grants, National Endowment for the Humanities, for grants in 1977 (RC 25568–76–1156) and 1979 (RO 32485–78–1612); the Sociology Program, National Science Foundation, for grants in 1977 (SOC 76–

20069) and 1979 (SOC 79–07128); and the Center for Population Research, National Institute for Child Health and Human Development, for a 1979 grant (HD 12413).

Although financial support provided the necessary foundation for the PSHP, only the efforts of people—a great many of them—ensured the completion of the research agenda. Many different constituencies were involved in our efforts. Close to 500 undergraduates from Work-Study programs at the University of Pennsylvania and other East Coast colleges and universities were employed at the PSHP since it began in 1969. In a variety of capacities, they performed the tedious clerical chores which are a necessary part of converting historical information to a machine-readable form and preparing so extensive a data base for computer analysis.

Christopher Sobotowski, Mary Jane Fitch, Gary Cope, and most recently Willam Kreider wrote the many computer programs used in PSHP research. From them I learned the meaning of the term "GIGO"—"Garbage In, Garbage Out"—which users of computer technology forget only at great risk. They also taught me a useful rule of thumb; in order to arrive at an accurate date for the completion of computer jobs, simply double the length of time that your programmers tell you it will require. There is a corollary: if the job is vitally important, triple the projected time involved. In a more serious vein, I want to thank these talented individuals for their efforts in the face of extremely demanding circumstances.

The support staff included many other people in a variety of roles. The data processing activities, through which literally millions of records were made machine-readable—using for data entry key-to-card, key-to-tape, and key-to-disk equipment, was led successively by Brenda King, Jackie Williams, and, most recently, by Gwendolyn Talford and Linda Jeffries. Administrative assistance and business management were ably rendered by Karen Shapiro, Deborah Hardy, Ann Carper, Andi Coyle, Rochelle Goldstein, Karen Parrington, and Margaret Burwell. Word processing technology supported the multiple revisions of our manuscripts, and in this task we were fortunate to have two talented typists, Jo Ann Tolbert and Elizabeth De Marco, the latter of whom typed more revisions than either of us would care to recall. Valuable support was provided by Robert Ulle in archival research and by Barbara Steinberg and Richard Greenfield in social science research methods. Several of the essays included in this volume benefited from the careful editing of Kim Holmes.

We come finally in citing our support staff to Henry Williams, Assistant Director of the PSHP. There is no one with whom I have worked since the start of research who deserves more praise, appreciation, and respect. His combination of rare intellect, quality work, and sustained dedication to the PSHP's long-term goals make him a specially valued colleague, confidant, and friend. This volume, with its many contributors, required multiple drafts and a sizable correspondence; its completion is in large part the result of Mr. Williams's tireless efforts.

Over the years, I have worked closely with and learned much from the many PSHP Research Associates representing different disciplines and institutions. I wish to thank Harold Cox (transportation history), John Crum (institutional history), Jay Feinman (law), Richard Fishbane (education history), Eudice Glassberg (social work), Claudia Goldin (economics), John Gruenstein (economics), John Holley (sociology), Leslie Kawaguchi (ethnic history), Dale Light, Jr. (ethnic history), Stephen Putman (city planning), Jeffrey Roberts (urban history), Mark Schmitz (economics), Allen Steinberg (social history), Mark Stern (social history), George Thomas (architectural history), Leonard Wallock (labor history), and William Whitney (economics).

I benefited especially from the close contact I had with Alan Burstein (demography) and Stephanie Greenberg (sociology), the first two students to complete doctoral dissertations at the PSHP. My collaboration on several articles with Frank F. Furstenberg, Jr. (sociology), Bruce Laurie (labor history), and John Modell (social history) taught me much that I value. The latter two each spent two years at the PSHP while on leave from their respective universities and were our first scholars-in-residence; during these years they became valued friends and colleagues. Our understanding of work and family in nineteenth-century Philadelphia is in large part a measure of their many valuable contributions to PSHP research. I look forward to continued collaboration with sociologists William L. Yancey and Eugene P. Ericksen from whose study of contemporary Philadelphia I have learned a great deal.

The PSHP benefits from the intellectually stimulating presence of our current full-time professional research staff: Gretchen Condran (demography), Michael Haines (economics), Jeff Seaman (sociology), and especially Michael Frisch (urban history), whose creative and critical mind, good humor, generosity, and friendship have been the source of much for which I am grateful. I also wish to thank Seymour Mandelbaum, Michael Zuckerman, and Alan Kors, once my colleagues in the Department of History at the University of Pennsylvania, for their decade-long substantive interest in and encouragement of PSHP activities.

Several senior scholars served as consultants to the PSHP for a NEH-sponsored conference held at the University of Pennsylvania in 1977. To J. Morgan Kousser who originally suggested the conference at an earlier site visit for NEH, and to the consultants—Stanley Engerman, Michael Frisch, Michael Katz, Eric Lampard, Allan Pred, and Charles Tilly—who reviewed our work to-date and attended, I wish to express my sincere appreciation. Their suggestions guided and their confidence inspired subsequent PSHP efforts.

My intellectual debt to several of the scholars who pioneered the "new" urban history will be made clear in the essays which follow; but I have learned so much from their work that I wish to note it here as well. Stephan Thernstrom, Eric Lampard, Sam Bass Warner, Jr., and Michael B. Katz richly deserve the praise given them by a grateful profession.

A note of appreciation is in order for the support given by Oxford

University Press in bringing this lengthy volume to press. Victoria Bijur gave the entire manuscript a painstaking reading. Sheldon Meyer was willing to publish a collection of this size and technical nature and to provide counsel and patience over several years during which it was delayed by numerous revisions.

I close these lengthy acknowledgments with an expression of gratitude to three special persons. David M. Potter, that remarkable man under whom I studied in graduate school, was responsible for introducing me to the social sciences and encouraging my search for a more systematic and interdisciplinary history. I regret that he is not alive today to see the fruits of a labor he did so much to inspire. Elliot Liebow appreciated the PSHP's goals from the outset. He realized the potential of this approach to the study of history for understanding issues of contemporary social policy. His support and friendship sustained me through difficult times. To Michael B. Katz I owe my greatest intellectual debt. His work on the history of education, on social structure, transiency and family in Hamilton, on the rise of the institutional state, and most recently on the social origins of early industrial capitalism serves both as an example of impeccable scholarship and as a guide to substantive PSHP research. As a friend and colleague, none surpass him.

Philadelphia   T.H.
June 1980

NOTES

1. Bruce M. Stave, "A Conversation with Eric E. Lampard," *Journal of Urban History,* 1 (August 1975), 449.

2. Michael B. Katz, *The People of Hamilton, Canada West: Family and Class in a Mid-Nineteenth Century City* (Cambridge, Mass.: Harvard University Press, 1975), 316.

3. Stuart Hampshire, "The Future of Knowledge," *New York Review of Books,* 24 (March 31, 1977), 14.

4. The first of these is Theodore Hershberg's doctoral dissertation (History, Stanford University, 1973); the second is T. Hershberg, guest editor, *Historical Methods Newsletter,* 9 (March–June, 1976).

Contents

Introduction

1. The New Urban History:
Toward an Interdisciplinary History of the City

THEODORE HERSHBERG

> If the urban historian is to be more than a historian who happens to do
> his research and writing on the subject of cities, it will be necessary to
> show that the term "urban" explains something in history that cannot be
> better explained by recourse to other frames of reference. In short, "urban"
> must signify not subject matter alone but a scheme of conceptualization
> in much the same manner as "economic" or "culture" history.
> ERIC LAMPARD
> *American Historical Review*, 1961[1]

Although almost two decades of research in urban history have now
passed, the basic thrust of Eric Lampard's challenge remains unmet. A
"scheme of conceptualization" for the study of the urban experience has
not been formulated. Nor is the nature of the role that *urban* plays in historical explanation widely understood. In fact, in fundamental ways, it is
not known whether an urban frame of reference matters, for what it might
matter, and which procedures might be followed to make these determinations. Perhaps in focusing on *urban* rather than on other explanatory categories such as capitalism, class, or culture a serious error is made. Some
recent scholarship considered below suggests that this may be the case.

What is certain at this point is that little progress will be made until the
conceptual confusion that thus far has clouded the field of urban research
is cleared up. So long as urban history remains a rubric under which can
be placed all things that happened in cities, progress is more than likely
to be impeded. To move ahead it will be necessary to grasp the fundamental distinction between the treatment of *urban as site* and *urban as
process,* to differentiate the study of the city as a dependent and an independent variable, to systematically explore the relationships between behavior and environment, and to understand the consequences arising from
the failure to distinguish between urban and social history.

Responsible in the largest measure for all of these failings is the com-

This essay was originally prepared for a PSHP conference, "Interdisciplinary Re-
search at the Philadelphia Social History Project: Work, Space, Life Course and
Group Experience in the Nineteenth-Century Industrial City" (Philadelphia, Pa.:
August 1–4, 1977) and appeared in a slightly different form in the *Journal of Urban
History* 5 (November 1978), 3–40. It is reprinted here with minor revisions and
additions. I am particularly grateful to Henry Williams for his help in its preparation.

partmentalized manner in which the city has been studied. Despite appearances to the contrary, our current understanding of urban processes and their consequences is badly fragmented and without historical perspective. What is worse, the organization of research at major universities emphasizes individual rather than group effort and hence operates to prevent the kind of research that is most likely to win a measure of real understanding from the complexities of the urban world in which we live. Since urban realities cannot be fully comprehended given our current organization, they cannot, I contend, be adequately dealt with.

Urban History

"We need fewer studies of the city in history," Oscar Handlin wrote some years ago, "than of the history of cities."[2] A review of the literature in urban history makes clear that so apparently straightforward a prescription as writing the "history of cities" meant different things to different historians. A number of writers have tried their hand at categorizing this literature, and building on their efforts, I would like to offer my own. Three categories emerge. One consists of *Urban Biographies*. Unlike the earliest multivolume works written by newspapermen or librarians in the 1880s and 1890s, "with an interest in local history and eye for sales," younger professional historians in the 1930s began to look at the total experience of individual cities.[3] Monographs in this group are exemplified by Constance Green's study of Holyoke and later Washington, D.C.; Bessie Pierce's Chicago; Blake McKelvey's Rochester; and Bayrd Still's Milwaukee.[4] These urban historians were not concerned with the general process of urbanization examined through the case study approach, but with writing a narrative that chronicled the growth and development of a specific city. Most studies, in this genre, though carefully researched and well written, lack any significant conceptual framework or fail in their periodization schema to distinguish adequately between urban and national history.[5]

A second group of studies falls into an omnibus category that can be called *Urban as Site*. No formal geographic meaning is intended by the term *site*. As used here, *site* is meant to imply the conceptual treatment of the city as a passive backdrop to whatever else is the subject of central concern. The disparate works in this genre share one particular attribute in common: they all focus on something that happened in cities. These "social-cultural, economic and political studies," all deal with "cities, or with life in cities, but rarely with urban history as distinguished from social, economic, or political history in the context of cities."[6] The main point to keep in mind about these works, however, is their treatment of the city as incidental, as a convenient setting to study the topic at hand. Little or no attempt is made to conceptualize the behavior being examined as affected by or interacting with some aspect of the urban environment. This is especially evident, as we shall see, in studies of social and geographic mobility recently undertaken by social historians.

The third group of studies may be listed under the rubric, *Urban as Process*. These works are concerned directly with the process of urbanization. Unlike the *Urban as Site* category, in this research the city occupies center stage and is not reduced to a passive role. The actual study of the historical urbanization process, however, has been troubled by conceptual difficulties. "There is need to differentiate the study of the city as a dependent and as an independent variable. Much of the apparent conflict in the literature . . . " wrote Philip Hauser for the Committee on Urbanization of the Social Science Research Council, "lies in the failure to make this distinction clear."[7]

Perhaps more than any writer in recent years, Eric Lampard has attempted to bring a measure of clarity to the field of urban studies. He expressed the critical distinction in this way:

> How do cities grow and how does a population, to a greater or lesser degree, become resident in cities? This is the study of urbanization as a dependent variable.
> What difference does it make (and to whom) that some activity or other aspect of population is "urban"? This is the study of urbanization as an independent variable.[8]

The study of urbanization as a dependent variable can be undertaken at either the macro- or micro-level. In the former, it is conceived of, following Tisdale and Lampard, as a "broad societal process" that resulted in the formation of cities.[9] This process began in the late eighteenth and early nineteenth centuries, building on significant and accelerating changes in technology and transportation, and led to the transformation of America from a rural to an urban society. The definition of this process is straightforward: as the number and size of cities grow, an increasing proportion of the total population becomes urban. As a historical process, little research in any discipline has been undertaken. We know little more than the rough sequence of "population concentration, the multiplication of points of concentration, or of the relations among concentrations of different size and density in various parts of the country at different times in our history."[10] As a contemporary process, research has been carried out by social scientists whose focus has been on the "classification" of cities by type and function and on "systems" of cities related to each other in a variety of ways on a regional or national basis.[11]

The study of the historical urbanization process as a dependent variable and at the micro-level has only recently begun. The societal perspective is replaced by focus on a particular city. Its purpose is to examine the process by which the urban environment, broadly conceived, is formed. In the words of Roy Lubove, it is "the process of city building over time." A "city," according to this view, should be conceived of as an artifact or a "physical container":

> This physical container of environment consists of a structure ("the spatial organization of key functional areas and essential service facilities . . . in response to certain fundamental living needs and activities of human society") and a form ("the visually perceptive features of the city which this structure produces, both the two-dimensional and three-dimensional forms created by surface, spaces, structures and circulatory systems in a defined natural setting").[12]

The city building process over time, argued Lubove, offers students of urban history a range of exciting possibilities not found in other formulations: it provides a framework for analyzing social organization and change; it clarifies the elusive relationship between personality, social organization and environment; it mandates greater emphasis upon, following Geddes and Mumford, the role of technological development in the urbanization process; and it explores the important relationships between communications and urban growth.[13]

In many respects, then, Lubove's notion is similar to ideas found in human ecology. This approach grew out of the work done by Robert Park, Ernest Burgess, and other sociologists at the University of Chicago in the 1920s and 1930s. Its formulation as a theory of community structure, however, was the accomplishment of Amos Hawley. The general approach has been expressed most recently in the work of Otis Duncan, Leo Schnore, and Stanley Lieberson.[14] Both Lubove and the ecologists pay considerable attention to the "key variables" in the ecological complex: population, organization, environment, and technology. Lubove, however, parts company with the ecologists because they are "critical of any behavioral, cultural analysis of social organization which focuses on the individual, on small group inter-personal relationships, on values, or on culture 'traits.' "[15] Lampard, while agreeing with the ecologists that "urbanization and community structure" are the result of a "changing balance between population and environment moderated by technology and organization," aligns himself more closely with Lubove's point of view by specifically including "the contingencies of events and personalities."[16] In other words, environmental determinism is avoided by assigning an important role in explanation to "subjective and attitudinal variables." In the last analysis, according to

Lubove, the city building approach views the urbanization process far less abstractly than the ecologists by conceiving of the city as a concrete entity whose form and structure are determined by human decisions that affect the use of land. Focus, therefore, is on the composition and growth of the urban environment: for example, its economy, industrial structure and industrial geography, population composition and distribution, terrain, transportation technology, communications network, housing and capital markets, and a host of variables exogenous to the particular city (trade, transportation, in- and out-migration, business organization) that link it to the wider regional, national, and international setting of which it is inextricably a part.

Urbanization can also be studied as an independent variable. In this formulation we are asking not what creates the urban environment, but how the urban environment, at one point in time or over time, affected things that occurred within it. These *things* need not be limited to cities; that is, they need not be urban *per se*. Rather our concern is quite simply with how they were affected by the variety of environments. It is here that we must look to answer the question "does urban matter?" and it is here that we can ultimately assess whether a framework other than urban provides a more satisfactory explanation for the phenomena we study. We may be interested in learning how the *city* affected simple behaviors such as birth, death, and marriage, or changes in jobs, neighborhood and wealth; or how the *city* affected processes such as social mobility, assimilation, socialization, the development of political and class consciousness; or how the *city* affected goals, values, and personality.

The Classification of Urban Environments

To arrive at a conceptual scheme for the study of urban history and to determine the explanatory value of an urban framework, we must recognize what is most obvious about cities: they are special types of environments. To utter this simple truth, however, does not get us very far, for the terms *urban* and *city* serve as proxies for a bewildering array of structures, behaviors, attitudes, and the processes that relate each to the other. The nature of our task requires that we find some way to differentiate urban environments, that we seize upon some means of classifying them.

Sociologists, who turned to the study of the city long before historians, devoted a generation to the task of systematizing what was meant by the terms *urban* and *city*. Their efforts began with an "urban-rural dichotomy," using as polar concepts of society the *Gemeinschaft/Gesellschaft* categories formulated by Toennies and most popularly expressed in the works of Louis

Wirth and Robert Redfield. Although their well-known identifications of the elements of life in each setting were offered as *ideal types* in the Weberian sense, many other sociologists took these all-inclusive character-izations as *given*.[17] Once accepted as the results of, rather than as guides to empirical research, it required only logic to envision a *continuum* be-tween the poles. All communities could thus be assigned locations, and their degree of *urbanness* or *ruralness,* it was believed, would vary more or less systematically along the continuum.

Over the last thirty years the continuum approach has come under so sustained and devastating a criticism that few writers today take it seri-ously. It has been found to be culture-bound, for it was "inapplicable to developing areas of the world," difficult to test empirically "because it combined culture and population concepts," failing such tests when con-ducted, and tautological in construction, for "the attributes of the types were reaffirmed by definition" rather than by evidence.[18] The multidimen-sional classification of communities for location on the continuum should be replaced, Eric Lampard argued, with a "simple demographic" measure of urbanization based on population concentration that allows "organiza-tional and behavioral characteristics . . . to vary independently." Such a simplified continuum approach, what is more, has real possibilities of succeeding if applied to the past rather than the present, for contemporary differences between city and country have been vanishing. For example, only half a century ago "urban areas were considered *sui generis* from rural ones" in rates of fertility and mortality, infant death, and longevity. The spread that separated these rates in urban and rural areas "has been narrowing precipitously" as the culture and technology associated with ur-banization has reached every corner of modern society.[19] It is not surpris-ing, therefore, to learn that even the simple demographic measure fails to correlate significantly with a range of behaviors on a contemporary "urban-rural continuum."

Another approach is to characterize cities by stages in their develop-ment. The periodization schema developed by an earlier generation of urban historians has to some extent been unfairly criticized. There is much less than generally believed of what can be referred to as "urban-irrelevant" stages such as "The City in the Age of Jackson" or "The Progressive City."[20] On the other hand, the stages they identified served to explicate their particular narrative rather than to illuminate a larger urban process.

In his new volume, *The Urban Wilderness,* Sam Bass Warner, Jr., our leading urban historian, suggests that we look to three general periods: 1820–1870, 1870–1920, 1920–. These, Warner believes, reflect the "im-pact of transportation and technological innovation upon the system of

American cities . . . because it is from a particular technological climate and a particular configuration of transportation that the form of cities and our business institutions . . . and our local jobs and local housing . . . inevitably takes shape."[21] Hand tools, water and horsepower, canals, steamboats, and railroads characterize the first period; mechanized production techniques, electricity, a national system of railroads, cheap mass transit, and the introduction of the motor-truck and auto characterize the second; while the modern period is distinguished by highly sophisticated advances in all forms of technology, especially communications and the introduction of atomic energy, a national system of highways, the emergence of the trucking industry, and intensive use of the auto, airplanes, and pipelines. It is from these innovations and their impact on the urban environment, argues Warner, that our research should proceed.[22]

A separate, but closely related approach to the classification of urban environments is the functionally differentiated *community-type*. Throughout our history, American communities have been of many different types. We have had agricultural villages, mercantile trading towns, handicraft manufacturing centers, great industrial cities, mill, mining, frontier and "boom" towns, modern metropolises, and suburban satellites. Some of these emerged in direct response to changes in industrial technology (Birmingham, Alabama's growth when new methods affected steel production) or in transportation technology (Chicago and scores of other cities that benefited from the shipment of goods by railroad). Some communities, such as resort, college, or governmental towns, continued their functions relatively independent of the major shifts in technology identified by Warner. Yet other communities, especially older ones such as Philadelphia, evolved gradually through successive types—trading, commercial and handicraft manufacture, industrial—in response to these same technological changes.

A potentially significant development in this last category emerges from Michael Katz's study, *The People of Hamilton, Canada West: Family and Class in a Mid-Nineteenth-Century City*. Among Katz's important contributions to our understanding of urban and social history is the notion that Hamilton represents a distinctive city-type. Hamilton is seen as a "commercial city," the interim product of a longer transition from a "preindustrial to an industrial society, or from a rural to an urban society." More recently, Katz expanded on this notion and called for the use of a three-stage, rather than a two-stage, paradigm in which mercantile capitalism, in the form of the commercial city and the wage-labor system, necessarily predated industrial capitalism.[23] In a perceptive review of the Hamilton study, Carl Kaestle urged Katz to "make clearer the 'causal nexus' " that might explain how the environment of the commercial city (broadly conceived) might influence the experience of its inhabitants. Kaestle wanted to know what the argument is "that links the modes of productive activity with people's private or social behavior."[24] Are differences that might be found in the experience of people living in commercial and industrial cities the result of differences in the nature of work itself or in the different ecological patterns associated with each city type?

These are critically important questions and equally valuable explanatory categories to pursue. They recognize *jobs and housing* or *work and residence* as the basic building blocks of the physical and social environment. People spend most of their lives on the job or at home (or on the block or in the neighborhood), and their experiences at these sites exert an enormous influence on their behavior and attitudes. The nature of work in which one engages, an immense sociological and economic literature documents, is tied to a vast range of topics. By the *nature of work* at the individual level, I refer to both the *setting* in which the work takes place and the *content* or particular tasks involved in the production process itself. Changes in the modes and means of productive activity affected both of these directly, first in the transition from an agricultural community to the commercial town and later from this intermediate stage to the industrial city. In the *separation of home and work,* the household was stripped of its endogenous economic functions, while *increases in scale* brought people into larger and larger work groups. The *specialization of tasks* meant that work was broken down into separate functions, which *diluted skills* as individual steps were performed by different persons. Work was *reorganized* and *discipline* maintained through the growth of *hierarchical differentiation* that brought layers of foremen, supervisors, managers, and bureaucracy. In exposing people to entirely new environments, these changes gradually affected identity, roles, values and expectations, social networks, class consciousness, and so on, through an almost endless list of human experience. "The arrangement of most economic activities of a city into work groups," Sam Bass Warner, Jr., has argued, "is as much of a revolution in the environments of cities as the introduction of the automobile or electricity."[25]

As with the *nature of work,* the relationships between the ecology of cities and the experience of their inhabitants is the subject of an extensive literature. The ecological linkage to behavior and attitudes suggests that next to the family, the relevant unit of socialization is the neighborhood or the patterning of people, housing, institutions, and organizational activities proximate to each individual's place of residence. The literature of many disciplines, especially sociology and geography, makes clear the existence of a strong relationship between residential patterns and human behavior.

Many aspects of behavior throughout the life course have been tied to residential patterns. The contemporary neighborhood is viewed as critical to the personality development and socialization process of young people through the institutions of family, play groups, and school. Propinquity has also been tied to adult friendship and kin networks and to marriage selection. Location in space is closely linked with institutional access to jobs, education, and housing. Studies have suggested the relationship between the sociocultural characteristics of neighborhoods and such social pathologies as crime, delinquency, and mental illness. There is a debate as to the impact of segregation and homogeneous residential patterns on the social mobility, assimilation, and integration of ethnic groups and on social conflict. Other studies have focused on the use of space, territory, and distance to express self-identity and to symbolize values and expectations.[26]

The argument offered, then, is that changes in the "modes of productive activity" brought about by industrialization altered both the nature of work (its setting and content) and the ecology of cities (the spatial arrangements of the environment). Not only did areas within cities experience segregation in economic function, resulting in pronounced industrial and commercial land use specialization, but social differentiation and spatial differentiation proceeded in tandem. Social differences wrought by industrialization—the emergence, for example, of a white-collar/managerial class—were expressed in new residential patterns. Differences that set people apart at work, most obviously the growing distinction between manual and nonmanual labor, were now extended to the residential setting and etched physically into the spatial forms of the city. The confluence of the streams of upward social mobility and residential mobility, aided by breakthroughs in transportation technology (beginning with the horsecar and accelerated by the introduction of the electrified trolley) produced modern neighborhood types characterized by segregation along class, racial/ethnic, and life-cycle lines. The emerging theoretical perspective accords spatial differentiation more than the passive role of manifesting changes in the larger social and industrial structure. Although most white-collar suburbs would become truly homogeneous only after World War II, it was in the late nineteenth century that they began to express a new ideology, social life, and consumption patterns and to embody the life style of new social groups.[27] Thus the spatial patterns that developed functioned themselves as dynamic forces in determining future social relationships and urban form. People living in different types of cities, or in cities at different stages in their economic development—commercial and industrial, for example—can be hypothesized to display different behavioral and attitudinal characteristics, and their collective patterns should lend themselves to documentation and measurement.

The New Urban History

In November 1968, a group of roughly forty students of the urban experience gathered at Yale University to discuss life in cities of the last century. The conference on the "Nineteenth-Century Industrial City" was marked by considerable intellectual excitement. Professional friendships made there led to frequent exchange of ideas and collaboration in research over the years. Those present represented varying intellectual backgrounds: half had been trained in history and the others in the social sciences. Despite their different training, they shared a desire to link historical data to sociological theory and to the social sciences in general; to use quantitative materials and techniques; and "to broaden the scope of urban studies to embrace the social experiences of ordinary, unexceptional people."[28] In short, they represented a generation of younger scholars determined to write a *new urban history*.

Given their interest in the micro-level experience of the masses of common people, and the impossibility of individual scholars pursuing such a topic on any but a case-study basis, the research challenges that awaited them were essentially three. *First,* they could examine the process of city building with an emphasis on the creation of the actual environment. *Second,* they could investigate how the wide range of human experience in which they were interested was affected by the variety of urban environments. Here they would not only observe the rates of variation in given behaviors, but explain how the city affected the behavior in question; that is to say they would not only describe, but identify the mechanisms through which the urban environment affected behavior. *Finally,* they could demonstrate the dialectical nature of the interaction between behavior and environment: how the sum of individual actions shaped the environment and how, in turn, the new environment shaped subsequent actions.

When Stephan Thernstrom and Richard Sennett edited *Nineteenth-Century Cities,* a collection of papers presented at the conference they organized, their prefatory note about the essays was encouraging: "They all aim at deepening our understanding of the lives of men and women living in dense urban settlements undergoing explosive growth and structural transformation."[29] Thus it appeared that the "New Urban History," as the volume was subtitled, would systematically explore the interactions between behavior and environment within the dynamic context of urbanization and industrialization. The prospects for urban history looked bright indeed.

With few exceptions, however, the decade of scholarship that followed the Yale Conference had very little to do with cities. Although the many studies that appeared all identified cities as the setting for their historical research, their subject matter, to borrow a phrase, though found *in* cities was curiously enough not *of* them. In these studies, by and large, the city was simply treated as the convenient location for the particular topic at hand. In short, they were studies that treated *urban as site,* not *urban as process.*

Sam Bass Warner recognized the limitations of the literature described as the "new urban history." In a recent interview for the *Journal of Urban History* conducted by Bruce Stave, Warner was asked whether he believed there was such a thing as the "new urban history." "There could be," Warner conjectured, "but I don't think it has come about yet." Although *Nineteenth-Century Cities* "seems to be about . . . cities . . . it's really largely social history in which the impact of whatever is cityness is not measured or talked about or really dealt with. There are things that take place in cities . . . but most of the material there is not urban history. . . . So," he concluded, "I think our subspecialty is in deep trouble, because the most active things being done are the mobility studies, in which there isn't much urban content yet."[30]

The mobility studies, of course, were sparked by Stephan Thernstrom's enormously influential and pioneering work on Newburyport.[31] They now constitute a sizable literature that includes some ten books and an even greater number of articles.[32] Although our knowledge of American history has been enriched by these studies, the gains for the student of urban history have been substantially less than the expectations raised at the Yale Conference. In reviewing these studies as a group, one cannot avoid being struck by their treatment of urban setting as almost incidental to the analysis of mobility taking place. This lack of concern with local setting grows in part from the intellectual milieu that spawned them. They grew out of an interest in comparing American with European society and in answering questions about inequality that were generated by the Civil Rights Movement of the 1950s and 1960s. In neither instance was the focus on cities: in the first comparison, focus was on nations differentiated by political and economic systems; in the second, focus was on ethnic and racial groups differentiated by degrees of access to an opportunity structure. It is clear from the questions that lay at the center of the mobility studies— how open was American society? How fluid was its population movement and its class structure? How true was its "rags to riches" dream?—that the analytic focus was not on the city *per se.* Their concern was not with the city building process nor with how the urban environment may have affected those who resided in the variety of such settings, but with a particular dimension of their behavior: mobility.

The explanation of their popularity does not seem obscure. That historians rallied to the mobility rather than to the urban banner must lie, at least in part, with the ideology of American culture, for in no other country has there been so great a preoccupation with mobility studies.[33] Writing "history from the bottom up," moreover, was new and exciting. Thernstrom's example in *Poverty and Progress* was bold and provocative. It not only raised a host of questions that touched indirectly upon new topics of pressing concern to American historians—race, ethnicity, class, industrialization, and social justice—but it offered a methodology that opened the field to all willing to venture their energies. In a discipline characterized by the lack of a method other than the critical reading of source documents, historians were delighted to learn that they could emulate Thernstrom's efforts in their own communities. All they needed was close at hand: manuscript population schedules, city directories, tax lists, and the like. What is more, computer technology was becoming widely available; regardless of the machine type, size, or configuration, most schools were able to offer historians the ability, never before possible, to manipulate large bodies of information.

What have we learned from these studies of geographic and social mobility? Although it is not possible to do justice to this voluminous research in a few paragraphs, any attempt to summarize the work would likely include the following observations. The last century was above all characterized by population volatility. Indeed, Michael B. Katz considered "transiency" as one of the two major themes of the nineteenth century.[34] The remarkable turnover in population has been expressed as the proportion of persons who could be found resident in the same community for at least one decade. Yet this figure, ranging from 40 to 60 percent in almost all studies, is dwarfed by the far greater magnitude of persons who flowed in and out of cities between census enumerations, estimated by Thernstrom and Knights to be between six and twelve times the number present at the start of a decade.[35] The composition of these restless numbers, it appears, has also changed over the last century. White-collar workers have replaced blue-collar workers as the more likely group to be on the move, although all studies have stressed that nineteenth-century migration streams—into, out of, and within cities—were swelled by people from all ethnic groups and from all ranks of society.

The careers of those who remained in one community at least long enough to be found in two successive censuses, provided the raw material for the analysis of change over time, or what historians have called occupational, residential, and wealth mobility or more deceptively, "social mobility." The evidence seems to indicate that most men remained stable within their occupational ranks, with more moving up than down, while many were able to make modest gains in property-holding, amounting to the purchase of their own home. Although the experience of their sons has been documented far less frequently, the emerging patterns were much the same as those of the previous generation: most sons began at the same level as their fathers and remained stable in that position with more moving up than down, though overall there appears to have been more inter- than intra-generational mobility. Unlike the case of geographic mobility, important differentials in ethnicity and race are found in social mobility. Native whites, Jews, and Germans rose faster and fell less frequently than did the Irish, Italians, and Poles, and all white groups enjoyed the rewards of the system to a vastly greater extent than did blacks.

The form assumed in almost all the mobility research by historians to date has been the case study—the examination of mobility experience in individual communities. Given the individualistic nature of historical research, the problems of data collection and data processing encountered in this type of micro-history make detailed research in more than one community at a time virtually impossible. Comparative analysis, therefore, must be synthetic, carried out on an *ad hoc* basis. An outstanding attempt to pull together the findings from these disparate studies is Thernstrom's now well-known chapter, "The Boston Case and the American Pattern," in his latest study of social mobility, the prize-winning *The Other Bostonians*.[36]

The dominant pattern that Thernstrom found in his review of this literature is the general lack of significant variation in either geographic or career mobility across time and across communities that differed greatly in "life styles, residential patterns, ethnic composition, city size, timing of growth, rates of growth and the like. . . . "[37] Thernstrom readily acknowledges the wide range of methodological problems that make these comparisons problematic, but finds the "striking consistency" that emerged persuasive enough to conclude that "the patterns of mobility that existed in Boston were not peculiar to that city, but rather were products of forces which operated in much the same way throughout American society in the nineteenth and twentieth centuries."[38] This is, without question, an extraordinary conclusion. Where geographic and career mobility are concerned, *urban* appears to account for little variation. Thernstrom may ultimately prove to be correct—and if he is we have a finding of real value. Yet such a conclusion is simply too important to accept, given the methodological problems, evidence, explanatory variables, and conceptual schema found in the mobility studies.

Anyone familiar with the implications of methodology for empirical results must recognize the remarkably weak foundations on which the results of the mobility studies rest. The techniques of record linkage, for example, directly underlie the calculations for both population persistence and career mobility. The techniques used to trace specific individuals through successive census manuscripts, city directories, and the like not only differ, but are far too often suspect and productive of sharply biased results. Based on the experience of the Philadelphia Social History Project (PSHP) it is likely that substantial proportions of the persons "linked" have nothing more in common with each other than the same name.[39] When one considers, moreover, how the use of widely differing sampling procedures, data sources, and classification schema for the vertical ranking of occupations can all operate to compound the bias and error, the basis for generalization is at best tenuous.

Thernstrom agrees that widely divergent approaches were used in the disparate mobility studies, but he concludes that this state of affairs supports his conclusion: the general agreement of results somehow proves that the differences must cancel each other out. This argument is not compelling; it appears to confuse the lack of concern produced by random error distributed over a great many observations on the one hand, with a problem more akin to comparing apples and oranges on the other. "The multiple hedges around the comparisons grow so high," Michael Frisch observed in reviewing Thernstrom's work, "as to leave us in something of a maze of highly informed hunches."[40] Thernstrom's intellectual efforts to synthesize so many independently conducted studies resulted in a remarkably persuasive essay; only familiarity with the genuinely problematic methodological foundations on which these studies rest suggests that we should remain skeptical. This skepticism, moreover, is supported by evidence made available in more recent studies of mobility by JoEllen Vinyard and David Doyle. These authors find much greater opportunity for the Irish in Midwestern communities than in older Eastern cities. And Thomas Kessner has found that Italian immigrants in New York City enjoyed greater upward mobility than Thernstrom suggested based on the evidence from Boston. Perhaps the dynamic economy of New York provided immigrants with a broader range of opportunities for advancement than were available in the sluggish economy of Boston.[41]

The analytic strategy that characterizes the mobility literature—the choice of dependent and independent variables—is the source of much dissatisfaction. Mobility is used in the former, but never in the latter capacity. By treating geographic or career mobility only as dependent variables, historians sought to explain variations in their rates, not the effect of mobility upon other dimensions of behavior or social structure. Thus the implication is that we know, for example, what accompanied a rate of persistence that was 20, 40, 60, or 80 percent; that we are aware of what happened when the rates moved sharply up or down. Yet nothing is further from the truth. We know precious little of the correlates or consequences of mobility rates. And, if we do not know what different rates of population turnover affected, it is somewhat misleading to speak of a given rate or change in the rate as "significant."

The central rationale of the initial mobility studies, as Thernstrom noted, was the "venerable cliché" that "the more fluid the composition of the working class of a society and the greater the opportunity to climb from lower to higher rungs of the class ladder, the less the likelihood of sharply class conscious collective working-class protest."[42] The mobility studies, however, assume the validity of this proposition rather than document its existence. Instead of continuing the proliferation of studies that describe the rates of mobility, Gilbert Shapiro urged that a higher priority be assigned to the study of the *relationship* between mobility and a variety of political consequences. In other words, the test of such a hypothesis requires a new *dependent* variable—"radicalism of belief, political stability or disorderly political action, however the *explicandum* is defined." Unfortunately, there are few studies "which measure both mobility and its supposed political effects."[43]

The little evidence that is available suggests what appears to be contradictory consequences: workers residing in the same community over a relatively long period of time have been portrayed as the source of both little and much militancy. Yet, as Michael Katz explained, this contradiction is more apparent than real. "The crux of the matter is *context:* the opportunities for economic success within a particular setting."[44] The political behavior of stable workers will vary according to the economic circumstances found in communities of different types.

Unfortunately, even when geographic or career mobility are used as dependent variables, the choice of independent variables undercuts this attempt to associate mobility or political behavior with the larger setting. The only independent variables used are those that describe the *personal attributes* of the individuals whose mobility behavior is being scrutinized. Thus the explanatory variables are those that describe age, sex, race, ethnic background, birthplace, address, occupation, property ownership, literacy, and education; some studies include as well religion, marital status, and family characteristics.

What is strikingly clear about this approach is the limited nature of the explanatory context. The "men" are indeed "in motion": they move up and down status ladders and into, out of, and within towns; but their movement is treated as if it occurred within a vacuum. We are not given a sense of how the particular places in which they lived influenced their behavior. This is not to say that most monographs in the mobility literature fail to set the scene by including an opening chapter that provides a brief overview of the local setting (yet some lack even this); but a general description is not a systematic specification of the relationships, for example, between mobility and the local or regional economy.[45]

With focus narrowly on career mobility along only a vertical axis defined by levels of skill and manual/nonmanual distinctions, and with the use of data sources such as the population census and city directories that report only the occupational title, the broader range of explanatory variables that could link mobility to the opportunity structure go unexamined. The proportions of "climbers and sliders" that serve as dependent variables and form the basis for comparisons across time and space, it is important to realize, are *averages* for each community. But what component parts made up the overall rates? Did mobility vary within different sectors of the economy, in industries that were old and new, that produced capital or consumer goods, that manufactured for local or export markets? Did mobility vary in large or small firms, among those with or without mechanization, between journeymen and craftsmen? Did mobility vary according to work setting and ecological patterns? Exclusive focus with vertical movement has all but obscured the rich details of horizontal movement within the local economy. Yet it is precisely these components of the overall rate that we must study in order to interpret the significance of Thernstrom's conclusion that mobility varied little across communities. If further research proves Thernstrom correct, it will likely be due to the fact "that the occupational structures of American communities of various sizes and types varied less than is commonly believed."[46] This was almost certainly truer for most cities throughout the nineteenth century and in the early twentieth century than for those of today. Without the large business corporation and the support of national markets and advanced transportation technologies, the urban economies of earlier cities (with some exceptions in a limited number of goods and markets) were unable to specialize in products that would provide them with comparative advantage. Thus the economies—and hence the occupational structures—of most big cities of the past century may well have resembled each other.

In any case, the limited nature of the explanatory frameworks used in the mobility studies is especially evident in examinations of intra-urban migration. While studies of social mobility can only speculate about the fate of those who left the community being examined, the study of residential mobility permits the tracing of people who moved to another section of town. Thus it is possible to learn what happened to them over time.

The explanatory base can be broadened to assess the impact of the environment on the twin decisions first to move and second to relocate. Yet such studies do not demonstrate the systematic relationship between mobility and the characteristics found at the origin and destination of the migration stream. Above all else, we should like to know for each of these two settings the nature of the housing stock, the job opportunities available, and the socioeconomic and demographic composition of the population. In contemporary studies of residential mobility, for example, the percentage "nonwhite" in census tracts explains a substantial proportion of the observed variation in mobility. We should also like to know about the effect of available transportation and shopping facilities and especially access to churches, schools, other institutions, and voluntary associations, and to basic services such as water, sewage, and gas. Contextual variables that describe the environment, considered in addition to the personal attributes of the individual mover or nonmover, serve fundamentally to expand the explanatory framework.

Without contextual variables, explanatory efforts are futile. When the personal attribute variables were considered *additively* in the only study of historical intra-urban migration to employ a multivariate analysis, they were found to explain only 10 percent of the observed variation in mobility rates.[47] In the absence of the ecological variables described above, how should this finding be interpreted? Is the decision to move—so central to a host of questions linked to the stability of the community or the body politic—rooted in caprice, societal norms, individual personality, or structural factors? It is critical to grasp that without the addition of ecological variables, the determinants of residential mobility cannot be identified.

By now it should be apparent that the kind of history provided in the mobility studies differed markedly from that proposed at the Yale Conference. Our " . . . understanding of the lives of men and women living in dense urban settlements undergoing explosive growth and structural transformation," although deeper, has not lived up to its promise because these studies have not related mobility to any aspects of the environment in which it took place.

Thernstrom was right in 1971 when, in reflecting on the *new urban history,* he doubted that the rubric accurately described the work taking place; he was right again in 1975 when, in an interview for the *Journal of Urban History,* he rejected the existence of the *new urban history;* and he was right once more when he told Bruce Stave that he "had stopped labeling" himself "as an urban historian at all." But I believe that he was seriously wrong when he remarked that he saw as unimportant the necessity to define "what is social history or urban history or rural history. . . ."[48]

The limited nature of the explanatory variables used in the mobility studies flows directly from flaws in their conceptual framework. Following Thernstrom's lead, they viewed *urban as site* rather than *urban as process,* treated their particular communities as incidental, and made little effort to understand mobility as an *urban process.* Thernstrom argued that since such topics as "the flow of population from country to city . . . (and) patterns of social mobility . . . are not confined to the city," they "should not be treated as if they were."[49] This argument is difficult to grasp. It is one thing to realize that mobility occurred throughout society; it is quite another properly to conceptualize the study of mobility as it took place in cities and to build an explanatory framework through which we can explore how the mobility was affected by urban environments. All historians who study behavior such as mobility have a responsibility to establish the links between that behavior and the setting in which it takes place. The point, then, is not simply that the mobility studies failed as urban history, but that in general they left a good deal to be desired as historical explanation. For some reason the conceptual confusion remained powerful, and this literature never developed hypotheses to link mobility to the environment in which it occurred. The mobility studies, in other words, neither adequately explained the mobility behavior they set out to study nor provided urban historians with a viable model to follow.

The hopeful beginnings of a model for urban historians were put forward in 1968, the same year as the Yale Conference. In an important article that proposed a "scaffolding for urban history," Sam Bass Warner, Jr., urged historians to undertake a full accounting of the relationships between environment and behavior as suggested by the early promise of the "new urban history." He described Philadelphia in three successive "periods in urban growth," each characterized by distinctly different environments. The setting of work and the ecological patterns of the city changed greatly between Warner's temporal cross-sections: 1770–80, 1830–60, and 1920–30. "Research on the historical interactions between the group organization of work and urban residential environments is not yet fairly begun," Warner accurately argued, "yet such research seems to hold great promise for extending our comprehension of the processes of urban history."[50] These relationships were potentially so significant that they had to be pursued by historians. The change in the average size of manufacturing firms, Warner hypothesized, could be linked to such important events as "the rise and decline of unions and strikes, epidemics of street violence, and the development of isolated mill-town culture in one quarter of Philadelphia as opposed to the suburban/downtown white-collar culture of another quarter." Changes in "social geography," Warner maintained, had important implications for "political institutions, communications within the city, and informal associations."[51]

Warner's model, however, was not followed, and his attempt "to call people's attention to the systematic relationships . . . " was ignored. This puzzled him. "Everybody reads the article and they think, 'yeah, that's a good article,' " he complained recently, "but it doesn't seem to tell people what to do."[52] Warner's self-appraisal was correct. His work took historians to the vista's edge for a look at how social change in the city took place, but he neither went down himself nor showed other historians how to reach the promised land.

Why the model Warner offered in the "scaffolding" article was not followed by urban historians is explained, in part, by the fact that he never implemented the model in his own prize-winning book, *The Private City,* which appeared the same year as his article. Warner's purpose was to explain why "the cities of America still lack full employment, racial integration, decent housing for the poor, safe streets, good schools, good clinics and hospitals, adequate recreation facilities, an abundance of small-community urban life, and a government which could begin to achieve these long-missing goals."[53] The explanation for these ills was "privatism." Privatism, Warner explained elsewhere, was actually "capitalism" and the culture it spawned. He did not use that word in *The Private City,* for he wished readers to reflect dispassionately on his message, rather than react with the knee-jerk response that such an emotionally charged word as "capitalism" would have prompted.[54]

With the "ills" of urban society as the story's "end" and "privatism" as its "means," the successive environments that Warner described played an analytically irrelevant role in *The Private City.* There was, in other words, a glaring disjuncture between his article and his book. The "scaffolding" that looked so promising in the former proved sadly disappointing in the latter. The collection of comparable data for a single city over 150 years presented in the article was a valuable descriptive contribution, but it is important to understand that these data documented only the different work settings and ecologies that characterized Philadelphia at three points in its historical development. When used in *The Private City* they described only changes in the environment, not the relationship between environment and behavior correctly hypothesized in the "scaffolding" article.

As a model for case studies, *The Private City* is a dead end for another reason. If "Philadelphia's history has been repeated, with minor variation, again and again across the nation, in Cincinnati, in St. Louis, in Chicago, in Detroit, in Los Angeles, and in Houston," then why study it again? If you've seen one city, Warner seems to be saying, and as Thernstrom said in regard to mobility, then you've seen 'em all. He offers us an analytic model with "urban ills" as the dependent variable and "privatism" as the single independent variable, but it is an independent variable without variation. Privatism is a holistic culture concept, not peculiar to Philadelphia, but characteristic of American society. With this type of research design, Warner should have conducted his study across cities in different cultures where the independent variable could have variation. As he confessed later, however, "I guess I never considered whether they (systematic structural relationships) would exist under a different value system."[55]

Some important clues as to why Warner's model was not followed by other urban historians can be found in his own subsequent work. Warner ignored his own advice to pursue the systematic relationship between behavior and environment not only in *The Private City*, but also in his next book. In *The Urban Wilderness*, Warner abandoned the case-study for higher levels of generalization. The "repeated interactions" that largely determined the end products of the entire system—the jobs and residential structure within cities," Warner observed, are ". . . an enormously complex subject requiring great expertise. . . . "[56] Is it not reasonable to conclude that such expertise is not found among historians?

Once again an ambitious beginning proved a dead end. The same reason, it seems to me, explains why mobility historians did not systematically relate mobility to features of the urban environment and why neither Warner nor other urban historians have been able to explore systematically the relationships between behavior and a changing urban environment.

These failures are not the result of individual shortcomings. On the contrary, the efforts of historians working as individuals to master new methods and techniques and read in the literature of other disciplines has on the whole been as entirely commendable as it has been hopelessly insufficient. Nor are these failures simply a function of the conceptual confusion that for so long has clouded urban studies. Indeed, this confusion is but a manifestation of the larger problem. Mobility historians did not seek an explanation of mobility in the characteristics of urban environment, and urban historians did not test relationships between behavior and environment because they quite simply did not possess the expertise required to do so. So long as research is conducted on an individual basis, historians like scholars in other disciplines, will be unable to put together the pieces of the urban puzzle. How many more decades will pass before we face the crux of the problem: the current organization of historical research.

The Organization of Research:
A Perspective from the Sociology of Knowledge

The "New History" is escaping from the limitations formerly imposed upon the study of the past . . . it will avail itself of all those discoveries that are being made about mankind by anthropologists, economists, psychologists and sociologists—discoveries which during the past fifty years have served to revolutionize our ideas of the origin, progress and prospects of our race.

JAMES HARVEY ROBINSON
The New History, 1912

The argument offered is simple: a fundamental relationship exists between how knowledge is sought and the nature of the learning obtained. The ways in which we organize to conduct our research have a necessarily profound impact on what we are likely to find. This relationship owes its power to the revolution in the sociology of knowledge that has characterized the past century.

The half-century to which James Harvey Robinson referred witnessed dramatic changes that affected not only what was known, but how it came to be known. Although the "Renaissance Man" may have remained the ideal for the well-educated baccalaureate, he was discarded then as an unacceptable model for the new professional, specialized research scholar. Guided by theories, concepts, and methods developed in newly created branches of learning, the frontiers of knowledge were rapidly expanded. Within a remarkably brief span of years in the last third of the nineteenth century, no less than two hundred learned professional societies formed. The pursuit of knowledge was formalized in history (1884), economics (1885), political science (1903), and sociology (1905). These efforts were consolidated by the early twentieth century as each emerging discipline successfully completed passage through a sequence of developmental stages that brought it full "professionalization." Each set aside an area of substantive inquiry, standardized a program for graduate training and certification, established national journals and organizations, and adopted a service ideal to ensure that it would be self-policing and would serve the public.[57]

If Robinson recognized long ago the necessity for historians to incorporate the learning being acquired rapidly in other fields, the need has become infinitely greater after almost seven decades of research have so enormously expanded the frontiers of knowledge. Yet because these advances came through a division of labor with ever increasing specialization and further subdivision, the study of society in the past and present was fragmented.

So while it is undeniable that this reorganization in the pursuit of knowledge produced extraordinary gains, it is equally true that these have not come to us as an unmixed blessing. Indeed, in important respects, professional specialization has progressed to the point of diminishing societal returns. So accelerated was the rate of accumulation all along the peripheries of the specialized disciplines that today the staggering amount of knowledge generated can barely be digested within a given isolated field, much less be made visible to others. "We may not know, in the sense that we may not realize, how much we now know," philosopher Stuart Hampshire recently pointed out, discussing the consequences of proliferating but unintegrated knowledge. "And if we do not know what we know, then our first order knowledge is apt to be unused, almost as if it did not exist."[58] Even more seriously, disciplinary boundaries have tended to become barriers preventing us from seeing the contours of enormously complex problems in a real world that resists compartmentalization. Interdisciplinary effort can thus become not simply desirable for maximizing integrated knowledge, but an absolute necessity if problems are to be correctly understood and engaged.

This problem of fragmented knowledge and narrow disciplinary boundaries has long been recognized by students of the city. Indeed, urban problems are perhaps the most frequently cited illustration of the more general necessity of interdisciplinary study. They can usefully be considered a microcosm of the larger problem in the sociology of knowledge.

As awareness of an "Urban Crisis" began to emerge in the 1950s, American historians contemplated a design for urban research. Their response was a thoughtful lament about the constraining narrowness of a disciplinary perspective. "The city is too complex a world to be understood from a single vantage point alone . . . ," R. Richard Wohl noted in a characteristic statement. "The full discovery of what has passed in a city's history can only be called forth by cooperative, interdisciplinary inquiry." "To study the city," Allen Davis argued, "means to cut across the artificial lines of departments and disciplines." The frustration growing out of research confounded by the existence of these "artificial lines" was captured well in the remarks of A. Theodore Brown. "There is no sense in which I can pursue studies in city history as a practitioner of a self-sustained 'discipline' called history," Brown complained; " . . . if the approach is worth anything at all it needs a great deal of reinforcing from other so-called disciplines."[59] Virtually every survey of urban history in the last two decades has come to precisely the same conclusion.[60]

But given this unanimity, the record of actual achievement in interdisciplinary work is disheartening. Social scientists and historians have been unable to generate new modes of research organization, whatever their commitment to the ideal of a new interdisciplinary scholarship. This can be indicated by looking at the inadequacies of the usual responses to the call for innovation. There is first of all the interdisciplinary conference. Scholars from most of the disciplines relevant to the study of the city— geography, sociology, demography, economics, political science, anthropology, and history—meet, discuss, and prepare essays describing the efforts underway in their respective fields. The essays are usually published shortly afterwards. The best and most familiar example of these is certainly *The Study of Urbanization* edited by Philip Hauser and Leo Schnore. While all students interested in urbanization are better off for being apprised of the latest scholarship underway in disciplines other than their own, the research itself remains fragmented, and the theories, concepts, and methods developed in other fields are rarely implemented with success. When they finally make their way into another discipline, it is usually many years later, long after being discredited or discarded by scholars in the discipline in which it originated. Interaction at the conferences benefits the participants to be sure, but the trickling down of wisdom rarely has a significant impact. Readers of such volumes are still left to face their research problems without the training necessary to undertake the promising new approaches underway in other disciplines.

The second and more frequent response is that of the individual scholar who strives to absorb the relevant literature of ancillary disciplines. The noble intention is one inevitably doomed owing to the limitations of what any individual can accomplish. Caroline Ware explained the failure of Robinson's pleas for a "New History" this way: "Challenging though this call to intellectual adventure might be, its very comprehensiveness left scholars aghast . . . it was a life's work to become an expert in any one of these fields."[61] Rather than a scholar with depth and breadth, such an approach was likely to make good the time-honored wisdom implied by the quip, "Jack of all trades, Master of none." As a result, few programs of graduate study in any discipline leave room for significant work to be done in other fields. While it is surely better to be at home in two disciplines (though few can be expected to achieve even this), it does not appear possible to stretch such an approach further.[62] Given the current organization of research, the individual scholar who wishes to work across disciplinary lines confronts a profound dilemma. "To ignore the contributions of the social sciences," according to Lawrence Stone, "is clearly fatal; to master them all, or even any one, is clearly impossible."[63]

Response of a third type is the proliferation of interdisciplinary studies programs (black, women, ethnic, and so on) and pan-professional associations. But interdisciplinary programs do not have departmental status in their colleges and universities and therefore cannot determine either their own fate or the fate of their faculty; but more to the point, offering a variety of undergraduate courses is not the same as promoting and sustaining active research across disciplinary lines. Such programs will always be the *consumers* rather than the *producers* of interdisciplinary knowledge.

Pan-professional associations formed when historians began to move beyond impressionistic approaches and evidence to rely upon process-produced data and social science methods, and social scientists began to move beyond correlation and contemporary cross-sectional analyses to use time-series data and historical perspective in their research. The warm response that accompanied the formation of the Social Science History Association and the publication of its journal, *Social Science History,* provides a real measure of the increasingly popular desire to engage in inter-disciplinary research. Commendable though it is to advocate bridging the gaps between the disciplines, efforts such as the SSHA cannot by them-selves succeed. They can cross-fertilize ideas, establish personal contacts across disciplines and institutions, and expose scholars to ideas and ap-proaches not part of their own disciplinary paradigm. These are to be sure valuable functions. Ultimately, however, interdisciplinary associations, like the other responses to the call for interdisciplinary research, are without mechanisms capable of integrating the disparate research they encourage. They sustain interdisciplinary communication, but not interdisciplinary process.

The failure to accomplish more than this despite laudable intentions is not accidental. It is traceable, rather, to a combination of *structural factors* —the system of rewards, especially of hiring and promotion, which gov-erns the current organization of research in American universities—and *cultural factors*—that set of values which sanctify individual accomplish-ment while de-emphasizing the collaborative efforts necessary to form the organizational base for interdisciplinary research.[64] How these reward structures operate to prevent the emergence of new organizational re-search forms in the humanities and social sciences—and what concrete steps can be taken to change these circumstances—are the focus of our Epilogue, "Sustaining Interdisciplinary Research."

Here it is necessary to qualify the argument, for it does not apply to the "hard" and "applied" sciences; thus it serves as a sufficient rather than a necessary explanation for the lack of interdisciplinary research. The same structural and cultural factors that have impeded such research in the "soft" sciences and the humanities, after all, have not inhibited the de-velopment of interdisciplinary research elsewhere in our universities. What explains the emergence of collaborative research in these areas? What is responsible here for facilitating the integration of disparate knowledge across disciplinary lines? The reason is simply that they must do so if they are to succeed. Putting a man on the moon and finding a cure for cancer, for example, are not tasks that a discipline, let alone an individual, can accomplish in solitary fashion. Concerned with the real world, the actual workings of which are not compartmentalized along departmental lines, there is no other choice but to bring together the requisite knowledge and expertise.

The selection of research topics and the sequence in which they are investigated, what is more, differ significantly between these divergent intellectual traditions. Scholars in the hard and applied sciences depend upon each other's efforts; but whereas they are accustomed to working collaboratively across disciplines, and assume the importance of systematically expanding knowledge built on the base of previous research, in the humanities emphasis has been on originality and creativity, often purchased at the expense of cumulative scholarly advancement. The argument is not with the quality of results which derive from individual efforts, but with the persistent failure to integrate them.

The challenge is thus to develop mechanisms capable of transcending both structural and cultural obstacles in the humanities and social sciences, mechanisms that will have to work, moreover, without the integrating features that characterize research in the hard and applied sciences. A different sort of mechanism to facilitate the integration of knowledge must be found.

Urban research remains the best ground on which to construct such a mechanism. As A. J. Dyos has pointed out, "There is a widening awareness of the possibility . . . that in the study of the way in which urban society has organized itself spatially and structurally and has developed such a variety of social systems, there exists an incomparable arena in which to bring together more explicitly a number of these converging disciplines." Such a focus "lends itself so well to fruitful exchanges among the disciplines," O. D. Duncan and Leo Schnore accurately observed, "because of its strong empirical base and its relatively concrete view of society."[65]

The experience of the PSHP suggests that it is possible to construct and operationalize the needed mechanism. A common data base that includes both ecological and behavioral information about the city serves as the necessary facilitating device, and computer technology and the methodologies developed to manipulate the data can support the efforts of scholars trained in separate disciplines to integrate their knowledge about the city.

Such an approach provides a working model of an interdisciplinary *structure,* and even more, a collaborative and interdisciplinary research *culture.* To be sure, formidable obstacles face those who would emulate this approach, and the current financial crisis makes it clear that solutions may have to be found in cross-institutional and perhaps regional and national cooperation as well. The technology of electronic data processing will support these efforts.

Historians studying the sociology of knowledge understand the relationship between organization and scholarship; it is time to apply such a critique to the present structure of research. To ignore it further dooms us to continued frustration. Unless new institutional mechanisms are developed to support interdisciplinary collaborative research, our knowledge about cities will remain hopelessly fragmented.

Urban as Process

Our goal in the new research is to conceive of the city in active terms. We must move beyond static cross-sections and disconnected pieces of the urban experience. Once the requisite research environment is constructed, it will be possible to see the simultaneity, the complex feedback loops, and the unanticipated consequences that issue from change in a given corner of the urban system. Only then will we be in a position to understand the interplay of personalities, political decisions, major events, institutional behavior, and impersonal, large-scale, socioeconomic and demographic forces. When our research is approached in this manner, it is likely that our sense of causality will be radically altered as well, an inevitable consequence of seeing urban complexities more wholly. *Urban as process* should be thought of as the dynamic modeling of the interrelationships among environment, behavior, and group experience—three basic components in the larger urban system. Research might focus on three things. First, how the urban environment changed over time. Second, what social experience was correlated with different aspects of urban settings; neither relatively simple behaviors such as intermarriage nor complex processes such as assimilation occurred in a vacuum. Finally, what were the mechanisms through which environmental and social change were effected.

In this task, we will do well to return to the pioneering yet uncompleted work of Sam Bass Warner, Jr., and consider most carefully both his suggested stages of city development, defined largely by technological change, and his implicit notion of jobs, housing, and transportation as the fundamental building blocks of the urban experience. PSHP research, for example, suggests quite clearly that the residential fabric of the nineteenth-

century city was influenced to a major extent by the distribution of manufacturing jobs. Thus, factors that determined the location of industrial
plants such as changing transportation, production, and communications
technologies were in large part responsible for the city's changing residential patterns (rich with implications for socialization and subsequent experience). The availability and concentration of housing and jobs was
integrally related to the formation of the immigrant ghettoes, and thus explains much of the different residential experience of the "Old" and "New"
immigrants and post–World War II black urban migrants (who were characterized, respectively, by low, moderate, and high levels of segregation).
Building practices engaged in by developers and contractors, such as row
housing, where all units were similarly priced, played an important role
in the process through which the city became socially and spatially differentiated. These are but a few examples of the many mechanisms through
which changes in the urban environment affected the lives of its diverse
population groups.[66] It is through linkages such as these and many others
like them that our understanding of "urban as process" will take shape.

NOTES

1. Eric Lampard, "American Historians and the Study of Urbanization," *American Historical Review* 67 (October 1961), 61; (hereafter cited as "American Historians").

2. Oscar Handlin, "The Modern City as a Field of Historical Study," in Oscar Handlin and John Burchard, eds., in *The Historian and the City* (Cambridge, Mass., 1966), 26.

3. Bruce Stave, "A Conversation with Bayrd Still," *Journal of Urban History* 3 (May 1977), 330.

4. Constance McLaughlin Green, *Holyoke: A Case History of the Massachusetts Industrial Revolution in America* (New Haven, Ct., 1939); Bessie L. Pierce, *A History of Chicago,* 3 vols. (New York, 1937–1957); Blake McKelvey, *Rochester,* 4 vols. (Cambridge and Rochester, 1945–1961); Bayrd Still, *Milwaukee: The History of a City* (Madison, Wisc., 1945).

5. Roy Lubove, "The Urbanization Process: An Approach to Historical Research," *Journal of the American Institute of Planners* 33 (January 1967), 33; (hereafter cited as "Urbanization Process").

6. *Ibid.*

7. Philip Hauser, "Urbanization: An Overview," in Philip Hauser and Leo Schnore, eds., *The Study of Urbanization* (New York, 1966), 41.

8. Eric Lampard, "The Dimensions of Urban History: A Footnote to the 'Urban Crisis,'" *Pacific Historical Review* 39 (August 1970), fn., 268.

9. Hope Tisdale, "The Process of Urbanization," *Social Forces* 20 (March 1942), 311–16.

10. Lampard, "American Historians," 50.

11. Brian J. L. Berry, ed., *City Classification Handbook: Methods and Applications* (New York, 1972).

12. Roy Lubove, "Urbanization Process," 33.

13. Patrick Geddes, *Cities in Evolution* (London, 1915); Lewis Mumford, *Technics and Civilization* (New York, 1934); and *The Culture of Cities* (New York, 1938).

14. Robert E. Park *et al.*, *The City* (Chicago, 1925); Ernest W. Burgess, "The Growth of the City," *Publications of the American Sociological Society* 18 (1924), 85–97; Amos Hawley, *Human Ecology: A Theory of Community Structure* (New York, 1950); Otis D. Duncan and Leo Schnore, "Cultural, Behavioral and Ecological Perspectives in the Study of Social Organization," *American Journal of Sociology* 65 (September 1959), 132–49; Stanley Lieberson, *Ethnic Patterns in American Cities* (New York, 1963).

15. Lubove, "Urbanization Process," 36; Duncan and Schnore, "Perspectives," 135–36, 142, 144.

16. Lampard, "American Historians," 60; Lampard, "Urbanization and Social Change: On Broadening the Scope and Relevance of Urban History," in Handlin and Burchard, eds., *The Historian*, 237.

17. Ferdinand Toennies, *Community and Society* (1887), translated by C. F. Loomis (New York, 1963); Robert Redfield, *Tepoztlan: A Mexican Village* (Chicago, 1930). Redfield characterized "folk" or "rural" society as "small, isolated, non-literate and homogeneous, with a strong sense of group solidarity. The ways of living are conventionalized into that coherent system which we call a 'culture.' Behavior is traditional, spontaneous, uncritical, and personal: there is no legislation or habit of experiment and reflection for intellectual ends. Kinship, its relationships and institutions, are the type categories of experience and the familial group is the unit of action. The sacred prevails over the secular; the economy is one of status rather than of the market. These and related characterizations may be restated in terms of 'folk mentality.' " See "The Folk Society," *The American Journal of Sociology* 52 (January 1947), 293–308.

Wirth characterized "urban" society as "a relatively large, dense, and permanent settlement of heterogeneous individuals. Large numbers account for individual variability, the relative absence of intimate personal acquaintanceship [and] the segmentalization of human relations which are largely anonymous, superficial, and transitory. . . . Density involves diversification and specialization, the coincidence of close physical contact and distant social relations, glaring contrasts, a complex pattern of segregation, the predominance of formal social control, and accentuated friction. . . . Heterogeneity tends to break down rigid social structures and to produce increased mobility, instability, and insecurity and the affiliation of the individuals with a variety of intersecting and tangential social groups with a high rate of membership turnover. The pecuniary nexus tends to displace personal relations, and institutions tend to cater to mass rather than to individual requirements. The individual thus becomes effective only as he acts through organized groups. . . ." See "Urbanism as a Way of Life," *American Journal of Sociology* 44 (July 1938) 1; 1–24.

18. These four criticisms appear in Philip Hauser, "Observations on the Urban-Folk and Urban-Rural Dichotomies as Forms of Western Ethnocentrism," in Hauser and Schnore, eds., *The Study of Urbanization*, 513; Charles T. Stewart, "The Urban-Rural Dichotomy: Concepts and Uses," *American Journal of Sociology* 63 (September 1958), 157; Otis D. Duncan, "Community Size and the Rural-Urban Continuum," in Paul K. Hatt and Albert J. Reiss, eds., *Cities and Society* (Glencoe, Ill., 1957), 35–45; and Lampard, "American Historians," 56. Other excellent critiques are found in Horace Miner, "The Folk-Urban Continuum," *American Sociological Review* 17 (October 1952), 529–37; Richard Dewey, "The Rural-Urban Continuum: Real but Relatively Unimportant," *American Journal of Sociology* 66 (July 1960), 60–66; and Otis D. Duncan and Albert J. Reiss, Jr., *Social Characteristics of Urban and Rural Communities, 1950* (New York, 1956).

19. Janet Abu-Lughod, "Urban-Rural Differences as a Function of the Demographic Transition," 69, reprinted in Charles Tilly, ed., *An Urban World* (Boston, 1974).

20. Bruce Stave, "Conversation with Bayrd Still," 334–35.

21. Sam Bass Warner, Jr., *The Urban Wilderness* (New York, 1972), 60–62.

22. We differ somewhat from Warner in assigning technologies to the second and third periods, in particular the placement of the auto and the motor truck. Although they were introduced during the second period, it was not until intra-urban expressways and the interstate highway system were constructed after World War II that the auto and motor truck had their greatest impact.

23. (Cambridge, 1975); "The Origins of Public Education: A Reassessment," *History of Education Quarterly* (Winter 1977).

24. Carl F. Kaestle, "Mobility and Anxiety in a Commercial City," review of Katz, *People of Hamilton* in *Reviews in American History* 4 (June 1976), 510–11.

25. Sam Bass Warner, Jr., "If All the World Were Philadelphia: A Scaffolding for Urban History, 1774–1930," *American Historical Review* 74 (October 1968), 39; David Ward, *Cities and Immigrants: A Geography of Change in Nineteenth-Century America* (New York, 1971), makes the same point.

26. See the review of the literature on neighborhood and behavior in D. W. G. Timms, *The Urban Mosaic: Towards a Theory of Residential Differentiation* (Cambridge, England, 1971); J. S. Plant, "The Personality and an Urban Area," in Hatt and Reiss, eds., *Cities and Societies;* J. B. Mays, *Education and the Urban Child* (Liverpool, 1962); J. M. Mogey, *Family and Neighborhood* (Oxford, 1956); Elizabeth Bott, *Family and Social Network* (London, 1957); Michael Anderson, ed., *Sociology of the Family* (London, 1971); Peter Willmott and Michael Young, *Family and Class in a London Suburb* (London, 1960); H. S. Bossard, "Residential Propinquity as a Factor in Marriage Selection," *American Journal of Sociology* 38 (September 1932), 219–24; T. Caplow and R. Forman, "Neighborhood Interaction in a Homogeneous Community," *American Sociological Review* 15 (June 1950), 357–66; L. Festinger, S. Schachler, and K. Back, *Social Pressures in Informal Groups* (London, 1950); Herbert Gans, *The Levittowners* (New York, 1967); Suzanne Keller, *The Urban Neighborhood* (Princeton, N.J., 1968); Wendell Bell and M. D. Boat, "Urban Neighborhoods and Informal Social Relations," *American Journal of Sociology* 62 (January 1957), 391–98; Wendell Bell and Maryanne Force, "Urban Neighborhood Types and Participation in Formal Association," *American Sociological Review* 21 (February 1956), 25–34; Scott Greer, *The Emerging City: Myth and Reality* (New York, 1962); Scott Greer and Ella Kube, "Urbanism and Social Structure: A Los Angeles Study," in Marvin Sussman, ed., *Community Structure and Analysis* (New York, 1959); David Harvey, "Society, The City, and the Space Economy of Urbanism," *Commission on College Geography*, Resource Paper No. 18 (Washington, D.C., 1972); for a review on the literature of neighborhood and deviant behavior see Timms, *The Urban Mosaic*, 14–30; Lieberson, *Ethnic Patterns in American Cities* (New York, 1963); Lieberson, "The Impact of Residential Segregation on Ethnic Assimilation," *Social Forces* 40 (October 1961), 52–57; Milton Gordon, *Assimilation in American Life* (New York, 1964); Walter Firey, "Sentiment and Symbolism as Ecological Variables," *American Sociological Review* 10 (1945), 140–48; Gerald Suttles, *The Social Construction of Communities* (Chicago, 1972); and *The Social Order of the Slum* (Chicago, 1968).

Some of the relevant literature in geography includes P. H. Rees, "Concepts of Social Space," in B. J. L. Berry and F. E. Horton, eds., *Geographic Perspectives on Urban Systems* (Englewood Cliffs, N.J., 1970), 30–37; L. A. Brown and E. G. Moore, "The Intra-Urban Migration Process: A Perspective," *Geografiska Annaler B* 52 (1970); F. E. Horton and D. R. Reynolds, "Effects of Urban Spatial Structure on Individual Behaviour," *Economic Geography* 47 (1971), 36–48; G. Rushton, "Behavioural Correlates of Urban Spatial Structure," *Economic Geography* 47 (1971), 49–58; J. F. Kain, "The Journey-to-Work as a Determinant of Residential Location," *Papers of the Regional Science Association* 9 (1962), 137–60; Kevin Lynch, *The Image of the City* (Cambridge, England, 1960).

27. John Modell, "Suburbanization and Change in the American Family: Their Connection," *Journal of Interdisciplinary History* 9 (Spring 1975), 621–46.

28. Stephan Thernstrom and Richard Sennett, eds., *Nineteenth-Century Cities: Essays in the New Urban History* (New Haven, Ct., 1968), vii–viii.

29. *Ibid.*, viii.

30. Bruce Stave, "A Conversation with Sam Bass Warner, Jr.," *Journal of Urban History* 1 (November 1974), 92.

31. Stephan Thernstrom, *Poverty and Progress: Social Mobility in a Nineteenth-Century City* (Cambridge, Mass., 1964).

32. *Ibid.;* Peter R. Knights, *The Plain People of Boston, 1830–1860: A Study in City Growth* (New York, 1971); Howard Chudacoff, *Mobile Americans: Residential and Social Mobility in Omaha, 1880–1920* (New York, 1972); Stephan Thernstrom, *The Other Bostonians: Poverty and Progress in the American Metropolis, 1880–1970* (Cambridge, Mass., 1973); Howard M. Gitelman, *Workingmen of Waltham: Mobility in American Urban Industrial Development, 1850–1890* (Baltimore, Md., 1974); Edward Pessen, *Three Centuries of Social Mobility in America* (Lexington, Mass., 1974); Michael B. Katz, *The People of Hamilton, Canada West: Family and Class in a Mid-Nineteenth-Century City* (Cambridge, Mass., 1975); Josef J. Barton, *Peasants and Strangers: Italians, Rumanians, and Slovaks in an American City, 1890–1950* (Cambridge, Mass., 1975); Dean R. Esslinger, *Immigrants and the City: Ethnicity and Mobility in a Nineteenth-Century Midwestern Community* (Port Washington, N.Y., 1975); Michael P. Weber, *Social Change in an Industrial Town: Patterns of Progress in Warren, Pennsylvania, From the Civil War to World War I* (University Park, Pa., 1976); Thomas Kessner, *The Golden Door: Italian and Jewish Immigrant Mobility in New York City, 1880–1915* (New York, 1977); Herbert G. Gutman, "The Reality of the Rags-to-Riches 'Myth': The Case of the Paterson, New Jersey, Locomotive, Iron, and Machinery Manufacturers, 1830–1880," in Thernstrom and Sennett, eds., *Nineteenth-Century Cities*, 98–124; also, in *Nineteenth-Century Cities*, see Stephan Thernstrom, "Immigrants and WASPS: Ethnic Differences in Occupational Mobility in Boston, 1890–1940," 125–264; Stuart Blumin, "Mobility and Change in Ante-Bellum Philadelphia," 165–208; Clyde Griffen, "Workers Divided: The Effect of Craft and Ethnic Differences in Poughkeepsie, New York, 1850–1880," 49–97; see Stephan Thernstrom and Peter Knights, "Men in Motion: Some Speculations about Urban Population Mobility in Nineteenth-Century America," *Journal of Interdisciplinary History* 1 (Autumn 1970), 7–36. See also Paul B. Worthman, "Working-Class Mobility in Birmingham, Alabama, 1880–1914," in Tamara K. Hareven, ed., *Anonymous Americans: Explorations in Nineteenth-Century Social History* (Englewood Cliffs, N.J., 1971), 172–213; Richard J. Hopkins, "Status, Mobility, and the Dimensions of Change in a Southern City: Atlanta, 1870–1910," in Kenneth T. Jackson and Stanley K. Schultz, eds., *Cities in American History* (New York, 1972), 216–31; Richard J. Hopkins, "Occupational and Geographic Mobility in Atlanta, 1870–1896," *Journal of Southern History* 34 (May 1968), 200–213; Michael P. Weber, "Occupational Mobility of Ethnic Minorities in Nineteenth-Century Warren, Pennsylvania," in John E. Bodnar, ed., *The Ethnic Experience in Pennsylvania* (Lewisburg, Pa., 1973), 144–74; Edward Pessen, "Did Fortunes Rise and Fall Mercurially in Ante-Bellum America? The Tale of Two Cities: Boston and New York," *Journal of Social History* 4 (Summer 1971), 339–58; Gordon W. Kirk, Jr., and Carolyn Tyirin Kirk, "Migration, Mobility and the Transformation of the Occupational Structure in an Immigrant Community: Holland, Michigan, 1850–

1880," *Journal of Social History* 7 (Winter 1974), 142–64; William G. Robbins, "Opportunity and Persistence in the Pacific Northwest: A Quantitative Study of Early Roseburg, Oregon," *Pacific Historical Review* 39 (August 1970), 279–96; Herman R. Lantz and Ernest K. Alix, "Occupational Mobility in a Nineteenth-Century Mississippi Valley River Community," *Social Science Quarterly* 51 (September 1970), 404–8; Alwyn Barr, "Occupational and Geographic Mobility in San Antonio, 1870–1900," *Social Science Quarterly* 51 (September 1970), 396–403. Glenna Matthews, "The Community Study: Ethnicity and Success in San Jose," *Journal of Interdisciplinary History* 7 (Autumn 1976), 305–18.

Clyde and Sally Griffen's recent study of social mobility in Poughkeepsie, *Natives and Newcomers: The Ordering of Opportunity in Mid-Nineteenth-Century Pough-keepsie* (Cambridge, Mass., 1979), is one of the most comprehensive studies in the mobility genre.

33. Michael B. Katz, *The People of Hamilton*, ch. 3.

34. Katz, *ibid.*, 44; for a full elaboration see 44–175.

35. See Thernstrom and Knights, "Men in Motion," 264.

36. (Cambridge, Mass., 1973).

37. Thernstrom, *The Other Bostonians*, 240.

38. *Ibid.*, 220.

39. A lengthy discussion of the problems encountered in record linkage and a guide to other relevant literature can be found in Theodore Hershberg, Alan Burstein, and Robert Dockhorn, "Record Linkage," in Theodore Hershberg, guest editor, "A Special Issue: The Philadelphia Social History Project," *Historical Methods Newsletter* 9 (March–June 1976), 137–63.

A few brief notes drawing on our experience are in order here. It is not commonly understood that not all persons can be linked with the same degree of certainty: nor is the degree of error this procedure introduces well known. Since PSHP linkage is done by computer rather than by hand, and since our "probabilistic" approach assigns each link a weight roughly corresponding to the degree of certainty in the match, we have been able to divide our linked records into two groups: the least and most confident matches among all records we considered initially to be accurately linked. When the socioeconomic characteristics of these two groups are compared, the differences are significant and striking. For example, we found 30 percent less residential mobility among our high confidence links than among our less confident links, a finding that reveals the effect of including as linked records persons who shared nothing more than the same name.

40. "Ladders, Racing and Forest Trails," a review of *The Other Bostonians* (Cambridge, Mass., 1973) in *Labor History* 15 (Summer 1974), 463.

41. Bruce Stave, "A Conversation with Sam Bass Warner, Jr.," 101; David N. Doyle, *Irish-Americans, Native Rights and National Empires: The Structure, Divisions, and Attitudes of the Catholic Minority in the Decade of Expansion, 1890–1901* (New York, 1976); JoEllen M. Vinyard, *The Irish on the Urban Frontier: Detroit, 1850–1880* (New York, 1976); and Thomas Kessner, *The Golden Door* (New York, 1977).

42. Stephan Thernstrom, "Working Class Social Mobility in Industrial America," in John M. Laslett and Seymour Martin Lipset, eds., *Failure of a Dream? Essays in the History of American Socialism* (New York, 1973), 509.

43. Gilbert Shapiro, "Prospects for a Scientific Social History," *Journal of Social History* 10 (Winter 1976), 200–201.

44. Katz, *The People of Hamilton*, 113.

45. For an excellent example that argues for a fuller economic context, see the critical review of *The Other Bostonians* by Roberta Balstad Miller, "The Historical Study of Social Mobility: A New Perspective," *Historical Methods Newsletter* 8

(June 1975), 92–97; in many respects Katz's *The People of Hamilton* is an exception to this general criticism of the mobility studies.

46. Thernstrom, *The Other Bostonians*, 240–41.

47. Alan N. Burstein, "Residential Distribution and Mobility of Irish and German Immigrants in Philadelphia, 1850–1880" (Ph.D. dissertation, Demography, University of Pennsylvania, 1975); and his "Immigrants and Residential Mobility: The Irish and Germans in Philadelphia, 1850–1880," in this volume.

48. Stephan Thernstrom, "Reflections on the New Urban History," *Daedalus* 100 (Spring 1971), 359–75; Bruce Stave, "A Conversation with Stephan Thernstrom," *Journal of Urban History* 1 (February 1975), 198–99.

49. Thernstrom, "Reflections . . . ," 361.

50. Sam Bass Warner, Jr., "If all the World Were Philadelphia," 42.

51. *Ibid.*

52. Bruce Stave, "A Conversation with Sam Bass Warner, Jr.," 94–95.

53. Sam Bass Warner, Jr., *The Private City: Philadelphia in Three Periods of Its Growth* (Philadelphia, 1968), ix–x.

54. Bruce Stave, "A Conversation with Sam Bass Warner, Jr.," 93.

55. *Ibid.*, 94.

56. Sam Bass Warner, Jr., *The Urban Wilderness*, 57.

57. Burton Bledstein, *The Culture of Professionalism* (New York, 1976); Henrika Kuklick, "The Organization of Social Science in the United States," *American Quarterly* 23 (Spring 1976), 124–41; Thomas L. Haskell, *The Emergence of Professional Social Science: The American Social Science Association and the Nineteenth-Century Crisis of Authority* (Urbana, Ill., 1976).

58. Stuart Hampshire, "The Future of Knowledge," *New York Review of Books* 24 (March 31, 1977), 14.

59. R. Richard Wohl, "Urbanism, Urbanity, and the Historian," *University of Kansas City Review* 22 (Autumn 1955), 57; A. F. Davis, "The American Historian vs. The City," *Social Studies* 56 (1965), 134; R. Richard Wohl and A. Theodore Brown, "The Usable Past: A Study of Historical Traditions in Kansas City," *Huntington Library Quarterly* 23 (May 1960), 237–59.

60. No useful purpose can be served by presenting .urther testimony. Suffice it to say that all surveys of the urban history field, most notably those by Eric Lampard, Charles Glaab, Charles Tilly, and Roy Lubove have made the same point. Sentiments of this nature were voiced not only by American urban historians, but by their European colleagues as well. *The Study of Urban History*, a widely respected collection of essays by scholars in Great Britain edited by A. J. Dyos, was filled with calls for cooperation across disciplinary lines; similar appeals regularly appear in the French journal *Annales;* the QUANTUM group in West Germany and scholars in the Scandinavian countries have also supported the idea of interdisciplinary research. And, at least at the level of rhetoric, such sentiments are shared by scholars in disciplines other than history. For example, one of the four major recommendations made by the Social Science Research Council's Committee on Urbanization was to work toward the advancement of multidisciplinary research in the process of urbanization. Eric E. Lampard, "American Historians"; C. Glaab, "The Historian and The American City: A Bibliographic Survey," in Hauser and Schnore, eds., *The Study of Urbanization;* Charles Tilly, "The State of Urbanization," *Comparative Studies in Society and History* 10 (October 1967), 100–113; Roy Lubove, "The Urbanization Process"; H. J. Dyos, ed., *The Study of Urban History* (New York, 1968); also see a special edition of *Annales* devoted to research on the city (1970), especially the remarks of O. Zunz; for work in Norway, see Sivert Langholm, "The Ullenshaker and Kristiania Projects at the University of Oslo," paper presented at the QUANTUM-SSHA Conference (Cologne, August 10–

12, 1977); for work in Sweden, see Kurt Agren, David Gaunt, Ingrid Eriksson, John Rogers, Anders Norberg, Sune Akerman, *Aristocrats, Farmers, Proletarians: Essays in Swedish Demographic History* (Uppsala, 1973); also see Bo Ohngren, *Folk: Rorelse: Samhallsutveckling, Flyttnings-monster Och Folkrorelser: Eskilstuna, 1870–1900* (Uppsala, 1974). For earlier work in Sweden, see the results of the conference organized by Carl Goran Andrae (Uppsala, June 1973) and reported in a special issue, "History and the Computer," *Historical Methods Newsletter* 7 (June 1974). Philip M. Hauser, "Urbanization: An Overview," in Hauser and Schnore, eds., *The Study of Urbanization*, 41.

61. Caroline F. Ware, "Introduction," in Caroline F. Ware, ed., *The Cultural Approach to History* (Port Washington, N.Y., 1940), 7.

62. This may be overstated. Precious few graduate programs are consciously designed to train students for interdisciplinary research in history and the social sciences (Carnegie-Mellon University's program "Applied History and the Social Sciences" is a recent exception). Despite the real limitations of individuals, it is likely that such programs could make a valuable contribution in the effort to integrate knowledge.

63. Lawrence Stone, "History and the Social Sciences in the Twentieth Century," in Charles E. Delzell, ed., *The Future of History: Essays in the Vanderbilt University Centennial Symposium* (Nashville, Tenn., 1977), 19.

64. See Theodore Hershberg, "The Organization of Historical Research," *AHA Newsletter* 12 (October 1976), 5–6.

65. H. J. Dyos, "Agenda for Urban Historians," in H. J. Dyos, ed., *The Study of Urban History,* 4; Otis D. Duncan and Leo Schnore, "Cultural, Behavioral and Ecological Perspectives in the Study of Social Organization," 145.

Different disciplines assign different meanings to the term "behavior." As used by sociologists Duncan and Schnore, "behavior" refers to the realm of the attitudinal; as used by social historians (and in PSHP research) "behavior" refers to human actions—to what people did. Studies of behavior by social historians thus include fertility, marriage, occupational and residential mobility, mortality, etc.

66. Most of the urban "mechanisms" alluded to above are developed in the essays collected from PSHP research; in this regard, the work of historical geographer David Ward has been pioneering. See his "The Emergence of Central Immigrant Ghettoes in American Cities, 1840–1920," *Annals of the Association of American Geographers* 58 (1968), 343–59; "Some Locational Implications of the Ethnic Division of Labor in Mid-Nineteenth-Century American Cities," in Ralph E. Ehrenberg, ed., *Pattern and Research in Historical Geography* (Washington, D.C., 1975), 258–70; "The Victorian Slum: An Enduring Myth?" *Annals of the Association of American Geographers* 66 (June 1976), 323–36. Kathleen Conzen's work, *Immigrant Milwaukee, 1836–1860: Accommodation and Community in a Frontier City* (Cambridge, Mass., 1976), is one of the first works in the "new" history to provide readers with a sense of urban process, linking the individual behavior and experience with the ecological unit.

However useful a general theory of the city may be, only the detailed tracing of an immense range of variables, in context, will illuminate the dynamics of the processes here outlined. We can readily enough associate such gross phenomena as the growth of population and the rise of the centralized state, as technological change and the development of modern industry, as the disruption of the traditional household and the decline of the corporate life. But *how* these developments unfolded, what was the causal nexus among them, we shall only learn when we make out the interplay among them by focusing upon *a* city specifically in all its uniqueness.

OSCAR HANDLIN
The Historian and the City, 1963

PART I

WORK

The starting point for those who wish to write either the history of urban development or "history from the bottom up" is the city's economic system. Although simultaneous change, then as now, best describes reality, we can usefully conceive of industrialization as the engine that drove changes through the larger urban system. Transformations in the economy affected everything—individual work environments, spatial arrangements, family life, and group experience. Thus we open with two essays that examine the structure and performance of the economy and the organization and composition of the labor force in nineteenth-century Philadelphia.

Each stage in the evolution of capitalism from commercial and handicraft manufacture to industrial and monopoly forms was manifested in the structure of the economy and the labor force. The major theoretical challenge at the local level is to learn how structural transformations in the economy affected the organization of work. Quite recently sociologists and economists have made several conceptual contributions that hold considerable potential for understanding the social consequences of capitalism's development. Although these studies focus on a slightly later period than directly concerns us here, they remain valuable both as an example of the linkages that must be made for the nineteenth century and as a substantive guide for new research.

As the laissez-faire economy of the early nineteenth century gradually changed during the course of industrialization, monopolies developed in capital-intensive industries where production and profits responded well to large capital outlays. The monopoly sector thus emerged in industries where technology transformed the production process and became by far the most profitable area of the economy. The competitive sector, in contrast, emerged in industries that were labor-intensive and required limited investment capital. Wages and profits in these industries were constrained and, for these reasons, were ignored by monopoly enterprise.[1]

The labor force in each of these sectors of the economy had quite different characteristics. The standard categories—blue and white collar—will no longer suffice because they mask more fundamental distinctions. Although the new "segmented" labor force divisions differ from each other and have been variously termed "dual" or "split," the new theorists share in common a belief: that the essential defining characteristic of work was not whether it was performed in the office or on the shop floor, but whether it paid high wages, offered real opportunities for career advancement, and provided important measures of stability and job security. Jobs with these positive attributes form the "primary" labor market and those lacking them characterize the "secondary" labor market.[2]

It is here that the new "segmented" labor force theories merge with the new economic sector theory, for it is in the competitive sector where secondary labor markets disproportionately emerged. With the establishment of linkages such as this we can see how structural changes in the economy were mirrored in the organization and social experience of the labor force. We need to learn more about how economic changes affected the ethnic, racial, demographic, and life-cycle profiles of workers in the primary and secondary labor markets.

More such linkages are needed. It is not enough to list the familiar component parts of the larger transformations in the economy over the last century and a half: the separation of home and work; increased scale and productivity; the decline of the skilled crafts; the emergence of hierarchy in management and bureaucracy; the rise of organized labor; major technological advances in transportation, communications, and marketing; sophisticated capital, credit, and incorporation arrangements; and the restructuring of market forces through the growth of monopoly forms and the public sector.

Because each of these areas has been the subject of much scholarly study, there is a reassuring sense that most of the work is behind us. Yet this is only an illusion. An older set of discrete preoccupations—of economists with the factors of production, of sociologists with occupational status, of business historians with firm biographies, and labor historians with the rise of unions—is fortunately in decline. These disparate concerns and the isolation in which scholars conducted their research prevented us from seeing the process that linked major economic transformations. We require careful studies which demonstrate how these changes were timed, sequenced, and interrelated. The major thrust of the most recent scholarship on industrialization has been in this direction as disciplinary specialists have grown dissatisfied with the narrowness of previous studies.

The two essays that follow examine how structural changes in the economy affected productivity and the organization of work. In "Manufacture and Productivity: The Making of an Industrial Base," labor historian Bruce Laurie and econometrician Mark Schmitz consider the performance of the economy. They build on earlier PSHP research by economist William Whitney.[3] After locating Philadelphia within a national economic context and describing its position of dominance, they focus on the subject of productivity. As technology impacted the production process and the supervisory role of foremen grew on the shop floor, skilled workers complained about the "degradation of labor" and their loss of control over the process of production. To disentangle the independent effects that scale, technology, labor force composition, organization, and management had on productivity, the authors use econometric procedures to estimate production functions on an inter- and intra-industry basis.

Their rather dramatic finding turns neoclassical economy theory on its head: with few exceptions, Philadelphia's industries showed no economies of scale. Constant returns or diseconomies characterized production throughout the period. Scale was a "liability" in both mechanized and unmechanized firms. Small factories were the most efficient: the use of power increased productivity more effectively at lower levels of employment; and industries which mechanized "throughput" from end to end, such as fuel, were the most efficient. When power is held constant, value added per worker declined with increasing firm size. In general, the adoption of power tended to raise productivity, but scale and other factors mitigated against efficiency. All of these rich empirical findings support the argument posited by Alfred D. Chandler in his new and important study, *The Visible Hand: The Managerial Revolution in American Business*. Businesses grew larger despite diseconomies of scale, Laurie and Schmitz maintain, because employers were concerned with the *amount*—not the *rate* of return.

They call attention to the fact that Philadelphia, in contrast to most other cities, had disproportionately fewer immigrants and more women and children in its labor force. To estimate the effect of labor force composition on productivity, the authors implemented a PSHP "labor shed" methodology which joins the data found in the manufacturing and population census manuscripts using spatial proximity for work and residence locations. This approach permitted the testing of the relationships between ethnicity and work habits: was the background of immigrant laborers out of step with the industrial discipline required by the emerging factory system? The analysis revealed no systematic evidence to support the view that immigrant workers had productivity levels that differed significantly from that of native whites; in a similar fashion, worker's age, used as a proxy for industrial experience, did not show a positive relationship with productivity, suggesting that the fruits of industrial discipline were not realized with increased exposure to factory working conditions.

Laurie and Schmitz also examine how structural changes in the economy affected the organization of work. They challenge the validity of the "textile" paradigm which has long dominated the way the scholars have thought about the industrialization process. They caution against confusing industrialization with mechanization. In place of a smooth transition in which work moved from homes and small shops to large factories and individual craftsmen were converted to mechanized factory operatives, they argue for a view of "the unfolding of industrial capitalism as a complex process rather than an event with a discrete beginning and end." Their examination of the organization of work revealed considerable variation across and within industries and even within individual firms which characterized Philadelphia's economy throughout this period. An adequate understanding of the "unfolding of industrialism" requires an alternative capable of capturing and ordering this complexity. Their provisional replacement is an exciting five-part model of work environments—factory, manufactory, artisan shop, sweatshop, and outwork. Their work environment schema is based on dimensions of scale and power and has considerable value for explaining patterns of industrial location.

The second essay in this section is Bruce Laurie, Theodore Hershberg, and George Alter's "Immigrants and Industry," written in 1973. In important respects it laid the groundwork for "Manufacture and Productivity" and for much of the PSHP's subsequent conceptual efforts. It follows rather than precedes the latter because "Manufacture and Productivity" offers a more thorough introduction to the structure and performance of the city's economy which, in turn, provides the appropriate context for the extended discussion of the ethnic differentials in the city's labor force found in "Immigrants and Industry." By combining evidence from the manuscript schedules of the manufacturing and population census, the authors were able to analyze how Philadelphia's industrial structure changed over the thirty-year period and how these changes affected the experience of the city's ethnic groups. To deal with a remarkably diversified economy which manufactured "everything from silk handkerchiefs to iron rails" and was characterized by "unevenness in industrial development," the manufacturing sector, which accounted for more than one of every two jobs, was divided into two groups. Firms in the major "Producer" and "Consumer" industries were compared in their use of mechanized power, capital investment, number of employees, hours worked, profits, and wages.

Several of the empirical results challenge a good deal of the conventional wisdom regarding the "Age of Industrialization." The detailed wage data reported on a firm-by-firm basis, for example, lead to a series of important revisions in our understanding of the industrial and occupational structure. The best work settings in terms of career opportunities, security, working conditions, and wages were large factories, not small shops. For skilled workers, the larger the firm, the higher the wage; this was only somewhat less true for unskilled laborers. So considerable was the variation in wages paid to workers, both within the skilled job category and between the skilled and unskilled categories, that the empirical validity of the occupational ranking schema used in the mobility studies genre was called into question. Indeed, it is for this reason—despite the PSHP's initial developmental interest in social mobility—that no essay focusing primarily upon individual career mobility is included in this volume.

Instead, the essay argues cogently for the importance of understanding work setting and work content—that is, the placing of individual occupational titles within the appropriate industrial context—before undertaking the actual study of mobility. Our understanding of career mobility should be reexamined in light of the evidence presented regarding existing stereotypes of "laborers" and the "unskilled" ranks in general; "informal apprenticeship" and "career potential," depending upon firm size and sector of the economy, are offered as possible new categories.

The ordinary person of the last century did not embark upon a career without constraints. The most severe handicaps were faced by blacks. They were so excluded from the broad range of opportunities generated by industrialization that figures on black employment were not included in the essay's data tables.[4] On the other hand, the job data constitute unmistakable evidence that considerable opportunity awaited *whites* who settled in a city with an expanding economy. Though the job distributions of the immigrants changed little between 1850 and 1880, their initial patterns were relatively impressive: roughly one-third of the Irish and two-thirds of the Germans held skilled jobs throughout the thirty years. The Germans began and ended the period in a position much superior to the Irish in the occupational hierarchy. American-born sons of immigrants considered as a group, however, did much better than their fathers; their occupational profiles came increasingly to resemble those of native whites. The second generation Irish did best. They closed the gap that had separated their fathers and German immigrants in 1850 and 1880 and in the latter year were better off than German immigrants had been in either year. Yet, as the authors remind us, "although each group rapidly deserted the sphere of its fathers . . . Irish immigrants were so dependent upon casual labor and Germans so concentrated in the older crafts that their sons could not help but remain heavily represented in those occupations."

The economy of the particular city in which all persons pursued their careers was a mediator of a different sort. It supplied the raw materials, as it were, from which careers were forged. In economic terms, it constituted the "demand" side, and the labor force, the "supply" side, of the career arena. It was the specific nature of a changing industrial structure, and the opportunities it generated interacting with the socioeconomic and demographic characteristics of the labor force that set the stage for the historical drama we study.

NOTES

1. James O'Connor, *The Fiscal Crisis of the State* (New York: St. Martin's Press, 1973); Harry Braverman, *Labor, Monopoly and Capital* (New York: Monthly Review Press, 1974); Eugene P. Ericksen and William L. Yancey, "Immigrants and Their Opportunities: Philadelphia, 1850–1936," paper presented at AAAS (Houston, Texas: January 1979).

2. See David M. Gordon, *Theories of Poverty and Underemployment*, ch. 4, "Dual Labor Market Theory" (Lexington, Mass.: D. C. Heath, 1972); Michael J. Piore, "The Dual Labor Market: Theory and Implications," and Bennett Harrison, "Education and Underemployment in the Ghetto," both in D. M. Gordon, ed., *Problems in Political Economy: An Urban Perspective* (Lexington, Mass.: D. C. Heath, 1971); and Edna Bonacich, "A Theory of Ethnic Antagonism: The Split Labor Market," *American Sociological Review* (October 1972).

3. Whitney reported his initial findings, "Manufacturing Location at Mid-Century," paper presented at Social Science History Association (Philadelphia: October 1976).

4. The occupational structure of blacks is discussed in separate detail in several of the essays in *Group Experience* and is the subject of systematic comparison with immigrants and native whites in T. Hershberg, A. Burstein, E. Ericksen, S. Greenberg, W. Yancey, "A Tale of Three Cities: Blacks and Immigrants in Philadelphia, 1850–1880, 1930 and 1970," *The Annals* 441 (January 1979), 55–81; also in this volume.

2. Manufacture and Productivity:
The Making of an Industrial Base, Philadelphia, 1850–1880

BRUCE LAURIE   MARK SCHMITZ

Introduction

The purpose of this essay is threefold. As the opening article in this section, it attempts to lay the groundwork for much of what follows by
examining the industrial base of mid-nineteenth-century Philadelphia. The
first part is dedicated to this task and to drawing comparisons between local industry and that of the nation as a whole. The second part attempts
to provide an alternative to conventional views of industrial change as
represented in what historians call the "textile paradigm." Here we show
that industrial growth proceeded far more unevenly than the textile paradigm would have us believe. Traditional and transitional forms of production existed along with factories as late as 1880, and the character of
production in the factories themselves varied significantly among industries.
This part seeks to capture such variation by treating work environments as
ideal types. The third part, an exercise in econometrics, presents findings
on the productivity of local industries. Using Cobb-Douglass production
functions, it reports the labor, capital, and total factor productivity of a
wide range of industrial categories, and, in keeping with the themes developed in the second part, shows striking variation within and among
them. It also attempts to account for the observed patterns by invoking
the work environments sketched out in the second part.

We wish to thank Professor Theodore Hershberg, Director of the Philadelphia
Social History Project, who conceptualized this paper and was its most inspiring
critic. We also express our appreciation to Stanley Engerman, Alfred D. Chandler,
David Montgomery, Louis Galambos, and Mark Stern for their helpful comments.
Finally, we acknowledge our intellectual debt to Dean William F. Whitney of the
University of Pennsylvania, whose pioneering work on productivity identified dis-
economies of scale and inspired much of what follows.

Philadelphia and the Nation

Though Philadelphia's colonial reputation as a commercial port and distributor of European manufactures carried over into the nineteenth century, few chroniclers of the antebellum city failed to comment on the importance and diversity of manufacturing. These themes emerge as early as 1811 when resident demographer John Mellish reported a mix of artisanal and industrial pursuits, and added, with some admiration, that local manufactures were "rising into great importance. . . ."[1] Twenty years later the McLane Committee uncovered evidence of brisk industrial development, stressing the recent proliferation of textile mills on the banks of the Schuylkill, and by the time Edwin T. Freedley published his exhaustive survey of area firms and industries in the middle of the 1850s, Philadelphia had achieved unquestioned industrial prominence.[2] Men of industry gradually displaced the heralded merchant princes in popular lore.

It was difficult to find a Pennsylvanian more rhapsodic over Philadelphia's industrial maturation than Daniel J. Morrell. Premier iron founder and leading radical Republican, Morrell rarely lost the opportunity to promote the interests of domestic manufacture or industrial Pennsylvania whether in public or private life. He had occasion to combine both causes in the 1870s upon presenting fellow Congressmen with a memorial from Philadelphia public officials urging the location of the upcoming Centennial Exhibition in their city. Repeating the paeans of previous boosters, Morrell proclaimed: "If it is conceded that an industrial exhibition is to be made in the city where the industries are found in greatest variety and perfection, no further enumeration of Philadelphia's advantages or claims need be made. New York may justly claim to be the commercial capital, but Philadelphia is certainly the industrial capital of America. Today Philadelphia is the first manufacturing city on this continent, and the second in the world, London being the first." Local industry, he emphasized, "is varied to suit all tastes and capacities. . . ."[3]

Carried away by his own partisanship and engulfed perhaps in the period's penchant for excess, Morrell distorted the record. As New Yorkers were fond of reminding rivals, their city won the race for industrial supremacy at mid-century and retained industrial leadership thirty years later. No urban center boasted a larger manufacturing labor force or greater gross product, but Philadelphia was a close second in both categories and among the leaders in others. By the Civil War only a few of New England's textile counties and Essex County, New Jersey, the home of Newark, had a higher proportion of industrial workers, and Philadelphians contributed more than their share to the nation's commodity pool.[4] Making up about 2 percent of the population in 1850, they fabricated 6 percent of the national prod-

Table 1.   Total Employment by Industry, 1850 and 1880

Industry	1850		1880		Percent Change
	Number	% of Total	Number	% of Total	
Food	1494	2.6	5366	3.1	259
Refined Food	696	1.2	1321	0.8	89
Shoes & Boots	6249	10.8	8362	4.8	34
Hats & Caps	1837	3.2	2940	1.7	60
Clothing	10532	18.2	34548	19.8	228
Textiles	10422	18.0	37741	21.6	262
Iron & Steel	1203	2.1	3657	2.1	204
Machine Tools & Hardware	3920	6.7	12549	7.2	220
Lumber & Wood	2357	4.1	4878	2.8	107
Furniture	1417	2.4	3661	2.4	158
Construction	3884	6.7	12914	7.4	232
Shipbuilding	949	1.6	2739	1.6	189
Fuel	298	5.1	3328	1.9	1017
Chemicals	629	1.1	3283	1.9	422
Glass	465	0.8	535	0.3	15
Paper	323	0.5	3216	1.8	896
Printing & Publishing	2096	3.6	7710	4.4	268
Blacksmiths	569	1.0	509	0.3	−11
Traditional Metals	545	0.9	2259	1.3	314
Others	8073	13.9	23248	13.3	188
TOTALS	57958	100	174,764	100	202

Source: U.S. Manuscript Censuses of Manufactures, 1850 and 1880.

uct, and they held their own in the ensuing years despite the frenzied economic activity and meteoric rise of manufacturing towns across the United States. In 1880 they accounted for less than 2 percent of the nation's population, but nearly 5 percent of its product.[5]

No one could fault Morrell, however, for accenting the city's remarkably broad industrial base. Unlike the shoe and textile towns of New England, the iron and mining hamlets of East and West Pennsylvania, and other locales specializing in a single product, Philadelphia was a virtual emporium of commodity production in 1850 and 1880. Workers fashioned an endless roster of goods and, as Table 1 shows, no one industry dominated. Textiles and the needle trades, the leaders in both years, hired about a third of the labor force in 1850 and slightly more than 40 percent in 1880. The building trades, boot and shoe manufacture, heavy industry and metallurgy absorbed between 5 and 11 percent, and five more trades, including hat making and printing, employed between 2 and 4 percent. A laundry list of business had under 2 percent (see Table1). Local manufacturers led the nation in many products according to an 1880 study which ranked the seven major industrial centers by gross product in thirty-seven categories. This survey placed Philadelphians first in six designations—bricks and tiles, drugs and chemicals, shipbuilding, mixed textiles, woolens, dying and finishing—second in twelve, and third in five. They were eclipsed only by Lynn, Massachusetts, shoe manufacturers in footwear and only by New Yorkers in nine categories, the most notable of which were men's and women's clothing, foundry and machine-shop products, and printing and publishing.[6]

These industries had mixed histories in this thirty-year period. Trades rooted in the colonial past, or what historians loosely refer to as the handicrafts, showed a bimodal pattern of growth. They either failed to keep pace with the 202 percent increase in the labor force or modestly outstripped this standard. Sluggish crafts, which seem to have lost out to competitors in other cities, included boots and shoes (34), hats and caps (60), skins (56), jewelry (85), and furniture and home furnishings (158). Growth trades, chiefly suppliers of local necessities and largely immune to outside competition, encompassed food processing (259), printing and publishing (268), clothing (228), and building construction (232). Apart from such prospering handicrafts, the pursuits that kept the city in the vanguard of expansion were the offspring of the industrial revolution itself. These newer industries without colonial legacies or the weight of craft traditions embraced machine tools and hardware (220), fuel (1017), textiles (262), chemicals (422), and paper (896). With the emergence of these businesses and the selective growth of the old crafts, Philadelphia began to exchange its suit of handicraft clothing for the garb of modern manufacture (see Table 1).

The national origins and sex of those who staffed the mills and workshops differed from the national aggregate. Immigrants of Irish, English, and German birth, whose numbers grew to 42 percent of the national labor force by 1880, did not bulk as large in Philadelphia. West Europeans were only 29 percent of the population in 1850 and 31 percent in 1880, which gave the city one of the most native-born working classes both in the nation and in the Northeast. Only five industrial towns and cities in the region—Camden, New Haven, Lynn, Reading, and Wilmington—had a higher proportion of native-born wage earners.[7] The reverse was true with regard to women gainfully employed. Single and married women constituted about a fourth of the national labor force in 1880, but made up at least 30 percent of Philadelphia's industrial workers. And few cities outside of New England textile towns, which customarily relied heavily on

Table 2. Adult Women in Industry, 1850 and 1880

Industry	1850		1880	
	Number of Females	% of Adults in Industry	Number of Females	% of Adults in Industry
Food	88	5.9	539	10.9
Refined Food	0	0	1	0
Shoes & Boots	1514	24.2	2532	32.2
Hats & Caps	1213	66.0	1510	53.3
Clothing	6422	61.0	19,555	59.5
Textiles	4110	39.4	18,194	49.0[a]
Iron & Steel	0	0	43	1.3
Machine Tools & Hardware	26	0	230	2.0
Lumber & Wood	203	8.6	239	5.4
Furniture	133	9.3	156	4.5
Construction	10	0	44	0
Shipbuilding	0	0	10	0
Fuel	5	1.7	0	0
Chemicals	84	13.5	517	16.1
Glass	0	0	23	4.7
Paper	197	60.1	1843	60.0
Printing & Publishing	600	28.6	1412	21.4
Blacksmiths	13	2.3	0	0
Traditional Metals	1	0	113	5.0
Others	1001	9.8	4010	17.6
Totals	15620	26.2	51,033	30.5

Source: U.S. Manuscript Censuses of Manufactures, 1850, 1870, 1880.

[a]Number of employees is based on percentage of females in 1870 returns. The 1880 textile figures derived from the manuscript schedules are inaccurate because many of these firms are not found on the extant documents, though they were counted in the published statistics. A subsequent survey by Blodget provides data on total employment but does not differentiate by sex. Thus, the 1870 proportions are used. See Lorin Blodget, *Census of Manufactures of Philadelphia* (Philadelphia: 1883).

women, surpassed the Quaker City in this regard. Of the twenty-five principal manufacturing centers in 1880 only New York, Boston, and Baltimore had a larger share of women in industry (see Table 2).[8]

The Process of Industrialization

The industrial revolution once evoked lively exchanges among European scholars over the social origins of the proletariat, the changing standard of living, and the decline in fertility and mortality. This pungent discourse had no counterpart in the United States and has receded in Great Britain as scholars have turned from the issues that preoccupied two generations of academicians. Beneath the debate, however, there was an unspoken consensus on how industrialization took shape if not on how it affected the pocketbooks of those who sweated over the machines. Writers on both sides of the Atlantic generally agreed that the shift to mass production involved the consolidation of labor into larger units, the incorporation of power-driven machinery and abridgement of hand techniques, and the coordination and integration of several work processes, and that these developments took place concurrently or in rapid succession. This convention, as Raphael Samuel observes, is an artifact of early scholarship's concentration on the textile industry and the subsequent extrapolating of the textile paradigm to industry as a whole.[9] If the industrial revolution was born in the shops of Lancashire, so was the study of it. The pioneering works on industrialization, whether cast in satanic Lancashire or paternalistic Lowell, told the familiar tale in which production shifted from home and small shop to the factory and hand techniques yielded to mighty machines. There were variations on this plot. Early New England textile bosses who organized mills in advance of the power loom had to give out yarn spun on machines to outworkers (just as merchant capitalists and general store proprietors in the shoe and clothing trades supplied cottagers with cloth and leather cut in central shops). But this awkward arrangement, born out of necessity, was a brief interlude in an otherwise smooth and linear progression to higher forms of production and organization. Outwork and small business died a quick death or were relegated to marginal importance when technological advances brought weaving and its equivalents up to par with spinning, and entrepreneurs outfitted mills and workshops with the latest machines. This centralization of tasks previously performed in disparate work settings drew growing streams of men and women from farm and small town to city and textile village where they were transformed from farmer and artisan to machine tender.[10]

Recently scholars have begun to question the wisdom of extrapolating this model beyond the beaten path of textiles. Writing in the neoclassical and Marxian traditions, they read the record from polar perspectives, but are at one in envisioning the unfolding of industrial capitalism as a complex process rather than an event with a discrete beginning and end.[11] One of the more holistic and intriguing contributions to the mounting literature of revisionism is Alfred D. Chandler's treatment of the rise of the large multiunit corporation. Contrary to those who would homogenize the history of factory production, Chandler stresses interindustry variation in the growth of scale, the application of powered machinery, and the coordination of work processes or "throughput." Early and mid-nineteenth-century entrepreneurs, he tells us, faced different constraints which dictated diverse

Table 3. Percentage of Workers in Firms Using Power,
by Industry, 1850 and 1880

Industry	Percentage of Workers	
	1850	1880
Fuel	88.3	98.5
Iron & Steel	85.4	95.1
Refined Food	61.8	93.4
Shipbuilding	2.5	91.2
Textiles	64.0	87.9
Machine Tools & Hardware	62.5	86.5
Chemicals	62.8	86.0
Printing & Publishing	30.5	74.5
Paper	61.6	64.1
Traditional Metals	32.2	56.8
Lumber & Wood	19.0	55.5
Clothing	10.3	52.9
Furniture	9.6	44.9
Food	15.4	44.5
Glass	3.9	37.2
Hats & Caps	3.3	35.8
Shoes & Boots	0.1	28.1
Construction	19.7	26.1
Blacksmiths	2.1	7.4
Others	32.0	57.7
Totals	27.6	63.5

Source: U.S. Manuscript Censuses of Manufactures, 1850 and 1880.

tactics in gearing production to mass consumption. Master craftsmen in most trades simply took on additional workers; merchants and some manufacturers of shoes and clothing resorted to the putting out system and, to some extent, to the division of labor; textile and metallurgical entrepreneurs alone deployed power-driven equipment in addition to inflating employment rolls. Industrial changes in the following decades altered this pattern somewhat, but such variations in the scale and mechanization of antebellum production foreshadowed Gilded-Age arrangements.[12]

The broad outlines of Philadelphia industry at mid-century confirm this impression of unevenness in firm size and use of power sources. In 1850 only 10 percent of all employers, employing one-third of the labor force, utilized steam engines or water wheels, and these innovators were confined chiefly to textiles and heavy industry. Entrepreneurs and masters

Table 4. Distribution of Workers by Firm Size, 1850 and 1880

Industry	1850				1880			
	1-5	6-25	26-50	51+	1-5	6-25	26-50	51+
Food	65.5	25.6	8.9	0	42.7	15.5	13.8	28.0
Refined Food	24.6	59.8	15.6	0	8.1	59.9	32.0	0
Shoes & Boots	17.5	35.3	11.3	35.8	9.8	17.9	10.2	62.0
Hats & Caps	15.6	41.0	15.8	27.5	5.4	21.3	17.7	55.6
Clothing	3.1	26.4	14.6	55.8	2.1	6.7	6.9	84.1
Textiles	2.6	12.0	13.8	71.6	1.0	7.1	9.8	82.1
Iron & Steel	2.6	16.1	14.8	66.5	1.1	7.7	16.0	75.2
Machine Tools & Hardware	11.5	23.0	12.8	52.7	4.5	16.1	16.5	62.8
Lumber & Wood	24.8	48.3	14.8	12.1	14.3	30.6	15.8	39.2
Furniture	19.4	38.7	21.6	20.3	11.0	24.2	19.3	45.0
Construction	9.4	34.7	29.0	26.8	17.4	32.6	14.1	35.9
Shipbuilding	7.9	29.4	11.6	51.1	1.6	7.2	1.7	89.4
Fuel	25.8	74.2	0	0	0	3.5	5.2	90.7
Chemicals	14.9	48.6	17.3	19.1	3.8	17.2	10.2	68.7
Glass	2.8	7.5	37.0	52.7	7.7	42.2	10.2	29.9
Paper	2.8	57.0	22.0	18.3	0.5	11.2	12.4	75.9
Printing & Publishing	3.6	26.1	28.6	41.2	2.9	17.2	21.2	58.7
Blacksmiths	70.1	29.9	0	0	74.2	20.0	5.9	0
Traditional Metals	42.2	25.9	17.2	14.7	17.2	27.2	16.5	39.1
Others	17.4	35.1	17.8	29.7	10.7	23.8	14.1	51.3
Totals	12.4	28.4	16.1	43.1	7.0	15.1	11.9	65.9

Source: U.S. Manuscript Censuses of Manufactures, 1850 and 1880.

in the handicrafts were a study in contrast. Regardless of calling, they ran workshops without power-driven machinery and often without foot-powered equipment or sophisticated hand tools (see Table 3). Big business was not yet dominant or very much in evidence. Ownership was still in the hands of individuals and partners—incorporation required a special act of the legislation until 1875 when a general incorporation law was passed—and existing large firms concentrated on production. The corporately owned, multiunit industrial giant awaited the 1880s and the merger movement of the 1890s. Firms with less than twenty-six employees hired as many workers as those with more than fifty (about 40 percent of the work force), and consolidation, much like mechanization, was largely the province of newer industry (see Table 4). The largest textile and metallurgical plants absorbed one-half to three-quarters of their respective workforces, while the equivalent handicraft operations claimed between a tenth and a half of their labor forces.

Technological advances in the next thirty years armed entrepreneurs thirsting to expand and modernize with decided advantages over their forebears and laid the groundwork for large-scale, machine-powered production. Urban population growth and industrial development itself enriched local demand for consumer and capital goods, and the spread and integration of the rail matrix opened up regional and national markets. Greater exploitation of coal seams in the western hinterland offered bountiful supplies of cheap fuel; and new technologies as well as improved devices of every description—from better steam engines to versatile lathes and McKay stitchers—were widely advertised. Prohibitively expensive or simply unavailable in the past, this battery of machines and equipment was brought within the budgets of entrepreneurs, and many took advantage of declining costs and accessibility.[13] By 1880 one manufacturer in five, twice as many as in 1850, used power, and such employers hired two-thirds of the labor force, compared with a third at mid-century. The concentration of ownership and consolidation of labor into larger units also proceeded apace, as firms with more than fifty workers jumped from 4.5 to 7.6 percent of all businesses, while the proportion of small and medium-sized business hardly changed at all. The labor force, meanwhile, grew by a hefty 202 percent, the largest relative gain (72.5 percent) occurring in the 1850s, but the largest establishments captured a disproportionate share of the increase. Where in 1850 they hired two-fifths of the workers, in 1880 they claimed two-thirds (see Table 5).

The fact remains, however, that the leaps in scale and mechanization recorded in these decades narrowed without completely closing the gap between new and old enterprise. Mechanization advanced uniformly among pursuits already wedded to powered machinery in 1850 and among the newest industries, so that in 1880 upward of 87 percent of the textile, metallurgical, paper, fuel, and chemical workers found employment in plants fitted with water wheels or, more likely, steam engines. Progress was slower and more uneven among the handicrafts where the range of workers in powered factories varied from three-fourths of the printers to under a third of the shoemakers. Variation between the old and new, or craft and industrial, also persisted to some extent with regard to the distribution of workers across small, medium, and large firms. The overwhelming majority of textile, metallurgical, fuel, and other industrial workers concentrated in the largest establishments in 1880, but craftsmen migrated there with less alacrity or not at all. Printers and compositors resembled industrial workers in this respect, and they were untypical craftsmen. Furniture workers were equally divided between the large and small firms, and shoe and clothing workers were deceptively concentrated in big businesses. Though most were employed by large manufacturers, goodly shares of them worked

Table 5. Distribution of Firms and Employees by Firm Size, 1850–1880

(Row %s) Year	(a) Number of Firms Firm size by employees 1-5	6-25	26-50	51 +	Total
1850	2621 (57.7)	1458 (32.1)	257 (5.7)	206 (4.5)	4542 (100.0)
1860	3678 (58.1)	1893 (29.9)	372 (5.0)	387 (6.1)	6330 (100.0)
1870	5146 (61.5)	2158 (25.8)	515 (6.2)	547 (6.5)	8366 (100.0)
1880	5713 (62.3)	2181 (23.8)	569 (6.2)	700 (7.6)	9163 (100.0)
	(b) Number of Employees				
1850	7182 (12.4)	16472 (28.4)	9319 (16.1)	24985 (43.1)	57958 (100.0)
1860	9969 (10.0)	22099 (22.1)	13610 (13.6)	54315 (54.3)	99993 (100.0)
1870	11699 (8.7)	26345 (19.6)	18864 (14.0)	77593 (57.7)	134501 (100.0)
1880	12300 (7.0)	26455 (15.1)	20861 (11.9)	115,148 (65.9)	174,764 (100.0)

Source: U.S. Manuscript Censuses of Manufactures, 1850–1880.

at home under the putting out system as late as 1880. Virtually no black-smith employed outside of heavy industry plied his trade in a large establishment (see Table 4).

This unevenness in the deployment of power sources among industries existed within industry and within a given firm. Precious few large employers, including those who replaced waterwheels with steam engines or boosted horsepower capacity with more powerful or multiple engines, mechanized the production process from end to end or, in Chandler's words, completely coordinated the throughput. Their establishments hosted a mix of new, middle range, and old technologies and were a far cry from the paradigms of modernization depicted in conventional historiography. Pockets of hand techniques and labor-intensive work, survivals of the past and creations of the industrial revolution, could be found in the most advanced work settings. Workers who tended machines, moreover, were not necessarily reduced to semiskilled automatons, captives of steam power. They confronted intensified and heavily scrutinized work routines and experienced the erosion of skills, but as revisionist historians insist, it is time to discard the romantic notion that artisans and hand workers were the sole repositories of skill, expertise, and autonomy at the workplace. The machine tender, whom traditional historians demote to the ranks of the semiskilled, emerges in recent scholarship as a skilled worker in new clothing, exercising judgment in his work and some control over output.[14] Mid-nineteenth-century production arrangements were far more complex than the partisans of the textile paradigm would suggest. Employers rarely ironed out the bottlenecks and discontinuities in production, and small business and outwork, though on the decline, lasted long after historians pronounced their passing.

A comprehensive view of the unfolding of industrialism thus requires an alternative to the textile paradigm—an alternative that captures this complexity. A helpful, though provisional, replacement is a model positing the coexistence of five discrete but occasionally overlapping work settings—factories, manufactories, sweatshops, outwork, and artisanal or neighborhood shops—distinguished by scale and mechanization as the first order of differentiation and market orientation as the second. Each setting engaged different shares of the workforce at various points in time, and some of them cut across trades and industries, so that fellow tradesmen often went about their work in vastly dissimilar surroundings.

Factories. Factories refer to any industrial plant equipped with power sources in the form of waterwheels, steam engines, or any combination of these. Factories dominated the industrial landscape of single-industry towns in New England, upstate New York, and western Pennsylvania, but in the diversified economy that was Philadelphia, they cast a modest net. In 1850, they enmeshed most metallurgical workers, perhaps half the textile hands, and only handfuls of craftsmen, who collectively totaled about a third of the manual labor force. This small and relatively homogeneous group doubled in the following decades, but in 1880 factory workers still hearkened from essentially the same trades as they had three decades before. Textile and metallurgical workers alone were fully half the factory corps; fuel and chemical workers contributed another 5 percent; and craftsmen, drawn disproportionately from various trades, made up the rest.

The ethnic and sexual composition of these workers and the character of their work depended heavily on the industry in question and on the period under study. Textile mills were powerful magnets for West European immigrants by mid-century when the Irish numbered about three-fourths of the male operatives. Contrary to demographic patterns observed elsewhere, however, native-white Americans (of American and Irish parentage) gradually displaced immigrant cotton and woolen workers (see Table 6). Sixty percent of the men were native-born Americans in 1880, but males were a bare majority in the industry. Women of various nationalities accounted for about half of the operatives (see Table 2). There was strict sexual and age-based division of labor that assigned the skilled

Table 6. Distribution of Industrial Employment by Ethnic Group, 1850 and 1880
(Males only; Manufacturing sector only)

	Blacks			Irish		
	% 1850	% 1880	% Change	% 1850	% 1880	% Change
Food	1.0	0.7	−30.0	13.3	6.0	−54.9
Refined Food	0.7	0.5	−28.6	19.2	11.7	−39.1
Shoes & Boots	1.6	1.4	−12.5	22.1	22.6	+2.3
Hats & Caps	0.1	0.5	+400.0	18.5	10.1	−45.4
Clothing	1.4	0.7	−50.0	23.4	13.3	−43.2
Textiles	0.2	0.3	+50.0	77.8	26.3	−66.2
Iron & Steel	0.4	0.3	−25.0	16.3	20.3	+24.5
Machine Tools & Hardware	0.3	0.4	+33.3	13.0	11.9	−8.5
Lumber & Wood	0.8	0.5	−37.5	10.0	9.7	−3.0
Furniture	1.6	1.8	+12.5	8.3	3.9	−53.0
Construction	2.3	2.5	+8.7	17.8	13.1	−26.4
Shipbuilding	1.1	0.3	−72.7	3.5	6.3	+80.0
Fuel	0.4	1.7	+325.0	11.8	18.6	−57.6
Chemicals	0.0	1.2	—	11.1	14.7	+32.4
Glass	0.0	0.1	—	22.9	12.0	−47.6
Paper	0.0	0.3	—	13.8	18.1	+31.2
Printing & Publishing	0.2	0.5	+150.0	9.2	4.6	−50.0
Blacksmiths	0.5	0.3	−40.0	22.0	27.8	+26.4
Traditional Metals	0.0	0.0	0.0	12.0	9.1	−24.2
Others	0.6	0.7	+16.7	14.5	3.7	−74.5
Total Industrial Sector‡	1.2	1.0	−16.7	22.9	13.5	−41.0

Source: U.S. Censuses of Population, 1850 and 1880.

*Includes second-generation Irish and Germans, i.e., those born in United States having foreign fathers.

†These totals differ from those in Table 1 because they enumerate only males and because the sources from which they are derived are different. The Censuses of Manufactures provide better estimates of industry size by employment than the Censuses of Population because many occupations listed in the population schedules are not clearly associated with a par-

Germans			Native-White Americans*			TOTAL N†	
% 1850	% 1880	% Change	% 1850	% 1880	% Change	1850	1880
43.1	40.1	− 7.0	42.6	53.3	+ 15.7	2,240	6,993
65.9	56.9	− 13.7	14.2	30.8	+ 116.9	422	1,342
21.4	30.9	+ 44.4	55.0	45.2	− 17.8	6,398	6,574
6.4	13.0	+ 103.2	75.0	76.4	+ 1.9	704	1,013
32.3	41.9	+ 29.7	42.9	44.1	+ 2.8	3,121	4,615
8.6	13.1	+ 52.3	13.4	60.4	+ 350.7	4,863	11,059
4.9	5.6	+ 14.3	78.4	73.8	− 5.9	719	3,585
13.3	11.0	− 17.3	73.4	76.7	+ 4.5	2,961	10,180
10.6	15.9	+ 50.0	78.6	73.9	− 6.0	2,558	5,433
32.1	35.7	+ 11.2	58.0	58.7	+ 1.2	1,708	2,653
4.0	5.4	+ 35.0	76.0	79.0	+ 3.9	10,732	21,077
0.9	2.4	+ 166.7	94.4	91.0	− 3.6	960	1,078
5.5	6.2	+ 12.7	82.4	73.5	− 10.8	255	1,225
13.2	25.0	+ 89.4	75.8	59.2	− 21.9	190	593
13.3	15.7	+ 18.0	63.8	72.2	+ 13.2	301	935
3.2	7.1	+ 121.9	83.0	74.5	− 10.2	188	701
6.4	6.2	− 3.2	84.2	88.7	+ 5.3	1,539	4,517
11.8	12.9	+ 9.3	65.6	59.0	− 10.1	1,765	2,869
12.3	11.0	− 10.6	75.6	79.9	+ 5.7	698	2,027
15.8	18.1	+ 14.6	69.1	77.6	+ 12.3	4,332	9,520
14.9	16.7	+ 12.1	61.1	68.8	+ 12.6	46,654	97,989

ticular industry type. For example, a person listed as a "laborer" in the manuscript population census may work as a textile operative but there is no way of assigning that individual to the textile industry on the basis of that occupational designation.

‡Excludes workers listed as "laborers" in the Censuses of Population.

jobs of mule spinning, dying, and printing to men, carding, ring spinning, and most weaving to women, and various menial tasks to youths. The term "skilled" is used advisedly, since most textile jobs were something less than trades. None involved formal apprenticeship or extended instruction, and all were passed on to aspiring spinners and dyers with relative ease through on-the-job training.[15]

Production itself conformed closely to the textile paradigm. The sequential tasks that turned fiber into cloth were harnessed to machinery before 1850. This expedited the centralization of work and left little room for hand work in the mill apart from loading and unloading materials and delivering stock and bobbins from room to room. The lone outposts of non-machine work in 1850 were weaving and, to a lesser extent, dying. Hand-loom weavers hired by merchant capitalists worked at home or in sheds, and dyers toiled in independently owned small shops. Otherwise, all operations—including carding, spinning, most weaving, and some dying and finishing—were performed on power-driven machines under the same roof.[16]

Here lay the uniqueness of textile mills and the key to their development. Since the sweeping mechanical innovations occurred before 1850, Gilded-Age entrepreneurs were relieved of pushing forward the frontiers of technology. Some effort and capital were invested in completing the integration of processes heretofore given out to contractors and outworkers. Most producers, however, concentrated on expanding their operations without changing existing methods of production. In addition to hiring more workers and building larger physical plants, they increased spindlage and loom capacity, shifted from water to steam power, and speeded up the machinery.[17]

Metal and machinery production differed from cloth manufacture in a number of particulars. The work demanded far more skill and training, and factories hired a wide range of highly skilled workers, apprentices and helpers, and large numbers of unskilled laborers. Immigrants of Irish and German birth moved into unskilled jobs and, as will be shown in the following essay, some of their sons gained access to skilled positions by 1880. But native-born Americans monopolized the skilled work throughout the period (see Table 6).

Mid-century metallurgical plants bore only a superficial resemblance to textile mills. Instead of occupying a single building of three or four stories, they encompassed vast complexes that consumed entire city blocks. Alfred Jenks's machine works, which was representative of the largest shops, included a foundry (130 × 50 feet), a blacksmith shop (120 × 50 feet), a brass foundry with cleaning and storage rooms (190 × 32 feet), a huge machine shop of three stories (225 × 30 feet), and storage bins, sheds, and yards covering 160,000 square feet. Each department or room housed groups of skilled workers who plied their trades simultaneously with the assistance of apprentices, helpers, and unskilled laborers and who used both hand tools and some of the most modern machines and equipment in the world. Lathes were found along with chisels and crude grinding wheels in the machine shops; steam-powered hammers and old anvils were within arm's reach of the blacksmiths; cranes began to compete with hand hoists in the assembly rooms.[18]

This was but prologue to a burst of innovation during the Civil War and the post-war era. Jenks and his counterparts, exercising their voracious appetite for technological improvement, designed their own machines and installed a litany of inventions.[19] Matthias Baldwin and his successors transformed their famous locomotive works into a gallery of machinery replete with railroad tracks that shuttled box cars laden with raw materials between storage yards and production rooms, and mammoth steam-powered cranes that swept the floors of foundry and machine shop, lifting bulky iron plate and castings heretofore jockied by hand. Three smith shops contained no less than eighty-seven fires, three lusty trip hammers, and huge mechanical sheers. The machine shop was remodeled into a web of belting that connected turret lathes, modern milling machines, and other devices with multiple steam engines.[20]

Impressive though they were, these innovations did not uniformly abridge manual labor or erode all skilled work. Metallurgical entrepreneurs, unlike textile bosses, deployed powered machines sequentially and selectively, leaving islands of hand techniques in a sea of modernity. The late nineteenth-century machine shop, wrote an engineer, is a "model of excellence in the way of modern tools," but the foundry is "the same old kind with which we are familiar, filled with broken flasks, with no system of heating, and ventillated only through broken windows. . . ."[21] Amid the rubble of the foundry at Baldwin and elsewhere worked the craft-proud molder, bane of the modernizers, plying his trade exclusively by hand. Many of his skilled comrades were stationed behind machines and were assigned to standardized work. They lost some autonomy and skill in the process, but hardly fit the stereotype of the semiskilled factory hand. Machinists still "guided the tool rather than the other way around . . . ,"[22] which left considerable latitude for judgment and the need for a trained hand. Precise or close work was beyond the scope of machinery, and the machinist and blacksmith who used lathes and trip hammers for roughing would turn to trusty files and chisels for finishing.

This mix of machine and manual techniques also characterized segments of the crafts that reached the factory stage of production between 1850 and 1880. The versatile printer-publisher who wrote and edited his own copy, set the type, manned the press, and hawked his own product was as rare as knee britches and powdered wigs by mid-century. Employers had already separated mental from manual work and had increasingly divided the latter into specialized tasks. Press rooms in the largest publishing houses closely mirrored the floors of textile mills, as owners recruited "half-trained" youths and, sometimes, women to run power-driven presses. Typesetting, however, continued to be a skilled hand trade and honorable calling in every sense.[23] The manufacture of the type combined a series of relatively menial and mechanized tasks with highly skilled hand procedures demanding painstaking patience and staggering manual dexterity. Punch cutters, for example, used precision instruments, including magnifying glasses and gauges, to fashion letters on thin strips of soft metal.[24] Makers of popular home furnishings, "cottage furniture" as it was widely known, carried on along the lines of James W. Cooper's employees. Cooper commenced business in the late 1850s with a few journeymen in a small rented room. Born in the perils of the 1857 depression, this modest shop quickly grew into one of the largest and most advanced furniture firms in Philadelphia. Within a decade Cooper abandoned his cramped quarters for a new factory consisting of a five-storied main building (50 × 200 feet) flanked by two wings of 25 square feet, and a rear annex (25 × 143 feet), and by 1880 he amassed a labor force of 150 men and women. The women did clerical work and escorted customers through the showrooms lined with bedsteads, cabinets, and other pieces. The men turned out the furniture in production rooms with different technologies. Saw room workers cut wood, and planers and turners made the components of furniture on modern machines powered by steam engines; but gilders, ornamenters, carvers, and other finishers worked strictly by hand.[25]

Manufactories. Nineteenth-century Americans used the term "manufactory" interchangeably with "factory" to refer to any large industrial establishment. In this context, however, it has a different meaning. It describes workshops with more than twenty-five workers but without power-driven machinery, or stated differently, manufactories are nonmechanized factories.

Manufactories were to shoemakers, tailors, printers, and furniture workers in 1850 what factories were to textile operatives. Though not as dominant in these crafts as factories were in newer industries, they were the most important work environment (see Table 7). Manufactories owed their existence to the unique strategies followed by producers of light con-

Table 7.   Distribution of Workers by Work Environment, 1850 and 1880

Industry	Year	Artisan		Sweat Shop		Manufactory		Factory	
		Number	%	Number	%	Number	%	Number	%
Food	1850	930	62.2	231	15.5	103	6.9	230	15.4
	1880	2178	40.5	519	9.7	282	5.2	2387	44.5
Shoes	1850	1091	17.4	2207	35.3	2964	47.1	5	0
& Boots	1880	805	9.6	1474	17.6	3737	44.7	2346	28.0
Hats	1850	284	15.5	734	40.0	759	41.3	60	3.2
& Caps	1880	157	5.3	574	19.5	1156	39.3	1053	35.8
Clothing	1850	324	3.1	2635	25.0	6483	61.6	1090	10.3
	1880	730	2.1	2133	6.2	13639	39.5	18046	52.1
Textiles	1850	176	1.7	826	7.9	3790	36.3	5628	54.0
	1880	270	0.7	1247	3.3	3053	8.1	33171	87.9
Iron	1850	21	1.7	54	4.5	100	8.3	1038	86.3
& Steel	1880	36	0.9	68	1.9	73	2.0	3480	95.2
Machine Tools	1850	395	10.1	416	10.6	660	16.8	2449	62.5
& Hardware	1880	364	2.9	806	6.3	549	4.3	10990	86.5
Furniture	1850	265	18.7	504	35.6	512	36.1	136	9.6
	1880	389	10.6	744	20.3	883	24.1	1615	44.9
Construction	1850	355	9.1	1151	29.6	1611	41.5	767	19.7
	1880	2158	16.8	3692	28.7	3634	28.3	3367	26.2
Ship-	1850	71	7.5	259	27.3	595	62.7	24	2.5
building	1880	45	1.6	167	6.0	0	0	2527	92.2
Fuel	1850	10	3.4	25	8.3	0	0	263	88.3
	1880	14	0.4	35	1.1	0	0	3279	98.5
Chemicals	1850	71	11.3	121	19.2	42	6.7	395	62.8
	1880	99	3.0	181	5.5	180	5.5	2823	86.0
Glass	1850	10	2.2	20	4.3	417	89.9	17	3.7
	1880	39	7.3	177	33.2	118	22.1	199	37.3
Paper	1850	4	1.2	80	24.8	40	12.4	199	61.6
	1880	14	0.4	230	7.2	911	28.3	2061	64.1
Printing &	1850	76	3.6	515	24.6	866	41.3	639	30.5
Publishing	1880	173	2.3	730	9.5	1054	13.7	5746	74.6
Blacksmiths	1850	398	70.0	158	27.8	0	0	12	2.1
	1880	346	69.3	86	17.2	30	6.0	37	7.4
Traditional	1850	218	40.0	98	8.0	26	4.8	203	37.2
Metals	1880	383	18.2	432	20.1	101	4.8	1193	56.8

Source: U.S. Manuscript Censuses of Manufactures, 1850 and 1880.

sumer goods. As Chandler observes, such employers eschewed mechanizing the production process for dividing up the labor and for enlarging their work forces. Most of them pursued both courses simultaneously, but, as far as one can gauge, at different rates and with idiosyncratic twists. Shoe and clothing manufacturers proved the most zealous and thorough devotees of the division of labor. By 1850 they effectively carved up their crafts into a range of repetitive tasks distinguished by quick and easy mastery of simple techniques, such as binding shoe uppers and stitching precut cloth, or by the need for training and expertise, such as shoe lasting and leather and garment cutting. Next came furniture makers who separated the primary stages of manufacture from producing components, assembly, and finishing. They were followed by printers and publishers who simply detached compositing from running the press.[26] Whatever the trade, the process was quite similar and rather divergent from that which prevailed in newer industries. These entrepreneurs assembled large labor forces and reorganized the work before introducing powered machinery or, in some instances, even hand tools. This debasement of skills, however, did not level all job designations to semiskilled tasks. Instead, it created a new occupational pyramid of skilled jobs at the top, semiskilled occupations in the middle, and menial ones at the base. The extent of centralized production was, in a rough way, inversely proportionate to the division of labor. Publishers and furniture manufacturers thus employed large workforces at the manufactory. Shoe and clothing producers, however, hired skeletal, if growing, groups of cutters and packers at the manufactory, but employed the bulk of their workers off the premises by contracting with garret bosses and by farming out work to cottagers.[27]

The equipment of manufactories could be and often was quite advanced, even though it was not mechanized. Shoe manufacturers installed pedal-operated sewing machines as well as hand- and foot-powered devices and simple hand tools. Leather cutters who wielded sharp knives in conformity with paper molds in the antebellum years stamped out stock with metal dies and leather mallets by the 1860s. Bottomers who once worked by hand gave way to McKay operators who performed the work of eighty men in an hour. These innovations intensified the division of work in a trade already fragmented into upward of thirty distinct tasks. Eyelet machines converted the punching of holes into a separate job, just as the McKay broke down the preparation of bottoming into several steps. Each job in shoe and clothing production was performed in a separate room or department, an arrangement that was carried to extremes when manufacturers marketed their own wares, as in the case of Wanamaker's.[28]

Philadelphia's premier clothing firm was hatched inauspiciously in 1861 when young John Wanamaker formed a partnership with his brother-in-law, Nathan Brown, and leased three rooms in a large building at Sixth and Market Streets. War contracts and shrewd advertising turned the fledgling business into a thriving enterprise and sent the partners scurrying for more space and additional workers. They first rented additional rooms and then purchased the entire building as well as two adjoining structures, which were refurbished with an elegant façade and fittingly renamed "Oak Hall." Brown's death in 1867 ended the partnership, but Wanamaker's enterprising spirit lived on. In 1869 he founded John Wanamaker and Company, a fashionable shop for the Chestnut Street trade, and he held the grand opening of the Grand Depot, his gargantuan department store at

Thirteenth and Juniper, coincident with the Centennial Exhibition in 1876. His combined labor force at Oak Hall and Wanamaker and Company jumped to 1,000 in 1870 and mushroomed to nearly 3,000 a decade later. Three in four Wanamaker employees were women, and many of them were methodically positioned behind counters in orderly sales rooms featuring everything from children's clothes to "mourning garments" and "Black suits." The specialization and regimen of sales suffused production as well. Whole floors and departments were the scenes of closely supervised garment cutters, trimmers, washers, spongers, buttonhole makers, and, of course, seamstresses stitching garments by machine.[29]

Yet the modernization of production was not as thorough as these changes imply. No manufacturer of shoes or clothing completely eliminated skilled work or hand labor any more than his counterpart in metallurgy. Some tools and machines mistakenly seen by conventional historians as substitutes for skill were more akin to aides or complements. Dies for stamping leather lightened the travail of the cutter, but he was the judge of where to place the tool in order to prevent stretching and ensure maximum use of the hide. Leather (and garment) cutting, said an early twentieth-century observer, "is an expert process and requires two or three years of experience before it can be mastered."[30] McKay operators still had to feed the machine and guide the material, and they did not bcome proficient workers without training. Some jobs never were digested by machines in this period. Shoelasting, the analogue of iron molding, persisted as a hand technique into the twentieth century.[31] Nor did manufacturers centralize all production processes. Shoe bosses still hired about a fifth to a fourth of the binders as outworkers in the 1870s, and clothing manufacturers were even slower to centralize. Wanamaker and other large clothiers gave out the lion's share of the sewing to subcontractors and outworkers as late as the 1870s.[32]

Sweatshops. Sweatshops, the third work environment, present nagging definitional problems. It is difficult to know where to draw the lines of scale between them and manufactories at their upper end and artisanal shops on their lower end. The setting of any parameters must be somewhat arbitrary, but impressionistic evidence and inferences drawn from the manuscripts of the industrial census, support treating sweatshops as unmechanized firms with six to twenty-five workers.

Sweatshops are usually thought to have evolved in the needle trades during the late nineteenth century when former journeymen and petty proprietors set up on their own and subcontracted with manufacturers. There is little doubt, however, that there were antebellum versions and that they reached beyond clothing manufacture. Early-day sweatshops took shape in three ways. Small producers of boots and shoes would purchase raw materials and would sell in bulk to downtown retailers;[33] merchants would advance capital or materials to petty proprietors and would demand shipment of finished goods by fixed deadlines;[34] or merchant capitalists and manufacturers operating out of central shops would give out portions of the work, usually binding and stitching, to subcontractors.[35] Proprietors of the first type were already on the wane by mid-century because of the competition of large retailers and because of the havoc wrought by repeated downturns in trade. The depression of the early forties was credited with bringing down over 2,000 garret bosses, and the panics of the late fifties and early seventies further winnowed their ranks.[36] The second type probably survived the 1850s in attenuated form in many trades, including light metals. The third, which was peculiar to shoe, clothing, and cigar making, became the prototypical Gilded-Age garret, and it had a longer if checkered career. Having emerged and flourished in the antebellum years under the impetus of merchant capitalism, it suffered in the second half of the century with the centralization of production in manufactories. This reduced the corps of workers employed in sweatshops from 10 to 20 percent of the shoe and clothing trades. But these establishments died hard; clothing garrets, in fact, enjoyed a rebirth in the 1880s and 1890s.

Sweatshops differed from manufactories in ways other than scale. Creatures of merchants and manufacturers, "sweaters" organized production in accordance with imperatives imposed from above. They rarely owned raw materials or sold their own products, and they were headquartered in homes or tenements often in close proximity to contractors. Unlike large manufacturers who had no direct role in production and who transferred supervision to foremen and room bosses, they combined manual and managerial functions by driving workers in order to meet contractual obligations and working alongside them in hopes of cutting costs. Workers themselves were disproportionately male of all nationalities, but as time wore on women became an important source of labor. They toiled exclusively by hand until the 1860s and 1870s when many "sweaters" outfitted tenements with foot-powered sewing machines, but innovation ended here. Since sweatshops were supplied with precut cloth and leather and were responsible for a limited range of tasks, they were spared the technological variability of manufactories.

Outwork. Outwork, which thrived in the early nineteenth-century countryside, is often considered an intermediate stage of production. It was exported to rural America by urban merchants and general store owners who mined the backlands for farm families willing to spin yarn, make brooms, hats, or buttons, and above all else, bind shoes in the manner of Whittier's nimble-fingered "Nell." The environs of Philadelphia had more than their share of "Nells," but so did the city proper. Outworkers there practiced many trades and were more resilient than their rural counterparts who passed into memory by the 1850s. Philadelphia households buzzed with the activity of handloom weavers, shoemakers, tailors, hat makers, and numerous other workers even as textile mills studded the banks of the Schuylkill and manufactories crowded the downtown in the first half of the century. On the eve of the Civil War when weavers in other locales worked in factories, there were over 5,000 handloom tenders in Philadelphia working at home or, to an increasing extent, in manufactories.[37] This large force of domestic weavers stubbornly refused to desert their arcane craft, and many loom tenders were still weaving yarn in Kensington and Moyamensing cottages during the 1860s. Outwork also enveloped the majority of the city's shoemakers and tailors in the 1830s, and these craftsmen did not gravitate to manufactories and other settings until the late 1840s and 1850s. By the middle of the seventies many shoe and clothing workers (as well as untold numbers of hatters, cigarmakers, and other tradesmen and marginal workers) continued to toil at home under the putting out system.[38]

Outworkers constituted a unique labor force working in a world of their own. Most appear to have been Irish males as well as women of every nationality who, in all likelihood, were the wives and daughters of outworkers themselves and poorer wage earners unable to make ends meet without secondary breadwinners. Entire families often worked together or shared responsibilities through an informal division of labor. Male handloom weavers, for example, tended the frames, while wives and daughters spooled and wound yarn for the family loom and for unmarried weavers. Hand methods prevailed in all trades except among some shoe and clothing workers who either purchased sewing machines or rented them from manufacturers in the late 1860s and early 1870s.

Employers clearly recognized the liability of hiring workers at home far from the watchful eye of manager and overseer. They tried tightening the work discipline by slashing piece rates, fining tardy work, withholding the pay of those who failed to return finished goods by fixed deadlines, and other negative incentives.[39] These methods and the press of the busy season exacted a fitful work rhythm, but never did destroy the autonomy of the outworker. A cynical observer of the city's handloom weavers, whose remarks apply to all domestic workers, was probably close to the mark in claiming that: "persons engaged in the production [of cloth] have no practical concern with the ten hour system, the factory system, or even with the solar system. They work at such hours as they choose in their own homes, and their industry is mainly regulated by the state of the larder."[40]

Artisan Shops. The final nonmechanized work settings are artisan shops or neighborhood stores. The smallest of all work settings, they could hire in excess of ten workers in 1850 and up to thirty in 1880, but most employed fewer than six in both years. These were already in eclipse by mid-century when they accounted for a paltry 12 percent of the labor force, but this figure is misleading, since it includes industrial workers who never labored in small shops. In 1850 most of the butchers, bakers, and traditional metal workers (blacksmiths, tinsmiths, and coppersmiths) and about a fifth of the shoemakers, cabinetmakers, and harnessmakers were located in such settings (see Table 7). The concentration of ownership in the following decades pared down small shopmen from 12 to 8 percent of the labor force, a modest decline by any standard and one that fell unevenly across the crafts. Food and light metal proprietors either gained workers or experienced moderate losses, and in 1880 they still claimed between 40 and 70 percent of their respective labor forces. Shoe, clothing, and furniture-makers, who had smaller shares of their trades to begin with, were left with less than 10 percent of their crafts. This differential decline is easily explained. These artisans produced either necessities for ordinary folk or custom goods for proper Philadelphia. These who turned out luxuries were driven from business by large manufacturers who invaded custom markets;[41] those who provided necessities proved more resilient because of the realities of the walking city. Philadelphians of all classes needed food on a daily basis and the products and services of blacksmiths and metalworkers with some frequency. This steady demand and the prohibitively high cost of public transportation, which tethered shoppers to neighborhood stores, gave small butchers, bakers, and metal tradesmen a lease on life. Nearly every block had such tradesmen who, dispersing throughout the city with the spread of population, offered the convenience of proximity to neighborhood customers.

Production arrangements in mid-century artisanal shops contrast sharply with garrets and sweatshops. The pace of work was decidedly more casual and irregular, especially in baking, and there was virtually no division of labor. Journeymen were among the most versatile and accomplished craftsmen in Philadelphia, and they fashioned the entire commodity from beginning to end. They were native-born American or German and almost always male. Women rarely figured in the production end of these businesses, and those who did work, usually the wives and daughters of

Table 8. Number of Firms and Current Value Added by Industry, 1850 and 1880

Industry[a]	Firms		Value Added ($1000)[c]	
	1850	1880	1850	1880
Food (02)	530	1430	1314	5799
Refined Food	68	38	1107	2225
Shoes & Boots (0801)	623	615	2123	4824
Hats & Caps (0802)	175	142	824	1553
Clothing (0803-4)	410	702	3235	10442
Textiles (09)	284	709	3308	b
Iron & Steel	34	73	767	2774
Machine Tools & Hardware	244	504	2192	10887
Blacksmiths	167	199	297	419
Lumber & Wood (13)	344	459	1431	3824
Furniture (1401)	152	291	942	2799
Construction (15)	271	1332	1865	8453
Shipbuilding (16)	52	41	1154	1686
Fuel (17)	13	22	404	8413
Chemicals (18)	63	122	840	6111
Glass (19)	16	43	265	389
Paper (21)	20	62	193	2111
Printing & Publishing (24)	93	263	1523	6203
Others	983	2116	5531	21666
Total	4542	9163	29315	100,578[b]

Source: U.S. Manuscript Censuses of Manufactures, 1850 and 1880.

[a]Numbers in parentheses represent two- or four-digit industry codes described in *Historical Methods Newsletter*, Vol. 9, Nos. 2 and 3 (March–June 1976), 82–89. All firms in the industry were included except for the following: Food: sugar and vinegar omitted; Fuel: fixtures omitted; Chemicals: drugs omitted. Refined food includes sugar, vinegar, and liquors.

[b]Value added data were available for only 158 of 709 textile firms in the city. The value added for those 158 firms are included in the "all other" category and the total. The total value added has not been adjusted for the textile omissions.

[c]Current prices used in both years.

masters, were confined to waiting on customers and keeping accounts. Small businessmen who survived the growing concentration of ownership in the following years instituted some changes in work methods. Many shoemakers and tailors, for example, installed sewing machines, but it is impossible to know whether and the extent to which they divided up skills. Most were probably content to perform manual labor and to have journeymen carry on in the old style, fitting customers and making the entire product. Masters in the other trades are equally mysterious and, one suspects, every bit as traditional as shoemakers. The bulk of them did not even use foot-powered machines in 1870.[42]

Table 9. Average Employment and Capital by Industry, 1850 and 1880

| Industry | Employment | | | Capital | | |
	1850	1880	% Increase	1850 (Mean)	1880 (Mean)	% Increase
Food	2.8	3.8	36	2,604	5,640	116
Refined Food	10.2	35.7	250	24,197	241,869	900
Shoes & Boots	10.0	13.2	32	2,043	5,387	164
Hats & Caps	10.5	20.8	98	4,050	10,612	162
Clothing	25.7	43.4	69	6,768	19,558	189
Textiles	37.0	53.2	44	14,052	a	a
Iron & Steel	35.4	50.1	42	35,637	64,038	80
Machine Tools & Hardware	16.1	25.1	56	10,578	36,816	248
Blacksmiths	3.4	2.6	−23	1,232	1,329	8
Lumber & Wood	6.9	10.6	54	3,986	10,391	161
Furniture	9.3	12.1	30	4,166	11,836	184
Construction	14.3	9.7	−32	4,865	15,045	209
Shipbuilding	18.3	68.4	274	25,753	57,472	123
Fuel	22.9	150.5	557	105,084	634,061	503
Chemicals	10.0	27.1	171	19,708	121,814	518
Glass	30.9	12.7	−59	21,073	9,901	−53
Paper	16.1	51.9	223	7,860	56,592	620
Printing & Publishing	22.5	29.5	31	13,308	27,576	107
Totals	12.9	15.6[b]	66	7,078	18,442	161

Source: U.S. Manuscript Censuses of Manufactures, 1850 and 1880.

Note: Employment is sum of "Average Number of Male Employees" and "Average Number of Female Employees" from the census returns. Capital is the reported value from the census. Calculations include only firms with non-zero values for employment, capital, and value added.

[a] The 1880 textile figures derived from the manuscript schedules are inaccurate because many of these firms are not found on the extant documents, though they were counted in the published statistics. A subsequent survey by Blodget provides data on total employment but not capital or value added. See Lorin Blodget, *Census of Manufactures of Philadelphia* (Philadelphia: 1883). (Also see Appendix II.)

[b] Equal to 19.1 if all firms with no reported output are included. The other figures are largely unaffected by this change.

Productivity

Such unevenness of growth and maturity within and between industries has larger implications for the study of urban life in late nineteenth-century Philadelphia. The aggregate shift from small business and handicraft manu- facture to mass production in factories and manufactories, for example, helps account for the differing locational needs and strategies of firms and for the variations in the journey to work between industries; the persistence of outwork, a bailiwick of women's employment, sheds light on the high frequency of women's participation in the labor force and on the workings of the household economy; the numerical superiority of small business deepens our understanding of the structural basis of the alliance between journeymen and small producers that recurred in third parties and labor reform organizations of the period such as the Knights of Labor. Most of these matters are examined in detail in the ensuing essays, and there is no need to anticipate the themes of other authors here.

It is appropriate at this juncture, however, to draw attention to the separate but related issues of expansion and productivity. Tables 5 and 8 present data on various dimensions of growth in this period. The data indicate general expansion, but in keeping with the theme outlined above, they also show that growth was neither linear nor consistent across industries. The number of firms thus increased by 39 percent in the 1850s, 32 percent during the Civil War decade, and only 9 percent in the depression-plagued 1870s. Total employment followed a similar pattern, increasing by 81, 24, and 20 percent respectively, which clearly distinguishes the 1850s as the boom period. The number of firms increased in most sectors, especially in machine tools and hardware, textiles, and printing, but not at all in ship building, clothing, and hats. None of the industries failed to expand value added but, again, there was uneven growth, with fuel, chemicals, and machine tools and hardware having the highest proportionate increases.

Another dimension of growth is identified in Table 9. Here we see that the average workforce per firm increased by 21 percent (to 15.6 employees), although this figure is misleading because it excludes many large textile firms which were not recorded in the 1880 industrial census. (Including such firms brings the mean increase to 49 percent.) Industries such as refined food, fuel, chemicals, and paper, however, more than doubled their mean labor forces during the period. The same four industries also increased their capitalization by over 500 percent, far surpassing the substantial aggregate increase of 161 percent.[43] By way of contrast, the average construction, printing, glass, and food processing firm had only slightly more or even fewer employees than in 1850, and the capitalization of these firms lagged well behind the aggregate figure.

Historians and economists of productivity have seldom been troubled by the variations within and exceptions to general trends in scale, mechanization, and value added. Most have worked at the aggregate level with all that implies, and those of a neoclassical perspective have viewed the larger trends not only as descriptions of industrial growth, but as *explanations* for it and for observed gains in productivity. Rooted as it is in neoclassical orthodoxy, this argument pivots on the assumptions that economies accrue from scale and mechanization and that singly or in combination both yield greater returns per unit of input.

Though some writers have questioned these propositions, none has registered a more forceful dissent than Chandler. His contention is that scale and mechanization did not necessarily realize internal economies and that, in some instances, scale was a liability leading to diminishing returns. Chandler locates the key to efficiency in the increased volume and velocity of production. Or as he puts it, "In modern mass production . . . economies resulted more from speed than size. It was not the size of the manufacturing establishment in terms of the number of workers and amount and value of capital equipment but the velocity of throughput and resulting increase in volume that permitted economies that lowered costs and increased output per worker per machine." This evening out of bottlenecks on shop floors brought about by the application of machine technology, coupled with the "skills and abilities of managers and workers and the continuing improvement of those skills over time," triggered higher productivity per worker.[44]

It is too early to know how critics will receive Chandler's argument. It is safe to assume, however, that they will demand supportive evidence and with good reason. Chandler invokes thick description and logic rather than empirical tests to weigh the relative importance of the variables. This is understandable, partly because the critical parameters of his argument, apart from scale, do not (or at least did not) easily lend themselves to statistical calculation. Our own data on the labor force, however, can be used as proxies for the skills and experiences of workers, and the work environments outlined above can be seen as proxies for various states of the coordination of production. The purpose in this section, then, is to subject Chandler's contentions about efficiency to empirical tests.

The efficiency of manufacturing production can be discussed in a number of ways. The most popular measure is the partial productivity of labor, or value added per worker. Value added per unit of capital is an equally valid measure, but is usually less preferred because of the problems involved in defining a "unit of capital"—a problem that is complicated here by the inflation premiums biasing the reported capital values. Nevertheless, both indexes are reported in Table 10. Looking first at labor productivity it is not surprising to find fuel and chemicals with the highest output per worker in both years and textiles and apparel with the lowest. This is unsurprising because the major determinant of labor productivity is the amount of capital each worker uses, and industries with relatively more inputs in machines and equipment will have more output per unit of labor, although not necessarily more output. An example may be instructive here. In digging a ditch, it may be possible to do one hole per week either by using ten men with ten shovels or one man with a steam shovel. Both processes provide the same ditch, but in the latter labor productivity (in

Table 10.   Labor, Capital, and Total Factor Productivity, 1850 and 1880

	Labor				Capital				Total Factor[c]		
	1850		1880		1850		1880		1850		1880	
Code[a]	V/N	Code[a]	V/N	Code[a]	V/K	Code[a]	V/K	Code[a]	TFP	Code[a]	TFP
5	1446	17	2544	8s	1.668	8s	1.456	16	96.1	17	139.1
17	1357	5	2181	14	1.488	8h	1.042	5	95.4	18	98.0
18	1335	18	1863	15	1.415	19	.935	18	94.3	5	83.4
16	1216	2	1084	24	1.232	8c	.876	2	80.7	2	76.9
2	879	14	834	21	1.229	24	.862	24	77.9	14	73.4
24	727	24	806	8h	1.169	9	.837[b]	17	70.9	24	73.4
14	665	13	786	8c	1.162	14	.813	14	69.4	8s	72.6
13	607	19	727	13	1.044	13	.804	21	68.5	19	70.7
21	597	11	709	2	.957	16	.723	13	65.4	13	70.6
19	570	9	689[b]	16	.862	2	.717	15	62.5	9	65.7[b]
11	578	15	668	19	.839	17	.630	19	58.2	8h	59.7
15	480	21	656	11	.780	21	.602	11	57.2	11	59.3
8h	449	16	616	9	.757[b]	11	.592	8h	55.8	16	58.1
8s	340	8s	596	18	.687	15	.424	8s	52.9	21	56.6
9	315	8h	528	5	.612	18	.414	8c	43.7	15	50.8
8c	307	8c	397	17	.296	5	.249	9	38.7	8c	46.7

Source: U.S. Manuscript Censuses of Manufactures, 1850 and 1880.

[a] Industrial Codes: 2, Food; 5, Refined Foods; 8s, Shoes & Boots; 8h, Hats/Caps; 8c, Clothing; 9, Textiles; 11, Metals (includes Iron and Steel and Machine Tools and Hardware from above and excludes Blacksmiths); 13, Wood; 14, Furniture; 15, Construction; 16, Shipbuilding; 17, Fuel; 19, Glass; 18, Chemicals; 19, Glass; 21, Paper; 24, Printing & Publishing. V = Value added, N = number of employees, K = capital. All calculations include firms with positive values for all three variables.

[b] See Notes to Tables 8 and 9.

[c] Total factor productivity = $V/(N^{.65}K^{.35})$

ditches per man-month) is ten times higher. The single worker need not work more diligently than the ten, nor be more experienced or better managed, but he will appear more productive. This illustration is also relevant across industries in which dollars are substituted for ditches and shovels. Industries such as fuel and chemicals whose value of capital per worker exceeded $4500 in 1880 rank highest, while shoes and clothing, whose capital-labor ratio was below $500, had the lowest observed labor productivities.

This relationship also works in reverse and explains why the ranking of labor and capital productivity is inverted. In the ditch digging example, if the steam shovel was more expensive than the hand shovels, it would also have a lower measured productivity. Industries with relatively little capital per worker had high capital productivity rankings, while the capital-intensive heavy industries ranked quite low. Since additional factors also influence the partial measures, the inverse ordering will not be exact. This also holds for the relationship between the capital-labor ratio and labor productivity. These factors can be best understood after defining the concept of total factor productivity.

This concept in turn requires the introduction of a production function. The separate production functions for each industry provide a technical relationship between output and inputs and give the maximum amount of product which can be obtained from any combination of inputs. The analysis that follows employs a Cobb-Douglas production function which in its simplest form can be written as:

$$V = A L^a K^b \qquad (1)$$

where V is value added, L is labor, K is capital, and a and b are the output elasticities of labor and capital respectively. The latter are coefficients measuring the proportionate changes in V that will result from proportionate changes in L or K. The "A" term is total factor productivity. Rewriting the function provides:

$$A = V/(L^a K^b) \qquad (2)$$

and indicates that A is the ratio of output to the geometric mean of the inputs.[45] This parameter provides a measure of differences in overall efficiency. Industries that produce more output per total input (rather than per unit of labor or capital) are in some sense more efficient.

Examination of Table 10 discloses a rank order similar to that of labor productivity. However, limited consideration should be given to these figures. In a world free of measurement errors and market disequilibria, interindustry differences should disappear. Ethnic, sex, and age variations in the work force, temporary price changes, or the failure of resources to move to sectors of greater reward will result in such differences.[46] Nonetheless, productivity variations still exist across industries, and part of our task is to identify the variables that explain the observed differences.

Total factor productivity is most salient when studied across time. Here it is a measure of technological change or the increasing ability to obtain more output from the same inputs. From this perspective it is evident that only five industries had declines in this index. The declines were minor in printing and refined foods (21 and 5), but unexplained falls in capital productivity led to large reductions in construction and paper. On the other hand, large increases were observed in the fuel and shoes industries among others. Also, the shipbuilding industry alone—in which one firm employed two-thirds of the workers—failed to increase labor productivity between 1850 and 1880, the leaders in this expansion being fuel, refined foods, and chemicals. However, as noted by Schmookler and others, technological advances are concentrated in growing industries.[47] The identification of the causes of these gains provides an additional line of inquiry.

In general terms, manufacturing growth may be represented as resulting from concurrent shifts in the supply and demand curves for a particular product. From 1850 to 1880 (and before and after these dates as well) the supply curves for most industries probably shifted outward. At the same time, demand rose, leading to an increase in output but having an indeterminant effect on the relative price of the product. One goal of our discussion will be to identify the factors affecting each curve, but at this point it is sufficient to note that neither an independent shift in supply or demand would be likely to induce a substantial increase in the quantity of output. A supply shift alone would simply move production along the old demand curve, and a change in demand would only pull additional resources into the industry, moving output up along the supply curve. Rapid industrial expansion thus requires concurrent shifts in supply and demand, and the experience of particular industries will depend on the relevant strengths of their market shifts. We turn, therefore, to the factors most often identified as responsible for these changes.

Our major concern is with the supply side of manufacturing development. This emphasis is consistent with historical interpretations surrounding the role of technological change and productivity gains across time. There are two ways to increase the supply of manufactured goods. First, more resources can and were directed toward the sector. We have already discussed the growth in manufacturing employment and capital that occurred during this period. In addition, even with the same level of resources, supply can increase through efficiency gains, which is a recognized feature of nineteenth-century development.

The role of capital appears to be crucial in each type of change. Not only did growing investment lead to a larger capital resource by 1880, it also represented the vehicle for introducing a substantial portion of the technological improvements of the period. For most industries, more capital also meant better capital and more efficient production techniques. Regardless of the causes of mechanization, the thrust of the past interpretation is that enormous productivity gains resulted from the capital investments. Quite obviously, more capital per worker led to greater labor productivity. Increasing capital intensity was also a likely factor in boosting total factor productivity, since a large share of investment was earmarked for the incorporation and modernization of power sources.[48] The use of power in turn has been traditionally viewed as an independent source of productivity gains which resulted in the lowering of unit costs. The effect of the shift to power on the supply of industrial products is therefore evident.

Economies of scale have also been proffered as a cause of productivity gains and manufacturing expansion. The notion of economies of scale is simply that larger firms were more efficient than small firms even when endowed with equivalent factor proportions and input quality. Adam Smith's pin factory is the classic representation of efficiency gains accruing from the specialization of tasks. As firms in most industries moved into larger size categories, we would expect them—like Smith's pin producer—to reap greater productivity from scale alone.

The above discussion briefly sketches what we view to be the traditional causes of output and productivity increases during this period. The following sections draw upon microeconomic data from the 1850 and 1880 manuscript censuses to test these hypotheses. Our technical arguments are presented in the context of the Cobb-Douglas production function introduced above. We concentrate first on the issue of scale economies and then turn our attention to the issue of power.

Formally, economies of scale exist if a proportional increase in all inputs leads to a greater than proportional increase in output measured here as value-added. In the function, the output elasticities (a and b, above) are additive, and hence increasing both L and K by x percent will lead to an x (a + b) percent increase in V. Economies of scale exist when a + b exceeds unity, and these hypotheses can be tested by estimation of the parameters.

There are varying interpretations of how power affects the production function and the data allow the testing of two hypotheses. First, the use of powered rather than nonpowered equipment should increase output, other things equal. That is, if two firms have equal labor forces, capital, and management, but only one has powered equipment, we would expect it to have a greater output. This hypothesis can be tested by introducing a dummy variable for power as follows:

$$V = A\, L^a\, K^b\, e^{cP} \tag{3}$$

where P represents a dummy variable having a value of one for firms with steam or water power and zero for all others. The coefficient c is expected to be positive and represents the efficiency differential between nonpowered and powered firms. An estimated value for c of .05 means that a powered firm will produce 5 percent more output than the equivalent nonpowered firm.

Alternatively, power can be viewed as a separate continuous input with its own output elasticity. Letting HP represent horsepower, we can estimate:

$$V = A\, L^a\, K^b\, HP^d \tag{4}$$

Each x percent increase in horsepower will cause a d(x) increase in V. The hypothesis is that firms could continuously raise output by adding more horsepower. It is difficult to imagine how this could be done, however, without changing the total capital stock as well. The colinearity of capital and horsepower is thus expected to make these estimates less reliable and more difficult to interpret.

The production functions were estimated using firm data collected from the manuscript censuses on manufacturing. The data were grouped according to industrial categories, and they were supplemented by locational data from the PSHP grid unit pattern. These data are discussed below. The variable definitions at this stage are based on unadjusted categories reported in the census. First, output was defined as value added, or the difference between the values of total product and materials. (An alternative definition is simply the gross value of production; the value-added figure was chosen in order to be consistent with our productivity analysis and for a number of economic reasons.)[49] Materials may be viewed as having a fixed relationship with output, since it is difficult to conceive of an increase in "material productivity" comparable to those found for labor. It is thus preferable to omit materials from the model.[50]

Labor is recorded in the census as the "average number of male employees" and the "average number of female employees." Youths are reported separately beginning in 1870. Data are also available on monthly wages, the maximum number of employees, and the "number of hours in an ordinary day" for both May to November and November to May. The employee data can be used in a number of ways to calculate the labor force of a given firm. We opted to use the sum of the average number of workers reported in the male, female, and youth categories as the measure of the labor force.[51]

As the capital input we used the value of capital as reported in the census. Although other studies have adjusted for price changes, this is not necessary here because deflation of the capital values by a constant price index will not affect the relevant parameters. With the Cobb-Douglas function, only the relative level of inputs across firms is relevant in the estimates of a and b.

Information on power and machinery is available in a number of forms. The 1880 census contains detailed information on waterwheels and steam boilers including the amount of horsepower generated by each, and for this year it is possible to introduce power as a continuous variable measured in total horsepower, or a dummy variable as discussed above.[52]

Tables 11 and 12 display estimates of Equation 3 for seventeen industries in 1850 and 1880. The estimates appear quite sound in a statistical sense and provide a number of interesting results. The R^2 statistics are high, indicating that our specification explains over 75 percent of the variation in output for most industries. The results are also encouraging

Table 11. Production Function Estimates by Industry, 1850

Industry	A	a	b	a+b	c	R^2	Sample Size
				Coefficients[a]			
Food	5.38	.76 (.03)	.19 (.02)	.945* (.035)	.22* (.10)	.65	530
Refined Food	4.57	.66 (.11)	.35 (.07)	1.008 (.079)	−.16 (.22)	.84	68
Shoes & Boots	5.13	.73 (.02)	.18 (.01)	.914* (.014)	.41 (.35)	.87	623
Hats & Caps	4.11	.51 (.04)	.38 (.04)	.894* (.032)	.69* (.24)	.83	175
Clothing	4.61	.65 (.03)	.26 (.03)	.916* (.022)	.20* (.13)	.82	410
Textiles	6.27	.75 (.05)	.11 (.05)	.861* (.036)	.66* (.11)	.73	284
Iron & Steel	4.68	.50 (.12)	.32 (.11)	.821* (.057)	.39* (.19)	.92	34
Machine Tools & Hardware	5.23	.69 (.05)	.21 (.04)	.897* (.037)	.06 (.08)	.86	149
Lumber & Wood	4.87	.70 (.04)	.25 (.03)	.951* (.029)	.10 (.10)	.79	444
Furniture	4.70	.70 (.05)	.29 (.04)	.994 (.040)	−.14* (.16)	.82	152
Construction	5.82	.70 (.03)	.14 (.03)	.838* (.023)	.14* (.80)	.85	271
Shipbuilding	5.63	.92 (.12)	.14 (.09)	1.061 (.072)	.07 (.41)	.83	52
Fuel	5.48	.50 (.34)	.25 (.20)	.747* (.185)	.75* (.41)	.86	13
Chemicals	5.78	.87 (.12)	.14 (.06)	1.012 (.107)	.26 (.21)	.76	63
Glass	5.25	.56 (.22)	.27 (.13)	.838 (.111)	.84 (.82)	.89	16
Paper	5.43	.79 (.19)	.10 (.22)	.891* (.144)	.81* (.49)	.81	20
Printing & Publishing	4.76	.71 (.07)	.27 (.06)	.984 (.049)	.06 (.16)	.86	93

Source: U.S. Manuscript Census of Manufactures, 1850.

Note: Only observations with positive values for V, L, and K were used. Firms with no employees have been recoded to have one employee. The function and definitions are discussed in the text.

[a]Standard errors in parentheses.

*Asterisks represent rejection of null hypotheses at 10 percent level (one-tailed test) that a + b = 1 or c = 0. Tests are implicit for a and b.

Table 12. Production Function Estimates by Industry, 1880

Industry	ln A	a	b	a+b	c	R^2	Sample Size
			Coefficients				
Food	5.73	.64 (.03)	.20 (.02)	.833* (.030)	.09 (.10)	.46	1429
Refined Food	4.93	.61 (.48)	.21 (.35)	.823* (.337)	.69 (.99)	.27	38
Shoes & Boots	5.28	.71 (.04)	.20 (.03)	.910* (.027)	.21 (.22)	.69	615
Hats & Caps	5.33	.50 (.09)	.22 (.07)	.727* (.070)	.57* (.32)	.52	142
Clothing	4.46	.48 (.03)	.36 (.03)	.841* (.031)	.07 (.10)	.86	537
Textiles (1870)	4.23	.45 (.06)	.42 (.04)	.869* (.028)	.11 (.30)	.73	474
Textiles (1880)	4.55	.59 (.07)	.33 (.05)	.920* (.061)	.10 (.12)	.83	146
Iron & Steel	5.28	.60 (.07)	.28 (.05)	.888* (.044)	−.20* (.14)	.91	73
Machine Tools & Hardware	5.75	.72 (.06)	.16 (.04)	.882* (.035)	0.03 (.10)	.65	380
Lumber & Wood	5.32	.64 (.05)	.24 (.04)	.875* (.035)	−.13 (.10)	.66	459
Furniture	4.42	.44 (.08)	.39 (.05)	.824* (.052)	.04 (.20)	.59	291
Construction	5.38	.58 (.03)	.23 (.02)	.818* (.024)	−.09 (.11)	.54	1332
Shipbuilding	5.08	.84 (.30)	.21 (.21)	1.053 (.199)	.15 (.78)	.62	41
Fuel	4.06	.61 (.15)	.43 (.16)	1.031 (.111)	−.41 (.44)	.47	21
Chemicals	5.84	.85 (.13)	.16 (.09)	1.010 (.072)	.06 (.22)	.75	122
Glass	5.96	.78 (.10)	.14 (.05)	.918 (.077)	−.02 (.27)	.84	43
Paper	4.10	.47 (.07)	.40 (.06)	.871* (.048)	.16 (.18)	.90	62
Printing & Publishing	2.81	.47 (.06)	.55 (.05)	1.020 (.038)	−.02 (.11)	.82	263

Source: U.S. Manuscript Censuses of Manufactures, 1870, 1880.

Note: See notes to Table 11.

in that the a and b estimates are quite stable across time. This is especially true where a large number of observations were available. In the shoe industry, for example, the a and b estimates for 1880 differ by only .02 from the 1850 estimates. The only cases of significant change occur in the industries with small sample sizes in 1850, and these are the only cases in which the a and b estimates are not significantly different from zero. Finally, the estimated A values and their changes are generally consistent with our calculations of relative total factor productivity and the general rise in productivity noted above.

The results do not support the hypotheses of increasing returns to scale. In only seven of thirty-four estimates is the scale parameter above unity, and only in shipbuilding is it greater than one in both years. Moreover, none of those seven estimates is statistically different from unity, which is suggestive of constant returns to scale for those industries. On the other hand, twenty-three of the scale estimates are significantly *less* than unity. Rather than scale economies, therefore, the results are more consistent with diseconomies, so that proportional increases in inputs did not lead to an equivalent expansion in output. Some industries exhibit significant diseconomies in both years. This is true for the clothing trades, metal industries, construction, and for wood and paper production. Such results would indicate that for these industrial sectors, size was actually a deterrent to efficiency.[53] This view is given further support below.

Is it possible that the use of power neutralized the apparent disadvantages of size in these industries? The coefficient for power is positive for each of the above industries in 1850 and in five cases in 1880. These estimates are statistically significant at the 10 percent level for four industries in 1850 but only for hats and caps in 1880. Overall, fifteen of the 1850 estimates have positive values, with seven of these statistically significant. In 1880, there are eleven positive signs, but only two are significant. The range of estimates, moreover, is quite large. In 1850, the estimate for the paper industry is .80, although only twenty observations were available, and the parameter value declines to .16 in 1880. Another sector with a high estimated value is hats and caps, and the two values are quite similar. Clothing and textiles also show substantial estimated differentials between powered and nonpowered firms, but the differentials decline from an average of 25 percent in 1850 to less than 10 percent in 1880.

Estimates of the continuous horsepower input for 1880 are not reported here, but they are quantitatively consistent with the results in Table 12. Only three sectors—wood, construction, and fuel—have negative estimated values for d, and these are not statistically significant. These sectors also have negative c estimates. The positive coefficients are significant in only three cases—hats, other metals, and paper—and the maximum value is .22

Table 13.   Labor Productivity by Firm Type, 1850 and 1880[a]

| Industry | Year | Firm Type[b] | | | | | |
		Artisan	Sweat Shop	Small Factory	Manufactory	Large Factory	All
Shoes & Boots	1850	405	379	810*	285	—	340
	1880	786	615	960*	534	605	596
Clothing	1850	430	397	430*	207	322*	306
	1880	720	687	1478*	350	371	414
Textiles[c]	1850	532	318	622	199	366	315
	1870	998	—	3530	—	885	689
Lumber & Wood	1850	626	517	1363	442*	473*	607
	1880	668	668	1151	1034	1149	983
Metals[d]	1850	769	734	787	526*	484	578
	1880	912	991	888	855	927	970
Fuel	1850	1037*	1054*	2689*	—	1071*	1357
	1880	1452*	2000*	2363*	—	2557*	2544
Chemicals	1850	952	1178	1652	3571*	734*	1335
	1880	1710	1685	2017	1986*	1847	1863
Paper	1850	470*	269*	837*	1127*	794*	598
	1880	959*	267	940*	542	736	656
Printing & Publishing	1850	730	555	607*	677	952	727
	1880	709	651	726	858	886	842

Source: U.S. Manuscript Censuses of Manufactures, 1850, 1870, and 1880.

*Less than 10 observations.

[a] All calculations for firms reporting non-zero value added and capital. For firms with zero employees, total employment was set equal to one.

[b] Definitions: Artisan shops: 1–5 Employees, no power; Sweatshops: 6–25 Employees, no power; Manufactory: 26 or more employees, no power; Small factory: 1–25 Employees, power; Large factory: 26 or more Employees, power.

[c] See Notes to Tables 8 and 9.

[d] Includes Iron and Steel and Machine Tools and Hardware from above.

(hats and caps). Only one other estimate exceeds .10. The results thus imply that additional power had positive, albeit limited, impact on productivity, but the evidence is stronger in 1850.

The findings indicate that the most efficient type of firm organization within many industries was likely to be the small factory. This conclusion gains additional weight from data on labor productivity (see Table 13). The effect of power can be seen by comparing sweatshops and small factories, work environments covering the same range of employment (up to 25 workers), but distinguished by the latters' use of power. In all but one instance, the small factory evinces higher labor productivity than the sweatshop, and the exception is not statistically significant. A comparison can also be made between the mechanized and nonmechanized firms with over twenty-five employees. Here the factory has greater productivity in six cases, but in none is the difference significant. The use of power, it seems, raised productivity more effectively at lower levels of employment.

Secondly, when power is held constant, value-added per worker declines with size in a number of industries. Small factories were more productive than large ones in all but two cases, and sweatshops outperformed manufactories in four of the six cases where comparisons could be made. The combined result of the positive power and negative scale effects is that small factories tended to have the highest value-added per worker. These firms were able to capture the gains from power without succumbing to the apparent diseconomies of large scale production. Moreover, the small unmechanized firms, or what we have referred to as sweatshops and artisan shops, were often more productive than manufactories and large factories. Small shoemakers, to cite just one example, far outstripped larger unmechanized firms and rivaled small factories with regard to value added per worker. Scale, in other words, was a liability in nonmechanized as well as in mechanized shops.

This accords with Chandler's observation on the importance of scale. What of his contention that firms which mechanized the throughput from end to end, such as fuel producers, were more efficient than those which were highly mechanized but had bottlenecks in the production process, such as machinery manufacturers? Table 13 provides some supportive evidence for this. Capital intensive fuel firms were in fact the most efficient with regard to labor productivity, while large metal firms, which were among the most highly capitalized but unevenly mechanized of all plants, were among the least productive. Although not shown in the table, the same conclusion also holds with respect to total factor productivity.

These results disclose that the large factory was not the efficiency leader in the mid- to late nineteenth century. The adoption of power tended to raise productivity and undoubtedly facilitated technological innovation across time, but other factors apparently worked against the factory's operational efficiency. Increasing the scale of operations, therefore, is not the crucial factor in explaining growth over time.

Labor Force Analysis. The preceding analysis has focused exclusively on technical variables. Yet it is clear that efficient factories required the coordination of workers as well as of instruments of production. Such coordination was likely to be hindered by the fact that the work force was not a set of homogeneous units that could be shifted from task to task or forced to work in tandem without objection or friction. This is one implication of recent scholarship on the interplay between industrialization and what wage earners bring to their jobs in the way of work habits and expectations. E. P. Thompson and Herbert Gutman thus argue that the unfolding of industrialization involved the conditioning of artisans and rural-urban migrants to new modes of work and tighter work disciplines.[54] Artisans, former farmers, and peasants surrendered their independence gradually and grudgingly, and their resistance to organizational and technological innovations unquestionably represented a restraint on firm efficiency. The initial stages of industrialization might thus be considered a period of training and indoctrination for an unwieldy labor force.

The operationalization of this argument requires the identification of the characteristics that affected worker performance. Gutman argues that the most important negative attribute is the lack of industrial exeprience—an attribute that was shared by immigrants of rural background and the Irish in particular, by rural-urban migrants, and by women, whose relatively abbreviated careers might have obstructed the "indoctrination period." Native-white Americans with urban backgrounds, on the other hand, would be expected to be the most productive workers. Age may be relevant as well, since it is suggestive of industrial experience. But it can be argued, as David Montgomery shows, that the most experienced (or the older) workers "learned the ropes" and understood how to foil the system and to resist change.[55]

Inadequate data prevent testing these hypotheses directly. Federal censuses do not specify an individual's tenure in a given locale, and while employee lists are available, they are neither systematic nor numerous enough to allow statistical analysis. Part of this data gap can be filled, however, by merging information from the population and manufacturing censuses in order to construct proxies for the labor force characteristics of different firms.

Our approach to measuring the impact of labor force characteristics involves the concept of the labor shed. We define a firm's labor shed as the geographical area from which it would draw employees. The boundary to this area was largely determined by transportation and walking distances. In 1850 we used a radius of one-half mile around a firm as the appropriate area, and in 1880 we increased this range to one mile.[56]

For each firm all individuals were identified who lived within the given distance and reported an appropriate occupation. Hats and caps, for example, were one of the four-digit industries (0802). For a company such as Marks' Brothers, a millinery manufacturer located at 108 North 8th Street in 1880, we selected out all individuals within one mile who listed occupations in the 0802 group. This process establishes a pool of potential employees for each firm. While it is obvious that this method cannot link individual workers to specific employers, it does capture the labor force and employee characteristics of a given firm.

For each firm we computed the ethnic configuration and average age of the labor shed. The ethnic categories included Irish, German, and black in

1850 and 1880, and second generation German and Irish in 1880. Under the assumption that each firm drew a representative sample of workers from its labor shed, the newly defined variables represent the qualities of its workers. In simple terms, we are arguing that firms in predominately German neighborhoods had a large percentage of German workers.

What we are doing, therefore, is allowing for variation in labor force characteristics *within* each industry. This is preferable to the use of intra-industry data where the simultaneous effects of technology, capitalization, and discrimination outweigh labor force differences. For example, we know that the Irish were heavily represented in low wage industries such as textiles and clothing. It could be argued that this is *prima facie* evidence that the Irish lacked industrial skills and were the cause of the low output per worker. Such an assertion would miss two important points. First, as shown above, labor productivity depends heavily upon the amount of capital available to each worker. More importantly, the issue is not whether the Irish or any other group had fewer industrial skills, but whether their attitudes and work habits prevented them from being effectively utilized in a factory environment. Hence, in discussing Irish textile workers, the proper basis for comparison is not native chemical producers but other textile workers. It is probable that the Irish were drawn into textiles because they lacked the requisite skills for other sectors, but it is improbable that this selection process also drew them to the least productive firms within the textile industry. For example, if firms with high proportions of Irish workers are associated with low output per worker, we can be more certain that this is due to the composition of the labor force.

The hypotheses are formalized within a production function framework. Adding the percentage of male employees from the census returns to the labor shed variables, we used a stepwise regression program to estimate the following extended Cobb-Douglas function.[57]

$$V/L = AL^{a+b-1} (K/L)^b P^c \exp [m\,\%\text{Male} + g\,\%\text{German} + r\,\%\text{Irish} + s\,\%\text{Black} + t\,\text{Age}] \qquad (5)$$

Given the cost of the labor shed analysis and the low variation in the variables for some industrial sectors, we have estimated the functions for only nine industries in each year. In our formulation the native-white American worker represents the standard of comparison.[58] A negative sign for any of the ethnic coefficients means that the group has lower productivity than the native-white Americans. A negative sign for the age coefficient indicates that older workers produced less, and the expected positive sign for m implies that firms with a higher percentage of male workers produced more per worker. Our other expectations are that r and g will be

negative, although the industrial background of Germans and their specialization in some trades suggests that violations of the latter hypothesis will
occur. For the second generation ethnic percentages available in 1880, we
expect no difference from the native-white Americans. The failure of blacks
to secure employment even with their great access to jobs makes it difficult
to theorize about the value of s, and given the ambiguity of the role of age,
we offer no set hypothesis for the value of t.

Our estimates of Equation (5) are reported in Tables 14 and 15. The
only consistent result is the significant positive signs for the percent male
variable. (The only exceptions are chemicals, in which over 80 percent of
the employees were male, and metals and hats in 1880, in which the low
number of female workers left little variation in the variable.)[59] There are
several possible explanations for this, one of which has to do with the nature of the female labor force. As is now well known, women workers had
attenuated careers, which may have limited their industrial training and accumulation of human capital. It is also noteworthy that women were relegated to the most menial jobs within the occupational hierarchies of these
industries. The limited range of occupations open to them glutted "wom-
en's" labor markets, and this, coupled with what appears to be discriminatory pay scales, kept their wages low. Poor earnings, in turn, contributed
to lower productivity.

The ethnicity parameters provide little support for our hypotheses.[60] The
German coefficient is positive in six cases, negative in four, and insignificant
(at the 20 percent level) for the remaining six. The only consistent results
across time are the positive value in the shoe and boot industry and in textiles. The former result is expected, given the traditional domination of the
trade by German craftsmen. The Irish estimates include six positive and
five negative values with no consistent pattern. Only in the furniture industry is the sign the same in both years; in textiles the sign goes from
negative to positive; in chemicals it goes in the opposite direction. Such results provide no systematic evidence that the Irish or Germans had levels of
productivity different from native whites. The same is true for blacks. In no
case was the coefficient statistically significant. Finally, the results show no
impact of average age on labor productivity in 1850 and mixed values for
1880 which precludes any conclusive statement on the effect of age on
efficiency.

These results cast some doubt on the hypotheses, except with regard to
women, but they should not be regarded as definitive. Although they are
based on data that are far more comprehensive than the available alternatives, several simplifying assumptions had to be made in order to conduct
the tests. The possibilities remain that labor in general was intractable and

Table 14. Production Functions with Laborshed Variables by Industry, 1850

Industry	Coefficients[a]								
	b	a + b	Power	% Male	% German	% Irish	Average Age	R^2	Sample Size
Food	.279 (.030)	.936 (.045)	.386 (.168)	.0020 (.0018)	—	—	—	.29	269
Boots & Shoes	.169 (.017)	.920 (.018)	.394 (.339)	.0037 (.0009)	.0098 (.0031)	.0040 (.0018)	—	.31	446
Hats & Caps	.310 (.042)	.945 (.032)	.296 (.249)	.0053 (.0010)	.0347 (.0112)	.0045 (.0030)	—	.61	134
Clothing	.226 (.026)	.956 (.020)	—	.0067 (.0001)	−.0032 (.0015)	—	—	.41	311
Textiles	.264 (.054)	.836 (.041)	.268 (.147)	.0029 (.0021)	.0114 (.0073)	−.0023 (.0014)	—	.47	124
Metals[b]	.303 (.069)	.922 (.035)	—	.0109 (.0037)	−.0070 (.0040)	−.0075 (.0050)	—	.35	73
Furniture	.258 (.042)	.910 (.043)	—	.0027 (.0021)	—	.0380 (.0096)	—	.37	115
Chemicals	.031 (.074)	.745 (.124)	1.120 (2.92)	—	—	.0085 (.0054)	—	.31	32
Printing & Publishing	.296 (.094)	.987 (.073)	−.222 (.179)	.0036 (.0036)	—	—	—	.33	33

Source: U.S. Manuscript Censuses of Manufactures and Population, 1850.

[a] Dependent variable is ln(V/L). The coefficient b is for the variable ln(K/L) and is capital's share. The term "a + b" is for ln(L) and is the scale parameter. Standard errors are reported in parentheses. Except for the labor and capital terms, variables were omitted with t-statistics less than unity.

[b] Includes Iron and Steel and Machine Tools and Hardware from above.

that immigrant workers were no more so than their native-born counterparts.

Conclusion

These findings raise the separate but ultimately related questions of why there was such unevenness in mechanization between and within industries and why scale did not yield greater returns per unit of input. There is no simple answer to either of these issues. Both require additional research, but a few possibilities suggest themselves at this writing.

The dualism in mechanization between new and old pursuits stemmed from a variety of factors. One of these was the state of the technology pool available to entrepreneurs at different points in time. As we have already seen, mid-century manufacturers of textiles, metal and metal products, fuel, chemicals, and paper had access to a broader and deeper range of capital equipment than their counterparts in the handicrafts. Endowed with this advantage, they had a head start, as it were, and outfitted their plants with

Table 15. Production Functions with Laborshed Variables by Industry, 1880

Industry	b	a + b	Power	% Male	% German	% Irish	Average Age	R^2	N
				Coefficients[a]					
Food	.191 (.018)	.841 (.029)	.356 (.092)	.0063 (.0013)	−.0049 (.0012)	−.0069 (.0026)	—	.24	802
Shoes & Boots	.171 (.023)	.933 (.021)	—	.0012 (.0012)	.0037 (.0036)	—	.0126 (.0122)	.15	438
Hats & Caps	.387 (.108)	.912 (.091)	.432 (.318)	—	−.0560 (.0375)	−.1028 (.0293)	−.1717 (.0800)	.77	29
Clothing	.332 (.025)	.871 (.018)	.099 (.098)	.0041 (.0007)	—	.0122 (.0039)	−.0108 (.0108)	.42	521
Textiles[b]	.295 (.051)	.849 (.040)	.175 (.136)	.0036 (.0019)	.0046 (.0042)	—	—	.46	129
Metals[c]	.236 (.003)	.895 (.025)	—	—	−.1459 (.0067)	—	.0249 (.0187)	.24	227
Furniture	.241 (.033)	.908 (.033)	.175 (.121)	.0049 (.0020)	—	.0183 (.0136)	−.0267 (.0150)	.25	230
Chemicals	.337 (.081)	.936 (.052)	—	—	−.0031 (.0026)	−.0094 (.0036)	—	.24	87
Printing & Publishing	.283 (.059)	.961 (.041)	.120 (.106)	.0053 (.0020)	.0177 (.0170)	—	—	.27	128

Source: U.S. Manuscript Censuses of Population and Manufactures, 1870, 1880.

[a] See Notes to Table 14.

[b] This result is for 1870. A laborshed radius of .75 miles was used.

[c] Includes Iron and Steel and Machine Tools and Hardware from above.

powered equipment much earlier than the craftsmen. They continued to modernize plants and equipment in the following thirty years as new inventions flooded the market and costs declined. Improvements came more slowly in the crafts, and while innovation picked up after 1850, employers in most trades, with the notable exception of publishers, still lagged behind entrepreneurs in newer industries.

This differential access to improved capital goods helps account for the variation in mechanization, but is not the sole explanation. To emphasize technology alone is to reduce the complexity of growth to vulgar technological determinism and to assume that entrepreneurs had complete freedom in their actions. No employer enjoyed such freedom. Each faced market conditions and forces beyond his immediate control, which placed constraints on the organization of production. The scope of markets and nature of demand, for example, could encourage or deter the deployment of machines and power sources, for as Raphael Samuel reminds us, mechanization was sensible and profitable only when "geared to large scale production."[61] Newer industries and segments of the handicrafts that reached out for regional and city-wide markets were in fact the most capitalized and mechanized, but such pursuits tended to be even more advanced than the crafts as a whole. One reason for this lies in the character of demand. Irregular and erratic trade plagued all industry, but was especially pronounced in certain consumer goods industries.[62] Shoe and clothing production suffered not only from long- and short-term fluctuations, but also from seasonal cycles. Firms ran part-time or shut down entirely in the dull season, and the wild fluctuations in trade probably deterred mechanization. Rather than tie up capital in machines which were sure to lay idle during the frequent downturns, employers preferred to hire more workers and subcontract in the busy season. When trade slowed, they could always cut costs by slashing employment rolls and refusing to let out contracts—options that were less available to those with highly mechanized plants.

The labor supply itself has been seen as a major incentive to mechanization in American industry. The dearth and dearness of labor, it is argued, caused employers to deploy machines in order to reduce labor costs. The extent of the labor shortage in Philadelphia has not yet been determined, but there is reason to believe that labor was not consistently scarce or expensive across the spectrum of industry. Workers were surely in short supply among industries still dependent on highly skilled labor, which is why manufacturers of metals, machines, and heavy equipment—to cite the most well-known examples—sought to undermine union rules and work practices that restricted the journeyman to apprentice ratio.[63] In the sweated trades, however, there appears to have been an adequate supply, if not a surplus, of inexpensive workers. Comprised chiefly of women, this force of cheap semiskilled labor was pressed into service as markets warranted and thus served as a substitute for mechanization.

Some forces deterred mechanization in old and new industry. Protracted downturns such as the long depression of the 1870s unquestionably halted growth and thus slowed down the deployment of machinery. Worker resistance to machines, though difficult to measure, played a role, as did the fact that some tasks did not easily lend themselves to machinery. For example, entrepreneurs and engineers alike threw up their hands in frustration over their inability to "formulate and to reduce" molding "to a system."[64] Even when molding machines and other devices appeared on the market, employers did not automatically take advantage of them, partly because inventors refused to guarantee the performance of their inventions, and partly because traditional managers could be every bit as resistant to mechanization as the most craft-proud worker. The role of managers and foremen in this process remains to be explored, but Daniel Nelson's recent study of foremen sheds some light on the issue. Nelson argues that the foreman was the "undisputed ruler of his department, gang, crew, or shop."

He hired and fired, laid out the work, disciplined the workers, and made sure that production quotas were met, but the latitude of his authority could extend beyond recruitment and supervision. Those in small batch and more backward industries, and possibly those with forceful personalities in most pursuits, often made decisions customarily attributed to owners and higher-level managers.[65] An engineer-inventor writing in the early 1890s put it this way:

> We have a case where the manager of a large iron foundry came to see a machine making castings similar to his own. He was especially interested when he saw a duplicate of one of his patterns on the machine, and, tons of machine-made castings in the yard for his inspection. There was no doubt, in his mind, of the value of molding machines in his business, and he wanted to introduce them. The question was left to his foreman, who decided against the purchase after seeing a machine in operation, and admitting the work was much better and cheaper than he could produce by hand. Here was a case where prejudice, or fear of a change in methods, overruled judgment. In another case, parties who are engaged in a competitive business, noted for low-priced castings, sent their foreman on a similar mission; on his return he insisted that one be furnished him, and their order for a machine followed. We have more than one instance on record of a foreman demanding machines. Such cases, however, are not the rule.[66]

The diseconomies of scale, our second major finding, can be traced to a combination of factors whose weights are still unclear. Mid-century entrepreneurs presiding over large scale enterprises were pioneers of a sort, feeling and sometimes stumbling their way through uncharted terrain. They were the first generation of American manufacturers to come to grips with managing unwieldy work forces, allocating substantial resources, arranging and rearranging the methods and instruments of production, delegating authority, and exercising other responsibilities for which there were few guideposts. Relying upon rule of thumb and trial and error, they evidently encountered some difficulty in one or more of these areas. Those who hired in excess of twenty-five workers faced the monumental organizational and managerial challenges inherent in any large-scale endeavor, and those who recruited inexperienced workers compounded the problem. Their foremen and subordinates who did the actual recruiting and supervising were not always up to the task. Some were pitifully corrupt. Instead of seeking the most productive and efficient workers, they often used favoritism and friendship to fill positions or tried to fill their own pockets by selling jobs to the highest bidders.[67]

If scale and inexperienced management confounded manufacturers, so did the organization of work. It was one thing to divide up the labor and install machines; it was quite another to restructure the components of fragmented work into an integrated whole, a point raised time and again by late nineteenth-century industrial engineers and scientific managers. Expansion was not simply a matter of adding proportionate increases in labor and capital as posited in a neoclassical production function. Growth apparently created as many problems as it allegedly solved. The scores on labor productivity are instructive in this regard (see Table 13). There was some variation among industry, but in most instances small factories with less than twenty-six workers outranked the largest firms, both mechanized and unmechanized. The glaring exception was fuel refining, and this is easily explained. Fuel refiners were among the only entrepreneurs who all but eliminated manual work and completely mechanized the production process. Having ironed out the bottlenecks and coordinated the throughput by the 1870s, they did not sacrifice efficiency upon hiring more workers, though there was probably a threshold beyond which even they could not venture without jeopardizing returns. Bottlenecks and discontinuities persisted in other industries and seem to have been especially troublesome in those with many different stages and steps in production. They were part of a broader problem in shoe and clothing manufacture. Manufacturers of footwear and apparel not only failed to synchronize the work-flow within the shop, they also were beset by the inefficiency and waste that accompanied farming out tasks to cottagers and subcontractors. It is noteworthy in this context that artisan shops and sweatshops—work settings without the technological variability of factories and manufactories—were nearly as efficient as small factories.

One last point deserves some mention. The discovery of decreasing returns to scale in a number of industries—clearly the most important empirical finding of this essay—seems to be "counter-intuitive." Because it goes against the grain of a vast body of historical scholarship, many scholars will be tempted to dismiss the finding out of hand. Such a dismissal would be unjustified. The traditional argument is appealing for two reasons. It is logically sound in that the most efficient firms should have been the surviving firms, and it has been supported by economists working with data for the twentieth century. But the argument has little or no empirical support for the earlier period. Jeremy Atack, perhaps the first scholar to estimate firm-level production functions for the mid-nineteenth century, came to the "acceptable" conclusion that "there did exist substantial economies of scale in antebellum manufacturing."[68] Yet this study is based on a data set far smaller than the Philadelphia samples, covers a shorter period of time, and reports on only five industries. It also shows just how far one must stretch the data to arrive at this conventional con-

clusion. A much fairer interpretation of Atack's production function results is that scale economies existed only in flour and lumber milling and
in western boot manufacture. The results for clothing and cotton textiles
conform with our own conclusion. In one of the few empirical works pur-
porting to show scale economies, therefore, the findings are mixed. This
study, on the other hand, uncovers a consistent pattern of nonincreasing
returns across twenty industries in a thirty-year period. And in spite of
its "counterintuitive" character, it is the most comprehensive examination
of efficiency differentials across size and work environment. It is hoped
that the relative strength of the results and the validity of our hypotheses
will be considered in future work.

The results imply that the typical large entrepreneur was best advised to
operate a single plant or a series of plants with around twenty-five workers
instead of a large factory with fifty or more employees. Yet we know that
many owners rejected this strategy for one of continued expansion. Why,
then, did businesses grow larger? Limited space and incomplete data pro-
hibit the resolution of this issue one way or another, if indeed so volatile
an issue can ever be resolved. But future researchers might find it useful to
pursue E. J. Hobsbawm's investigation of worker and employer attitudes
toward production. Such an approach would posit one or more strategies
and would seek to link them to employer and worker thinking. A complete analysis would consider both sides; here we posit a scenario from
the employer's perspective along the lines envisioned by Hobsbawm. It is
Hobsbawm's contention that rationalistic marketplace behavior—the "rules
of the game"—is learned.[69] Customary conceptions of workload and payment informed the thought and expectations of European employers well
into the nineteenth century. They clung to the notion that the lowest wages
and longest hours reduced labor costs per unit of time, and they paid little
or no attention to wage incentives and managerial practice until the late
Victorian period.

Customs, of course, died quicker in the United States, and it is still unclear whether traditional or older views had any currency among entrepreneurs on this side of the Atlantic. But an analogous phenomenon might
have been at work. In this connection one is reminded of the remark of a
lowly but informed cotton spinner who complained of his employer's
habit of purchasing poor cotton which repeatedly broke in the machine
and thereby reduced his earnings. Such employers, he griped, were ap-
pallingly ignorant of production methods. "True," he conceded, "they
understood the business of making money, but comparatively nothing
about machinery."[70] Contemporary industrial engineers expanded this
critique of Gilded-Age manufacturers. It was the engineers, and not en-

trepreneurs, it should be recalled, who studied plant organization, management, and payment methods and who put forth schemes in all such areas that were designed to increase both efficiency and returns per unit of input.[71] But few employers paid much attention at first. No "young upstart" fresh from college or "outsider" was going to tell *them* how to run their *factories*.

All of this suggests that employers were ignorant of or unconcerned with the rate of return. More than likely, they were chiefly concerned with the amount of return and blindly accepted the older, if not traditional, formulation of "so many hands, so many dollars."[72] Those who hired more workers, after all, accumulated more revenue and more profit, if not greater returns per unit of input. To them, enlarging workforces was a profit-maximizing strategy which strikes the modern observer as wrong-headed and misguided but which stands as the most reasonable explanation for the growth of scale in the precorporate age.

NOTES

1. J. Thomas Scharf and Thompson Westcott, *History of Philadelphia* (Philadelphia: L. H. Everts, 1884), III, 2231–32.
2. Louis McLane, "Report on Manufacturers," *Documents Relative to the Manufactures in the United States,* House Document No. 308, 22nd Congress, 1st Session (Washington: 1833); Eastern Pennsylvania in Document No. 13, vol. II, 195–234; Edwin T. Freedley, *Philadelphia and Its Manufactures* (Philadelphia: Edward Young, 1858).
3. Scharf and Westcott, *Philadelphia,* III, 2239.
4. William G. Whitney, "The Uses of Urban Space in Nineteenth-Century Philadelphia: Manufacturing Location at Mid-Century," paper presented at the Social Science History Association (Philadelphia, Pa.: October 1976), 1.
5. *Ibid.;* and Department of the Interior, Census Office, *Report on the Manufacturers of the United States at the Tenth Census* (Washington: U.S. Government Printing Office, 1883), xxiv.
6. Census Office, *Tenth Census,* xxvi.
7. *Ibid.,* xxxviii.
8. *Ibid.,* xxxiii, xxxviii.
9. Raphael Samuel, "The Workshop of the World: Steam Power and Hand Technology in Mid-Victorian Britain," *History Workshop Journal* 3 (Spring 1977), 6–72.
10. See, for example, Caroline Ware, *The Early New England Cotton Manufacture* (Boston and New York: Houghton Mifflin, 1931); Vera Shlakman, "Economic History of a Factory Town: A Study of Chicopee, Massachusetts," *Smith College Studies in History* 20 (October 1934; January, April, July, 1935), Nos. 1–4; Hannah Josephson, *The Golden Threads* (New York: Russell and Russell, 1949). Also, see Edward Kirkland, *Industry Comes of Age: Business, Labor and Public Policy* (Chicago: Quadrangle Books, 1967), esp. 163–80; and Thomas C. Cochran and William Miller, *The Age of Enterprise: A Social History of American Industry* (New York: Macmillan, 1942), esp. 129–53, 228–48.
11. For example, Samuel, "Workshop of the World"; Herbert G. Gutman, "Work,

Culture, and Society in Industrializing America, 1815–1919," *American Historical Review* 78 (June 1973), 531–88; David Montgomery, "Workers' Control of Machine Production in the Nineteenth Century," *Labor History* 17 (Fall 1976), 485–509; Michael P. Hanagan, "The Logic of Solidarity: Social Structure in Le Chambon-Feugerolles," *Journal of Urban History* 3 (August 1977), 409–26; and Brighton Labour Process Group, "The Capitalist Labour Process," *Capital and Class* 1 (Spring 1977), 3–26.

12. Alfred D. Chandler, Jr., *The Visible Hand: The Managerial Revolution in American Business* (Cambridge: Harvard University Press, 1977), 50–80, 240–83.

13. On the importance of coal, see Chandler, *Visible Hand*, 52, 76, 244–45; on transport and regional markets, see Diane Lindstrom, *Economic Development in the Philadelphia Region, 1810–1850* (New York: Columbia University Press, 1978), 93–151; on the declining cost of technology, see Dorothy Brady, "Relative Prices in the Nineteenth Century," *Journal of Economic History* 24 (June 1964), 145–203.

14. See, for example, Montgomery, "Workers' Control."

15. Robert Baird, *The American Cotton Spinner and Managers' and Carders' Guide: A Practical Treatise on Cotton Spinning* (Philadelphia: A. Hart, 1851). See also Freedley, *Philadelphia and Its Manufactures,* 234–39, 250–63.

16. *Ibid.;* and David Jeremy, "Innovation in American Textile Technology During the Early Nineteenth Century," *Technology and Culture* 14 (January 1973), 40–76. On the persistence of handloom weaving see Freedley, *Philadelphia and Its Manufactures,* 241–42.

17. Chandler, *Visible Hand*, 242–43.

18. Freedley, *Philadelphia and Its Manufactures,* 427–29; Scharf and Westcott, *History of Philadelphia,* III, 2253–54; Nathan Rosenberg, ed., *The American System of Manufactures* (Edinburgh: Edinburgh University Press, 1969), 1–86, 273–77.

19. On the inventiveness of local machine builders, see Freedley, *Philadelphia and Its Manufactures,* 130; and Bruce Sinclair, *Philadelphia's Philosopher Mechanics: A History of the Franklin Institute* (Baltimore, Md.: Johns Hopkins University Press, 1974), 293–95, 322-25. Helpful histories of machine tools are L. T. C. Rolt, *A Short History of Machine Tools* (Cambridge: M.I.T. Press, 1965); Nathan Rosenberg, "Technological Change in the Machine Tool Industry, 1840–1910," *Journal of Economic History* 23 (December 1963), 414–43; and E. G. Parkhurst, "Origin of the Turret, or Revolving Head," *American Machinist* 13 (May 24, 1900), 489–91.

20. See, for example, Isaac Vansant, ed., *The Royal Road to Wealth: An Illustrated History of the Successful Business Houses of Philadelphia* (Philadelphia: Samuel Loag, n.d.), 5–20, 76–107; United States Census Office, *Census of the United States, Manufacturing Schedule, County of Philadelphia, 1850 and 1880* (Microfilm, MSS, National Archives, 1850 and 1880). *Hexamer General Surveys* contain floorplans of the major industrial plants in the second half of the nineteenth century. Plans of the Baldwin works are in v. I, 7, and v. VI, 287. The *Surveys* have been indexed by Joyce A. Post, *A Consolidated Guide to the Hexamer General Surveys* (Philadelphia: n.p., 1974).

21. On molding, see Harris Tabor, "Machine Molding," American Society of Mechanical Engineers, *Transactions* 13 (1892), 537–56. The quotation is on 539.

22. Samuel, "Workshop of the World," 40. See also Montgomery, "Workers' Control."

23. Benson Soffer, "A Theory of Trade Union Development: The Role of the Autonomous Workman," *Labor History* 1 (Spring 1960), 141–63. See also, *Public Ledger,* July 30, 1849. Hereafter cited as *P.L.*

24. Vansant, *Royal Road,* 49–61.

25. Charles Robson, *The Manufactories and Manufacturers of Pennsylvania* (Philadelphia: Galaxy, 1875), 201–2; and Census Office, *Tenth Census, Manufactur-*

ing, MSS, 1860, 1870, 1880. For an excellent account of custom furniture production see George Henckels, *An Essay on Household Furniture: Its History, the Materials Used in Its Construction* . . . (Philadelphia: n.p., 1850).

26. For evidence of the division of labor before 1850 in shoemaking, see John R. Commons, "American Shoemakers, 1648–1895: A Sketch of Industrial Evolution," *Quarterly Journal of Economics* 24 (November 1909), 39–84; and protests of journeymen cordwainers in *Pennsylvanian*, Apr. 4, 1835, and (Letter signed "ONE OF THE CRAFT"), Mar. 28, 1850; in tailoring, see Freedley, *Philadelphia and Its Manufactures*, 22–23; Marcus T.C. Gould (reporter), *Trial of Twenty-Four Journeymen Tailors, Charged with Conspiracy* (Philadelphia: n.p., 1827), esp. 142 and passim; and *P.L.*, Sept. 9, 1850, May 31, 1851, which contains notices of meetings of garment cutters; in cabinetmaking see, *Pennsylvanian*, Apr. 22, 1835; *United States Gazette*, Jan. 15, 1835, Jan. 9, 1839; in printing, see *United States Gazette*, July 6, 1835; and *P.L.*, July 30, 1849.

27. The proportion of outworkers to shop workers at any point in time is difficult to gauge. One of the largest clothing manufacturers in New York hired 3,672 workers in 1850, but only 72 of them, mostly male and probably cutters and packers, worked on the premises. The remaining 3,600 employees, mostly young women, worked at home under the putting out system. See *Hunt's Merchants' Magazine* 20 (March 1849), 347–48. Other New York and Philadelphia clothiers may not have been so dependent on outworkers, but smatterings of evidence indicate that the system was quite common and probably embraced a majority of the tailors and shoemakers in the early antebellum years. See *P.L.*, Aug. 21, 23, 1843, and Dec. 4, 6, 1847, for trial proceedings of shopworkers accused of harassing scabbing outworkers during strikes.

28. *Atlantic Monthy* 51 (December 1877), 669–74; "Description of the Principal Occupations in the Shoe Industry," Extracts from *Vocational Pamphlet No. 2* (Cincinnati Public Schools), reported in Augusta Emile Glaster, *The Labor Movement in the Shoe Industry with Special Reference to Philadelphia* (New York: The Ronald Press, 1924), 201–7; and Robson, *Manufactories and Manufacturers*, 506.

29. Vansant, *Royal Road*, 143–44; Joseph H. Appel, *The Business Biography of John Wanamaker, Founder and Builder* (New York: Macmillan, 1930), 3–135; Herbert Adams Gibbons, *John Wanamaker*, 2 vols. (New York: Harper and Bros., 1926), I, 50–182; and Census Office, *Tenth Census, Manufacturing, MSS*, 1870 and 1880.

30. Galster, *Labor Movement*, 205.

31. *Atlantic Monthly*, "Modern Shoemaking"; Galster, "Principal Occupations in the Shoe Industry," esp. 203, 205–6. On garment cutting, see Freedley, *Philadelphia and Its Manufactures*, 221.

32. An account of Wanamaker and Brown in 1869 thus notes that "the employees of this large establishment, numbering over 1500 persons, *are paid regularly on the delivery of their work* . . ." (emphasis added). See *Royal Road*, 144. Shirley and Thornton, one of the largest manufacturers of ladies' and children's shoes in Philadelphia, employed five hundred workers in the 1870s, "all but fifty of whom are in the manufactory on Market Street, and the balance do the work at their homes." See Robson, *Manufactories and Manufacturers*, 376.

33. See Freedley, *Philadelphia and Its Manufactures*, 188. Also letter of John Herran, *P.L.*, Oct. 10, 1846.

34. See Elva Tooker, *Nathan Trotter: Philadelphia Merchant, 1783–1853* (New York: Arno Press, 1972 ed.), esp. 115.

35. See Commons, "American Shoemakers"; and letters in *Fincher's Trades Review*, May 14, 1864, 94; Feb. 11, 1865, 42, complaining of "sweating" in the needle trades.

36. *P.L.*, Oct. 10, 1846.

37. Freedley, *Philadelphia and Its Manufactures*, 241–42; David Montgomery, "The Shuttle and the Cross: Weavers and Artisans in the Kensington Riots of 1844," *Journal of Social History* 5 (Summer 1972), esp. 412–19.

38. See footnote 32.

39. *P.L.*, Mar. 2, 1846.

40. Freedley, *Philadelphia and Its Manufactures*, 241–42.

41. Vansant, *Royal Road*, 140. Numerous advertisements in local newspapers confirm the impression that many large manufacturers of consumer goods produced both mass market goods and custom goods.

42. The industrial census of 1870 recorded the number of machines per firm (up to three machines) as well as the motive power. This allows distinguishing firms using no machines from those with machines but without external power sources and those with machines and power. A preliminary analysis discloses that the range of workers in firms without machines or power plants ran from a low of 15 percent of the clothing workers to a high of half the construction workers. The overwhelming majority of the smallest firms, moreover, had neither machines nor power sources.

43. Some of these capital figures are misleading, however, especially in industries with relatively more fixed and permanent capital. This results from the Civil War inflation which pushed up capital costs and book values along with other prices. Since many companies apparently reported the original value of capital assets rather than a depreciated or replacement figure, real capital values are overstated. This is made obvious by noting the mean capital stocks for 1860, 1870, and 1880. In 1860, the average was $11,634, or 64 percent above the 1850 average. By 1870 the average had risen another 106 percent to $23,965. The 1880 value actually represented a decline of 33 percent but probably still includes an inflation premium. This conclusion is consistent with the observed 30 percent decline in capital productivity from 1850 to 1880. As expected, the most dramatic declines were in fuel, chemicals, and paper sectors where relatively more permanent capital was found.

44. Chandler, *Visible Hand*, 242, and passim.

45. The definition will vary with the functional form, but this is the basic definition. See M. Ishaq Nadiri, "Some Approaches or the Theory and Measurement of Total Factor Productivity," *Journal of Economic Literature* 8 (December 1970), 1137–77. Note that we can also write $A = (V/L)^a (V/K)^b$ if a and b sum to unity.

46. For example, the finding that A was higher in shoes than in textiles may be due to our equal weighting of male and female workers which overestimates the relative labor input in textiles if females are less productive. This input overestimate leads us to underestimate productivity in textiles.

47. Jacob Schmookler, *Invention and Economic Growth* (Cambridge: Harvard University Press, 1966).

48. In formal terms, a higher capital-labor ratio represents a substitution effect along given production isoquants, reducing the amount of labor used for any given level of output. In addition, labor-saving shifts in the production function were also occurring leading to new and more efficient production functions.

49. See Z. Griliches and V. Ringstad, *Economies of Scale and the Form of the Production Function* (Amsterdam: North-Holland, 1973). Our conclusions were unaffected by the choice of definition.

50. Materials remain a relevant factor in manufacturing. For instance, the cost of cotton surely affected textile prices and output.

51. With regard to the male-female aggregation, this will lead to biases in our estimates if male exceeded female (or vice versa) productivity and if there was a systematic variation in the ratio of males to females across the size of firms.

52. Since only nonzero values are allowed for continuous inputs, we assigned an arbitrary horsepower level of one to each firm without power. The alternative is to omit the many firms without power.

53. Alternative functional forms and input specifications were also used, but no significant scale economies were found. We examined the generalized Cobb-Douglas function that Atack used to find limited returns to scale in some manufacturing sectors for 1850 and 1860 but could not reject the simple Cobb-Douglas as being appropriate. See Jeremy Atack, "Return to Scale in Antebellum United States Manufacturing," *Explorations in Economic History* 14 (October 1977), 333–59. While Atack's paper emphasizes the identification of scale economies at the lower end of production, a fairer interpretation of the results is that in no industry was there an advantage to "large scale" production.

54. Gutman, "Work, Culture, and Society"; E. P. Thompson, "Time, Work-Discipline, and Industrial Capitalism," *Past and Present* 38 (1967), 56–97.

55. Montgomery, "Workers' Control."

56. Theodore Hershberg, Harold Cox, Dale Light, Jr., and Richard Greenfield, "The 'Journey-to-Work': An Empirical Investigation of Work, Residence and Transportation, Philadelphia, 1850 and 1880"; in this volume.

57. The percentage of native-white Americans is omitted from each equation to prevent perfect multicolinearity (the percentages would always add to 100). Hence, they represent the standard. A negative value for another group would mean their productivity was lower than the native whites, all other things equal.

58. Native-white Americans, of course, are not the best standard. As Gutman observes, immigrants from the countryside to the city were as unaccustomed to modern work rhythms as European peasants. Unfortunately, the population censuses do not distinguish rural- from urban-born peoples.

59. Also, the 1880 file for hats and caps included only twenty-nine observations.

60. The relative inconsistency of the ethnic parameters versus the sex parameter is to be expected from the relative accuracy of the data. The male-female ratio was directly measured. As an aside, it is interesting that the micro results for the total sample of nine industries nearly duplicate the interindustry results. Hence, the Irish coefficient was negative in both years and the German coefficients positive. Therefore the prior results probably were simply capturing the effects of the industries in which the two groups were employed.

61. Samuel, "Work Shop of the World," 54.

62. There is some evidence for this. The industrial census of 1880 recorded for each firm "months in operation" according to "full time only," "3/4th time only," "1/2 time only," and "1/4th time only." A preliminary analysis shows a rough correlation between undermechanized industries, such as clothing, and part-time operation.

63. See, for example, *F.T.R.*, Oct. 17, 1863, 79, and May 28, 1864, 103.

64. Harris, "Machine Molding," 537.

65. Daniel Nelson, *Managers and Workers: Origins of the New Factory System in the United States 1880–1920* (Madison: University of Wisconsin Press, 1975), 34–54. The quote is on 42.

66. Harris, "Machine Molding," 550.

67. Galster, *Labor Movement in the Shoe Industry,* 54–55.

68. Atack, "Return to Scale," 357.

69. E. J. Hobsbawm, "Custom, Wages and Work-Load," in Hobsbawm, *Labouring Men: Studies in the History of Labour* (New York: Basic Books, 1964 ed.), 344–70.

70. Massachusetts, Bureau of the Statistics of Labor, *Thirteenth Annual Report* (Boston: Rand, Ahern, 1882), 311.

71. See, for example, Nelson, *Managers and Workers,* 55–87. Also see, David R. Noble, *America by Design: Science, Technology and the Rise of Corporate Capitalism* (New York: Alfred A. Knopf, 1977).

72. Alan Dawley, *Class and Community: The Industrial Revolution in Lynn* (Cambridge: Harvard University Press, 1977), 74.

3. Immigrants and Industry:
The Philadelphia Experience, 1850–1880

BRUCE LAURIE THEODORE HERSHBERG
GEORGE ALTER

Shortly after Stephan Thernstrom published *Poverty and Progress* (1964), the first study by an American historian of social mobility in an urban setting, interest in the mobility patterns of the past century mushroomed. "Nowhere, perhaps," was "there a more obvious fit between national ideology and scholarly preoccupation," Michael Katz reminds us, than with "this American concern with making it."[1] In our haste to "get on with it," however, historians turned to the sociological literature. And, in being "more attentive initially to the sociologists who developed this field than to economic and labor historians pursuing changes in the composition and experience of the work force in particular occupations or in the economy as a whole," we were guilty of a time-consuming false start.[2]

Studies of occupational mobility, in particular studies which attempt to

This essay was originally presented at a conference, "Immigrants in Industrial America, 1850–1920," sponsored by the Eleutherian Mills Historical Library and the Balch Institute (November 1–3, 1973). The paper was revised in 1974 and presented to the Sixth International Congress on Economic History (Copenhagen, Denmark: August 19–23, 1974). It was revised again in 1975 and appeared in the *Journal of Social History* 9 (December 1975), 219–48. It is reprinted here with only minor revisions and additions.

The reader will note some disparities between the data presented here and that in Bruce Laurie and Mark Schmitz, "Manufacture and Productivity: The Making of an Industrial Base, Philadelphia, 1850–1880," also in this volume. These are the result of changes in the components of a few industries and of different definitions of the labor force. In particular, "Manufacture and Productivity" includes men, women, and youths in its definition of the labor force; in this essay, we consider men only.

Bruce Laurie wishes to thank the National Endowment for the Humanities for supporting his research with a post-doctoral fellowship.

describe social mobility, *require* the construction of vertical stratification schema for the classification of occupations according to skill, income, status, and so forth. Mobility is frequently thought of as connoting improvement, but movement among strata can be in three directions: from lower to higher, from higher to lower, or horizontally between two positions on the same level. The role assumed by the stratification scheme in such studies is crucial. The empirical findings will be seriously flawed if the strata *at each point in time* do not reflect the accurate ranking of occupations.

Sociologists who study social mobility concentrate primarily on status. They are able to construct classification schema which are justifiable empirically. "Some individual titles apparently have shifted their relative position," surveys of public opinion have shown, "but the overall transformation of the hierarchy in the last fifty years has been glacial in nature."[3] Unfortunately, historians do not have comparably firm data about occupational status for the nineteenth century. Extrapolating the current trend backward in time to a period which was dissimilar in important respects (such as income, education, skill levels, and industrial structure) would be dubious at best and fundamentally ahistorical. The occupational stratification schema used by sociologists scrutinizing the twentieth century cannot simply be appropriated by historians who wish to understand the nineteenth.

In retrospect this should not be surprising. Industrialization in the nineteenth century had a significant impact on the occupational universe; it altered occupational patterns perhaps more fundamentally, and certainly differently, than it did in the twentieth century. Radical changes were brought about through the reorganization of work and the introduction of labor-saving technologies. The problem of constructing occupational stratification schema in such an environment should not be underestimated or ignored.

If, for example, both the shoemaker who worked with his hands to fashion a pair of shoes in 1850 and the shoemaker who worked with the aid of a pegging machine to complete only part of the work required to make a pair of shoes in 1880 were classified in the same stratum (vertical category), no change would be recorded by the historian. Yet significant change did occur. There was a clear dilution of skill, a possible drop in income, and probably a decline in status as well. Classification schema based on skill, income, and status, therefore, would consider the change in the work done by the shoemaker as downward mobility, regardless of the fact that the occupational designation "shoemaker" remained the same in both years. A useful occupational classification scheme must take all of these factors into account.

Where does one acquire such detailed knowledge about nineteenth-century occupations? Even for those occupations about which we know a great deal, such as shoemaking, the required information seems almost impossible to find. General studies are available which describe the industry in England and Massachusetts, but are of limited value. Like most industries, shoemaking varied greatly from place to place, and knowledge of how the industry or occupation generally operated will not suffice when it is necessary to know the state of the industry or occupation for a *specific locale at a given time*. And if this is true for the few occupations and fewer industries about which we know relatively much, what about those of which we know little or nothing at all?

A considerable body of recent scholarship has produced important refinements in our understanding of the occupational structure by using the now familiar sources of the "new" social history—manuscript population censuses, city directories, and tax lists. Clyde Griffen argues, for example, that the line separating skilled craftsmen from proprietors is a blurred line, movement across which connotes as much downward as upward mobility.[4] Michael Katz suggests that the division between manual and nonmanual work was not as "firm or noticeable" as has been assumed.[5] Furthermore, it is now apparent that the category of "semiskilled" workers has rested on too little knowledge of work content to make it analytically useful. While these insights are valuable, the sources of the new social history suffer from several limitations: they cannot be employed systematically to devise strata sensitive to industrial changes in specific settings at specific dates; they can *describe,* but not *explain* the changing occupational patterns observed.

There is a source of information, however, which provides the requisite data. The manuscript schedules of the U.S. Census of Manufactures report wage rates, number and sex ratios of employees, mechanization, capital investment, and values of raw materials and finished products.[6] This detailed information for each firm makes possible the differentiation of industries and their ranking by *desirability* for the working man. When used in conjunction with the population manuscripts and impressionistic sources, they permit the description of the impact of industrialization on the occupational universe.

Systematic use of these data reveals how industrialization affected incomes, working conditions, and opportunities for career advancement. Specifically, the data point to further shortcomings in traditional occupational ranking schema. They reveal a considerable amount of variation in the objective conditions of skilled occupations which are usually assigned to a *single* category and indicate that the line separating skilled from unskilled workers blurs when one considers firm size and industry type. Above all, they demonstrate that industrialization shuffled the distribution of occupations within the occupational hierarchy. Traditional occupational ranking schema are static and, therefore, unable to capture the subtle changes in the occupational universe wrought by the process of industrialization.

What began for us as an attempt to improve the occupational stratification schema borrowed from sociologists has resulted in the determination that such schema are inappropriate to the tasks we have assigned them and that it makes sense to abandon the practice of using *a priori* occupational stratification schema as the *means* to the study of social mobility. For the time being we should concern ourselves with understanding the ways in which nineteenth-century occupations were actually stratified. Our new *means* might include socioeconomic and demographic profiles of individual occupations over time and sophisticated techniques of record linkage in order to reconstitute the actual careers of individuals. Our new *end* should be the accurate stratification of the nineteenth-century occupational universe.

To demonstrate both the opportunities and pitfalls inherent in such a reorientation of scholarly efforts, we focus in this paper on changes in the fourteen largest manufacturing industries in Philadelphia between 1850 and 1880. We seek to explain both how the industrial and occupational hierarchy changed and how this change affected the distribution of selected ethnic groups in the manual labor force.[7]

Patterns of Industrial Change

The fourteen industries under examination have been divided into manufacturers of consumer goods and manufacturers of producer goods.[8] The first group encompasses industries important in Philadelphia since the days of Dr. Franklin, namely shoemaking, clothing, baking, building construction, blacksmithing, printing, and traditional metal crafts. Included in the second group are textiles, hardware, machine tools, and iron and steel. With the exception of textiles, which appeared in colonial times but showed little growth before the Jackson period, these industries were new to the city. They emerged in the 1820s and 1830s when entrepreneur-inventors like Samuel Merrick, Matthias Baldwin, and Alfred Jenks opened foundries and machine shops and pioneered in the production of metal and metal products.

Though they were newer than the consumer industries, the producer industries developed more quickly and displayed greater industrial maturity in 1880. As Table 1 demonstrates, they were far more mechanized than the older industries both in 1850 and 1880. By 1880 nearly four-fifths of the firms in iron and steel and almost two-thirds of the firms in textiles

Table 1.   Percentage of Firms Using Steam or Water Power

Rank	1850		1880	
1.	Iron & Steel	76.3	Iron & Steel	79.1
2.	Textiles	50.6	Machines & Tools	67.4
3.	Machines & Tools	47.8	Textiles*	57.8
4.	Hardware	17.6	Hardware	39.2
5.	Printing	15.1	Printing	38.8
6.	Metal	7.4	Furniture	12.3
7.	Building Construction	5.5	Metal	8.7
8.	Furniture	4.6	Clothing	6.2
9.	Clothing	2.2	Meat Processing	4.6
10.	Baking	1.2	Blacksmithing	4.0
11.	Shoes	0.2	Baking	3.2
12.	Harnesses	0	Building Construction	2.6
13.	Meat Processing	0	Harnesses	2.5
14.	Blacksmithing	0	Shoes	2.4

Source: United States Census Office, *Census of the United States, Manufacturing Schedule, County of Philadelphia, 1850* and *1880* (Microfilm MSS, National Archives).

*Lorin Blodget's 1882 survey of area industrial firms revealed that the extant manuscript schedules of the 1880 United States Census of Manufactures are missing about 80 percent of Philadelphia's textile producers. The aggregate statistics for the textile industry published in the 1880 census compendium, however, provide a reasonably accurate gross picture of the city's textile industry, thus indicating that the federal census contained a fairly comprehensive enumeration of textile firms but that the data for many of these companies has since been lost. To remedy this data deficiency, we added the firms listed in Blodget's survey to those already taken from the federal census, but this was done subsequent to the initial 1975 publication date. We have revised Table 1 to incorporate the textile firms in Blodget's census. Other tables in the article could not be updated, however, because Blodget listed only the firm's name, type of product, location, number of employees (not differentiated by sex), number of engines and horsepower, and number and type of machines. Thus, the following tables are based on the original federal census manuscripts which now include about one-fifth of the city's textile establishments. We are not certain that these firms constitute an adequate sample of the textile industry. The data on power taken from Blodget's census do not sharply diverge from the information provided in the federal census and give us confidence that the missing firms are not grossly different from those found in the federal survey. Nevertheless, readers are urged to use caution in interpreting the other tabular data for textiles found in this text, especially that contained in Tables 2, 3, 4, and 5. See Lorin Blodget, *Census of Manufactures of Philadelphia* (Philadelphia: 1883).

and machine tools produced wares with the aid of steam or water power. Firms in the older industries were primitive by comparison. Printing and publishing houses showed the most advancement, but only 38.8 percent of them in 1880 boasted power-driven presses. Furniture makers rank a distant second: less than 12 percent of them were equipped with steam or water power, while less than 10 percent of the firms in each of the remaining industries used steam engines or water wheels.

The predominance of steam power in the newer industries helps account for the striking disparity in capitalization between them and the older industries (see Table 2). Median capitalization of these firms surpassed consumer industries in 1850 and 1880, and median capitalization in each producer-goods industry increased in the period. Capitalization also increased

Table 2.   Median Capitalization (in $)

	1850		1880	
1.	Iron & Steel	10,867	Iron & Steel	29,750
2.	Textiles	4,833	Textiles*	9,194
3.	Hardware	4,500	Hardware	5,461
4.	Machines & Tools	3,250	Machines & Tools	5,250
5.	Printing	3,125	Printing	5,232
6.	Clothing	2,958	Clothing	2,487
7.	Furniture	1,538	Furniture	2,200
8.	Metal	1,375	Meat	1,479
9.	Meat	1,350	Metal	1,288
10.	Harness	1,030	Baking	1,036
11.	Building Construction	948	Building Construction	975
12.	Baking	839	Harness	780
13.	Shoes	690	Shoes	681
14.	Blacksmithing	582	Blacksmithing	492

Source: See Table 1.

*See Note for Table 1.

Table 3.   Median Number of Male Employees Per Firm*

	1850		1880	
1.	Textiles	19.50	Iron & Steel	31.88
2.	Iron & Steel	13.00	Printing*	9.75
3.	Clothing	9.69	Textiles*	9.50
4.	Printing	9.50	Hardware	6.92
5.	Machines & Tools	6.08	Machines & Tools	6.86
6.	Furniture	4.96	Clothing*	6.06
7.	Building Construction	4.92	Furniture	3.98
8.	Hardware	4.71	Building Construction	3.39
9.	Shoes	4.55	Metal	2.52
10.	Harness	3.75	Shoes*	2.14
11.	Metal	2.73	Blacksmithing	1.92
12.	Blacksmithing	2.65	Baking	1.61
13.	Baking	2.05	Harness	1.46
14.	Meat	1.41	Meat	1.39

Source: See Table 1.

*The data in Tables 3, 4, and 5 do not include female employees or youths and thus underrepresent firm size for industries having a significant proportion of these workers, in particular printing, textiles, clothing, and shoes. For the proportion of female operatives in these industrial categories, see Table 2 in Laurie and Schmitz, "Manufacture and Productivity," in this volume.

Moreover, as indicated in the Note for Table 1, Blodget's 1882 census does not differentiate employees by sex; thus we cannot include the textile firms added from this survey in the computations for Tables 3, 4, and 5 which present data for male employees only.

in printing and furniture-making, but they are exceptional. Capital costs of most consumer industries either remained constant between 1850 and 1880 or actually declined as in clothing, blacksmithing, harnessmaking, shoemaking, and metal crafts.[9]

Firms in the newer industries not only required more capital and used more power-driven machinery; they also employed more workers than firms turning out consumer goods. As Table 3 shows, the rank order did not change appreciably between 1850 and 1880. Table 4 analyzes shop size another way; it distinguishes firms with 1 to 5 employees, firms with 6 to 50 employees, and firms with more than 50 employees. The aggregate picture conforms to our expectations in that categories 1 and 2 lost ground to category 3. Where in 1850 the largest firms employed 51 percent of the labor force, in 1880 they employed 61 percent. The one exception to this is hardware, in which the largest firms lost some ground to the medium-sized operations, but the largest hardware manufacturers still employed 60.2 percent of their labor force in 1880. In the consumer industries the trend toward larger firms is unmistakable, but even more striking is the persistence of small shops, especially in meat, baking, and blacksmithing. Even in shoes and clothing, where most of the labor force was located in large firms, there were still large numbers of small shops in 1880 (see Table 5).

Data contained in the industrial census of 1880 confirm the suspicion that firms with less than five employees were not the proverbial handicraft shops of bygone days whose journeymen and masters produced custom goods on flexible work schedules and enjoyed relatively cordial relations. Instead, they were sweatshops characterized by frequent layoffs, the division of labor, and long hours under the rigid hand of severe taskmasters. Table 6 offers some insight into the abysmal working conditions in "sweated" industries—meat, baking, clothing, and shoemaking. The table shows that they were the most flagrant violators of the standard ten-hour day, operating in excess of ten hours as well as running on "short time" and capriciously shutting down in the middle of the day.

We are also skeptical of the view put forth by some historians that large firms and heavy industry were the bane of the skilled worker. It is misleading to equate nineteenth-century foundries and iron and steel mills with modern factories and to envision those who labored in such settings as an undifferentiated mass of semiskilled workers. The production of iron, steel, and heavy machinery entailed a range of intricate processes. The various craftsmen, semiskilled workers, and unskilled workers who performed this labor were linked in an elaborate occupational hierarchy. The work environment could be disagreeable, the work itself was often dangerous, but

Table 4. Percentages of Workforce by Number of Male Employees Per Firm*

| Industry | Number of Employees Per Firm | | | | | |
| | 1850 | | | 1880 | | |
	1–5	6–50	50+	1–5	6–50	50+
Iron & Steel	1.7	34.1	64.2	0.7	16.9	82.4
Textiles*	1.8	20.2	78.0	2.4	39.6	58.0
Hardware	11.8	23.9	64.3	3.9	35.9	60.2
Machines & Tools	6.2	38.2	55.6	4.8	38.2	57.0
Printing*	5.0	51.2	43.8	3.6	37.7	58.7
Building Construction	22.6	54.0	23.4	24.0	45.7	30.2
Clothing*	4.8	44.3	50.9	2.8	17.3	79.9
Furniture	17.9	62.1	20.0	11.7	45.5	42.8
Metal	48.6	33.0	18.3	22.2	41.3	36.5
Meat	67.2	32.8	—	59.7	27.3	12.9
Harness	15.8	41.0	43.2	15.3	30.5	54.2
Baking	71.1	28.9	—	45.2	34.8	19.9
Shoes*	16.9	46.6	36.5	8.5	28.6	62.8
Blacksmithing	61.0	28.4	10.6	78.3	21.7	0
All 14 Industries	11.2	37.7	51.1	9.5	29.6	60.8

Source: See Table 1.

*See Notes for Tables 1 and 3. For a breakdown by the number of *all* employees, see Table 4 in Laurie and Schmitz, "Manufacture and Productivity," in this volume.

skilled workers in large firms were well compensated for their endeavors. Cross tabulations of the wages of skilled workers by size of firm demonstrate that there was a direct relationship between firm size and average daily wage, so that *by 1880 the larger the firm, the higher the wage* (see Table 7). Some skilled workers, no doubt, objected to what one historian calls the "impersonal and mechanical" relations with employers.[10] Yet it is not entirely clear that factory work in heavy industry was as degrading in the eyes of the skilled worker as many historians believe. The perceptions of workers obviously deserve more treatment than is possible here, but it appears that some skilled workers found decided advantages in working for large employers, quite apart from the fact that they earned higher wages. One such worker, a machinist by trade, though not a Philadelphian, tells us that

> Large firms can hire help to better advantage than small ones. The mass
> of workingmen like to feel that their situations are as permanent as pos-
> sible, and this they cannot do when employed in a small shop. For one
> of limited means to secure the services of an expert and really valuable
> assistant, extra considerations must be offered, and even these will not
> retain such labor if the work seems likely to fail. The highly paid assistant
> hired in this small way, must be frequently employed upon a class of work
> which in a large shop would be done by the most unskilled, inexperienced,
> and, of course, poorly paid labor. . . .[11]

Table 5. Number of Firms by Number of Male Employees Per Firm*

Industry		1850				1880		
		Number of Employees Per Firm						
	0–5	6–50	50 +	Total	0–5	6–50	50 +	Total
Iron & Steel	6	13	3	22	6	20	17	43
Textiles*	46	87	53	186	25	59	8	92
Hardware	76	42	7	125	114	122	27	263
Machines & Tools	42	44	6	92	96	113	19	228
Printing*	36	60	10	106	105	148	36	289
Building Construction	83	59	3	145	588	227	18	833
Clothing*	165	294	43	502	301	255	93	649
Furniture	84	66	3	153	185	105	20	310
Metal	83	11	1	95	166	47	5	218
Meat	81	3	0	84	458	23	2	483
Harness	32	15	3	50	96	21	2	119
Baking	384	29	0	413	910	73	8	991
Shoes*	339	224	20	583	441	139	34	614
Blacksmithing	141	18	1	160	187	12	0	199

Source: See Table 1.

Note: Due to the fact that the census only recorded firms producing more than $500 per year, there may be serious undercounting of firms with one or no employees.

*See Notes for Tables 1 and 3.

When we translate daily wages into average yearly earnings, we begin to appreciate the plight of the small master craftsman and his journeymen under the stress of industrialization. Calculations of average yearly earnings of each industry are presented in Table 8. The table suggests that in 1850 handicraft producers enjoyed an enviable position in the marketplace, since their journeymen earned the highest incomes. And while there was a considerable gap among industries, the range within industries was nominal. Thirty years later, however, industrialization undermined the small producer, who could not compete with larger, more efficient firms and whose workers held the least remunerative jobs. Workers employed by the largest and medium-sized employers, whether they were in the consumer or the producer group, secured the best incomes. In the consumer industries, for example, workingmen employed by the *largest* printers and publishers, boot and shoe manufacturers, and construction bosses, earned the highest incomes, as did workers in the remaining industries who found employment in the medium-sized firms. In the producer industries, workers employed in the largest firms (with the exception of textiles) garnered the best incomes.

In this thirty-year period, moreover, the disparity in earnings within industries increased considerably. To take a few examples, the range in incomes between wage earners in small and medium-sized shoemaking shops

Table 6. Percentage of Firms by Hours Worked per Day May to November

Industry	Under 10 Hours	10 Hours	Over 10 Hours
Iron & Steel	2.3	97.7	0
Textiles*	14.1	81.5	4.4
Hardware	3.0	94.7	2.3
Machines & Tools	3.9	94.7	1.3
Printing	18.3	81.0	0.7
Building Construction	4.3	95.0	0.7
Clothing	14.8	81.4	4.0
Furniture	4.8	93.9	1.2
Metal	3.2	95.4	1.5
Meat	21.9	38.5	39.5
Harness	1.7	95.8	2.5
Baking	10.3	36.4	53.3
Shoes	8.4	85.4	6.4
Blacksmithing	1.5	93.5	5.0

Source: See Table 1.

*See Note for Table 1.

in 1850 was only $2, but widened to $84 in 1880. In the meat-packing and baking firms, the disparity between incomes was $31 and $10 respectively in 1850, $55 and $133 thirty years later. The same pattern holds for the new metal trades in which the margin between the smallest and largest iron and steel mills and machine shops was $26 in both in 1850 and $196 and $75 in 1880. This period also witnessed the development of major differentials between the incomes of workers in the producer and consumer groups. Table 9, which ranks each industry by average yearly income, shows that in 1850 neither group dominated; representatives of each were dispersed randomly in the rank order. But in 1880 the producer industries achieved superiority and occupied three of the top four positions in the ranking. The average yearly income of manual workers in these industries ranged between $468 and $631, while the range within the consumer groups, if we exclude printing for the moment, was between $359 and $469. Or, to put it another way, by 1880 the highest average earning in the consumer group was the lowest in the producer group.

These developments in industrial Philadelphia closely parallel the findings of Eric Hobsbawm in his brilliant study of the "Labour Aristocracy" in nineteenth-century Britain.[12] In both cases metal trades developed rapidly. Iron and steel mills, foundries, and machine shops proliferated and employed a highly diversified labor force comprised partly of iron puddlers, rollers, machinists, and other skilled workers who formed the aristocracy of labor, partly of semiskilled workers who toiled alongside the aristocrats, and partly of unskilled workers who performed menial tasks.[13]

Table 7. Average Daily Wages Paid by Number of Employees per Firm in 1880

Skilled Mechanic	1-5	1880 6-50	51+	Ordinary Mechanic	1-5	1880 6-50	51+
Iron & Steel	1.97	2.30	2.48	Iron & Steel	1.25	1.35	1.42
Textiles*	1.84	1.99	2.00	Textiles*	1.24	1.31	1.31
Hardware	2.04	2.25	2.44	Hardware	1.24	1.28	1.39
Machines & Tools	2.09	2.29	2.47	Machines & Tools	1.15	1.40	1.34
Printing	2.03	2.45	2.70	Printing	1.14	1.27	1.48
Building Construction	2.07	2.18	2.29	Building Construction	1.39	1.93	1.45
Clothing	1.90	2.14	2.55	Clothing	1.10	1.19	1.30
Furniture	2.08	2.18	2.27	Furniture	1.23	1.42	1.34
Metal	2.00	2.18	2.40	Metal	1.25	1.28	1.27
Meat	1.57	1.80	2.00	Meat	0.99	1.31	1.38
Harness	1.78	2.07	2.00	Harness	1.16	1.23	—
Baking	1.65	2.20	2.50	Baking	1.20	1.26	1.30
Shoes	1.65	2.06	2.54	Shoes	0.93	1.32	1.67
Blacksmithing	1.86	2.38	—	Blacksmithing	1.14	1.38	—

Source: See Table 1.

Note: Entries in this table have been weighted by the number of male employees in each firm.

*See Note for Table 1.

Puddlers, rollers, machinists, and other skilled metal workers earned the highest incomes of all tradesmen, though superior earnings alone did not distinguish them from other workers. As Hobsbawm notes, a number of nonwage factors—conditions of work, relations with other workers and other social classes, styles of life—also figure in the equation. Historians are only beginning to treat those complex matters, but some evidence suggests that skilled metal workers occupied a more advantageous position in the workshop than most handicraft workers. Not the least of their advantages was considerable autonomy, despite the impressive advances in technology. They often combined managerial functions with manual skills, hiring their own crews and frequently determining the quantity and quality of outputs. It was precisely such autonomy that would inspire a determined effort by large employers and scientific managers to wrest control of the workplace from skilled workers in the 1890s and the early twentieth century. But in the third quarter of the nineteenth century, as David Montgomery demonstrates, skilled metal workers were the vanguard of tradesmen who exercised "control over the actual use of . . . implements in the productive process. . . ."[14] Few if any of them could realistically aspire to become employers because of the enormous capital requirements, but they commanded considerable status and respect, both from employers

Table 8.   Average Yearly Wages Paid to Males by Number of Employees per Firm

1850	1–5	6–50	51+	Total	1880	1–5	6–50	51+	Total
Boots & Shoes	272	274	263	270	Boots & Shoes	378	462	492	469
Harness	322	339	378	353	Harness	440	484	n.a.	469
Textiles	268	226	197	206	Textiles*	436	491	436	468
Clothing	319	333	236	287	Clothing	409	449	329	359
Baking	271	281	—	273	Baking	393	526	400	435
Meat	305	336	—	306	Meat	385	440	422	405
Furniture	373	335	374	351	Furniture	457	489	433	462
Blacksmithing	300	268	—	300	Blacksmithing	448	466	—	452
Printing	355	370	372	370	Printing	398	445	578	518
Building	375	340	159	307	Building	453	446	508	467
Hardware	391	329	320	330	Hardware	498	418	609	534
Metal	383	319	330	352	Metal	414	466	444	446
Machines & Tools	354	326	328	329	Machines & Tools	469	464	544	509
Iron & Steel	319	394	345	361	Iron & Steel	474	454	670	631

Estimation procedure for 1880:
(Average male wages) = (Total wages paid)/
([#males] + .4 [#females] + .3 [youths])

Source: See Table 1. Entries in this table have been weighted by the number of male employees in each firm.
*See Note for Table 1.

who relied heavily on their skill and judgment and from wage earners below them in the occupational hierarchy.

Workers performing semiskilled tasks and ordinary labor in the new metal trades, moreover, were better off than their counterparts in the older industries. They earned slightly more per day than most ordinary workers in consumer industries and had more access to skilled jobs atop the occupational hierarchy because these industries had a greater ratio of skilled to unskilled jobs than did the old crafts. In the crafts, on the other hand, the division of labor diluted skills, and mobility held less promise for the ordinary workers who competed for a diminishing number of "skilled" jobs.

Within the consumer group certain industries expanded, namely printing and to a lesser extent, building construction. These industries contained their own occupational hierarchy with a sizable labor aristocracy, paid relatively high wages, and offered skilled workers considerable job satisfaction and prestige.[15] In fact, "aristocrats" could be found in most older industries, as in cabinetmaking, where a select few fashioned expensive furniture, or in clothing, where garment cutters whose ability to ruin employers with a fatal slip of the knife earned them prestige, respect, and high wages.[16]

Table 9. Average Yearly Wages Paid to Males

1850		1880	
Printing	370	Iron & Steel	631
Iron & Steel	361	Hardware	534
Harness	353	Printing	518
Metal	352	Machines & Tools	509
Furniture	351	Boots & Shoes	469
Hardware	330	Harness	469
Machines & Tools	329	Textiles*	468
Building Construction	307	Building Construction	467
Meat	306	All 14 Industries	464
Blacksmithing	300	Furniture	462
All 14 Industries	288	Blacksmithing	452
Clothing	287	Metal	446
Baking	273	Baking	435
Boots & Shoes	270	Meat	405
Textiles	206	Clothing	359

Source: See Table 1.

Note: Entries in this table have been weighted by the number of male employees in each firm.

*See Note for Table 1

In the main, however, working people found consumer industries less rewarding and less desirable between 1850 and 1880. These pursuits lacked the elaborate occupational hierarchy of the newer industries, which provided a career ladder for workers within a given firm. The alternative to rising within a firm was opening a small shop, which was still possible in many industries whose capital costs were not prohibitively high. Such was the case in meat processing, clothing, shoemaking, and baking, where shops capitalized at $500 were still common as late as 1880.

Yet it is improbable that journeymen bettered themselves by opening small shops. Small producers usually operated on the fringe of their industry as subcontractors producing specialized goods for large manufacturers.[17] The intense competition of subcontracting forced small employers to "sweat" journeymen and even to work alongside them in the hope of cutting costs. This arrangement necessarily blurred the functional line between employer and employee in the shop, but the risk remained squarely on the shoulders of the employer who operated on a thin profit margin and was constantly haunted by the specter of ruin. Many, and perhaps most of them, did fail, and those who succeeded earned little more than the people they hired and less than many factory foremen (see Table 10).[18]

Table 10.   Average Gross Profits of Firms Reporting Capital of $500 or Less

| | 1850 | | 1880 | |
	N	Average ($)	N	Average ($)
Boots & Shoes	261	427	287	520
Harness	15	341	50	482
Textiles*	14	428	5	818
Clothing	73	529	148	674
Baking	147	552	308	914
Meat	15	650	154	1665
Furniture	34	477	82	637
Blacksmithing	75	413	116	744
Printing	15	816	18	1058
Building Construction	50	780	333	877
Hardware	11	638	41	620
Metal	21	323	70	631
Machines & Tools	10	283	21	687
Iron & Steel	0	—	0	—
All 14 Industries	741	482	1633	907

Source: See Table 1.

*See Note for Table 1.

Patterns of Occupational Change

Changes in the ethnic composition and occupational distribution of the male labor force accompanied the transformation of Philadelphia's industrial activity.[19] Population doubled between 1850 and 1880, but the city's principal nativity groups—Irish and German immigrants and native-born whites—did not contribute equally to the population growth. Table 11 shows that Philadelphia's male work force grew from 100,404 in 1850 to 215,686 in 1880, an increase of over 100 percent. During this period the Irish maintained their standing as the city's largest immigrant group with 27,152 adult males in 1850 and 39,428 in 1880. But Irish immigration failed to keep pace with the city's expansion, and the Irish fell from 27 percent of the male work force in 1850 to 18 percent in 1880. German immigrants, on the other hand, increased at the rate of 137 percent, from 11,427 in 1850 to 27,099 in 1880. The number of native white males in Philadelphia increased from 56,754 to 139,716, an increase of 147 percent. Less than half of the native white entrants into the labor force in this period, however, were of native-born parentage. In 1880 there were 24,399 native-born sons of Irish immigrants and 13,860 native-born sons of German immigrants. (The columns headed "Irish 2," "German 2," and "Other 2" in Table 11 give the number of native-born sons with foreign-born parents.)

Table 11.   Male Workforce* by Ethnicity

1850	Black	Irish	Irish 2	German	German 2	NWA	Other 2	Total
N =	5071	27152		11427		56754		100,404
% of total	5.1	27.0		11.4		56.5		100.0
1880								
N =	9443	39428	24399	27099	13860	87930	13527	215,686
% of total	4.4	18.3	11.3	12.6	6.4	40.8	6.3	100.0
% increase	86.2	45.2		137.1		54.9		114.8

Source: United States Census Office, *Census of the United States, Population Schedule, County of Philadelphia, 1850* (microfilm MSS, National Archives).

*Males 18 years and older

The proportion of each group that found employment in manufacturing declined between the two census years. The Germans showed the smallest decrease (64.1 to 61.1 percent), followed by the Irish (40.7 to 33.8 percent), and the native whites (53.7 to 44.0 percent). The sons of German immigrants were just about as heavily concentrated in manufacturing as their fathers in 1880 (59.7 percent). The sons of Irish immigrants, however, reversed the trend of their fathers and entered manufacturing, so that 47.3 percent of them worked in that sector of the economy in 1880.

What concerns us here are the skilled and unskilled workers employed in our fourteen industries.[20] Occupations in these industries account for slightly less than half the skilled labor force in 1850, slightly more than half of it in 1880. Occupations in the consumer industries—shoemaker, tailor, butcher, and the like—represent a much larger segment of the "skilled" labor force in both census years than those in the producer industries. In the ensuing three decades, however, they declined from 25.3 percent of the labor force to 23.2 percent, while the occupations in the producer industries increased from 6.9 to 8.2 percent of the labor force. And there is every reason to believe that this trend continued, since the metal trades and other producer industries expanded dramatically in the following three decades.

Four consumer industries—meat, baking, printing, and the old metal crafts—increased their share of the labor force. All others lost ground, usually in the neighborhood of 0.5 percent of the total male work force. The most dramatic declines occurred in shoes, whose share of the laboring population fell from 6.2 to 3.4 percent, and in clothing, which declined from 3.4 to 2.7 percent in 1880 (see Table 12). Conversely, the producer industries grew, the only loss coming in textiles which dropped 1 percent of the labor force between 1850 and 1880 when the handloom weaving industry virtually disappeared.

Table 12.   Percentage of Ethnic Group by Industry

Industry	Irish	Irish 2	German	German 2	NWA	Total
Iron & Steel						
'50	0.3		0.3		0.9	0.6
'80	1.4	2.2	0.6	1.3	1.6	1.4
Textiles						
'50	13.0		2.9		0.8	4.3
'80	4.0	6.4	3.2	2.6	1.9	3.3
Hardware						
'50	0.4		0.7		0.9	0.7
'80	1.1	1.6	0.8	1.8	1.2	1.2
Machines & Tools						
'50	0.6		1.4		1.8	1.3
'80	1.1	2.4	2.3	2.4	2.9	2.3
Printing						
'50	0.6		0.9		2.3	1.6
'80	0.7	3.2	1.3	3.1	3.3	2.4
Building Construction						
'50	4.2		2.6		10.2	7.4
'80	4.4	6.7	3.0	5.7	11.0	7.3
Clothing						
'50	2.9		8.6		2.9	3.4
'80	1.9	1.3	8.3	3.9	1.6	2.7
Furniture						
'50	0.5		4.7		1.7	1.7
'80	0.4	0.6	3.7	1.7	1.3	1.4
Metal						
'50	0.3		0.5		0.8	0.6
'80	0.4	1.4	0.9	1.3	0.9	0.9
Harness						
'50	0.3		0.5		0.7	0.5
'80	0.3	0.1	0.4	0.1	0.3	0.3
Baking						
'50	0.9		7.8		1.0	1.7
'80	0.6	0.3	7.7	5.1	0.7	1.8
Boots & Shoes						
'50	5.2		11.6		5.9	6.2
'80	4.2	2.1	8.1	3.1	2.4	3.4
Blacksmithing						
'50	1.4		1.7		2.0	1.7
'80	2.1	1.8	1.4	1.5	1.1	1.4
Medical/Legal						
'50	0.3		0.4		2.0	1.3
'80	0.3	1.4	0.5	1.3	2.9	1.7
Street Trades						
'50	4.3		1.0		1.2	2.1
'80	5.1	6.4	1.6	3.1	2.7	3.5

Source: See Table 11.

Table 13 displays the occupational distribution of the Irish, German, and native-born groups, and it reveals few surprises. Even by a crude occupational rank order the Irish fare the worst of the three groups in 1850, for nearly half of them were located in day labor (30.3 percent), handloom weaving (11.6 percent), and carting (3.3 percent). Less than a third of them worked at "skilled" trades (excluding handloom weavers). The Germans also fulfill our expectations. We know that many of them arrived in America as skilled workers, and it is not surprising to find them less dependent upon unskilled labor and more heavily represented in the skilled trades than the Irish. In 1850 only 11.6 percent of them toiled as day laborers and nearly two-thirds worked at skilled trades. They were especially prevalent in shoemaking, tailoring, and baking, which together account for one-fifth of the German male labor force (see Table 13). The occupational superiority of the native-born whites requires little elaboration. Suffice it to note that they were much less involved in unskilled labor than the other groups and less evident than the Germans in clothing and shoemaking, but more concentrated in the prestigious building trades and printing and disproportionately represented in commerce and the professions.

Thus at mid-century, native-white Americans and German immigrants dominated the most desirable skilled occupations. Heavily involved in printing, building, clothing, and shoemaking, they plied trades which promised fairly high wages and whose skills were just beginning to be diluted by segmentation of work or by machinery. Many of them were extremely articulate, a talent which they often parlayed into leadership positions in social organizations, trade unions, and local political parties. Local leaders of some prestige, they easily qualified as the labor aristocracy of their day.[21]

The occupational distribution of the immigrants in 1880 looks much as it did in 1850. Only two changes stand out. About 10 percent of the Irish ceased operating handlooms as weaving finally moved into the factory, and the proportion of German day laborers fell from 11.6 to 6.4 percent, an impressive change by any measure. Otherwise there were no striking changes. The Irish were still mired in unskilled labor, the Germans still employed chiefly in traditional crafts.

Upon closer examination, however, Table 13 indicates a trend barely perceptible among the immigrants, but apparent in the native whites and native-born sons of immigrants. These groups began to abandon traditional trades in the consumer industries (excluding printing and building trades), though they did so at slightly different rates. The desertion of sons of Germans is most impressive, for only 15.7 percent of them plied these

Table 13. Percentage of Ethnic Group by Occupation

Occupation	Irish	Irish 2	German	German 2	NWA	Total
Laborer						
'50	30.3		11.6		3.7	13.0
'80	30.0	14.7	6.4	6.1	5.8	12.6
Weaver						
'50	11.6		2.4		0.4	3.6
'80	1.6	1.7	1.1	0.9	0.2	0.9
Dyer						
'50	0.7		0.5		0.2	0.4
'80	0.4	1.1	0.6	0.3	0.3	0.5
Molder						
'50	.02		0.1		0.5	0.4
'80	0.4	1.2	0.1	0.6	0.6	0.5
Iron Molder						
'50	0.0		0.0		0.0	0.0
'80	0.2	0.4	0.1	0.3	0.3	0.3
Boiler Maker						
'50	0.1		0.1		0.1	0.1
'80	0.5	0.3	0.2	0.2	0.2	0.2
Machinist						
'50	1.5		3.3		2.7	2.3
'80	1.0	2.2	2.0	1.8	2.4	2.0
Printer						
'50	0.3		0.3		1.2	0.8
'80	0.3	1.5	0.4	1.3	1.5	1.1
Stone Mason						
'50	0.7		0.3		0.3	0.4
'80	0.8	0.2	0.6	0.2	0.2	0.4
Plumber						
'50	0.1		0.0		0.2	0.1
'80	0.3	1.1	0.1	0.3	0.8	0.6
Carpenter						
'50	2.7		1.6		6.5	4.6
'80	1.9	1.7	1.6	2.1	4.3	2.8
Painter						
'50	0.6		0.7		1.6	1.1
'80	0.6	1.2	0.6	1.3	2.0	1.3
Bricklayer						
'50	0.4		0.1		1.6	1.1
'80	0.4	1.2	0.2	0.3	0.9	0.7
Plasterer						
'50	0.3		0.0		0.9	0.6
'80	0.4	0.6	0.0	0.3	0.7	0.5
Tailor						
'50	2.4		7.4		1.9	2.6
'80	1.3	0.2	6.4	2.0	0.5	1.5
Turner						
'50	0.1		0.7		0.3	0.3
'80	0.0		0.1	0.2	0.1	0.1
Varnisher						
'50	0.1		0.1		0.1	0.1
'80	0.1	0.2	0.2	0.4	0.1	0.1
Cabinet Maker						
'50	0.4		4.0		1.1	1.2
'80	0.1	0.2	2.9	1.2	0.6	0.8

Table 13.   (cont'd) Percentage of Ethnic Group by Occupation

Occupation	Irish	Irish 2	German	German 2	NWA	Total
Locksmith						
'50	0.1		0.6		0.1	0.2
'80	0.0		0.4	0.2	0.1	0.1
Tinsmith						
'50	0.1		0.3		0.2	0.2
'80	0.3	1.0	0.6	0.5	0.6	0.6
Butcher						
'50	0.1		1.0		0.7	0.5
'80	0.3	0.7	3.5	3.5	1.5	1.5
Harness Maker						
'50	0.1		0.1		0.1	0.1
'80	0.2	0.1	0.3		0.2	0.2
Saddler						
'50	0.2		0.4		0.6	0.4
'80	0.1		0.1	0.1	0.1	0.1
Baker						
'50	0.8		6.3		0.5	1.2
'80	0.5	0.3	5.4	3.5	0.3	1.2
Shoemaker						
'50	3.5		7.4		4.2	4.2
'80	3.2	1.3	6.5	2.2	1.4	2.4
Blacksmith						
'50	1.4		1.8		2.0	1.7
'80	2.0	1.8	1.4	1.4	1.1	1.3
Lawyer						
'50	0.1		0.0		0.9	0.6
'80	0.1	0.6	0.0	0.3	1.0	0.5
Doctor						
'50	0.1		0.3		1.1	0.7
'80	0.1	0.3	0.4	0.6	1.5	0.8
Clerk						
'50	1.5		1.2		5.0	3.4
'80	0.3	2.3	0.4	2.4	3.8	2.2
Drayman						
'50	1.0		0.4		0.1	0.4
'80	0.3	0.1	0.0		0.0	0.1
Ostler						
'50	0.6		0.7		0.2	0.4
'80	0.6	0.0	1.0	0.2	0.2	0.4
Carter						
'50	3.3		1.4		0.9	1.6
'80	1.0	0.6	0.2	0.6	0.2	0.5
Teamster						
'50	0.0		0.0		0.1	0.0
'80	1.2	1.6	0.4	1.3	0.9	1.0

Source: See Table 11.

trades compared to 30.1 percent of the 1850 immigrant cohort, a shift of 52.7 percent. The sons of Irish immigrants and native-born whites followed close behind and displayed shifts of 47.5 and 29.4 percent respectively. In 1880 only 5.7 percent of the sons of Irish immigrants and 6.6 percent of the native whites worked at these trades. It is perhaps ironic, but in the occupations of the consumer industries, the Irish sons and the native whites resemble one another more than the Germans. German immigrants were so concentrated in these crafts in 1850 and 1880 that their native-born sons constituted a sizable residual force despite the alacrity with which they abandoned the handicrafts.

An even broader parallel between the occupational distributions of the sons of immigrants and native whites emerges when we examine the ethnic composition of printing and the building trades. Unlike other older crafts, these trades still commanded relatively high wages in 1880. All of the groups entered the expanding printing industry in this period, but setting type was more of a magnet for the immigrant sons. The proportion of printers in the native-white population increased by only 0.3 percent (from 1.2 to 1.5 percent, Table 13), and the immigrant proportions hardly changed at all. The sons of immigrants, however, entered printing more rapidly than the native whites and more easily than their fathers and achieved parity with the native whites by 1880. In building construction the three native-born groups began to converge. The percentage of native whites declined from 11.1 in 1850 to 8.9 in 1880, while large numbers of immigrant sons became building tradesmen. Six percent of the Irish sons, for example, worked at skilled construction trades compared to 4.8 percent of the 1850 Irish cohort; the proportion of German sons in building was 4.6 percent, almost two percentage points higher than the Germans in 1850.

The sons of Irish immigrants also gained access to the prestigious jobs in the new metal industries. Slightly over 4 percent of them, compared to 1.8 percent of the 1850 cohort, plied skilled trades in machine shops, iron foundries, and rolling mills. Indeed, they had a higher proportion in these trades in 1880 than both the native whites (3.5 percent) and the sons of German immigrants (2.9 percent).

By 1880 German immigrants and their sons had as low a proportion of their numbers in casual labor as the native whites (roughly 6 percent). The percentage of native-white day laborers actually increased between 1850 and 1880 (from 3.7 to 5.8), probably as a result of in-migration from rural areas. A sizable share of Irish-born Philadelphians (30.0 percent) still worked as unskilled laborers in 1880, but casual labor was not as appealing to their sons. Only 14.7 percent of them were so employed in 1880. It appears, then, that the position of unskilled Irish sons paralleled that of skilled German sons in the traditional consumer crafts. Each group rapidly deserted the sphere of its fathers, but Irish immigrants were so dependent upon casual labor and German immigrants so concentrated in the older crafts that their sons could not help but remain heavily represented in those occupations.

Conclusion

The evidence presented here warrants two concluding observations and invites speculation about the relationship between immigrants, occupations, and industrial change. First, it is evident that the occupational distribution of Irish and German immigrants did not change significantly between 1850 and 1880. Aside from the Irish retreat from handloom weaving, which was not a matter of choice but a necessity, since the industry disappeared, and the German shift out of day labor, each group clustered in the same occupations in 1850 and 1880.

The occupational distribution of these immigrants had less to do with the conditions in America than with prior experience in the Old World. Rural, underdeveloped Ireland bequeathed her sons very little in the way of industrial experience or skill, which forced Irish immigrants in Philadelphia to assume positions at the bottom of the occupational hierarchy. They entered day labor, occupations easily learned such as handloom weaving or shoebinding, and street trades which required no skill and small capital investment. Germans who left their country in the midst of the industrial revolution brought skills with them, and it is fitting that we find the majority of them in skilled trades in 1850 and 1880, especially in shoemaking, tailoring, and baking.

A combination of factors made it difficult for immigrants to take advantage of opportunities and shift into more rewarding occupations. Nativist feelings, which ran high in Philadelphia after the anti-Catholic riots of 1844 and which were directed chiefly against the Irish, probably inspired some employers to reserve the most remunerative jobs for native-born Americans. Germans could have been victimized by nativism to some extent as well, though one suspects that they had peculiar reasons not to seek new opportunities. Many of them came to America expressly to practice trades which were threatened by technology in the homeland. Wedded to the traditional crafts by habit and custom, they were not especially disposed to forsake the trades they valued so highly.[22] Shifting into new occupations also necessitated learning and acquiring skills, which took time and commitment, and German and Irish immigrants were much older than the native-born population in 1880. Well into their careers, they could not easily shift into more desirable jobs.

Second, our analysis of industrial change runs counter to the view held by many historians who see this period as an "Age of Industrialization," animated by the rapid and wholesale application of steam power and technological improvements.[23] This essential misunderstanding derives from equating industrialization with mechanization. The use of mechanized production techniques constitutes only a single *stage* (with greater import for the economics than the sociology of industrialization) which occurred relatively late in the process of industrialization. John R. Commons's classic study of the shoe industry made clear that significant changes in the organization of work, authority relationships, and production techniques transformed the role of the craftsman long before mechanization was introduced.[24]

Towns like Fall River, Massachusetts, or Johnstown, Pennsylvania, which housed textile factories and iron and steel mills, shifted to mechanization early and rapidly. Perhaps the dramatic nature of the industrial change experienced by towns dominated by a single industry explains why some historians have mistakenly equated industrialization and mechanization. But in a large city with a diversified economy like Philadelphia, which produced everything from silk handkerchiefs to iron rails, the complexity and unevenness of industrial development precludes such a view.

In Philadelphia, mechanization did not reach much beyond heavy industry and textiles, which we referred to earlier as producer industries. Modern though they were, these pursuits employed a relatively small proportion of the manual labor force. Most of the city's male manual workers were located in the consumer industries, which were not as mechanized as we have been led to believe. Still, significant changes did occur. Between 1850 and 1880 these industries underwent considerable division of labor, used the latest hand tools, employed larger numbers of workers per firm, and produced their goods in factories even though they did not rely upon independent power supplies. It was not unusual in the 1870s, for example, for 150 shoemakers to be working under one roof without steam power.

Such transformations in the premechanized stages of work occurred at different times in different industries in different cities. A host of factors influenced these changes: the state and cost of local technology and the expertise of local craftsmen in fashioning new tools and machines; the strength of organized labor; the level of skills, availability, and ethnic composition of the labor force. In some industries innovations were so gradual that workers experienced no great or abrupt changes in procedures and work methods. Other industries changed more rapidly, which forced workingmen to make major adjustments to new methods. Whichever the case, it seems that the most important developments in authority relationships and work roles occurred prior to mechanization. The independent craftsman or skilled worker, in other words, was not reduced to the factory operative in one fell swoop. A major challenge facing historians will be to comprehend the socioeconomic consequences of such incremental changes for those who worked in this period of premechanized industrialization.

The nature of industrial change in Philadelphia, coupled with the occupational careers of its immigrants, sheds some light on our limited understanding of occupations and job mobility. All too often we treat skill as an absolute and assume that an occupation is either skilled or it is not, that a man who calls himself a tailor, carpenter, or butcher is a skilled worker. It should be clear, however, that skill is relative in that one skilled occupation may require more skill than another, though we hasten to add that measuring the differences is extremely difficult. It should also be evident that the skill level of an occupation changes over time, as do wage rates and the immediate environment of the workplace. We know, for example, that occupations such as butchering, tailoring, and shoemaking changed considerably relative to newer occupations in Philadelphia between 1850 and 1880. Division of labor diluted skills, sweatshops with rigorous work routines emerged, wages declined, and career opportunities for workingmen were limited because these operations lacked an articulate occupational hierarchy. The reverse occurred in the new metal trades, where both skilled and unskilled workers commanded relatively high wages, skill was at a premium, and career opportunities were probably good because of the developed occupational ladder.

All of which is to say that we must not assume that all skilled occupations were equally desirable or inherently *better* than unskilled occupations. Skilled jobs generally commanded higher wages in the period under discussion, but the wage differential between skilled and unskilled labor is not as great as we have been led to believe for the labor force overall. The line between these occupational groups blurs when we introduce the variable of shop size, for we find that wages of "skilled" workers in small shops in select consumer industries were hardly better than wages of "ordinary" workers in the largest shops in the new metal trades. Judging from wage rates presented in Table 7, moreover, it appears that there was as great a differential among rates paid to skilled workers as there was between the wages of the lowest paid skilled workers and unskilled laborers. Jobs in the consumer industries were even less desirable from the standpoint of career potential. Many of them were a *cul de sac,* and no one realized this more than the sons of immigrants.

If we regard career potential as an important component of occupation then it behooves us to rethink our stereotype of unskilled labor. We might consider the possibility that German immigrants were not that much better off than their Irish counterparts simply because they were more likely to be "skilled" workers.[25] German immigrants were locked into declining crafts. Just as large numbers of Irish sons remained in day labor where their fathers were so heavily concentrated, the sons of German immigrants were still located principally in the crafts in 1880. But many of these first generation Americans perceived that better opportunities lay in the developing industries and assumed skilled jobs in printing, building construction, and heavy industry.

The means by which the sons of immigrants moved into these occupations is not known since we have not yet traced the careers of individuals. But we cannot resist the temptation to speculate that the Irish immigrants' lack of skills was not so great a disadvantage to their sons as has been thought.[26] It seems that the crucial occupational designation is *laborer,* which we normally associate with deprivation—low status, low wages, and limited career potential—and usually locate at the bottom of the occupational rank order. The problem with this assessment is that it fails to consider the career potential of some day laborers employed in building construction and the metal trades.[27] These laborers may have been engaged in on-the-job training, or what we should like to call "informal apprenticeship."[28] Toiling beside skilled workers on construction sites and in foundries and machine shops, they probably learned how to perform highly skilled jobs, which they later practiced as skilled workers. German sons followed a similar career pattern, but did so more slowly, partly because they did not have as much access as their Irish counterparts to the informal training ground of unskilled labor.[29]

By 1880 then, we find that the sons of Irish and German immigrants have begun to abandon occupations in the consumer industries and have gained a foothold in skilled occupations in printing, building construction, and the new metal industries. By entering these trades, they established themselves as labor aristocrats, an honor previously held by native-born Americans and some German immigrants. In abandoning the older crafts, they made room for the "new" immigrants who flocked to meat packing, the needle trades, and to unskilled positions in the iron and steel industry at the turn of the century.

NOTES

1. Michael B. Katz, *The People of Hamilton, Canada-West: Family and Class in a Mid-Nineteenth-Century City* (Cambridge: Harvard University Press, 1975), ch. IV.

2. Clyde Griffen, "Occupational Mobility in Nineteenth-Century America: Problems and Possibilities," *Journal of Social History* 5 (1972), 310–30.

3. David L. Featherman and Robert M. Hauser, "On the Measurement of Occupation in Social Surveys," *Sociological Methods and Research* 2 (1973), 241.

4. Griffen, "Occupational Mobility," 324–27.

5. Katz, *op. cit.,* ch. IV.

6. These documents report richly detailed information for each firm whose annual product was valued at $500 or more. The schedules for 1850 and 1860 are identical. Variables include name of corporation, company, or individual; name of business, manufacture, or product; capital invested; raw materials used; quantities, kinds, value; kind of motive power, machinery, structure, or resources; average monthly rate of male labor; average monthly rate of female labor; annual products: quantities, kinds, values.

The schedule for 1870 dropped some valuable detail, especially the separate reporting of average monthly wages paid to male and female employees, replacing them with a lump sum paid to all employees for the entire year, but added important information describing the kinds and numbers of machines used and the number of months the firm was in active operation. Variables include name of corporation, company, or individual; name of business, manufacture, or product; capital invested; motive power: kind of power, if steam or water, number of horsepower; machines: name or description, number of; average number of hands employed: males above 16, females above 15, children and youth; total amount paid in wages during year; number of months in active operation reducing part time to full time; materials: kinds, quantities, value; production: kinds, quantities, value.

The schedule for 1880 changed more dramatically, dropping information on the specific kinds, quantities and values of raw materials and finished products, but adding a host of new detailed information including an invaluable distinction in wages paid to "skilled" and "ordinary" labor. Variables include name of corporation, company, or individual; name of business, manufacture, or product; capital invested; greatest number of hands employed: males over 16, females over 15, children and youth; number of hours in ordinary day of labor: May to November, November to May; wages and hours of labor: average day's wages for a skilled mechanic, average day's wages for an ordinary laborer, total amount paid in wages during the year; months in operation: on full time, on 3/4 time only, on 2/3 time only, on 1/3 time only, idle; value of material; value of product; power used in manufacturing: if water used, on what river or stream, height of fall in feet, wheels: number, breadth in feet revolutions/minute, horsepower; if steam power used; number of boilers, number of engines, horsepower. (Also see Appendix II.)

7. Our discussion focuses on three distinct groups of males above the age of 18: a) the "Irish and Germans," foreign-born immigrants identified by their place of birth; b) "second-generation Irish and Germans," American-born sons of Irish and German fathers; and c) "native-white Americans," American-born sons of native-white parents. Second-generation males can be differentiated from native whites only for the year 1880. The 1850 census identified the place-of-birth for the individual *only,* while the 1880 census reported the place-of-birth for the father and mother as well as for the individual. The 1850 figures for native-white Americans, then, include all native-born whites regardless of parental birth (see Table 3).

Although we have data available for all black males above the age of 18 as well, they have not been included in this analysis. Blacks were so excluded from the industrial sector of the economy that discussing their occupational patterns within the context of this paper would be counterproductive. Their occupational patterns are treated in Theodore Hershberg, "Free Blacks in Antebellum Philadelphia: A Study of Ex-slaves, Freeborn, and Socioeconomic Decline," *Journal of Social History* 5 (1972), 191–92, 198–200; also in this volume. The occupational distribution of Philadelphia's Negro community is discussed in Theodore Hershberg and Henry Williams, "Mulattoes and Blacks: Intra-Group Color Differences and Social Stratification in Nineteenth-Century Philadelphia"; in this volume.

8. It should be added that these are crude categories constructed to facilitate our discussion. As will become evident, there are exceptions in each group, the most conspicuous of which are printing and building construction in the consumer group and textiles in the producer group.

9. Because of an undercounting of small firms in the 1850 manufacturing census, the figures for median capitalization presented in Table 2 may be somewhat inflated, masking a slight increase in capitalization by 1880. Any increase which might have occurred, however, remains small by comparison with the increases observed in the producer industries.

10. Edward C. Kirkland, *Industry Comes of Age: Business, Labor and Public Policy, 1860–1897* (Chicago, 1967), p. 351.

11. Massachusetts Bureau of the Statistics of Labor, *Report* (Boston: Wright and Potter, 1870), pp. 338–39.

12. E. J. Hobsbawm, *Labouring Men* (New York, 1964), pp. 272–315.

13. For an example of the range of wage rates and occupations in the metal industries, see *Annual Report of the Secretary of Internal Affairs of the Commonwealth of Pennsylvania, Part 3, Industrial Statistics*, vol. 4, 1875–1876 (Harrisburg, 1877), pp. 546, 621, and ff. See also *Ibid.*, vol. 6, 1877–1878, passim.

14. David Montgomery, "Trade Union Practice and the Origins of Syndicalist Theory in the United States" (Paper delivered at the Sorbonne, 1968), p. 3; United States Senate, *Report of the Committee of the Senate upon the Relations Between Capital and Labor*, 5 vols. (Washington, D.C., 1885) 2: 2–3; David Brody, *Steelworkers in America: The Non-Union Era* (Cambridge, Mass., 1960), p. 52.

15. Seymour M. Lipset, Martin Trow, and James S. Coleman, *Union Democracy* (Glencoe, Ill., 1956), pp. 1–76; and Robert Christie, *Empire in Wood* (Ithaca, N.Y., 1956), pp. 25–28.

16. See Montgomery, "Trade Union Practice"; and Edwin T. Freedley, *Philadelphia and Its Manufactures* (Philadelphia: Edward Young, 1858), p. 221.

17. Blanche E. Hazard, *The Organization of the Boot and Shoe Industry in Massachusetts Before 1875* (Cambridge, Mass., 1921), pp. 87–126. See also Charles Booth, *Labor and Life of the People* (New York, 1970), 1st ser., vol. 4, pp. 37–156 and 2nd ser., vol. 3, pp. 9–50.

18. A foreman blacksmith from Philadelphia reported to Pennsylvania's Secretary of Internal Affairs that his yearly income for 1880 was $900 (*Industrial Statistics*, vol. 8, 1879–1880, p. 247). This compares favorably with the average profit of small blacksmith firms, which was $744 in 1880 (see Table 10). The same source indicates that foremen in various industries earned daily wages ranging from $2.25 to $6.00 (annual incomes of $675 to $1800). See *Industrial Statistics*, vol. 4, 1875–1876, pp. 546–49; and vol. 9, 1880–1881, pp. 163–65.

19. Although we have collected data on the occupational patterns of women, they were not available for use in this essay. The discussion in this section, therefore, is based on the male work force above the age of 18.

20. "Unskilled" labor is of two types: *specified* occupations such as "watchman," and *unspecified* occupations such as "laborer," "day labor," "laboring man," etc. Our discussion here focuses on the *unspecified* category "laborer"; that is, occupations whose designation in the population manuscripts does not allow for categorization into an industry group.

21. See Bruce Laurie, "The Working People of Philadelphia, 1827–1853" (Ph.D. diss., University of Pittsburgh, 1971), chs. 7, 8, and Appendix C.

22. Mack Walker, *Germany and the Emigration, 1816–1885* (Cambridge, Mass., 1964), p. 69.

23. See, for example, Thomas C. Cochran and William Miller, *The Age of Enterprise*, rev. ed. (New York, 1961), p. 223; Ray Ginger, *Age of Excess* (New York,

1965), pp. 35–36; and Carl N. Degler, *The Age of the Economic Revolution 1876–1900* (Glenview, Ill., 1967), p. 34.

24. John R. Commons, "American Shoemakers, 1648–1895," *Quarterly Journal of Economics* 24 (1910), pp. 39–84.

25. If the ownership of real property is considered as a measure of "well-being," this possibility gains support. Although the proportion of Germans who were "skilled" workers was *twice* that of the Irish, the Germans were only 20 percent more likely to own real property. In 1870, 16.2 percent of the Germans and 13.6 percent of the Irish owned real property (these figures are age-standardized).

26. Stephan Thernstrom, *Poverty and Progress* (Cambridge, Mass., 1964), pp. 99–102, 109–11, and 155–57.

27. The problem, of course, is how operationally to differentiate among this large group of workers. The population census manuscripts do not provide any information beyond the designation "laborer" which can be used to resolve this problem. Although the manufacturing census manuscripts contain information which explicitly and implicitly describes the work environment, they do not list by name the individuals employed by each firm. Taken alone neither of these two sources of information is useful in overcoming the problem. But if they can be combined in some fashion, it may be possible to differentiate among laborers.

The Philadelphia Social History Project has worked out a method ("industrial geography") which links the residence of the individual worker to the location of the individual firm in which he may have worked (this method is not limited to laborers, but can be used in the linkage of any worker to any firm). Laborers who lived within roughly a two-block radius (empirically derived) of the firm are identified as likely to have worked in the firm, and their careers are treated separately in analysis. A profile of their well-being, including ownership of real and personal property and whether wives worked and children attended school, can be constructed and compared to profiles of other groups of laborers. The profiles of laborers who are identified as employed by firms paying high wages, for example, should be better than those of laborers who were linked to firms paying low wages or to undifferentiated laborers who probably were employed on a very casual basis. This method of linking individuals to the firms in which they may have worked will be most successful in the outlying areas of the city where heavy industry was located and where identification of potential employees will not be complicated by the dense concentration of people and firms at the city's center. "Industrial geography" is discussed in greater detail in Theodore Hershberg, "The Philadelphia Social History Project: A Methodological History" (Ph.D. diss., Stanford University, 1973).

28. See, for example, Robert Tressell (pseud., Robert Noonan), *The Ragged Trousered Philanthropists* (London, 1971), p. 15; and Sidney Pollard, *A History of Labour in Sheffield* (Liverpool, 1959), p. 84.

29. See the proportion of Irish and German sons with occupations in building construction, new metal trades, and printing (Tables 12 and 13).

PART II

SPACE

"Urban studies, historical or contemporary," Charles Tilly reminds us, "is about human settlements—people in space."[1] Indeed, this volume's opening essay argued that the major weakness of the "New Urban History," as well as much that came before it, was its failure to understand that above all else cities are "peculiar environments." Lacking conceptual frameworks which elaborate the linkages between behavior and environment, these earlier studies treated *urban* as *site* not *process*. Without understanding how "the spatial distribution of people, institutions, activities and artifacts influences, or is influenced by" what else happens in cities,[2] little progress will be made in the effort to determine whether and for what the category "urban" matters.

Central to the processes of urbanization and industrialization which shaped our cities is the socioeconomic differentiation of urban space. The American city of the late eighteenth and early nineteenth centuries, except for specialized areas along the waterfront, was characterized by "ill-defined and overlapping" commercial and industrial districts. Work and residence were combined at the same address, rich and poor lived side by side, and residential segregation among racial, ethnic, and socioeconomic groups was allegedly uncommon. The city of today, in striking contrast, is characterized by the sharply differentiated use of urban space. Commerce and industry are found in clearly defined areas removed from residential neighborhoods. Work and residence are entirely separated. Neighborhoods reflect marked segregation along family stage, class, and ethnic-racial lines.

But how did these changes come about? It is important to bear in mind that these *then* and *now* capsule characterizations of spatial form in

American cities are only historical snapshots, not the active processes through which urban spatial differentiation actually occurred. It is not that we lack *any* historical perspective, in other words, but that the existing one is static rather than dynamic. Present knowledge, therefore, is descriptive rather than explanatory. Spatial differentiation has been used to describe differences in a wide range of city types across cultures, but it has rarely been treated as a process through which urban spatial arrangements were transformed.

Between 1850 and 1880, the size of Philadelphia's population and the space that it inhabited doubled. The spatial patterns of the city at the end of this period, however, were not a duplication of those extant at its beginning. In 1850, Philadelphia's urban form was clearly rooted in its colonial past: it was geographically compact and contained a heterogeneous mix in industry, business, and residence. By 1880, the spatial structure of the city had begun to assume the unmistakable dimensions of the modern metropolis: it had pronounced retail, commercial, financial, governmental, and cultural functions in a central district;[3] industrial concentrations and working-class communities in specific sections of the city; and purely residential neighborhoods, relatively homogeneous and middle- and upper-class in composition at its peripheries.[4]

Although it is true that "large American cities have always grown chiefly by peripheral accretion," it is important to bear in mind that the "deconcentration" of population which began in the nineteenth century was part of a larger process through which population and the urban space it inhabited became differentiated.[5] It is not merely that the city expanded, but that its basic spatial structure changed.

Significant changes in economic and social structure wrought by industrialization were expressed physically in the spatial form of the city. Spatial and socioeconomic differentiation proceeded in tandem. Spatial differentiation, from this theoretical perspective, does more than passively reflect changes in the larger social and industrial structure. New spatial patterns themselves functioned as dynamic forces in determining future social relationships and urban form.[6] Explanations for Philadelphia's multifaceted transition from a commercial to an industrial city are found in advances in technology—production, transportation, communications, and building construction—and in human decision-making—political activities, land speculation, and capital markets. Although these changes were underway between 1850 and 1880, they would not be clearly seen until well into the twentieth century.

At any point in Philadelphia's economic development, the city's ecological form can be understood as the spatial manifestation of its "structure of opportunities"—the nature of available jobs, housing, transportation, and the like. In its most basic sense, then, location in urban space, especially in the "walking city" of the nineteenth century, must be understood as *access* to a broadly defined range of opportunities.

Here it is useful to think of the urban space as a stage on which the historical actors played out their roles. However, the stage is not an incidental setting for the drama; it very much affects what takes place upon it. "It is because social relations are so frequently and so inevitably correlated with spatial relations; because physical distances so frequently are, or seem to be, the indexes of social distances," Robert Park argued half a century ago, "that statistics have any significance whatever for sociology."[7] The composition of the stage and where upon it people settled (and why) conditioned the full range of life experiences: socialization, schooling, and contact with "significant others"; kin, friendship and job networks; marriage patterns, mobility, assimilation, and the like. Consider, for example, the consequences likely to issue, on the one hand, from heterogeneous residential patterns, with a mix of different social classes and ethnic groups, and, on the other hand, from homogeneous residential patterns, composed of people whose socioeconomic characteristics closely resemble each other. Many hypotheses could be posed: in the heterogeneous setting, assimilation to the values and expectations of the host society should be more rapid; rates of intermarriage should be higher; and membership in schools, churches, and voluntary associations should be more pluralistic.

It follows from this that the forces that affected the composition of the stage played a major part in explaining the process through which urban space was differentiated. The PSHP has begun to examine some of these forces and the changes they wrought. The three essays included in this section provide some valuable clues with which to understand the spatial changes that occurred in the industrializing city of the mid-to-late nineteenth century.

The "Journey-to-Work" essay, by Theodore Hershberg, Harold Cox, Dale Light, Jr., and Richard Greenfield, provides an overview of the organization in Philadelphia of work, residence, and transportation. It finds that only a very short distance separated the workplace and residence of most Philadelphians. Although the city developed an extensive transportation network of horse-drawn streetcars during the period, the fare structure and wage levels precluded widespread use of the system among the working classes. Most of the passenger volume was accounted for not in daily commuting between home and work, but in shopping, entertainment, and intercity travel; only the wealthy were able to use the horsecars regularly in their journey-to-work. Further advances in transportation technology were necessary before workers were freed from the necessity of living close to their places of employment. It was not until the introduction of the electric streetcar in the 1890s, the stabilization of fares, and the rise in real wages that the working classes found it possible to move to the "streetcar" suburbs which mushroomed at the city's residential peripheries.

In "Immigrants and Residential Mobility," demographer Alan Burstein examines the applicability to mid-to-late nineteenth-century Philadelphia of the spatial models developed by human ecologists Robert Park and Ernest Burgess and sociologist Gideon Sjoberg. Complexity at the microlevel abounds, but Burstein identifies elements that both undercut and support the Chicago School model of urban structure and those which characterize both the preindustrial and modern city.[8] He finds spatial patterns that upset long accepted notions of immigrant settlement. His study of the residential patterns and residential mobility of the Irish and Germans makes clear that ethnic ghettoes did *not* form in this large nineteenth-century city. At this phase in Philadelphia's development, there simply was not available the requisite stock of cheap housing close to jobs in which the immigrant groups could have clustered in dense homogenous concentrations. They settled instead across the face of the city. The segregation levels of the "Old" immigrant groups were thus substantially lower than— roughly half—those of the "New" immigrants who came to Philadelphia at the turn of the twentieth century.

Burstein's examination of the patterns of intra-urban migration draws upon the PSHP's "linked" population files—individual careers that have been reconstructed from successive decennial censuses. He sensitizes us to the intellectual benefits of a multivariate statistical approach in explaining who moved and who stayed. The simple tabular percentages used in most of the "new" histories appear to account for the behavior of the "movers and stayers." The multivariate method, however, leads to a very different conclusion. Because the individual-level variables (such as age, occupation, and property) are so closely correlated with each other, they explain very little of the total variation in mobility. This finding reinforces the argument put forward in our introductory essay that explanatory frameworks must be broadened to include ecological variables (such as housing, jobs, transportation) if we are to arrive at a satisfying explanation.

Burstein demonstrates that change in an individual's industrial affiliation was more significant than change in his occupation in explaining residential mobility. This finding underscores the role of work-related moves in generating the high rates of intra-urban mobility observed by all students of nineteenth-century cities, and it provides an exciting linkage to the work done by sociologist Stephanie Greenberg. Examining 1880 Philadelphia,

Greenberg focuses on the relationships between "Industrial Location and Ethnic Residential Patterns." She finds industry more important than ethnicity in explaining residential patterns.[9]

Among her most important findings is that the spatial characteristics of industries defined the residential context in which their workers were likely to live; if an industry was centralized, dispersed, or decentralized but clustered—so were the residences of its workers. The residential distribution of the Irish and Germans was explained by the spatial distribution of the industries in which they were concentrated; German residences were more clustered than those of the Irish because most of the industries in which Germans worked were spatially more clustered. The residential characteristics of ethno-industrial groups were more homogeneous by industrial affiliation than by ethnicity; for example, the residential patterns of German shoemakers had more in common with those of other shoemakers than with those of other Germans. Without cheap mass transportation to support commuting long distances to work, the location of industry dominated the residential patterning of the nineteenth- and early twentieth-century city. When economic and technological change altered the locational imperatives of firms, the composition of the urban stage changed in significant ways with profound consequences for urban society.

Greenberg's other major finding concerns the one ethnic group that was an exception to the ecological generalization noted above: black Americans. The ecological "rules" that governed access to job opportunities were "suspended" for blacks. The pattern persisted well into the twentieth century, but this part of the story as well as a fuller explanation of the process of spatial differentiation will be told in "A Tale of Three Cities," this volume's closing essay.

NOTES

1. Charles Tilly, *An Urban World* (Boston: Little, Brown, 1974).

2. John B. Sharpless and Sam Bass Warner, Jr., "Urban History," *American Behavioral Scientist* 21 (November–December, 1977), 225.

3. Jeffrey Roberts, "The Central District," paper presented at Social Science History Association (Philadelphia: October 1976); and "Railroads and the Growth of the Downtown: Philadelphia 1830–1900," in Howard Gillette and William Cutler, eds., *The Divided Metropolis: Social and Spatial Dimensions of Philadelphia, 1820–1940* (Westport, Ct.: Greenwood Press, 1980).

4. The role of land speculators and the ways in which building construction was financed played an especially important part in this process. Roger Miller and Joseph Siry treat some of these topics in "The Emerging Suburb: West Philadelphia, 1850–1880," *Pennsylvania History* 46 (April 1980), 99–145. See also Roger Miller, "Time-Geographic Assessment of the Impact of Horse-Car Transportation in Philadelphia, 1850–1860" (Ph.D. dissertation, Geography, University of California, Berkeley,

1979); and Susan M. Drobis, "Occupation and Residential Differentiation: A Historical Application of Cluster Analysis," in Theodore Hershberg, guest editor, "A Special Issue: The Philadelphia Social History Project," *Historical Methods Newsletter* 9 (March–June, 1976), 114–34.

5. Kenneth Jackson, "Urban Deconcentration in the Nineteenth Century: A Statistical Inquiry," in Leo F. Schnore, ed., *The New Urban History: Quantitative Explorations by American Historians* (Princeton: Princeton University Press, 1975).

6. Two essays by John Modell develop these themes as they relate to family life: "Suburbanization and Change in the American Family: Their Connection," *Journal of Interdisciplinary History* 9 (Spring 1979), 621–46; and "Suburbanization, Schooling, and Fertility in Philadelphia, 1880–1920: Toward an Ecology of Family Decisions," paper presented at United States Department of Housing Conference, "The Dynamics of Modern Industrial Cities" (Storrs, Ct.: September 1979).

7. Robert Park, "The Urban Community as a Spatial Pattern and Moral Order," in Ernest Burgess, ed., *The Urban Community* (Chicago: University of Chicago Press, 1926).

8. Extended discussion of the Burgess model as it applies to post-1880 Philadelphia is found in Eugene P. Ericksen and William L. Yancey, "Work and Residence in Industrial Philadelphia," *Journal of Urban History* 5 (February 1979), 147–82.

9. Extensive evidence supporting this conclusion is found in the work of PSHP research associate Richard Greenfield, "The Determinants and Dynamics of Intra-Urban Manufacturing Location: A Perspective of Nineteenth-Century Philadelphia," paper presented at Social Science History Association (Columbus, Ohio: November 1978).

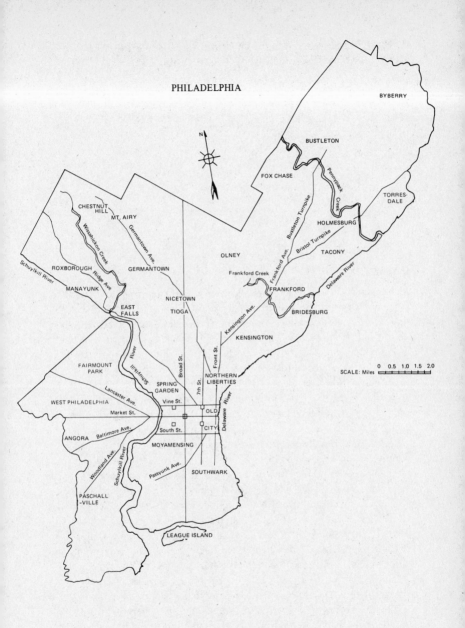

PHILADELPHIA

N

BYBERRY

BUSTLETON

FOX CHASE

Pennypack Creek

TORRES-
DALE

CHESTNUT
HILL

MT. AIRY

Bustleton Turnpike

HOLMESBURG

Wissahickon Creek

Germantown Ave.

OLNEY

Frankford Ave.

Bristol Turnpike

TACONY

ROXBOROUGH

Ridge Ave.

GERMANTOWN

Frankford Creek

Delaware River

MANAYUNK

Schuylkill River

FRANKFORD

NICETOWN

BRIDESBURG

EAST
FALLS

TIOGA

Kensington Ave.

KENSINGTON

River

Broad St.

Front St.

FAIRMOUNT
PARK

Schuylkill

SCALE: Miles   0   0.5 1.0 1.5 2.0

Lancaster Ave.

SPRING
GARDEN

7th St.

NORTHERN
LIBERTIES

WEST PHILADELPHIA

Vine St.

Delaware River

Market St.

OLD

ANGORA

Baltimore Ave.

South St.

CITY

Schuylkill River

MOYAMENSING

Woodland Ave.

Passyunk Ave.

SOUTHWARK

PASCHALL
-VILLE

LEAGUE ISLAND

4. The "Journey-to-Work": An Empirical Investigation of Work, Residence and Transportation, Philadelphia, 1850 and 1880

THEODORE HERSHBERG   DALE LIGHT, JR.
HAROLD E. COX   RICHARD R. GREENFIELD

Introduction

Most everybody today recognizes how the world has shrunk as a result of modern transportation and communications technology. From the invention of the internal combustion engine to the development of supersonic jet aircraft, from the first successful telegraph message to the placement of communications satellites in earth orbit, scientific advancements have greatly increased the ability of individuals to know of and interact with the wider world about them. Today we speculate about the impact of this exposure on the development of personality, group behavior, political and economic systems, and the emergence of the multinational corporation.

There is also a tendency to see equally parallel developments on the local level. Yet, despite the presence of expressways, mass transit, and the nightly TV news, modern technology has not transcended all the constraints imposed by time and distance. Location in urban space remains a significant factor in the organization of daily activities. As the increasing cost of energy curtails travel by automobile, we will come rather painfully to appreciate the implications of spatial location. Location in urban space must be understood as "access to opportunities"—to people and jobs, to shopping and leisure time activities, to quality of housing, sanitation, and other public facilities, and to schools, churches, institutions, and services. When spatial location is treated in neighborhood terms, it becomes the site at which socialization occurs; where goals, values, expectations, and behavioral norms are inculcated in the young; and where immigrants undergo a process of acculturation and assimilation into the host society.

An earlier version of this paper was presented at the American Historical Association (Chicago, Ill.: December 1974).

If location in urban space plays so important a role today, despite modern transportation systems and communication media, its significance in the nineteenth-century city with only rudimentary forms of these technologies was vastly greater. We know that the city of the nineteenth century was a "walking city," but to say this leaves much that is unknown. Who walked and who had access to transportation? How did the constraints of walking affect the form and content of life's activities? Were the distances covered by pedestrian travel great or small? Did they vary systematically by class, ethnicity, or industry? Did walking take people through a variety of neighborhood types, exposing them to life styles and behavior different from their own?

To proceed, let us conceptualize the "walking city" as contemporaries may well have, as a series of "journeys" that took people to work, recreation, shopping, church, school, and voluntary associations. In this paper, we are concerned with the first of these journeys—the "journey to work" (JTW).[1] The separation of home and work was among the earliest and most important changes brought about by the process of industrialization. After describing the data and methods used in this study, we document the JTW in 1850 and 1880. Although many people still combined home and work, for those who labored outside their homes the JTW doubled over the thirty-year period. We then shift from description to explanation, less concerned with the significance of the increased distance in the JTW *per se* than with the complex interplay of factors that account for it. The explanatory section opens with a consideration of the impact of the new transportation technology—the horse-drawn streetcar—and makes clear that the new technology alone did not account for lengthening the JTW distance, for an expensive fare structure precluded its widespread use.

Next we identify the separate component parts that do account for the increased JTW: the housing construction boom at the close of the Civil War decade that led to the deconcentration of population and the development of new neighborhoods; the emergence of the downtown central district which combined a multitude of nonresidential land uses; the increasingly significant shift toward larger firms in the industrial sector of the economy; and, despite a sharp increase in manufacturing employment over the period, the more rapid spatial expansion of population than industrial jobs. All operated to leave people further from their places of employment in 1880 than in 1850. The explanatory section closes with a discussion of the results obtained from the application to nineteenth-century Philadelphia of a contemporary city planning model that helps us assess the relationships between jobs and housing and enables us to estimate the impact of the new transportation technology. The essay concludes with speculations about the implications of these changes for the experience of nine-teenth-century Philadelphians.

This study of the JTW was also undertaken for an important method-ological purpose. A variety of topics—occupational and residential mo-bility among them—depend upon an empirically derived estimate of the distances that separated workplace and residence. In recent years a grow-ing literature has recognized the limitations of the Federal Population Manuscript Schedules when used in isolation.[2] These data report only the occupational title for each gainfully employed person; they describe neither the work *content* nor the industrial *context* in which work took place; nor do they tell us the composition of the environs in which resi-dential mobility occurred. They do not tell us, for example, whether the individual worker labored at home, in a small shop or in a factory, was self-employed or worked for others, labored by hand or with the aid of a machine; nor do they tell us about wages, or with whom the individual worked, or about the hierarchy of responsibilities, authority relationships, or opportunities for advancement; they reveal nothing about the larger in-dustrial structure responsible for generating jobs for the economy as a whole; finally, in regard to residential mobility, the data do not describe—for both the origin and destination end of the migration stream—the na-ture of the housing market, the availability of employment opportunities, or the socioeconomic and demographic composition of the population. Yet all of these considerations are central to the study of occupational and residential mobility.

A great deal of information relevant to these concerns can be found in data other than the population census schedules. Data used for the study of work content and industrial context can be found directly in or inferred from city business directories or other historical documentary sources whose information can be spatially located. Especially useful in this regard are the Federal Manufacturing Manuscript Schedules. The methodology we devised seeks to join these rich data describing individual firms with information contained in the population schedules describing individual workers. Unfortunately, as valuable as the manufacturing schedules are, they do not contain employee lists that provide the names of individual persons; thus another means of linking these two data sets had to be found. Our strategy was to construct the "labor shed" boundaries within which firms were likely to have drawn their employees.

The determination of labor shed parameters required the reconstruction of the JTW across the industrial spectrum. With empirically derived esti-mates for the labor sheds, we are able to associate individual workers with the firms in which they likely worked by matching their occupational title to the product manufactured in individual firms. The labor shed boundaries also make it possible, using other data described below, to associate an individual's location in space with the full range of opportunities and services available there. The labor shed estimates were used in other PSHP research.[3] They will also make it possible in future research to interpret changes in occupational and residential mobility in light of the specific work content, industrial context, and environmental characteristics in which the work occurred.

Data and Methods

Data. The empirical information contained in this paper are drawn from a number of different sources which describe individual-level and ecological characteristics of the county of Philadelphia from 1850 to 1880. All data were converted to machine-readable form and are now a permanent part of the large body of information collected by the PSHP. All of these data are more fully described in Appendix II.

To undertake spatial research at the PSHP, a grid system was constructed covering the total area of Philadelphia County (130 square miles). This was done by imposing a set of vertical and horizontal lines across a map of the county; each of the areal units was a consistent 1.25 city blocks in area (660 by 775 feet) and uniquely referenced by an X-Y grid coordinate system.[4] All data for this paper and for other files in the PSHP data base are coded for precise grid unit location whether they consist of, for instance, firms, families, adult males, or transportation lines. These unchanging boundaries and the small size of the grid areal unit overcome many of the problems associated with the use of wards, enumeration districts, or other politically created and impermanent spatial units. Thus it is possible to select out of the data files, for instance, the firms which cluster along Market Street, east of Seventh Street, or those individuals who lived within a specified distance of a specific firm.

For this particular study we have utilized data for the years from 1850 to 1880 from a variety of sources: 1. The Manuscript Schedules of the U.S. Census of Population; 2. Manuscript Schedules of the U.S. Census of Manufacturing; 3. City Business Directories; 4. City Street Directories; and 5. Records of the individual intra-urban transportation companies.

While the population census schedules and city directories have been used repeatedly, albeit on a small scale, by "new" social historians, the other files may not be as familiar to many students of urban history. For each manufacturing firm whose annual product was valued at $500 or more, the federal census of manufacturing recorded information such as the name of the company, type of business or product, amount of capital invested, average wage, number and sex of employees, the raw materials used, and the kinds, quantities, and values of the annual product. The business directories, published yearly and paid for by those who advertised within their pages, closely resemble today's "yellow pages," lacking only telephone numbers; these directories listed the business name (usually that of the proprietor), business product or service, and street address. The data set on transportation consists of the block-by-block reconstruction of the omnibus and street railway lines found from 1850 to 1880 in Philadelphia along with figures (largely for streetcars in the latter decades) on passenger volume, fares, and daily operating revenue receipts on a company-by-company, line-by-line basis.[5]

Methods. Measuring the JTW quite obviously requires the prior establishment of the worksites at which individuals labored.[6] This was accomplished in several different fashions which varied with intellectual purpose and types of data. Initially, five industries—morocco leather finishing, ship building, sugar refining, iron rolling, and banking—were selected for detailed study because they met three criteria: they employed large numbers of workers; the individual firms in each industry were highly clustered, facilitating measurement procedures; and they differed from each other in important ways, providing representativeness. The first three industries were old and well established in Philadelphia in 1850, and two of these industries—morocco leather finishing and sugar refining—were major industries in Philadelphia throughout the thirty-year period of study. The latter two industries—iron rolling and banking—greatly expanded their workforces from 1850 to 1880, thus providing a comparison between old and new industry as well as between industrial and commercial activities. The locations of the five industries also offer a high degree of spatial contrast. Ship building and morocco leather changed their location within the city only slightly, moving a few blocks further from the city center in 1880 than they had been in 1850. Banking, on the other hand, moved to an east-west axis along Chestnut Street from the older north-south axis centering on the Exchange. The sugar and iron industries also altered their location over the period.

The workforces of the five industries, moreover, offer a striking contrast in ethnic composition. Sugar refining was heavily dominated by first generation immigrants, particularly Germans. Ship building, banking, and iron rolling were dominated by native-white Americans. Morocco leather presented a rather even balance between first and second generation workers and native whites. Wage rates and working conditions also varied considerably. Morocco leather and sugar refining were among the least desirable occupations in the city from both standpoints, while iron rolling and ship building were comparatively high status industries. These numerous differences enable us to determine whether and how the JTW differed in varying socioeconomic, demographic, and spatial circumstances.

Occupational title as designated in the population manuscript schedules played a critical role in this study. Only occupational titles which made explicit their relationship to work performed *in* the production processes reported in the manufacturing schedules were included. Sugar dealers and iron merchants, for example, were *not* included because their efforts, and wholesaling and retailing in general, were carried out away from the manufacturing firms.[7] A computer-generated map was made showing the home residence for *all* persons with selected occupational titles, and the location of the firms in the corresponding industry was derived from the manufacturing schedules and business directories and added to these maps by hand.

The measurement of any adult male's journey-to-work in these five industries (and in others described below) involved calculating the distance from the centroid of the grid unit in which the individual resided to the centroid of the grid unit that contained the nearest firm whose industrial classification was consistent with the occupational designation of that individual worker. While the JTW is expressed in tenths of a mile, distances were measured in feet, and diagonal distances were calculated using the Pythagorean theorem. A question arose as to whether the nearest firm strategy underestimated the actual or average distance traveled from home to place of employment. Since firms similar to the nearest firm selected were often found individually or in separate clusters throughout the city, it would have been difficult to select that firm or group of firms that best represented the destination of the worker. What is more, the distances that resulted from such alternative measurement procedures were on their face unreasonable: median and mean distances were grossly inflated by "journeys" from a residential neighborhood to an industrial area across the length of the occupied urban plain.

Although measurements to the nearest firm can be used confidently to provide *relative* measures which are valid for comparisons across the five industries and between census years, we also wanted an accurate measure of the *absolute* distances traveled in the JTW to estimate the actual parameters of the "labor shed"—the contiguous area from which firms were likely to draw their employees. To test whether the calculations based on the nearest firms accurately approximated the distances traveled in the actual JTW, we set up a series of other measurements which enabled specific links to be made between individuals and the firms in which they worked. The first of these focused on single firms separated by several miles from other firms in the same industry and surrounded by a cluster of workers whose occupational titles corresponded to the work being performed at each firm. These included an iron rolling mill in Manayunk, a distant community in the northwest of the city, a similarly located carpet factory in the Falls of Schuylkill, and a brickyard in Frankford Borough, far to the city's northeast. Other measures involved unique workplaces, such as the Customs House or the U.S. Mint. In several cases, we were able to locate the actual employee lists. In yet other instances, the names of employees working at a variety of city government posts were found at the end of the business directories and traced to the street directories for home addresses.[8]

Each person sampled was looked up in the business and city directories. We determined first whether workplace and residence were in fact separated for such occupations as lawyers, confectioners, and others; and second, if they were separated, what were the distances between home and work. Since the addresses listed in the respective directories described the same individual, there was little margin for error. The JTW distances derived from the two sets of directories, moreover, provide the basis for useful comparisons, on the one hand, among professionals, proprietors and artisans, and on the other, among industrial workers, clerical employees, and public servants derived from the other sources.

The calculations from all these diverse sources, as will be seen below, corroborated the essential accuracy of the distances which had been computed using the nearest firm.[9] For workers in the five sample industries these distances were then used to establish labor shed parameters. Using these boundaries, we formulated still other ways to measure the JTW. In these instances, we located industrial firms which employed large numbers of workers and imposed the labor shed boundaries around them. Next, we computed the proportion of each firm's workforce (matching occupational title from the population census with industrial product from the manufacturing census) that resided within the same grid unit as each firm and within concentric rings of grid units surrounding it.

Empirical Findings

The JTW was remarkably short for most people in 1850, and although it nearly doubled by 1880, the absolute distances traveled at the later date remained small. Most workers in both years lived well within walking distance of their worksites; the vast majority of the 4,000 persons (see Table 1) whose JTW was reconstructed lived within a radius of six-tenths of a

Table 1. Number of Cases Studied

	1850 Total	1850 NWA*	Other Total	Other NWA*	1880 Total	1880 NWA*	Total Cases	Weighted Cases†
Industries								
Sugar Refining	119	1			174	4	293	330
Morocco Finishing	338	53			424	83	762	1961
Ship Building	270	118			282	89	552	1854
Iron Rolling	13	5			172	19	185	362
Banks	17	8			136	48	153	577
Specific Firms								
Harding Printers (1860 data)			14	n/a			14	14
Bricks (Frankford)					28	2	28	44
Carpets (Falls of Schuylkill)					12	7	19	75
Iron Rollers (Manayunk)					50	1	50	58
Public Services								
N. Lib. Gas Works (1853 data)			21				21	21
Customs House	11	9			14		25	70
U.S. Mint	9	8			13		22	86
City Offices (1870 data)			47		27		74	74
Business Directories								
Physicians	40				40		80	80
Lawyers	40				40		80	80
Confectioners	115				765		880	880
Cabinet Makers	67				129		196	196
Bookbinders	33				54		87	87
Blacksmiths	78				112		190	190
Carpenters	77				115		192	192
Totals							3711	6769

*NWA refers to native-white Americans.

†Numbers in this column give the total number of individuals represented rather than the number of cases studied. To obtain these figures, the number of NWA's were weighted up by a factor of 6 for the 1850 samples and by a factor of 9 for the 1880 samples.

mile from where they worked in 1850 and within a radius of one mile in 1880.[10]

There were, however, significant variations in the distances traveled to work between and to some extent within different occupational groups. The two professional groups differed considerably in their JTW. Physicians combined work and residence in both years. None separated their offices from their homes in 1850, and less than 5 percent did so in 1880. Lawyers, on the other hand, did separate home and work, and this separation became far more pronounced over the period. Half of all lawyers in 1850 worked away from home, and they did so at a median distance of roughly two-tenths of a mile. By 1880, however, fewer than one-fifth of all lawyers still combined work and residence, and the median distance they traveled

Table 2.   The Journey to Work, 1850 and 1880
Professionals, Proprietors, Artisans†
Cumulative Percentage at Specified Distances from Worksite (in miles)

	% Combining Home & Work	0.1	0.2	0.3	0.4	0.5	0.6	0.7	0.8	0.9	1.0	Median D (in miles)
Physicians												
1850	100.0	—	—	—	—	—	—	—	—	—	—	
1880	95.0	97.5	97.5	97.5	97.5	97.5	97.5	97.5	97.5	100.0	—	
Lawyers												
1850	52.6	63.2	78.9	89.5	89.5	89.5	89.5	89.5	89.5	94.7	100.0	.18
1880	17.6	17.6	23.5	23.5	23.5	29.4	29.4	35.3	41.2	47.1	47.1	1.30
Confectioners												
1850	91.1	92.4	94.9	92.6	97.5	97.5	100.0	—	—	—	—	.25
1880	90.6	92.1	93.3	93.7	93.7	94.2	94.9	95.1	95.5	95.9	96.2	.73
Bookbinders												
1850	30.3	30.3	36.4	36.4	42.4	48.5	57.6	63.7	69.7	75.8	75.8	.73
1880	9.3	9.3	11.1	11.1	14.8	14.8	20.4	20.4	33.3	33.3	48.1	1.14
Blacksmiths												
1850	23.7	39.8	60.5	71.0	76.3	76.3	86.8	89.5	89.5	94.7	94.7	.21
1880	23.0	48.0	63.2	68.4	71.0	76.3	77.0	78.9	80.3	80.9	81.6	.19
Cabinetmakers												
1850	64.2	71.7	74.6	76.1	77.6	82.1	86.6	86.6	92.5	95.5	95.5	.50
1880	54.3	59.7	65.1	67.4	70.5	74.4	77.5	79.8	82.2	83.7	86.8	.58
Carpenters												
1850	39.0	44.2	48.0	51.9	57.1	63.6	68.8	74.0	77.9	83.1	84.4	.61
1880	53.0	58.3	66.1	71.3	73.0	76.5	81.7	83.5	86.1	87.0	87.0	.50

*Median distance calculations exclude individuals not separating home and work.

†Based on addresses listed for the same individual in the city's business and street directories.

increased sharply to 1.3 miles (see Table 2). The differences between these professionals reflect the nature of their respective work. Physicians followed the population exodus from the Central Business District (CBD), living and practicing medicine, in many instances, largely in residential neighborhoods just outside the CBD. Almost all lawyers maintained their offices in the CBD and shifted their residences to areas considerably removed from the downtown area. In so doing lawyers were among a small vanguard of white-collar personnel who, in separating home and work, abandoned the city's core for more desirable residences in its surrounding rings.[11]

Public servants, with the exception of the U.S. Mint employees in 1850, lived at considerable distances from their worksites. Expensive rents for housing in the CBD, where the Customs House and other city offices were located, might have influenced employees to reside outside the city's center (see Table 3). Many of these positions were likely doled out as patronage, and the scattered residential patterns of employees may reflect this practice. With tenure in such posts unstable, few employees may have made the effort to relocate their homes closer to their work.

Bank employees, as white-collar workers in the private sector, lived on the periphery of the CBD in 1850. They spread into newly developed residential areas to the north, west, and south of the city center during the next three decades (see Table 4). They had somewhat longer journeys-to-work than most blue-collar workers, and some of the riders on street railways by 1880 may well have been clerks and tellers traveling to and from their work in the CBD.

Philadelphia's class of small proprietors is represented in this study by confectioners and bookbinders (see Table 2). The difference in the JTW of these two groups relates quite directly to the services they provided. Confectioners served a neighborhood market and, consequently, had little reason to separate their work and residence. Bookbinders, conversely, served a city-wide market and had good reason to locate their enterprises in the center city, while maintaining residences outside the CBD. In this respect they parallel the differences observed within the professional ranks between physicians and lawyers. A similar differentiation was found by Allan Pred who studied bakers and engravers in Manhattan at a somewhat earlier time.[12]

The JTW for artisanal proprietors such as blacksmiths, cabinetmakers, and carpenters provide interesting and challenging patterns which are likely related to the model of different work settings elaborated by Laurie and Schmitz.[13] The separation of home and work was apparently tied to the

Table 3. Employees Traced to Specific Worksites, Cumulative Percentage at Specified Distances (in miles)

	0.1	0.2	0.3	0.4	0.5	0.6	0.7	0.8	0.9	1.0	Miles Median	No. Cases
William Harding Print Shop												
1860	—	—	—	27.3	—	45.5	54.6	72.7	90.9	100.0	.64	11
Frankford Brickyards												
1880	—	—	—	19.0	—	38.0	—	—	98.0	100.0	.56	28
Falls of Schuylkill Carpets												
1880	5.3	21.1	47.4	52.6	73.7	78.9	89.5	—	—	94.7	.35	19
Manayunk Iron Rollers												
1850	—	61.0	63.6	81.8	—	100.0	—	—	—	—	.28	11
1880	1.9	37.7	43.4	49.1	86.8	88.7	—	—	90.6	—	.51	50
U.S. Mint												
1850	—	36.7	—	73.5	87.8	—	100.0	—	—	—	.34	9

	.5	1.0	1.5	2.0	2.5	3.0	3.5	4.0	4.5	5.0		
				(in miles)*								
U.S. Mint												
1880	7.7	38.5	46.2	53.8	69.2	—	—	76.9	—	—	1.75	13
U.S. Customs House												
1850	—	1.8	36.8	78.9	—	—	89.5	—	—	—	1.07	12
1880	—	14.3	50.0	57.1	—	85.7	—	—	—	—	1.00	14
City Office Employees												
1870	12.8	27.7	55.3	72.3	76.6	80.8	87.3	91.5	—	—	1.90	47
1880	7.4	11.1	25.9	40.7	74.1	77.8	85.2	88.9	—	—	2.28	27

*Please note the increased scale of these distances.

Table 4. Disperson of Work Force Around Potential Worksites, 1850 and 1880
Cumulative Percentage at Specified Distances (in miles)

1850:	0.1	0.2	0.3	0.4	0.5	0.6	0.7	0.8	0.9	1.0
Sugar	25.8	55.0	62.5	70.8	81.6	93.3	94.1	96.6	98.3	—
Morocco	23.4	71.2	80.4	84.8	90.1	93.6	94.7	97.4	97.8	98.7
Ships	27.0	71.5	79.1	82.1	88.2	90.9	94.4	—	95.3	96.3
Iron Rollers	9.0	81.8	—	100.0	—	—	—	—	—	—
Banks	22.2	33.3	66.7	—	77.8	—	88.9	—	—	—
1880:										
Sugar	3.0	32.5	46.7	50.9	62.1	69.8	74.0	76.9	82.8	84.6
Morocco	24.0	59.8	68.1	71.4	75.4	78.8	83.7	86.4	88.2	88.7
Ships	7.9	33.3	37.1	42.6	46.4	55.5	69.7	76.3	77.5	80.5
Iron Rollers	21.1	54.5	64.9	74.4	74.4	91.3	92.1	—	93.8	—
Banks	1.9	22.2	28.4	44.3	44.3	65.3	80.1	84.3	85.6	—

scale of labor—the decline, persistence, or growth over the thirty-year period in small and large firms. Small firms in these crafts served local markets, were distributed across the city and were low-profit operations, all of which combined to reinforce the combination of work and residence under one roof. The enormous expansion of the building construction industry between 1850 and 1880 included the proliferation of small firms (1–5 employees) which grew from 57 to 71 percent and may explain why the proportion of carpenters combining home and work increased from 39 to 53 percent. Cabinetmakers offer a more complex, yet not contradictory, pattern. Although the proportion combining home and work declined between 1850 and 1880 (64 to 54 percent) while the proportion of small firms increased (55 to 60 percent), the similarity in both years of the proportions of craftsmen living where they worked and in small firms suggests an association between JTW and scale.[14] Blacksmiths, however, found in all neighborhoods in both years (confirming the continuing importance of horse transportation in Philadelphia), seem the exception to this paradigm. The proportion of master blacksmiths who separated home and work remained low in both 1850 and 1880 (about 23 percent), although the proportion of small firms was quite high (88 and 94 percent). Smithing appears to have been an anomalous trade because, in spite of its small scale, the industry's space requirements and "nuisance" characteristics may well have prevented craftsmen from combining work and residence.

The JTW for industrial workers increased over the thirty-year period (see Tables 3 and 4). In the sugar, morocco, ship building, and iron rolling industries in 1850, a JTW of a half mile or less was the common experience of 80 to 90 percent of the workforce. By 1880, similar proportions within each of these industries traveled to work at distances of roughly one mile. Although the JTW had nearly doubled over the period, the absolute distances remained short and industrial workers continued to walk to work.[15]

Wage differentials and the differing ethnic composition of the workforce in the four industries had no discernible impact on the JTW. Differences in the age of the industry and geographical location, on the other hand, had some effect. Iron rolling was a new industry in Philadelphia in 1850, and the intense clustering of its workers in the immediate vicinity of its firms was unique: 82 percent of its workers lived within 0.2 miles. No longer a new industry thirty years later, the distribution of iron rolling workers more closely resembled the patterns observed in the other industries. Location along the waterfront also affected the JTW. Over the period, this area was more developed industrially and offered far less residential housing. In 1880, workers in ship building lived further from their work than did workers in morocco and iron. The same was true for sugar workers. The move of the industry from the CBD in 1850 to the Southwark waterfront forced its workers to live further away.

The most significant variation in the JTW is found in the different distances traveled by white- and blue-collar workers. The former lived further away from their worksites than the latter. It can be argued that this generalization, which derives from the data presented in Tables 2 thru 4, is an artifact of measuring the JTW to the nearest firm which reports distances for a largely blue-collar workforce. The generalization, however, is supported by three findings which are not subject to this possible bias. First, the JTW for banking employees was calculated in the same manner as for industrial workers, and a greater proportion of bank employees, with a few exceptions, were found living at further distances. Second, the same kind of variation is observed within the industrial workforce itself. Although hampered by lack of vertical differentiation in the occupational titles associated with each industry, there are enough cases in the sugar and morocco industries in 1880 to document that white-collar workers lived further from their worksites than blue-collar workers (see Table 5). Third, when we consider only those persons who lived more than one mile from their worksites, the predominance of white-collar over blue-collar is plainly evident (see Table 6). Despite the possible bias in the way the JTW was computed for industrial workers, in other words, the finding holds that the JTW was greater for white-collar than blue-collar workers.[16]

Finally, there do not appear to be any significant and consistent variations in the JTW across individual characteristics of workers such as age, ethnicity, and ownership of real property. Whatever minor differences existed in 1850 disappeared by 1880. There is some evidence to suggest that boarding may have been used by workers to live closer to their work-

Table 5. Median Journey-to-Work by Occupational
Status, 1880 (in miles)

| | Vertical Code | | | |
Industry	1	2	3	4
Sugar Refining	—	.61	.34	.37
Morocco	—	.25	.19	.20
Banks	.60	.39	—	.55

The vertical codes represent occupations categorized and ranked by a combination of inferred skill and status: Vertical 1 (professional and high white-collar); Vertical 2 (proprietors and low white-collar); Vertical 3 (skilled); Vertical 4 (unskilled with the nature of their work specified, e.g., ditch digger). Vertical 5, "laborers," are not included because they cannot be assigned a worksite. For the development of these codes, see T. Hershberg and R. Dockhorn, "Occupational Classification," *Historical Methods Newsletter*, 9:2–3 (March–June, 1976), 66–71.

sites: the median distances traveled by boarders and relatives in 1880 are shorter than the median distances for all workers in four of the five industries studied (see Table 7).

There is also some evidence—but only suggestive—that individual firms in the same industry may have had workforces dominated by members of one ethnic group. We know from city-wide figures that the ethnic composition of the workforce at the industry level differed considerably.[17] We know, too, that although there were no massive and distinctly defined ethnic ghettoes, there was spatial differentiation in ethnic residential patterns.[18] The residential patterns of workers in the morocco industry provide an example of ethnic clustering around different firms in the same industry. We do not yet know whether this pattern was widespread, but

Table 6. Percentage of Blue- and White-Collar Workers Living More Than
One Mile from the Nearest Potential Worksite, 1880

			White-Collar	Blue-Collar
Sugar	N*	206	28	178
	n**	32 (15.5)	10 (35.7)	22 (12.4)
Morocco	N	1088	50	1038
	n	123 (11.3)	9 (18.0)	114 (11.0)
Ships	N	994	26	324
	n	194 (19.5)	8 (30.8)	186 (19.2)
Iron	N	324	0	324
	n	22 (6.8)	0	22 (6.8)
Banks	N	520	489	31
	n	75 (14.4)	73 (14.9)	2 (6.5)

*N = total in workforce
**n = number living in excess of one mile from the nearest potential worksite

Table 7. Median JTW by Relationship to Head of Household, 1880 (in miles)

Industry	Total	Head of Household	Relative of Head	Boarder
Sugar	.47	.42	.55	.44
Ships	.50	.52	.44	.48
Morocco	.18	.21	.19	.14
Iron	.22	.23	.18	.17
Banks	.45	.60	.33	.52

more to the point, without employee lists, it is not possible to document whether the observed residential clustering was reflected in individual firms.

Nineteenth-Century Intra-urban Transportation: The Street Railway System

We turn from our description of the JTW to consider a range of possible explanations for its doubling over the thirty-year period. The most obvious factor to examine is the city's transportation system. What technological changes affected the city's intra-urban transportation system in this period? Did improved transportation make it possible for a large segment of the population to commute to work on a regular basis? Were improvements in transportation, therefore, responsible for the lengthening of the JTW?

The form of public transportation available to Philadelphians in 1850 was the omnibus. Based on the French model and introduced in American cities in the 1830s, the omnibus replaced the hackney coach. The omnibus was a fairly large vehicle, seating as many as ten to twelve passengers. Unlike the hackney coach, it operated over a fixed route of city streets for a standard fare regardless of distance traveled by a particular passenger. In Philadelphia the omnibus became an important means of transportation for the wealthy and for better-off merchants and businessmen.[19] By 1848 there were 18 separate lines over which about 130 omnibuses traveled. When the first street-railway line was begun a decade later, about 320 omnibuses were active on as many as 30 routes. Although the omnibus provided the primary means of public transportation in Philadelphia for about twenty-five years, it was never an adequate solution to the problem of moving large numbers of people. The vehicles were slow, gave a bone-jarring ride over cobblestone streets, and served only limited sections of the city.

Shortly after the consolidation in 1854 of the County's twenty-seven municipalities into a single governmental unit (the City of Philadelphia), private contractors introduced a new form of transportation technology—the horse-drawn streetcar—which characterized public transit in the city to the mid-1890s.[20] The first street passenger railway operation in the United States was in New Orleans in 1835. Similar operations began in New York in 1851 and in Boston in 1853. The operation of horse passenger cars over regular railroad tracks in Philadelphia dated from about 1834; however, these were limited operations, chiefly for summer recreational traffic, and regular passenger railway service did not begin until the opening of the Frankford and Southwark line on January 20, 1858.

The design of this new form of transportation was extremely simple: iron rails were laid in the streets over which vehicles seating up to twenty or twenty-five passengers were pulled by one or two horses. Since the wheels struck rail rather than rough stone, mud, or earth, the degree of friction was greatly reduced, and speed was increased to a maximum of 6 to 8 miles per hour. Two horses could now pull three to five times the load at about 1.5 times the speed of the omnibuses. Heavy traffic on many of the city's downtown streets, of course, reduced the actual speed of the streetcar. However, due to the economies of scale obtained from the horse-car, the omnibus quickly disappeared from the face of major American cities within only a few years after the first appearance of the streetcar. In Philadelphia, for example, the use of the omnibus declined sharply. Virtually none were in operation in 1860 when some 340 streetcars served the city; some 500 cars were in use in 1870 and roughly 800 by 1880.[21]

The growth of the street-railway system in Philadelphia was rapid both in terms of passengers and miles of track. Although the first company did not begin to lay track until the fall of 1857, six million passengers had been carried over 50 miles of track by the end of 1858. In the year before the Civil War came to an end, roughly 44 million passengers used the system with 129 miles of track. By 1880, fifteen companies operated thirty-five lines that accounted for some 99 million passenger rides over some 298 miles of track.

The shape assumed by the streetcar system in 1860 would characterize it well into the twentieth century: routes radiated out from the city's core in six directions along Philadelphia's major roads (see the map introducing the "Space" section of this volume and Maps 1 and 2). The proportion of inhabited grid units through which streetcars passed remained constant throughout the period. What changed significantly was the density of transportation; it increased from 1.9 to 2.7 lines per inhabited grid. In other words, passengers were served by a growing number of cars representing new lines of competing companies, rather than new directional routes. Only the Depression of 1873 and a change in the state law in 1875 regu-

Table 8.   Transportation Developments: 1860–1800
                 Growth of Horse Car Lines

Year	# of Inhabited Grids	% with Horse Cars	# Grids w/Any Horse Cars	% Increase	Total Lines Through Grids	% Increase	Ratio Lines/ Grid*
1860	1,205	45.8	552		1,058		1.92
1865	NA		601	8.7	1,285	21.5	2.14
1870	1,397	49.1	686	14.1	1,551	20.7	2.26
1875	NA		808	17.8	2,065	33.1	2.56
1880	1,996	42.1	840	4.0	2,262	9.5	2.69

*Ratio based on grids with at least one line.

lating the incorporation of street railway companies slowed the transportation boom (see Table 8 and Maps 1 and 2).

When the 1860 routes are imposed on maps showing the 1860 and 1880 distributions of population, commerce, and industry, it is clear that transportation led the way to these land use patterns. The uneven growth of residential and commercial construction at the periphery of Philadelphia's densely built-up areas was the partial result of cooperation and collusion between the owners of street-railway lines and land developers and the need of upper-middle class, white-collar residents in these new neighborhoods to have efficient access to the downtown core of the city.[22]

Yet, despite this marked improvement in transportation over the thirty-year period, the vast majority of Philadelphians did not use the system of street railways in their JTW because of an expensive fare structure and the locations of the routes themselves. Although the JTW doubled between 1850 and 1880, most people continued to live within a short walk of their workplaces. Those who could afford to ride the horsecars did so to gain access to recreational facilities, to shop in the CBD, and to reach the city's train stations and ferries. As we shall see, these uses accounted for a far greater proportion of passengers than did commuting to work on a regular basis.

The prohibitive cost of public transportation for most Philadelphians was not a new problem. The transportation network provided by the omnibus lines in 1850 was characterized by individuals operating without franchises and adequate corporate or financial support. Lines which might exist on marginal streets one day might well disappear the next, since the operator had no investment in tracks or franchises and could simply take his horses and bus to a more lucrative routing. The service they offered was at times irregular and unpredictable in fares. Costs ranged from three cents up, but the majority of lines charged a one-way fare of six and a

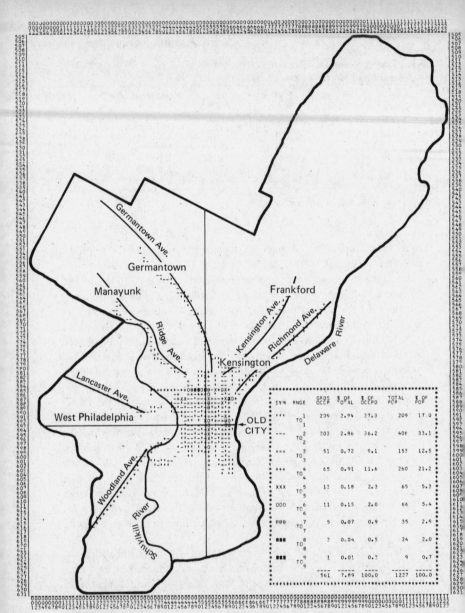

SYM	RNGE	GRDS OCCP	% OF TOTAL	% OF OCCPD	TOTAL POP	% OF POP
'''	1 TO 1	209	2.94	37.3	209	17.0
---	1 TO 2	203	2.86	36.2	406	33.1
===	2 TO 3	51	0.72	9.1	153	12.5
+++	3 TO 4	65	0.91	11.6	260	21.2
XXX	4 TO 5	13	0.18	2.3	65	5.3
000	5 TO 6	11	0.15	2.0	66	5.4
ᵇᵇᵇ	6 TO 7	5	0.07	0.9	35	2.9
■■■	7 TO 8	3	0.04	0.5	24	2.0
▓▓▓	8 TO 9	1	0.01	0.2	9	0.7
		561	7.89	100.0	1227	100.0

Horse Car Lines, 1860

The computer-generated DENPRINT maps display variables by distribution and density. Each character represents a grid unit (660' by 775') which contains at least one occurrence of the display variable; distinct characters represent nine different density levels which increase at equal increments. The inset of tabular information presents statistical data for each density level.

The first two columns describe the density symbol (SYM) and the range of its numeric equivalent (RNGE). The next three columns refer to the geographic *distribution* of the display variable. GRDS OCCP is the number of grids occupied at each

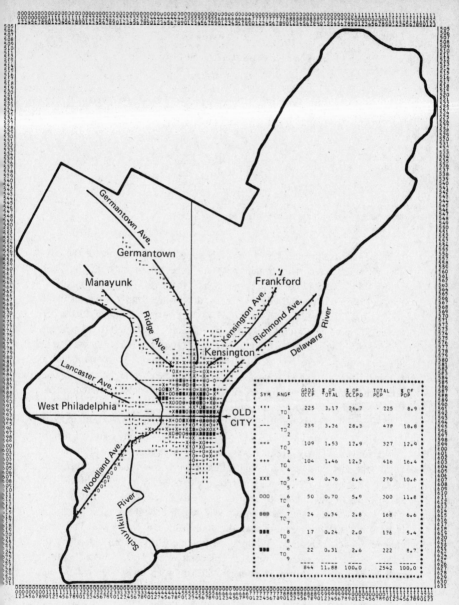

SYM	RNGE		GRDS OCCP	% OF TOTAL	% OF OCCPD	TOTAL POP	% OF POP
'''	TO	1 / 1	225	3.17	26.7	225	8.9
---	TO	2 / 2	239	3.36	28.3	478	18.8
===	TO	3 / 3	109	1.53	12.9	327	12.9
+++	TO	4 / 4	104	1.46	12.3	416	16.4
XXX	TO	5 / 5	54	0.76	6.4	270	10.6
OOO	TO	6 / 6	50	0.70	5.9	300	11.8
888	TO	7 / 7	24	0.34	2.8	168	6.6
▓▓▓	TO	8 / 8	17	0.24	2.0	136	5.4
▓▓▓	TO	9	22	0.31	2.6	222	8.7
			844	11.88	100.0	2542	100.0

Horse Car Lines, 1880

density level; % OF TOTAL is the proportion these girds form of all grids in the
county (roughly 7,100); % OF OCCPD is the proportion these grids form of all
grids containing the display variable. The final two columns describe the *density* of
the display variable. TOTAL POP reports the absolute frequency of the display variable at each density level; and % OF POP reports the proportion of the display
variable frequency found at each density level. Summary totals are provided in the
final row of the table.

Table 9. Fares and Daily Wage Rates, 1850, 1880 and 1980

	Average Daily Wages ($)	Round-Trip Fare One-Vehicle		Round-Trip Fare with Exchange	
		Cost ($)	% Wage	Cost ($)	% Wage
1850					
Unskilled	1.00	.13	13.0	.26*	26.0
Skilled	1.50	.13	8.7	.26*	17.3
1880					
Unskilled	1.30	.12	9.2	.18	13.8
Skilled	2.01	.12	6.0	.18	9.0
1980					
Federal Min. Wage	24.80	1.00	4.0	1.10	4.4
$20,000/year	76.00	1.00	1.3	1.10	1.4

*No exchange agreements providing reduced fares.

half cents for a ride generally within the older built-up sections of the city. The cheapest fares were found in those areas where most of the lines competed for available traffic; and, while the evidence is fragmentary, they appear to have varied upward or downward with the intensity of competition. To the average unskilled worker earning roughly $1.00 per day, a single vehicle round-trip ride on a streetcar amounted to 13 percent of his daily wages, and for a skilled worker, almost 9 percent (see Table 9). Since there were no interline transfer agreements, a job requiring a multivehicle ride would have resulted in considerably higher fares. The fare structure for the omnibuses and later the street-railway system effectively denied access to most members of the working classes.[23]

The system of street railways that replaced the omnibus was rationalized somewhat between its introduction and the end of our study in 1880. While maverick lines would lower fares on occasion, the fare structure within the city was generally controlled through the Board of Presidents of City Passenger Railways. The fare for a one-way ride, established at seven cents in 1865, was lowered to six cents in 1877. A system of "exchanges" and "transfers" was introduced which brought greater flexibility to passengers requiring more than one line in their daily travels. The "exchange" ticket, purchased for three cents (one-way), permitted riders to travel to points served by two different companies. The "transfer" was a free exchange and permitted riders to shift between lines operated by the same company. The free transfer was little used in Philadelphia before 1880, except on the Union Passenger Railway lines.

Despite these improvements, the cost of using public transportation to journey to work in 1880 remained beyond the means of most working people. Although, on average, unskilled and skilled workers now earned $1.30 and $2 per day, respectively, round-trip fares on the streetcars still meant spending too much (9 and 6 percent) of their daily wages. With exchanges, the proportions of their daily wages required to use public transportation was the same as in 1850: 13 and 9 percent respectively.[24] In contrast, in 1980 an unskilled worker employed at the federal minimum wage ($3.10 per hour) taking an equivalent ride in Philadelphia would spend only 4.0 percent of his daily wage for his JTW (see Table 9). Given an already serious gap between income and the cost of living, even at subsistence levels, it is quite clear that the typical workingman could not afford so costly an expenditure. Living within walking distance of one's workplace was a form of behavior dictated more by economic necessity than by choice.[25]

The layout of the routes themselves also helps to explain why transportation did not play an important role in the JTW. The omnibuses of 1850 were virtually useless as a means of transport from home to work. The entire omnibus system was established with a common terminus at the Exchange, the center of the city's financial district. The lines' outer ends were found only at railroad stations and major places of amusement. Adequate service was found along streets which were already heavily built up or which led to some major source of business.

Things were not much better in 1880. The narrowness and grid pattern of the city's streets combined to generate an eccentric system. The narrowness of the streets necessitated one-way traffic flows, and inbound and outbound trips were on streets as much as four blocks apart. The grid street pattern, emulated in in many other cities, had a disastrous effect on efficient transport because it prevented diagonal travel and forced riders traveling in such directions to use costly and time-consuming exchanges.[26] But even the recourse to exchanges was limited by the refusal of some companies to enter into exchange agreements with their competitors as well as termination of exchange agreements on short notice. So in addition to the slowness and geographical limitations of the transportation network, passengers requiring rides on two different lines were usually forced to pay full extra fares in order to reach their destinations.

Despite these drawbacks, some 99,000,000 passenger rides on the street railways were taken in 1880. To determine who the passengers were, and why they rode the horsecars, we have used an "accounting" approach which involves making rough estimates of the proportion of passengers riding for purposes other than the JTW. The proportion of rides unaccounted for establishes the upper limits for those who may have used the streetcars regularly in the JTW.[27]

The street railways were used by Philadelphians to provide access to recreational facilities. With the sole exceptions of the lines serving Frankford and Southwark along the Delaware River waterfront, every company attempted to secure an entrance to Fairmount Park, then and now the largest municipally maintained park in the world. Of fifteen companies in Philadelphia in 1880, six served the main entrance to the Park, getting within a short walk of 25th and Green Streets, while five served the Centennial Exposition entrance at 44th and Elm Avenue.[28] At the same time, only four companies operated cars direct to the Exchange, still the financial center of the city.

Sunday traffic on most lines showed disproportionately high volume which varied according to the weather and the season; an early afternoon storm or an all-day rain on a Sunday could cut traffic in half.[29] It rained all day on July 31, 1880. That day Columbia Avenue line cars brought in a total income of $491 while on the 17th, a clear day with temperatures rising to 82 degrees, passenger revenues totaled $1,023. The Peoples line served the waterfront district at Market Street, ran through Philadelphia's worst slum and an upper-middle-class residential district before terminating at the Park. It served no part of the CBD, and it is doubtful that it carried many shoppers. Its summer traffic was considerably different from that of the rest of the year averaging 160 percent more on Sundays, 60 percent more on Saturdays, and 30 percent more on weekdays than during other seasons (see Table 10).[30]

Newspapers of the period corroborate the importance of Fairmount Park to the public on days other than Sundays. Records of many business establishments indicate that the average employee worked until 5 p.m. most of the year and only half a day on Saturdays. There was, in other words, ample time to attend some special event. The sharp rise of traffic during a circus held in the Park in April of 1880 documents that the public did ride the horsecars on weekday evenings. The circus accounted for a 30 percent rise in traffic on the Thirteenth and Fifteenth Street railway while it was in town (see Table 11). Our estimate is that passengers riding the street railways for recreational purposes on Sundays, Saturdays, and weekdays account for 25 percent of all riders.

A considerable amount of weekday and especially Saturday traffic must be attributed to shoppers traveling to and from the CBD. By 1880, the business enterprises of the city had begun to differentiate sharply. While bakeries, confectioners, ice cream parlors, and groceries were to be found scattered among the residences on the neighborhood level, the larger dry goods and general merchandise stores had begun to concentrate in the same general area they occupy today along Market and Chestnut Streets. The volume of passengers on the Germantown line, which served the CBD, for example, fluctuated regularly with weather. If the cars were being

Table 10. Index of Saturday/Sunday Traffic, 1880*

Week Beginning	Girard Sat	Girard Sun	Germantown Sat	Germantown Sun	Peoples Sat	Peoples Sun	Notes on Weather	Sat/Sun
5 January	112.8	138.0	121.3	80.8	123.9	82.9	39–53 Clear	33–54 Cloudy from 3 PM
12 January	104.4	128.2	110.8	76.6	106.8	73.1	29–47 Fog	33–49 Cloudy to 2 PM
9 February	112.2	87.4	110.1	60.9	121.8	62.6	37–54 Clear	33–39 Cloudy, Snow
16 February	102.5	137.8	108.9	79.9	116.3	77.9	26–42 Snow to 2 PM	33–46 Clear
23 February	107.9	137.6	116.4	78.4	138.2	80.9	56–56 Lt. Rain PM	48–66 Cloudy AM
31 May	135.6	185.0	111.6	95.1	119.8	129.9	61–79 Cloudy PM	63–82 Cloudy AM
7 June	115.4	185.8	116.2	91.3	128.0	140.4	71–92 Rain 2–3 PM	72–88 Cloudy 2–3 PM
14 June	135.8	191.9	113.8	95.2	125.2	127.4	64–86 Clear	65–87 Clear
21 June	113.1	158.5	119.5	86.6	117.5	120.3	74–90 Threatening	72–90 Clear
28 June	124.1	173.8	119.7	87.1	124.5	118.2	63–81 Clear	63–84 Clear

Girard Avenue served Fairmount Park and the Richmond industrial district, but no shopping district.

Germantown served Germantown suburbs and the CBD, but no major parks or recreational facilities.

Peoples served Fairmount Park, middle-class-residential, working-class and waterfront industrial districts.

Sources: Germantown Passenger Railway Company, Cash Book C, 1874–1893; Peoples Passenger Railway Company, Cash Book 1, 1875–1881. Philadelphia *Public Ledger*.

*The index for Saturday and Sunday is based on the average passenger volume (100) for the preceding five weekdays.

Table 11. Thirteenth and Fifteenth Streets Passenger Railway Company: Effects of Circus upon Passenger Traffic, 1880

Week Beginning	Weekdays	Saturday	Sunday	Income Index Weekdays	Income Index Saturday	Income Index Sunday	Notes
5 April	$ 817.15	$1097.58	$643.23	100.0	100.0	100.0	Circus unloading Sat.
12 April	1067.78	1224.82	737.22	130.7	111.6	114.6	Circus opened Monday
19 April	1083.20	1025.73	606.33	132.6	93.8	94.3	Circus closed Friday
26 April	818.41	962.67	664.76	100.2	87.7	103.3	

Sources: Thirteenth and Fifteenth Streets Passenger Railway Company, Cash Book, 1880–1885; Philadelphia *Public Ledger*.

regularly ridden to work rather than to shopping, passenger volume should have either remained constant or increased in bad weather; instead, as Table 10 shows, passenger volume decreased in inclement weather and rose with good weather, suggesting quite clearly that the street railways were used for optional purposes, such as shopping in the CBD. We estimate that riding the horsecars for this purpose accounts for roughly 28 percent of all passengers.

Intercity travelers required public transportation from the city's seven major railroad stations and ferries across the city's two rivers. The Pennsylvania Railroad station, for example, was located at 32nd and Market Streets, over two miles from the CBD; the closest station, the Philadelphia and Reading, located at Broad and Callowhill, was roughly one mile away. When, in 1881, a new station was established in the center of the city at Broad and Market Streets, the line that had carried passengers several miles to and from the original station in West Philadelphia suffered a 13 percent decline in business.[31] Because there was no shift in the location of ferry stations of which we are aware, it is difficult to determine directly the volume of traffic generated by this source. The Philadelphia City Passenger Railway Company, however, estimated that its chief competitor, the West Philadelphia Company, may have derived as many as one million passengers each year from a single ferry station located at Market Street and the Delaware River. We estimate that the use of the street railways for these purposes accounted for roughly 10 percent of all riders.

Combining our estimates for recreational users (25 percent), shopping users (28 percent), and railway station and ferry transit users (10 percent), an upper limit of 37 percent can be established as the proportion of all riders (99 million) who might have used the street railways for their JTW. If the JTW consisted of two daily rides six times a week throughout the year, then a maximum of 58,702 persons could have regularly ridden the horsecars to and from work. Expressed as a proportion in 1880 of all employed persons and as a proportion of the total population, only 17 and 7 percent, respectively, could have regularly ridden on the street railways in their JTW (see Table 12).

Who were these people? They were likely those who lived more than one mile from their worksites. Since they had to have an income sufficiently high to afford the cost of daily commuting, they had to consist largely of nonmanual workers. Since roughly one quarter of the city's adult male labor force in 1880 was in fact engaged in nonmanual efforts, our estimate of one person in six regularly riding the horsecars to work fits well within the pool of potential riders. The estimate is also supported

Table 12. Accounting of All Passengers, 1880

Total Passengers		99,000,000
Estimated proportion of passengers using street railways for non-JTW purposes		
Shopping	28%	27,720,000
Recreation	25%	24,750,000
Railroad Station & Ferries	10%	9,900,000
TOTAL	63%	62,370,000
Estimated maximum number of passengers using street railways in their JTW		36,630,000
Number of rides per year for regular JTW (round-trip 2 rides daily x 6 days per week x 52 weeks per year).		624
Estimated total regular passenger rides (26,630,000 divided by 624)		58,702
Expressed as proportion of		
Total workforce (348,900)		16.8%
Total population (841,343).		7.0%

Note: These estimates are based upon analysis of rider income from horse railway lines with special characteristics (served parks but not the CBD, served CBD but not parks, served railroad stations, served special recreational centers such as ball parks, etc.). These figures have been compared with general income statistics of other lines to arrive at the stated percentages. The statistics so derived compare favorably with the estimates of workers living more than one mile from their employment. The true totals may be as much as ten percent higher.

by evidence for 1880 which indicates that the only large occupational group living in relatively homogeneous areas away from the CBD were those in high white-collar jobs.[32]

In closing this section, it should be noted that the per capita increase in general riding in Philadelphia after 1880 (it was one ride per week in 1880) was still far below what might have been expected even after the reduction of fares, electrification, and the introduction of rapid transit. The available evidence on per capita rides suggests that the use of public transportation for commuting to work on a regular basis by most workers did not become the primary purpose of the system until after the reorganization of the services in the years after 1910 (see Table 13).[33]

Population Deconcentration and Industrial Development

The "lengthening of the journey-to-work," Kenneth T. Jackson has carefully documented, was part of a larger process of population deconcentration. It "occurred in the largest American cities before the introduction of the electric street car in the 1890's" and included as well: ". . . higher peripheral rates of growth, leveling of densities, absolute loss of population at the center (and) movement of the upper and middle class to the periphery. . . ."[34] The development of the horse-drawn streetcar cannot directly account for the increase of the JTW, for, as we have seen, most people continued to walk to work. But the new transportation technology operated indirectly to lengthen the JTW by catalyzing the city's residential, industrial, and commercial expansion.[35] To explain the increase in the JTW, we must examine a series of changes—in housing, residential densities, the central business district, the scale of manufacturing, and the distribution of manufacturing jobs relative to population across the urban plane—each of which was a component part of the larger process of spatial differentiation.

The city's population grew rapidly in the years between 1840 and 1880.

Table 13. Philadelphia Public Transportation—Patterns of Growth, 1862 to 1920

Year	Population	Passengers	Rides per Capita Round Trip	Route Miles	Fare/Exch.		Notes
1862	580,000	25,250,000*	23.49	114	$.05	$.08	Service began in 1858
1870	674,022	61,000,000*	45.25	177	.07	.10	Fare raised in 1865
1880	874,170	99,045,515	58.46	298	.06	.09	Fare reduced in 1877
1890	1,046,964	164,542,586	78.58	351	.05	.08	Fare reduced in 1887. Consolidation begins
1900	1,293,697	292,237,924	112.95	470	.05	.08	Lines electrified 1894–1897 Suburban fares eliminated
1910	1,549,008	397,497,191	128.31	628	.05	.08	Subway opened in 1908. Service inadequate
1920	1,823,779	699,169,281	191.68	677	.05	.08	Free transfers extended

Sources: Frederic Speirs, "The Street Railway System of Philadelphia, Its History and Present Condition," *Johns Hopkins University Studies in Historical and Political Science,* Fifteenth Series, III–IV–V (March–May, 1897). *Reports of the Several Railroad and Canal Companies of Pennsylvania Communicated by the Auditor General,* 1858–1874. Title varies. *Annual Report of the Secretary of Internal Affairs, Part IV, Canal and Telegraph Companies,* 1875–1900. *Annual Report, Union Traction Company of Philadelphia,* June 30, 1900. *Annual Report of the Philadelphia Rapid Transit Company,* June 30, 1910. *Philadelphia Rapid Transit, Stotesbury-Witten Management,* 1911–1920.

Note: Exchanges were additional-fare inter-company transfers. Transfer and exchange passengers are excluded from statistics. Route miles indicate single track miles because of predominance of one-way street operation.

*Figures estimated.

Table 14. Population, Dwellings, Households and Grid Units, 1850 and 1880

	1850	1880	% Change
Population	408,081	840,584	+106.0
Grid Units	1,050	1,996	+90.1
Dwellings	61,866	148,671	+140.3
Households	73,010	175,976	+141.0
Ratios			
Population/Grid	388.6	421.1	+8.4
Population/Grid (Mean Individual)	1,384.0	1,150.0	−16.9
Population/Dwelling	6.6	5.7	−13.6
Population/Household	5.6	4.8	−14.7
Household/Dwelling	1.18	1.18	0.0
Dwelling/Grid	58.9	74.5	+26.5
Dwelling/Grid (Mean Dwelling)	212.4	207.9	−2.1

The introduction of canals, steamboats, and railroads opened large new markets in Philadelphia's hinterland. As production increased to meet a rising demand for the city's manufactures, many new jobs were created; thousands of Irish and German immigrants fleeing economic and political dislocation along with native migrants from the surrounding countryside flocked to Philadelphia seeking work. As a result, the population doubled in the decades before the Civil War, reaching 565,000 in 1860; and it increased by half again reaching 841,000 by 1880 (see Table 14 and Maps 3 and 4).

On the eve of the Civil War, Philadelphians lived in dense, crowded fashion in and near the city's center. The available housing stock was simply outstripped by the rapid increase in population. Although building construction increased in the late 1850s in response to sharply rising demand, the Civil War intervened, deterring capital investment as it promoted capital accumulation. A few years after the War, the building construction industry responded vigorously to the demand for new housing. So rapid was the housing boom that one-third of all buildings extant in 1880—roughly 50,000 dwellings—had been built in the preceding ten years. In fact, the construction industry enjoyed the most significant growth of all industries over this period, registering a three-fold increase in workers and firms and a sevenfold increase in capital investment.

While the industry remained largely the province of small builders, the carpenter who erected individual buildings on demand was joined by contractors and speculators who developed sizable tracts of land along the expanding routes of the new streetcar network. The reorganization of the

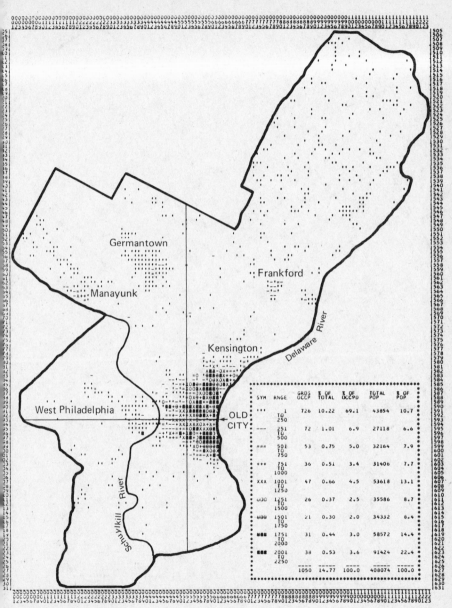

Philadelphia Population, 1850

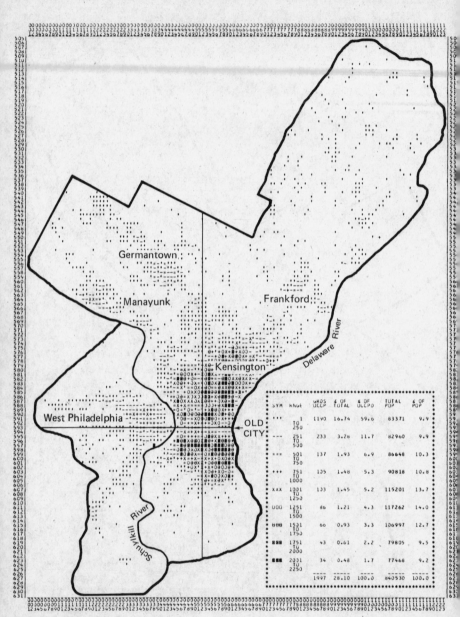

Philadelphia Population, 1880

SYM	RANGE	GROS UCCP	% OF TOTAL	% OF UCCPO	TOTAL POP	% OF POP
''	1 TO 250	1190	16.74	59.6	83371	9.9
---	251 TO 500	233	3.28	11.7	82960	9.9
===	501 TO 750	137	1.93	6.9	86648	10.3
+++	751 TO 1000	105	1.48	5.3	90818	10.8
XXX	1001 TO 1250	103	1.45	5.2	115201	13.7
OOO	1251 TO 1500	86	1.21	4.3	117262	14.0
⊟⊟⊟	1501 TO 1750	66	0.93	3.3	106997	12.7
▐▐▐	1751 TO 2000	43	0.61	2.2	79805	9.5
▮▮▮	2001 TO 2250	34	0.48	1.7	77468	9.2
		1997	28.10	100.0	840530	100.0

Table 15. Residential Housing Construction by Type, 1850–1874

	1850	1851	1853	1867	1869	1870	1872	1873	1874
2-story	6	7	4	1149	2200	2706	2456	2801	2553
3-story	303	315	135	1827	2599	1776	1900	1589	1744
4-story	105	150	86	32	88	62	44	4	13
5-story	6	7	1						
6-story		1							
Total	420	480	226	3008	4887	4554	4400	4394	4310
Nonresidential*	164	110	146	758	621	649	884	827	730

Source: This table is based on evidence collected by John Modell (Research Associate, PSHP, and Professor of History, University of Minnesota) from nine reports made by the Building Inspector and published in Reports of the *Common and Select Councils* (Philadelphia City Archives). The figures in the table below, prior to 1854, refer to the "old" City of Philadelphia; after that date, the figures refer to the entire county. See *Journal of the Common Council, 1850–51*, Appendix XII, 18–19; *Journal of the Select Council, 1851–52*, Appendix XIII, 21–23; *Journal of the Common Council, 1853–54*, Appendix XXXI, 199–200; *Journal of the Select Council, 1868*, V. I, 1034; *Journal of the Select Council, 1870*, V. I, 645–46; *Journal of the Select Council, 1871–72*, V.I, 152–53; *Journal of the Select Council, 1873*, V.I, 759; *Journal of the Select Council, 1874*, V. I, 832–33; *Journal of the Select Council, 1875*. V. I, 1497. Data could not be located for the other years.

*Excludes additions and back buildings.

construction industry after the Civil War led to two significant changes: four-story residential buildings gradually disappeared; and the two-story row home replaced the three-story dwelling as the modal housing type. Two-story houses accounted for roughly six of every ten new houses constructed between 1868 and 1874 (see Table 15). Using standardized building materials and techniques of construction together with the duplication of architectual design, houses were built inexpensively ($700 to $800) and sold at prices (about $1,200) within the reach of the newly emerging middle- and upper-middle classes. The boom continued through the next decades; in the five-year period ending with 1891 more new buildings were erected in Philadelphia than in New York, Boston, and Baltimore combined.[36] These efforts altered the face of the city, leaving Philadelphia with one of its most enduring nicknames, "The City of Homes."

The rate of housing growth caught up with and surpassed population growth. Despite the addition of 150,000 persons to the city's population between 1870 and 1880, the new transportation technology and the housing boom led to declining residential densities. At the height of crowding in 1860, the proportion of the entire population living in the densest grid units (those with more than 170 persons per acre) was one in four; by 1880 it was only one in eleven. Similarly 25 percent more people in 1880 than in 1850 lived in low density areas of the city (less than 30 persons per acre). In order to understand the level of density experienced by the population, we must consider not the average density for occupied grids, but the weighted mean density. According to this "experiential" measure, the average individual in 1850 lived on an acre with 120 other residents; while in 1880 he resided with about 100 persons per acre of land. The ratio of new population to new housing units fell sharply over the period —from 8 to 1 during the 1840s to 4 to 1 in the 1870s.

The declining population densities were also reflected in changes in the number of persons occupying dwellings and households—the building and "apartment" units, respectively—that were enumerated by the U.S. census marshals. Both increased far more rapidly than did the population —141 percent compared to 106 percent—with most of the growth oc-curing in the 1870s. Although the ratio of households to dwellings re-mained identical in both years, the ratio of persons per household and per dwelling declined by nearly one: from 5.6 to 4.8 and from 6.6 to 5.7 respectively (see Table 14).[37] The process of population deconcentration over the thirty-year period, in other words, involved a dispersion of more people over a considerable area of newly developed land, housed in a greater number of smaller buildings, with fewer persons living in each household and dwelling.

Another factor which affected the JTW was the expansion of the central district, itself an early and significant component in the larger process of spatial differentiation.[38] Over the thirty-year period the central district experienced a massive outflow of residential population and an equally impressive inflow of businesses and manufacturing firms and jobs. Between 1850 and 1880, while the city as a whole gained 433,000 persons (a 106 percent increase), the CBD lost roughly 29,000 persons (a 30 percent decline). Meanwhile, business and industry moved into the area in sub-stantial numbers. A count of central district firms of all types listed in the business directories in 1850 and 1880 indicates a 91 percent increase: from 7,196 to 13,724. The growth of manufacturing activity in this sec-tion was equally striking. Where in 1850 there were 1,567 firms with 25,512 employees, by 1880 there were 2,249 firms with 68,458 employees (see Table 16). The ratio of adult males to jobs decreased from almost four to one in 1850 to less than parity in 1880.[39]

The exodus of population and the mass entry of business and industry reflects the increasingly expensive cost of downtown land use for resi-dential purposes. The same process observed in other cities was operative in Philadelphia. The economic advantages of central place location—ac-cess to markets, other firms, and transportation (what economists call "ex-ternalities" and "agglomeration effects")—made downtown location highly

Table 16. Population, Firms and Industry in the Central District, 1850–1880

Area	Year	Population	Firms Listed in Business Directories	Manufacturing* Firms	Employees
Central District	1850	95,590 (23.4)	7,196† (70.0)	1,567 (49.4)	25,512 (51.2)
	1860	87,169 (15.4)	11,690 (41.7)	2,198 (46.0)	50,252 (58.0)
	1870	72.439 (11.0)	13,308 (34.1)	2,757 (38.3)	55,327 (43.1)
	1880	67,070 (7.8)	13,724 (29.4)	2,249 (30.2)	68,458 (40.5)
County	1850	408,081	10,275†	3,170	49,833
	1860	564,586	28,031	4,779	86,621
	1870	656,808	38,972	7,194	128,277
	1880	840,584	46,705	7,440	169,157

*Includes only manufacturing establishments for which addresses could be determined (see Appendix II).

†The 1850 business directory included firms within the "old" City of Philadelphia and its surrounding districts. After consolidation of all the County's political subdivisions in 1854, coverage in the business directories was County-wide. Because the central district lies largely within the "old" City, the 1850 business directory provides an accurate count of firms in that area. The directory, however, fails to accomplish this task for the County. Thus, the stated increase in the number of Philadelphia County businesses from 10,275 firms in 1850 to 28,031 in 1860 is partially due to the lack of complete coverage in the earlier year (see Appendix II).

desirable. The ensuing competition led to increased demand which drove land rents sharply upwards and forced residential users of CBD space to locate elsewhere in the city. Faced with high rents, many persons who earlier combined work and residence in the downtown now began to separate them. Although in 1880 three among four of the city's businesses were located outside of the CBD—most were small firms expanding along with the population—the growth of the CBD over the period played an important role in the overall increase in the JTW. With fewer persons living where a substantial portion of employment was located, the distances traveled to work had to be greater.

Changes in the industrial sector of the economy also played a significant role in increasing the JTW. Other essays in this volume document that manufacturing employment in 1880 accounted for a greater proportion of all jobs than it had in 1850 (52 percent as compared to 32 percent) and that manufacturing employment increased 202 percent over the thirty years. What concerns us in the discussion of the JTW, however, is the vastly disproportionate growth of the industrial workforce employed in large firms. While the number of employees in firms with 1 to 25 workers grew 64 percent, firms with 26 to 50 workers grew 124 percent, and firms with 51 to 150 workers grew 195 percent, the largest firms—those employing more than 151 workers—grew 585 percent. In 1850 firms with

Table 17.   Growth in the Size of Manufacturing Firms, 1850–1880

Firm Size (# of Employees)	1850	% of Workforce	1880	% of Workforce	% Growth
1–25	23,654	40.8	38,755	19.8	63.8
26–50	9,319	16.1	20,861	15.4	123.9
51–150	14,348	24.8	42,250	24.9	194.5
151+	10,637	18.3	72,898	39.9	585.3
Total All Firms	57,958	100.0	174,764	100.0	201.5

Source: U.S. Manuscript Censuses of Manufactures, 1850, 1860, 1870, 1880.

more than fifty workers accounted for four workers in ten—by 1880 they accounted for six workers in ten. Where at the start of the period the typical worker labored in a firm that employed 74 persons, at its end he or she labored along with 117 others(see Table 17).

While spatial differentiation was manifested most clearly in the growth of the CBD, it was also evident in the differential expansion of population and manufacturing from the city's center. Over the thirty years, population spread faster and further than did manufacturing jobs. Where a quarter mile separated the typical person from the typical job in 1850, a half mile separated them in 1880. By the end of the period, the typical person had moved 0.6 miles and the typical job only 0.4 miles from the city's center (see Table 18). The evidence arrayed in Table 19 demonstrates the differential growth and distribution of all jobs and population in yet another way. In 1850, slightly less than one-third of all the city's manufacturing jobs were within one mile of the home of the average adult male; by 1880, this proportion had fallen to one-sixth.[40] The doubling of both the population and the urban space it inhabited between 1850 and 1880, in other words, did not result in a duplication of the relationships which characterized the spatial distribution of jobs and population in the antebellum city. It is within this broader context that impact of the growth in firm size upon the JTW must be understood. With more workers in 1880 than in 1850 employed in large individual firms, and with lower population densities surrounding these firms, the distances traveled to work had to increase.[41]

The impact that changes in transportation, building construction, the central district, and manufacturing scale had on residential dispersion and industrial employment location can be examined in work done by Stephen Putman. The results of Putman's application to our data base of a simulation model of land-use allocation, DRAM[42], developed in his city planning research, corroborate the distances we found in our study of the JTW. More importantly, however, they enable us to infer the timing and extent

THE "JOURNEY-TO-WORK" 161

Table 18. Distance of Population and Manufacturing Jobs from City Center, 1850–1880* (in miles)

Year	Population	Manufacturing Jobs
1850	1.05	0.80
1860	1.21	0.81
1870	1.39	0.93
1880	1.63	1.17
30-year growth	0.58	0.37

Source: U.S. Manuscript Censuses of Manufactures, 1850, 1860, 1870, 1880; U.S. Manuscript Censuses of Population, 1850, 1860, 1870, 1880.

*Excludes the outlying communities of Frankford, Germantown and Manayunk. The "city center" is defined here as 7th & Market Streets.

of the impact that transportation might have had on the overall relationship between jobs and housing. The computer model assumes that the length of any trip between employment location and residence is determined by two opposing constraints: housing opportunities increase with distance from worksites; and the propensity to travel decreases with distance from worksites. DRAM begins with the location of jobs and determines how far workers had to travel before "encountering opportunities" for housing to terminate their work-to-home trip. As used here the model measures not the JTW trips of specific individuals, but the aggregate patterns of residential and employment location.[43]

The fine calibrations of DRAM permit us to see graphically, in two computer-generated plots of the opportunity and travel propensity constraint functions, when the relationships between jobs and housing changed. In 1850 housing opportunities (see Figure 1) diminished with increasing

Table 19. Number and Percentage of Jobs per Unit Distance from Average Adult Male, 1850–1880

Year	Distance in Miles					
	0.0–0.5	0.5–1.0	1.0–2.0	2.0–5.0	5.0–10.0	10.0+
1850	2055	10711	13569	6171	3228	190
	5.7	29.8	37.8	17.2	8.9	0.5
1860	2236	15413	23697	12245	5951	278
	3.7	29.7	39.6	20.4	9.9	0.5
1870	2335	16615	32092	25973	8587	336
	2.7	19.3	37.3	30.2	10.0	0.4
1880	2559	18288	38419	49435	16545	405
	2.0	14.5	30.5	39.3	13.2	3.2

Source: U.S. Manuscript Censuses of Manufactures, 1850, 1860, 1870, 1880; U.S. Manuscript Censuses of Population, 1850, 1860, 1870, 1880.

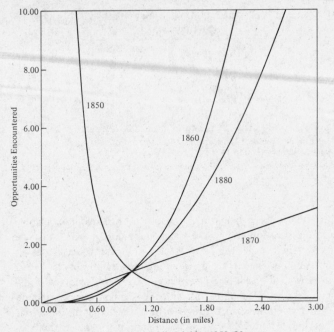

Figure 1. Opportunity Function: Philadelphia, 1850–80.

distance from the trip's origin—the place of employment. Jobs and housing in the central city and other built-up areas such as Germantown were so compactly organized that traveling only a half-mile or more from workplaces generally resulted in declining housing opportunities; in other words, one would soon encounter sparsely populated or vacant areas of the city. This inverse relationship between distance and opportunities for housing has never resulted in applications of DRAM to twentieth-century cities. The curve for 1860 displays the normal or "modern" relationship; opportunities to terminate the "work-to-home" trip increased with greater distance from the origin.

The slope of the travel function in Figure 2 is near zero in 1850, indicating that individuals were indifferent to the length of a JTW trip. Since all trips were of so short a duration, it is logical that individuals did not have a preference for trips of 0.1 miles as opposed to ones of 0.4 or 0.5 miles. The 1860 curve, in contrast, displays a "modern" form; it was beginning to be possible for people to make relatively long trips. The shape of the curve, however, suggests that individuals were disinclined to make them.

In both Figures 1 and 2, the 1870 curve is anomalous, appearing be-yond the 1880 curve. The anomaly is explained by a burst of housing and transportation construction after the Civil War that led to a relatively sparse distribution of new homes along the routes of the new horsecar lines. The return of the 1880 curve to a point between the 1860 and 1870 curves reflects, in turn, the spectacular expansion of housing in the 1870s; most of the new housing constructed in that decade "filled-in" the areas be-tween the streetcar lines which reached their outer limits in 1870 (see Tables 13 and 15). The flattening out of the opportunities curve in 1870 and 1880 together with the less sharply declining travel function strongly suggests that one had to travel farther to obtain the same housing oppor-tunities (urban deconcentration) and that many people were willing to travel greater distances between home and work by the 1870s than they had in 1860.

It is difficult to isolate the independent effect of the new transportation technology on the relationship between work and residence. Could the horse-drawn streetcar have had a profound impact in merely the two

Figure 2. Travel Function: Philadelphia, 1850–80.

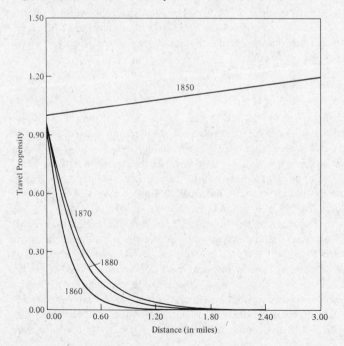

years following 1858 when the system was initiated? On the one hand, it is unlikely. It can be argued that the shift in the opportunities function between 1850 and 1860 reflects less the impact of the transportation system than the burst of building construction at the decade's close (see Table 18). The appearance of new housing sufficiently in advance of new job opportunities at the peripheries of the built-up areas of the city increased the number of residences available to workers at further distances from their factories or businesses. On the other hand, the new building on the outskirts might itself have been stimulated by the knowledge that transportation would be available for potential residents, many of whom would be able to afford the high costs of regular commuting.[44] The new transportation system, it is useful to bear in mind, with its routes radiating out from the city center like so many spokes on a wheel, was clearly established by 1860; in that year it consisted of seventy-five miles of track and is estimated to have carried 15 million passengers. However, Putman concludes that it was not until the end of the Civil War decade that the impact of the transportation sysem was fully felt. He emphasizes that it is the shift to the right of the travel propensity function between 1860 and 1870 (indicating that many more people were willing to travel further distances to work), rather than the inversion of the opportunity function between 1850 and 1860, that constitutes the more significant effect of the new transportation system on the relationship between workplace and residence.

Conclusions

These changes in the social and spatial differentiation of the city were the result of the industrialization process. Transportation played a critical role in the transformation of urban space, its impact increasing with more advanced technologies. Other PSHP research focuses on how new technologies freed industry from its historic dependence on water as its major source of power and transport and enabled firms to assume new patterns of distribution and concentration across urban space.[45]

Our major concern in this essay has been with the JTW. Allan Pred has explored this subject in Manhattan during the first four decades of the nineteenth century. In this era of the horse-drawn omnibus, Pred found that "virtually nobody divorced his place-of-work from his place-of-residence by more than a mile," and that the population commuting considerable distances to work was limited to an insignificant number of merchants and artisan proprietors.[46] Sam Bass Warner, Jr., examined the JTW in the last three decades of the nineteenth century. In the "streetcar suburbs" of Boston, Warner found that the proportion of the population commuting increased from roughly 20 percent in the 1870s to 50 percent by the 1890s. The commuters were largely middle-class, and their use of the streetcars led to the development of residentially homogeneous suburbs.[47]

Advances in transportation technology made it possible for white-collar workers to choose where they wished to live, constrained to be sure, by considerations of taste, cost, and discrimination. As we have seen, these constraints were not randomly distributed among the population. It is fair to say that in 1880 Philadelphia was composed of two population groups that roughly reflected the distinction between manual and nonmanual work being emphasized by industrialization.[48] The first of these groups consisted of a small, but growing, number of wealthier citizens who commuted to work on the horsecars and steam-driven railways from new neighborhoods developing at the city's edges. They emerged as a result of the industrialization process that altered the city's occupational and social structure. These processes of social and spatial differentiation went on simultaneously, each reinforcing the other. People of similar socioeconomic backgrounds, whether representative of the older, established classes or newly emerging ones, began to move to new areas of the city where they could reside with others more like themselves. Social differences, in other words, were being physically expressed in the spatial patterns of the city as well as in the architecture of their homes. These new and increasingly homogeneous sections, however, did more than passively reflect social differences; they influenced future social and spatial arrangements. In embodying a new life style distinguished by different consumption patterns and ideologies, they provided for emulation an example that is inextricably bound up with the contemporary American dream of suburban living. Unlike most Philadelphians whose limited incomes all but eliminated their residential options, confining them to locations close to their workplaces, these citizens were able to combine residential and social mobility, moving into better sections of the city as their fortunes dictated; they were also able to move when life cycle considerations, such as marriage and children, called for more appropriate housing and location.

The second group of Philadelphians in 1880 represented the bulk of the labor force whose residences were by necessity tied to the blocks surrounding the firms in which they earned their livelihood. This helps to account for the high rates of urban population fluidity found by all researchers of the nineteenth-century city.[49] Most studies have been long on description and short on explanation. Modern demographic theory posits two explanatory categories for contemporary geographic mobility: job-related and family-related moves. The assumption underlying this theory is that the automobile and cheap mass transit make it possible for workers to maintain a fixed local residence and commute to any job available in the city. *Intra*-city moves, according to theory, are made only in response to different housing needs necessitated by changes in the life cycle. Because the city is viewed as a single, large labor market within the reach of all workers, all job-related moves must be *inter*city in nature.

The realities of urban life in the last century require that we revise these theories of geographic mobility. The large nineteenth-century city has to be conceptualized as consisting not of one, but of multiple labor markets. The absence of cheap mass transit meant that workers had to move if their employment shifted from one local labor market to another. Given the nature of employment in the nineteenth-century economy, a reasonable hypothesis can be presented to explain why urban populations were so volatile. An irregular business cycle with many up-and-down turns, frequent layoffs, seasonal fluctuation, little job security, and the lack of institutional supports such as unemployment insurance meant that workers had to change residences when the location of their employment shifted substantially. With many already living at the margins of subsistence, there was precious little time to spare in finding a new job. If employment was not immediately available in the area of the city where they lived and if work could be found elsewhere that necessitated a move, they had little choice but to relocate without delay.[50] It is in this context that the evidence presented earlier on the JTW for boarders and lodgers takes on special significance. Although the evidence is still fragmentary, it appears that one of the important functions of boarding was to allow workers a quick and efficient means of locating close to their new workplaces. Closely related to this discussion are the factors that determined the location of industrial firms. These factors and the locational decisions they influenced would dominate the residential patterns of the city; this is a significant topic that deserves careful attention.[51]

When the results of our research on the JTW and transportation are considered along with those on geographic mobility, we confront a major paradox of nineteenth-century urban life. The proximity of most persons to their jobs, schools, churches, shopping, and the like suggests an insulated, rarely changing environment; while the volatility of the population movement into, out of, and within the city suggests an ever-changing setting for most people. On the one hand, we envision stable neighborhoods, strong friendship, and kin networks, and limited exposure to the world beyond with its different ethnic and religious groups, culture, and behavior; on the other, we see change as the hallmark of the society with continuous uprooting and relocation, limited opportunity to develop enduring ties to kin, friends, and fellow laborers, constant exposure to new people, values, and ideas, and different ways of life.

What shall we make of this paradox? To understand it first requires that we learn more about the serial environments that people moved through. Were these circumscribed areas in which urban workers and their families lived and labored, and through which they moved with considerable frequency, similar or contrasting environments? If, excluding the new and more homogeneous neighborhoods developing to meet the needs of a wealthier class of citizens, the industrializing city of the late nineteenth century was a collection of reasonably self-contained, heterogeneous communities that by and large closely resembled each other, then frequent movement through working-class neighborhoods may have placed people in successive environments that differed not in their particulars, but only in the identity of the specific persons who lived there. The kinds of people one worked with, drank with at the local tavern, met and talked with on the streets; the employment opportunities and types of housing, shops, and services; the variety of institutions and voluntary associations present; all may have been similar to what was left behind. The cultural milieu and the organization of life, in other words, might have remained pretty much what it had been before the move to a new job and neighborhood.

If, in contrast, the city's working-class communities were differentiated in important respects by local economic and industrial structures which functioned as separate labor markets and attracted people of different demographic, ethnic, and occupational characteristics, then the consequences of frequent residential mobility would be different indeed. Each of these possibilities has serious implications for our understanding of the development and maintenance of working-class culture and consciousness, rates and patterns of intermarriage and assimilation, labor organizing and political activities. And each of these topics—the study of local working-class areas within the larger city and the consequences arising from the interaction between behavior and environment—requires further yet finer-grained analysis.

NOTES

1. Kate Liepmann was one of the first scholars to perceive the importance of these journeys for urban society; her empirical investigation of the relationship between residential and employment location was first published in a now classic study, *The Journey to Work* (New York: Oxford University Press, 1944).

2. See Clyde Griffen, "Occupational Mobility in Nineteenth-Century America: Problems and Possibilities," *Journal of Social History* 5 (Spring 1972), 310–30;

Michael Katz, "Occupational Classification in History," *Journal of Interdisciplinary History* 3 (Summer 1972), 63–88; see Bruce Laurie, Theodore Hershberg, and George Alter, "Immigrants and Industry: The Philadelphia Experience, 1850–1880," *Journal of Social History* 9 (December 1975), 219–48, also in this volume; and T. Hershberg and R. Dockhorn, "Occupational Classification," in Theodore Hershberg, guest editor, "A Special Issue: The Philadelphia Social History Project," *Historical Methods Newsletter* 9 (March–June, 1976), 59–98; the issue containing this essay is hereafter cited as "PSHP: Special Issue."

3. In this volume, for example, see the use of the labor shed parameters by Laurie and Schmitz to study worker productivity and by Greenberg to study job access. Bruce Laurie and Mark Schmitz, "Manufacture and Productivity: The Making of an Industrial Base, Philadelphia, 1850–1880"; Stephanie W. Greenberg, "Industrial Location and Ethnic Residential Patterns in an Industrializing City: Philadelphia, 1880."

4. The rationale for these particular dimensions is explained in T. Hershberg, "The Historical Study of Urban Space," in "PSHP: Special Issue," *op. cit.*, 100–101; and in Hershberg, "The Philadelphia Social History Project: A Methodological History" (Ph.D. dissertation, History, Stanford University, 1973), ch. III and V, section 2; hereafter cited as "The PSHP." See, too, Appendix II.

5. The literature available on public transportation in Philadelphia can be found in the original records of the Philadelphia Rapid Transit Company (P.R.T.) and its predecessors. These include reports to public authorities and articles of the muck-raking period around 1900, some of which appeared in scholarly publications. The majority of the minute books and cash books of the original companies survive and both are of considerable value in determining what types of business the companies considered particularly desirable. In addition, there were various records maintained over the years that provide specialized information on traffic, routings, and fare structures. The most important of these are noted below.

An untitled notebook contains comparative costs on operations and the effect of service changes and alterations in patterns of public travel as well as other data on operations and fares; the notebook was maintained by the Philadelphia City Passenger Railway Company from 1876 to 1902 (P.R.T. Corporate History). Other important sources include unpublished manuscripts on blueprint paper (P.R.T. Routing History) and unpublished spirit-duplicated manuscripts. The last of these has severe limitations in the period before 1911 and has been revised and expanded from other sources; see Harold E. Cox, *Electric Street Railway Routings of the City of Philadelphia, Pennsylvania, 1892–1958* (unpublished spirit-duplicated manuscripts, December 1958); see, too, an untitled unpublished typescript of horse, cable, and steam railway routings.

Published sources of data include *Reports of the Several Railroad and Coal Companies of Pennsylvania Communicated by the Auditor General*, title varies (the relevant years cover 1858 to 1874); *Annual Report of the Secretary of Internal Affairs* (of Pennsylvania), *Part IV, Railroad, Canal and Telegraph Companies*—this is valuable for routes, income, and operating practices from 1875 to 1900, but must be used with caution since the reports were not checked and contain unintentional errors as well as what appear to be deliberate efforts to mislead. Information for both of the above items is incomplete for earlier years and requires estimations from the data given, particularly in the area of passenger traffic; *Annual Reports of the Union Traction Company of Philadelphia, 1896 to 1901; Annual Reports of the Philadelphia Rapid Transit Company, 1902 to 1910; Philadelphia Rapid Transit Company, Stotesbury-Mitten Management, 1911 to 1920;* Speirs, *Report of the Transit Commissioner*, City of Philadelphia, July 1913, 2 vols., n.p.; Ford, Bacon, and Davis, *Pennsylvania State Railroad Commission* (in the matter of complaints against the volumes), March 7, 1911; Chandler Brothers and Company, *The Philadelphia Rapid*

Transit Company: A Descriptive and Statistical Analysis of the Consolidation and Development of the Street Railway Properties of Philadelphia, 1904.

All of the above are to be found in the P.R.T. Collection, Wilkes College, Wilkes Barre, Pa.

6. Data on women and youths, although part of the larger PSHP data base, were not available for use in this study. There is no evidence to suggest, however, that their JTW, when computed, will be significantly different than that of adult males. What differences emerge will likely be in the direction of a shorter distance traveled. See E. E. Pratt, *Industrial Causes of Congestion of Population in New York City* (New York: Columbia University Press, 1911), 116–88.

7. Also, occupational titles such as "laborer," which did not make explicit the industry in which work was performed, could not be included in this study. However, once the spatial boundaries for the labor shed are computed, we intend to determine whether the socioeconomic profile of laborers residing close to large firms (which, for example, paid high wages to unskilled workers) is superior to the profile of all laborers.

8. See Peter Knights, "City Directories as Aids to Ante-Bellum Urban Studies: A Research Note," *Historical Methods Newsletter* 2 (September 1969), 1–10.

9. Several contemporary studies provide evidence that in fact people tend to live as close as possible to their workplaces. See Stephen N. Putman, "Calibrating a Disaggregated Residential Allocation Model—DRAM," in D. B. Massey, P. W. J. Batey, eds., *London Papers in Regional Science, 7. Alternative Frameworks for Analysis* (London, 1977), 108–24; and "Calibrating a Residential Model for Nineteenth-Century Philadelphia," *Environment and Planning A* 9 (1977), 449–60.

10. Measuring to the nearest firm in both 1850 and 1880, despite other possible biases, makes clear that the JTW at minimum doubled over the period.

11. For a map locating the respective geographic centers of work and residence for lawyers, see T. Hershberg and A. Burstein, "A Research Note on New PSHP Techniques for the Study of Space," in "PSHP: Special Issue," *op. cit.,* 136.

12. *The Spatial Dynamics of U.S. Urban-Industrial Growth, 1800–1914: Interpretative and Theoretical Essays* (Cambridge: M.I.T. Press, 1966), 196–213.

13. See Laurie and Schmitz, "Manufacture and Productivity," *op. cit.;* and Laurie *et al.,* "Immigrants and Industry," *op. cit.*

14. We can offer no compelling explanation for the different patterns among carpenters and cabinetmakers. Perhaps carpenters moved to new areas under construction, combining work and residence, while cabinetmakers began to prefer the maintenance of separate shops for fixed construction.

15. We have checked our estimates of the JTW in two additional ways. The first of these consisted of drawing boundaries corresponding to the estimated JTW (0.6 miles in 1850; 1.0 miles in 1880) around the major firms in an industry. We then counted the proportion of that industry's workforce living within the boundaries. The results were as follows:

Industry	Year	% of Workforce Within Estimated JTW
Boiler Makers	1850	87.9
Boiler Makers	1880	87.0
Glass Makers	1850	84.8
Glass Makers	1880	88.6
Lamp & Gas Fittings	1850	64.6

No calculation was made for lamp and gas fitters for 1880 because by that time the industry had dispersed too greatly for the measure to be meaningful.

A second check was made upon highly dispersed industries. In this case some indication of clustering close to the firms was obtained by calculating the proportion of the industry's workforce residing in grid units occupied by major firms or in grids adjacent to the major firms. In 1880 the grid units adjacent to or occupied by major firms making lamp and gas fittings constituted only 6.7 percent of the grids occupied by the labor force, yet they contained 14.5 percent of that workforce. Clearly, clustering near the major firms was taking place. Similarly, large brickyards occupied or were adjacent to only 11.1 percent of the grid units occupied by the workforce in that industry. Yet, these grids contained 19.5 percent of the workforce.

16. See, too, Stephanie Greenberg, "Industrial Location and the Residential Patterns of Occupational Groups: Philadelphia, 1880," paper presented at Social Science History Association (Columbus, Ohio: November 1978). Among factory owners, it is also apparent that the owners of the largest firms lived furthest from work. In an unpublished PSHP paper, Timothy Cook and Andrew Pollott find that the mean JTW of the owners of the city's largest morocco firms in 1880 was .85 miles, in contrast to a median of .2 miles for morocco manufacturers as a whole (see Table 5). They also discover that 46 percent of the morocco "elite" lived over a mile from their worksites as compared to 18 percent of the PSHP sample of morocco white-collar workers (see Table 6). Cook and Pollott measured the *actual* JTWs of their elite, and the PSHP estimated the JTW by calculating the distance to the nearest firm; it is thus possible that the differences between the two groups are somewhat exaggerated. The sharp divergence between the JTWs of these white-collar groups, however, indicates that industrial scale, serving as a proxy for wealth, strongly influenced an owner's choice of residence. See "A Fronting Block Analysis of the Residential Patterns of Late Nineteenth-Century Philadelphians: Morocco Workers, 1880, as a Test Case," unpublished manuscript in possession of PSHP.

17. Laurie and Schmitz, "Manufacture and Productivity," *op. cit.,* Table 6.

18. In this volume, see Alan Burstein, "Immigrants and Residential Mobility: The Irish and Germans in Philadelphia, 1850–1880"; see also his "Residential Distribution and Mobility of Irish and German Immigrants in Philadelphia, 1850–1880" (Ph.D. dissertation, Demography, University of Pennsylvania, 1975); and "Patterns of Segregation and Residential Experience," in "PSHP: Special Issue," *op. cit.,* 105–13.

19. J. Thomas Scharf and Thompson Westcott, *History of Philadelphia* (Philadelphia: L. H. Everts, 1884), 2144–2200; George R. Taylor, "The Beginnings of Mass Transportation in Urban America," *Smithsonian Journal of History* 1 (Summer 1966), 35–50; 1 (Autumn 1966), 31–54. Roger Miller has completed extensive research on the city's transportation system; see his "Time-Geographic Assessment of the Impact of Horsecar Transportation in Philadelphia, 1850–1860" (Ph.D. dissertation, Geography, University of California, Berkeley, 1979).

20. For a discussion of the consolidation movement, see Howard Gillette, "Corrupt and Contented: Philadelphia's Political Machine, 1865–1887" (Ph.D. dissertation, American Studies, Yale University, 1970); and his "The Emergence of the Modern Metropolis: Philadelphia in the Age of Consolidation," in H. Gillette and William Cutler, eds., *The Divided Metropolis: Social and Spatial Dimensions of Philadelphia, 1820–1940* (Westport, Ct.: Greenwood Press, 1980).

21. It should be noted, however, that omnibuses continued to run on Broad Street where streetcars were not permitted. Additionally a line ran to the Navy Yard after it moved to League Island in the early 1870s.

22. For discussion of the role played by land speculators and large steel producing firms in these developments, see Gillette, "Corrupt and Contented," *op. cit.*

23. Further detail on the fare structure is provided in Roger Miller, *op. cit.*, 259–93.

24. Suburban operation charged higher fares ranging up to twelve cents for a one-way ride. Discounts were offered by some companies (e.g., five rides for twenty-five cents), but these did not apply to exchanges.

25. Working-class families did not include transportation costs as an item in their budgets. For a general discussion of family budgets, see John Modell, "Patterns of Consumption, Acculturation and Family Income Strategies in Late Nineteenth-Century America," Tamara K. Hareven and Maris A. Vinovskis, eds., *Family and Population in Nineteenth-Century America* (Princeton, N.J.: Princeton University Press, 1978); and Michael Haines, "Industrial Work and the Family Life Cycle, 1889/1890," *Research in Economic History* 4 (1979). For Philadelphia, see Eudice Glassberg's discussion of family budgets, "Work, Wages and the Cost of Living: Ethnic Differences and the Poverty Line in Philadelphia, 1880," *Pennsylvania History* 66 (January 1979), 17–58; in this volume, see the essays by Haines, "Poverty, Economic Stress and the Family in a Nineteenth-Century American City: Philadelphia, 1880"; and by Claudia Goldin, "Family Strategies and the Family Economy in the Late Nineteenth Century: The Role of Secondary Workers."

26. Only one company provided remotely adequate service. The Union Passenger Railway had terminals at Fairmount Park, Kensington, the Old Navy Yard, and the Market Street Ferries. It gave free transfers between all of its own lines. That the lack of diagonal streets led to frequent transfers to a second line can be seen in the fact that one-fourth of the passengers carried by the Union Passenger Company in 1880 were transfer passengers.

27. Estimates of riding proportions contained in the subsequent text and Table 12 were derived from an analysis of the riding characteristics of streetcar lines that had clearly definable service areas such as heavy factory districts, recreational facilities, and CBD shopping facilities. Much of this data is available in manuscript form in the studies made by the Philadelphia City Passenger Railway Company in an untitled notebook in which it estimated its railroad and park business. Using data reported for special purpose lines and the impact of the weather and special events upon traffic, as shown in Tables 10, 11, and 12, we estimated the volume of traffic generated by shopping, recreation, and railroad stations and ferries. These estimates were then weighted proportionately to the other lines of the city according to their function and traffic loads. Although these totals can only be approximations, the resulting percentages assigned to the work force for regular JTW use compare favorably with the proportion of the work force living at a distance of more than one mile from their place of employment. They are also consistent with the proportion of commuters reported for Boston in 1870 by Sam Bass Warner, Jr., in *Streetcar Suburbs: The Processes of Growth in Boston, 1870–1900* (Cambridge: Harvard University Press, 1962). Estimations were deliberately understated so that the already small proportion of traffic assigned to the JTW may actually have been even lower.

28. The Centennial lines were built for special purposes in 1876, but remained after the close of the Exposition as a means of reaching the western portions of the Park, an area which previously had been virtually inaccessible from the center-city area.

29. Riding on Sunday was originally prohibited, but new legislation after the Civil War (November 9, 1867) opened the transportation system for Sunday travel; see Harold Cox, "Daily Except Sunday: Blue Laws and the Operation of Philadelphia Horsecars," *Business History Review* 39 (September, 1965), 228–42.

30. The data in Table 10 are index values computed to allow comparisons of weekend and weekday riding. The percentage differences reported for the Peoples

Line are based on the actual volume of passengers recorded in the company ledgers; see note 5.

31. Untitled Record Book, Philadelphia City Passenger Railway Company; Commonwealth of Pennsylvania, *Annual Report of the Secretary of Internal Affairs, Part IV, Railroad, Canal, and Telegraph Companies*.

32. Susan Drobis computed indices of segregation for several occupational groups in 1880. High white-collar jobs had by far the highest measure (0.61); the others were low white-collar (0.31), skilled (0.29), and unskilled (0.35). Working paper, PSHP, November 1974; also see her essay, "Occupational and Residential Differentiation: A Historical Application of Cluster Analysis," in "PSHP: Special Issue," *op. cit.*, 114–34.

33. We have not yet estimated the proportion of the population using private means of transportation, but since "few people could afford the expense or nuisance of maintaining a horse and carriage," it is unlikely that such a form of transportation was a significant factor. Kenneth T. Jackson, "The Crabgrass Frontier: 150 Years of Suburban Growth in America," in Raymond A. Mohl and James F. Richardson, eds., *The Urban Experience* (Belmont, Cal.: Wadsworth, 1973), 158.

34. See Kenneth T. Jackson's valuable essay, "Urban Deconcentration in the Nineteenth Century: A Statistical Inquiry," in Leo Schnore, ed., *The New Urban History: Quantitative Explorations by American Historians* (Princeton, N.J.: Princeton University Press, 1975), 110–42.

35. Walter Isard, "Transport Development and Building Cycles," *Quarterly Journal of Economics* 57 (November 1942), 90–112.

36. John N. Gallagher, "Real Estate Holdings and Valuations," in Frank H. Taylor, ed., *The City of Philadelphia* (Philadelphia: George S. Harris and Sons, 1893), 83.

37. This decrease, it must be remembered, was also part of the larger fertility decline that characterized the Western world throughout the nineteenth century.

38. Jeffrey Roberts discusses many changes in his work, "Continuity and Change in Downtown Land Use: The Evolution of Philadelphia's Central District, 1850–1880," paper presented at Social Science History Association (Philadelphia: 1976); and "Railroads and the Growth of the Downtown: Philadelphia, 1830–1900," in Gillette and Cutler, eds., *op. cit.*

39. If nonmanufacturing jobs, a growing component in the expansion of financial, retailing, and other commercial activities of the downtown district, were included in these calculations, the ratio would decrease still further.

40. To determine the average adult male's access to jobs, the grid units were aggregated into 363 zones, each consisting of a four-by-five grid unit area. Next, the distance of each zone to all other zones and the number of jobs within specified distances of each were calculated. Finally, each zone's job-distance vector was weighted by the number of adult male residents and the mean for each distance category across all zones was determined.

41. The shortening of the work day from an average of eleven hours in 1850 to ten hours in 1880 may also have had an important effect on the distances laborers were willing to walk to work. In his detailed study, E. E. Pratt found "a close relation between hours of labor and the distribution of the workers by residence." This relation appeared "so intimate" to Pratt that he concluded that the "long day necessitated the nearby residence of workers, while a short working day permits a wider distribution by residence." See *Industrial Causes of Congestion of Population in New York City, op. cit.*, 198.

42. DRAM—disaggregated residential allocation model—is discussed in the two papers by Stephen Putman, "Calibrating a Disaggregated Residential Allocation Model," *op. cit.*; and "Calibrating a Residential Model," *op. cit.*

43. DRAM uses a minimum likelihood procedure to simultaneously maximize opportunities while minimizing travel distances. The resultant functional form can be thought of as a probability distribution of JTW trips. The procedure does not explicitly model the JTW trip, but allows estimations to be made of the distributions of such trips.

44. For a case study of the impact that new transportation had on land speculation and housing construction, see Gilbert Osofsky, *Harlem: The Making of a Ghetto, Negro New York, 1890–1930* (New York: Harper & Row, 1963).

45. See David Ward's excellent discussion of the elements involved in this process, *Cities and Immigrants: A Geography of Change in Nineteenth-Century America* (New York: Oxford University Press, 1971); and in this volume see Theodore Hershberg, Alan N. Burstein, Eugene P. Ericksen, Stephanie Greenberg, and William L. Yancey, "A Tale of Three Cities: Blacks and Immigrants in Philadelphia, 1850–1880, 1930 and 1970," *The Annals* 441 (January 1979), 55–81, also in this volume; and the work of Eugene P. Ericksen and William L. Yancey cited there.

46. Pred, *Spatial Dynamics, op. cit.,* 208.

47. Sam Bass Warner, Jr., *Streetcar Suburbs, op. cit.,* 52–64.

48. Alan Burstein, "Immigrants and Residential Mobility," *op. cit.;* and Susan Drobis, "Occupation and Residential Distribution," in "PSHP: Special Issue," *op. cit.*

49. Stephan Thernstrom and Peter Knights, "Men in Motion: Some Data and Speculations About Urban Population Mobility in Nineteenth-Century America," *Journal of Interdisciplinary History* 1 (Autumn 1975), 7–36. Thernstrom has summarized a variety of studies that bear on this subject in chapter 10 of his *The Other Bostonians: Poverty and Progress in the American Metropolis, 1880–1970* (Cambridge: Harvard University Press, 1973).

50. The role of extended family and kin-networks located nearby may have temporarily mediated the exigencies arising from loss of work; the extent of assistance thus rendered remains speculative. In this volume, see John Modell, Frank F. Furstenberg, Jr., and Theodore Hershberg, "Social Change and the Transitions to Adulthood in Historical Perspective," *Journal of Family History* 1 (Autumn 1976), 7–32; Haines, "Poverty," *op. cit.;* Goldin, "Family Strategies," *op. cit.*

51. This topic is the subject of the essay on manufacturing location by Richard Greenfield, "The Determinants and Dynamics of Intra-Urban Manufacturing Location: A Perspective on Nineteenth-Century Philadelphia," paper presented at Social Science History Association (Columbus, Ohio: November 1978). Greenberg discusses this topic in "Industrial Location and Ethnic Residential Patterns in an Industrializing City: Philadelphia, 1880," in this volume; in "The Relationship Between Work and Residence in an Industrial City," in Gillette and Cutler, eds., *op. cit.;* and in her "Industrialization in Philadelphia: The Relationship Between Industrial Location and Residential Patterns, 1880–1930" (Ph.D. dissertation, Sociology, Temple University, 1977). John Gruenstein outlined an econometric approach in "Dynamic Models of Employment and Population Location for Philadelphia, 1850–1880," paper presented at Social Science History Association (Philadelphia: 1976). See, too, Theodore Hershberg *et al.,* "A Tale of Three Cities," *op. cit.,* especially the pages on "The Nineteenth-Century City: 1850–1880."

5. Immigrants and Residential Mobility: The Irish and Germans in Philadelphia, 1850–1880

ALAN N. BURSTEIN

Immigrants and Residence: The Chicago School and Beyond

While a half century has passed since Burgess presented his model of urban spatial structure characterized by concentric zones, the basic framework retains a sufficient degree of viability to continue to influence our study of the city, both present and past.[1] The framework which Burgess's model provides is particularly valuable if we go beyond the exercise—often futile—of merely attemtping to empirically test for the existence of the five concentric zones in any chosen city at a given point in time. Indeed one may be better served by the model by understanding that regardless of the existence of the specific circularly shaped zones which Burgess described, development of the study of the city by the Chicago School stressed not a specific shape, but rather the operation of certain processes. Most important of these processes in shaping the city were invasion, succession, and outward movement concurrent with industrialization, formation of the modern central business district, and aging of the central housing core resulting in formation of the "zone in transition," the most heterogeneous and hence least precisely defined of the five concentric zones.[2] The result of these processes is that demographic variation can be

This research is based on a larger work, Alan N. Burstein, "Residential Distribution and Mobility of Irish and German Immigrants in Philadelphia, 1850–1880" (Ph.D. dissertation, Demography, University of Pennsylvania, 1975). An earlier version of this paper was presented at the Social Science History Association (Philadelphia: October 1976). The advice and support of Theodore Hershberg and of the PSHP research associates and administrative staff are gratefully acknowledged.

174

observed with increasing distance from the center of the city, most typically an increasing of socioeconomic status with increasing distance from the center. The residential pattern of immigrant groups is placed in the perspective of the Burgess model by Park:

> It has been observed . . . that immigrant peoples primarily settle first in or near the centers of cities, in the so-called areas of transition. From there they are likely to move by steps (perhaps, one might better say by leaps and bounds) from an area of first to areas of second and third settlement, generally in the direction of the periphery of the city and eventually into the suburban areas—in any case, from a less to a more stable sector of the metropolitan region. To these movements, seeing in them the effects of natural tendencies in the life of the urban community, students have applied the term "succession."[3]

This view of immigrant residential patterns—initial central settlement, assimilation and outward movement, and eventually suburbanization—is widely held.

Clearly a model of immigrant residential patterns based on Park's and Burgess's view of the city is most appropriate to the twentieth century. An urban form characterized by central immigrant and ethnic ghettoes and affluent suburbs cannot always have existed. Sjoberg provides a model of the preindustrial city where the variation of socioeconomic status with distance from center is reversed from the modern pattern.[4] In which framework—the preindustrial or the modern—are we to view nineteenth-century Philadelphia? Blumin finds evidence of the preindustrial pattern in Philadelphia prior to 1850, and full emergence of the modern pattern does not occur until the early twentieth century.[5] The thirty years between 1850 and 1880, then, are neither preindustrial nor fully modern.

As decades of industrialization, this period marked a transition in urban form. On the one hand we find the transportation system evolving such that some individuals were able to move away from the center while on the other hand the vast majority of the population still needed to live close to their places of work. The process of invasion and succession which resulted in twentieth-century ethnic ghettoes had clearly not run its course by 1880.[6] Nevertheless, immigration from Ireland and Germany had become a major demographic force in Philadelphia by 1850.

The many ecological studies of nineteenth-century cities that have appeared during the last decade have provided little detail on the consequences of immigration on the city's residential pattern during this period. Previous spatial studies have in general not focused on these crucial decades. Blumin's studies of Philadelphia and Kingston, Conzen's on Milwaukee, Handlin's and Knights's on Boston, Katz's on Hamilton, and Thernstrom's on Newburyport all deal with the period prior to 1860.[7] Thus their studies cover a few years after the first major wave of nineteenth-century immigration. Chudacoff's study of Omaha, Kessner's of New York, and Weber's of Warren all deal with the period after 1880 when the major origin of immigration was shifting to Eastern and Southern Europe and the twentieth-century models were becoming increasingly appropriate.[8] Only Gitelman's study of Waltham and Esslinger's of South Bend have turned attention to the transition period from 1850 to 1880.[9] Ward's work is most directly concerned with the impact of immigrants on urban spatial structure, and he considers the different experiences of the "old" and "new" immigrants. His valuable comparative analysis, however, lacks the kind of detail that can be gained from a more microscopic examination of a single city.[10] Additionally, most of these studies have examined residential patterns without analyzing intra-urban mobility. Only Knights, Chudacoff, Kessner, and Blumin have attempted to study empirically *both* residential patterns and residential mobility, but these studies do not cover the period between 1850 and 1880. Other authors have "described" intra-urban movement by examining residential patterns at periodic intervals and then inferring the processes that apparently generated them. Thus, whatever understanding of nineteenth-century residential patterns we have acquired has generally been without the benefit of direct examination of intra-urban mobility patterns.

Despite such deficiencies, these studies do at least suggest the nature of the transition from the preindustrial to the modern urban ecological form. Blumin and Conzen indicate that Sjoberg's model for the pre-industrial city, positing high status core and lower-status periphery, may be applicable to the city at mid-century.[11] It is evident, however, that a high level of social differentiation did not exist. These studies also imply that whatever concentrations existed were not uniform or static entities but rather grew and declined over time, depending on the particular city, the stage of its urban-industrial development, and the socioeconomic or ethnic group studied. By the late nineteenth century, however, class-segregation became sharper and, with the arrival of the "new" immigrants, ethnic differentiation also became more pronounced.

Nevertheless, we have detailed understanding of neither the transition in the urban ecological pattern nor the role of immigration in that transition. It is within the context of this transition that we consider the residential mobility of Irish and German immigrants in nineteenth-century Philadelphia. The differing experiences of the two groups will be seen to reflect the transition situation quite well.

Philadelphia between 1850 and 1880

Transition in Philadelphia's Spatial Structure. The distinct differentiation and segregation of the twentieth-century American city was not to be found in late nineteenth-century Philadelphia. Warner's description of spatial patterns in Philadelphia between 1830 and 1860 clearly emphasizes this point:

> Social and economic heterogeneity was the hallmark of the age. Most areas of the new big city were a jumble of occupations, classes, shops, homes, immigrants, and native Americans. Although by 1860 there were the beginnings of concentrations which reflected the future economic and social articulation of the city—a downtown, three manufacturing clusters, a small slum, a few black blocks, and occasional class and ethnic enclaves—these concentrations did not dominate the spatial patterns of the city. The full development of the segregated metropolis was yet to come.[12]

While Warner's characterization continues to appear generally correct, our own data have provided a more microscopic view which indicates a degree of differentiation. Across Philadelphia's landscape of the late nineteenth century, changes indicative of the transition from preindustrial to modern can be clearly discerned. In the absence of efficient, convenient public transportation in the city's early development, the most affluent segments of the population tended to reside in the city's early central district, close to the Delaware River. By the middle of the nineteenth century, increasing congestion and industrialization resulted in somewhat diminished desirability of areas in close proximity to the river for residential use. Expensive homes began to be built in the western section of the old city, toward the Schuylkill River. Whatever public transportation existed followed the regular rectangular grid of the city; the early expansion of the affluent population to the west reflected the fact that the best transportation to the emerging central business district was along the east-west axis.

The most important change in the technology of public transportation between 1850 and 1880 centered about the laying of rails on streets over which fewer horses could move more people; hence the horse-drawn rail car was the dominant form of transportation within the densely populated area of the city in 1880. Fares were high for the average laborer, who would have needed to spend 9 percent of his wages in order to commute to work.[13] The spatial pattern of the transportation network remained troublesome, following the city's rectangular grid. If two points were not on the same east-west or north-south street, it was often necessary to transfer between lines, thus doubling the cost of the ride.[14] In 1880, then, most laborers continued to find it necessary to reside close to their work. Schedules and dependability had improved over the thirty years, though, and in-

Table 1. Occupational Composition of Major Areas in Philadelphia, 1850 and 1880
(Disproportionality based on citywide occupational composition shown in parentheses)

	1850 Professional, Proprietary, and White Collar Workers	1850 Craftsmen, Artisans, and Skilled Workers	Unskilled Laborers	1880 Professional, Proprietary, and White Collar Workers	1880 Craftsmen, Artisans, and Skilled Workers	Unskilled Laborers
Areas in Old City						
CBD	34.9 (1.47)	44.0 (.84)	21.0 (.88)	35.8 (1.24)	31.8 (.73)	32.3 (1.17)
Southwest	19.2 (.81)	43.7 (.83)	37.1 (1.56)	26.4 (.91)	28.5 (.66)	45.1 (1.63)
West	34.5 (1.45)	43.1 (.82)	22.4 (.94)	41.3 (1.43)	31.3 (.72)	27.4 (.99)
Areas Adjacent to Old City						
Southeast	17.2 (.72)	58.7 (1.12)	24.2 (1.02)	26.3 (.91)	41.5 (.95)	32.2 (1.17)
Northeast	21.0 (.88)	63.0 (1.20)	16.0 (.67)	29.9 (.86)	46.6 (1.07)	23.5 (.85)
Northwest	24.6 (1.03)	58.1 (1.11)	17.3 (.73)	36.3 (1.28)	41.0 (.94)	22.6 (.82)
South	15.6 (.66)	46.5 (.83)	37.9 (1.59)	20.9 (.72)	49.2 (1.13)	29.9 (1.08)
Southwest*				23.6 (.82)	43.6 (1.00)	32.9 (1.19)
Outlying Areas						
Near Northeast	1.30 (.55)	63.1 (1.20)	23.9 (1.00)	19.8 (.69)	58.2 (1.34)	22.0 (.80)
Near Northwest	15.6 (.66)	52.1 (.99)	32.2 (1.36)	37.6 (1.30)	46.9 (1.08)	15.5 (.56)
Northeast	33.7 (1.42)	42.0 (.80)	24.3 (1.02)	22.0 (.76)	41.8 (.96)	36.3 (1.32)
Northwest	25.7 (1.08)	46.9 (.90)	27.4 (1.15)	34.6 (1.20)	37.0 (.85)	28.4 (1.03)
West	24.1 (1.01)	40.3 (.77)	35.6 (1.50)	27.9 (.97)	40.1 (.92)	32.0 (1.16)
Total City	23.8 (1.00)	52.4 (1.00)	23.8 (1.00)	28.9 (1.00)	43.5 (1.00)	27.6 (1.00)

*This area is included in the "South" area in the first two decades.

dividuals of higher socioeconomic status were increasingly able to utilize the rail lines for commuting, permitting them to live at increasing distance from the central district.

A slowly emerging trend toward reversal of the relationship between distance from center and socioeconomic status can be seen through an examination of the occupational characteristics of broad sectors of the city in 1850 and 1880. Table 1 presents these data. Using a modified version of the Philadelphia Social History Project occupational coding system, the occupational composition of a sample of adult males is shown for areas of the city defined according to distance and direction from center.[15] While the size of the areas employed obscures some spatial detail, the general trend of transition in the spatial structure is evident. The proportion of the sample in the central district who are in the highest occupational category remains relatively stable over the thirty-year period, but the proportion who are laborers shows a marked increase, by more than half, indicating some deterioration in the socioeconomic status of the central district during the three decades. In 1850, the area containing the highest proportion of professional and proprietary workers was the central district, but by 1880 the area with the highest proportion of such workers had shifted to the northwest, an area beginning to emerge as an early affluent suburb.

The trend toward transition becomes clearer when the disproportionalities presented in Table 1 are examined. While the proportion of workers in the highest status residing in the central district remained relatively stable over time, it is seen that throughout the city, the proportion of individuals in this category increased during the three decades from 23.8 percent to 28.9 percent. Based on this city-wide percentage, professionals and proprietors were overrepresented in the central district in both 1850 and 1880, but the degree of disproportionality declined over time, from 1.47 to 1.24, while the laborers, underrepresented in the central district in 1850, were clearly overrepresented there in 1880. In outlying sectors to the northwest, changes in proportional representation of the highest and lowest occupational status groups were reversed; representation of the highest group increased while that of the lowest group decreased. While the general pattern of heterogeneity which Warner describes remains prevalent even when small spatial units are observed, the shift of the affluent to the west and northwest and the influx of the poor to the central areas is a major feature of the early process of differentiation in Philadelphia.

Immigrants in Mid-Nineteenth-Century Philadelphia. The population of Philadelphia more than doubled between 1850 and 1880, as is indicated in Table 2. While it is no simple task to estimate the relative importance of natural increase and migration in contributing to the growth of Philadelphia's population in the nineteenth century, it is likely that net migration was a very important component of the city's population growth.

Regardless of the magnitude of internal, rural-urban in-migration, immigration from Europe, particularly from Ireland and Germany, was substantial. Table 2 shows the number of Irish and German-born individuals in the four census years. Growth of both groups was most rapid during the decade of the 1850's. While the Irish-born population grew at a pace somewhat slower than that of the total population, the German immigrant population grew more than twice as rapidly as the total, increasing by 91.5

Table 2. Total Population, Irish Immigrants and German Immigrants
in Philadelphia, 1850, 1860, 1870, and 1880

Year*	Total Population		Irish Immigrants			German Immigrants		
	Population	Percent Change	Population	Percent of Total	Percent Change	Population	Percent of Total	Percent Change
1850	408081		71,787	17.6		22,788	5.6	
1860	564586	38.4	94,443	16.7	31.6	42,247	7.5	85.4
1870	656808	16.3	94,730	14.4	0.3	48,660	7.4	15.2
1880	840584	28.0	99,975	11.9	5.5	55,572	6.6	14.2

*Figures for 1850 through 1880 are from PSHP tallies of the census manuscripts.

percent during the decade. Growth of the Irish immigrant population diminished markedly following 1860 as did growth in the number of German immigrants, with the German immigrant population growing somewhat more rapidly than the Irish during the twenty years between 1860
and 1880.

The residential patterns displayed by the two immigrant groups were
quite different from one another. Map 1 shows the distribution of the
German-born population in 1850 by Philadelphia Social History Project
grid units, rectangular units of 660 feet by 775 feet (see Appendix II).
When this figure is compared with that for the total population (see page
155), a clustering pattern of the Germans in the northeast sector of the
city is immediately apparent. While the area to the northeast of the central district was the most densely populated part of the city, the maps
show that the German immigrants were clustered in that area to a disproportionate degree. The only other part of the city showing a cluster of
German immigrants in 1850 is the densely populated heterogeneous area
south of the central district, and many of the Germans in that area appear to have been German Jews.[16] Map 2 shows the distribution of the
German-born population in 1880. The appearance of the concentrated
distribution of the Germans in the northeast remains, and as the German
population has grown, the area of concentration has expanded to the north.
Additionally, over the thirty-year period, a number of German immigrants
appear to have dispersed, so that at least some German immigrants are
now found in almost all the inhabited areas of the city.

Initial inspection of the maps showing the residential patterns assumed
by the German immigrants may indeed indicate a situation similar to the
twentieth-century pattern of initial settlement in centralized ghettoes and
dispersion over time. However, the German concentration in the northeast was *not* an ethnic ghetto. Rather, as the most densely populated area

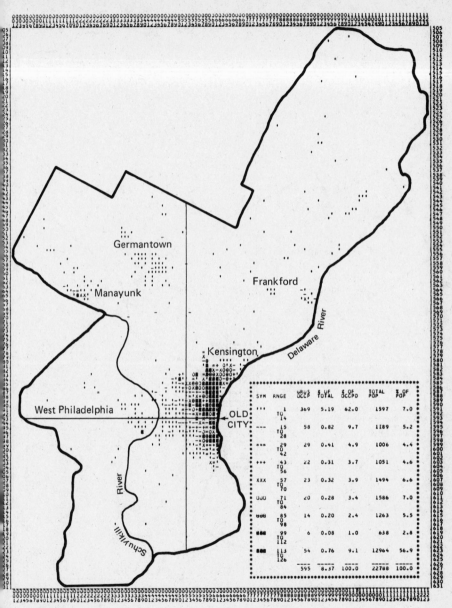

German Immigrants, 1850

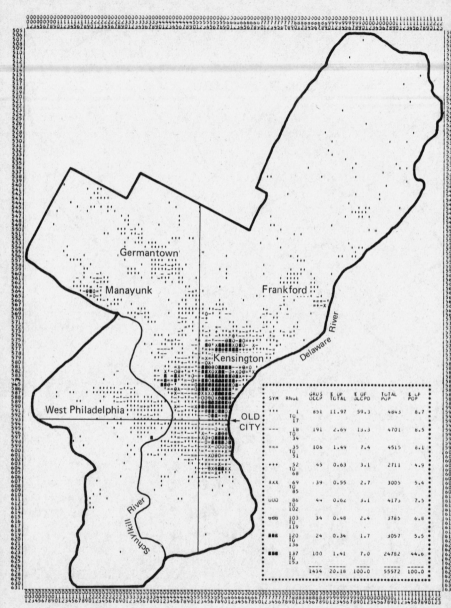

German Immigrants, 1880

of the city, it was shared by the German immigrants with a large number of individuals from other ethnic groups. The distinction between a German *concentration* and a German *ghetto* is important in comparing the experience of the German immigrants with those who came later. The term "ghetto" refers not only to an area containing a concentration of a particular group, but also to an area which is proportionately dominated by members of that group. Thus while the German immigrants were clustered in the northeast, they did not numerically dominate the area in which they were clustered. The northeast, then, was not an area characterized by ethnicity as much as it was characterized by the presence of craftsmen and artisans, an occupational group to which the majority of German immigrants belonged.

A more succinct view of the Germans' residential patterns can be gained through an examination of segregation indices measuring their distribution. The most commonly used measure, showing the proportion of German immigrants who would have to change their residence to match the distribution of the remainder of the population, is 0.41 in 1850 and 0.38 in 1880, representing a moderate level of segregation. Segregation measures in the moderate range can result from different patterns of clustering, the degree to which a group is concentrated in a compact area of the city, and dominance, the degree to which a group resides in areas in which they constitute a high proportion of the population. The degree to which German immigrants lived in areas that were primarily German can be measured by an index of dominance showing the proportion of the population which is German in the grid unit inhabited by the "average" German immigrant. For German immigrants, this index measures 0.11 in 1850 and 0.12 in 1880, indicating that in those two years, the "average" German immigrant lived in a grid unit which was 11 percent and 12 percent German respectively. Very few grids, in fact, housed a population which was composed of more than 20 percent German immigrants.[17]

Maps 3 and 4 show the residential patterns assumed by the Irish immigrants in 1850 and 1880. In 1850, the Irish immigrants are clearly more dispersed than the Germans, residing to some extent in all inhabited areas of the city. The number of Irish immigrants in Philadelphia was quite large by 1850, but no immigrant ghetto could form in the absence of a large, cheap, and centralized housing supply. The prevalence of alley dwellings was particularly important in distributing Irish immigrants throughout the old city. In comparing the map of the Irish immigrants with that of the total population in 1850, however, small concentrations of Irish immigrants are seen to have existed, particularly to the south and southwest of the central district. As Map 4 indicates, in 1880 Irish immi-

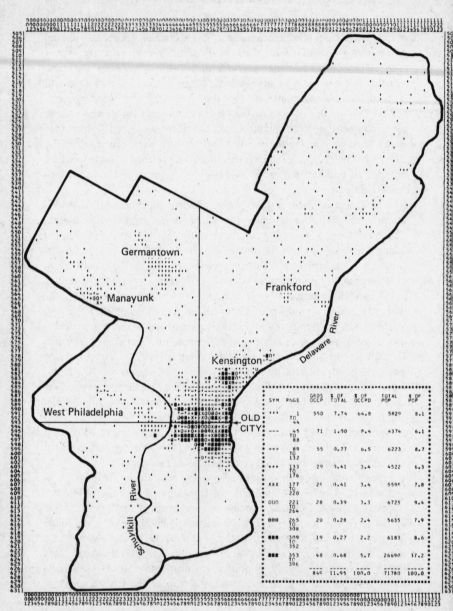

SYM	RNGE	GRDS OCCP	% OF TOTAL	% OF OCCPD	TOTAL POP	% OF POP
'''	1 TO 44	550	7.74	64.8	5829	8.1
---	45 TO 88	71	1.00	8.4	4374	6.1
===	89 TO 132	55	0.77	6.5	6223	8.7
+++	133 TO 176	29	0.41	3.4	4522	6.3
XXX	177 TO 220	29	0.41	3.4	5599	7.8
000	221 TO 264	28	0.39	3.3	6725	9.4
888	265 TO 308	20	0.28	2.4	5635	7.9
▓▓▓	309 TO 352	19	0.27	2.2	6183	8.6
███	353 TO 396	48	0.68	5.7	26690	37.2
		849	11.95	100.0	71780	100.0

Irish Immigrants, 1850

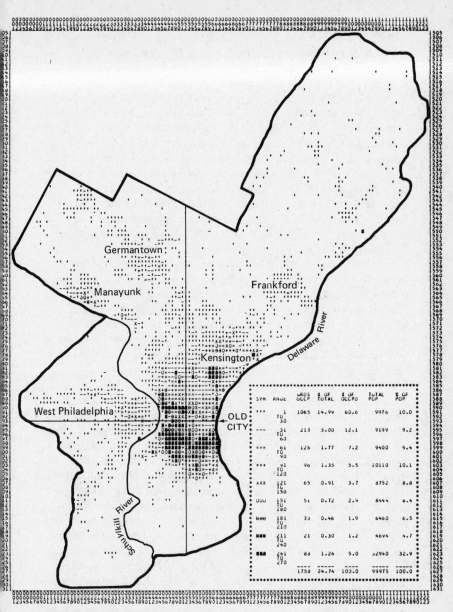

SYM	RNGE	GRDS OCCP	% OF TOTAL	% OF OCCPD	TUTAL POP	% OF POP
•••	1 TO 30	1065	14.99	60.6	9976	10.0
---	31 TO 60	213	3.00	12.1	9199	9.2
===	61 TO 90	126	1.77	7.2	9400	9.4
+++	91 TO 120	96	1.35	5.5	10110	10.1
XXX	121 TO 150	65	0.91	3.7	8752	8.8
OOO	151 TO 180	51	0.72	2.9	8444	8.4
⊕⊕⊕	181 TO 210	33	0.46	1.9	6460	6.5
▓▓▓	211 TO 240	21	0.30	1.2	4694	4.7
■■■	241 TO 270	88	1.24	5.0	32940	32.9
		1758	24.74	103.0	99975	100.0

Germantown

Manayunk

Frankford

Kensington

Delaware River

West Philadelphia

OLD CITY

Schuylkill River

Irish Immigrants, 1880

grants still resided in all inhabited areas of the city; however, the most striking feature of the map is the greatly enlarged Irish concentration to the southwest of the central district. In terms of city-wide distribution, the Irish were more dispersed than the Germans, but those Irish who did reside in the major Irish residential concentration in the southwest lived in an area more similar to an ethnic ghetto than did the Germans. As development of the southwest involved widespread construction of inexpensive houses, the area became dominated by Irish immigrants and their descendants. Thus while many Irish immigrants by 1880 did reside in a relatively centralized ethnic ghetto, the distinction of their pattern from the twentieth-century model should be made clear. Although the peak of Irish immigration occurred in 1851, the Irish ghetto did not appear until somewhat later; clearly it could not have been the area of first settlement for the largest body of Irish immigrants. Finally, it is important to bear in mind that only one Irish immigrant in six lived in their largest single concentration.

Like the Germans, the Irish immigrants showed a moderate degree of segregation as measured by the standard dissimilarity index, which was 0.36 in 1850 and 0.31 in 1880. However, a measure of clustering for the Irish immigrants, showing the concentration of the Irish immigrant population relative to that of the total population, actually increased slightly over the thirty-year period, from 1.45 to 1.52, indicating that dispersion of the Irish population proceeded at a pace that was slower than that of the total population.

Hypotheses Concerning Residential Mobility. While the residential patterns assumed by the Irish and German immigrants in mid-nineteenth-century Philadelphia do not conform well with twentieth-century models, it is nevertheless possible that some of the models' basic processes were in operation. Specifically, while the Germans did not initially reside in an ethnic ghetto, they did settle in a centralized and concentrated pattern. Dispersion over time may indeed have been governed by assimilation and upward socioeconomic mobility. The pattern displayed by the Irish immigrants raises a more complex set of questions. Some decentralization occurred, and it is reasonable to hypothesize that the more affluent Irish immigrants were following the trend of the general population by moving to the west and northwest. But which of the Irish immigrants contributed to the formation of the large, ethnically dominated area in the southwest? Irish immigration did continue into the late nineteenth century, but much of the later Irish immigration consisted of domestic servants, whose residential patterns would have been spatially similar to those of the more affluent native-white Americans. In any case, it seems unlikely that the later Irish immigration would have been numerically large enough to create an area of first settlement of the size found in the city's southwest cluster. It can be hypothesized, therefore, that an important segment of the Irish immigrant population did not residentially disperse over time, but rather moved together as a large area of inexpensive housing became available.

The question raised concerning the processes underlying the residential patterns of the immigrant groups, particularly that of the Irish, cannot be adequately approached through examination of change over time in the cross-section, "snapshot" views of the residential patterns. Thus it is valuable to examine change in residence of groups of individuals. Most studies of residential mobility within nineteenth-century cities have traced individuals' addresses through city directories.[18] An alternative, but methodologically more complex approach, is through census manuscripts. City directories have an important advantage over census manuscripts for the study of residential mobility in that they are published annually and movement over short periods of time can be observed. Census manuscripts can show the residence of individuals only at points in time which are fully ten years apart. Nevertheless, the use of census manuscripts entails certain important advantages. First, while city directories provide only the occupation and address of an individual, the census manuscripts contain a wealth of additional information such as age, real and personal property, place of birth, and marital status, which can provide more detail on the specific characteristics of movers. Additionally, the enlarged spectrum of attributes included for each person increases the number of individuals that can be accurately linked over time. If our concern is with the general patterns of residential mobility, then the analysis need not suffer excessively through a lack of detail concerning intercensal mobility. We are given the residence of an individual at two points in time, and regardless of movement which occurred between those two points in time, we can legitimately test hypotheses concerning change in residence which might have occurred over ten years given the individual's specific characteristics.

Philadelphia is a fortunate choice of cities for the study of nineteenth-century residential mobility owing to its large area. Early outlying towns are within the boundaries of Philadelphia County, which comprised the city boundaries as well after consolidation in 1854. The post-consolidation boundaries are used throughout the study, and thus most decentralization would have occurred within the area covered. Few movers would be lost through suburbanization in the political sense, that is, through movement to nearby areas across the city boundaries.

Street address is not available in the census manuscripts until 1880.

Table 3. Residential Mobility Rates of Linked German-born Adult Males by Change in Occupational Status

Decade	(N)	Total File Percent mobile	Percent of those stable in occupational status who moved	Percent of those undergoing upward change in occupational status who moved	Percent of those undergoing downward change in occupational status who moved
1850–1860	616	65.1 (401)	64.1 (289)	60.7 (54)	76.3 (58)
1860–1870	1843	61.4 (1131)	58.3 (746)	68.7 (230)	68.0 (155)
1870–1880	3078	54.3 (1672)	52.2 (1140)	60.0 (321)	58.8 (211)

However, through a time-consuming process of cross-referencing samples from the manuscripts with city directories, we have been able to assign all individuals in each of the four census manuscripts between 1850 and 1880 to their appropriate grid unit.[19] Additionally, through automated nominal record linkage, we have constructed longitudinal data files of Irish and German male immigrants over the age of eighteen for each of the three decades.[20] Thus for the study of residential mobility, operationally we consider a person in the linked files to have moved if a change in grid unit shows him to have resided in different locations at the beginning and the end of the decade.[21]

The analysis will pose two broad questions. First, we shall ask what the characteristics were of those who moved as opposed to those who did not move. The main interest here is in socioeconomic mobility, for which change in occupational status will be employed as an indicator. The second broad question to be explored involves the spatial pattern of residential mobility. This question will be approached through a consideration of the residential distribution of movers at the begining and end of each decade and through an examination of differential destinations according to the occupational status of movers at the end of the decade.

Residential Mobility of the German-born Adult Males

Residential Mobility Rates. Mobility rates are shown in Table 3 for the German-born adult males as a group and according to occupational mobility for each decade. Residential mobility rates declined over the thirty-year period, a change which will be further considered in the context of the German immigrants' pattern of dispersal.

The notion that residential mobility rates were greater with occupational mobility appears to be verified by the differential mobility rates. While during the first decade of the study, those individuals who were occupationally stable underwent more residential mobility than those who moved upward in occupational status, the pattern is reversed in the next two decades, when residential mobility among those individuals moving upward in occupational status was considerably higher than for those who were stable in status. In all cases, those undergoing a downward shift in occupational status displayed considerably higher residential mobility rates than those who were occupationally stable.

Change in occupational status has been emphasized, since it is important in our twentieth-century models as a determinant of residential mobility. Occupational status, of course, is but one personal characteristic that may be related to residential mobility and may be correlated with other variables that are more powerful in determining residential mobility. For example, an individual's age might also be expected to play a role in determining mobility; mobility rates are generally higher among younger adults than for those who are older. However, a similar relationship may exist between occupational mobility and age. It is only through examining the relationship between occupational mobility and residential mobility while statistically controlling for age that we can measure the actual effect of occupational mobility. As a wide spectrum of variables is available to us in the census manuscripts, it is important to subject residential mobility to a multivariate analysis in order to determine whether or not occupational mobility remains important in explaining residential mobility when other variables are controlled.

The relationship of five independent variables with residential mobility has been examined. Those variables are change in occupational status, change in industry, marital status, ownership of real property, and age. The techniques for multivariate analysis developed by Andrews, Morgan, and Sonquist provide a straightforward way of dealing with correlated independent variables such as residential mobility.[22] The results of multiple classification analysis can be viewed at two levels. First, we can examine differences in mobility rates for different subclassifications of the German immigrant group. Such results are provided in Table 4. For each decade, we can note the observed mobility rates for German immigrants classified according to different values of each variable included in the analysis. For occupational status, for example, the observed mobility rates are identical to those reported in Table 3. In general, differential observed mobility rates for other variables are as would be expected. Those who were married, who owned property, who did not change industry, or who were older tended to display lower mobility rates than those who were not mar-

Table 4. Differential Rates of Residential Mobility Adjusted by Multiple Classification Analysis: German Immigrants in Philadelphia, 1850-1880

| | 1850–1860 | | | 1860–1870 | | | 1870–1880 | | |
| | | Percent Who Moved | | | Percent Who Moved | | | Percent Who Moved | |
	N	Observed	Adjusted	N	Observed	Adjusted	N	Observed	Adjusted
Total Sample	616	65.1		1843	61.4		3078	54.3	
Change in Occupational Status									
Stable	541	64.1	65.9	1280	58.3	59.8	2184	52.2	54.5
Upward	89	60.7	54.8	335	68.7	65.0	535	60.0	52.4
Downward	76	76.3	72.6	228	68.0	65.0	359	58.8	56.3
Industry									
Stable	380	60.8	61.8	1132	57.1	58.3	2070	48.8	49.6
Change	236	72.0	70.4	711	68.2	66.3	1008	65.7	63.9
Marital Status									
Unmarried-unmarried	20	75.0	64.1	57	66.7	61.4	113	57.5	46.7
Unmarried-married	28	78.6	71.9	103	76.7	68.4	122	78.7	65.0
Married-married	562	64.1	64.8	1644	60.0	60.7	2774	53.0	54.0
Married-unmarried	6	66.7	64.5	39	69.2	69.8	69	60.9	62.1
Real Property*									
No prop.-no prop.	368	69.8	68.1	1101	62.8	61.7	2238	62.0	60.3
No prop.-prop.	160	63.1	63.8	461	67.0	66.4	840	33.9	38.4
Prop.-prop.	71	45.1	52.4	213	43.7	49.7			
Prop.-no prop.	17	64.7	65.4	68	55.9	51.8			
Age in First Year									
18–19	4	100.0	81.2	14	78.6	68.0	30	66.7	95.3
20–24	47	72.3	67.5	114	81.6	79.1	150	74.7	67.4
25–29	118	76.3	74.8	343	69.7	68.4	357	72.8	67.1
30–34	163	71.8	72.0	443	65.2	64.5	478	64.9	63.4
35–39	110	63.6	65.5	381	55.4	56.2	611	53.9	54.3
40–44	83	45.8	46.8	260	58.9	59.4	521	49.9	51.8
45–49	52	57.6	57.6	141	49.7	52.6	483	43.3	46.9
50–54	22	45.5	51.5	109	41.3	43.2	261	40.6	42.3
55–59	10	40.0	39.3	38	52.6	55.3	108	37.0	40.0
60+	0			0			79	32.9	38.9

*Because property was not recorded in the 1880 census, the figures in the 1870–1880 column reflect only 1870 property status and do not indicate the subsequent property experience of the linked German males.

Table 5. Summary of Multiple Classification Analysis on Residential
Mobility of German-born Adult Males

	1850–1860	1860–1870	1870–1880
Mobility rate	65.1	61.3	54.2
Number of cases	616	1893	3078
Changes in Occupational			
Status			
eta	0.09	0.07	0.02
beta	<u>0.10</u>	0.05	0.02
Change in Industry			
eta	0.11	0.11	0.16
beta	0.09	<u>0.08</u>	<u>0.13</u>
Marital Status			
eta	0.07	0.08	0.10
beta	0.03	0.04	<u>0.06</u>
Ownership of Real			
Property			
eta	0.16	0.14	0.25
beta	0.10	<u>0.10</u>	<u>0.20</u>
Age			
eta	0.24	0.19	0.24
beta	<u>0.21</u>	<u>0.16</u>	<u>0.17</u>
Multiple R	0.293	0.249	0.340
Multiple R²	0.086	0.062	0.115

Underscored beta statistics are significant at the 0.05 level.

ried, did not own real property, changed industry, or were younger. As has
been noted, however, several of the independent variables tend to correlate with each other. For example, older individuals are more prone to
owning real property than younger ones; individuals who underwent
change in occupational status were more likely to change industry than
those who did not. The adjusted residential mobility rates correct for the
effect of correlations between the independent variables. Thus looking
again at occupational status, the adjusted rates are those which would result after industry, marital status, real property ownership, and age are
accounted for. When the differentials according to change in occupational
status are compared with that for change of industry in the last two
decades, it can be seen that mobility differentials according to change in
industry are substantially higher than those according to change in status.
Considering the adjusted mobility rates, then, it would appear that change
in industry is a more powerful determinant of residential mobility than is
change in occupational status.

This notion can be more precisely tested by examining the strength of
each independent variable's effect on residential mobility.[23] Table 5 presents summary results of the multiple classification analysis of the German

immigrants' residential mobility during each of the three decades. Implications of the analysis concerning the importance of change in occupational status in determining residential mobility are quite striking. Considered alone, change in occupational status does account for a significant amount of variation in residential mobility rates during each of the three decades. However, when all given variables are included in a multivariate analysis, occupational status is a statistically significant correlate of mobility only in the first decade. It is important to note that this finding does not suggest that occupation itself is insignificant as a determinant of residential mobility. Rather, the single dimension of occupation we are considering— change in occupational status—is of decreasing importance over the thirty-year period.[24] Noteworthy are the relative effects on residential mobility of change in occupational status and change in industry. In the last two decades, it is seen that change in industry, not change in status, is a significant determinant of residential change. The inclusion of change in industry in the analysis substantially diminishes the effect of change in occupational status.

That change in industry is generally as important as or more so than change in occupational status in determining residential mobility is vital to our understanding of immigrants' residential mobility in nineteenth-century Philadelphia, for it indicates that proximity to workplace remained a more important determinant of residence than assimilation as measured through social mobility.

Examination of the degree to which all five independent variables account for residential mobility particularly reveals the lack of conformity of the nineteenth-century immigrant groups to our modern view of residential change. The five variables included in the MCA should account for a substantially higher amount of variation in the mobility rates than is the case here. The multiple correlation coefficients, while statistically significant, are not large, and for the German immigrants, the five variables account for no more than 11.5 percent of the variation in residential mobility rates. Change in occupation, then, does not have strong explanatory power in considering residential change. That change in industry is often more important than change in status as a determinant of mobility suggests that changes in the ecological characteristics of different areas of the city, particularly with respect to employment opportunities, may explain residential mobility better than changes in individual characteristics.

Residential Mobility Patterns. While change in occupational status was not an important determinant of mobility *rates,* it is still important to examine the extent to which status affected mobility *destinations.* Table

Table 6.   Distribution of Destinations of Mobile German Adult
Males by Occupational Status at End of Decade

	Professional, Proprietary, White Collar			Craftsman, Artisan, Skilled			Unskilled		
	1850–60	1860–70	1870–80	1850–60	1860–70	1870–80	1850–60	1860–70	1870–80
Areas in Old City									
CBD	5.7	7.4	4.3	5.0	4.4	2.0	3.5	0.0	1.9
Southwest	4.8	0.6	1.2	0.8	0.5	0.4	1.8	0.6	0.5
West	9.6	7.1	4.1	4.2	2.7	2.5	1.8	2.4	1.0
Areas Adjacent to Old City									
Southeast	1.9	5.3	4.5	10.0	6.7	3.2	5.3	4.8	3.9
Northeast	22.8	11.7	9.4	10.9	11.5	10.4	7.0	9.1	6.8
Northwest	18.0	14.5	13.8	11.7	13.3	8.8	12.3	9.7	4.8
South	2.9	3.7	3.7	5.4	4.2	4.1	3.5	3.0	4.8
Southwest*			2.5			2.6			2.9
Outlying Areas									
Near northeast	12.4	26.1	22.8	31.4	33.0	36.1	40.4	36.0	28.4
Near northwest	9.5	15.4	18.1	13.0	13.2	14.7	3.5	10.4	10.6
Northeast	1.0	2.5	5.1	1.7	4.4	6.9	7.0	10.4	11.1
Northwest	10.5	4.3	7.9	3.8	4.4	5.3	12.3	11.0	17.3
West	1.0	1.5	2.7	2.1	1.9	2.8	1.8	2.4	6.2
Total	100.0	100.0	100.0	100.0	100.0	100.0	100.0	100.0	100.0

*This area is included in the "South" area in the first two decades.

6 classifies those German adult males who underwent residential mobility
into their occupational status groups at the end of each decade and presents the distribution of destination areas for each of the occupational
status groups in each decade. Most mobility of German immigrants, of
course, ended in the northeast and northwest sectors of the city, reflective
of the overall distribution of the German immigrants. However, certain
differentials in destination between the occupational groups should be
noted. Particularly interesting is the difference between the groups regarding movement to the northeast and the northwest. An individual in the
professional, proprietary, or white-collar group was more likely to move
to the northwest than was a craftsman or artisan, who more frequently
moved to the northeast. This differential mirrors the emergent occupational characteristics distinguishing the northeast from the northwest.
Among the German immigrants, then, many who were most successful
were dispersing away from the German concentration. It is noteworthy,
however, that just as proprietors and professionals were more likely than
artisans or craftsmen to move to the outlying northwest, so also were laborers, at the lowest end of the occupational status scale. This pattern indicates the importance of laborers living close to their places of work, for
the construction industry in the developing northwest was an important
source of employment.

Also of interest is the movement of the more affluent German immigrants to the western part of the old city, the earliest affluent area away from the central district. During the decade of the 1850s, a considerably higher proportion of the German professionals, proprietors, and white-collar workers moved to that area than individuals of lower occupational status. Development of the area was already in an advanced stage by 1850, and, therefore, construction did not provide a source of employment to laborers in the western old city. As time went on, the trend in distribution of the affluent was away from the western old city toward the northwest, which is reflected by a decreasing proportion of mobile German proprietors, professionals, and white-collar workers, who moved to the western old city. Finally, the central district in the eastern old city remained a destination for mobile professionals and proprietors, but the number of such individuals who moved there was small compared to the number of individuals moving to the northwest.

In some ways, residential mobility of the German immigrants was not unlike the pattern that would emerge among the "new" immigrants in the twentieth century. Much of the Germans' mobility ended in their primary concentration in the northeast, but such mobility declined proportionately during the three-decade period. Many of the more successful German immigrants moved away from the concentration and dispersed toward the affluent northwest. It was the mobility of the laborers which was most discrepant from the modern pattern, since suitable employment opportunities were often in more outlying areas where construction was occurring, and in nineteenth-century Philadelphia, it was clearly necessary for the laborer to live close to his place of work.

Residential Mobility of the Irish-born Adult Males

Residential Mobility Rates. Table 7 shows the residential mobility rates for the Irish-born adult males in each of the three decades. As was the case with the Germans, the overall mobility rate for the Irish immigrants declined during the thirty-year period. Variation in residential mobility rates with change in occupational status, however, displayed a more regular pattern than with the Germans, which was consistent with hypotheses concerning the relationship between residential and social mobility. In all decades, occupationally stable Irish-born adult males experienced substantially less residential mobility than did those whose occupational status changed. Furthermore, those undergoing a downward shift in occupational status showed considerably higher rates of residential mobility than those undergoing an upward shift.

Table 7.   Residential Mobility Rates of Linked Irish-born Adult
Males by Change in Occupational Status

| Decade | Total File | | Percent of those stable in occupational status who moved | Percent of those undergoing upward change in occupational status who moved | Percent of those undergoing downward change in occupational status who moved |
	(N)	Percent mobile			
1850–1860	2227	61.9 (1378)	57.2 (833)	68.0 (280)	74.0 (265)
1860–1870	2357	54.3 (1280)	49.9 (810)	62.7 (252)	66.0 (219)
1870–1880	2625	53.6 (1408)	49.7 (940)	60.6 (281)	69.5 (187)

As was the case with the German immigrants, however, the multiple classification analysis shows that the strength of change in occupational status as a determinant of residential mobility decreases when other variables are introduced. Table 8 shows the differential mobility rates, both observed and adjusted, for different subclassifications of the sample, while Table 9 shows the MCA summary statistics. While differential mobility rates can be observed according to change in occupational status, the beta statistic for change in industry is higher than for change in status in all decades except the last, where it is only slightly lower than for change in status.

Again the multiple correlation coefficients, while significant, are low; the five personal characteristics considered as independent variables account for no more than 8.3 percent of the total variation in residential mobility rates. Again the implication is that occupational change is not a powerful predictor of residential change. Where occupation does matter, however, it is seen that change in status is generally no more important than change in industry, again implying the importance of proximity of workplace as a determinant of residence.

Residential Mobility Patterns. Although the movement of the linked Irish males displays some dispersion, a striking feature of the pattern is the tendency of many to come together and cluster to the southwest of the central district. Consisting of a population that was more than half Irish immigrants and their children, here we find Philadelphia's first large, ethnically dominated area. Primarily residential in character, the city directories indicate that the area was laced with small business establishments and services, usually owned by individuals of Irish surname, whereas industry was located on the periphery of the area, within walking distance

Table 8. Differential Rates of Residential Mobility Adjusted by Multiple Classification Analysis: Irish Immigrants in Philadelphia, 1850–1880

| | 1850–1860 | | | 1860–1870 | | | 1870–1880 | | |
| | | Proportion Who Moved | | | Proportion Who Moved | | | Proportion Who Moved | |
	N	Observed	Adjusted	N	Observed	Adjusted	N	Observed	Adjusted
Total Sample	2227	61.9		2357	54.3		2625	53.6	
Change in Occupational Status									
Stable	1457	57.2	60.2	1623	49.9	52.0	1892	49.7	51.3
Upward	412	68.0	63.3	402	63.7	57.6	464	60.6	55.6
Downward	358	74.0	67.3	332	66.0	61.4	269	69.5	66.5
Industry									
Stable	1186	55.1	57.3	1276	47.5	49.5	1538	48.2	50.5
Change	1041	69.7	67.1	1081	62.4	60.0	1087	61.4	58.1
Marital Status									
Unmarried-unmarried	30	70.0	64.2	65	75.4	65.3	73	60.3	53.9
Unmarried-married	16	68.8	72.9	21	90.5	78.8	17	58.8	51.3
Married-married	2171	61.9	61.9	2248	53.4	53.9	2515	53.3	53.6
Married-unmarried	10	30.0	35.8	23	47.8	43.9	20	65.0	64.7
Real Property*									
No prop.-no prop.	1596	64.9	64.0	1561	57.1	56.1	2050	59.1	58.2
No prop.-prop.	403	61.1	62.0	402	58.7	58.4	575	34.1	37.4
Prop.-prop.	154	29.2	35.4	274	31.0	35.8			
Prop.-no prop.	74	68.9	70.5	120	56.7	59.2			
Age in First Year									
18–19	12	75.0	70.4	11	90.0	75.6	1	50.0	44.9
20–24	201	70.7	67.8	130	66.2	60.5	96	74.0	68.0
25–29	433	74.6	72.6	433	65.8	64.0	349	66.5	62.1
30–34	500	63.8	63.6	540	58.0	57.4	454	60.6	58.7
35–39	368	57.9	58.8	458	53.3	53.8	540	53.7	54.2
40–44	304	54.6	55.7	313	46.7	48.8	410	49.5	50.9
45–49	200	52.0	53.0	214	46.7	49.7	363	48.2	50.0
50–54	170	47.7	51.6	204	35.3	36.8	229	41.5	45.3
55–59	39	53.9	55.7	54	64.2	46.9	97	38.2	40.8
60+	0	—	—	0	—	—	85	34.1	38.7

*Because property was not recorded in the 1880 census, the figures in the 1870–1880 column reflect only 1870 property status and do not indicate the subsequent property experience of the linked Irish males.

Table 9. Summary of Multiple Classification Analysis on Residential
Mobility of Irish-born Adult Males

	1850–1860	1860–1870	1870–1880
Mobility rate	61.8	54.3	53.6
Number of cases	2227	2357	2625
Changes in Occupational Status			
eta	0.14	0.13	0.14
beta	0.05	0.07	0.09
Change in Industry			
eta	0.15	0.15	0.13
beta	0.10	0.11	0.08
Marital Status			
eta	0.05	0.10	0.03
beta	0.05	0.06	0.02
Ownership of Real Property			
eta	0.19	0.17	0.21
beta	0.15	0.14	0.17
Age			
eta	0.18	0.19	0.19
beta	0.14	0.15	0.13
Multiple R	0.280	0.287	0.288
Multiple R^2	0.078	0.083	0.083

Underscored beta statistics are significant at the 0.05 level.

but removed from the residences. While clearly an area characterized by an Irish presence, the southwest did not house the Irish immigrants of the lowest socioeconomic status. Rather, the Irish in the southwest tended to be relatively older, more skilled, more literate, and more likely to own property than were the Irish settling north of the central district. The area was typified, then, by immigrants who had achieved some degree of social stability.

The clustering rather than dispersion of the mobile Irish immigrants is most evidenced during the first decade. During succeeding decades, the change in distribution of the mobile Irish males shows movement away from areas in immediate proximity to the central district and toward both the Irish concentration in the southwest and to more dispersed locations in all sectors. Thus the overall pattern movement of the linked Irish males is similar to that of the total Irish immigrant population.

The wider range of areas in which Irish immigrants were to be found compared with the Germans is further indicated by the distribution of mobile Irish immigrants' destinations shown in Table 10. Clearly the south was the destination of the largest groups of Irish immigrants, but not until the last decade did the proportion of Irish immigrants moving to the south

Table 10. Distribution of Destinations of Mobile Irish Adult Males by Occupational Status at End of Decade

	Professionals, Proprietary, White Collar			Craftsman, Artisan, Skilled			Unskilled		
	1850–60	1860–70	1870–80	1850–60	1860–70	1870–80	1850–60	1860–70	1870–80
Areas in Old City									
CBD	6.4	5.0	4.8	2.8	3.4	0.8	4.0	4.7	2.0
Southwest	6.7	8.1	2.5	8.4	6.5	2.3	8.3	6.3	2.8
West	15.3	7.7	5.1	11.3	8.2	2.9	12.8	11.3	5.5
Areas Adjacent to Old City									
Southeast	18.0	15.4	7.9	17.0	15.2	8.2	12.5	11.6	8.3
Northeast	2.2	1.2	1.9	1.6	1.7	1.6	2.2	2.8	1.6
Northwest	11.6	12.4	9.1	11.1	12.5	8.8	12.2	11.1	7.7
South	8.6	6.2	7.9	9.2	11.4	6.3	12.2	7.3	6.2
Southwest*			13.6			18.2			15.7
Outlying Areas									
Near northeast	14.2	15.0	15.2	22.1	19.8	22.4	18.1	16.4	13.0
Near northwest	5.2	8.1	5.7	3.1	4.6	5.6	3.0	2.5	4.6
Northeast	2.2	5.4	9.8	3.3	4.8	8.1	3.7	7.6	10.9
Northwest	3.7	6.5	7.6	6.3	6.0	5.7	5.1	10.2	11.7
West	5.6	8.8	8.9	3.7	5.8	9.2	5.6	7.4	9.9
Total	100.0	100.0	100.0	100.0	100.0	100.0	100.0	100.0	100.0

*This area is included in the "South" area in the first two decades.

match the proportion of German immigrants settling in the northeast. Indeed, during the thirty-year period, it is clear that movement into the growing Irish-dominated area was on the increase. Furthermore, the data on differential destinations according to occupational status at the end of each decade refute the notion that the emerging "ghetto" was the destination of the least successful Irish immigrants. As time went on, movement to the south by the skilled craftsmen more than matched that of the laborers. It can be shown, in fact, that the immigrants who most typically moved to the southwest were skilled craftsmen, slightly older than the mainstream of Irish adult males, who appear to have been in the process of family formation and childraising. The Irish "ghetto," then, was not an area of first residence for newly arrived immigrants, but rather was the location of a more stable segment of the immigrant population who had achieved a moderate degree of success.

Mobility patterns of the Irish immigrants are less distinct than those of the Germans. A pattern of dispersion from an initial concentration is clearly not evidenced by the Irish to the extent displayed by the Germans. On the contrary, a major feature of the Irish pattern is clustering of the group over time toward the southwest. Despite a weak degree of differentiation in the spatial pattern of mobility, certain trends do appear. First, while the professionals, proprietors, and white-collar workers maintain movement to the central district, there is an increasing tendency for these individuals to move to outlying areas in the west and northwest. Second is movement of the laborers; as they would have been most dependent on proximity to their places of work, they tended to move to the most diverse areas of the city, but of particular interest is an early pattern of mobility to the outlying areas, preceding that of the more affluent. Movement of the skilled craftsmen falls into two patterns. Many of them tended to move to the northeast, an area that attracted a high proportion of skilled craftsmen of all ethnicities. A larger proportion of the skilled moved to the southwest in the most significant pattern of Irish mobility seen in the data, whereby a large proportion of more settled Irish immigrants tended not to undergo residential dispersion but rather to cluster together in an area increasingly dominated by the Irish.

Conclusions

During the course of transition from a preindustrial to a modern spatial pattern, spatial differentiation was not sharp by twentieth-century standards. While differentials in the pattern of mobility are evident, they are not strongly pronounced. Yet in our view, the mobility patterns indicate spatial change. The central district of the city, originally containing the residences of the most affluent, displayed a decline in desirability, while the outlying areas began their transformation into early suburbs. Among the two immigrant groups whose residential mobility has been examined, two occupational extremes are of most interest in the context of transition of the spatial structure. Laborers preceded the more affluent to more outlying areas where construction of dwellings took place. As the area underwent development, movement of the more affluent from central to outlying areas could be observed. The mainstream of the German immigrants and of the more established Irish immigrants were the skilled workers, however, and these individuals tended to reside in areas of intermediate distance from the center. An exchange of residential areas between the most and the least affluent would indeed have left the craftsmen in the middle. The old German concentration in the northeast and the emerging Irish concentration in the southwest, intermediate in distance from the central district, were thus dominated by the more stable skilled workmen. Here we are reminded of Burgess's zone of workingmen's residences, perhaps the first of the modern types of urban residential areas to distinctly emerge.

Clearly the residential experience of immigrants in the mid-nineteenth century was different from that of the later immigrants as characterized by the Chicago School model of initial settlement in centralized ghettoes with outward movement reflecting assimilation over time. The ecological structure was inappropriate for such a pattern in the nineteenth century. No large, cheap, centralized housing supply existed in which ethnic ghettoes could form. Equally important was the primitive nature and high costs of the transportation system which mandated proximity of home to workplace. While improvements in transportation during the thirty years between 1850 and 1880 permitted decentralization of some of the affluent into emerging suburbs, for the ordinary workingman Philadelphia remained a "walking city" throughout the period.

Thus the location of workplace had an important effect on residential mobility, making it difficult to deal with mobility in twentieth-century terms involving residential satisfaction and individual change. Personal characteristics such as occupational status, age, marital status and property ownership explain only a small proportion of mobility. In the twentieth century, we make the distinction between long distance migration and short distance moving in that the former involves a change in labor market while the latter does not. This distinction is not so clear for the nineteenth century; the requirement that home be close to work results in the possibility that a move across the face of the city may indeed involve a change in labor market. In order to explain such moves, we need to look not only at characteristics of *individuals,* but at characteristics of *areas* as well. Thus, our findings suggest further research that examines structural characteristics of small areas as well as individual characteristics as determinants of residential mobility. The PSHP data base, containing addressed information on business, industry, and the urban infra-structure in general as well as on individuals, is facilitating expanded research. Through such research we shall gain valuable new understanding of how distinct urban ecologies affected the residential patterns of the "old" immigrants.

NOTES

1. Ernest W. Burgess, "Urban Areas," in T. V. Smith and L. D. White, *Chicago: An Experiment in Social Science Research* (Chicago: University of Chicago Press, 1971), 114–23.

2. Amos Hawley, *Human Ecology: A Theory of Community Structure* (New York: Ronald Press, 1950), 400–402.

3. Robert E. Park, *Human Communities* (Glencoe, Ill.: Free Press, 1952), 213.

4. Gideon Sjoberg, "The Preindustrial City," *American Journal of Sociology* 60 (1955), 438–45.

5. Stuart M. Blumin, "Residential Mobility Within the Nineteenth-Century City," in Allen F. Davis and Mark H. Haller, eds., *The Peoples of Philadelphia: A History of Ethnic Groups and Lower-Class Life, 1790–1940* (Philadelphia: Temple University Press, 1973), 37–52.

6. William Yancey and Eugene Ericksen, "The Organization of Residence in the Industrial City," unpublished manuscript (1976). ·

7. Blumin, *op. cit.;* Stuart M. Blumin, *The Urban Threshold: Growth and Change in a Nineteenth-Century American Community* (Chicago: University of Chicago Press, 1976); Kathleen Neils Conzen, *Immigrant Milwaukee, 1836–1860: Accommodation and Community in a Frontier City* (Cambridge: Harvard University Press, 1976); Kathleen Neils Conzen, "Patterns of Residence in Early Milwaukee," in Leo F. Schnore, ed., *The New Urban History: Quantitative Explorations by American Historians* (Princeton, N.J.: Princeton University Press, 1975); Oscar Handlin, *Boston's Immigrants: A Study in Acculturation* (New York: Atheneum, 1970); Peter R. Knights, *The Plain People of Boston, 1830–1860: A Study in City Growth* (New York: Oxford University Press, 1971); Michael B. Katz, *The People of Hamilton, Canada West: Family and Class in a Mid-Nineteenth-Century City* (Cambridge: Harvard University Press, 1975), see especially Appendix 1, written by Ian Davey and Michael Doucet, 319–42; Stephan Thernstrom, *Poverty and Progress: Social Mobility in a Nineteenth-Century City* (New York: Atheneum, 1972).

8. Howard P. Chudacoff, *Mobile Americans: Residential and Social Mobility in Omaha, 1880–1920* (New York: Oxford University Press, 1972); Thomas Kessner, *The Golden Door: Italian and Jewish Immigrant Mobility in New York City, 1880–1915* (New York: Oxford University Press, 1977); Michael P. Weber, *Social Change in an Industrial Town: Patterns of Progress in Warren, Pennsylvania, from Civil War to World War I* (University Park, Pa.: Pennsylvania State University Press, 1976).

9. Howard M. Gitelman, *Workingmen of Waltham: Mobility in American Urban Industrial Development, 1850–1880* (Baltimore, Md.: Johns Hopkins University Press, 1974); Dean R. Esslinger, *Immigrants and the City: Ethnicity and Mobility in a Nineteenth-Century Midwestern City* (Port Washington, N.Y.: Kennikat Press, 1975).

10. David Ward, *Cities and Immigrants: A Geography of Change in Nineteenth-Century America* (New York: Oxford University Press, 1971).

11. Blumin, *op. cit.;* and Kathleen N. Conzen, "Patterns of Residence in Early Milwaukee," *op. cit.*

12. Sam Bass Warner, Jr., *The Private City: Philadelphia in Three Periods of Its Growth* (Philadelphia: University of Pennsylvania Press, 1968), 50.

13. Theodore Hershberg, Harold Cox, Dale Light, Jr., and Richard R. Greenfield, "The 'Journey-to-Work': An Empirical Investigation of Work, Residence, and Transportation in Philadelphia, 1850 and 1880"; in this volume.

14. *Ibid.*

15. Details of the PSHP occupational coding scheme can be found in Theodore Hershberg and Robert Dockhorn, "Occupational Classification," in Theodore Hershberg, guest editor, "A Special Issue: The Philadelphia Social History Project," *Historical Methods Newsletter* 9 (March–June, 1976), 59–98; hereafter cited as "PSHP: Special Issue."

16. James Finkelstein, "The German Jewish Immigrants to Philadelphia, 1850–1880," unpublished manuscript in possession of PSHP.

17. For a detailed discussion of clustering and dominance as dimensions of segregation and the residential pattern, see Alan N. Burstein, "Patterns of Segregation and the Residential Experience," in "PSHP: Special Issue," *op. cit.,* 105–13.

18. For example, Blumin, "Residential Mobility," *op. cit.;* Chudacoff, *Mobile Americans, op. cit.;* Stephan Thernstrom, *The Other Bostonians: Poverty and Progress in the American Metropolis* (Cambridge: Harvard University Press, 1973).

19. This process is fully described in Theodore Hershberg, "The Philadelphia Social History Project: A Methodological History" (Ph.D. dissertation, History, Stanford University, 1973).

20. Details on the procedure used in constructing the linked files are found in Burstein, "Residential Distribution," *op. cit.;* and in Alan N. Burstein, Theodore Hershberg, and Robert Dockhorn, "Record Linkage," in "PSHP: Special Issue," *op. cit.,* 137–63.

21. In order to ensure that those individuals classified as movers had actually changed their residences, we employed an operational definition of mobility based on "leapfrog" changes in grid. That is, an individual was classified as a mover if his residence at the end of a decade was at least two grids away from that at the beginning of the decade. This definition was employed since a small degree of unavoidable imprecision in the addressing procedure resulted in the possibility that an individual could be identified as residing in two adjacent grids at two points in time without actually having moved. Our study confirms the prevalence of high mobility rates as found by others. Residential changes over very short distances have been observed, and such mobility can be missed by the operational definition of mobility employed here. We have undertaken a pilot study to determine the extent to which our procedure underestimates the extent to which actual residential change was occurring and find whether the actual rate of residential change, determined by examining a sample of our linked pairs in the city directories, may have run 10 to 20 percentage points higher than the mobility rates based on change in grid unit. The rates of residential mobility over a decade reflect changes in the size of the areal unit used for measurement. For example, the rate of residential mobility for the Irish in the 1850–1860 decade could be reported as grid (82.8 percent); "leap frog" grid (61.9 percent); ward (41.2 percent). Since the interest here is in the relationship between mobility and large-scale changes in the residential pattern of the city, the omission of very short distance moves from the analysis need not be of concern.

22. Frank Andrews, James Morgan, and John Sonquist, *Multiple Classification Analysis* (Ann Arbor: Institute for Social Research, University of Michigan, 1969). Their main analytic tool is called Multiple Classification Analysis (MCA), yielding results similar to those of multiple regression analysis with dummy variables, but more easily accommodating nominal scale variables. It should be noted that the use of a dichotomous dependent variable has been sometimes criticized since the homoscedasticity assumption, necessary for statistical inference in regression analysis, is clearly violated by such a variable and estimates of the effects of independent variables can be inefficient, subject to high variation from sample to sample. However, these problems are severe only where the sample mean of the dependent variable, in this case represented by the proportion of the immigrants who moved, is very close to zero or very close to one, resulting in excessive skewness in the dependent variable. In simple terms, an analysis in such circumstances would produce results which would frequently yield predicted mobility rates outside of the zero-one range. In this analysis, however, the mobility rates are not extreme, in general falling between 50 percent and 65 percent, and the samples are large. Only rarely do the results produce combinations of independent variables' categories which would yield predicted mobility rates outside the zero-one range, and even then the combination would be a very unusual one. Thus the MCA analysis is quite useful in describing differences between mobility rates for different groups of individuals. Also see John L. Goodman, Jr., "Is Ordinary Least Squares Estimation with a Dichotomous Dependent Variable Really Bad?" working paper, The Urban Institute (Washington, D.C.: 1976).

23. Two statistics are of interest here for each independent variable. First, MCA produces an eta statistic, the unbiased correlation ratio yielded by one-way analysis of variance. When squared, the eta coefficient shows the amount of variation in the dependent variable explained by any one independent variable when the effects of the other independent variables are not controlled. The beta statistic, also produced

by MCA, can be interpreted as a correlation ratio controlling for the effects of other independent variables. Thus our interest will be in the relative sizes and significances of the beta statistics, particularly for change in occupational status as a correlate of residential mobility. Additionally, MCA produces a multiple R and multiple R squared which indicate the degree to which all of the independent variables combined explain variation in the dependent variable.

24. Status and industry are two of nine dimensions which the PSHP assigns to each occupation. See Hershberg and Dockhorn, "Occupational Classification," *op. cit.*

6. Industrial Location and Ethnic Residential Patterns in an Industrializing City: Philadelphia, 1880

STEPHANIE W. GREENBERG

Introduction

Social scientists and historians have often assumed that culture, a shared set of norms, values, and institutions, explains a wide range of behavior, including residential. This paper attempts to determine whether the structural contraints of the late nineteenth-century city inhibited people's ability to live among those with a common cultural heritage. The goal is to see to what extent the traditional view of urban residence should be modified, or perhaps even rejected.

Review of the Literature

The study of life in ethnic communities has been an important part of sociological research since the 1920s. Beginning with Burgess's and Park's seminal theoretical statement in *The City* and Louis Wirth's early applied study of the Jewish ghetto in Chicago, traditional social ecology has viewed the ethnic community as the embodiment of a culture transplanted from the country of origin onto new soil.[1] The basic premise in this literature seems to be that the high concentration of a group into one homogeneous

This research is based on a larger work, Stephanie W. Greenberg, "Industrialization in Philadelphia: The Relationship Between Industrial Location and Residential Patterns, 1880–1930" (Ph.D. dissertation, Sociology, Temple University, 1977). An earlier version of this paper was presented at the Social Science History Association (Philadelphia, Pa.: October, 1976). The author would like to express her appreciation to Professors Eugene Ericksen, Theodore Hershberg, William Yancey, and David Elesh for their many helpful comments.

area, typically near the center of the city, is the product of the desire of group members to carve out their own readily identifiable neighborhoods and to establish primary relationships with others of the same religion or nationality within the anonymity of the metropolis. Such areas provide the stage upon which the transplanted culture is played out. As the group becomes assimilated into American society, it becomes residentially integrated with the native population. The ghetto gradually disappears, and with it, much of the culture. Hence, by studying the growth, organization, and eventual dissolution of immigrant ghettos, it is believed that much can be learned about the process of assimilation, and by extension, the structure of the larger society.

This view of urban residence as a reflection of cultural tastes was challenged by Pratt in a study of the residential patterns of manufacturing workers in New York in roughly the same period as the Chicago School sociologists were conducting their research.[2] Pratt found that the location of employment opportunities was critical in determining the residence of workers. Immigrant workers tended to be the lowest paid and to work the longest hours, and hence were constrained to live in dense clusters close to factories, wherever those factories were located. This study suggested that the relative lack of choice in residence among immigrants, combined with the spatial concentration of manufacturing in the early twentieth century, produced the high levels of immigrant segregation observed in cities during this period.

Despite Pratt's findings, the Chicago School view of urban residence remains a dominant theme among students of the city.[3] However, a number of recent scholars have questioned this approach and turned increasingly to Pratt's argument. They posit that physical space as a reflection of social space is not a universal feature of urban ecology and that cultural groups have not always been able to carve out "urban villages." They suggest that ethnic segregation is a response to a specific set of conditions that prevailed in large cities between the turn of the century and World War II. These conditions are the concentration of a large stock of inexpensive, old housing near the urban core, and centralized workplaces.[4] In the nineteenth century, it is argued, the urban population was also distributed according to the availability of housing and jobs, both of which were thought to be dispersed. This discouraged the formation of centralized ethnic ghettos.

The need to reexamine assumptions about the residential structure of cities in the early industrial period and the limitations of commuter transportation in this era have raised the question: did culture operate independently of structural constraints in organizing residence in the walking city? In the present study, we examine the effect of one major structural variable, the location of work opportunities, on the residential organization of ethnic groups. The following question is explored: to what extent can the residential patterns of ethnic groups be explained by the spatial distribution of jobs? That is, to what extent did job location intrude upon shared cultural background in the determination of residence?

Several specific questions follow from the general question. It is commonly believed that immigrants from northern and western Europe and their children are more residentially integrated with native whites than immigrants from southern and eastern Europe because the former groups are more assimilated into American society. They are more assimilated because they have been in America much longer than the "new" immigrants. The largest wave of immigration of the northwest Europeans took place in the mid-nineteenth century. Hence, by the time the "new" immigration occurred in the early twentieth century, the "old" immigrant groups, primarily the Germans and Irish in the northeastern cities, had achieved a substantial measure of economic and cultural assimilation. When these groups first arrived, however, during the middle third of the nineteenth century, they occupied a position in the social structure analogous to that of the southeastern Europeans at the turn of the century. If the cultural explanation of differences in ethnic residential patterns in twentieth century cities is correct, then it is expected that the Germans and Irish should be much more segregated from native whites in 1880 than they were in the early twentieth century.

Given the limitations in transportation and housing in this period, we may then ask: if high segregation of immigrant groups from the native population existed, can it be viewed as a function of the closer ties between work and residence for immigrants than for natives, as Pratt's study showed? Since it is expected that immigrants had fewer economic resources than others, they would be more constrained to locate close to work opportunities, resulting in residential segregation. Or, during this period, did the entire urban population cluster in those areas with a large number of work opportunities? The result of this would be residential integration. If this were the case, then it may be that the integration of the "old" immigrants observed in twentieth-century cities is a retention of ecological patterns developed years earlier rather than a reflection of assimilation.[5]

While recent studies of nineteenth-century cities indicate that immigrant ghettoes, such as those observed by Wirth and Pratt, do not appear to have developed, some differences in the residential patterns of ethnic groups have been noted.[6] Warner and Burstein both report that the Germans in Philadelphia were more segregated from the rest of the population, more clustered, and lived in more densely populated areas than the Irish. Is it a trait of German culture to prefer living in clustered, densely populated conditions? Or can this difference be accounted for by a greater tendency for Germans to work in more spatially concentrated industries than the Irish? In other words, can residential differences between ethnic groups be explained by differences in their industrial composition?

Related to this question is the issue of commonality in residential location. A number of studies of urban life have concluded that geographic propinquity has a profound impact on a variety of social relationships, such as friendship formation, spouse selection, voluntary association membership, and access to various institutions.[7] All of these are strongly linked to social mobility and assimilation into American society; with whom one associates is critical in determining success or failure in society.[8] In addition, in an era with limited transportation and communication, spatial proximity may have been a prerequisite for the organization of labor and the formation of ethnic institutions. Thus, the composition of residential areas assumes major importance in the understanding of mobility and assimilation. For this reason, it is necessary to determine whether people lived primarily among those with a shared cultural background or with a common workplace.

These questions are explored in 1880, a point in time just prior to both the large wave of immigration from southeastern Europe and full industrialization.

Data and Methods

The research is carried out in three steps which include an examination of 1. the relationship between the location of jobs and residence among workers in manufacturing industries; 2. the relative importance of ethnicity and industrial affiliation in determining residence; and 3. the degree to which the ethnic composition of industries explained differences in ethnic residential patterns.

The two major data sources are the original manuscripts from the U.S. Census of Population and the U.S. Census of Manufactures of 1880. The latter provides the location of manufacturing jobs. The most detailed population information, including residential location, ethnicity, occupation, sector of the economy, and industrial affiliation is currently available for adult males only.[9]

The population for which the most detailed data are available consists of all German and Irish male immigrants over the age of seventeen, all black adult males, and a one-in-nine sample of native-white adult males.

Since native whites are thereby underrepresented, they are weighted by a factor of nine in all analyses.

Beginning in 1870 the population census collected detailed information on the occupations of gainfully employed persons, from which sector of the economy and industrial affiliation were inferred. When industrial affiliation of the population is used in this study, only adult male workers in manufacturing were included. Manufacturing accounted for one of every two male jobs in 1880. This decision was made since there are very few data in 1880 on nonmanufacturing workplaces; the city's business directories can provide only location, not the number of persons employed at a given site. The industries were grouped into forty-four categories in order to examine the relationship between work and residence. These categories were derived from a more detailed coding scheme primarily on the basis of comparability both with the scheme used in a recent study of manufacturing location in Philadelphia in 1930[10] and with the Standard Industrial Classification used today by the Census of Manufactures. Eleven of the largest industries in terms of male workers and male jobs were selected for a more detailed analysis of the residential patterns of ethnic groups within industries.

The individual level data on population and jobs were aggregated into areal units. The roughly 7,300 one by one and one-quarter block grid units adopted by the Philadelphia Social History Project were grouped into the 404 census tracts into which the city was divided in 1930 (see Appendix II). Each individual and job was assigned to the tract he (it) would have occupied had the city been tracted in 1880. It is assumed that jobs and population were located at the centroid of each tract. The purpose of using census tracts rather than grid units is to permit direct comparisons of spatial measures and to trace change systematically in one city over a period of time spanning 1850 to 1970.

Workplace accessibility is expressed by measuring the total number of manufacturing jobs within one mile of a census tract.[11] The distance of one mile is used, since it is a good approximation of the likeliest maximum distance for a one-way daily trip on foot, as described in the "Journey-to-Work" essay in this volume.

The spatial distribution of the population is expressed through several measures. Two commonly used measures to express locational dissimilarities are the *indices of dissimilarity and segregation*. The former indicates the proportion of one group that would have to change its location in order to be distributed identically with another group, and the latter shows the proportion of a group that would have to move in order to have the same distribution as the rest of the population. Burstein has developed measures that tap several other dimensions of spatial distribution that are as important as segregation in the description of residential context.[12] The *index of relative clustering* shows the degree to which a group is clustered into one areal unit, on average, compared to the amount of clustering in the entire population. The *index of density* shows the population per acre in the areal unit inhabited by the group's mean individual.

Findings

Work and Residence in Forty-Four Industries. As a first step in the analysis, the work-residence relationship for manufacturing workers is examined. Demonstrating the extent to which workers in a given industry clustered around jobs in those industries will make it possible to test the relative effects of industry and ethnicity in residential patterns in a later section of this paper. The two dimensions of the work-residence relationship that are examined in this section are 1. the degree of residential concentration of workers around potential workplaces and 2. the extent to which the spatial patterns of industries correlated with the residential characteristics of workers.

One way of measuring the work-residence relationship is to compare the average number of jobs in an industry within a mile of workers in that industry to the average number of jobs in the same industry within a mile of the entire population. The resulting ratio shows the relative degree of concentration of workers around potential workplaces compared to the population as a whole. A ratio greater than one indicates that there are more jobs, on average, in an industry within a mile of workers in that industry than there are for the general population. A ratio of one or less shows that workers in an industry are no more oriented and possibly even less oriented to job location than the entire population.

It can be seen (see Table 1) that for thirty-two out of the forty-four industries, there were more jobs in a given industry, on average, within a mile of workers in that industry than there were in the total population. For example, there were over three times as many ship building jobs within a mile of the homes of ship builders, on the average, as there were within a mile of the entire population. In the remainder of cases, there was either an approximately equal number of jobs within local access to workers in those industries and the rest of the population or a slightly lower number of jobs proximate to workers in the given industry. This suggests that with few exceptions, workers were drawn to areas with high accessibility to their particular type of workplace. This is not to say, for example, that all woolen workers living within a mile of a woolen mill

Table 1. Relative Access of Workers to Jobs in Forty-Four Industries,
Philadelphia, 1880

Industry	A_i	A_t	R	Male Workers
Apparel	1730	1250	1.44	1622
Baking	302	280	1.08	2953
Beverages (brewed)	70	55	1.26	842
Blacksmith	61	66	0.92	3013
Boots, shoes	1396	936	1.49	6877
Brass	106	85	1.25	547
Carpets	2480	956	2.59	2947
Chemicals	594	504	1.18	1045
Confection	202	127	1.60	773
Construction	1114	1156	0.92	17,715
Copper, other metal	97	64	1.51	237
Cotton goods	377	374	1.01	1673
Dyeing of textiles	239	174	1.38	1167
Food, NEC	222	230	0.97	931
Furniture	830	666	1.24	3636
Hardware, other fabricated metal	556	479	1.16	2082
Harnesses, saddles	70	65	1.08	619
Hosiery, knits	699	385	1.82	637
Instruments	388	238	1.63	867
Iron, steel	562	556	1.01	3635
Leather	1479	508	2.91	2052
Locomotives	714	165	4.34	42
Lumber, wood products	677	689	0.98	4257
Machinery	543	585	0.93	6514
Meat	84	111	0.75	3346
Miscellaneous textiles	520	436	1.19	3080
Paper	193	57	3.38	591
Paper boxes	104	29	3.60	118
Petroleum refining	202	136	1.49	216
Precious metals, jewelry	190	133	1.43	1412
Printing, publishing	1197	757	1.58	5003
Railroad cars, parts	418	95	4.38	190
Rope, twine	84	42	2.02	233
Ships	916	300	3.05	1089
Shirts	239	131	1.83	198
Silk	216	161	1.34	216
Stone, clay, glass	599	455	1.32	4446
Stoves, boilers	187	171	1.10	907
Sugar refining	390	124	3.15	235
Tailor	148	98	1.52	3291
Tin	161	175	0.92	1263
Tobacco products	548	421	1.30	2141
Tools	591	468	1.26	800
Woolen goods	279	170	1.65	1506
Total	15,391	15,391	1.00	100,503

A_i = number of male jobs in industry i within one mile of the mean male worker in industry i

A_t = number of male jobs in industry i within one mile of the mean individual in the total male
population

R = A_i/A_t

Total includes miscellaneous manufacturing.

Sources: Original manuscripts, U.S. Census of Population, U.S. Census of Manufactures,
Philadelphia, 1880.

worked in that mill. Without employee lists, such a statement would not be possible.[13] But given the difficulties involved in commuting long distances and the fact that workers had local accessibility to more jobs in their industry than other workers, it is not unreasonable to suggest that workers tended to cluster near job opportunities.[14]

Factors that might account for differences in the work-residence relationship were examined in a more detailed analysis of these data.[15] Briefly, it was found that proximity of jobs to the central district, degree of spatial clustering of jobs, and degree of environmental pollution (noise, odor) all had an effect. Industries close to the center, such as printing and publishing, shoes, and apparel, did not have as close a work-residence relationship as most other industries; by 1880, the concentration of economic activities in the center displaced residence.[16] There was a strong relationship among spatially clustered industries, particularly if they were far from the center. Industries such as textiles and paper may have created a mill town effect within the city. Finally, industries that polluted the surrounding area—chemicals, primary metals, machinery, food processing—tended to prevent worker concentrations. Differences in the work-residence relationship among the forty-four industries were not explained by the wage level of an industry.

The findings thus far suggest that urban residence late in the nineteenth century cannot be understood without reference to job access. However, there is a second dimension in the analysis of the work-residence relationship other than access to jobs. The spatial characteristics of neighborhoods have been found to have considerable impact on a wide variety of social processes. Therefore, it is important to find the degree to which the spatial distribution of industries predicted the residential characteristics of workers in those industries. It is expected that during this period the spatial context of residence corresponded closely to the geographic distribution of jobs.

Four spatial measures are used to define the spatial context of jobs and residence: mean distance from the center and the indices of segregation, relative clustering, and density. For each of the forty-four industries, the locational characteristics of the residence of workers are regressed on the corresponding characteristics of jobs.

The relationship between the spatial distribution of jobs and workers is a close one (see Table 2). Over half of the variance in the centrality and clustering of workers, almost three-quarters of the variance in segregation, and over a third of the variance in the average density in which industrial workers lived were accounted for by the corresponding spatial characteristics of jobs. For example, industries in which the workplaces were the

Table 2. Spatial Distribution of Jobs and Workers in Forty-Four Industries, Philadelphia, 1880

Industry	Mean Distance from Center—mi.		Index of Segregation		Index of Rel. Clustering		Index of Density	
	Jobs	Workers	Jobs	Workers	Jobs	Workers	Jobs	Workers
Apparel	0.61	1.57	59.25	34.60	6.75	1.92	56	25
Baking	1.43	1.85	49.80	21.85	0.58	1.38	15	23
Beverages (brewed)	1.04	2.02	79.55	58.20	2.73	5.28	17	20
Blacksmith	1.86	2.37	53.90	29.15	0.77	1.15	12	19
Boots, shoes	0.70	1.68	51.35	25.00	3.97	1.64	45	25
Brass	0.76	1.61	61.65	50.35	4.41	2.47	50	25
Carpets	2.69	2.65	85.85	66.30	2.64	5.20	12	19
Chemicals	1.38	1.97	49.20	42.05	2.10	1.75	28	22
Confection	0.80	1.53	52.20	41.35	2.39	2.12	27	25
Construction	1.51	2.23	42.10	18.40	0.79	1.03	21	20
Copper, other metals	2.48	1.60	62.40	58.55	2.69	3.62	26	26
Cotton goods	3.53	3.87	63.10	59.15	1.32	3.15	18	13
Dyeing of textiles	2.97	3.12	72.90	62.45	1.73	2.88	13	16
Food, NEC	1.24	2.08	63.05	44.45	6.05	1.65	19	22
Furniture	1.00	1.86	41.15	26.90	1.70	1.54	28	24
Hardware, fab. metal	1.47	1.88	62.55	33.90	2.08	1.60	22	23
Harnesses, saddles	0.99	2.07	51.45	44.45	2.66	2.23	37	23
Hosiery, knits	3.01	2.77	73.30	70.45	1.55	4.76	12	19
Instruments	0.81	1.64	63.15	49.20	2.45	2.31	28	25
Iron, steel	1.39	2.18	54.30	30.85	1.64	1.71	23	21
Leather	0.98	1.56	81.35	61.50	3.52	7.00	18	28
Locomctives	1.12	1.65	97.60	89.75	20.16	15.49	24	20
Lumber, wood products	1.43	2.08	41.65	25.15	0.68	1.24	18	21

1. Spatial measures are based on male jobs and workers.

2. Index of Segregation $= \frac{1}{2} \sum_{j=1}^{404} \left| \frac{g_{tj} - g_{ij}}{G_t - G_i} - \frac{g_{ij}}{G_i} \right|$, where G_t = total jobs or population;

G_i = total jobs or workers in industry i; g_{tj} = total jobs or population in tract j; g_{ij} = jobs or population in industry i located in tract j.

3. Index of Relative Clustering: $C_i = \frac{1}{G_i} \sum_{j=1}^{404} \left(g_{ij} \cdot \frac{g_{ij}}{G_i} \right)$; $C_t = \frac{1}{G_t} \sum_{j=1}^{404} \left(g_{tj} \cdot \frac{g_{tj}}{G_t} \right)$; $I_{rc} = C_i / C_t$

4. Index of Density: $\frac{1}{G_i} \sum_{j=1}^{404} \left(g_{ij} \cdot \frac{g_{tj}}{acres} \right)$.

Sources: See Table 1.

Industry	Mean Distance from Center—mi.		Index of Segregation		Index of Rel. Clustering		Index of Density	
	Jobs	Workers	Jobs	Workers	Jobs	Workers	Jobs	Workers
Machinery	1.62	2.15	43.65	22.80	1.61	1.15	26	21
Meat	1.43	2.46	45.25	40.70	1.34	1.54	24	18
Misc. textiles	2.21	2.53	71.80	56.00	1.71	5.02	12	17
Paper	2.51	4.68	70.80	74.35	3.91	6.79	25	12
Paper boxes	0.54	1.04	74.80	76.65	11.40	10.43	65	37
Petroleum refining	1.04	1.71	76.60	72.50	9.89	4.37	23	19
Precious metals, jewelry	0.62	1.54	60.90	41.05	4.18	1.91	42	25
Printing, publishing	0.58	1.69	61.05	27.20	5.16	1.49	44	25
Railroad cars	2.00	2.02	90.55	72.10	9.92	4.95	9	19
Rope, twine	1.46	2.40	78.60	73.80	11.31	4.20	22	14
Ships	2.10	1.78	90.65	64.45	6.78	8.01	10	22
Shirts	0.86	1.45	75.55	67.95	11.87	4.73	27	26
Silk	1.28	1.80	64.55	63.80	5.14	3.57	46	21
Stone, clay, glass	2.06	2.15	61.70	33.40	0.57	1.31	13	19
Stoves, boilers	1.01	1.96	57.20	47.40	2.72	2.46	33	23
Sugar refining	1.84	1.21	86.95	56.20	9.14	4.00	21	27
Tailor	1.00	1.59	55.15	31.90	3.32	2.01	38	26
Tin	1.04	2.09	45.80	41.15	2.74	1.66	37	20
Tobacco products	1.11	1.66	45.95	33.95	1.87	1.88	24	26
Tools	1.31	3.43	81.35	67.85	5.97	3.97	22	18
Woolen goods	3.92	4.52	81.00	69.80	2.08	3.82	9	9
Total	1.62	2.07	—	—	—	—	26	21
		$R^2 = .5598$		$R^2 = .7298$		$R^2 = .5268$		$R^2 = .3575$

most centralized, such as apparel, boots and shoes, publishing, and jewelry, also had the most centralized workers. By the same token, workers in decentralized industries—textiles and paper—lived the greatest distance from the center. Industries with jobs that were the most segregated from other jobs, many of which were located far from the center, had workers who were the most segregated from the rest of the population. The findings were similar with regard to relative clustering. In industries where the work-residence relationship was particularly close, both jobs and workers were highly clustered relative to all jobs or the entire population, respectively; they also tended to be decentralized. These results suggest that employment centers located far from the core were likely to have developed autonomously, almost as separate entities. Finally, there is a close association between job density and residential density; workers in industries located in dense manufacturing areas lived in dense residential areas. It should be noted that the relationship between the density of jobs and workers is not as strong as the other spatial measures. In several cases, workers lived in dense areas but there were few other manufacturing jobs per acre. The explanation may be that workplaces in these industries were located in areas with little manufacturing but a great many other jobs that would attract population, such as dockworking in water-oriented industries like sugar refining and ship building and warehousing for a variety of industries.[17]

The evidence suggests a close relationship between work and residence. Areas with access to jobs in a given industry also had large numbers of workers in those industries. In addition, the industry in which one was employed defined the spatial context in which one was likely to live. With this basic set of relationships in mind, let us now look at the relative effects of ethnicity and jobs on the residence of workers.

Ethnic Segregation. If the cultural argument of ethnic residential patterns holds true, it is expected that the Germans and Irish should be much more segregated from the native whites in 1880 than they were in the early twentieth century. It is just prior to the earlier period that the wave of German and Irish immigrants arrived and hence the period when these two groups were the least assimilated. The level of segregation should therefore be similar to the high levels observed for the southeastern European immigrants several decades later. But the results in the previous section show that workers in most manufacturing industries concentrated around job opportunities. If this is true regardless of ethnicity, then ethnic segregation from native whites should be low.

The index of dissimilarity shows that approximately one-third of first

Table 3.   Index of Dissimilarity of Non-Native Ethnic Groups from Native
Whites, Philadelphia, 1880 and 1930

Group	1880 Index of Dissimilarity		Total	
Blacks	53	(53)	9412	(30,405)
Irish 1	35	(33)	39,805	(100,004)
Irish 2	34	(32)	25,776	(126,569)
German 1	37	(37)	27,550	(55,605)
German 2	31	(33)	14,958	(80,677)

Group	1930 Index of Dissimilarity	Total
Blacks	62	219,599
Ireland	29	115,146
Germany	33	131,278
Great Britain	25	167,819
Italy	60	182,433
Poland	55	77.377
U.S.S.R	57	176,002

1. In 1880, the data refer to the adult male population, with the total population in parentheses. In 1930 the data refer to the total population.

2. Index of Dissimilarity $= \frac{1}{2} \sum\limits_{j=1}^{404} \left| \dfrac{g_{ij}}{G_i} - \dfrac{g_{kj}}{G_k} \right|$, where G_i = total number in group i; G_k = total

number in group k; g_{ij} = number in group i living in tract j; g_{kj} = number in group k living in tract j.

3. Irish 1—foreign-born Irish; Irish 2—native born with Irish-born father; German 1—foreign-born German; German 2—native born with German-born father; Native White—native-born white of native parentage. In 1930, the ethnic groups refer to foreign stock, i.e., foreign born or native born of foreign parents.

Sources: 1880—Original manuscripts, U.S. Census of Population, Philadelphia, 1880. 1930—W. L. Yancey and E. P. Ericksen, "The Industrial Causes of Ethnic Segregation, Philadelphia, 1910–1970," (1976).

and second generation Irish and Germans would have to relocate in order to be distributed identically with native whites (see Table 3). This proportion is far lower—almost half—than that observed for the "new" immigrants from Poland, Italy, and U.S.S.R. in Philadelphia in 1970[18] and in other cities in the first half of the twentieth century.[19] For these groups, the index typically varies between one-half and two-thirds. These findings indicate that segregation from the native population is not a basic feature of the immigrant residential experience, but rather is specific to period.

The degree of segregation of the Irish and Germans from native whites between 1880 and 1930 in Philadelphia is quite stable. Some research suggests that immigrants from northern and western Europe were not highly segregated from the native population in the early twentieth century, because by this time, the "old" immigrant groups had been assimilated into the dominant culture. However, our evidence shows that these groups were *never* highly segregated. During the period in which the largest numbers of German and Irish immigrated to the cities of the northeast, workers tended to live in areas with high access to jobs. In this light, as Yancey *et al.* and Hershberg *et al.* suggest, it may be more reasonable to interpret the low segregation observed in later periods as a continuation of an established ecological pattern rather than as a sign of assimilation.[20]

In contrast to the Germans and Irish, the blacks were markedly segregated from native whites. It was found in another analysis of these data that blacks were far more centralized than any other group.[21] This pattern of both high segregation from native whites and centralization is similar to that observed for blacks in present-day cities. It is clear that this phenomenon is not the product of the abandonment of the inner city by both industry and the middle class that has been described in the city of the post–World War II period. Rather it has been a feature of urban residence for at least a century.[22]

Ethnicity and Industry in the Location of Residence. The evidence indicates that industrial workers concentrated around job opportunities and that white ethnics were not highly segregated from native whites. But when the two variables of industrial affiliation and ethnicity are examined together, which emerges as more important in the determination of residential distribution? That is, were workers more likely to live among those with the same industrial affiliation or the same ethnic background? Given the importance that has been attached to spatial proximity as an influence on many social relationships, the answer to this question may provide valuable clues to the nature of interaction in the late nineteenth-century city.

This issue may be addressed by calculating the index of dissimilarity between pairs of ethnic industrial groups and comparing the degree of dissimilarity between each ethnic industrial group and all others in the same industry (Irish shoemakers and German shoemakers, Irish shoemakers and native-white shoemakers, and so on) and between each ethnic-industrial group and all others in the same ethnic group (Irish shoemakers and Irish leather workers, Irish shoemakers and Irish apparel workers). Let us take one ethnic-industrial group, German leather workers, as an illustration of this approach. If ethnicity is more important than industrial affiliation in distributing the population across space, then German leather workers should have a relatively low index of dissimilarity from Germans working in other industries and a high index score from Irish, native-white, and black leather workers. If, on the other hand, industrial affiliation is more important, then German leather workers should be less segregated from non-Germans working in this industry than they are from Germans working on other industries. Only workers in the eleven major industries are used in this analysis because the number of ethnic-industrial groups in all manufacturing industries is prohibitively large.

Table 4 shows the summary frequency distributions of the Index of Dissimilarity between pairs of ethnic-industrial groups within each ethnic group and each industry. (The index values upon which this summary table is based are found in Appendix Table 1 at the back of this essay.) Most of the index values are fairly high, none going below 30 percent. However, the *relative* rather than the absolute sizes of the index values are of primary interest. The lowest indices of dissimilarity are between white ethnic-industrial groups and other whites in the same industry and between blacks across industries. Seventy percent of the ten black industrial groups have index values below sixty, indicating that less than 60 percent of the members of each of these groups would have to relocate in order to have the same distribution as blacks in another industry. The percentage distribution of index values is similar for white ethnic groups from other whites in the same industry, such as German leather workers from Irish leather workers. Far higher index values occurred among blacks from whites in the same industry and between white ethnics from members of the same ethnic group who worked in different industries. Between one-quarter and one-third of the Germans, Irish, and native whites had index values below sixty from groups of the same ethnicity but different industrial affiliation. This compares to almost 70 percent among Germans, Irish, and native whites from different white ethnic groups in the same industry. Thus, Irish apparel workers, for example, are less segregated from German and native white apparel workers than they are from Irish woolen weavers or Irish leather workers. The highest index values are found in the dissimilarity of black industrial groups from whites in the same industry; 100 percent of black industrial groups had an index of sixty or greater from whites in the same industry.

While the dissimilarity of white ethnics from others of the same ethnicity but different industrial affiliation tends to be quite high, there are some instances where this is not the case. This usually occurs when jobs in the two industries are located close to one another. For instance, printing and publishing and shoemaking are both located near the center of the city. The index of dissimilarity between the Irish in these two industries is 35.5 percent; between German printers and German shoemakers, it is 31.2 percent; and between native whites in these industries, it is 43.5 percent. In contrast, printing and publishing firms are usually far from woolen mills.

Table 4. Frequency Distribution of Indices of Dissimilarity Between Pairs of Ethnic-Industrial Groups in Eleven Major Industries, Philadelphia, 1880 (Summary)

Index of Dissimilarity Between Ethnic-Industrial Groups	Blacks from Whites Within Same Industry	Whites from Other Whites Within Same Industry	Blacks from Other Blacks	Irish from Other Irish	Germans from Other Germans	Native Whites from Native Whites
30–39	0.0%	10.0%	20.0%	7.3%	10.9%	3.6%
40–49	0.0	21.2	10.0	5.5	12.7	14.6
50–59	0.0	36.4	40.0	12.7	12.7	10.9
60–69	46.7	21.2	30.0	23.6	21.8	10.9
70–79	26.7	12.1	0.0	32.7	20.0	27.3
80–89	26.7	0.0	0.0	16.4	16.4	21.8
90+	0.0	0.0	0.0	1.8	5.5	10.9
	100.0%	100.0%	100.0%	100.0%	100.0%	100.0%
30–59	0.0%	67.6%	70.0%	25.5%	36.3%	29.1%
60+	100.0	33.3	30.0	74.5	63.7	70.9
	100.0%	100.0%	100.0%	100.0%	100.0%	100.0%
Total Number of Pairs of Ethnic-Industrial Groups	15	33	10	55	55	55

1. The two generations of Irish and Germans are combined; see Table 3 for definition of ethnic groups.

2. Table is based on adult male workers in eleven major industries. These industries are 1. leather, 2. boots and shoes, 3. apparel, 4. machinery, 5. stone, clay, and glass, 6. construction, 7. ship building, 8. printing and publishing, 9. woolen goods, 10. cotton goods, 11. carpets. These represent about half of all male manufacturing workers and of all male manufacturing jobs.

3. See Appendix Table 1 at the end of this essay for complete table.

4. See Table 3 for definition of Index of Dissimilarity.

Source: See Table 3.

The index between Irish, German, and native-white workers in these two industries is 80.9 percent, 69.3 percent, and 90.4 percent, respectively. This suggests the possibility that homogeneous ethnic enclaves had the potential of forming among members working in different industries located in the same area of the city. However, the size of these communities would be limited by the fact that they would not include many members working in distant industries. Thus, small ethnic neighborhoods may well have developed among workers in the same industry or a few industries if the jobs were located close to one another.

The evidence strongly suggests that, with the exception of blacks, it was industry rather than ethnicity that best predicted the residential location of workers. Once employment in a given industry was obtained, the physical location of workers was far more similar to other workers in the same industry than to workers of the same nationality, at least among whites. Of course, it is clearly not possible to make a statement of causality unequivocally. In order to do so would require employee lists and a close temporal analysis of the movement of firms and workers. But given the limitations in transportation and housing, the causal inference is not unwarranted. The fact that blacks were an exception to this general rule implies that even when members of this group did obtain manufacturing jobs, they were not as free to orient their residences to their workplaces as whites apparently were.

The Effects of the Ethnic Composition of Industries on Residential Patterns. Another way of looking at the relative contribution of industrial affiliation and ethnicity in determining residential patterns is to ask the questions, what would be the spatial distribution of ethnic group members if industrial affiliation completely determined residence, and to what extent did the actual distribution differ from this "expected" distribution? The previous section examined the degree of segregation of ethnic-industrial groups from members of the same ethnic group compared with members of the same industry. In this section, we look at the contribution that industrial affiliation made to the residential characteristics of ethnic groups.

Burstein found that the residential patterns of German and Irish immigrants in Philadelphia between 1850 and 1880 differed in several important ways, despite their similarly low degree of segregation from native whites.[23] The Germans were more clustered and lived in areas that were more densely populated than the Irish. Earlier in the present analysis, it was found that the residential patterns of workers bore a strong resemblance to the spatial distribution of the industries in which they worked. The questions which emerge from these two sets of findings are:

To what extent did differences in industrial composition account for differences in residential patterns among ethnic groups? Were Germans, for example, overrepresented in spatially clustered industries? Did the Irish concentrate in dispersed industries?

These questions are addressed by the following method. If industrial affiliation were completely responsible for residential location, then it is expected that if Germans, for instance, account for 10 percent of all workers in industry x, then they should do so in every census tract; that is, 10 percent of the workers in industry x living in tract j should be German. The total expected number of Germans in each tract can be obtained by applying this assumption to each industry and summing the resulting numbers.[24] This calculation was carried out for adult male manufacturing workers in the six ethnic groups. (See Appendix Table 2 at the end of this essay for the composition of industries by ethnicity.)

Looking first at the actual residential patterns of ethnic groups, we find that the blacks had the most distinct distribution (see Table 5). Black manufacturing workers were the most segregated and clustered and lived in the densest areas, followed in order by the Germans, Irish, and native whites.[25] While there were clear differences among the five white groups, they were generally quite small when viewed in juxtaposition to the blacks. The sons of both the German and Irish immigrants were distributed similarly to their fathers, but they tended to be slightly less segregated from the rest of the population, less clustered, and in the case of second generation Germans, lived in areas that were less centralized and dense. In both groups, differences between fathers and sons represent an increase in similarity on the part of the sons to the distribution of native whites. This suggests that as the sons moved away from the traditional crafts or low-skilled manual work of their immigrant fathers, their residential distribution began to take on the characteristics of the native population.[26]

The index of dissimilarity is calculated between the actual manufacturing workers in a given ethnic group and expected workers in that group. The difference between the observed and expected distribution is the portion of the observed distribution that is unexplained by industry. For example, if the index of dissimilarity between the expected and observed is ten for group i, 10 percent of the observed members of this group would have to move to be distributed identically to the expected number.

The results in the first row of Table 5 show that the residence of blacks diverged by the greatest amount from what it would be if industry totally explained residence. Over half of all blacks would have to relocate in order for their spatial distribution to be consistent with their industrial composition. These percentages are far lower for every white ethnic group, ranging

Table 5. Standardized Spatial Distribution Compared with Observed Spatial Distribution of Ethnic Groups in Manufacturing, Philadelphia, 1880

Spatial Measures	Blacks	Irish 1	Irish 2	Ger. 1	Ger. 2	Native White
$\stackrel{\wedge}{\text{I.D.}}$ Between Observed and Expected Members of Each Group	55.20	28.05	25.40	20.85	21.15	13.05
Observed Mean Distance from Center	1.80	2.13	2.07	1.92	2.01	2.34
Expected Mean Distance from Center	2.08	2.24	2.26	2.00	2.03	2.14
(Observed-Expected)/ Observed	−.156	−.052	−.092	−.042	−.010	−.085
Observed Index of Segregation	52.75	28.90	27.35	34.85	31.45	22.40
Expected Index of Segregation	12.30	16.55	14.55	15.40	13.85	13.10
(O-E)/O	.767	.427	.468	.558	.560	.415
Observed Index of Relative Clustering	3.71	1.36	1.30	1.98	1.80	0.98
Expected Index of Relative Clustering	1.06	1.23	1.13	1.26	1.21	1.08
(O-E)/O	.714	.096	.131	.364	.328	−.102
Observed Index of Density	23.8	20.0	20.3-	23.9	23.4	19.5
Expected Index of Density	21.2	21.1	20.7	22.5	22.3	21.4
(O-E)/O	.109	−.055	−.020	−.059	.047	−.097
Total	962	13,827	12,461	16,905	8186	40,848

1. Standardized spatial measures are based on the number of adult male ethnic group members expected in a census tract if industrial affiliation completely determined residential distribution.

Expected number of group i in tract j = $\stackrel{\wedge}{g_{ij}}$ = $\sum\limits_{x=1}^{45} (t_{xj} \cdot \dfrac{g_{ix}}{t_x})$, where t_{xj} = number of workers in industry x living in tract j, g_{ix} = total number in group i working in industry x, t_x = total workers in industry x.

2. I.D. = $\frac{1}{2} \sum\limits_{j=1}^{404} \left| \dfrac{g_{ij}}{G_i} - \dfrac{\stackrel{\wedge}{g_{ij}}}{G_i} \right|$, where $\stackrel{\wedge}{g_{ij}}$ = number in group i living in tract j, g_{ij} = expected number in group i living in tract j (see Note 1), G_i = total number in group i.

3. Index of Segregation = $\frac{1}{2} \sum\limits_{j=1}^{404} \left| \dfrac{g_{tj} - g_{ij}}{G_t - G_i} - \dfrac{g_{ij}}{G_i} \right|$, where G_t = total population; G_i = total number in group i; g_{tj} = total population in tract j; g_{ij} = number in group i living in tract j.

4. Index of Relative Clustering: $C_i = \dfrac{1}{G_i} \sum\limits_{j=1}^{404} (g_{ij} \cdot \dfrac{g_{ij}}{G_i}); C_t = \dfrac{1}{G_t} \sum\limits_{j=1}^{404} (g_{tj} \cdot \dfrac{g_{tj}}{G_t}); I_{rc} = C_i/C_t.$

5. Index Density = $\dfrac{1}{G_i} \sum\limits_{j=1}^{404} (g_{ij} \cdot \dfrac{g_{tj}}{acres}).$

6. Observed spatial measures are based on total adult male manufacturing workers in each ethnic group.

7. See Table 3 for definition of ethnic groups.

Source: See Table 3.

from about a quarter for the Irish to a little over 10 percent for native whites. Even though there are differences among the whites, the findings indicate that the vast bulk of their variation across tracts—almost 90 percent for the native whites, 80 percent for the Germans, and 75 percent for the Irish—is explained by their industrial composition. This is not the case for blacks. Factors other than industry obviously operated to determine their residence.

The expected number of each ethnic group is used to calculate the spatial measures of centrality, segregation, relative clustering, and density. The expected index values are then compared to the observed to show the proportion of the observed value that is unexplained by industry. Again, the results show that, without exception, black residence was least affected by the industrial composition of this group. Black manufacturing workers were far more centralized, segregated, clustered, and lived in denser areas than would be expected on the basis of industry. The only two industries that contained more than a few blacks were construction and building materials. These industries were dispersed and decentralized, the exact opposite of the residential characteristics of blacks.

The residential patterns of the white ethnic groups were far more consistent with their industrial composition. The expected measures show that native whites were overrepresented in industries whose workers were not highly segregated or clustered, decentralized, and lived in areas of only moderate density. Examples of these industries are construction and machinery. The spatial characteristics of these industries are closely associated with the actual residential patterns of native whites, although this group is even less centralized and clustered than would be expected on the basis of industry alone.

The expected patterns of the Irish indicate that this group was overrepresented in industries whose workforces were decentralized, lived in sparsely populated areas, and were less clustered than those in which the Germans were overrepresented. Such industries were construction, stone, clay, glass, and blacksmithing. But the Irish were also concentrated in industries with highly clustered workforces—iron and steel, leather, boots and shoes, miscellaneous textiles, and particularly carpets. This may be one important reason why the difference in expected clustering between the Irish and Germans was not greater, given the heavy participation of the former in many dispersed industries.

The industrial composition of the Germans was substantially different from that of the Irish and native whites. This difference is reflected in German residence. Germans were far more oriented toward skilled hand trades, specifically boots and shoes, furniture, leather, tailoring, baking, butchering, and brewing. These industries all tended to locate either in the center or one ring out, and most were clustered and located in moderate to high density areas. These characteristics are all consistent with the residential patterns of Germans. While this group was more segregated and clustered than would be expected on the basis of their industrial composition, their residence was similar to what it would be if industrial affiliation determined the distribution of workers.

The evidence indicates that the spatial distribution of white ethnic groups was highly consistent with their industrial composition. In most cases, the residential pattern deviated by only a small proportion from what would be expected if the location of industrial groups completely accounted for residence. The major exception to this rule was the segregation index. The deviation between expected and observed was greater here than for the other spatial measures; ethnic groups were more segregated from the rest of the population than would be expected on the basis of industry alone. However, the difference was much greater for blacks than for the white ethnic groups. While industrial affiliation explains about half of the segregation of white manufacturing workers, it explains only a quarter for blacks. This is consistent with the general pattern. There is always some portion of the observed residential patterns that cannot be explained by industrial composition, but this residual is much smaller for whites than for blacks. Knowledge of a group's industrial characteristics was much more critical to the understanding of white ethnic residential patterns than black residential patterns in this period.

At this point, one might ask why ethnic groups tended to concentrate in certain industries. Isn't this a sign of a cultural proclivity to favor specific types of work? Evidence indicates that this tendency is not as much a matter of cultural tastes as of the interaction between the occupational structure of the country of origin and that of the adopted country.[27] It has been suggested that those immigrants who came to this country with a skill were more likely to find "matching" jobs than were unskilled immigrants.[28] Since highly skilled occupations were often industry-specific and low-skilled occupations were not as tied to a particular industry, this meant that highly skilled immigrants were more likely than others to find employment in the industry which demanded those skills. In contrast, unskilled workers had to find jobs in industries that were rapidly expanding and therefore had a high demand for labor. Such industries typically had a greater need for unskilled than skilled labor. Since a greater proportion of the Irish were unskilled than of the Germans, the former were more likely to be attracted to such expanding industries as construction and building materials. The Germans, in contrast, were seemingly able to obtain jobs in industries in which they had experience in Germany, such as furniture making and brewing. A similar line of reasoning has been used to explain differential ethnic concentrations between cities.[29]

Thus, in the explanation of ethnic residential patterns, we start with the industrial structure of a city at a given point in time which defines the types and amounts of labor demanded. Next, the match-up process between demands and skill levels results in the differential industrial composition of ethnic groups. Finally, the differences in the residential distribution of ethnic groups correspond to the spatial distribution of jobs.[30]

Summary and Conclusions

The following is a summary of the major findings of this study:

1. In three-quarters of manufacturing industries, workers in a given industry lived in areas that had local access to a greater number of manufacturing jobs in this industry than the population as a whole.
2. There was a strong relationship between the spatial characteristics of manufacturing industries and the residential context in which their workers were likely to live.
3. The segregation of German and Irish immigrants and their sons from the native population was low relative to that of the "new" immigrants in the early twentieth century and was similar to levels observed for these two groups in later periods.
4. White ethnic-industrial groups had more in common residentially with whites in the same industry than others in the same ethnic group. The residential distribution of blacks was more like that of other blacks than whites in the same industry.
5. The differences in the residential distribution of native whites, Irish, and Germans could be accounted for by differences in their industrial composition. This was not the case for blacks.

The evidence presented here suggests four concluding points. First, the ghettoization of a large proportion of any ethnic group into homogeneous areas was not likely to develop in the nineteenth-century city. Rather, if identifiable ethnic communities existed at all, they would probably develop within a larger industrial context. That is to say, workers in a particular industry lived around workplaces in that industry, and within that larger industrial cluster, small, homogeneous ethnic enclaves may have evolved. However, by necessity, these would have had to be narrowly delimited, perhaps spreading no further than one or two blocks. An analysis of the residential patterns of leather workers in Philadelphia during this period suggests that this is precisely what happened.[31] A large concentration of morocco leather workers lived around factories of this type, but the concentration was divided into German and Irish segments. Given the residential constraints of nineteenth-century cities, it is not unreasonable to expect there to be many such areas, each developing within the context of accessibility to a particular industry. Hence, in terms of community formation, industrial affiliation seems to have been the primary organizing factor, with ethnicity emerging as a secondary factor.

The findings presented here should not be interpreted as meaning that in the nineteenth-century city, culture was of no importance in the determination of behavior, either residential or otherwise. The existence of ethnic newspapers, voluntary associations, and the like suggests that shared ethnicity played an important role. What is being argued is that in terms of residential patterns, structural variables seemed to form the first-order explanation. But culturally determined behavior may well have emerged within a specific structural context. Thus, the argument is not culture versus structure, but rather whether culture exerted an effect independently of or only within the context of structural constraints. The conclusion of this study is that the former is not true. The validity of the second proposition remains an empirical question.

Second, these findings are relevant to the process of network formation. In an era in which communication beyond areas within walking distance was limited, it would be difficult to interact on any regular basis with people living several miles away. If it were the case that neighborhoods formed within the context of accessibility to workplaces, then the development of networks based on ethnicity would be undercut by the necessity of living among those with the same industrial affiliation but not necessarily the same cultural affiliation. When ethnic networks did develop, they would be unlikely to draw from the entire population of group members but rather would probably be limited to ethnics living in the local area—people who had been attracted by jobs of a specific type. In a study of contemporary Philadelphia, it has been found that members of an ethnic group who live in ethnically homogeneous areas of the city are more likely to form networks with others of the same group than are members of that group who live in ethnically heterogeneous areas.[32] True at the present, it is even more likely to have been the case in 1880. The fact that residence tended not to be ethnically homogeneous in this period would work against the formation of a large ethnic network.

Third, the evidence presented here speaks to the assimilation process among blacks. Some contemporary scholars have argued that blacks (and more recently, Hispanics) are the last of the immigrants. Just as the Northwestern Europeans, and later the immigrants from Southern and Eastern Europe, merged with the mainstream of American society, they contend, so too will the blacks. It is only a matter of time and perseverance. But blacks in their long history in Philadelphia were never like other immigrants in terms of either occupation or residence. Few managed to secure jobs in manufacturing, despite proximity. Those who did work in manufacturing did not live close to other workers in the same industry, as was the case with white workers. Thus, even when the city contained a great many manufacturing jobs with which to employ low- and semiskilled labor, blacks were not integrated into the mainstream of immigrant laborers. Their situation is much more difficult today when blacks find themselves residing in the central areas of large cities that are rapidly losing their concentration of manufacturing jobs.[33]

Finally, the findings suggest that urban neighborhoods are not simply the product of either the abstract, natural laws put forth by the classical ecologists or the desire of people with a common cultural heritage to live close to one another. Rather the social composition of neighborhoods is linked to decisions made in the local, regional, and national economies that determine the location of industries. The present study suggests this to be true in the nineteenth century; others have presented evidence of this in contemporary settings.[34] One of the fundamental decisions in our society, affecting a whole host of social relationships, including neighborhood composition, is the type and location of investment made by private enterprise. While this is not the only factor influencing community composition, it is a fundamental one and too often ignored by urban scholars.

NOTES

1. Robert E. Park, Ernest W. Burgess, Roderick D. McKenzie, *The City* (Chicago, 1925); Louis Wirth, *The Ghetto* (Chicago, 1928).

2. Edward E. Pratt, *Industrial Causes of Congestion of Population in New York City* (New York, 1911).

3. Otis D. Duncan and Stanley Lieberson, "Ethnic Segregation and Assimilation," *American Journal of Sociology* 64 (1959), 364–74; Avery Guest and James A. Weed, "Ethnic Residential Segregation: Patterns of Change," *American Journal of Sociology* 81 (1976), 1088–1111; Stanley Lieberson, *Ethnic Patterns in American Cities* (New York, 1963); Karl Taeuber and Alma Taeuber, *Negroes in Cities* (Chicago, 1972).

4. David Ward, *Cities and Immigrants* (New York, 1971); Sam Bass Warner, Jr., and Colin B. Burke, "Cultural Change and the Ghetto," *Journal of Contemporary History* 4 (1969), 173–87; W. L. Yancey, E. P. Ericksen, and R. N. Juliani, "Emergent Ethnicity: A Review and Reformulation," *American Sociological Review* 41 (1976), 391–403.

5. W. L. Yancey et al., "Emergent Ethnicity," *op. cit.*

6. Alan N. Burstein, "Residential Distribution and Mobility of Irish and German Immigrants in Philadelphia, 1850–1880" (Ph.D. dissertation, Demography, University of Pennsylvania, 1975); Howard P. Chudacoff, *Mobile Americans: Residential and Social Mobility in Omaha, 1880–1920* (New York, 1972); Ian Davey and Michael Doucet, "The Social Geography of a Commercial City, ca. 1853," Appendix 1 in

Michael B. Katz, *The People of Hamilton, Canada West* (Cambridge, Mass., 1975), 319–42; Clyde Griffen, "Workers Divided: The Effect of Craft and Ethnic Differences in Poughkeepsie, New York, 1850–1880," in Stephan Thernstrom and Richard Sennett, eds., *Nineteenth-Century Cities* (New Haven, Ct., 1969), 49–97; Peter R. Knights, *The Plain People of Boston, 1830–1860: A Study in City Growth* (New York, 1971); Sam Bass Warner, Jr., *The Private City* (Philadelphia, 1968); S. B. Warner and C. B. Burke, "Cultural Change and the Ghetto," *op. cit.*

7. Wendell Bell and Maryanne Force, "Urban Neighborhood Types and Participation in Formal Associations," *American Sociological Review* 21 (1965), 25–34; J.H.S. Bossard, "Residential Propinquity as a Factor in Marriage Selection," *American Journal of Sociology* 38 (1933), 219–24; T. Caplow and R. Forman, "Neighborhood Interaction in a Homogeneous Community," *American Sociological Review* 5 (1950), 357–67; William H. Michelson, *Man and His Urban Environment: A Sociological Approach* (Reading, Mass., 1976); Michael Young and Peter Willmott, *Family and Kinship in East London* (London, 1957); Elizabeth Bott, *Family and Social Network* (London, 1957).

8. E. P. Ericksen and W. L. Yancey, "Using Connections: Antecedents and Consequences of Personal Networks in the City," paper presented at the Annual Meetings of the American Sociological Association (New York, 1976); Mark S. Granovetter, "The Strength of Weak Ties," *American Journal of Sociology* 78 (1973), 1360–80.

9. For a more detailed discussion of the data sources, see S. W. Greenberg, "Industrialization in Philadelphia," *op. cit.;* and Theodore Hershberg, guest editor, "A Special Issue: The Philadelphia Social History Project," *Historical Methods Newsletter* 9 (March–June, 1976). (Also see Appendix II.)

10. E. P. Ericksen, "The Location of Manufacturing Jobs in a City: Changes in the Pattern, 1927–1972," manuscript, Department of Sociology, Temple University (1976).

11. E. P. Ericksen and W. L. Yancey, "The Organization of Residence in an Industrial City," manuscript, Department of Sociology, Temple University (1976).

12. A. N. Burstein, "Residential Distribution and Mobility," *op. cit.*

13. The "Journey-to-Work" essay, which utilizes the employee list of one firm along with several indirect measures of the work trip, also suggests that workers clustered around the places in which they worked or were likely to work, although there were some differences by economic status and industry. See T. Hershberg, Harold Cox, Dale Light, Jr., and Richard Greenfield, "The 'Journey-to-Work': An Empirical Investigation of Work, Residence and Transportation, Philadelphia, 1850 and 1880"; in this volume.

14. That the accessibility of jobs to workers seems to be more important in 1880 than in the early twentieth century can be inferred from the fact that the ratios observed in the former year are generally higher than those in a comparable study of Philadelphia in 1930. See E. P. Ericksen and W. L. Yancey, "The Organization of Residence," *op. cit.,* for the 1930 analysis. Ericksen and Yancey used the same measure of job accessibility and the same areal units as are used in the present study, basing their analysis on data from the 1930 population census and the 1928 Pennsylvania Industrial Directory. They calculated the job access ratio for eleven industries. The highest ratio they found was 2.80, for auto workers, and all but four industries had ratios below 1.50.

15. S. W. Greenberg, "Industrialization in Philadelphia," *op. cit.*

16. See the "Journey-to-Work" essay for a discussion of the expansion of the central business district. T. Hershberg *et al.,* " 'Journey-To-Work,' " *op. cit.*

17. It is impossible to measure total job density, since there are no data on the location of wholesale, retail, or service jobs.

18. W. L. Yancey and E. P. Ericksen, "The Industrial Causes of Ethnic Segregation, Philadelphia, 1910–1970," paper presented at the Annual Meetings of the American Sociological Association (New York, 1976); T. Hershberg, A. N. Burstein, E. P. Ericksen, S. W. Greenberg, W. L. Yancey, "A Tale of Three Cities: Blacks and Immigrants in Philadelphia, 1850–1880, 1930 and 1970," *The Annals* 441 (January 1979); also in this volume.

19. O. D. Duncan and S. Lieberson, "Ethnic Segregation and Assimilation," *op. cit.*; S. Lieberson, *Ethnic Patterns in American Cities, op. cit.*

20. W. L. Yancey *et al.*, "Emergent Ethnicity," *op. cit.*; T. Hershberg *et al.*, "A Tale of Three Cities," *op. cit.*

21. S. W. Greenberg, "Industrialization in Philadelphia," *op. cit.*

22. It remains true, however, that the levels of segregation experienced by blacks were considerably higher after 1945 and that the degree of dominance blacks achieved has increased steadily since 1850. See T. Hershberg *et al.*, "Tale of Three Cities," *op. cit.*

23. A. N. Burstein, "Residential Distribution and Mobility," *op. cit.*

24. Beverly Duncan and Otis D. Duncan, "The Measurement of Intra-City Locational and Residential Patterns," *Journal of Regional Science* 2 (1960), 37–54; Seymour Spilerman and Jack Habib, "Development Towns in Israel: The Role of Community in Creating Ethnic Disparities in Labor Force Characteristics." *American Journal of Sociology* 81 (1976), 781–812; Karl Taeuber, "Residential Segregation," *Scientific American* 213 (1965), 12–19.

25. The measures of segregation, clustering, and density calculated by Burstein for Irish and German immigrants using as the areal unit the PSHP grid (one block by one and a quarter) differ only slightly from those (based on the 1930 census tract) in the present study of manufacturing workers. This indicates that even though larger and nonuniform areal units are used here, there is no substantial masking of intra-tract differences.

26. It is interesting to note briefly the differences in industrial composition between the first and second generations of the two foreign-born ethnic groups. The sons of both the Irish and German immigrants had a much smaller representation in the skilled hand trades than did their fathers. Irish handloom weavers traditionally dominated the carpet industry in Philadelphia, and the Germans were well known for their skill in cabinetmaking, brewing, baking, and shoemaking. But skilled craftsmen operating small shops were increasingly supplanted by large factories requiring semi- and unskilled labor, and many of the traditional craft industries actually left Philadelphia after this conversion. As this occurred, the second generation began to search for greater opportunities for advancement in other industries. Such rapidly growing industries as building materials, metals, and printing and publishing may have provided the answer for the second generation. This transition between the first and second generations represented a greater departure from past traditions for the Germans than for the Irish, since the latter were found in very few of the skilled trades to begin with. See Bruce Laurie, Theodore Hershberg, and George Alter, "Immigrants and Industry: The Philadelphia Experience, 1850–1880," *Journal of Social History* 9 (1975), 219–48; also in this volume.

27. S. Lieberson, *Ethnic Patterns in American Cities, op. cit.*

28. W. L. Yancey *et al.*, "Emergent Ethnicity," *op. cit.*

29. Caroline Golab, "The Immigrant and the City: Poles, Italians, and Jews in Philadelphia, 1870–1920," in Allen F. Davis and Mark H. Haller, eds., *The Peoples of Philadelphia* (Philadelphia, 1973), 203–30.

30. On the level of the individual, it may well have been that a newly arrived immigrant with a given set of skills was helped in obtaining employment in an industry requiring those skills by friends, relatives, and the like who had lived in the

city for some time. This information network was likely to be based on common ethnicity. Here, ethnicity became a tool which the individual had at his or her disposal in transferring from the occupational structure of the country of origin to the occupational structure of the adopted country. In this sense, ethnicity would reinforce the effects of industrial affiliation in determining residence and would function within the overall necessity of living close to work. See Bruce Laurie and Mark Schmitz, "Manufacture and Productivity: The Making of an Industrial Base, Philadelphia, 1850–1880"; in this volume.

31. Timothy Cook and Andrew Pollott, "A Fronting Block Analysis of the Residential Patterns of Late Nineteenth-Century Philadelphians: Morocco Workers, 1880," unpublished manuscript in possession of the Philadelphia Social History Project (Spring 1975); T. Hershberg *et al.,* "The Journey-to-Work," *op. cit.*

32. W. L. Yancey, personal communication.

33. See T. Hershberg *et al.,* "A Tale of Three Cities," *op. cit.*

34. David Harvey, *Social Justice and the City* (London, 1973); John R. Logan, "Industrialization and the Stratification of Cities in Suburban Regions," *American Journal of Sociology* 83 (1976), 333–48; Harvey Molotch, "The City as a Growth Machine: Toward a Political Economy of Place," *American Journal of Sociology* 82 (1976), 309-32; S. Spilerman and J. Habib, "Development Towns in Israel," *op. cit.*

Appendix Table 1. Index of Dissimilarity Between Pairs of Ethnic-Industrial Groups in Eleven Major Industries, Philadelphia, 1880

Index of Dissimilarity Between Pairs of Ethnic-Industrial Groups Within Same Industry

Apparel

	Germans	Natives
Irish	58.6	69.4
Germans		58.7

Boots and Shoes

	Irish	Germans	Natives
Blacks	65.1	72.7	76.3
Irish		55.2	52.4
Germans			40.8

Carpets

	Germans	Natives
Irish	33.5	68.5
Germans		65.6

Construction

	Irish	Germans	Natives
Blacks	62.2	68.2	60.7
Irish		49.9	43.0
Germans			39.4

Cotton Goods

	Germans	Natives
Irish	71.7	60.1
Germans		78.8

Leather

	Germans	Natives
Irish	33.7	55.8
Germans		54.9

Machinery

	Irish	Germans	Natives
Blacks	85.2	83.5	82.2
Irish		52.6	45.1
Germans			44.7

Printing and Publishing

	Irish	Germans	Natives
Blacks	74.5	78.1	80.3
Irish		58.1	44.7
Germans			47.5

Ships

	Germans	Natives
Irish	79.1	56.3
Germans		79.5

Stone, Clay, and Glass

	Irish	Germans	Natives
Blacks	67.1	69.5	65.5
Irish		52.1	54.4
Germans			53.7

Woolen Goods

	Germans	Natives
Irish	63.8	68.3
Germans		67.2

Index of Dissimilarity Between Pairs of Ethnic-Industrial Groups Within Same Ethnic Group

Blacks

	Printing	Construction	Machinery	Stone, etc.
Boots, shoes	55.6	35.8	53.5	47.8
Printing		55.6	66.2	62.9
Construction			54.2	39.3
Machinery				61.4

Irish

	Apparel	Printing	Leather	Wool	Cotton	Carpets	Constr.	Ships	Machines	Stone, etc.
Boots	50.9	35.5	74.9	80.9	61.5	77.6	35.2	63.1	45.9	50.3
Apparel		62.8	73.6	83.5	69.5	67.1	59.1	72.4	59.3	60.3
Printing			79.1	82.5	71.5	81.6	43.6	65.4	51.6	55.3
Leather				81.5	80.5	68.6	72.1	85.4	72.5	74.4
Wool					62.8	73.9	74.8	91.5	76.3	75.4
Cotton						72.0	57.4	82.1	60.2	62.8
Carpets							72.5	80.3	73.7	69.9
Constr.								70.3	34.8	36.0
Ships									67.5	72.3
Machines										46.1

Germans

	Apparel	Printing	Leather	Wool	Cotton	Carpets	Constr.	Ships	Machines	Stone, etc.
Boots	34.2	31.2	49.6	69.3	77.7	63.7	32.5	78.2	35.9	51.5
Apparel		37.3	49.3	72.0	81.8	72.3	44.0	80.3	43.8	60.0
Printing			58.7	73.1	81.0	72.0	41.4	81.4	48.5	53.6
Leather				69.0	82.3	66.2	57.0	91.4	53.5	70.4
Wool					63.0	61.0	62.0	93.5	64.5	68.1
Cotton						83.1	78.2	90.5	76.1	80.8
Carpets							60.5	77.1	62.1	55.0
Constr.								80.6	31.5	47.6
Ships									81.0	72.9
Machines										53.2

Native Whites

	Apparel	Printing	Leather	Wool	Cotton	Carpets	Constr.	Ships	Machines	Stone, etc.
Boots	43.1	43.5	59.6	90.4	83.6	74.4	40.6	66.7	42.2	52.3
Apparel		50.8	67.6	87.3	80.9	76.5	49.6	73.1	51.0	59.3
Printing			72.0	89.3	82.8	84.0	35.6	71.2	41.0	54.4
Leather				96.2	89.2	79.8	70.0	64.6	68.2	72.9
Wool					76.2	93.2	84.6	95.8	86.3	84.2
Cotton						87.0	78.6	93.1	79.2	83.9
Carpets							77.0	90.1	77.6	78.4
Constr.								68.2	31.2	43.5
Ships									65.7	71.8
Machines										43.5

1. Table is based on adult males.

2. The two generations of Irish and Germans are combined; see Table 3 for definition of ethnic groups.

3. See Table 3 for definition of Index of Dissimilarity.

Source: See Table 3.

Appendix Table 2.   Ethnic Composition of Forty-Five Industries, Philadelphia, 1880

Industry	Blacks	Irish 1	Irish 2	Ger. 1	Ger. 2	Native Whites	Total
Apparel	0.6%	9.4%	8.9%	17.3%	10.1%	50.3%	1,611
Baking	0.3	7.0	2.1	58.6	18.0	10.0	2,957
Beverages (brewed)	0.2	10.5	2.1	67.9	8.6	9.6	842
Blacksmith	0.3	29.1	16.7	12.4	5.7	32.5	3,015
Boots, shoes	1.3	21.8	7.8	30.3	7.1	28.8	6,880
Brass	0.0	7.1	16.4	7.5	9.9	52.6	548
Carpets	0.5	42.0	21.7	15.4	4.0	10.1	2,948
Chemicals	2.0	16.7	10.3	21.0	14.6	28.4	1,046
Confection	0.6	4.1	3.5	34.7	18.6	31.4	773
Construction	1.3	12.1	11.4	5.6	4.5	58.1	17,777
Copper, other metals	0.0	15.4	7.3	15.0	22.0	29.3	246
Cotton goods	0.2	18.8	22.5	11.7	5.9	23.1	1,677
Dyeing of textiles	0.3	19.2	24.7	17.4	3.9	22.3	1,168
Food, NEC	1.8	11.5	8.7	11.3	5.8	54.1	931
Furniture	1.3	4.2	6.2	30.8	9.7	41.9	3,628
Hardware, fab. metal	0.1	8.2	16.4	13.8	7.3	46.9	2,091
Harnesses, saddles	0.8	17.1	5.8	16.8	5.8	45.0	620
Hosiery, knits	0.0	7.2	24.0	8.0	9.9	25.4	637
Instruments	0.0	2.5	8.3	21.9	24.9	34.2	869
Iron, steel	0.3	20.3	16.5	5.6	6.7	43.0	3,644
Leather	0.5	19.8	12.7	22.2	18.4	21.5	2,052
Locomotives	0.0	11.8	0.0	0.0	0.0	52.9	51
Lumber, wood prods.	0.6	10.5	13.5	14.9	8.6	45.3	4,267
Machinery	0.5	11.7	11.4	10.3	5.5	51.4	6,532
Meat	0.8	3.6	5.6	29.6	14.5	41.3	3,357
Misc. textiles	0.0	25.4	21.6	13.1	7.0	23.0	3,090
Paper	0.3	23.3	10.7	5.8	1.5	50.3	591
Paper boxes	0.0	3.4	7.6	12.7	22.9	45.8	118
Petroleum refining	1.4	14.4	8.3	5.1	12.5	54.2	216
Precious metals	0.1	4.2	8.2	14.5	16.5	43.1	1,420
Printing, publishing	0.5	4.5	14.2	6.1	8.3	55.5	5,012
Railroad cars	0.0	15.3	18.9	4.2	0.0	52.1	190
Rope, twine	0.0	8.6	11.6	14.2	11.6	46.4	233
Ships	0.3	6.4	9.1	2.4	3.3	71.2	1,089
Shirts	0.0	5.6	13.7	16.8	13.7	36.5	197
Silk	0.5	4.1	4.1	45.6	8.3	20.7	217
Stone, clay, glass	6.4	16.9	25.5	7.1	4.2	35.2	4,450
Stoves, boilers	0.3	24.9	13.9	10.3	8.9	32.7	907
Sugar refining	0.9	24.7	3.8	55.3	3.8	7.7	235
Tailor	0.9	15.7	1.9	51.9	8.7	17.5	3,294
Tin	0.0	8.6	24.2	11.6	5.0	42.0	1,263
Tobacco products	0.7	2.4	8.0	18.7	20.1	41.9	2,150
Tools	0.0	6.9	4.4	8.3	9.9	57.3	817
Woolen goods	0.1	18.2	18.5	7.6	4.8	31.7	1,507
Miscellaneous	0.5	8.5	13.0	14.0	9.9	46.8	3,538
Total	1.0	13.7	12.4	16.8	8.1	40.7	100,701

1. The percentages do not add to 100 because of the small number of native-born whites of non-Irish or non-German foreign parentage that are not included as a separate ethnic group.

2. See Table 3 for definition of ethnic groups.

Source: See Table 3.

PART III

FAMILY

The last decade witnessed a virtual revolution in the writing of American family history. In his 1962 Presidential Address to the American Historical Association, Carl Bridenbaugh characterized family history as a "neglected field," and a 1969 survey of the literature lamented that these circumstances "had not altered."[1] Yet today research in all aspects of family history is booming. New learned journals are devoted to the subject, scholarly conferences abound, and scores of books, articles, and doctoral dissertations have appeared. The sources of this explosion in interest are multiple. Among the most salient are the issues raised by the feminist movement, the vicissitudes of the contemporary family, concern with social justice, debates over modernization theory, and developments in the social sciences. Given the diverse motives for the research it is not surprising that no theoretical, conceptual, or methodological consensus unites the field. Like other branches of the "new" history, however, the emerging literature focuses on the experience of all families, especially the masses of ordinary families, not merely those of the rich and powerful, and is concerned with such basic human realities as birth and child rearing, marriage and kinship, work and play, aging and death.

The family deserves its recent popularity and centrality in the new historical research. "The ultimate theoretical question," according to Charles Rosenberg, involves "the relationship between change in social structure, ideological change, and the tendency of intra-familial roles and functions to reshape themselves in consistency with such changes."[2] The degree to which this relationship is reciprocal—that the family not only responds to but influences external forces—is open to question. Perhaps it is appropriate to agree with the observation of Christopher Lasch that the family is "the missing link between cultural and intellectual history on the one hand, and politico-economic history on the other; between the study of culture and the study of social structure, production and power."[3]

Although the three essays that follow were not prepared as a unit, they are closely related. They move modestly toward understanding the pivotal role played by the family. They see the family mediating between external forces and internal roles and experience. Operating within the structure of opportunities afforded by the larger urban economy, the family determined who worked, who stayed at home, and who went to school. The first two essays, set in 1880 Philadelphia, examine the familial circumstances in which such critical decisions were made; they make clear that the starting point was the family, for it—rather than the individual person—was the essential decision-making unit. The third essay, ranging over a century, compares the ways in which the life-course was organized and how "growing up" differed in the vastly altered social, economic, normative, and institutional conditions of 1880 and 1970.

Much of the initial research in the new family history was concerned with the notion advanced by Talcott Parsons and other sociologists that the nuclear family emerged as a response to industrialization's need for small, mobile, emotionally bonded familial units. The search for evidence to date the decline of the extended family led to a cross-sectional, static research design that focused on household structure and composition. The results of this research make clear that the nuclear family existed in the West long before the onset of industrialization. Although some research continues along these lines, most students of the family understand the theoretical and practical limitations of this approach and have moved toward "a developmental rather than a static perspective." More recent studies in family history, therefore, have examined generational experience and used family-cycle models and life-course perspectives.[4]

The three essays in this section are characteristic of these more recent developments, not only in their focus on the experience of the inarticulate, but in their use of innovative conceptual, methodological, and statistical approaches. They move well beyond the cross-sectional to examine how the family life-cycle affected consumption and income; how a "family strategy" perspective provides a better analytic framework to understand a host of family behaviors; and how a life-course approach can highlight changes in the transition to adulthood over a century.

The first essay, "Poverty, Economic Stress and the Family," by economic historian Michael Haines, has three objectives: to derive a poverty measure based on actual behavior rather than normative judgments; to assess the effects that family demographic and life-cycle variations had on household income and consumption; and to determine the behavioral response (labor force participation and boarding) to conditions of "economic stress" (identified as "shortfall" between family expenditures and the income of the family head).

Haines introduces a wholly new approach to the subject of poverty. He begins by building upon the careful studies of previous scholars to determine basic "cost of living" budgets.[5] These identified the composition of the period's typical family, estimated the family's consumption requirements, calculated family income and determined whether adequate income was available to meet basic family needs. Haines points out that these earlier efforts involve too much normative judgment. They are based more on what people should have consumed than on what they did consume; on what they might have earned rather than on what they did earn. Moreover, because such studies are cross-sectional rather than longitudinal in approach, they have difficulty in dealing with life-cycle effects on family consumption and family income. Not only is consumption affected by income, but both depend upon family composition, and composition, in turn, depends upon stage in the family's life-cycle.

To identify families in poverty Haines turns to the budget studies of working-class families done in 1889–90 by Carroll Wright, U.S. Commissioner of Labor. To determine family income, he uses the actual age-earning profiles of individual occupations; to determine family consumption, he uses actual expenditures among these families. These income and consumption profiles are then applied to a sample of white working-class families in 1880 Philadelphia.

The major behavioral response of families to economic stress was the provision of additional labor, almost entirely by their children; poorer families sent their children to work with greater frequency. White married women rarely worked for wages outside the home, a response that varied little with economic circumstances. Poorer families did not take in boarders and lodgers in large numbers. Demographic and life-cycle variations influenced consumption and income in significant ways. Children were the source both of the "problem"—in their consumption needs—and the "solution"—in their income contributions. The farm was not the only setting where children proved to be a family economic asset. Finally, if poverty is measured by a behavioral response such as child labor, no sharp "cut-off" line can be identified; quite the opposite—a smooth continuum of labor force participation emerged instead.

The second essay, "Family Strategies and the Family Economy: the

Role of Secondary Workers," by economic historian Claudia Goldin, be-gins where Haines leaves off. Goldin explores the determinants of labor force participation—those particular conditions that affected the work be-havior of wives and children among native-white, immigrant, and black households in 1880 Philadelphia.

The determination of who worked, who stayed at home, and who went to school depended not only upon the characteristics of each individual (age, sex, race, literacy, etc.), but upon the characteristics of his or her household (size, stage in family cycle, composition, birth order of siblings, etc.). The number of possible ways in which these individual and house-hold characteristics combined to influence labor force participation were vast. The labor force experience of individuals with identical personal characteristics depended upon both sets of variables. In Table 5 of her essay, Goldin provides an excellent example of the problem's complexity. She employs a multi-variate regression technique for dichotomous de-pendent variables (probit) to explore the determinants of labor force participation.

Her findings are many and important. Perhaps the most striking among them concerns the functioning of the household as a unit. Although the likelihood of a child to enter the labor force was similarly affected by in-come earned through the efforts of an uncle or boarder as by his or her father, it is the compositional rather than the purely economic factors which emerge most significantly. Child labor force participation, in other words, was more responsive to the complex composition of the household —for example, the presence and sex of younger or older siblings and non-nuclear family members—than to income. This "substitutability" among children, as economists refer to it, was a central feature of the late-nine-teenth-century family.

Immigrant and native-white families had different child labor force participation rates. Explanations for the differences among white families tell us a good deal about the meaning of ethnicity in the late nineteenth-century city. The work and school behavior of Irish, German, and native-white boys was different, to be sure, but the reasons why are rooted not in cultural differences—attitudes about work and school embedded in an ethnic culture—but in structural differences which distinguished the groups. When the economic, demographic, and educational characteristics of their households were controlled, the behavioral differences among boys disappeared. This was not the case for immigrant girls. Even when these factors were held constant, immigrant and native-born girls still be-haved differently. It is fascinating to observe, however, that when the work behavior of native-born daughters of immigrant parents was compared to that of native-born daughters of native parents, the differences were eliminated. One dimension of assimilation, as Goldin speculates, was withholding daughters from the labor force.

The differences between black and white families were far more striking than those found among immigrant and native-white families. Their family structures and the labor force behavior of women and children were different: the subtenanting of unrelated persons was far more common; blacks had far lower child-woman ratios; their children, especially their daughters, left home earlier; they had far more female-headed families; black women, widows in particular, were found in the labor force far more often than white women. Black family strategies were different as well: the characteristics of a mother played a more important and different role; children responded differently to sibling age hierarchy (in which older children worked and younger ones stayed at home or went to school); women and children reacted differently to the wage rate and unemployment of husbands and fathers. In other words, even when the internal characteristics of their families were similar to those of whites, black families appeared to be following a different set of rules. This suggests a very different world view. The opportunities generated by industrialization were not equally available to all Philadelphians. When black families observed the city and the narrow range of options available to them, they apparently behaved differently, creating short- and long-run family strategies very much unlike those of whites.

The third essay in this section is "Social Change and Transitions to Adulthood in Historical Perspective" by historians John Modell and Theodore Hershberg and sociologist Frank F. Furstenberg, Jr. The life-course approach is a powerful tool for historical analysis, for, as Glen Elder writes, it "brings sensitivity to the continual interchange between the family and other institutional sectors, to the interdependence of individual life history and family history, and to the impact of historical change in life patterns."[6]

The authors provide a new method for analyzing the development of the life course. Five statuses in the transition from childhood to adulthood were studied. Two are "nonfamilial"—leaving school and entering the labor force. Three are "familial"—leaving home, getting married, and becoming a household head. Five measures to study changes in these statuses were constructed: prevalence, timing, spread, age-congruity, and integration. The evidence indicates that there has been a substantial change in the pattern of the transition to adulthood over the last century: a more rigidly defined life course has replaced the broad latitude of choice which characterized growing up in the nineteenth century; prevalence has increased for most transitions; spread has narrowed; the moving together of nonfamilial and familial statuses due to changes in timing has created a considerable overlap in status spreads.

Because most urban families in nineteenth-century America were able to operate within a margin of comfort only to the degree that they could count on a steady contribution from their laboring children of both sexes, children deferred marriage and remained at home to support their families at the later stages in the family life cycle when economic stress was most acute: the median age of marriage in 1880 for men was twenty-six; in 1970 it was twenty-two.[7] In 1880, "everybody" entered the labor force before getting married; today there is much overlap in statuses. Contemporary cohorts are far more likely to face serious and more irreversible decisions about sequencing and combining statuses. "Growing up" today, as the authors contend, "has become briefer, more normful, bounded and consequential—and thereby more demanding on the individual participants."

These essays offer a new perspective on the massive entry of women into the post-1950 labor market. Using a variety of poverty measures, Steven Dubnoff has argued that the wages paid to the typical blue-collar worker in the U.S. were not sufficient to support his wife and family until the 1920s or 1940.[8] The response of American families well into the twentieth century was to send children—not wives—into the labor force. Less than 4 percent of married women in 1880 Philadelphia worked, and the income shortfall was made up largely through the money earned by working children.

Working wives today have assumed the role played by children during the last century. The 1950s can thus be understood as the momentary fulfillment of a major aspect of the American Dream: a single income capable of supporting a spouse and children. Such a perspective permits us to see that the egalitarian aspects associated with the mass entry of women into the contemporary work force mask what is equally significant: the clear erosion of economic progress as a minimum standard of family living once again requires the income of more than one breadwinner.

NOTES

1. Carl Bridenbaugh's address, "The Great Mutation," appears in the *American Historical Review* 68 (January 1963); Edward N. Saveth, "The Problem of American Family History," *American Quarterly* 21 (Summer 1969), 311.

2. "Introduction: History and Experience," Charles Rosenberg, ed., *The Family in History* (Philadelphia: University of Pennsylvania Press, 1975), 11.

3. Christopher Lasch, "The Family in History," *New York Review of Books* 22 (November 13, 1975), 33.

4. Maris Vinovskis, "From Household Size to Life Course: Some Observations on Recent Trends in Family History," *American Behavioral Scientist* 21 (November 1977), 264; Lutz Berkner, "The Use and Misuse of Census Data for the Historical Analysis of Family Structure," *Journal of Interdisciplinary History* 4 (Spring 1975), 721–38; Peter Laslett, *Household and Family in Past Time* (Cambridge, England: Cambridge University Press, 1972); and "Characteristics of the Western Family Considered Over Time," *Journal of Family History* 2 (Summer 1977), 89–115.

5. Eudice Glassberg, "Work, Wages, and the Cost of Living: Ethnic Differences and the Poverty Line, Philadelphia, 1880," *Pennsylvania History* 66 (January 1979), 17–58, is an especially useful effort done at the PSHP.

6. Glen Elder, Jr., "Family History and Life Course," *Journal of Family History* 2 (Winter 1977); and "Approaches to Social Change and the Family," in John Demos and Sarane Spence Boocock, eds., *Turning Points: Historical and Sociological Essays on the Family, American Journal of Sociology* 84 (Supplement, 1978); and Tamara K. Hareven, ed., *Family Transitions in the Life Course in Historical Perspective* (New York: Academic Press, 1979).

7. John Modell, Frank F. Furstenberg, Jr., and Douglas Strong, "The Timing of Marriage in the Transition to Adulthood: The Continuity of Change, 1860–1975," in Demos and Boocock, eds., *Turning Points, op. cit.*

8. Steven Dubnoff, "Long Term Trends in the Adequacy of Individual Incomes in the United States, 1860–1974," paper presented at Social Science History Association (Columbus, Ohio: 1978).

7. Poverty, Economic Stress, and the Family in a Late Nineteenth-Century American City: Whites in Philadelphia, 1880

MICHAEL R. HAINES

Introduction

Poverty is neither a new problem nor one that has been ignored histori- cally. It has been argued that the Mercantilists of seventeenth- and eigh- teenth-century England were fundamentally concerned with alleviating unemployment and reducing poverty.[1] Early studies of consumer behavior were often motivated, in part, by concern for the poor,[2] and the first Brit- ish census, taken in 1801, appears to have been related to measuring the extent of poverty in that country.[3]

Nineteenth-century United States citizens inherited a tradition of con- cern about the poor from their English forebears.[4] At that time relief activities were almost exclusively confined to action by state and local gov- ernment, or to private philanthropy, but interest and investigation did con- tinue under various auspices. Carroll D. Wright, one of America's greatest empirical statisticians, undertook a pathbreaking study of Massachusetts's working-class budgets in 1875 in order to investigate the apparent declin- ing condition of workers and to discover the adequacy of wages.[5] By the late nineteenth century, although the United States had made considerable progress toward industrial development and higher per capita incomes, the fact of poverty was still highly visible.[6]

Today contemporary social scientists and policymakers are dealing with

The author wishes to thank Claudia Goldin for providing the Philadelphia wage data, an accurate 1880 Philadelphia family file, and extensive criticisms. Helpful criticisms were also furnished by Theodore Hershberg, Michael Katz, Stanley Enger- man, Mark Stern, John Modell, Jeff Seaman, Henry Williams, Gretchen Condran, and Elaine Allen. Able research assistance was given by Michael Strong.

the tantalizing prospect that economic and social developments may offer the means for alleviating or even eliminating poverty. It is essential for the realization of this goal, however, to begin with a functional definition of the problem: the description must be insightful and distinct and the phenomena susceptible to measurement. By combining techniques of statistical analysis with computerized data currently available, a more accurate and perceptive analytical picture should be produced. This paper addresses the issues of the measurement and nature of poverty, relying predominantly on observed behavior to achieve empirically rather than normatively derived judgments.

Location and the Problem of Measurement

Late nineteenth-century Philadelphia provides an excellent focus for the study of poverty and economic distress; it was the second largest urban area in the United States in 1880, one of the early centers of industrialization and immigration,[7] and had an extensive and ethnically varied city-dwelling workforce. Philadelphians experienced the urban and industrial revolutions of that period with the concomitant exacerbation of the magnitude, if not the relative amount, of economic stress on wage earners.[8] The data base of the Philadelphia Social History Project affords the opportunity to make a detailed evaluation of economic position at the family level using samples of the enumerators' schedules from the 1880 census.

One standard method for the measurement of poverty has been to estimate a "minimum" budget for a family of some fixed composition in order to establish a "poverty line."[9] This is the approach adopted by Glassberg in her recent study of poverty in late nineteenth-century Philadelphia. It was also used by the Social Security Administration in its early efforts to calculate a poverty "threshold" in the mid-1960s.[10] This approach seeks some absolute standard of poverty, adjusted for price changes and possibly for changes in the market basket of goods and services used for the basic budget, but it is rather restrictive.

Glassberg, for example, surveyed much of the available price and budget information and attempted to compute such a poverty line for a "typical" family: father, mother, boys aged ten and four, and a daughter aged six. The result was a poverty budget of $643.[11] A similar result of approximately $600 was reported by Carroll Wright for Massachusetts in 1875.[12] These budgets, however carefully derived, do not allow for variation in family composition and reflect a great deal of normative judgment about what constitutes an "adequate" standard of living.

The Social Security Administration has modified its method to allow for demographic variation by providing a "look-up" table that provides poverty lines for families of different types and sizes.[13] The calculation is still rather arbitrary, however, in that it computes a minimum food budget for families of differing sizes and compositions and then multiplies this value by three, on the assumption that approximately one-third of a "poverty" budget is spent on food.[14]

Another common approach to the measurement of poverty is that which discusses relative (as opposed to absolute) poverty. Examples of this include summary measures of distribution of income or wealth, such as the Gini coefficient, coefficient of variation or variance of income and wealth, or the share of income or wealth received or held by the highest "x" percent (e.g., 5 percent) or the lowest "y" percent (e.g., 20 or 25 percent) of the population.[15] Current research in economic and social history has devoted some effort in this direction, calculating summary measures of inequality of income, wages, or wealth.[16] Other scholars have treated the problem of inequality through revision of our views on social stratification.[17] While the study of inequality has value in and of itself (e.g., as a means to study social structure), it solves only part of the problem of identifying poverty. In particular, although the share of the lowest group or groups may not improve relatively, the level of living may increase for all as growth occurs. Poverty may still exist in both an absolute material sense and a relative subjective one, but it becomes difficult to follow over time.

There is no "correct" way in which to assess poverty; absolute and relative types of measures embody many different sets of assumptions and highlight different aspects of the problem. An assessed level of poverty is frequently quite sensitive to the measure chosen. Steven Dubnoff, for example, found in surveying the period from 1890 to 1950 that the point at which a "typical" American family crossed the income adequacy threshold varied depending on the poverty measure used.[18]

In the attempt to work out an accurate and useful scheme for discovering minimum comfort levels, it has been show that demographic and life cycle variations in families make a notable difference in the total evaluation of economic position. As Morton Paglin has pointed out for the United States, inequality of income, as measured by the Gini coefficient, improves markedly when adjusted for life cycle stage.[19] More striking are the findings of Dubnoff which reveal that in the United States, since 1860, poverty has been significantly related both to family composition and the life cycle. The number and sex of family members bore significantly on economic position, and age was an even more complex factor. During the early and middle years of the family life cycle, when basic consumption needs were greatest, income was inadequate while resources were the most limited; children who were too young to work were not only consumers and non-contributors but might also require the attention of a potential wage earner. As children grew older and shared in income providing, their participation could relieve economic stress, but salaries for heads of families who had become older were then typically lower. Dubnoff's work also points to the potential biases (for an absolute measure of poverty) of excluding life cycle effects.[20]

One may logically conclude from the foregoing that it is frequently better to use fewer normative judgments and to adopt an approach that concentrates more on what people actually do when confronted with expenditure choices and a very restricted income.[21] Such an economic measure of poverty would focus on "the means for pursuit of happiness rather than happiness itself,"[22] and examine household or individual behavior when income and time constraints exist. It would stress the functioning unit—the family as an entity but with interacting changing elements—and consider its performance over time.

The purpose of this paper is to explore, in an historical context, the issues of identifying poverty, utilizing empirical findings on white, working-class families in 1880 Philadelphia. It is hoped that the behavioral approach used here, which stresses empirical evaluation rather than normative judgments, will add insight into our understanding of the phenomenon of poverty, and will overcome some of the shortcomings of the more normative, poverty line measurement. Incomes estimated from occupations, wages, and age of wage earner were used,[23] but an alternative could have been to work from occupational titles. The more elaborate estimation procedure was used because it was felt necessary to condense the diverse occupational categories into money income terms.

The focus was on actual behavior as an index of economic stress; this term was adopted in preference to poverty because it more accurately captures the concept of a constraint. Incomes were estimated for male heads of families in industrial employment taken from a sample of the Philadelphia census of 1880; these incomes were then compared to estimated "minimum adequacy" expenditures for the same families. Expenditures were estimated from budget data in an 1889/1890 survey conducted by Carroll D. Wright while he was U.S. Commissioner of Labor.[24] Income of the male family head was compared to expected "minimum adequacy" expenditures, dependent on the demographic composition of the family; and the behavior of families with a shortfall was compared to that of families with a surplus on the assumption that the differences in behavior would demonstrate the results of "economic stress." No attempt was made to estimate a "poverty threshold." The basic premise was that some families would feel economic stress, as defined by contemporary standards of behavior, and that the best means of measuring this was to see if the families took steps to alleviate the pressure placed upon them.

Findings revealed that the major behavioral response to financial inadequacy was the provision of additional labor, almost entirely by the children of the family. The fact that a family had children in the labor force was by no means a sure indicator of straightened circumstances, but poorer families sent their children to work with greater frequency.

This finding should not be wholly surprising. Working-class families in nineteenth-century American cities were faced by severe economic constraints.[25] With the exception of homes, which were often mortgaged, there was little wealth to furnish nonlabor income. Male heads of family were usually as fully employed as economic conditions would permit. For a variety of reasons, married women did not work in the wage labor market outside the home.[26] One way in which a wife might have contributed to family income without leaving the home was to take in boarders, but poorer families do not seem to have taken in boarders in large numbers, perhaps because they simply did not have the space to do so. Married women may have engaged in handicraft production in the home, but census data do not discriminate between work outside and inside the home. To the extent that work within the home was reported, it was classified here as market work. Overall, the provision of additional labor by children was virtually the only resource utilized by economically constrained families.

The Data

Two major data sources are used here. The first consists of a sample of households from the 1880 census for Philadelphia, taken by the Philadelphia Social History Project.[27] These samples comprise a random selection of 2,000 households headed by native white Americans, 2,000 households headed by Irish-born individuals, and 2,000 households headed by German-born individuals (see Appendix II).[28] A subfamily structure was imposed on each household by examining the individuals of each household by name, age, sex, marital status, relationship to head of household, place of birth, place of birth of parents, occupation, and order of enumeration. Subfamilies (which are called families here) were then separated out if there was a conjugal unit or the remains of a conjugal unit (e.g., a husband and wife, parent or parents and children) in the household.[29] In most cases, the household and family were identical, but enough extra families were discovered by this process to create a sample of 7,439 families from the original 6,000 households. This sample is the basic focus of analysis.

The second data set consists of a sample of 6,809 working-class families whose head labored in nine industries (pig iron, bar iron, steel, bituminous coal, coke, iron ore, cottons, woolens, and glass) from twenty-four states of the United States in 1889 and 1890.[30] The sample, based on a survey of selected "protected" industries in both the United States and Europe, was taken under the direction of Carroll D. Wright when he was United States Commissioner of Labor. Although the sampling procedures were not clarified, and it is uncertain if biases were introduced by selecting only families which were more responsive to being queried, the survey contains such a wealth of information (including the demographic characteristics of each family, the occupation, industry, ethnicity, and location of the head of family, and information about income, expenditures, and housing) that it was considered the most appropriate source of data.[31] This survey will be used, first to estimate age/earnings profiles for various occupations or occupational groups in order to assist in estimating incomes for male household heads in Philadelphia; and second, to estimate "minimum adequacy" budgets for the Philadelphia families in 1880.

Incomes and Expenditures among Philadelphia Families: 1880

Incomes were estimated for adult male family heads in selected occupations using wage data and information on age, occupation, and employment from the 1880 census samples of households headed by native-white Americans, Irish born, and German born. The occupations selected were almost entirely industrial and craft groups. The objective of this procedure was to compare income of the family head with estimated family consumption requirements and then to measure the shortfall and to assess its impact (i.e., "economic stress") on patterns of economic activity in the family. A major problem in using income as a variable in the study of nineteenth-century social and economic history is the lack of explicit census data. While questions on wealth were asked in the U.S. censuses of 1850, 1860, and 1870, no question on family income was asked until the census of 1940.[32] That is why the 1889/1890 U.S. Commissioner of Labor Survey, along with other data sources, had to be used to obtain income and wages.[33]

Table 1 presents age/earnings profiles for selected occupations in the form of indices (indexed to the mean income of the occupation)[34] calculated from the U.S. Commissioner of Labor Survey of 1889/90. There is

Table 1. Estimated Age/Earnings Profiles, Average Weekly Wages, Estimated & Actual Average Yearly Income, Selected Occupations: Philadelphia, 1880. (U.S. Commissioner of Labor Survey, 1889/1890.)

Occupation	Index for Age of Wage Earner						Average Weekly Wage (Dollars)	Estimated Yearly Income (Dollars)	Average Yearly Income 1889/90 (Dollars)
	10–19	20–29	30–39	40–49	50–59	60+			
1) Clerk	.700	.819	1.347	1.112	.589	.575	18	978	525
2) Carpenter	.800	1.316	1.174	.899	.850	.751	15	621	488
3) Blacksmith	.700	.952	1.077	1.018	.900	.861	14.5	742	599
4) Machinist	.700	.829	1.010	1.033	1.066	.937	15	738	671
5) Fireman	.700	.998	1.011	1.035	.803	.750	9.5	498	458
6) Stoker	.700	.998	1.011	1.035	.803	.750	9.5	470	—
7) Teamster	.700	1.357	1.123	.950	.930	.520	10	544	398
8) Driver	.700	.997	1.000	1.118	1.015	.720	9.5	500	390
9) Mason	.800	1.316	1.174	.899	.850	.751	21	878	541
10) Bricklayer	.800	1.316	1.174	.899	.850	.751	21	885	541
11) Laborer	.700	1.132	1.111	.988	.912	.844	7.3	336	341
12) Miner	.700	.958	1.016	1.044	1.034	.723	17	926	386
13) Puddler (Iron)	.600	.780	1.050	1.018	1.000	.848	19.6	993	758
14) Heater (Iron)	.600	.780	1.050	1.018	1.000	.848	20	1066	1180
15) Moulder (Iron)	.600	.780	1.050	1.018	1.000	.848	16	788	510
16) Roller (Iron)	.600	.780	1.050	1.018	1.000	.848	23	1255	1298
17) Blower (Glass)	.700	.931	1.036	1.003	.989	.843	18	920	994
18) Finisher	.700	1.196	1.235	1.017	.785	.718	16	886	536
19) Weaver (Textiles)	.600	1.000	1.065	.978	.930	.652	16	472	400
20) Spinner (Textiles)	.600	1.011	1.030	.980	.905	.718	10	552	461
21) Carder (Textiles)	.600	.986	1.093	.991	.897	.794	11.2	599	381
22) Watchman	.600	.957	.971	.986	1.084	.756	11	554	418

Occupation									
23) Guard	.600	.957	.971	.986	1.084	.756	11	524	—
24) Cutter (Glass)	.600	.933	1.046	1.088	.972	.778	15.5	784	995
25) Dresser (Textiles)	.600	.954	1.016	1.000	1.010	1.107	11	575	505
26) Dyer (Textiles)	.600	.860	1.098	.998	.975	.949	11	559	430
27) Packer	.600	.933	1.046	1.008	.972	.778	9.8	520	486
28) Sorter (Textiles)	.600	.862	1.048	1.067	.924	.808	11	550	608
29) Boxmaker	.600	.933	1.046	1.008	.972	.778	9	433	591
30) Foreman	.800	.992	1.003	1.009	.945	.900	23	1188	749
31) Engineer	.700	.867	1.034	1.092	1.002	.656	15.4	792	639
32) Spooler (Textiles)	.700	.986	1.093	.991	.897	.794	8	417	—
33) Trimmer	.700	.986	1.093	.991	.897	.794	14	704	—
34) Burner (Iron)	.600	.929	1.048	1.026	.978	.760	19.6	746	—
35) Smelter (Iron)	.600	.929	1.048	1.026	.978	.760	16	689	—
36) Forger (Iron)	.600	.929	1.048	1.026	.978	.760	17	933	—
37) Founder (Iron)	.600	.929	1.048	1.026	.978	.760	19	968	1027
38) Galvanizer	.600	.929	1.048	1.026	.978	.760	17	827	—
39) Gasman	.600	.929	1.048	1.026	.978	.760	16	862	644
40) Melter (Iron)	.600	.929	1.048	1.026	.978	.760	12	659	596
41) Plater	.600	.929	1.048	1.026	.978	.760	15	576	—
42) Refiner (Iron)	.600	.929	1.048	1.026	.978	.760	15	736	641
43) Caster (Iron)	.600	.929	1.048	1.026	.978	.760	19	1021	645
44) Miscellaneous Crafts	.700	.944	1.037	1.020	.950	.777	15	765	—

Source: Age/earnings profile indices and average annual yearly income 1889/90 calculated from data in U.S. Commissioner of Labor, *Sixth Annual Report* (1880), *Seventh Annual Report* (1890). Assumed average weekly wages were partly derived from data in the "Weeks Report" in, U.S. Bureau of the Census, *Tenth Census of the United States: 1880*, Vol. 20, "Report on the Statistics of Wages in the Manufacturing Industries with Supplementary Reports on the Average Retail Prices of Necessaries of Life and on Trades Societies, and Strikes and Lockouts," by Joseph O. Weeks (Washington, D.C.: U.S. G.P.O., 1886). Wages were taken as approximate averages in building trades and factory work. A full week of 5.6 days was assumed when the wages were given in wage per day (as was usual). When a wage was unavailable, it was assigned the value of a "next best" alternative.

Average estimated yearly income was calculated by methods described in the text.

ample contemporary evidence that earnings vary by age, and these 1889/90 survey data confirm that this was true in the late-nineteenth century.[85] The occupations listed in Table 1 were largely industrial operatives or craftsmen, most of whom were employed in factories or large establishments.

So, for example, carpenters and masons were not general construction workers but rather those employed by large industrial firms. The laborers were factory and industrial laborers and probably not common day laborers. It is assumed that the age/earnings profile of a given occupational title or description will be the same for Philadelphia in 1880 as for the Commissioner of Labor Survey for 1889/1890. This is not a particularly stringent assumption and says nothing about the *level* of income, only the pattern by age. Where the number of observations in the Commissioner of Labor Survey were limited for any particular occupation, or where the occupation was not directly given, the age/earnings profile for a similar occupation was used,[36] or the profile for the whole industry was assigned to a particular occupation within that industry.[37] Some of the profiles were irregular and so were arbitrarily smoothed,[38] and the lack of data for workers below age twenty led to arbitrary assignments of profile indices for family heads of that age group.

Table 1 also presents assumed average weekly wages for the selected occupations in the 1880 Philadelphia family sample. These wages were derived from a number of sources.[39] Average weekly wages were derived from average daily wages (when that was how wages were reported) on the assumption of an average work week of 5.6 days. Where a wage for a particular occupation was not available, the wage was assigned on the basis of a "next best" alternative. To expand weekly wages to annual income, it was then assumed that those employed in these selected occupations worked, on average, forty-eight weeks. Exceptions to this were carpenters, masons, and bricklayers (construction crafts) who were assumed to have more seasonal work and therefore were assigned a working year of forty weeks. Laborers were also assumed to work somewhat less than average and assigned an average working year of forty-four weeks. The question in the 1880 census manuscripts on number of months unemployed was also used, whenever information was given, to deflate annual earnings. Although these data were not consistently provided, they were reported frequently enough to justify their use. Biases introduced in these procedures would inflate estimated average annual income, since few people were likely to overstate their unemployment in the twelve months prior to the census while a substantial number of census respondents probably gave no response. It seemed justifiable to use a reasonably low estimate of unemployment, since there is no evidence that the census year of 1880 (i.e., June 1, 1879, to May 30, 1880) was characterized by high unemployment.[40]

Using these procedures, each male family head having an identified occupation (among our sample of 7439 total families) was assigned a weekly wage corresponding to that occupation. The wage was multiplied by the number of weeks employed (assumed or the number stated in the census) and by the index to adjust for age. The average estimated annual incomes are given in Table 1. In total, incomes were estimated for 2,238 heads of families with industrial occupations, 30.1 percent of the total sample of Philadelphia families. The largest groups were laborers (795), clerks (105), carpenters (178), blacksmiths (141), weavers (145), engineers (89), machinists (113), and drivers (105). Many of the occupations were represented by only a few individuals. The types of occupation which were omitted from this analysis included professionals, many craftsmen and artisans, and many self-employed proprietors. Examples would be bakers, tailors, salesmen, grocers, hotel keepers, lawyers, and physicians. Also, some industries (such as wood products, boots and shoes, food processing) were not well covered. Thus, the analysis here is really confined to a rather selective subset of industrial workers, those emphasized in the Commissioner of Labor Survey in 1889/90. The results below indicate that many of the professional and mercantile occupations, if fully occupied throughout the year, would have done relatively well. Anyone with a weekly income of about $15 or above would, if employed for forty-eight weeks out of the year, have achieved an income of $720 or more. This was true for a number of these professionals, artisans, and self-employed proprietors.[41] Although there is no guarantee that these occupations had employment any more stable than industrial workers, there is also no reason to believe that their employment was any less stable. Thus, focusing the analysis largely on industrial workers and laborers concentrates on those groups most likely to find themselves with low incomes and under conditions of economic stress.

There are some further problems in assuming the equivalence of occupational titles. A weaver, for example, might have been a handloom weaver or a person who worked the large mechanized looms in a factory. There was a wide difference between these groups in terms of status and pay, but fortunately we know that most of the handloom weavers had disappeared from Philadelphia by 1880.[42] Similarly, laborers might have been common day laborers or somewhat more highly paid factory laborers. Blacksmiths might have been proprietors of their own shops or employees. Carpenters might have been free-lance, working for a contractor, or employed regularly in a business or factory. Thus, a further simplifying assumption is that the occupational titles as given in the 1880 census represent average work with average pay.[43]

In the last column of Table 1 are given the average incomes for the same selected occupations in the 1889/1890 Commissioner of Labor Survey. It is clear that the averages do not coincide, but in many cases they are close. Of the thirty-three occupations in which there is a direct comparison,[44] however, only eight were higher in the 1889/1890 survey. This is rather surprising, but it must be remembered that the data from the survey were based on larger samples, more regularly distributed by age; that the survey contained data from some lower wage areas (such as the South); that the Philadelphia incomes were often estimated for only a few cases for some occupations; and that Philadelphia may well have been a high wage area.[45] Also, the estimates of the weeks employed may have been too optimistic for the Philadelphia wage earners. Overall, however, the low income groups in Philadelphia were generally also the low income groups in the Commissioner of Labor Survey and vice versa.[46] Skilled workers generally had high estimated annual incomes while semiskilled and unskilled workers (e.g., weavers and laborers) had low incomes. In sum, it must be remembered that the estimated Philadelphia incomes for male family heads might be closer to full-time annual equivalent earnings and therefore a bit high.

The next step was to calculate "minimum adequacy" budgets for each of the Philadelphia families for which income of head has been estimated. Using the expenditure data from the 1889/1890 Commissioner of Labor Survey, simple linear expenditure equations were estimated for families, taking into account the age of the husband and wife, the ages and sexes of the children, and the ethnicity of the family head.[47] Ordinary least squares regression was the fitting technique used. In this case, only families from the Northern states in the survey were used on the assumption that consumption levels might have been normatively different in the North than in the South. Further, it was necessary to decide which group would give the best approximation of some "minimum adequacy" level of consumption.

Several different selection criteria were considered: the families in the lowest "n" percent of the distribution of total income, head's income, income per capita, head's income per capita, and expenditures per capita. The per capita criteria seemed most useful because "economic stress" is generally experienced that way. Looking at the actual distributions of income and expenditure per capita, there appeared to be a level of resistance below which income and expenditure per capita would not go. This was in the range of $60–80.[48] Almost no families were located below this.

Table 2.   Equation for Estimating Total Family Expenditure (Families with Male Heads[a])

Variable	Lowest Quartile Families (Equation I)			Upper Three Quartile Families (Equation II)		
	Coefficient	t-ratio	Significance[b]	Coefficient	t-ratio	Significance[b]
Dependent Variable						
Total family expenditures						
Independent Variables						
Constant	376.660	NC[c]	NC	519.752	NC	NC
Age of male head	−.206	.264	n.s.	1.243	1.394	n.s.
Age of wife	−.274	.313	n.s.	−2.119	2.398	**
No. of children 0–4	30.201	6.859	***	40.842	7.434	***
No. of children 5–10	40.327	11.432	***	56.819	12.440	***
No. of male children 11–13	36.618	4.737	***	71.465	6.620	***
No. of male children 14–15	49.150	4.522	***	90.035	6.645	***
No. of male children 16–17	38.481	2.964	***	109.445	7.335	***
No. of male children 18 +	27.503	1.919	*	149.800	11.934	***
No. of female children 11–13	38.564	5.197	***	88.792	7.548	***
No. of female children 14–15	40.164	3.937	***	105.210	8.090	***
No. of female children 16–17	40.548	3.399	***	76.793	5.384	***
No. of female children 18 +	51.275	4.563	***	119.644	11.764	***
Male head native born	−24.991	3.407	***	24.369	3.128	***
Income from children	.397	9.996	***	.033	1.078	n.s.
R^2 adjusted		.533			.381	
F-ratio		95.784	***		142.196	***
Number of cases		1165			3207	

Source: Data were derived from U.S. Commissioner of Labor, *Sixth Annual Report* (1890); *Seventh Annual Report* (1891). Equations were estimated by ordinary least squares regression. The sample was of renters only and excluded those who owned their own homes.

[a] Equation I used all families with family income per capita in the lowest quartile (below $97).
  Equation II used all families with family income per capita in the upper three quartiles.

[b] ***$p < .01$ **$p < .05$ *$p < .1$

n.s. = not significant at least at a ten percent level.

[c] NC = not calculated.

Families at or near this level were felt to be "expenditure constrained." That is, they were in a situation where there was resistance to allowing expenditure to fall any further. These families were identified as all those with total income per capita in the lowest quartile (i.e., below $97). The results are presented in Table 2, which also includes the equation for the remaining upper three quartiles.

It should be noted in Equation I of Table 2 that total family expenditure (the dependent variable) becomes a function of the demographic composition of the family (i.e., the age and sex of the family members) and that one variable accounts for "tastes": the ethnicity of family head. One extremely important variable is omitted—the income of the family head. Expenditure equations generally include this as one of the central determinants of family spending. In this case it was not included because it was felt that these families were "expenditure constrained" with respect to income. That is, their expenditures were at a "minimum adequacy" level (as determined by contemporary tastes and norms, as well as basic biological needs) and depended largely on demographic composition.[49] In terms of the contemporary debate over measurement of poverty, this is an attempt to use a relative measure of poverty (i.e., families in the lowest quartile of family income per capita) to derive an absolute measure of poverty (i.e., a "minimum adequacy" budget) dependent only on family composition and ethnicity of head. What is important here is that the actual expenditure behavior of worker families in the 1889/1890 Commissioner of Labor Survey is used as a basis for the measurement of poverty, rather than some more arbitrary standard.

There is, however, one additional variable included in Equation I which requires explanation. Income from the children of the family was included as an independent variable to test whether or not the earnings of older children influenced family expenditure. Ideally, if only fully expenditure-constrained families had been chosen, then this coefficient would have been insignificant. It was not, and indeed had the largest B-weight[50] (and hence the largest effect) of any variable in the equation. It was clear that the availability of children's income did influence the expenditures of families with relatively low income of head. This posed real problems in estimation which were solved by truncating this variable from the equation and using the abbreviated equation, which was "purged" of the effects of children's earnings, to estimate a minimum adequacy budget. The estimated expenditures were then roughly equivalent to what the family would have spent if none of the children could have worked. When Equation I was estimated without children's income, the coefficients for older children were much larger, indicating that the effect of their earnings had been picked up by these terms.[51]

Equation I was moderately successful in "explaining" variation in total family expenditures in the sample: 53 percent of total variation was accounted for by age, sex, and ethnic composition alone. It was significant overall at least at a 1 percent level (as measured by the F-ratio). A problem with this equation was that the added consumption needs due to the presence of other dependents (and boarders) were not taken into account. This was, in turn, due to a lack of data in the Commissioner of Labor Survey.[52] It must, therefore, be considered that the extra consumption needs of other dependents will be underestimated, although the impact was apparently not great.[53] A final point concerning the two equations in Table 2 is that both were estimated only for renters, and excluded homeowners. This was because the Commissioner of Labor Survey did not include an item for imputed rent in expenditure or imputed value of housing services in income. Therefore, income and expenditures for nonrenters are downward biased.[54]

The estimated coefficients in Equation I (for families in the lowest quartile) had a few surprises but confirmed basic expectations. First, the ages of the male head of family and the spouse had little effect on total consumption expenditure. These coefficients were insignificant and actually negative, implying a declining marginal effect on consumption as the family head and spouse aged.[55] The impact of the husband and wife (if present) were taken up by the intercept term. Second, the effect of additional children was uniformly positive, significant, and relatively large. Young children (age group 0–4) had a generally smaller effect than older children. Among children aged five and older, however, there was little difference in the coefficients, apart from some slight tendency for expenditure for additional children to increase with age (with older males being an anomalous exception).[56] (Males and females were estimated together for the age groups 0–4 and 5–10, since it was felt that sex differences in consumption would not be important among young children but only among those over about age 10.) One surprising result was that, in these samples, families with a native-born head consumed less, on average, than families with a foreign-born head. The expected relationship might have been the opposite, assuming that norms among families headed by native-born males would have been toward higher consumption relative to the foreign born. Such was apparently not the case among these industrial families.

It is also instructive to compare Equation I with Equation II, which was estimated for the remaining three quartiles of families. For one thing, a test for the differences in regression coefficients revealed that the two equations were jointly different at a 1 percent level of significance.[57] For another, the earnings of children had a small and insignificant effect on family expenditures in the upper quartiles where the average head's income was much higher (see Table 6 below). It was quite evident that families under economic stress turned to children for additional income in order to maintain acceptable or desired expenditure levels, while better-off families would have felt much less pressure to send children to work.[58] The relatively lower adjusted R^2 in Equation II points to less importance in explaining expenditure by demographic patterns, ethnicity, and children's earnings alone. Equations like those in Table 2 were estimated including head's income as an independent variable. (These are not presented.) When head's income was included as a variable, the explanatory power (as measured by the adjusted R^2 value) of the expenditure equation for the upper three quartiles increased greatly (from .381 to .668), while that for the equation for the lowest quartile increased only a small amount (from .533 to .655). Thus, head's income played a more important role in explaining family expenditures in the upper three quartiles than in the lowest quartile. This is consistent with the idea that families in the lowest quartile were expenditure constrained while those in the upper quartiles were freer to choose greater consumption if the head's income permitted. Finally, the effect of ethnicity was reversed in Equation II relative to Equation I. While among the group under the most economic stress, the foreign born had higher "minimum adequacy" standards, the rest of the survey population showed that families headed by the native born were prone to consume more. Perhaps the foreign born felt relative deprivation more acutely in their new environment.

It would be useful to compare various "poverty line" calculations with the predictions from Equation I in Table 3. In particular, Glassberg's "minimum adequate standard of living" for a Philadelphia family of five (a husband, wife, boys aged ten and four, and a girl aged six) of $643 can be compared with the results in Table 3.[59] Also useful is a comparison with Wright's estimate of $600 for 1874 and Dubnoff's estimate of $657 for 1880, both for families of five persons.[60] In Table 3, Family I corresponds to Glassberg's average family in composition; but predictions based on Equation I of Table 2 are well below her "minimum adequate standard of living." It may be that the expenditure data for the Northern states in the Commissioner of Labor Survey in 1889/1890 were not the appropriate comparison. But this was probably not so important; most of the families in the 1889/1890 Survey were urban and all were industrial. In addition, between 1880 and 1890, real income per capita in the United States had increased. Prices did decline over the 1880s (which would tend to make 1890 budgets lower in nominal terms), but not by a great deal.[61]

Some effort was made to correct for this. All expenditure estimates were multiplied by the ratio of estimated average incomes among adult male industrial workers in the Philadelphia 1880 sample and actual average incomes among adult male industrial workers in the 1889/1890 Commissioner of Labor Survey. The averages were calculated as weighted averages of age-specific income levels, the weights being the proportions in each

Table 3. Predicted Minimum Adequacy Budgets and Incomes for
Selected Families: 1880–1890

Families[a]	Minimum Adequacy Budget[b]	Head's Predicted Full Employment Income
Family I		
a) Father Native Born	$447	—
	(464)	
b) Father Foreign Born	472	—
	(490)	
Family II	545	$ 755
	(566)	
Family III	535	936
	(555)	
Family IV	408	1107
	(424)	
Family V	445	398[c]

Source: Minimum adequacy budgets predicted using equation 1 in Table 2. Incomes predicted using data from Table 1 and assuming full employment as discussed in text.

[a] *Family I:* Glassberg's "average" family consisting of a father, mother, and three children (boys aged 10 and 4, girl aged 6). The ages of the parents were assumed to be 35 for the father and 32 for the mother.
Family II: Household #2153 from the 1880 PSHP family sample. Patrick McQuillen, father (age 49), occupation: brick mason; place of birth: Ireland. Wife: Elizabeth (age 43), keeps house. Daughters: Mary (17), Elizabeth (14), Bulah (12), all work in textile or garment factories. Sons: William (10), Frank (4).
Family III: Household #6087 from the 1880 PSHP family sample. Godfrey Reebman, father (age 43), occupation: iron founder; place of birth, Bremen, Germany. Wife: Catherine (age 42), at home. Sons: Godfrey (18, iron worker), Harry (10). Daughters: Agnes (16), Mary (14), Emmy (12), Loraine (3).
Family IV: Household #8499 from the 1880 PSHP family sample. David Atkinson, father (age 32), occupation: foreman; place of birth: Pennsylvania. Wife: Anna (age 28), keeping house. Son: Frederick (7). Daughter: Carrie (3).
Family V: Family #1203 from 1889 Commissioner of Labor Survey. Head (age 36), native born, laborer in a Pennsylvania bar iron firm. Wife (age 32), at home. Daughter (12), at school. Sons: age 10, at school; age 3, at home. Actual income: $397.80. Actual expenditures: $466.75. Did not own their home. Comments of interviewer: "In debt, house poorly furnished, but neat."

[b] Figures in parentheses are budgets adjusted for the difference in incomes between the 1889/1890 U.S. Commissioner of Labor Survey and 1880 Philadelphia.

[c] Actual income.

adult male age group in the 1880 Philadelphia sample. The rationale for this particular correction was that expenditure levels probably bore a close relation to income levels. At any rate, the correction ratio was small (1.038) and no large discrepancy appears to arise from this source.

The figures in parentheses in Table 3 are the predicted "minimum adequacy" expenditure levels adjusted for the income difference. The most likely explanation for the low levels of expenditures predicted for Glassberg's "average" family of five is that expenditure constrained families were making do on considerably less (24–30 percent less) than implied by a budget of $643. There must have been a good deal of hardship among these families. Comments by the interviewers who conducted the Commissioner of Labor Survey do point to this as does an eloquent letter from a woman who wrote to the Commissioner of Labor after having been interviewed.[62] It must also be borne in mind that these expenditure levels are net of the extra spending made possible by the earnings of children. Hence, in a sense, they really are closer to a social and physical minimum. It is clear that many families lived far below the levels calculated in "minimum adequacy" budgets, even while their children worked. Also observable from Table 3 is the fact that variations in demographic composition do indeed affect predicted "minimum adequacy" consumption.

Since one of the issues here is the effect of income shortfall on the family economic behavior, incomes for family heads were estimated for Families II, III, and IV. Actual income was available for Family V, while Family I had no specified occupation for the family head. For a full year of work, the head in Family II, Patrick McQuillen, a brick mason (assumed to work forty weeks), would have had predicted earnings of $775. If he had worked forty-eight weeks, he would have earned $906. Both were well above the predicted low-level consumption for his family. The iron founder in Family III, Godfrey Reebman, had a predicted income of $936 for forty-eight weeks' work, apparently enough to support his large family. Predicted annual earnings for David Atkinson, the thirty-two-year-old foreman who headed Family IV, was $1,107—enough to allow his family to live well above a minimum budget. Finally, the anonymous laborer in Family V actually earned only $397.80 for 1889—a sum insufficient to meet his predicted minimum consumption needs ($445) or his actual consumption expenditure ($467). This family was going into debt.

The major conclusion here is that, while "minimum adequacy" expenditure needs were very much dependent on family composition and size, income of the principal wage earner was influenced only by occupation, age, and regularity of employment. Family composition and size were, in turn, dependent on life cycle stage. "Minimum adequacy" expenditure needs did vary across the life cycle, but in a slow and predictable manner. Income of the principal wage earner was much more unpredictable and erratic. Overall, this leads to the quite unsurprising result that families with heads in low wage occupations or with irregular employment felt the press of economic stress. For instance, if the head of Family I had been a laborer and had worked forty-four weeks, he would have earned only $357. (His income would have only been $421 if he had the great luck to work all fifty-two weeks.) An older laborer would have been in still worse circumstances. The fact that this extensive analysis leads to a common-sense conclusion should not be taken to mean that the analysis was unnecessary. Indeed, the analysis has revealed other findings, particularly that family life

Table 4. Selected Characteristics of the Sample of Male-Headed Philadelphia Families, 1880, Used to Estimate Income and Expenditures

(1) Total Families	2238	
(2) Percentage of Families with Spouses Present	93.5	
(3) Place of Birth of Family Head		
(a) Pennsylvania	673	(30.1%)
(b) Other United States	72	(3.2%)
(c) Germany	471	(21.0%)
(d) Ireland and Britain	1022	(45.7%)
(4) Percentage of Families with Boarders	12.7	
(5) Percentage of Families with Servants	3.2	
(6) Percentage of Families with Unrelated Individuals	1.7	
(7) Percentage of Families with no Nonnuclear Family Members Present	83.9	
(8) Percentage of Spouses Working	2.3	
(9) Mean Estimated Income of Family Head	$567	
(10) Mean Estimated Expenditures[a]	$441	(458)
(11) Mean Age of Family Head	42.4	years
(12) Mean Age of Spouses	38.3	years
(13) Percentages of Children Working		
(a) Males 11–13	18.5	
(b) Males 14–15	58.2	
(c) Males 6–17	87.2	
(d) Males 18 and over	94.7	
(e) Females 11–13	12.6	
(f) Females 14–15	42.4	
(g) Females 16–17	55.0	
(h) Females 18 and over	63.1	
(14) Percentage of Male Household Heads Illiterate	6.7	

Source: Sample of census enumerator's manuscripts. Estimations of incomes and expenditures described in text.

[a]Figure in parenthesis is adjusted for the difference in incomes between the 1889/1890 U.S. Commissioner of Labor Survey and 1880 Philadelphia.

cycle and compositional effects were crucial determinants of economic stress.

The question then naturally arises as to what strategy families followed who had head's income less than some "minimum adequacy" expenditure level. A comparison of the estimated expenditures (based on family size and composition) and income of head (based on occupation, assumed wages, age, and assumed duration of employment) was done for the 2,238 families in the 1880 Philadelphia census sample for whom incomes were estimated. It must be remembered that these estimations are far from exact and, therefore, so must the comparisons be.[63]

Some characteristics of these selected families are given in Table 4. All the families were male-headed, and most (93.5 percent) had spouses present. Very few (2.3 percent) of those spouses were working, however. Many of the families took in boarders (12.7 percent), although this was less than the average for the whole city (approximately 20 percent). Relatively few of the families (3.2 percent) could afford servants. Even fewer (1.7 percent) had any unrelated individuals present. These families were, in fact, largely nuclear families, as may be seen by the fact that only 16 percent of the families had relatives other than nuclear family members present. Family heads averaged about forty-two years of age with spouses being about four years younger on average. Most of the family heads could read and write (93.3 percent). A disproportionate share of the family heads were Irish (45.7 percent), and relatively fewer than expected were German (21.0 percent).

Since the original samples were based on three groups of 2,000 households each headed by native-white Americans, Irish born, and German born, about one-third from each group could be expected in the sample.[64] The larger share of Irish family heads and smaller share of German family heads in this subsample can be attributed to the bias of the estimating procedure in favor of industrial workers and laborers (who were disproportionately Irish) and against mercantile proprietors and artisans (who were disproportionately German).[65] The mean estimated income for family heads was $567, while mean estimated "minimum adequacy" expenditure was $441 (or $458 if adjusted for the slightly higher Philadelphia wage/income structure). Finally, it is of note that large numbers of children were enumerated in the sample as employed. Overall, 69.3 percent of males and 45.8 percent of females aged eleven and over were employed. This compares with about 67 percent for male children in the full sample of white households and about 38 percent for female children.[66] Thus the subsample of largely industrial and manual workers' families used here showed higher rates of child labor force activity, particularly for females. As may also be seen in Table 4, older children worked more frequently than younger children, while males worked more than females. All this is not too surprising, but the proportion of children working, especially those aged fourteen and older, was substantial.

It is argued here that relative poverty, however defined, was related to family composition, as well as to income. These were both, in turn, related to the stage of the family's life cycle.[67] This may be seen in Table 5 which presents estimated incomes and expenditures for the 2,238 families classified by age of family head (a good proxy for life cycle stage). It may be observed that incomes were higher among younger male family heads and peaked at ages thirty to thirty-nine. This was a function of two things: the age/earnings profiles which also generally peaked at this point (see Table

Table 5. Average Estimated Incomes for Male Heads of Families and Average Estimated Expenditures for Families: Philadelphia, 1880 (By Age of Male Family Head)

		10–19	20–29	30–39	40–49	50–59	60 & Over	Total
				(Dollars)				
(1) Estimated Income of Male Head of Family (N)		340	595	647	566	505	411	567
		(3)	(310)	(678)	(619)	(392)	(236)	(2238)
(2) Estimated Family Expenditure[a]	(a)	356	385	436	468	464	423	441
	(b)	370	400	453	486	482	439	458
(3) Difference of Averages	(a)	−16	210	211	98	41	−12	126
	(b)	−30	195	194	80	23	−28	109

Source: Sample of enumerator's manuscripts. Methods of estimation of incomes and expenditures are explained in the text.

[a]Estimated expenditure (a) is unadjusted for differences in average incomes between the U.S. Commissioner of Labor Survey of 1889/1890 and Philadelphia in 1880. Estimated expenditure (b) is adjusted for the difference.

1), and the fact that a disproportionate share of younger men held the better paying occupations. At the same time, however, predicted expenditures increased for older family heads as family composition altered toward more and older children.[68] While on average, therefore, expected income of head was somewhat above expected expenditure, the pattern varied according to family composition and age of family head. In addition, little savings could be accomplished for the average family using only the earnings of the head, if that family wished more than a meager budget. Only younger families could have done so.[69]

A predictable response to this situation would have been to seek other sources of income. This is illustrated in Table 6, which gives a number of characteristics of families broken down into the quartiles of the difference between predicted income of head and predicted "minimum adequacy" expenditure. As may be seen, the families in the lowest quartile had a much higher proportion of older children working than those in the highest quartile (see rows 9, 10, and 12). The intermediate quartiles give an expected intermediate ranking. This result is partly due to the fact that a much higher proportion of the lowest quartile consisted of families with older heads who had older children. Approximately 76 percent of the lowest quartile had at least one child aged eleven and over while only about 34 percent of the highest quartile had at least one child eleven or older.[70] Thus, the older families had a higher proportion of the children above age eleven who were above age fourteen or eighteen and who, therefore, had a greater likelihood of working. When the age groups of children are examined separately, however, it may be seen that the families in the lower quartile had higher age and sex specific labor force participation rates

Table 6. Selected Characteristics of Families by Income/Expenditure
Quartiles: Philadelphia, 1880

	Lowest 25%	26–49%	50–74%	75% & Above	Total
				Quartiles Ranking Families by Difference of Estimated Income of Head and Estimated Minimum Expenditure[a]	
(1) Number of Cases	536	579	564	559	2238
(2) Cut Points (Income Minus Expenditure)	−80	90	320	—	—
(3) Mean Estimated Income					
(a) Unstandardized	$310	$427	$627	$897	$ 567
(b) Standardized[b]	304	430	630	873	567
(4) Mean Estimated Expenditure[c]					
(a) Unstandardized	$517	$444	$448	$426	$ 458
(b) Standardized[b]	513	446	453	420	458
(5) Place of Birth of Male Head					
(a) United States	55	142	236	312	745
[Row Percent]	(7.4)	(19.1)	(31.7)	(41.9)	
(b) Germany	90	106	149	126	471
[Row Percent]	(19.1)	(22.5)	(31.6)	(26.8)	
(c) Ireland and Britain	391	331	179	121	1022
[Row Percent]	(38.2)	(32.4)	(17.5)	(11.8)	
(6) Percent with Illiterate Heads	15.3	8.1	2.8	1.1	6.7
(7) Percent with Spouses Present	93.7	92.9	94.0	93.4	93.5
(8) Percent with Spouses Working (as percent of all families with spouses present)	2.2	2.1	2.3	2.7	2.3
(N)	(502)	(538)	(530)	(522)	(2092)
(9) Percent with Children Working (as percent of all families with children aged 11 and over)	77.2	66.8	70.6	50.3	68.7
(N)	(408)	(238)	(262)	(191)	(1099)
(10) Percent of Total Children Aged 11 and Over Who Were Working	65.2	53.1	55.7	44.1	57.7
(11) Percent of Total Families Having No Dependents Other Than Nuclear Family Members	85.3	84.8	84.2	81.4	83.9
(12) Age and Sex Specific Child Labor Force Activity Rates (Percent)					
(a) Males 11–13	26.9	19.4	8.7	10.2	18.5
(b) Males 14–15	66.3	54.3	57.1	41.9	58.2
(c) Males 16–17	89.1	91.4	86.1	76.2	87.2
(d) Males 18 and over	97.4	94.6	93.2	89.2	94.7
(e) Females 11–13	15.9	11.7	7.0	13.0	12.6
(f) Females 14–15	51.3	38.6	38.9	26.1	42.4
(g) Females 16–17	64.4	53.6	56.2	20.0	55.0
(h) Females 18 and over	74.5	54.8	58.8	32.6	63.1
(13) Percent of Families with Boarders	12.3	14.5	11.3	12.7	12.7
(14) Percent Distribution of Family Heads by Age					
(a) 10–19	0.4	0.0	0.2	0.0	0.1
(b) 20–29	2.6	16.6	19.1	16.5	13.9
(c) 30–39	18.1	33.7	23.8	45.1	30.3
(d) 40–49	35.8	23.5	25.4	26.5	27.7
(e) 50–59	23.9	16.2	20.0	10.2	17.5
(f) 60 and over	19.2	10.0	11.5	1.8	10.5
Total	100.0	100.0	100.0	100.1	100.0

Source: Sample of enumerator's manuscripts. Estimations of incomes and expenditures explained in text.

[a]Differences estimated from expenditure equation I from Table 2.

[b]Standardized to the age structure of all family heads.

[c]Adjusted for the difference in incomes between the 1889/1890 U.S. Commissioner of Labor Survey and 1880 Philadelphia.

among their children. Thus, even holding age and sex composition constant, the effect of a greater gap between husband's income and expected "minimum adequacy" expenditure was to induce greater labor supply by the children.

A similar result was not, however, true for women. Labor force participation among married women was so low in Philadelphia at that time that it is difficult to say whether the differences between the quartile groups were significant. At any rate, the variation across the quartiles was not striking. An alternative to married women working outside the home was to take in boarders. As Table 6 shows, however, there was no clear pattern of this across quartiles. One reason that the lowest quartile might have had a relatively low proportion of boarders was that the families with less income from husbands relative to "minimum adequacy" expenditures might have had less housing space to use for boarding.[71] But, overall, the gap between head's income and expected expenditure did not appear to have greatly influenced this type of family labor supply.

A few additional points concerning Table 6 are notable. First, the lowest quartile had a disproportionate share of Irish-born heads of families while the highest quartile had a much greater than expected representation of native-born heads of families.[72] The Irish born had a higher proportion of low-skill occupations (e.g., laborers), which lowered expected incomes, and also had larger families, which raised expected "minimum adequacy" expenditures, relative to the native born.[73] A similar result was seen with respect to literacy of family heads: the lowest quartile had more illiterate family heads who were also those more likely to have low skill jobs and have larger families and hence higher expected "minimum adequacy" expenditures.[74]

Conclusions

In conclusion, then, it appears that basic consumption needs, estimated by a "minimum adequacy" budget, interacted with the expected income of the head of family and induced a family labor supply response when income was close to or below this level of consumption need. The response was a greater probability that children would work. This was quite unlike the mid-twentieth century where the response of secondary family wage and salary earners is likely to consist of wives, and not children, working.[75] Thus equally important are the negative findings: married white women did not respond to economic stress in the late nineteenth century by entering the wage labor market in great numbers. Further, in this 1880 Philadelphia sample at least, families under economic stress did not take in boarders with any greater frequency than better-off families.

As may be seen in Table 6, however, the families experiencing the greatest amount of economic stress from a low level of head's income relative to basic family consumption needs were more likely to be older families. Aging of the family head had two effects. The first was to lower the income of family head because of declining earnings with age, usually after the 30s, and because a larger proportion of older industrial workers occupied less well-paid occupations.[76] The second was to increase the basic consumption needs of the family because the family was more likely to have more and older children. Income of head showed more variation than did family consumption needs over the family life cycle. In a sense, the economic stress implied by the measure used here has less to do with the specific methods used to estimate incomes and expenditure and more to do with family consumption and the life cycle. Larger and older families thus had a "built-in" path toward poverty which was alleviated by utilizing the labor of their children, a major source of the problem (i.e., large "minimum adequacy" expenditure needs), as part of its solution (i.e., securing additional income). Families may have adopted different fertility strategies precisely with the eventual economic value of older children in mind. This relates to the whole issue of the costs and benefits of children and the value of children as producers of family income and as sources of old age "social security" for the parents.[77] While there are doubts about the value of a child as an asset in the present day, even for agrarian populations in developing societies, the evidence here is consistent with the notion that children were valued as an economic asset in late nineteenth-century Philadelphia, especially among families experiencing economic stress.

There may also have been some interaction between the income of head and life cycle stage. Family heads in their 30s, with younger children and little additional family labor to offer the market, may have in fact worked harder (e.g., more hours) and caused the age/earnings profiles to peak at that point. Later, with the labor of the children available, there would be less need for such action.

A point of some importance in interpreting Table 6 is that there is a continuum of child labor force response from the lowest to the highest quartile, rather than an abrupt threshold. This casts doubt upon the validity of the notion of a "poverty line" and indicates that there is a wide variety of behavioral response to economic stress. A "poverty line" may be a necessary policy device for public officials who are required to allocate welfare and poverty funds. For them, it is necessary to define unambiguously who is, and who is not, "poor." But the results here indicate that, if behavior is any guide, identifying the "poor" is not a simple task. Indeed, one of the limitations of the finding is that, although families experiencing greater "economic stress" were more likely to send children out into the labor market, using child labor force activity as an indicator of who was "poor" presents difficulties because families from all quartiles had older children in the labor force, but only a portion of all families had older children. Finally, because of child labor laws, compulsory education laws, and changing social mores, child labor is no longer characteristic of families under economic stress. Labor force activity of married women is, but it is clear that many married women currently work for reasons other than inadequate income of the principal male wage earner. Thus behavior is now, as then, an incomplete guide to identifying the poor.

A behavioral, empirical method of discussing poverty has advantages over a more normative approach because it examines what people actually did and compares that behavior to hypotheses about possible responses to poverty and economic stress. The fact that the behavioral approach yields a relative continuum of response is noteworthy and indicative of the problem in identifying a poverty line and relating income to that. It must be conceded that the concept of "minimum adequacy" expenditure needs is not entirely free from normative value judgments; such a judgment was implicit in the choice of a sample to estimate the expenditure equations. The selection of a particular subgroup in the Commissioner of Labor Survey (i.e., those with family income per capita in the lowest quartile) made a judgment about those persons at or near some "minimum adequacy" level. On the other hand, the procedure attempted to stay as close to actual behavior as possible, rather than make arbitrary assignments of "need."

What does it mean that the "minimum adequacy" budget for Glassberg's "normal" family is $464, while her computation yielded a much higher "poverty line" of $643? The fact that "minimum adequacy" budgets based on observed behavior were below those based on more normative procedures does not mean that those families who would have been classed as poor were really not. The conclusion must be that large numbers of Philadelphia families were experiencing "economic stress" and that they were making do by contemporary standards.

Introducing demographic variation also increases the problem of any economic welfare interpretation of "minimum adequacy" budgets relative to income because of the inability to compare variations in preferences for children among families. This latter point indicates that the analysis is also not free of the problems of making welfare judgments about consumption. As Pollak and Wales[78] have recently pointed out, it is difficult to compare the welfare situation of different families because of the possibility of different preferences for number of children. That is, in a regime of at least partially effective fertility control, family size becames partly a matter of choice. These choices are presumably made taking individual family preferences into account. If, for example, two families have male heads with identical ages, occupations, and incomes, and have spouses the same ages, but have differing numbers of children, then the relationship between head's income and expected "minimum adequacy" expenditure will be different. In the terms used in this paper, the family with more children will be "worse off." But would it? Perhaps it actually feels better off because it has the extra children, if it had them as a matter of choice. Here again the issue of the costs and benefits of children arises. If children are valued differently (both as productive and social insurance assets and as family members) by different family heads and spouses, differing family compositions may be chosen simply because of differing preferences. Thus, welfare judgments are difficult to infer.

Finally, what has been done here is really an alternative to using multivariate analysis to discuss issues of labor force participation of secondary family members. Such analysis has been done elsewhere and produces many of the same answers.[79] This other work is not, however, directly concerned with the issue of poverty and consumption needs, which has been the direction of approach here. This paper has been restricted to industrial and manual workers in 1880 Philadelphia because of a desire not to overextend the results from the 1889/1890 Commissioner of Labor Survey. If the age/earnings profiles and the predicted expenditures were extended to professionals, white-collar workers (other than clerks), and particularly self-employed proprietors, most would have been found not to have been under conditions of economic stress.

Poverty, or economic stress, has been examined here from the perspective of behavior. Did families who had a low head's income relative to predicted "minimum adequacy" expenditures behave differently from those who did not? The answer was yes, with respect to child labor force activity. The same was not the case for two other likely responses: taking in boarders or having the wife enter the wage labor market. These findings are quite consistent with what we know about the nineteenth-century family economy and society. When earnings of the family head declined late in the life cycle, the slack was taken up by the children. This is dramatically demonstrated for the Commissioner of Labor Survey in Figure 1, which relates earnings of family head and earnings from children and other sources to total income and expenditures for the U.S. families. This is also ample confirmation of the relevance of family composition and life cycle effects to the phenomenon of economic stress. Clearly, families later in the life cycle were more subject to it than those in earlier stages.

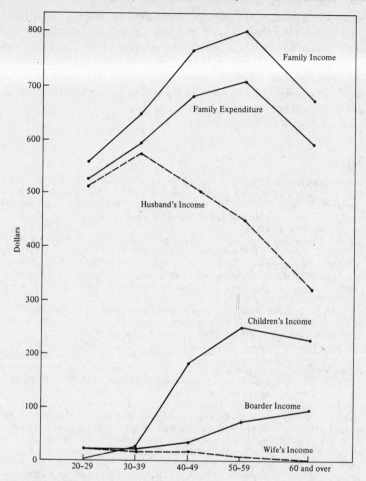

Figure 1. Composition of Family Income by Age of Family Head in Nine Industries, United States, 1889/1890.

The finding that poorer families sent their children to work is certainly not a startling one. But the fact that it appears to have been the main source of additional support for late nineteenth-century urban families under economic stress is not obvious. Also not immediately apparent was the importance of life cycle and family composition. These findings are also consistent with another aspect of late nineteenth-century demographic and social life: the late age of marriage. When children remained in the home for an extended period to assist in family support, late marriage is certainly expected.[80] Finally, although a major focus of this paper has been child labor force activity, there are many other important dimensions of child labor, such as variation by race, ethnicity, sex, age, occupation, and family composition, that are not treated in detail here. These will be explored in the following essay.

NOTES

1. Charles Wilson, "The Other Face of Mercantilism," *Transactions of the Royal Historical Society,* Fifth Series, 9 (1959). See also, John Maynard Keynes, "Notes on Mercantilism, the Usury Laws, Stamped Money and Theories of Under-Consumption," in *The General Theory of Employment, Interest, and Money* (New York: Harcourt, Brace, 1936), 333–71.

2. See George Stigler, "The Early History of Empirical Studies of Consumer Behavior," *The Journal of Political Economy* 17 (April 1954). Reprinted in *Essays in the History of Economics* (Chicago: University of Chicago Press, 1965), 198–233.

3. Michael Drake, "The Census, 1801–1891," in E. A. Wrigley, ed., *Nineteenth-Century Society: Essays in the Use of Quantitative Methods for the Study of Social Data* (Cambridge, England: Cambridge University Press, 1972), 8.

4. See, for example, Stanley K. Schultz, "Breaking the Chains of Poverty: Public Education in Boston, 1800–1860," in Kenneth T. Jackson and Stanley K. Schultz, eds., *Cities in American History* (New York: Alfred A. Knopf, 1972), 306–23.

5. Jeffrey G. Williamson, "Consumer Behavior in the Nineteenth Century: Carroll D. Wright's Massachusetts Workers in 1875," *Explorations in Entrepreneurial History* 4 (Winter 1967), 101–3.

6. Edward Young, *Labor in Europe and America,* Report of the Bureau of Statistics of the Treasury Department (Washington, D.C.: U.S. G.P.O., 1876), 820-21.

7. For a discussion of Philadelphia's early industrialization, see Diane Lindstrom, *Economic Development in the Philadelphia Region, 1810–1850* (New York: Columbia University Press, 1978), ch. 2. For the later period, see Bruce Laurie, Theodore Hershberg, and George Alter, "Immigrants and Industry: The Philadelphia Experience, 1850–1880," *The Journal of Social History* 9 (December 1975), 219–48; Bruce Laurie and Mark Schmitz, "Manufacture and Productivity: The Making of an Industrial Base, Philadelphia, 1850–1880"; both essays appear in this volume.

8. The issue of poverty in mid- to late nineteenth-century Philadelphia has been discussed in an earlier PSHP paper by Eudice Glassberg, "Work, Wages, and the Cost of Living: Ethnic Differences and the Poverty Line, Philadelphia, 1880," *Pennsylvania History* 66 (January 1979), 17–58.

9. See Stigler, "The Early History of Empirical Studies of Consumer Behavior," 199–213.

10. Glassberg, "Work, Wages, and the Cost of Living." The Social Security Administration poverty line calculation was particularly the work of Mollie Orshansky. See, for example, Mollie Orshansky, "How Poverty Is Measured," *Monthly Labor Review* 92 (February 1969), 37–41. Much of the literature and the debate on the subject is discussed in U.S. Department of Health, Education, and Welfare (DHEW), *The Measure of Poverty: A Report to Congress Mandated by the Educational Amendments of 1974* (Washington, D.C.: U.S. G.P.O., April 1976).

11. Glassberg, "Work, Wages, and the Cost of Living."

12. Massachusetts Bureau of Statistics of Labor, *Sixth Annual Report*, Public Document No. 31 (Boston: 1875), 447.

13. DHEW, *The Measure of Poverty*, 5–11.

14. Some adjustments were made for small households which do not realize some of the economies of scale of consumption experienced by larger households. Rural households were assigned lower poverty thresholds than urban households because of the feeling that housing is cheaper in rural areas while income in kind is also more prevalent there. The multiplier of three was based on a 1955 Household Food Consumption Survey by the USDA, which also furnished the economy food plan used to estimate the basic food costs. See DHEW, *The Measure of Poverty*, 6. For a recent criticism of the measurement of poverty as excluding the value of various welfare transfers in cash or in kind (e.g., food stamps or Medicaid), see Martin Anderson, *Welfare: The Political Economy of Welfare Reform in the United States* (Palo Alto, Cal.: Hoover Press, 1978).

15. See, DHEW, *The Measure of Poverty*, 69–72.

16. Peter H. Lindert and Jeffrey G. Williamson, "Three Centuries of American Inequality," *Research in Economic History* 1 (1976), 69-123; Lee Soltow, "Evidence on Income Inequality in the United States, 1866–1965," *Journal of Economic History* 29 (June 1969), 279–86; "Economic Inequality in the United States in the Period from 1790 to 1860," *Journal of Economic History* 31 (December 1971), 822–39; *Men and Wealth in the United States, 1850–1870* (New Haven, Ct.: Yale University Press, 1975).

17. One example, dealing with the Canadian city of Hamilton, may be found in Michael Katz, *The People of Hamilton, Canada West: Family and Class in a Mid-Nineteenth Century City* (Cambridge: Harvard University Press, 1975), ch. 2.

18. See Steven Dubnoff, "Long Term Trends in the Adequacy of Individual Incomes in the United States, 1860–1974," paper presented at the meetings of the Social Science History Association (Columbus, Ohio: November 1978), Graph 3. An historical discussion of these and other problems with calculating a poverty line may be found in Eugene Smolensky, "The Past and Present Poor," in Robert W. Fogel and Stanley L. Engerman, eds., *The Reinterpretation of American Economic History* (New York: Harper & Row, 1971), 84–96. A current and more quantitative view of the sensitivity issue is found in DHEW, *The Measure of Poverty*, Chapter 4. For a critique, see Anderson, *Welfare: The Political Economy of Welfare Reform in the United States.*

19. Morton Paglin, "The Measurement and Trend in Inequality: A Basic Revision," *American Economic Review* 65 (September 1975), 598–609.

20. Steven Dubnoff, "The Life Cycle and Economic Welfare: Historical Change in the Economic Constraints on Working-Class Family Life, 1860–1974," paper presented at the annual meetings of the Eastern Sociological Society (Philadelphia: April 1978). Dubnoff's thesis, on New England mill workers, also attempts some poverty line calculation. See Steven Dubnoff, "The Family and Absence from Work: Irish Workers in a Lowell, Massachusetts, Cotton Mill, 1860" (Ph.D. dissertation, Brandeis University, 1976). See also, Steven Dubnoff, "Long Term Trends in the Adequacy of Individual Incomes in the United States, 1860–1974"; Louise A. Tilly and Steven J. Dubnoff, "Families and Wage Earnings in Amiens and Roubaix, 1906: Measures of Income Adequacy and Household Response in Two French Cities," paper presented at the meetings of the Social Science History Association (Columbus, Ohio: November 1978).

21. Milton Friedman, "The Methodology of Positive Economics," in Milton Friedman, *Essays in Positive Economics* (Chicago: University of Chicago Press, 1953), 3–43.

22. Harold W. Watts, "An Economic Definition of Poverty," in Daniel P. Moynihan, ed., *On Understanding Poverty* (New York: Basic Books, 1969), 322.

23. Such an approach is implicitly adopted by Michael Katz, *The People of Hamilton, Canada West*, ch. 2.

24. U.S. Commissioner of Labor, *Sixth Annual Report* (1890); and *Seventh Annual Report* (1891). The survey and its nature and representativeness are discussed in Michael R. Haines, "Industrial Work and the Family Life Cycle, 1889/1890," *Research in Economic History* 4 (1979) and in Michael R. Haines, *Fertility and Occupation: Population Patterns in Industrialization* (New York: Academic Press, 1979), ch. VI.

25. The work of Steven Dubnoff cited in note 20 (above) emphasizes the notion of economic constraints on family behavior.

26. Robert W. Smuts, *Women and Work in America* (New York: Columbia University Press, 1959), ch. II.

27. For a description of the original samples and sampling procedures, see Theodore Hershberg, "The Philadelphia Social History Project: A Methodological History" (Ph.D. dissertation, Stanford University, 1973), ch. II. See also, Theodore Hershberg, guest editor, "A Special Issue: The Philadelphia Social History Project," *Historical Methods Newsletter* 9 (March–June, 1976), hereafter cited as "PSHP: Special Issue."

28. One of the major problems with these samples is that they do not, when combined, represent the population characteristics of the white population of Philadelphia in 1880. First, they exclude households headed by other than native whites, Irish, and Germans, and second, the sampling proportions do not approximate the total population. This must be kept in mind when interpreting the results. Another issue is that the black population (about 3.7 percent of the total population of Philadelphia in 1880) was not included here. This should be the subject for further inquiry. Census weights could be used to approximate the population characteristics. These will be used in future analysis, but the biases here should not affect the overall results.

29. This was done by hand by Claudia Goldin. Efforts to computerize this process are now underway.

30. U.S. Commissioner of Labor, *Sixth Annual Report* (1890); and *Seventh Annual Report* (1891).

31. See note 24.

32. A description of the data available in the United States Census schedules may be found in U.S. Bureau of Census, *Population and Housing Inquiries in the U.S. Decennial Censuses, 1790–1970,* Working Paper No. 39 (Washington, D.C.: U.S. G.P.O., 1973). Some recent work with wealth data from the censuses of 1850, 1860, and 1870 may be found in Lee Soltow, *Men and Wealth in the United States, 1850–1870* (New Haven, Ct.: Yale University Press, 1975).

33. This is not to say that there was a lack of interest in the issue of wages and incomes. Carroll D. Wright conducted several studies of incomes and budgets when he was Massachusetts Commissioner of Labor and later U.S. Commissioner of Labor. His first study, which covered 397 families of skilled and unskilled workers with two or more persons in 1874/1875, appears in Massachusetts Bureau of Statistics of Labor, *Sixth Annual Report* (1875). The second, which has already been mentioned, was much more comprehensive, covering 8,544 families in nine industries in the United States and Europe. It appeared in U.S. Commissioner of Labor, *Sixth Annual Report* (1890); *Seventh Annual Report* (1891). Another notable report is found in U.S. Commissioner of Labor, *Fourth Annual Report* (1888), "Working Women in Large Cities" (Washington, D.C.: U.S. G.P.O., 1889). For a biography of Wright, see James Leiby, *Carroll Wright and Labor Reform: The Origin of Labor*

Statistics (Cambridge: Harvard University Press, 1960). See also, Williamson, "Consumer Behavior in the Nineteenth Century," 100–106.

The 1889/1890 Survey covered nine industries (pig iron, bar iron, steel, bituminous coal, coke, iron ore, cottons, woolens, and glass) in twenty-four states of the United States (Alabama, Georgia, Illinois, Indiana, New York, Ohio, Pennsylvania, Tennessee, Virginia, West Virginia, Connecticut, Kentucky, Louisiana, Maine, Maryland, Massachusetts, Mississippi, New Hampshire, North Carolina, Rhode Island, South Carolina, Missouri, New Jersey, and Delaware), and five European countries (Belgium, France, Germany, Great Britain, and Switzerland). Of the 8,544 families, 6,809 were located in the United States. They were also not evenly distributed ranging from only ten in cotton textiles in Louisiana to 1877 in all nine industries in Pennsylvania. For a description and evaluation of the sample, as well as an analysis of the interaction of family income and expenditures, see Haines, "Industrial Work and the Family Life Cycle, 1889/1890."

Among the sources used to estimate wage data were U.S. Bureau of the Census, *Tenth Census of the United States: 1880*, vol. 20, "Report on the Statistics of Wages in the Manufacturing Industries with Supplementary Reports on the Average Retail Prices of Necessaries of Life and on Trade Societies, and Strikes and Lockouts," by Joseph D. Weeks (Washington, D.C.: U.S. G.P.O., 1886). (This is often known as the "Weeks Report.") "Report on Wholesale Prices on Wages, and on Transportation," Senate Committee on Finance, *52nd Congress, 1st Session*, Senate Report 986 (1892). (This is often known as the "Aldrich Report.") Edward Young, *Labor in Europe and America* (Philadelphia: S. A. George, 1875); Pennsylvania Department of Internal Affairs, *Seventh Annual Report* (1879–1880), "Industrial Statistics" (Harrisburg, Pa.: Lane S. Hart, 1881).

These wage series are summarized in Stanley Lebergott, *Manpower in Economic Growth: The American Record Since 1800* (New York: McGraw-Hill, 1964); and U.S. Department of Labor, Bureau of Labor Statistics, *History of Wages in the United States from Colonial Times to 1928*, Bulletin of the United States Bureau of Labor Statistics No. 604, Revision of Bulletin No. 499 with Supplement, 1929–1933 (Washington, D.C.: U.S. G.P.O., 1934).

34. An alternative procedure would have been to index one age group (e.g., 30–39), and then age structure would not influence the results (since age weights do influence the mean). But since the wages given for Philadelphia are implicitly averages, it was felt preferable to index the means for each occupation.

35. For contemporary evidence, see Henry Phelps Brown, *The Inequality of Pay* (Berkeley, Cal.: University of California Press, 1977), 263–69; Jacob Mincer, "The Distribution of Labor Incomes: A Survey with Special Reference to the Human Capital Approach," *The Journal of Economic Literature* 8 (March 1970), 1–26. For a review of this in the 1889/1890 Commissioner of Labor Survey, see Haines, "Industrial Work and the Family Life Cycle, 1889/1890."

36. For example, the profile for masons was used for bricklayers, that of watchmen for guards, and that of firemen for stokers. Iron puddlers, rollers, heaters, and moulders were all assigned a profile based on the joint, pooled data from all these occupations.

37. For example, among the metalworking occupations, the profile of the iron and steel industry was assigned. (This included burner, smelter, forger, founder, galvanizer, gasman, melter, plater, refiner, and caster.) Among some textile workers (trimmer, spooler), the profiles for the cotton and woolen industries were given. Finally, glass workers (cutters) were given the profiles for the whole glass industry.

38. One example was the profile for clerks. There was, for many groups, a lack of data for workers over sixty.

39. See note 33 above.

40. Such evidence as is available points to 1880 as a relatively normal year in a decade (the 1880s) characterized by a relatively low (ca. 4 percent) unemployment rate. See Lebergott, *Manpower in Economic Growth,* 164–90.

41. To provide a few examples, estimated weekly wages for adult males were: *Professional and White Collar:* Lawyer ($35), physician ($30), teacher ($33), agent ($23), salesman ($16), merchant ($45).

Proprietors and Artisans: Butcher ($14.50), grocer ($18), clothier ($15), cabinet-maker ($14.50).

Some examples of numerically important groups that were somewhat worse off would include shoemakers ($12.50), tanners ($9), servants ($8), bakers ($13.70), barbers ($12), hucksters ($11), tailors ($13).

42. Laurie, Hershberg, and Alter, "Immigrants and Industry," 234. This paper discusses the problem of occupational equivalence as well. On the problems of occupational equivalence, see Hershberg, "The Philadelphia Social History Project," 259–84; Clyde Griffen, "Occupational Mobility in Nineteenth-Century America: Problems and Possibilities," *Journal of Social History* 5 (Spring 1972); Stuart Blumin, "The Historical Study of Vertical Mobility," *Historical Methods Newsletter* 1 (September 1968), 1–13; Michael B. Katz, "Occupational Classification in History," *Journal of Interdisciplinary History* 3 (Summer 1972), 63–88; Theodore Hershberg and Robert Dockhorn, "Occupational Classification," in "PSHP: Special Issue," 59–98; Theodore Hershberg, Michael Katz, Stuart Blumin, Lawrence Glasco, and Clyde Griffen, "Occupation and Ethnicity in Five Nineteenth Century Cities: A Collaborative Inquiry," *Historical Methods Newsletter* 7 (June 1974), 174–216.

43. The sources cited in note 42 above also discuss some of the variation that may be found within a single occupational classification or title.

44. Several occupations were not given in the 1889/90 survey as such, and their Philadelphia equivalents were assigned industry average profiles.

45. Data in the "Weeks Report" tend to support this.

46. A zero order correlation between the incomes of the occupations for the two different samples was .697, which was significant at a .001 level.

47. There are some difficulties in estimating simple linear expenditure equations with total expenditures as the dependent variable. More complex models estimate equations in various specifications (e.g., linear, quadratic, translog) for individual expenditure groups (e.g., food, clothing, etc.). Not the least of the problems is that prices did vary geographically over the United States and did change, both relatively and absolutely, between 1880 and 1890. Fortunately, however, prices generally fell a bit overall in the 1890s, so an 1890 budget study will not generally overstate 1880 expenditure levels. For a recent treatment of the estimation of expenditure systems, see Robert A. Pollak and Terence J. Wales, "Estimation of Complete Demand Systems from Household Budget Data: The Linear and Quadratic Expenditure Systems," *American Economic Review* 68 (June 1978), 348–59.

48. Both the income and expenditure per capita tabulations revealed a roughly similar pattern.

49. A theoretical justification for this procedure is provided in an appendix to this paper.

50. The B-weight is defined as coefficient multiplied by the ratio of the standard error of the independent variable to the standard error of the dependent variable.

51. Yet another problem was posed by the possibility of interactions between the income of children and the number of children in various age/sex groups. An equation was specified with dummy variables for each age/sex group of children (1=one or more persons in the group, 0=otherwise), a dummy variable for income from children (1=some income from children, 0=otherwise), and interaction terms between the dummy income variable and the number of children in each age/sex

group. The results did not indicate any large or significant coefficients on the interaction terms, so that this specification was not used.

52. The 1889/1890 Survey gave data on the age and sex composition of the nuclear family but only gave the total number in an aggregate category "Boarders and Others" for each household.

53. An effort was made to assess the importance of other dependents to family expenditure in the Commissioner of Labor Survey. Since the survey only reported the total number of "Boarders and Others," a separate equation was run for the families who had no income from boarders and which included, as an additional independent variable, the total number of "Others." The assumption was that families reporting no boarder income would have no boarders and that the total number of persons in this category would be other dependents. The estimated coefficient for this number of other dependents was very small: about $4 per year in extra consumption per dependent. It therefore seemed that additional dependents had little effect on total expenditure and that their presence probably resulted more in changing composition and allocation of consumption within the household. On the positive side, however, the incidence of families having other dependents in the Philadelphia census sample was not particularly large, being 360 out of 2,238 families or 16.1 percent.

54. This would have some impact on the subsequent analysis, since a shortfall in head's income could be made up partly through income from wealth (i.e., housing services by wholly owned homes). The incidence of home-ownership is not available, however, in the 1880 census.

55. It was thought at first that the negative and insignificant coefficients might have been the result of a nonlinearity of the relationship of expenditure to age of male family head and spouse, but a quadratic specification did not yield any better results. Thus, the original specification was retained.

56. The odd result posed by the low coefficient for males 18 and over was troublesome. One would have expected a higher number from older males, particularly, but the result was taken as it stood in preference to some arbitrary adjustment.

57. The test is described in Gregory Chow, "Tests of Equality Between Sets of Coefficients in Two Linear Regressions," *Econometrica* 28 (1960), 591–605. The value of the Chow test was F=62.560 which is significant at a 1 percent level with 154,342 degrees of freedom.

58. This issue is discussed in much more detail in Haines, "Industrial Work and the Family Life Cycle, 1889/1890," where it is pointed out that children, and not wives, were the secondary wage earners of importance.

59. Glassberg, "Work, Wages, and the Cost of Living."

60. Massachusetts Bureau of Labor, *Sixth Annual Report*, 447; Steven Dubnoff, "The Life Cycle and Economic Welfare," 14.

61. Income per capita in the United States increased from $327 in 1877/1881 to $335 in 1887/1891. This was in current dollar prices. Prices declined over the same period: the Consumer Price Index from 29 in 1879 to 27 in 1889 (base: 1967=100) and the more volatile Warren-Pearson wholesale price index from 90 in 1879 to 81 in 1889 (base: 1910–14=100). Data derived from U.S. Bureau of Census, *Historical Statistics of the United States, Colonial Times to 1970* (Washington, D.C.: U.S. G.P.O., 1975), Part 1, Series F-71, A-7, E-135, E-52.

62. See comments in U.S. Commissioner of Labor, *Sixth Annual Report* (1890); *Seventh Annual Report* (1891), passim. The latter is reprinted in the *Sixth Annual Report*, 688–90. The following quote is both amusing and revealing: "I think sometimes in our efforts to make both ends meet we are like a kitten I once had who tried with all his might to catch his tail. He kept twirling round and round and

round, always with the end he so much wanted in view, but never quite reaching it."

63. One way to view the income and especially the expenditure estimates is as a form of standardization. The husband is assigned a standardized income based on occupation, age, and possibly, unemployment information. The family is standardized to a "minimum adequacy" predicted expenditure pattern based on the ages and sexes of family members.

64. The sample being used here is of families and not households. Households can consist of more than one family. Because the sample is of families and not households, the proportions headed by each ethnic group are no longer exact. This also accounts for the appearance of a few families with British-born heads.

65. See Laurie, Hershberg, and Alter, "Immigrants and Industry."

66. See the paper by Claudia Goldin, "Family Strategies and the Family Economy in the Late Nineteenth Century: The Role of Secondary Workers"; in this volume.

67. See Haines, "Industrial Work and the Family Life Cycle, 1889/1890"; Dubnoff, "The Life Cycle and Economic Welfare."

68. The decline in expected minimum adequacy expenditures for family heads above age 60 may be attributed to a reduction in family size as older children finally left home.

69. It is also to be noted that only for the age group 30–39 does the average estimated income of family head come close to the $643 poverty threshold calculated by Glassberg.

70. The age 11 was selected as appropriate for examining the population of children largely at risk of entering the paid labor force because of customary practices of school leaving and child employment.

71. There was always the possibility of renting larger quarters in the expectation that the extra space would be used for boarding and lodging. Thus, wealth was not necessarily a barrier. Also presumably some houses could be obtained through mortgages.

72. If all heads of household in each category of ethnicity were equally distributed according to a rectangular distribution, then one would expect something much closer to 25 percent in each cell (across the quartiles). This is approximately what did happen in the distribution of *total* families across the cells, but not to families in particular ethnic groups.

73. There is also the effect of ethnicity or consumption directly to be considered. The dummy variable for place of birth in the expenditure equations always assigned more consumption to families with foreign-born heads, holding all other things constant.

74. Fertility was generally higher among the illiterate. This has been shown true for the Pennsylvania anthracite region. See Michael R. Haines, "Fertility, Marriage and Occupation in the Pennsylvania Anthracite Region, 1850–1880," *The Journal of Family History* 2 (Spring 1977), Table 4. Research is currently underway to examine differential fertility and marriage in Philadelphia over this period.

75. Valerie K. Oppenheimer, "The Life Cycle Squeeze: The Interaction of Men's Occupational and Family Life Cycles," *Demography* 11 (May 1974), 227–45.

76. An example of this table may be seen in the Commissioner of Labor Survey data where 50.2 percent of puddlers, heaters, moulders, and rollers (i.e., skilled metal refiners) were below age 40 while 65.6 percent of laborers were *above* age 40. Similar results held in the case of Philadelphia.

77. This issue has attracted a good deal of attention in the literature on the economic demography of developing areas. See, for example, Robert A. Repetto, "Direct Economic Costs and Benefits of Children," and Eva Mueller, "The Eco-

nomic Value of Children in Peasant Agriculture," in Ronald Ridker, ed., *Population and Development: The Search for Selective Interventions* (Baltimore: Johns Hopkins University Press, 1976), 77–153. This, of course, assumes a demographic regime in which there is some choice as to completed family size.

78. Robert A. Pollak and Terence Wales, "Welfare Comparisons and Equivalence Scales," *American Economic Review* 69 (May 1979).

79. Haines, "Industrial Work and the Family Life Cycle, 1889/1890." See particularly the following essay in this volume by Claudia Goldin, "Family Strategies and the Family Economy in the Late Nineteenth Century."

80. See John Modell, Frank F. Furstenberg, Jr., and Theodore Hershberg, "Social Change and the Transitions to Adulthood in Historical Perspective," *Journal of Family History* 1 (Autumn 1976), 7–32; also in this volume.

Appendix: Some Theoretical and Empirical Problems in Estimating the Expenditure Equation

This appendix will present a simplified model of a family economy which will allow a discussion of some of the theoretical problems in estimating expenditure equations based on demographic information alone.

Assume every family has one parent (p) and one child (c), whose age (A) is a random variable. (Assuming more children and two parents does not add any conceptual difficulties. It only complicates the algebra.) The family has total income (Y), partly from the parent (Y_p), which is determined exogenously, and partly from the child (Y_c) determined endogenously as a product of the child's wage (W_c), assumed not necessarily to vary with age, and hours of work (H_c). Thus, in this simple model:

1. $Y = Y_p + Y_c$ [family income]
2. $Y_c = W_c \cdot H_c$ [child's income]
and 3. $H_c = \alpha_0 + \alpha_1 Y_p + \alpha_2 A$

This last equation (3) expresses child's hours of work (i.e., labor supplied) as a function of parent's income and age. It is assumed that $\alpha_1 < 0$ and $\alpha_2 > 0$.

The family's expenditures (E) might depend only on the family's income, or

4. $E = \beta_0 + \beta_1 Y$ [family expenditure]

where we expect $\beta_1 > 0$. Alternatively, there might exist some minimum adequacy expenditure standard for each family member—here dependent only on the child's age—below which one strongly resists falling. Then there would be some lower bound to E for each family, say $\bar{E}$. For $Y \geqslant Y_p \geqslant E \geqslant \bar{E}$, 4 would be relevant. But if $Y_p < \bar{E} = E$, then

5. $\bar{E} = \beta_0' + \beta_2' A$ [minimum adequacy budget]

is appropriate. Equation 5 expresses a poverty line—a subsistence expenditure for each family dependent only on its composition. As soon as $Y > \bar{E}$, you cannot estimate (in stochastic form) because families are then unconstrained. If $Y_p > \bar{E}$, then families can borrow, take in boarders, or send their children to work (i.e., $H_c > 0$). But, if this added income from children (or boarders) raises their income above $\bar{E}$, they are then in the regime given by 4.

Yet another specification of the expenditure function might be:

6. $E = \gamma_0 + \gamma_1 Y + \gamma_2 A$
   $= \gamma_0 + \gamma_1 (Y_p + Y_c) + \gamma_2 A$

where $\gamma_1 > 0$ and $\gamma_2 > 0$. This expenditure equation allows for both an effect of income (γ_1) and an independent effect for the presence and age of the child (γ_2), beyond that implied by the child's earnings. Solving for the reduced form of this expression (assuming that it is part of the structural system including equations 1, 2, 3, and 6), we obtain:

6′. $E = \gamma_0 + \gamma_1 Y_p + \gamma_1 (W_c) (\alpha_0 + \alpha_1 Y_p + \alpha_2 A) + \gamma_2 A$
    $= (\gamma_0 + \gamma_1 W_c \alpha_0) + \gamma_1 (1 + W_c \alpha_1) Y_p + (\gamma_1 W_c \alpha_2 + \gamma_2) A$

There are two empirical problems in this paper which may be discussed in the context of this equation. The first concerns the importance of children's earnings. If equation 6 were estimated (in stochastic form) *without* including the income from children (i.e., assuming that the earnings of children did not matter to the family in terms of expenditures), the coefficient of A, the age of the child, would always be upwardly biased. This is because $(\gamma_1 W_c \alpha_2 + \gamma_2) > \gamma_2$ since $\gamma_1 > 0$, $W_c > 0$ (and assumed constant), and $\alpha_2 > 0$. This would then overestimate the "pure" effect of an additional child of a given age on minimum family consumption. What is desired is an estimate of γ_2. This can be obtained by estimating

$E = \gamma_0 + \gamma_1 Y_p + \gamma_1 Y_c + \gamma_2 A$

and then dropping the term $\gamma_1 Y_c$. This would yield the "pure" effect of an additional child. Here it is assumed that the family cannot obtain earnings from the child, and the question is asked: what would the family spend even if it could obtain no earnings from the child? The actual estimation was done using a series of variables for children in various age/sex categories, instead of a single A, and also a variable for the earnings of all children together. It is encouraging that comparing estimated linear expenditure equations including and excluding children's earnings reveals that the coefficients for the age/sex groups were uniformly lower in the equations including children's income. Thus, the bias was in the predicted direction.

The second problem concerns the decision not to include the earnings of the head of the family in the expenditure equation. It is commonly assumed that income of the principal wage earner is the main determinant of family spending. For the entire renter sample from the Northern states in the 1889/1890 Commissioner of Labor Survey, this was indeed true. But by truncating the sample into a lower group (i.e., those in the lowest quartile of family income per capita) under conditions of "economic stress," it was felt the earnings of the head were not relevant to expenditure decisions for these constrained families. In terms of equation 6, this is equivalent to estimating

$$6''. \ E = [\gamma_0 + \gamma_1 \ \bar{Y}_p] + \gamma_1 \ Y_c + \gamma_2 \ A$$

where the first term in brackets is the constant term and where Y_p is income of the head of family held constant at the sample mean. This really tries to estimate expected expenditure if income of the head were constrained to be equal to that of the mean for the families in the lowest quartile. (This was $388 for the lowest quartile of family income per capita in the Commissioner of Labor Survey.) From the standpoint of estimation, it is encouraging that the income of head (Y_p), when included in the equations for the lowest quartile and for the top three quartiles, was much less important in terms of variation explained in the equation for the lowest quartile. (It was, however, not statistically insignificant.) One point to note is that when we look at the form of 6 which holds Y_p constant (i.e., $6''$) and estimate it for the lowest quartile of income per capita, the coefficients are significantly different for the specification between the equation for the lowest quartile and the equation for the upper three quartiles. We thus have some support for the notion that the families in the lowest quartile are "constrained." It is most likely that what is actually being estimated is something like $6''$ and, therefore, what must be assumed is what the expenditure behavior of the family would be if the head only earned roughly $390 per year. This is more than a laborer in Philadelphia in 1880 could earn in a year but much less than what could be earned by craftsmen, proprietors, skilled workers, professionals, and most white-collar workers. When the $\gamma_1 \ Y_c$ is eliminated, we get

$$7. \ E = [\gamma_0 + \gamma_1 \ \bar{Y}_p] + \gamma_2 \ A$$

which is the minimum expenditure of the family if the head were constrained to a low (average) income and if the family could not earn extra income from the child.

There are specification biases introduced by estimating equation 7 instead of equation 6 in one of its forms. This is because the income of the head of family (Y_p) does not turn out to be statistically unimportant (or uncorrelated with the other variables) for the lowest quartile. But, since actual income data are lacking for the 1880 Philadelphia families, these must be estimated. If these were then used on the right-hand side of an expenditure equation, this would introduce bias because of errors in variables. One is forced to choose between two econometric evils. The course chosen here was to estimate the "constrained" expenditure equation (i.e., equation 7) and compare the estimated results with the estimated incomes.

8. Family Strategies and the Family Economy in the Late Nineteenth Century: The Role of Secondary Workers

CLAUDIA GOLDIN

Family Strategies and the Family Economy: A Framework for Analysis

Families and households are the most fundamental decision-making units of the economy, determining a vast array of economic behavior, including labor supply, commodity demand, population growth, mobility, and savings. The family, by a complex set of processes, determines its size and composition, the allocation of each household member's time, its geographic location, and its expenditures. Few individuals ever make these decisions *in vacuo* during any part of their lives.[1] Most of these decisions are jointly determined within the family and are, as well, interrelated over time. For example, the labor force participations of various family members are the results of interconnected decisions and are also dependent upon future choices. A daughter might be asked to labor in the home rather than in the factory because remaining at home might enhance her potential marital status. The savings behavior of parents might be greatly affected by the assurance that their children will provide for them in their later years, and children might be encouraged to do so both by particular inheritance patterns and by other economic incentives to remain in their parents' household.

Sections of this paper were originally presented at the Social Science History Association (Ann Arbor, Michigan: 1977); and at the Conference on Regional Economic History, "Economy and Society: Philadelphia and Its Hinterland" (Wilmington, Del.: October 1978). Portions of the material on white households have been taken from the author's "Household and Market Production of Families in a Late Nineteenth-Century American City," *Explorations in Economic History* 16 (1979), 111–31.

I use the term "strategy" to describe a set of interrelated family decisions involving economic and demographic variables. Interrelations among such decisions can be highly complex. Strategies may require families to consider events in the distant future, as in the set of decisions made by parents to ensure security in their old age. A shorter range strategy might be the set of decisions governing how a family copes financially with the illness or unemployment of its prime income earner.

Families and households are the primary economic units in contemporary analysis. The late nineteenth century, however, provides an even richer period in which to explore the concepts of family strategies. In many respects, the decisions of families with regard to economic variables were more manifest in the late nineteenth-century urban economy in part due to lower levels of real per capita income and greater economic insecurity.[2] Secondary workers in a family in 1880, for example, included children, even relatively young ones, whereas families today typically have no more than two income providers. The joint determination of the labor supply of the husband and wife has been an important problem of contemporary labor economics. The late nineteenth century, in contrast, provides a more complex analytic problem—the joint determination of the labor supply of parents and children, where the number and characteristics of the children were also subject to choice.

In making decisions today and in the past, the family has taken cognizance of certain immutable facts of life, what economists generally term the "constraints." Constraints, which include both cultural and structural variables, were probably more numerous and more severe in times past. Societal norms, in particular, were probably sufficiently strong so that most families treated certain aspects of life as fixed. Fathers usually worked, and married white women rarely held jobs outside the home.[3] Hindrances were often imposed on the family from outside by the peculiarities of the late nineteenth-century city. Horse-drawn streetcars, though a convenient method of transportation, were far too expensive to be used by the vast bulk of working people on a daily basis. The average journey to work in Philadelphia was probably not over one mile and rarely as much as two in 1880.[4] Therefore, once located, the family's residence imposed considerable constraints.

Historians, in general, have stressed these constraints to the neglect of the decisions or choice variables and have attributed much of the observed behavior of families to the somewhat ambiguous term "culture." Economists, in comparison, have put far more emphasis on behavioral results as being generated by rational decision-making subject to tastes and constraints. Much of the emphasis by historians on constraints stems not merely from a somewhat different model of human behavior but, more importantly, from a concern with decision-making in past centuries. Ordinary people in times past were, indeed, faced with severe constraints—economic, cultural, and institutional—and were bound by tradition far more than today. But families, at some point in time, began to control more of their present and future lives and eventually were capable of planning long-run strategies of life. At what point meaningful long-run family strategies emerged is not known, but it is clear that many such strategies were the norm by the late nineteenth century.[5]

The analytic approach taken in this paper enables a partial sorting-out of the constraints, including cultural aspects, from the variables subject to choice. For example, the labor force participation of children was a choice variable that depended upon such considerations as the income and unemployment of the father, and that depended, as well, upon differences in tastes among families which may have varied systematically with factors such as ethnicity, race, and literacy. The heterogeneity of Philadelphia's late nineteenth-century population permits a cross-cultural analysis of family decision-making. Philadelphia contained about 850,000 people in 1880 and was an ethnically and economically diverse city. It was the second largest city in the United States both in terms of population and manufacturing activity. About 16 percent of its citizens lived in households headed by a German-born individual, and about 25 percent resided in Irish-headed households. Philadelphia, in addition, contained over 30,000 blacks, the most extensive group of Afro-Americans in any Northern city.

This article has two purposes: first and most importantly, to analyze the patterns of labor force participation among secondary workers; and second, to provide a framework for analyzing family strategies and the family economy. A small but related portion of the choice variables facing late nineteenth-century families will be described and analyzed. A brief outline describes one approach to the larger topic.

It is convenient to group economic decisions into three, somewhat simplified, categories. The first is the allocation of family members' time and income. The members of a family can allocate their time to the marketplace, to work in the household, to leisure broadly defined, and to education, including job-training. The allocation of time incorporates many short-run strategies, such as the response of children to a father's unexpected absence from the labor force, and it is also linked to longer-run strategies, such as the age of independence of children and the inheritance patterns of families. The age at which adult children leave their parents' household may be determined largely by their work and educational experiences when they were young. The expenditures or budgets of the famiilies also involve economic choices important both for aggregate economic activity and the personal well-being of individuals.

The second category of decisions concerns the size and composition of the household, a function of both demographic and economic variables. Marital fertility and the age at marriage demographically determine the number of children ever born; child mortality and the age of independence then determine the total number of children living in the household. Families also lived with nonnuclear related individuals, boarders, and servants. A complete study of family strategies would analyze the determinants of such living arrangements: in particular, the reasons why parents, especially widows, lived with their children; why married children stayed in the homes of their parents; and why other family members and unrelated individuals boarded.

Historical studies of families typically tabulated the size and composition of households, rather than analyzed their determinants.[6] An analysis of family strategies could remedy this deficiency by integrating size and composition into other aspects of family decisions. It is suggested in the empirical work that follows that nonnuclear, related family members and boarders were an integral part of the family economy and were particularly important in determining the work experiences of daughters.

A third category of decisions, not explicitly analyzed here, concerns the geographic location of the family. Nineteenth-century Philadelphia was primarily a "walking city." Convenience to friends, place of worship, and stores influenced the family's location, but proximity to work was probably of primary importance. Work meant not only the major breadwinner's job but also those of children and other family members. The location of the father's job may have determined the economic opportunities of the others but, most likely, family location decisions were made to optimize all resources. In the short run, family decisions took location as a constraint, but minimized its impact over longer periods through geographic mobility both within and from the city.[7]

The Data and Outline of the Paper

The data for this study originated in the 1880 U.S. Federal Population Census manuscripts for Philadelphia. These data yield detailed information on both individual and household characteristics. Ever since its inception in 1790, the census has been a tabulation of American households, amassing information on every household member, including boarders and servants. The census of 1880 was the first to list the relationship of these various household members to the "head" of the household. The information recorded for 1880 includes geographic (street address) location, full name, race, sex, age, relationship to the head of the household, marital status, occupation, number of months unemployed during the census year, infirmities, school attendance, literacy in any language, place of birth, and place of parents' birth (see Appendix II).

This article summarizes findings from two distinct but related projects, each using a different portion of the manuscript census data. The first, on working children in native-born white and immigrant families, uses the 1880 PSHP household sample. These data were grouped by families and subfamilies to allow analyses both at the family and the household levels. The second project, on secondary workers and family structure in black households, uses the PSHP's black population data. The PSHP coded the entire population of black residents of Philadelphia but, for various reasons detailed below, these data were sampled, "reconstituting" family and subfamily structures.

The primary question addressed in this essay is what determined the labor force participation of secondary workers in late nineteenth-century families; in particular, which children worked for pay outside the home. Several related issues that demand separate study cannot be entirely ignored in this research. Married white women rarely worked for pay on a full-time basis, although more than one-fifth of all black married women did. The analysis of white children does not directly address why their mothers chose not to work outside their homes, although that for black children does implicitly model the joint determination of children's and mother's work. Household structure can also be analyzed together with labor force decisions, for example, in terms of the living arrangements of widows and their children. The number and characteristics of children in the home are, as well, determined jointly with their labor force participation.[8] White and black families will be analyzed separately in view of the distinct differences in their family structures and in their intrafamily allocations of time. Comparisons among the ethnic and racial groups will be highlighted in the conclusions.

The White Family Economy: Children in the Labor Force

The Characteristics of White Families in 1880 Philadelphia. Philadelphia's white residents lived primarily in nuclear units but, as indicated by Table 1, a large percentage lived in expanded and extended households with family members other than their spouses and children. Over 23 percent of the dual parent families in which the head was a native-born white American had at least one family member outside the nuclear unit, and this figure increases to over 28 percent for the fifty to fifty-nine year-old age group. Ger-

Table 1.   Philadelphia's Families and Households, 1880, by Ethnicity and Race

| | | Households Headed by | | |
| | | | | Native-Born |
	Irish	German	White	Black[e]
(1) Average Number of Individuals[a,c]	4.743	4.687	4.237	
(2) Average Number of Children[a,b,d]				
(a) Age of father: 40–49 years	2.699	2.627	2.037	1.609
(b) Age of father: 50–59 years	2.674	2.428	2.090	1.602
(c) Age of father: 60–69 years	2.325	1.819	1.822	1.179
(3) Percent with Nonnuclear, Related Individuals[a,b]				
(a) Age of father: across all ages	16.1%	13.5%	23.6%	
(b) Age of father: 50–59 years	16.1	13.5	28.2	
(4) Percentage with Related Subfamilies[a]	3.55	4.11	6.47	
(5) Percentage with Boarders or Subtenants[a,b]	15.53	16.06	16.11	32.7
(6) Percent with Servants[a]	4.99	9.32	16.29	

[a] Primary families. The "primary family" is the nuclear or extended family of the head of the household, as listed by the census marshal.

[b] Both parents present.

[c] Excludes servants and boarders.

[d] Children living at home.

[e] Certain data that are less meaningful for black families and households have been omitted. See discussion in the text regarding subtenanting and reconstituting family relationships in the black sample.

man and Irish families, for obvious reasons related to immigration, had a lower percentage of expanded households, 13.5 percent and 16.1 percent, respectively. About one in six households across all ethnic groups boarded unrelated individuals, and other data indicate that such households were disproportionately female-headed and older.

Fully 30 percent of the Irish male heads between thirty to fifty-five years old were unspecified laborers, and 14 percent more were unskilled specified laborers not employed in industry. At the other extreme, possibly one-third of all German male heads were proprietors, that is bakers, dealers, grocers, tavern keepers, and owners of assorted small businesses, and over 40 percent were skilled or semiskilled craftsmen, such as tailors, shoemakers, cabinetmakers, and machinists. The Irish and German male heads occupied the two extremes of the skill and wage spectrum, whereas native-born white male heads were more evenly distributed, although disproportionately employed in professional and clerical jobs.

Although there were numerous constraints governing the economic lives of these nineteenth-century families, they did not face effective legal restraints in sending their children into the labor market. Several states had enforceable child labor laws by the 1880s, but Pennsylvania did not, and it was not until 1901 that it passed a compulsory education act, a necessary

Table 2. The Schooling and Labor Force Experiences of Children in Philadelphia, 1880

(Percentage of single children living at home, at work and at school by age, sex, race, and ethnicity for children in primary families.)

	Age	Native-Born Whites			Irish			German			Black[a]		
		Work	School	N	Work	School	N	Work	School	N	Work	School	N
M	11	3.0%	91.1%	84	6.0%	90.8%	92	3.9%	92.9%	127	0.0%	85.7%	21
A	12	9.4	83.0	106	11.7	82.7	124	9.0	85.1	117	7.7	84.6	26
L	13	15.5	76.1	71	30.4	62.8	117	29.3	58.2	97	22.7	72.7	22
E	14	32.0	55.6	89	36.3	51.9	109	60.8	25.8	123	33.3	61.9	21
S	15	45.6	45.6	68	59.9	30.7	96	68.8	19.4	93	45.8	41.7	24
	16	71.7	21.0	69	72.2	16.7	108	81.0	9.6	105	41.2	52.9	17
	17	72.6	16.1	62	87.7	8.1	93	85.5	4.5	110	90.0	10.0	20
	18	80.3	12.1	66	86.2	4.3	105	88.3	7.0	107	95.5[b]	0.1	67
	19	85.1	7.9	57	95.3	2.8	106	92.2	1.0	103			
	>20	91.8	2.2	451	95.9	0.7	604	94.5	1.8	509	79.4[c]	0.1	77
F	11	1.1	88.9	90	3.0	87.9	99	3.5	92.7	130	3.1	87.5	32
E	12	5.2	85.6	97	15.0	74.4	133	9.4	80.0	143	10.7	78.6	28
M	13	10.1	78.5	79	15.8	71.6	95	15.5	56.0	116	11.1	75.0	36
A	14	11.9	72.6	84	37.3	45.7	107	28.3	31.9	113	22.7	54.5	22
L	15	20.0	53.8	65	38.8	28.2	103	41.5	7.5	100	14.3	71.4	21
E	16	38.9	34.5	68	57.7	15.8	105	49.2	9.0	122	48.3	24.1	29
S	17	20.4	25.9	54	56.8	6.8	88	55.3	2.6	114	61.1	11.1	18
	18	40.8	2.8	71	58.0	6.7	119	51.9	3.3	109	61.1[b]	7.4	54
	19	34.3	0.0	70	68.2	0.0	88	56.7	1.9	104			
	>20	36.5	0.7	411	66.5	0.7	576	45.6	1.7	458	66.7[c]	0.0	57

Source: Federal Population Census Manuscripts, Philadelphia, 1880, sample collected by the Philadelphia Social History Project.

Note: Ethnicity refers to place of birth of household head; work (school) = percentage of children in age group at work (school); N = number of observations in each age group. The percentage at work and the percentage at school do not sum to 100%. The residual were listed in the census as "at home." The small number of those listed as having both an occupation and being at school were divided equally between these two categories, although they were assigned to the labor force category for the regression analysis.

[a]Includes all families, not only primary families.

[b]Includes 18 to 21 year-olds.

[c]Includes 22 year-olds and older.

prerequisite for effective child labor legislation.[9] Philadelphia's manufacturing sector provided an abundance of tasks which could be performed by children of all ages and, furthermore, families often employed their own children as apprentices and helpers. Children were a major economic resource in the nineteenth-century family, contributing income in normal times, and supporting their families in especially difficult situations.

Children's participation in the labor force varied with their age, sex, race, and the ethnicity of the household head (as shown in Table 2).[10] The children of immigrants, in this case the Irish and the Germans, labored in the market to greater degree than did the children of native-born household heads. The higher labor force participation rates of these Irish and German children reduced the disparities in the incomes of their families, with children in immigrant families contributing a larger percentage of family income than did native-born white youngsters. Irish children contributed between 38 percent and 46 percent of total family labor income in dual parent families where the father's age was between fifty and seventy. For German children, these percentages are 33 percent to 35 percent and for the native-born, 28 perecnt to 32 percent.[11] Boys worked in the market more than girls, and older children more than younger. What can explain why these children worked? What factors served to increase or decrease their participation? Which particular children in a family worked and which did not?

Qualitative evidence on these issues is not easy to obtain. Most magazines of the time, for example, appealed to families who were concerned that their daughters be educated "in a showy, superficial manner, [dressed] . . . as handsomely as . . . means will permit, and [passed] over to the young men, who are expected to have one or two or three servants. . . ."[12] There was scarcely a hint that over one-third of all native-born white daughters over fifteen years old worked outside the home and that a substantially greater percentage of the daughters of immigrant families did as well. Quantitative data on the characteristics of children, their families, and their households must be used instead to provide at least partial answers to these questions.

The Determinants of Child Labor Force Participation. Models of household and market production suggest a set of useful variables with which to explain the labor force participation of a particular family member.[13] These include the comparative advantage of the family member in the labor market or in household production, the income of the family, and the household demands of the family. The comparative advantage of a child's working in the labor market would depend, for example, on the child's wage rate, the characteristics of other children in the family, the absence of either parent, and the child's future vocation.

Wage data for 1880 Philadelphia and Pennsylvania, for example, indicate that girls less than fifteen years old earned about 86 percent of what boys of the same age did; this ratio decreased with age, reaching 70 percent by maturity in most occupations.[14] Sons, therefore, would be more likely to specialize in labor market work in families also containing daughters. Because the age-wage profile rose more sharply for males than for females, birth ordering should also have influenced time allocation decisions. One would expect, for example, that older brothers had a strong comparative advantage in the labor market over younger brothers, but that older sisters would have had little advantage over younger sisters in the labor market.

The variables explaining the labor force participation of the children should account for various household characteristics as well as those pertaining to the individual child. The variables relating to the children should proxy the child's comparative advantage in the market. Demands in the home and exogenously determined income and wealth should also be included. The information in the 1880 Federal Population Census has been supplemented with wage data from various nineteenth-century sources to construct family labor income from occupations.

Demographic Characteristics. The variables included to account for the individual characteristics of the child, its siblings, its parents, its family and other household members are given in Table 3. The characteristics of siblings—variables 2 through 5—are included to account for the comparative advantage of the child in the labor market. Older children would be more productive outside the home, but the above observations concerning relative age-wage profiles indicated that the extent of this comparative advantage would depend on the child's sex. The presence of younger siblings, variable 6, should account for increased household demands on older children. The absence of either parent—variables 7 and 8—would probably affect the labor force participation of children. One would expect that a girl without a mother would be more likely to remain at home, but that the absence of a father would increase the probability of all children being in the labor force.

Economic Characteristics. Variables 9 through 18 are included to account for some of the economic characteristics of the child's family and household. The father's labor income has been inferred from his occupation by matching it to nineteenth-century wage data for occupations in Philadelphia and Pennsylvania.[15] The father's occupation is assumed to be exogenously

Table 3. List of Variables, Definitions, and Sample Means for Tables 4 and 6

VARIABLE NAME	VARIABLE NUMBER		DEFINITION
	Table 4	Table 6	
AGECHILD	1		Age, in years
AGE11–15		1	Dummy = 1 if 11 to 15 years
#OLDBROS	2	2	Number of older brothers
#OLDSIS	3	3	Number of older sisters
#YNGBROS	4	4	Number of younger brothers over 10 yrs.
#YNGSIS	5	5	Number of younger sisters over 10 yrs.
CHILD6	6	6	Dummy = 1 if a sibling is 0–6 yrs.
MOM	7	7	Dummy = 1 if mother at home
POP	8	8	Dummy = 1 if father at home
WAGEPOP[a]	9	9	Yearly labor income of father x 10^{-3}
AGEFAM	10	10	Age of father if POP = 1; Age of mother if POP = 0
UNSKILL[b]	11		Dummy = 1 if father is unskilled
SKILL	12		Dummy = 1 if father is skilled or proprietor
UNPOP	13	11	Months unemployed for father
WAGEMOM[a]	14		Yearly labor income of mother x 10^{-3}
MOMINWORK[c]		12	Dummy = 1 if mother works for pay at home
MOMOUTWORK[c]		13	Dummy = 1 if mother works for pay outside home
ILLITMOM	15	14	Dummy = 1 if mother is illiterate
WAGEOFM[a]	16		Yearly labor income of other family members (nonnuclear) x 10^{-3}
SERVANT	17		Dummy = 1 if family has servants
BOARD	18	15	Dummy = 1 if family has boarders or subtenants
GERMAN	19		Dummy = 1 if head of household is German
IRISH	20		Dummy = 1 if head of household is Irish
NWA.FOR	21		Dummy = 1 if native-born parents with at least one foreign-born grandparent
RACE		16	Dummy = 1 if black; 0 if mulatto
PRIMARY		17	Dummy = 1 if primary; 0 if subtenant
POBIRTH		18	Dummy = 1 if born in South

[a] Constructed from occupations. See note #10.

[b] UNSKILL includes some service jobs, sea-related occupations, transportation jobs, and generally unskilled functions, such as helping or assisting.

[c] See text for fuller explanation.

[d] Note that sample means are for the sample of children, not separate families. Therefore any variables correlated with family size will have values that differ from the true family or household means. Note as well that these are uncondi-

determined and, therefore, so is his wage.[16] But because actual wages generally vary with age for a particular occupation, these constructed wages will not always account for changing productivity within an occupation. To make an explicit correction for this problem would involve adjusting the wage by the individual's age, and this adjustment would depend upon the

SAMPLE MEANS:[d]

WHITE		WHITE[e]			BLACK	
Male[f]	Female[f]	Irish	German	Native Born	Male[f]	Female[f]
18.52	18.43	18.20	17.76	18.63	18.39	17.47
					0.39	0.48
0.57	0.56	0.61	0.57	0.46	0.35	0.47
0.55	0.56	0.62	0.52	0.44	0.29	0.39
0.56	0.53	0.62	0.52	0.46	0.34	0.29
0.55	0.54	0.61	0.58	0.46	0.46	0.38
0.48	0.69	0.57	0.55	0.50	0.49	0.54
0.93	0.93				0.95	0.95
0.86	0.87				0.65	0.65
0.706	0.685	0.687	0.858	0.859	3.10	3.35
50.26	51.03	50.5	50.6	49.9	45.99	46.36
0.08	0.08					
0.27	0.27					
0.32	0.35	0.72	0.16	0.32	0.41	0.26
0.014	0.016	0.004	0.007	0.007		
					0.16	0.15
					0.09	0.10
0.05	0.05				0.22	0.19
0.050	0.057	0.049	0.038	0.100		
0.11	0.09	0.05	0.09	0.18		
0.14	0.15	0.12	0.14	0.17	0.30	0.31
0.36	0.37					
0.37	0.37					
0.17	0.16					
					0.78	0.76
					0.92	0.94
					0.25	0.19

tional means. For example, the actual average unemployment for black fathers is higher than the sample mean because 35 percent of all childen in the sample did not live with their fathers.

[e] These sample means include only those children with both parents present to standardize by family characteristics given the differences in age among ethnic groups. Irish and German families were somewhat older than the native-born and, therefore, had a higher incidence of single-headed families.

[f] Including only unmarried children.

age-wage profile for the particular occupation. Because such information is difficult to obtain, the age of the household head has been added to the equation.

Two occupational dummies were included for the father. The UNSKILL variable is for very low skilled occupations to account for parent's inability in locating jobs for their children. Parents with very low skilled jobs might have had few contacts to obtain jobs for their children or may have resided far from manufacturing jobs.[17] The SKILL variable is for skilled craftsmen and proprietors who might be hiring their own children. Families with high-wage fathers may have had, as well, high labor force participation rates for their children, if their children were apprentices. German fathers were disproportionately skilled craftsmen, and this variable was entered to adjust for the different occupational structures of the ethnic groups.

The presence of servants was added to proxy the family's wealth, and the presence of boarders was included because boarding increased both the family's income and the demands for household work. Variables 19 through 21 account for the ethnicity of the child's family which the empirical work will show was important in explaining the labor force participation of girls but not of boys.

The observations for this study are children over ten years old in families with at least one parent present. Children in subfamilies, that is families living within other households, were not directly included.[18] The entire sample consisted of 8,282 never married children, 4,113 females, and 4,169 males.

A child can be either in the labor force, as indicated by the listing of an occupation, or engaged in another activity, at school or at home. The dependent variable is, therefore, dichotomous; it can be either 1 or 0. There are several econometric problems that arise when the dependent variable is dichotomous. Such problems obviate the use of an ordinary least squares regression and necessitate the use of a procedure such as probit analysis.[19] One obvious consideration is that the predicted values of the dependent variable should be bounded on the zero to one interval, and ordinary least squares will not guarantee such a result. Note as well that the predicted value of the dependent variable is the probability of a child's being in the labor force, even though in actuality the child is either in or not in the labor force. One can also interpret these predicted probabilities as the percentage of a large sample of children with a given set of characteristics who are in the labor force.

The Results of the Analysis of Child Labor Force Participation. The probit regression results in Table 4 are presented separately for male and female children.[20] The coefficients of these equations must be interpreted first by constructing an index which is a linear function of the independent variables and then by getting the value of the standard normal cumulative distribution at the index. The procedure yields the probability of a child's being in the labor force, conditional on the given set of individual, family, and household characteristics. Mathematically, construct an index,

$$(1)\ \hat{I} = \hat{\beta}_0 + \hat{\beta}_1 \bar{x}_1 + \ldots + \hat{\beta}_n \bar{x}_n,$$

where the $\bar{x}$'s are the characteristics of a particular child and its family, e.g., age, number of siblings and income, and the $\hat{\beta}$'s are the estimated coefficients in Table 4. The index $\hat{I}$ is then evaluated by the standard normal cumulative distribution,

$$(2)\ \hat{Y} = F(\hat{I}),$$

to get the predicted value of the dependent variable. Note that this evaluation of the index guarantees that $\hat{Y}$, or the predicted value for the dependent variable, is bounded on the zero to one interval.

Both the economic and demographic features of the family appear to have had a strong impact on the family's decision to have its children work outside the home. Because the findings of this analysis are many, and because analyzing probit coefficients is a somewhat complicated procedure, a brief discussion will summarize the major results and illustrative examples will follow. The variables will be discussed in their order in Table 4, and the examples in Table 5 will underscore the most important findings.

Birth order of siblings was generally critical in determining which of the children worked in a family. The presence of older siblings living at home was important in explaining the labor force experience of a child. For example, a boy was almost equally deterred from working by the presence of either an older brother or sister. But a young girl stood a much lower probability of working had she an older brother than had she an older sister. These results are fully consistent with the statement of a fashionable woman's magazine of the day that a girl was expected to work "to relieve her hard-working father of the burden of her support, to supply [her] home with comforts and refinements, [and] to educate a younger brother."[21] The presence of younger, working-aged siblings increased the likelihood of a child's working but, as suggested by the wage data, this impact was stronger for the boys. The presence of very young children in the family decreased the probability of all children's working, probably reflecting the increased demands youngsters created in the home.

The absence of either the mother or father greatly influenced a child's activities. A family without a father was more likely to have both its sons and daughters in the labor force, although the impact was stronger for the sons. The absence of the mother, though, had a differential effect on the male and female children, revealing a strong substitutability between daughters and their mothers within the family economy. Girls were far less likely to work in the labor market had they no mother at home, even

Table 4. The Determinants of Child Labor: Probit Analysis of White Single Male and Female Children, Over Ten Years Old, in Primary Families with at Least One Parent Present

Variable[a] (variable number)	Maximum Likelihood Estimate	MLE/ Standard Error[b]	Maximum Likelihood Estimate	MLE/ Standard Error
	Males: mean of dependent variable = 0.678		Females: mean of dependent variable = 0.384	
Constant	−1.837	−8.094	−1.144	−5.941
AGECHILD (1)	0.053	11.420	0.012	2.996
#OLDBROS (2)	−0.133	−4.495	−0.215	−7.529
#OLDSIS (3)	−0.188	−6.450	0.028	1.013
#YNGBROS (4)	0.410	10.750	0.182	6.639
#YNGSIS (5)	0.346	9.272	0.280	10.224
CHILD6 (6)	−0.141	−4.924	−0.066	−2.313
MOM (7)	−0.264	−2.427	0.396	4.610
POP (8)	−0.256	−2.699	−0.194	−2.341
WAGEPOP (9)	−0.167	−3.270	−0.304	−6.060
AGEFAM (10)	0.038	11.532	0.006	2.096
UNSKILL (11)	−0.095	−1.079	−0.138	−1.670
SKILL (12)	0.031	0.539	0.046	0.896
UNPOP (13)	0.043	2.361	0.015	1.276
WAGEMOM (14)	0.414	1.247	−0.114	−0.401
ILLITMOM (15)	0.383	3.115	0.439	4.375
WAGEOFM (16)	0.001	0.063	−0.264	−2.417
SERVANT (17)	−0.610	−7.774	−0.857	−8.981
BOARD (18)	0.077	1.148	−0.171	−2.794
GERMAN (19)	0.119	1.429	0.274	3.498
IRISH (20)	0.001	0.009	0.464	5.802
NWA.FOR (21)	−0.079	−0.858	−0.079	−0.874
−2 times log likelihood ratio[c]	1543		813	
Number of observations	4169		4113	

[a]See Table 3 for variable definitions and sample means.

[b]Maximum likelihood estimate/standard error, which has a 't' distribution asymptotically.

[c]Distributed as chi-square with 21 degrees of freedom. The null hypothesis is that all coefficients are zero.

though their brothers were equally influenced to work by the absence of either parent.

The higher the father's wage, the lower the probability of a child's participating in the labor force. These responses to changes in full-time labor income are with respect only to changes in occupational titles because wages were assigned by occupations. Within an occupation, labor income can vary by productivity differences and by unemployment. Productivity has been partially proxied in the regressions by including the age of the father, and, as expected, this variable has a positive sign, implying that the older the father the more probable the labor force participation of the children.[22] The older the father, the more the assigned wage overstates the actual wage and, therefore, the more probable, given the occupation, the children will be in the labor force. The variables UNSKILL and

SKILL were entered to account for occupational differences not captured in the wage variables. The coefficients on these variables have the expected signs but are not highly significant, suggesting that the wage variable incorporates most of the important effects of occupational differences.[23]

The unemployment of the family's prime breadwinner was an additional economic factor in the labor force experiences of the children.[24] Because many nineteenth-century families were severely constrained by limited savings and the virtual absence of saleable assets, unemployment should have greatly increased the probability of a child's participating in the labor force.[25] Male children were extremely affected by their father's unemployment, although daughters were somewhat less influenced by this factor. A father's unemployment did provide a strong incentive to send sons into the labor market.

The illiteracy of the parents can indicate lower productivity for a given occupational title, in a manner similar to age. Illiteracy can, as well, measure the relative gains from a child's living with its parents, as against being employed outside the family. Children with more educated mothers might learn from them, an effect that was probably greater for girls than for boys, and become more productive individuals by remaining in the household. Educated parents might, as well, value more highly both education and leisure for their children. Illiteracy was entered in the equations separately for the mother and the father, although the impact of the latter was not significant and was omitted. Girls with illiterate mothers were far more likely to be in the labor force, and boys were similarly affected by this variable, although the impact was somewhat weaker.

Literary and impressionistic evidence from the nineteenth century has been insufficient in resolving whether nonnuclear but related household members formed an integral part of the family economy. The regression results indicate that these household members were indeed part of the family's decision-making unit. Daughters, but not sons, were very strongly affected by the presence of working relatives. A dollar from an uncle or grandparent, for example, had about the same impact as an additional dollar in wages from a father in reducing the probability of a daughter's working in the market. The impact of the income provided by other family members was reinforced by the greater demands placed on daughters by increased housework. But it was the income from other family members and not their presence that provided the deterrent effect to the labor force participation of daughters.[26] The presence of servants is a good proxy for wealth among nineteenth-century families, and both the male and female children whose families had servants stood a substantially reduced probability of working in the labor market.

The boarding of unrelated individuals was a common nineteenth-century urban phenomenon, and families generally housed boarders in rooms emptied by their grown children. Boarding was for many families a major way of supplementing labor income and providing support in parents' later years. Married and widowed women, not desiring to work outside their homes, could financially assist their families through the institution of boarding. The impact of boarding was, similar to that of income from other family members, primarily on the daughters, for whom it was a strong deterrent to labor force participation. The income provided the family by boarders most likely accounted for this effect, which was probably reinforced by boarding's increased demands on home duties.[27]

The economic and demographic variables included in the analysis account for many of the differences among the ethnic groups. They fully account for all differences among sons, as shown by the small and insignificant coefficients on the ethnicity variables. But all differences are not accounted for among daughters. In addition, neither the male nor female regressions were affected by the inclusion of a variable accounting for children with native-born parents but at least one foreign-born grandparent. The higher labor force participation of the immigrant's male children, therefore, has been fully accounted for by differences in the other independent variables. That for the female children was not, although the impact of "foreignness" wore away after only one generation in America. These results can indicate that one part of the assimilation process was "learning" not to send your daughters into the labor force and that this socialization process occurred quite rapidly. Irish immigrants, for example, seemed to have placed a great emphasis on acquiring their own homes and involved their daughters in pursuit of this goal. Whether this was a vestige of their peasant background and culture, or part of a longer-run strategy to make their latter years economically secure is not at present known.

Ethnicity has, thus far, entered the empirical work only as a constant, that is, it has not been interacted with other independent variables. Regressions have also been estimated for males and females by ethnicity, but the hypothesis that the ethnic groups were, econometrically speaking, part of the same population could not be rejected. These results are not presented because they are, on the whole, not significantly different from those in Table 4. Only one important difference did arise in that empirical work. German children had the strongest response to household variables, that is, the wages of other family members and the presence of boarders were both stronger deterrents to the labor force participation of German children than to those in other families. Even males had lower labor force participation rates in response to a working uncle or a boarder, for example, results in strong contrast to those of the aggregate. The household appears to have been more significantly the economic unit among German than among other families.

An important feature of Table 4 is that although boys and girls responded similarly to some of their family's characteristics, they reacted quite the reverse to many others. Several variables provided these opposite responses. For example, the presence of the mother, of boarders, of income from other family members, and of older and younger siblings, indicate obvious differences among boys and girls. Sons and daughters had differing relative productivities in the household and in the market and required differing training for their future occupations inside or outside the home. But the coefficients on other variables, such as the father's unemployment and wage, provide a new view of the divergent roles of boys and girls in late nineteenth-century families. Furthermore, ethnic differences in labor force participation, as shown in Table 2, are fully accounted for by the independent variables for boys but not girls. Irish and German girls stood apart from their native-born white counterparts of similar family characteristics in the degree of their labor force participation outside the home.

The coefficients in Table 4 can be used to construct predicted probabilities of participating in the labor force, conditional on a set of characteristics for the child, its family, and household. The above discussion of the estimated coefficients has stressed their signs, statistical significance, and relative magnitudes. Predicted probabilities, however, are more illustrative, although there are an immense range of possibilities. The sample means in Table 3 for children by sex and ethnicity give some indication of relevant magnitudes to use in constructing such probabilities. Table 5 was constructed with reference to these data and shows the predicted conditional probabilities of labor force participation for a daughter or a son, each sixteen years old, under eleven illustrative circumstances.

A sixteen-year-old Irish daughter, for example, with both parents present, one older sister (adding both one older brother and one younger brother would not change the results), and a father earning the mean income, had a 42.5 percent predicted probability of working (see line 1a). The addition of an uncle earning the mean income of the father or the addition of a boarder lowers the probability to 35.6 percent (see line 3a). The different responses of boys and girls to family characteristics can be seen, for example, by observing lines 2a and 2b in comparison to 1a and 1b. These data show the son's increased labor force participation in response to his father's unemployment but indicate no change for the daughter. The absence of the mother (lines 8a and 8b) also demonstrates the opposite reaction of the children, with the boys increasing their participa-

Table 5. Conditional Probabilities of Labor Force Participation Predicted from Probit Analysis: Some Examples

Sex and Age of Child		Conditional Probability of Labor Force Participation	FAMILY CHARACTERISTICS					
			Ethnicity[a]	Parents Present[b]	Siblings	Labor Income and Source	Unempl. of Father	Other Characteristics
16-year old: Daughter	(1a)	42.5%	Irish	Both	1 older sister	father with mean income	none	none
	(1b)	53.8	Any ethnicity[c]					
Son	(2a)	42.5					2 mos.	
	(2b)	57.2						
	(3a)	35.6					none	Uncle with mean income of father or a boarder
	(3b)	57.2						
	(4a)	50.0			1 younger brother			none
	(4b)	75.6						
	(5a)	66.7						Illiterate mother
	(5b)	86.0						
	(6a)	53.8				father with ½ mean income		none
	(6b)	77.4						
	(7a)	38.2			1 older brother			

	only father	only mother	none	no income from parents	Both		
(7b)	58.3						
(8a)	24.3						
(8b)	68.2						
(9a)		58.5					
(9b)				74.4			
(10a)						Native born	25.7
(10b)						Any ethnicity	61.2
(11a)							6.6
(11b)							37.2 servants

(10a) father with mean income — Both — Native born — 25.7
(10b) Any ethnicity — 61.2

Source: Tables 3, columns (1) and (2), and Table 4.

a Only white families.

b Parents are assumed to be of mean age in the sample.

c Ethnicity for males. Note that a change in ethnicity does not change the conditional probabilities for males but does for females.

Note: This calculation illustrates the use of the coefficients resulting from probit analysis and uses equations (1) and (2). Each coefficient is multiplied by the assumed value for that particular variable and the sum, or index, is evaluated using the standard normal cumulative distribution. In the case of line (1a):

$$-1.144 \quad + 0.192 \ (= 0.012 \times 16 \text{ yrs}) + 0.464 + \quad 0.396 \quad - \quad 0.194 \quad + 0.306 \ (= 0.006 \times 51 \text{ yrs}) - 0.208 \ (= -0.304 \times \$0.685) = -0.188$$
[constant]   [age]   [Irish]   [Mom present]   [Pop present]   [age of father]   [Father's labor income]

There is a 42.5 percent probability of observing a value of -0.188 or less. (See references in note 18 for a detailed justification of this mechanical explanation.) A "mean" value for a variable indicates values given in Table 3 from columns (1) or (2) depending upon the sex of the child. Only the variables that have been changed are indicated; the remaining variables are identical to those in the row directly above. These predicted probabilities are somewhat smaller than the actual probabilities given in Table 2 because there was a sharp rise in some of the labor force participation rates between ages 15 and 16.

tion probability from 58.3 to 68.2 percent and the girls lowering their participation from 38.2 to 24.3 percent. The remaining conditional predicted probabilities have been generated by changing, at each step, one or two of the more interesting or representative variables to observe each effect separately.

The Black Family Economy:
Women and Children in the Labor Force

The Data. Black families in late nineteenth-century Philadelphia had radically different household structures from those of white families, and their strategies of life appear equally distinct. The experiences of these families provide an illuminating comparison with the white data and are, as well, a critical link between the black experience in slavery and in twentieth-century cities. Certain unique data difficulties have arisen in analyzing black households in Philadelphia, and two characteristics of this population —subtenancy and domestic service—have forced a reworking of the manuscript census data. Because many black Philadelphians subtenanted, that is, rented space from the household's primary occupants, their relationship to the household head was often listed in 1880 as "unrelated" or "unknown," even though such individuals were frequently living with family members.

More than 20 percent of all blacks not living in white households resided as subtenants, and almost one-third (32.7 percent) of all primary families had at least one unrelated subtenant living with them. Subtenants usually shared rented dwellings which were accordingly cheapened and more crowded for all. The wide range of subtenanted situations is indicated by W.E.B. DuBois's comment, from his pioneering study of black Philadelphians, that the "practice . . . is found . . . in all degrees: from the business of boarding-housekeeper to the case of a family which rents out its spare chamber." Although white persons often boarded with other families, a feature discussed above, various aspects of the subtenanting arrangement make these two forms of residence quite distinct. DuBois noted that subtenanting was the result of both poverty and discrimination. "Whoever wishes to live in the centre of Negro population, near the great churches and near work, must pay high rent for a decent house. This rent the average Negro family cannot afford, and to get the house they subrent a part to lodgers."[28] Little is known about the characteristics of subtenants, their rate of turnover, and their living conditions. This study will suggest that many families subtenanted to find a job for the wife. The analysis of black families and households is complicated further by the residence of blacks in white households. Across all ages, 19 percent of all black females and over 8 percent of all black males resided in white households.

A substantial fraction of the subtenants who were not related to the household head, and some black residents in white households, actually lived with members of their own families; such relationships were indicated by, for example, last name, sex, age, and marital status. Families, therefore, were statistically "reconstituted" using algorithms based on known family characteristics.[29] Such a procedure obviously failed to recognize many relations, in particular those of the wife, adopted children, and, on occasion, children from a previous marriage; and these "reconstituted" data have been used only for those analyses where the drawbacks of this procedure would not create serious biases.

Characteristics of Black Families and Individuals in 1880 Philadelphia. Both the child-woman ratios and the average number of children living at home were substantially lower for blacks than for native whites in 1880 Philadelphia.[30] The average number of children under seven years old per married (husband present) black woman twenty to twenty-nine years old was 0.858 as opposed to 1.093 for native white women. Native-born white fathers fifty to fifty-nine years old living with their wives had an average of 2.090 children at home, but black fathers had only 1.602. Irish fathers with similar characteristics had 2.674 children in their households. Other information indicates that black children, especially daughters, left their parents' homes earlier than did white children.[31] DuBois has suggested that the low fertility of the black population in Philadelphia's 7th Ward could be explained by both a late age at marriage and selective migration. "The size of families in cities is nearly always smaller than elsewhere, and the Negro family follows this rule; late marriages among them undoubtedly act as a check to population; moreover, the economic stress is so great that only the small family can survive; the large families are either kept from coming to the city or move away, or, as is most common, send the breadwinners to the city while they stay in the country."[32]

Only 64 percent of all black families, that is, families with at least one parent and one "own" child, were couple-headed. Of the remainder, 30.8 percent had only the mother and 4.8 percent had only the father present. By comparison over 80 percent of native-born white families were couple-headed, and the difference between this figure and that for blacks is actually more extreme because the white heads of households were older.[33]

One in four black women in Philadelphia over fourteen years old was either widowed or married but not living with her spouse. Only one-tenth of these women lived with relatives in a household in which they were not the head, and over one-third lived alone, some of whom may have been boarding with friends. Almost 35 percent of these women headed families, and over 20 percent resided in white households. Widows who were not the household head of a black family rarely resided with relatives, in particular their children, although such living arrangements were far more common among white women. The transiency of the black population, their lack of home ownership, the lower incomes of their children, their lower fertility, and the possibility that black women were more willing to work for pay may all have contributed to these residence arrangements.

The Labor Force Participation of Secondary Workers in Black Families. Black married and widowed women had much higher labor force participation rates than did their white counterparts, native or immigrant. Of all women in the late nineteenth century, only black women participated in the labor force for a significant fraction of their married lives.[34] For individuals over fourteen years old about 75 percent of all single, 22 percent of all married spouse present, and 58 percent of all widowed black women listed an occupation in 1880.[35] Many of these women worked in their own homes for pay, for example as laundresses, and the analysis that follows underscores the importance of the location of their work.

Even though black family incomes were lower than those of whites, black children up to the age of sixteen years (see Table 2) worked in the labor force to a lesser degree than did the children of immigrant families and about equal to those of native-born white parents.[36] Therefore, the explanation for why black married women worked must involve not only family income, wealth, and other related variables but also the intrafamily allocation of time. It is possible that black families were more willing to send both their married and widowed women to work to enable their children to go to school. Black children in Philadelphia remained in school more years than did the children of immigrant families. Immigrants, in contrast, appear to have foregone their children's education rather than send their married women to work in the labor market.

DuBois has offered an alternative explanation to the differences between black and white working patterns. The "absence of child labor . . . is not voluntary on the part of the Negroes, but due to restricted opportunity; there is really very little that Negro children may do. Their chief employment, therefore, is found in helping about the house while the mother is at work." Textile mills and other industries did not, in fact, hire black children, although they did employ a substantial percentage of the white children who worked for pay. Differential relative discrimination, therefore, may have been the primary factor in encouraging black families to send their children to school and their mothers to work. Although DuBois's hypothesis is, most likely, partially correct, it is also possible that black women, having had a longer history of labor force participation, may have been less prejudiced against working outside the home than were white women.[37]

Although it is not a simple matter to confirm or reject the various hypotheses concerning the workings of the black family economy, sorting out the determinants of child and female labor force participation provides a good beginning. There are many problems in estimating labor force equations for these two groups. The time allocation decisions for children and wives were made interdependently, and additional problems can arise in considering, as well, the residence decisions of widows and older children. The labor force equations that follow are based on two, somewhat noncomparable, data sets: 1. single children, over the age of ten, living at home with at least one parent present (note that these are the identical characteristics of the white sample); and 2. married women and widowed heads of households. The noncomparability problem exists because the second group is not entirely coincident with the mothers of the children over the age of ten. Many of the women in the second group did not have children living at home. The dependent variable in all equations that follow is labor force participation, a dichotomous variable, and probit analysis has been employed as in the previous analysis.

Both the children and the married women are assumed to take the father's or husband's labor force decision, wage rate (occupation), and months unemployed as given. They do not, however, take each other's labor force decisions as given, that is as exogenous, but determine them jointly. Demographic characteristics of the children and the husband, as well as his labor force variables, have been included in the women's equation. A dummy variable was entered for widows so that the absence of a husband would not bias the other coefficients. The male and female children's labor force equations have been estimated separately for econometric reasons. The results from these three equations will be discussed in comparison with each other and in contrast to the findings on white children in 1880 Philadelphia. (Note that the variable names and definitions for Table 6 have been listed in Table 3, and that the form of the equations estimated is almost identical to that for white children.[38] Variables introduced for the mother's equation are defined in Table 7.)

Three types of variables have been entered in the children's equations: 1. those indicating intrafamily allocation decisions, for example, the characteristics of siblings; 2. the economic characteristics of the father; and 3. characteristics of the household that are attempts to proxy exogenous variables but that may have been jointly determined with the dependent variable. This third group has been omitted in one variant of the labor force equations in Table 6, columns (1) and (5). An example of such a variable is PRIMARY, which is a dummy variable equal to 1 if the family is a primary family and 0 if it is a subtenant or subfamily. This variable might be a proxy for wealth, that is, primary families may have been wealthier than other families. But it might as well be a measure of transiency, determined by the family's desire to locate work for the wife or the female head of household.

Both female and male black children were more influenced in their labor force decisions by their mother's characteristics and by the composition of their households than by the wage rate and unemployment of their fathers (see Table 6). The presence or absence of either parent was a very strong factor in a son's decision to work, while the presence of only the father was important for the daughters. The absence of either parent greatly increased a son's probability of being in the labor force, although it was only the absence of the father that increased this probability for a daughter. Similar signs for these two variables were found in the labor force equations for white children, but the intensity of impact was much smaller. In further contrast, white girls stayed home if their mothers were absent, whereas the presence of a mother had no impact on the labor force participation of black female children. The fact that a son had so greatly a decreased probability of working if his mother was present may indicate that mothers worked to allow their sons to attend school. An alternative explanation is that daughters may have had a greater chance to find jobs as servants, whereas their brothers, denied access to manufacturing pursuits, had severely limited opportunities. The presence of a mother may also indicate a home environment more beneficial to a child; or alternatively, the absence of a mother left a child with little reason to stay at home.

The variables accounting for the intrafamily allocation of labor among other children also have different signs from those for white children. There is no apparent hierarchy among the children, as was found for white families, whereby older children work and younger ones are enabled to go to school or stay at home. A black female with sisters of any age was much more likely to work in the market, indicating perhaps that daughters located jobs together or that family location was a factor for all. The presence of young siblings under seven years old had a positive and strong impact on the labor force participation of female and male children. These small siblings increased the demand for household help, thereby keeping mothers at home, and sending older children to work. The impact of young children was exactly the reverse of the white case, where their presence led to a decline in the probability of the older child's

Table 6. The Determinants of Child Labor: Probit Analysis of Black, Single Male and Female Children, Over Ten Years Old, Living with at Least One Parent

Variable[a] (variable number)	(1) MLE[b]	(2) MLE/SE[c]	(3) MLE	(4) MLE/SE	(5) MLE	(6) MLE/SE	(7) MLE	(8) MLE/SE
	Males: mean of dependent variable = 0.634				Females: mean of dependent variable = 0.352			
Constant	2.363	4.226	1.353	1.643	−0.107	−0.232	−1.673	−1.847
AGE11–15 (1)	−1.896	−8.328	−1.927	−7.636	−1.548	−7.044	−1.612	−6.662
#OLDBROS (2)	0.089	0.566	0.006	0.034	−0.031	−0.246	−0.057	−0.429
#OLDSIS (3)	−0.126	−0.834	−0.205	−1.264	0.270	2.404	0.279	2.373
#YNGBROS (4)	0.423	2.032	0.357	1.650	−0.080	−0.520	−0.152	−0.915
#YNGSIS (5)	0.009	0.064	−0.031	−0.197	0.200	1.746	0.212	1.774
CHILD6 (6)	0.158	1.383	0.195	1.597	0.253	2.371	0.309	2.666
MOM (7)	−1.095	−2.125	−1.265	−2.357	−0.055	−0.134	−0.049	−0.114
POP (8)	−0.683	−1.945	−0.971	−2.528	−0.492	−1.649	−0.313	−0.996
WAGEPOP (9)	0.190	0.359	0.370	0.652	0.600	1.401	0.590	1.344
AGEFAM (10)			0.026	2.171			0.014	1.359
UNPOP (11)	−0.012	−0.183	−0.008	−0.114	−0.088	−0.785	−0.075	−0.648
MOMINWORK (12)			0.278	1.006			0.453	1.708
MOMOUTWORK (13)			−0.680	−1.912			1.092	3.375
ILLITMOM (14)	0.688	2.977	0.462	1.608	0.581	2.325	0.615	2.564
BOARD (15)			−0.240	−1.059			0.220	1.072
RACE (16)			−0.118	−0.479			−0.361	−1.604
PRIMARY (17)			0.303	0.795			0.913	1.667
POBIRTH (18)			0.450	1.686			0.150	0.585
−2 times log likelihood ratio	149		164		104		123	
Number of Observations	284		284		290		290	

[a] See Table 3 for variable definitions and sample means.

[b] Maximum likelihood estimate.

[c] Maximum likelihood estimate/standard error, which has a 't' distribution asymptotically. The standard errors in this table are larger than those in Table 4 in part because of the much smaller number of observations in the black sample. The discussion of these results will allow a much lower level of significance than for those of the white equation.

working. The most probable reason for this difference is that white married women rarely held jobs outside their homes and there could be no substitution between mothers and their children in terms of who worked in the labor market. A black child with an illiterate mother stood an increased probability of being in the labor force, as was the case for white children. This result might reflect the lower wages paid to illiterate women, but it also suggests that children with illiterate mothers stood less to gain from remaining at home with them.

A second group of regressions adds variables that might bias the coefficients of those included in the first equation;[39] in particular, whether the mother worked for pay in the home (as a laundress, seamstress, boarding housekeeper) or outside the home.[40] The coefficients on these variables are striking. A daughter stood a much higher probability of working had she a mother who labored outside the home. Working mothers may have located jobs for their daughters or may have trained their daughters in their vocation. In sharp contrast, a son had a much reduced probability of working had he a mother who labored outside the home, indicating again that mothers may have worked to allow their sons to go to school.

The results from the equation using data on married and widowed women show their general responsiveness to economic variables. The coefficients on the husband's wage rate, literacy, and months unemployed, given in Table 7, are all of the expected signs. An increase in the husband's income, variable 9, decreased the probability of participating for a wife, as did an increase in his months unemployed, variable 10. The illiteracy of the husband, variable 8, dramatically increased the probability of a wife's working, possibly because illiteracy modifies the wage variable but also, perhaps, because illiteracy is monitoring differences in tastes across families. Young children, as expected, had a deterrent impact on a mother's working. The response of mothers to the age and sex characteristics of their older children indicates that women stayed out of the labor force had they young teen-aged daughters, but increased their participation somewhat with the presence of older daughters.[41]

Widowed women, of course, had higher labor force participation rates than did married women, but a widow who resided with her older children had a much reduced probability of working. Widows living with their daughters had a lower probability of working than those residing with a grown son, as can be seen by comparing the coefficients on the interaction terms, variables 5 and 6. These findings demand discussion beyond the scope of this essay concerning the residence decisions of widows and their children, and provide an illustration of the many interdependencies among family decisions.

Table 7. The Determinants of the Labor Force Participation of Married and Widowed[a] Black Women: Probit Analysis

Variable Name	(1) MLE	(2) MLE/SE	(3) MLE	(4) MLE/SE	Sample Mean	Variable Definition
	Mean of the dependent variable = 0.295					
Constant	−0.513	−3.537	−0.208	−1.215		
OLD (1)	−0.406	−2.183	−0.399	−2.134	0.07	Dummy = 1 if ≥ 55 years.
WIDOW (2)	0.908	5.647	0.843	5.186	0.25	Dummy = 1 if a widow
CHILD6 (3)	−0.345	−3.661	−0.342	−3.613	0.40	Dummy = 1 if children ≤ 6 yrs.
FEM11–13 (4)	−0.296	−1.699	−0.290	−1.647	0.08	Dummy = 1 if a female child 11–13 yrs.
WIDOWFCH (5)	−0.639	−1.904	−0.543	−1.605	0.02	Interaction of widow & female children ≥ 17 yrs.
WIDOWMCH (6)	−0.299	−1.098	−0.234	−0.855	0.04	Interaction of widow & male children ≥ 17 yrs.
LLIT (7)	0.149	1.292	0.164	1.423	0.21	Dummy = 1 if woman illiterate
LLITPOP (8)	0.269	1.958	0.291	2.105	0.13	Dummy = 1 if husband illiterate
WAGEPOP (9)	−0.430	−1.781	−0.360	−1.506	0.362	Husband's labor income x 10^{-3}
UNPOP (10)	0.086	2.458	0.087	2.492	0.26	Husband's unemployment in months
PRIMARY (11)			−0.413	−3.408	0.85	Dummy = 1 if primary family
−2 times log likelihood ratio	162		173			
Number of observations	1035		1035			

[a] Only widows who were household heads have been included.

Women in primary households, as shown by the second estimation, had a much reduced probability of working in the labor force. Primary families may have had higher wealth, but this finding might also reveal a particular characteristic of subtenants. Families may have subtenanted to allow wives to be within walking distance of work. The fact that children in primary families had higher labor force participation rates suggests that this latter explanation is highly likely.

The striking differences between the determinants of the labor force participation of black and white secondary workers merit further discussion. Decisions within these families appear to have been made in extremely different ways, and it is difficult to attribute this finding to disparities in the income levels of the two groups. Many Irish, for example, had equally low incomes and yet behaved in a similar manner with respect to most variables, as did the Germans and the native-born whites. Indeed, differences among ethnic groups with regard to the work experience of their daughters took the form of a differential and not as a function of the independent variables. That is, native-born white, Irish, and German families responded similarly to changes in economic and demographic variables, but black families behaved very differently. The key to these differences concerns the apparent barriers blacks faced in finding jobs for their children combined with the willingness of black married women to work for pay. The virtual absence of job opportunities in industry for single black women meant that many left their homes to become servants in white households or to become subtenants in search of work in other parts of town. Many who remained in their parents' households seemed to have done so only if they could work with their mothers in the paid labor force. The age at which children left home and the determinants of this age appear critical to understanding the family economy for both blacks and whites. It should be stressed that even though the labor force experiences of black children cannot be analyzed simply, the determinants of the labor force experiences of black mothers are of a more usual form with regard to husband and other family characteristics.[42]

Summary and Conclusions

This essay has analyzed secondary workers in the household economy in an effort to understand the complex process of household decision-making in the late nineteenth century. A brief summary of the salient results in this work will help integrate its many parts. White children across the ethnic spectrum participated in the labor force in a manner dependent on the economic and demographic characteristics of their families. Girls and boys responded differently to many variables, and this behavior has both reaffirmed and broadened our knowledge of the roles of sons and daughters in household economies of past time. But the similarities among white families of all ethnic backgrounds are more important than the differences between girls and boys. Changes in family income, unemployment, the number and characteristics of siblings, the presence of servants and of boarders, and the absence of either parent, to mention a few of the included variables, affected white boys and white girls similarly. Irish and German daughters had higher rates of participation than did native-born white girls, even after controlling for such variables, but the response of all daughters to their family's characteristics were the same.

An attempt to explain the labor force participation of black children using the same framework demonstrated that black families responded in extremely different ways to changes in these variables. There was little in the explanation for the white data that could be transferred to the black case. It was suggested that these differences resulted, in part, from labor market discrimination against black children combined with the fact that black married and widowed women seemed more willing to work than did their white counterparts. The empirical results do not allow one to reject

either the hypothesis that black women worked to enable their sons to remain in school or the hypothesis that they worked because their children
were discriminated against in the labor market.

The family decisions analyzed in this essay concern only a portion of
those decisions made over the family's entire life cycle. An integration of
these decisions was termed family "strategies," and it has been stressed
throughout this essay that labor force participation of children cannot be
divorced from related issues, such as the age of their independence and the
old age security of their parents. Preliminary results from an investigation
of the age of independence among white children of immigrant parents
demonstrate that children left their parents' homes earlier if their parents
had lower income, less wealth, higher unemployment, and if the child had
prior work experience.[43] Such results reaffirm the position that one should
not analyze in isolation portions of the family's life cycle. All decisions
made over the life cycle should be analyzed jointly, although this involves
complex modeling and estimation difficulties. This essay has begun that
task by analyzing the labor force participation of late nineteenth-century
children within the broader context of family strategies.

NOTES

1. Economists have long treated the family and the household as the primary
decision-making units in the economy. See, for example, Becker's pioneering piece
on fertility and the work that has followed on the quality-quantity trade-off in the
demand for children; Mincer on migration; and Mincer on the labor force participation of married women and the literature by G. Cain and R. Gronau, for example,
that has followed. Gary Becker, "An Economic Analysis of Fertility," in *Demographic Change in Developed Countries,* Universities-National Bureau Conference
Series No. 11 (Princeton, N.J.: Princeton University Press, 1960); Jacob Mincer,
"Family Migration Decisions," *Journal of Political Economy* 86 (1978), 749–73;
Jacob Mincer, "Labor Force Participation of Married Women," in H. Gregg Lewis,
ed., *Aspects in Labor Economics,* Universities-National Bureau Conference Series
No. 14 (Princeton, N.J.: Princeton University Press, 1962); Glen Cain, *Married
Women in the Labor Force: An Economic Analysis* (Chicago: University of Chicago
Press, 1966); Reuben Gronau, "The Intra-Family Allocation of Time: The Value of
Housewives' Time," *American Economic Review* 63 (1973), 634–51; Reuben
Gronau, "The Allocation of Time of Israeli Women," *Journal of Political Economy*
84 (1976), S201–20. See as well, articles in three special issues of the *Journal of
Political Economy,* March/April 1973, March/April 1974, and August 1976 for
numerous papers applying economic models of household behavior.

2. The variables subject to choice by the family, that is the endogenous variables,
were, most likely, fewer in 1880 than today, but decisions regarding these variables
were more manifest in the late nineteenth century. This paradoxical statement can
be resolved by considering that higher wealth, social security, and better insurance
markets today have obviated many of the decisions made by late nineteenth-century

families. In addition, incomes today would have to fall substantially for parents not to send their children to school. That is, there are many decisions for which contemporary families are at "corner solutions." M. Haines's article in this volume analyzes the income adequacy of a father's wages in the late-nineteenth century. See "Poverty, Economic Stress, and the Family in a Late Nineteenth-Century American City: Whites in Philadelphia, 1880."

3. Fewer than 4 percent of all white married women in Philadelphia in 1880 stated that they had an occupation other than household work. Robert W. Smuts has suggested that the low rate of married female employment in the nineteenth century is, in part, a measurement error because married women were reluctant to inform a census marshal of their occupation. Smuts has also claimed that married women did not inform marshals of part-time labor, because the instructions, at least for 1890, defined an occupation as that "work upon which [a person] chiefly depends for support." See Robert W. Smuts, "The Female Labor Force: A Case Study in the Interpretation of Historical Statistics," *Journal of the American Statistical Association* 55 (1960), 73. Smuts is probably incorrect in assuming that married women lied about their employment, although part-time and piece-work labor in the home may have been understated. Many married women did state an occupation, and the labor force participation of married women varied considerably by city and by race in 1880 and 1870. See Claudia Goldin, "Female Labor Force Participation: The Origin of Black and White Differences, 1870 and 1880," *Journal of Economic History* 37 (1977), 87–108. Furthermore, Carroll D. Wright's 1888 survey of 17,427 working women reported that only 745 were married, leading him to conclude that the "working women, then as a rule, are single women." See Carroll D. Wright, *Fourth Annual Report of the Commissioner of Labor, 1888: Working Women in Large Cities* (Washington, D.C.: U.S. G.P.O., 1889), 64. Black married women provide an important exception to these employment figures and are treated separately in this paper.

4. Hershberg *et al.,* have computed the mean journey-to-work for various occupations in nineteenth-century Philadelphia. Although their computation is occasionally a minimum journey-to-work, that for specific industries is highly reliable and indicates that about 90 percent of employees lived less than a mile from their place of employment. They also report that the round-trip fare for a streetcar was between 6 and 9 percent of a worker's daily wage, and that it increased to 9 to 13 percent after the inclusion of one exchange. See Theodore Hershberg, Harold Cox, Dale Light, Jr., and Richard Greenfield, "The 'Journey-to-Work': An Empirical Investigation of Work, Residence, and Transportation, Philadelphia, 1850 and 1880"; in this volume.

5. The works of Easterlin, David and Sanderson, and Sanderson suggest family fertility strategies in nineteenth-century America. See Richard A. Easterlin, "Population Change and Farm Settlement in the Northern U.S.," *Journal of Economic History* 36 (1976), 45–75; Paul David and Warren C. Sanderson, "Contraception Through Stochastic Learning Behavior: An Analysis of Adaptive Rhythm Method," Stanford University, mimeo (1976); Warren C. Sanderson, "New Interpretations of the Decline in the Fertility of White Women in the U.S., 1800–1920," Stanford University, mimeo (1977).

6. See, for example, the data, especially Table 1.1, in Peter Laslett, "Characteristics of the Western Family Considered over Time," *Journal of Family History* 2 (1977), 89–115; and various articles in Peter Laslett and Richard Wall, eds., *Household and Family in Past Time* (Cambridge: Cambridge University Press, 1972).

7. The location of the family was also subject to choice and, therefore, would have to be modeled separately from the labor force decisions. Location is explicitly considered in the black family equations in terms of the subtenanting arrangement.

8. One problem with the analysis that follows is that children are not only capable, at some time, of leaving the household, but most do in fact eventually exit. A child's decision to leave the household depends, in part, on the price of alternative lodgings, affective ties, ambiant conditions in the parent's household, and the child's ability to be financially independent. With a far more complicated model, the age of independence can be determined together with labor market decisions. In view of the enormous theoretical and empirical problems with such a model, the age of independence has been left for separate study. Research on this topic has been an integral part of the broader study of family strategies, and some of the findings from this work will be discussed in the conclusions to this essay. See Claudia Goldin, "Family Strategies in Late Nineteenth-Century Philadelphia," *Working Papers from the Regional Economic History Research Center*, vol. 2, no. 3 (1979), Eleutherian Mills-Hagley Foundation.

9. Ensign, Loughran, and Barnard give the histories of child labor and compulsory schooling laws in Pennsylvania and elsewhere. See Forest Chester Ensign, *Compulsory School Attendance and Child Labor* (New York: Arno Press and The New York Times, 1969; orig. ed., 1921); Miriam E. Loughran, *The Historical Development of Child-Labor Legislation in the United States* (Washington, D.C.: Catholic University of America, 1921); J. Lynn Barnard, "Factory Legislation in Pennsylvania: Its History and Administration," University of Pennsylvania Series in Political Economy and Public Law, Publication No. 19 (1907).

10. It is highly probable that some children worked part-time during the year but were not given an occupation in the census because they were not considered to be earning a living.

11. The data on labor income have been inferred from the occupational information. An appendix detailing these data and their sources can be obtained from the author. Note that the data on family income and the contributions of children have implicitly ignored the issue of how much children actually contributed to their families when living at home and how much after they exited from the household. See Claudia Goldin, "Household and Market Production of Families in a Late Nineteenth-Century City," *Explorations in Economic History* 16 (1979), 111–131, for a more detailed analysis of the contribution of children to family income.

12. *Arthur's Illustrated Home Magazine* 44 (January 1876), 126.

13. See Orley Ashenfelter and James Heckman, "The Estimation of Income and Substitution Effects in a Model of Family Labor Supply," *Econometrica* 42 (1974), 73–85; Gary Becker, "A Theory of the Allocation of Time," *Economic Journal* 75 (1965), 493–517; Farrell Bloch, "The Allocation of Time to Market and Non-Market Work Within a Family Unit," Inst. Mat. Studies Social Science, Technical Report No. 114, Stanford University (1973); Gronau, "The Intra-Family Allocation of Time," *op. cit.;* and "The Allocation of Time of Israeli Women," *op. cit.*, on models of household and market production.

14. The ratio of wages for children under 15 years old was computed for industry categories found in 1880 Philadelphia from data in Secretary of Internal Affairs of the Commonwealth of Pennsylvania, *Annual Report: 1879–80,* V. VII, Part II; "Industrial Statistics" (Harrisburg, Pa.: Lane S. Hart, 1881). The ratio for adult workers was computed from that source and data for Pennsylvania from Commissioner of Labor, *Eleventh Annual Report, 1895–96: Work and Wages of Men, Women and Children* (Washington, D.C.: U.S. G.P.O., 1897) using the data for one decade earlier. The relative wage rates of nineteenth-century boys and girls are, interestingly enough, consistent with data on hire rates for slaves. Young female slaves were somewhat more productive than were young male slaves, but mature men were far more productive than were women. See Robert W. Fogel and Stanley L. Engerman, *Time on the Cross: The Economics of American Negro Slavery* (Boston: Little,

Brown, 1974). Young girls were capable of greater dexterity and work discipline than were young boys but lost their efficiency advantage by their late teens. Although female wages in 1880 Philadelphia and Pennsylvania were about 70 percent of male wages for occupations in the same industries, females were not employed by certain high wage industries, such as iron and steel. Therefore, the overall average of female to male wages was lower than 70 percent.

15. See note 10. Note that all wage, that is, labor income, variables were constructed in the same way.

16. The census marshals in 1880 asked individuals for the occupations in which they worked and supported themselves. The assumption that the occupation is exogenously determined implies as well that the labor force participation and the wage rate are exogenously determined. The assumption about the labor force participation rate is not crucial because about 97 percent of all fathers in the sample listed an occupation.

17. See Table 3, footnote b, for the occupations comprising the UNSKILL and SKILL variables. Teenage unemployment among contemporary youths has been partially attributed, by some, to a failure of the labor market to clear because of informational problems. This logic suggests that the children of parents who have no access to jobs for their sons and daughters stand a much higher probability of being unemployed.

18. Children in subfamilies were included as other family members in the empirical analysis and were included in variable 16 if they contributed income. The determination of their work behavior would have to be analyzed jointly with their residence decision.

19. For a more complete discussion of qualitative dependent variables see A. Goldberger, *Economic Theory* (New York: John Wiley, 1971), 248–51; and H. Theil, *Principles of Econometrics* (New York: John Wiley, 1971), 630–31.

20. The hypothesis that all the coefficients of a regression with both males and females were equal to those of the unconstrained separate regressions was rejected at the 0.5 percent level.

21. *Arthur's Home Magazine* 44 (June 1881), 325–27.

22. If the father was either dead or not present for another reason, the age of the mother was used.

23. The UNSKILL variable is negative and significant for females, indicating, perhaps, that location was a factor in determining both a father's and his daughter's occupations.

24. Note that the measured response of children to their father's unemployment will be reduced, somewhat, by the way in which these variables have been measured. Unemployment for the father is given in months per census year, but the child's labor force participation is inferred only from the listing of an occupation. An occupation might not be listed if the child were working only during the months of the father's unemployment and not full-time or when the census marshal visited the family.

25. The unemployment variable captures the "transitory" component of income, whereas the wage variable, because it is assigned by occupation, is a good proxy for the "permanent" component. Mincer has shown, using contemporary data, that the labor force participation of wives is far more responsive to changes in the "transitory" than in the "permanent" component. He has used this information and estimates of the "own" elasticity of supply to resolve the apparent paradox between the time-series finding of rising labor force participation rates of married women and the cross-section finding of a strong, negative relationship between husband's income and wife's participation. See Mincer, "Labor Force Participation of Married Women," *op. cit.*

26. The number of other family members residing in the household was added to the equation, but the coefficient on this variable was insignificant in all estimations.

27. The decision to board individuals could be modeled and estimated separately, and might not belong in the child labor supply equation if both boarding and labor force participation were determined jointly by the family.

28. W. E. B. DuBois, *The Philadelphia Negro* (New York: Schocken, 1967; orig. ed., 1899), 194, 290–91.

29. Approximately one out of every six black households was sampled from the Philadelphia Social History Project's 1880 black household file, and these households were then "reconstituted." This procedure yielded 5,149 individuals out of the 1880 black population of 31,684. See Claudia Goldin, " 'The Philadelphia Negro' in 1880: Some New Findings and Comparisons," mimeo (1978), for a discussion of the sample and population means.

30. This leaves open the possibility that infant and child mortality were much higher among black families, a topic being explored at the Philadelphia Social History Project.

31. The age distribution of daughters living at home truncates sharply around age 18 for black families but not for whites.

32. DuBois, *Philadelphia Negro, op. cit.,* 165.

33. F. Furstenberg, Jr., T. Hershberg, and J. Modell, "The Origins of the Female-Headed Black Family: The Impact of the Urban Environment," *Journal of Interdisciplinary History* 6 (September 1975), 211–33, and in this volume, use the household rather than the family as their unit of analysis and find somewhat different results. Their use of the household implicitly omits more than 20 percent of all blacks in Philadelphia, many of whom were unrelated subtenants with extremely different demographic and economic characteristics from those of the household's primary family.

34. White married women, native or immigrant, had less than a 4 percent labor force participation rate in 1880 Philadelphia. To compare these numbers with similar findings for other cities and at other points in time, see Goldin, "Female Labor Force Participation," *op. cit.;* and Elizabeth Pleck, "A Mother's Wages: Income Earning Among Married Italian and Black Women, 1897–1911," in Michael Gordon, ed., *The American Family in Socio-Historical Perspective* (New York: St. Martin's Press, 1978).

35. These statistics are lower bound estimates, defining labor force participation as narrowly as possible. In particular they exclude "housekeepers," a category that could have included women who were paid to keep other people's homes.

36. The divergence between the percentage of black and white ethnic children under 17 years old in the labor force appears to be unaffected by variations in the age of independence. Comparisons after that age are probably greatly affected by differences in the age at which children exited from their households.

37. For a fuller discussion of such an hypothesis, see Goldin, "Female Labor Force Participation," *op. cit.;* DuBois, *Philadelphia Negro, op. cit.,* 111.

38. There are two obvious ways in which the forms of the equations in Tables 4 and 6 are different. Age was added as a dummy, AGE11–15, in the black equation but is a continuous variable in the white equation. The sharp change in the labor force participation of black children around age 15 necessitated this change. In addition, WAGEMOM from Table 4 is replaced in Table 6 by two dummy variables, MOMINWORK and MOMOUTWORK. The occupations of black women were not numerous, and the distinction between working inside and working outside the home was more important in the black than in the white case.

39. The regressions in columns (3) and (7) also add the variables RACE and POBIRTH.

40. The 1880 census made no distinction between working in the home for pay and working outside the home. The occupations selected seemed most likely to be those performed in the home for pay.

41. The standard errors of the variables accounting for the characteristics of other older children were too large for inclusion. The possibility that girls with nonworking mothers left their families to find work elsewhere in the city raises difficult problems in modeling and estimation. Note that the results on mothers and their daughters are fully consistent with those for female children which indicated that daughter's and mother's work were complementary.

42. See Mincer, "Labor Force Participation of Married Women," *op. cit.;* and Cain, *Married Women in the Labor Force, op. cit.;* and the extensive literature that has followed on the determinants of the labor force participation of married women.

43. These findings are consistent with Anderson, see chapter 9 in particular. Anderson concludes that children in Lancashire were conscious of the possibility of deserting their families and living on their own wages and that they "used it as a way of bargaining a highly independent relationship with their families." See Michael Anderson, *Family Structure in Nineteenth-Century Lancashire* (Cambridge: Cambridge University Press, 1971), esp. 135.

9. Social Change and Transitions to Adulthood in Historical Perspective

JOHN MODELL   FRANK F. FURSTENBERG, JR.
THEODORE HERSHBERG

Rules can be found in every society governing the passage to adulthood. In some social systems, this transition is sharply demarcated, highly routinized, and carefully coordinated, while in others, it is far less easy to chart the course through which social members come of age. Sociologists and historians have shown little taste for studying patterns of transition, relegating these problems to anthropologists or social psychologists instead. Remarkably little work has been done on the scheduling of critical life events in our society, and on the existence of and changes in social timetables.[1] How such scheduling is articulated with the requirements of other social institutions, though a subject of some speculation, has been generally neglected as a topic for empirical investigation.[2]

Although this paper explicitly addresses only the problem of youth, we regard the transition to adulthood as an illustrative case of a more general set of problems concerning how institutional constraints bear on the construction of the life course. The present paper may be seen as an exploratory study of some gross contrasts between youth "then"—in the late nineteenth century—and "now" in 1970. At the same time, it proposes a series of analytic distinctions and a methodology, the implications of which will be discussed more fully further on.

This paper was originally presented at the American Sociological Association (San Francisco: August 1975). It later appeared in the *Journal of Family History* 1 (Autumn 1976), 7–32. Except for the conversion to endnotes of textual source references, it is reprinted here without revision.

Youth and Uncertainty

Discomfort, even turmoil, commonly characterizes the period we have come to call youth, a stage of life during which major transitions of status are accomplished. These transitions, no doubt, are stressful in themselves, but our appreciation of the turmoil of youth typically rests on assumptions about the fit between the transition period and the society within which it occurs. It is widely held that this fit has changed substantially since industrialization. Most commentators have argued that the period of youth has been moved later in the life course,[3] extended,[4] removed for better or for worse from meaningful contact with the adult world,[5] and experienced as meandering and arbitrary. They contrast this to a vision of the past in which youth was a relatively brief period (lacking even a name) of substantial and near adult responsibility.[6]

As is often the case, our historical image is the product of no research in particular, but is instead based on nostalgia and the need for a contrasting image to our concept of youth today. Happily, in recent years a genuine historiography has developed. Joseph Kett's description indicates that the experience of rural youth in the nineteenth century was surely different from what we see today.[7] But it was anything but brief and consistently filled with adult-like responsibility.

Michael Katz's intensive study of family behavior in a mid-nineteenth-century Canadian city also finds growing up then to have been a qualitatively different process from what it has become.[8] His lucid exposition is the fullest treatment now available. "Most young people," Katz maintains, passed through "a semi-autonomous state," having entered some adult statuses but not having completed the entire set of transitions. Katz finds, moreover, that the length of this period of life—or even its occurrence at all—was quite responsive to local economic conditions, becoming rarer among youths during time of economic stringency.

Kett's account indicates that even within narrower segments of the population, fixed and regular patterns of transition were not much in evidence, and points out several ways in which the life course of the pre-adult was far less predictable. Early life in nineteenth-century America might be said to be "disorderly," to borrow Harold Wilensky's characterization of some types of work careers.[9] Youth was not a clearly progressive and irreversible status sequence, but was variable and seemingly capricious.

Many commentators on contemporary youth would dispute the claim that the transition to adulthood has become more orderly and predictable during the twentieth century. Some writers contend that it has now become more difficult to grow up because passage to adulthood has become *less* and not *more* clearly charted. Protracted schooling, economic dependency upon the family, and the complex nature of career decisions are taken as signs that the timing in the transition to adulthood has become more prolonged and the sequence of movement less clearly prescribed. Alienation follows from the lack of clarity; weak institutionalization rather than its excess is seen as a defect of American society today.

Needless to say, these varying interpretations are possible because we possess relatively little systematic information that bears directly upon the question of what kinds of changes have occurred in the organization of the life course. Indeed, we lack even a clear conceptual basis on which to conduct empirical inquiry, despite widespread agreement that the "latitude," "predictability," or "clarity" of the transition to adulthood may have varied over time.

Students of youth typically have stressed learning in their models of growing older. Gerontologists, by contrast, studying a population deemed progressively incompetent to perform their former tasks, have often seen growing older in terms of a reallocation of roles. Growing older, of course, empirically involves both learning and role allocation, at all ages. The gerontological perspective, however, should be appealing to those studying social change, since it suggests the inexorable but variable process of replacement, which the social demographer Norman Ryder has identified as a main feature of "social metabolism."[10] This bio-social process, Ryder argues, gives rise to a set of conventions for moving individuals in and out of social patterns.

The most enlightening statement of the nature of this problem, by Matilda Riley and her collaborators, divides the social-metabolic process into two conceptually distinct though empirically overlapped processes: "allocation"—the role-assignment and exchange process as seen from the structural point of view, and "socialization"—the motivation and instruction of role occupants.[11] The timing of any particular transition in our complex society is rarely a simple reflection of an age norm, but is rather the cumulative outcome of the allocational needs of the society (the whole set of roles available and their age-related definitions), the time required for adequate socialization for the performance of these roles, and individual volition. Social schedules, Riley and her collaborators argue, reduce dangerous conflicts and minimize incompetence. Age norms limit the field of contestants for desired positions to a manageable number of relatively well-prepared persons. Yet even if one accepts the premises, one need not necessarily endorse the assumption that this is desirable.[12]

The present paper has three purposes: 1. We wish to turn this gerontological-demographic perspective to the question of youth. 2. We will do so especially by examining the distribution, timing, and sequencing of a series of transitions, thereby suggesting the juncture between the societal perspective of allocation and the individual perspective of the career. And 3. we intend to do these things while developing the points historically, indicating thereby some long-term shifts in the meaning of "youth" in American society.

When we speak of the transition to adulthood, we are already dealing with a somewhat artificial construct. It is an open question whether individuals in any given society hold a common notion of adulthood. We can be reasonably certain that at the present time there would be imperfect agreement among Americans about when and how someone attains adult status in our society. One can, however, safely assume that both in the past and now, becoming an adult involves a *series* of changes in status which moves an individual from economic dependence upon parents or their surrogates to economic independence (or dependence upon a spouse), and from participation in the family of orientation to establishment of a family of procreation (or, far less commonly, to move out of the family of orientation into lifetime roles as spinster or bachelor). These events may not universally announce adulthood, but they certainly bear an overwhelming and apparent association with participation in the adult world. In our construction of the complex transition to adulthood, we shall center our attention on five particular transitions for which data are available: exit from school; entrance to the workforce; departure from the family of origin; marriage; and the establishment of a household.

Methods and Data

The purposes of this paper are exploratory, aiming to look at a large subject with a new perspective and fresh information. The data we press into service are admittedly crude, though, we think, not inadequate to the purposes to which they are put. The same might be said about the methods. Taken together, these cautions argue that only where findings are strong and mutually supporting can we speak with certainty. Though our arguments are ineradicably quantitative, they do not pretend to be precise or refined.

What little systematic information we possess on tempo and organization of the transition to adulthood has relied heavily on the methods devised by Paul Glick for depicting changes in the life cycle of Americans. Glick's life cycle approach presented a pioneering effort to describe the shifts which have taken place during the twentieth century in the spacing of critical family events such as marriage, childbirth, and family dissolution. Thus, for example, Glick was able to show that the domestic careers of women have become *increasingly concentrated* in the early portions of their lives, leaving a lengthy period of time within marriage after the last child has departed from the home.[13]

The application of the Glick method has brought some interesting findings to light, but it is a rough tool at best for characterizing the timing and arrangement of events over the life span. What Glick and his followers have done is to estimate mean ages at which certain events occur. These means taken in sequence are a convenient way of expressing years "of experience" in particular life cycle stages for the population taken as a whole. But if we wished to arrive at a typical life course by arranging these averages in chronological order, we would need to assume that all transitions take place at the mean age and that everyone undergoes all transitions.[14] Moreover, if variance is high (or changing) the notion of average intervals is highly suspect. Based on aggregate averages, the interval between entering marriage and setting up a household may be far smaller than when computed on the basis of individual experiences.[15] Or, a significant minority may delay household formation substantially, while for the majority it occurs simultaneously with marriage.

Throughout our analysis, we employ a rather simple quantitative device, the intent and assumptions of which should be discussed here. Our treatment of transitions differs from the usual "age-at" basis (seen most typically in examinations of marriage), for our concern is not so much with central tendencies as with dispersion in timing. Accordingly, our technique calls for the analysis of the *distribution* of ages at which members of a population make a given transition. But our data are not from a registration of life-course events for individuals (such as a marriage register). What we have, instead, is an enumeration of statuses occupied by individuals, classified by their age and sex (from a census). Our problem is to infer from this count what set of age-specific events might have produced it. We can do this by assigning equal sizes to all equally bounded age groups, and by assuming that only transitional events (which are irreversible) account for changes in distribution of statuses within succeeding age-groups, not death or migration.[16]

A source of uncertainty in inferring timing from a momentary distribution of statuses by age is the fact that entry into many statuses does not preclude subsequent exit; many transitions are, to a degree, reversible. Our nomenclature prevents us from thinking a widowed or divorced person "unmarried," but one could never know from age-specific labor-force participation rates that for males the process of youthful attachment and senescent detachment from work often involves a shuttling in and out of the work force. Were we to examine this feature of status transitions, longitudinal data would be required to measure reversibility. In a real sense, however, reversibility is not relevant, for our concern is with binding transitions—what Howard Becker calls "commitment."[17] To marry is to incur obligations and relationships that are generally lasting. While a casual job may not impose permanent obligation, commitment to regular work (even if at casual labor) does, and such commitment undoubtedly occurs close to the time of entry to the labor force.

If we had uniform, smooth data on these statuses for single years of age for men and women separately for 1880 and 1970, we would have no computational problems with the data (given the above operational assumptions). But we do not. Whereas we have all–United States data for 1970 from the published census,[18] only sometimes available with single-year-of-age detail, our data for 1880 are fresh tabulations from a large, every Nth sample of Philadelphia whites from the Federal Population Manuscript Schedules.[19] Wherever possible, we also present calculations based on age-by-status data available for other nineteenth-century American populations, for the sake of comparison. In the broad terms in which we cast our argument, these data validate the general applicability of our Philadelphia materials, though of course there are differences of detail.[20] Where interpolation is necessary, we have interpolated linearly, unless the result is absurd. Where we have had to smooth, we have used the simplest arithmetic methods that seemed to give reasonable figures. For the most part, we have been able to make our categories for 1880 line up pretty well with those for 1970, although we do not know precisely how often a person in the nineteenth-century census lacking an "occupation" was really out of the work force. There is no reason to believe, however, that the distribution by age is seriously biased.

As much as possible, we have tried to use techniques of data analysis which remain intuitively comprehensible, and to remain close enough to the data so that the approximateness of our procedures will not be forgotten. Thus, we rely heavily in the next section upon calculating the approximate ages at which increasing cumulative deciles of the population had completed certain transitions—when the first 10 percent were married, the next 10 percent, and so on—and deriving measures from this. These will be described in detail below. Only one measure could not be accomplished with this intuitive simplicity: the measure of the interrelatedness of a pair of statuses. Here we required a measure which would be applicable across age-groups in which marginal distributions for each of the statuses varied widely; a measure of association in which the effects of *both* sets of marginal frequencies are eliminated. Accordingly, we have computed Goodman's λ for the interaction of the two variables.[21]

The concepts we are developing are, perhaps, more complicated than our measurements. This is especially the case because the thrust of our argument is moving toward seeing experience as *longitudinal* and understood in *cohort* form. The ideal ending-point of this inquiry would be a distribution of careers, which might be categorized by starting age, sequence of transitions, and intervals among transitions. To know this distribution of careers would permit us substantial insight into how they were constructed. But our data permit us only to compare cross-sections, in order to draw implications for patterns of events within individual life courses.[22]

The concepts we will introduce here are designed to begin to bridge our present capabilities and our ambitions. We shall discuss five dimensions of status transitions. A sixth, reversibility, has not been introduced for methodological reasons. Within certain logical limits, these several dimensions of status passage are independent of one another. In reality, however, they form a coherent configuration linked to other features of a social system. Of these five dimensions, the first three are simple, referring to a property of a single status transition. The last two are complex, referring to the interrelationship of two or more status transitions. All five measures are meaningful at the aggregate level of analysis only.

1. The *prevalence* of a transition is the measure of the proportion of a population (ignoring mortality) which experiences a given transition. Some transitions are quite rare, others almost universal.

2. *Timing,* when considered in the aggregate, refers to typical points in the life course at which transitions occur. We shall employ three measures of timing: the age at which half the population has experienced the transition under question, and the ages at which the first and fifth deciles make the transition (the latter two based only on those who ever make the transition). Timing may be early or late.

3. *Spread* is the period of time required for a fixed proportion in a population to undergo a particular transition. As our measure of spread, we use the central 80 percent of those who make the transition, but some other figure would be equally appropriate. A transition can have a brief or protracted spread.[23]

4. The *age-congruity* of a pair of transitions refers to the degree of overlap of their spreads. A population will undergo a pair of congruous transitions over the same period. If the transitions are incongruous, the population first accomplishes one transition, then the next. This dimension is a joint property of a pair of aggregate distributions, and does not refer to the closeness in time of transitions of the individual level.

5. *Integration,* on the other hand, is a summary measure of individual-

level relationships. The dimension refers to the degree to which status transitions are contingent upon one another at the individual level, apart from their degree of age-congruity. (Without longitudinal data, we cannot measure directly the contingency of transitions, but we can measure the contingency of statuses. Goodman's λ, mentioned above, measures this interaction for narrow age-groups.) A pair of transitions may be consistently integrated or unintegrated, or its integration may vary with age.[24]

The Pace of Transition to Adulthood

In the analysis which follows, we take up several different ways of assessing whether the timetable for coming of age has changed. For each method of assessment, we shall consider the five events which we identified earlier as important transitions in the early life course.

Prevalence. We can assume even in the absence of data that a fraction of the population will not make certain transitions at any point in their lives. Some individuals (even ignoring mortality in youth or before) never enter and thus never leave school, never go to work, marry, or depart from the households of their families of origin. To the extent that these transitions have become more prevalent, we may conclude the social timetable of becoming an adult may have become more rigidly prescribed.[25]

Table 1 presents prevalence estimates for the five events at different points in time for males and females separately. Considering the fact that the census data from the nineteenth century are more likely to omit information, and hence fail to record occupancy of a status, the figures do not reveal striking differences. In both centuries most individuals attended school, entered the work force, married, and ultimately left their household of origin to establish one of their own. The drift of the figures, however, is toward generally greater prevalence.

Not surprisingly, the greatest difference occurs in the proportion showing up as school attenders. In the twentieth century, we discover that virtually all youth attend school at some age. The figure (99.7 percent) is identical for both males and females. The rates for the two sexes are similar, too, in the nineteenth century, but the figure is lower—between 80 and 90 percent. Again, we should caution the reader that the nineteenth century data undoubtedly understate the proportion of individuals who *ever* attended school, but even so, few would dispute the claim that what is today virtually universal was in the nineteenth century merely commonplace. In that sense, we now see greater uniformity in the process of growing up.

Entrance to the work force reveals a similar pattern for females, though it is questionable whether gainful employment for women has been a relevant part of the transition to adulthood. In both centuries nearly all males —over 95 percent—enter the work force at some point, while by contrast the figures for females are dramatically lower. Given the temporary nature of female participation in the work force, at least up until the present era, we must regard these prevalence estimates with some suspicion. Nevertheless, it does seem likely that a higher proportion of women in the nineteenth century never had an occupation other than housewife.

Looking at the departure from home, again we find greater uniformity in the twentieth century. According to the 1970 census, there are ages when virtually everyone lives as a child in a family. The pattern in the nineteenth century suggests that even at very early ages (under eight), nearly a tenth of the sample were not living in the households of their parents, presumably the result of orphanhood, separation from both parents, or residence in more complex households which their parents did not head.

For the other two statuses which we examined, marriage and household headship, we discovered little or no variation in prevalence between the pattern of a century ago and the contemporary mode. Roughly the same proportion—over 90 percent—married at some point in the life course.[26] Males and females differed little in this respect. Headship rates were also almost identical over time. Again, our estimate certainly understates the actual prevalence, yet indicates that in both centuries at least 86 percent of surviving individuals in the population set up their own household at some point.

With the exception of female participation in the work force, the prevalence data presented in Table 1 indicate that both males and females today more uniformly experience the five transitions. While this fact in itself does not necessarily imply a greater degree of determinacy in the process of entering adulthood, it is at least consistent with this interpretation.

Spread. Many commentators on the problem of youth in contemporary society have remarked on the extended nature of the transition to adulthood. It seems to take longer to grow up today than it did in times past. We have examined this supposition by looking at the typical ages at which most individuals have entered adulthood, but we must also measure the length of the transition process as it occurred in both centuries. Here we are not referring to the time it takes any one individual to pass from childhood, but the period of years it requires for an entire cohort to make the transition. In short, we want to know how many years it takes a cohort to leave school, enter the work force, and so on.

The spread of the five transitions we are discussing—exit from school,

Table 1. Prevalence, Spread, Timing of First and Fifth Deciles, and Population Median Timing of Transitions, by Sex, 1880 and 1970

	Leaving School			Entering Workforce		
	1880 Phila.	Other 19th C.	1970 US	1880 Phila.	Other 19th C.	1970 US
MALES'						
Prevalence	86.6%	82.0%[a]	99.7%	[b]	97.9%[c]	95.4%
Spread	5.0	7.5	7.5	6.9	9.6	8.1
Timing: 1st decile	11.9	11.4	16.4	12.4	12.4	14.5
Timing: 5th decile	14.4	14.9	19.1	15.3	16.5	17.3
Timing: Median	[g]	[g]	[g]	15.7	16.6	17.5
FEMALES						
Prevalence	88.0%	82.0%[a]	99.7%	[b]	42.3%[c]	58.3%
Spread	5.8	6.2	7.6	6.7	7.3	4.8
Timing: 1st decile	11.3	10.8	16.3	11.3	11.0	14.3
Timing: 5th decile	14.3	14.1	18.6	14.6	14.7	17.0
Timing: Median	[g]	[g]	[g]	never	never	19.8

[a] Selected areas of Dutchess County, New York. From Daniel Hovey Calhoun, *The Intelligence of a People* (Princeton: Princeton University Press, 1973), 348.

[b] The prevalence figure for Philadelphia is probably somewhat low because a small number of rare occupations had not yet received a code at the time we made our calculations. Persons thus occupied were temporarily recorded as though not in the work force. Occurrence of these miscoded people was essentially random by age (though not by sex).

[c] All United States, 1890. U.S. Department of the Interior, Division of the Eleventh Census, *Special Report on the Statistics of Occupations,* (1896), 21.

[d] "Child" prevalence is a function of orphanhood, not of abandonment of child status in the process of becoming adult. In a trivial sense, everyone surviving his parents ceases being a "child." No figures are presented.

[e] All United States, 1890. U.S. Census Bureau, *Fifteenth Census of the United States: 1900,* Special Reports, "Supplementary Analysis and Derivative Tables" (1906), 832.

[f] Massachusetts, 1885. (Massachusetts, Bureau of Statistics of Labor, *Census of Massachusetts: 1885,* I, part 1 (1887), 482–83. The unfortunately broad age groups available in this publication for household status by age and sex did not permit the calculation of sufficiently precise spread and timing figures to justify the enterprise. As nearly as can be seen, however, the figures conform to the Philadelphia nineteenth-century pattern, and diverge markedly from the twentieth-century pattern.

[g] The notion of half a population leaving a status which not all of them have ever occupied is self-contradictory. No figures are presented.

Leaving Household of Origin			Marriage			Establishing Own Household		
1880 Phila.	Other 19th C.	1970 US	1880 Phila.	Other 19th C.	1970 US	1880 Phila.	Other 19th C.	1970 US
d	d, f	d	88.7%	93.7%e	93.7%	86.5%	85.9%f	86.4%
16.0		12.4	17.1	19.7	7.1	18.1		13.6
17.7		15.8	21.2	19.9	19.6	21.6		17.0
23.2		20.1	26.0	26.4	21.8	25.8		23.9
g		g	26.8	26.9	22.3	27.7		25.7
d	d, f	d	80.3%	92.9%e	93.0%	83.8%	81.3%f	90.1%
19.0		12.7	11.7	15.0	7.9	17.0		12.4
17.0		16.1	18.5	17.4	17.1	19.1		16.8
20.1		20.5	22.7	22.3	20.2	24.0		22.0
g		g	25.0	23.0	20.5	25.7		23.8

entrance to the work force, departure from home, marriage, and establishing a household—changes a bit in the nineteenth century, but it is minor in comparison to the historical trends we shall discuss below. In other words, cohort behavior in the previous century was probably relatively stable.[27] A good deal of variation always occurs at the extremes— the points at which the transition begins and concludes—and, in order not to give undue weight to these two tails, we shall define the spread as the period it takes for 80 percent of a given population to achieve a particular transition. Since the prevalence figures are generally quite high at both periods, this causes no problem in comparing the transition spreads within or between periods.

As the figures in Table 1 reveal, the trend toward extended schooling is evident in the larger spread in the period during which the 1970 youth exit from school. It took 6.5 years for the central 80 percent of the population to complete the process of transition in 1970 whereas the comparable figure in nineteenth-century Philadelphia was only 4.3 years. Though the estimates of spread square with our intuitions about the prolongation of this transition, they are not quite as dramatic as we might have expected. Even in the nineteenth century, the transition from schooling was not sudden or abrupt in the sense that most individuals left school at just the same age. We have reason to believe that in certain localities, the transition was quite gradual; indeed, the spread was hardly different from what we find today. For example, in Dutchess County, New York in 1850, it took 7.5 years for the central 80 percent of the males to make the transition from schooling. Although schooling is more prevalent today and extends over a far greater proportion of the life span, the length of time required by individuals to depart from schooling was not very much more concentrated during the last century. Despite the greater institutional pressures to attend school today, the spread in the transition out of school has only been extended by about two years.

Turning to entrance to the work force, the historical trend in spread is less obvious, though Table 1 shows a slight increase for males. During the nineteenth century, the entrance to work revealed a great deal of variation. Some individuals had occupations listed while quite young, while others acquired them only in their late teens or early twenties. Nevertheless, it seems unlikely that the time required to enter the workforce was more extended in the past than now. In fact, there is some indication that the spread for males decreased in the mid-twentieth century, as entrance was delayed by child labor legislation but not deferred to the extent that it is today by prolonged schooling and the inability of young people to find work. In other words, the transition may have been more concentrated in the near past than the more distant past, when economic conditions both prescribed and favored the entrance of young people into the work force.

In the three familial transitions, there is a clear trend in the evidence we have assembled. Unquestionably, it now takes *less* time for young people to move out of their parents' household, marry, and set up their own home. Among both males and females there is a decidedly shorter pattern of departure from the family of origin. This corresponds to a strikingly different spread in the period over which marriage occurred. For both sexes the period in which 80 percent of the population marry is about half as long as was once the case.[28] Finally, setting up a separate household also occurs with more alacrity. Young people complete this transition in about two-thirds the time it took a century ago.

The narrowing of the spread in the years that it takes youth to make the transition from the family of orientation to the family of procreation is unmistakable. Like the figures presented earlier on prevalence, these findings reenforce the notion that the passage to adulthood has become more determinate, at least in respect to the familial transitions. In contrast to a century ago, young people today are more likely to be similar to one another in the age at which they leave home, enter marriage, and set up their own households. The greater rapidity of this transition is somewhat inconsistent with our notion that the stage of youth has become more protracted, though it is consonant with the view that this period of life has become more routinized.

Timing. The question of whether or not the period of youth has become more prolonged during the twentieth century cannot be completely settled by our measure of spread. Transitions may be concentrated into fewer years, as we have found, but that period in which the transition occurs may come later in the life course. In other words, most individuals may not arrive as early even if the passage takes less time because, in effect, they begin the movement later. Thus, the timing of the entrance to adulthood may be independent of the length of the period in which the transition takes place.

Certainly, what we know about the extension of schooling supports the supposition that entrance to adulthood has been delayed. Formal education has become more protracted for most young people today as compared to their forebears. Table 1 presents two sets of figures on the timing of the departure from school. The first is the age at which the first decile of the school population has left, broken down by historical period and sex. The second is the median point for leaving school, correcting for the fact that not all individuals in the population attend school. The figures in the table are all ages in years.

Regardless of which figure we examine, there is little doubt that the age of departure from school has risen dramatically during the past century. The median age of school departure for both males and females is roughly four-and-a-half years later today—19.1 in 1970 as compared with 14.4 in the nineteenth century. The same degree of variation is evident at the first decile.

It is easy to understand why so many observers have been persuaded that the extension of schooling has delayed the entrance to adulthood. Yet if we look at the other transitions, the picture is different. Not surprisingly, as schooling has lengthened, entrance to the work force has occurred later. The differences over time, however, are less than impressive. The census data reveal that entrance to the work force occurs only one to two years later today than it did in the latter part of the nineteenth cenury.

Clearly, there are certain problems in making these inferences. The concept and measurement of occupational status have changed, and, more importantly, the significance of entrance to the work force has altered. Part-time work may well have proliferated among youths. While we need to take note of these differences, we should not exaggerate them. Like their counterparts today, most working youth in the nineteenth century were not economically independent, but were contributing to the family economy. To be sure, their contribution may have been more substantial and more necessary than is now the case. Not only economic independence, but also the establishment of a family were portrayed in literary sources as essential components of adulthood in the late nineteenth century.[29]

As Table 1 reveals, the age pattern of family formation in the nine-teenth century was markedly different from current practice. As implied by our figures on the spread, many individuals delayed departure from the home a century ago. Although the pattern of boarding and lodging was quite common, most young people did not leave home until their early 20s, several years later than is the custom today. Even more disparity is apparent at the extremes. A fifth of the young people in the nineteenth century remained in the household of their family of origin until their late 20s; this pattern is extremely unusual today.

Age of marriage changed even more over the time period we are study-ing. Whereas at the present time, most of those who eventually marry do so by their early 20s, a century ago a substantial proportion of the females and most of the males did not wed until their late 20s or early 30s. There are, of course, certain variations according to the time and region, but the figures presented in Table 1 point to distinctly different configurations from those today.

Underscoring these patterns of family formation are the data on house-hold establishment. Again, we discover sharp contrasts in the age at which most individuals formed separate residential units. At the median point, this event occurred several years later in the previous century, and at the extremes the differences were far more pronounced. Frequently, house-hold formation did not occur until the early 30s for nineteenth-century males, and a delay between marriage and the establishment of a separate household was frequent. During this period, the newlyweds resided in the home of parents or boarded with another family. From the source ma-terial we have examined, there is good reason to suspect that many young people did not feel prepared to marry until after they had discharged ob-ligations to their family as well as accumulated some resources to support a family of their own. In that particular sense, the period of preparation for adult responsibility was extensive and often was characterized by a good deal of uncertainty.

We can summarize some of these differences by creating an overall measure of the period of youth, examining the time elapsed between the point when the first quintile passed through the first status transition (leav-ing school, or entering the work force) and the last quintile arrived at the final status transition—headship of a household. This measure reveals the degree to which the transition to adulthood has become more concen-trated. For males, the period was reduced by a third, taking 21.7 years in 1880, but only 14.4 years in 1970. While most of this concentration re-sulted from a truncation of the *end* of the period of "youth," some is at-tributable to a slightly later point of entrance to "youth" today. For nineteenth-century Philadelphia males, the period of youth extended from 12.6 years to 34.3 years. Their counterparts in 1970 entered youth at 14.2 and completed the series of transitions at 28.6. For females the duration was and is shorter (because it ends earlier) though the increase in concentration is nearly as great.

When looked at from this vantage point, it would be difficult to substantiate the position that growing up in contemporary America has become more problematic because it takes a longer period of time or because the expectations for becoming an adult are more blurred than was once the case. If anything, the information of the pacing of the transition to adulthood suggests that the process of growing up has become more prevalent, less prolonged, and more concentrated than it was a century ago.

Complex Measures: Age Congruity and Integration

There are two additional measures—age congruity and integration—which can be used to discover whether the transition to adulthood has become increasingly determinate over the last century. Unlike the "simple" measures, which dealt with the different dimensions of each status transition separately, these complex measures deal with two status transitions considered in conjunction.

Age congruity indicates the degree of overlap between the spreads of two transitions. To provide a summary measure, we have constructed an index of age congruity (Table 2). A value of 0.00 indicates complete incongruity or no overlap between spreads. In such an instance, almost all members of a cohort have completed one transition before beginning the other. A value of 1.00 indicates the opposite, complete congruity or overlap of spreads, or the simultaneous occurrence of the two transitions.

In our discussion of the five statuses considered separately, we noted that although the proportion of persons experiencing the statuses (prevalence) remained roughly the same in both centuries, there were significant changes in the spread and timing of the transitions. Two major findings emerged: the two nonfamilial status transitions (school leaving and workforce entry) started earlier in the nineteenth century (timing) and required slightly less time to reach completion (spread); second, the three familial transitions started later, and required considerably more years for completion.

Prior to these changes, significant age congruity for males and females was found in 1880 only in the three wholly familial or wholly nonfamilial type transitions. All six mixed pairs of transitions (involving statuses from both the nonfamilial and familial categories) were quite age-incongruous,

Table 2. Age Congruity of Transition Pairs, by Sex, 1880 and 1970

	Males		Females	
	1880	1970	1880	1970
Nonfamily transition:				
School/work force	.76	.79	.93	.45
Family transitions:				
"Child"/marriage	.72	.73	.80	.77
Marriage/head-spouse	.66	.69	.77	.78
Mixed transitions:				
School/"child"	.00	.75	.01	.75
School/marriage	.00	.59	.00	.91
School/head-spouse	.00	.64	.00	.71
Work force/"child"	.14	.60	.08	.34
Work force/marriage	.00	.39	.00	.31
Work force/head-spouse	.00	.51	.00	.27

Computing formula: $\text{Congruity} = \dfrac{2 \times \text{years overlapped (central 80\%) between two transitions}}{\text{transition}_a + \text{transition}_b}$

Sources: See Table 1. All 1880 figures based on Philadelphia data.

with the slight exception of workforce entry and leaving home (0.14 for males and 0.08 for females). Logic suggests that shorter spreads in 1970 should have resulted in reduced age overlap, yet we find the opposite: shorter spreads in the twentieth century were accompanied by increased overlap in spreads. What explains this apparent paradox is that the changes in spread did not occur in a vacuum. The reduction in spreads was more than offset by changes in timing which moved the spreads toward each other.

The movement toward each other of spreads in the mixed-pair category was brought about by legislation affecting the spread and timing of school leaving and workforce entry, and economic forces, which affected the spread and timing of leaving home, marriage, and headship. Yet it is important to note that these same forces did not produce a significant increase by 1970 in the degree of overlap of wholly nonfamilial or of wholly familial pairs of transitions. These remained age-congruous to roughly the same extent as they had been in the last century. In summary, family transitions are now (as they were not a century ago) mixed with non-familial aspects of the complex transition to adulthood. No longer do youth segregate into distinct phases the entrance into the world of work climaxed by the entrance into the family world of adults. Graphs 1a and 1b show how the development of rather massive overlap between marriage and labor-force entrance has at least formally *complicated* the sequencing decisions faced by contemporary youths.

The changes in spread and timing, then, had the effect by 1970 of collapsing or concentrating the transition to adulthood into a smaller number

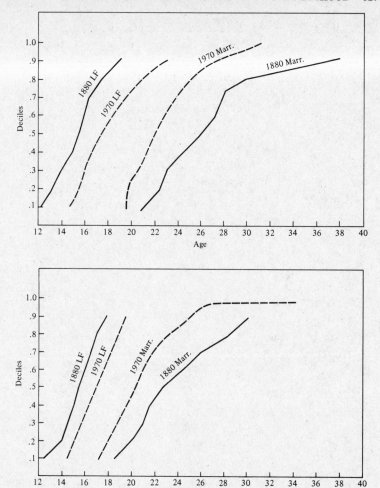

Graph 1. Age at Completion of First Through Ninth Deciles: Transition Spread, Workforce, and Marriage, 1880 and 1970. Top (a) Males; bottom (b) Females.

of years situated earlier in life. These changes raise questions about the nature of the organization of the life course today. Life-course organization in the nineteenth century was substantially the product of age-congruity. Most members of a cohort left one status before any entered another. Individuals today are forced to make more complex career decisions in a

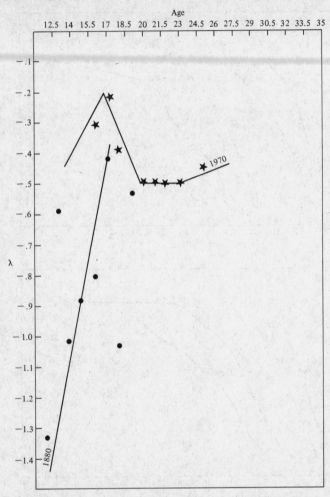

Graph 2. Integration Between School Attendance and Workforce Participation, 1880 and 1970. Left (a) Males; Right (b) Females. (Negative Lambda Indicates School Attendance Makes Workforce Participation Less Likely.)

briefer period of time because increased age-congruity, in theory, makes possible the holding of several statuses simultaneously. Considered in the abstract, increased age-congruity is not necessarily accompanied by greater determinacy in the life course. Age-congruity only makes possible simul-

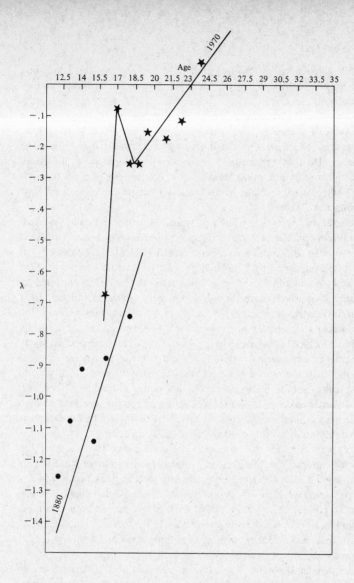

taneous occupancy of statuses; it does not by itself tell if or how status transitions will be coordinated with each other. We wish to learn, therefore, whether the process of decision making has become more helter-skelter or more orderly. Is the high degree of age-congruity today associated with a reduction in the determinacy of the path to adulthood; that is, with large numbers of individuals holding once incompatible statuses simultaneously?

This question bears directly on our understanding of the turmoil of youth today. To answer it we use a measure which we call *integration*. Here we are concerned with the degree to which *pairs* of statuses affect each other. Do they complement each other as do marriage and headship? Conflict with each other as do school and marriage? Or are they unrelated? Integration, in other words, indicates the degree of interaction—of contingency—between statuses.

To demonstrate how integration is measured, consider two age-congruous transition spreads, such as marriage and headship of household. Each of the variables is dichotomous (single/married and head/nonhead) and can be displayed in a 2 by 2 table. Here we discover that statuses at given ages can be compatible or incompatible. Incompatibility is manifested by a cell frequency which is significantly below what would be expected from the marginal distributions for the incidence of the two statuses.

Our measure of integration is Goodman's λ. This measure indicates the degree to which cell frequencies in an N by N table can be explained solely by the interaction between two variables entirely apart from the size and distribution of either set of marginal frequencies. When λ is high, we can better predict holding of one status by knowing the holding of another. Since we have calculated λ values for specific ages, we are also able to see whether the interaction between statuses varied with age for each sex, and how this interaction changed between 1880 and 1970.

Let us now consider the interaction between status pairs in the three categories: nonfamilial, familial, and mixed. In the one nonfamilial pair (school leaving and workforce entry), being in school, as one would expect, consistently and strongly precluded labor force participation. (Graphs 2a and 2b portray this visually.)[30] While this was true in both centuries, the interaction was considerably stronger in 1880 than in 1970. This relationship weakened decidedly with age for both sexes in 1880, and for females in 1970.

In the first familial pair of transitions, marriage and leaving home, we find a strong negative relationship; that is, knowing if someone was married increased significantly our ability to predict that he no longer resided in his parents' home. This was true in both centuries for both sexes, with contemporary patterns showing slightly greater predictive value. For the other wholly familial pair, marriage and headship, the two were related positively and strongly. Holding one status much increased the likelihood of holding the other; slightly more so in 1970 than in 1880. In addition, the interaction for males was sharply age-graded in both centuries, that is, predictive value declined with age, while for females the strength of the interaction increased until roughly 28–29, falling thereafter. In the instances noted above, both age-congruity and integration were found in both centuries, but while the degree of congruity remained constant over time, the degree of integration increased to an even greater peak in the twentieth century. We conclude that family decisions are highly orchestrated, especially through a very tight pattern of status integration.

Let us now consider the degree of integration found in the mixed category, among the six pairs each of which includes a nonfamilial and a familial status. The high congruity between school departure and marriage is one of the most dramatic instances of the increased complexity of transition to adulthood today.

Since this pair of transitions was age-incongruous in the nineteenth century, thus obviating the need for, or possibility of, integration, it is especially interesting to discover whether the transitions have by now become integrated. The two transitions might not now interact, even though they are simultaneous. What we in fact find to a significant degree is conflict between school and marriage in 1970 (though by no means so much as in some other pairs, like marriage and "child" family status). There is a striking difference between the sexes in integration: the degree of integration for women is generally twice as high as it is for men, though for both sexes λ declines steadily with age. For contemporary women (especially those at younger ages) school must be tightly meshed into the schedule of family transitions. For contemporary men, while school and marriage are still integrated, the greater instrumental worth of continued education to men means that more is to be gained by staying in school even when married. A common expression of this pattern is for a newly married wife to leave school and go to work, in order to permit her husband to remain in school.

The nature of integration between headship and school, and its change over the century, is sufficiently like that between marriage and school departure that we need not discuss it at length. School attendance and departure from the family of origin is another question. Indeed, the patterns shown for this pair of transitions are as perplexing as any revealed by our data. What is especially striking is that *lambda* is generally low, and unstable over the relevant age ranges. In 1880, there is something of a predominance of positive λ values, indicating that those youth not yet departed from their parents' households (most often into statuses like "boarder" or "servant" rather than to headship) were more likely to be in school. But these positive figures were low. In 1970, the strongest generalization

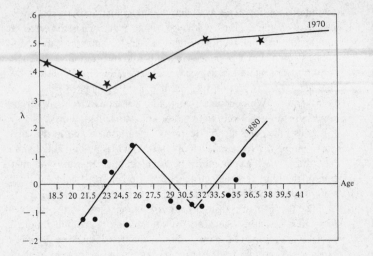

possible is that at the central transition ages, departure from family origin was almost unrelated to school attendance, although extreme ages show signs of a relationship. Residence at school may explain this in part.

Turning to the relationship between entrance into the work force and family transitions, it is important to remember that for women, workforce entry is by no means irreversible. Predictably, the patterns of integration break down quite differently by sex. For males, "child" status in 1880 had a rather unstable integration with workforce participation. In 1880, at all ages but the youngest (where sons were *less* prone to work) the relationship is small and essentially insignificant. For females, the pattern is consistent both by age and over time: daughters were more likely to work than women who had left their families of origin. The degree of integration between the two statuses is roughly similar over time.

Among males, integration between marriage and workforce entrance was almost absent in 1880 (Graphs 3a and 3b). By 1970, a strong and significant positive relationship between marriage and workforce participation existed. The responsibilities of marriage typically include employment for men: a greater proportion of young men's workforce participation can now be attributed to marriage than was formerly the case. Our supposition is that workforce participation in 1880 was so general by the age when people began to marry that nonworkers were usually disabled or disinclined men, conditions rarely affected by a change in marital status.

Similar patterns can be seen in the other family and workforce transitions for males. Headship and workforce participation were to a great

Graph 3. Integration Between Marriage and Workforce Participation, Males, 1880 and 1970. Left (a) Males; Below (b) Females. (Positive Lambda Indicates Marriage Makes Workforce Participation More Likely.)

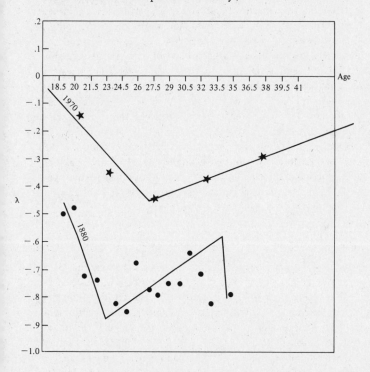

extent age-incongruous in 1880, but unlike the marriage/workforce relationship just examined, even at that early date there are some signs that the statuses were contingent upon each other. By 1970, this relationship between the two appears to have become even stronger, and is consistently more impressive than the marriage/workforce relationship. It would appear that the 1970 pattern was foreshadowed in 1880. Integration between work and family formation has been facilitated by institutional innovations. Thus, for example, for those in the workforce, housing (rented as well as owned) is now easier to come by, making family headship more feasible.

Headship of household is the last of our transitions in sequence, and in that sense for males usually the culmination of a series of earlier moves. For women in 1880, by contrast, *departure* from the workforce was often seen as the culmination of the transition to adulthood following marriage and household formation. Accordingly, in 1880, females displayed a strong integration between marriage and workforce participation, and between headship (most often "wife" status) and workforce participation, but in the *opposite* direction from that for males. The relationship, moreover, was remarkably stable across a wide band of ages. In 1970, major fragments of this convention remained, but it was not intact. The negative relationship is markedly weaker than in 1880, and is presently primarily at the younger ages. As women in 1970 entered their 30s, a new configuration took shape and a positive trend emerged between the married state and workforce participation.[31]

Leaving aside specific considerations, overall there is no doubt that the concentration of transition decisions in a briefer period of time has not resulted in a random or helter-skelter response. In contrast to the age-incongruity of the nineteenth century, an integrated mode has emerged in the twentieth century.

Conclusions

The burden of this paper has been to present evidence suggesting that over the last century has been change in the pattern of the transition to adulthood. As a result, the early life course today is to an important degree organized differently, with different consequences for youth. Our quantitative evidence expands and refines Kett's argument that the broad latitude of choice that characterized growing up in the nineteenth century has been replaced today by a more prescribed and tightly defined schedule of life course organization. The prevalence of the usual transitions has increased somewhat, and for most of the transitions, the spread has narrowed, sometimes markedly. The relative timing of the several statuses—notably the moving together of the familial and the nonfamilial transitions—has created a situation of far greater age-congruity. A far larger proportion of a cohort growing up today is faced with choices about sequencing and combining statuses.

We can perhaps understand the slight increase of prevalence and the narrowing of spread as an aspect of the homogenizing over time of the regional, urban/rural, and ethnic differences in this country, each subgroup in the nineteenth century putatively living within its own age-graded system. Only further research into the sources of variation of age-norming can determine to what degree this was actually the case. Surely, however, young people today face more complex sequencing decisions, rendered stressful by their very individuation and preferential basis. Our use of the individual level Philadelphia data (regionally and ecologically homogeneous), demonstrates that the change in the mechanisms of life course organization from the age-incongruity of the nineteenth century to the integration of the twentieth century represents a real historical development.

The distinction between familial and nonfamilial transitions has appeared in all our discussions to this point. Our understanding of how growing up has changed is bound up with this dichotomy. Characteristics of familial and nonfamilial transitions, distinct from each other in the nineteenth century, today have become increasingly alike. They resemble each other in spread and timing, and they are more age-congruous and integrated with one another. No longer are the family transitions the predominately consequential ones: today school departure and workforce entry are far more important in shaping the subsequent work career than a century ago. And today the familial transitions are not so enduring as was once the case. In the nineteenth century, the family was a unique institution, standing alone; in the twentieth, it is one of many; or rather, one of the many in and out of which individuals have to thread their way.

The past century witnessed a radical alteration in the nature and functioning of the household economy as the family passed through its developmental cycle. Notable in regard to the transition to adulthood we are discussing has been a major change in the function of the labor of "dependents." In the nineteenth century, most urban American families were able to operate with a margin of comfort to the degree that they could count on a steady contribution from their laboring children of both sexes. A young man or woman in 1880 Philadelphia typically would enter the workforce and contribute to a family income for about seven years (barring mortality). By contrast, the 1970 family economy depends upon husband and wife alone. Children, while they are briefly (2.5 years) of working age but still living with their parents, either spend the money they earn on consumption goods, or accumulate for their own subsequent families (usually by investing in their own education), rather than contributing their earnings to their families of origin.

Michael Anderson describes well the predictably unpredictable quality of nineteenth-century urban family life which made the family such a special institution.[32] His focus, rightly we feel, is on the exigencies brought on by premodern urban morbidity and mortality, and by the narrow economic marginality which characterized family life as early industrialization transformed society. Sudden death, maiming accidents, frequent and extended layoffs, sickness, and other such devastating events made it essential for families to have a reserve of obligations to aid at times of such calamities. If the family, with its small knowledge and limited risk pool, were to perform as actuary, it needed the ability to call upon able members over many years. This period extended beyond what "youth" subsumes today and would be incompatible with current standards of adult independence.[33]

A major historical development of the past century has been the creation of nonfamilial responses to meet the material exigencies of life. Public health clinics, workmen's compensation, unemployment insurance, pensions, and the like have rendered life far more predictable and the risk-balancing role of the family far less important. At the same time, the affluence of industrial society has created a surplus that frees families from dependence on the labor of their "dependents." Individuals now find that their course to adulthood is far more involved than before with nonfamilial institutions, especially those concerned with training and occupation, and relatively free from familial obligations. In short, affluence has made participation in the family economy unnecessary and children have the luxury of leaving home earlier and hence can afford to set up their own family at a much earlier point in the life course. Here we are not arguing the desirability of an earlier schedule for family formation, but stating that what was once uncommon in the nineteenth century has today become more nearly normative.

It is important to bear in mind that the legislation that raised the ages of leaving school and entering the workforce was *not* accompanied by other legislation governing the age-graded sequence of status decisions which constitute a social career. Indeed, if anything, to a larger extent than before, the career is for the individual to determine. Career decisions have in many cases become criteria for social evaluation, placing greater pressure on the individual to choose correctly.

Transitions are today more contingent, more integrated, because they are constrained by a set of formal institutions. The institutions with which individuals must increasingly deal call for and reward precise behavior. By contrast, the nineteenth-century family allowed for far greater latitude, providing individuals were prepared to satisfy their familial obligations. "Timely" action to nineteenth-century families consisted of helpful response in times of trouble; in the twentieth century, timeliness connotes adherence to a schedule.

Whatever the sources for the change in the mode of the transitions, it should be obvious enough that the shift to the contemporary pattern of allocation, the "integrated mode," has not been without stress. While we can make a case that in certain respects the current pattern of transition both allows more individual discretion and seems to display more articulation between statuses, the integrated mode does not in our way of thinking imply the reduction of strain. Growing up, as a process, has become briefer, more normful, bounded, and consequential[34]—and thereby more demanding on the individual participants.

Scholars who see today's period of youth as extended, normless, lacking bounds, and without consequential decisions are responding—we believe —not to its essential characteristics, but to the expressions of those experiencing the phase of life. They reflect rather than analyze turmoil.

NOTES

1. Bernice L. Neugarten, *Middle Age and Aging: A Reader in Social Psychology* (Chicago: University of Chicago Press, 1968).

2. Glen Elder, "Age Differentiation and the Life Course," in *Annual Review of Sociology* (Palo Alto, Cal.: Annual Reviews, 1975).

3. F. Musgrove, *Youth and the Social Order* (Bloomington: Indiana University Press, 1965); Kenneth Keniston, "Youth: A 'New' Stage of Life," in Thomas J. Cottle, ed., *The Prospect of Youth* (Boston: Little, Brown, 1972).

4. Richard Flacks, *Youth and Social Change* (Chicago: Markham, 1971); Panel on Youth of the President's Advisory Committee, *Transition to Adulthood* (Chicago: University of Chicago Press, 1974).

5. James S. Coleman, *The Adolescent Society* (New York: Free Press of Glencoe, 1961); Bennett M. Berger, *Looking for America: Essays on Youth, and Suburbia, and Other American Obsessions* (Englewood Cliffs, N.J.: Prentice-Hall, 1971).

6. John Demos and Virginia Demos, "Adolescence in Historical Perspective," *Journal of Marriage and the Family* 31 (1969), 632–38.

7. Joseph Kett, "Growing up in Rural England, 1800–1840," in Tamara K. Hareven, ed., *Anonymous Americans: Explorations in Nineteenth-Century Social History* (Englewood Cliffs, N.J.: Prentice-Hall, 1971); "Adolescence and Youth in Nineteenth-Century America," in Theodore K. Rabb and Robert I. Rotberg, eds., *The Family in History: Interdisciplinary Essays* (New York: Harper & Row, 1973); and "Part I," in Panel on Youth of the President's Science Advisory Committee, *Transition to Adulthood* (Chicago: University of Chicago Press, 1974).

8. Michael Katz, *The People of Hamilton, Canada West* (Cambridge: Harvard University Press, 1975).

9. Harold Wilensky, "Orderly Careers and Social Participation: The Impact of Work History on Social Integration in the Middle Mass," in Bernice L. Neugarten, ed., *Middle Age and Aging: A Reader in Social Psychology* (Chicago: University of Chicago Press, 1968).

10. Norman B. Ryder, "The Cohort as a Concept in the Study of Social Change," *American Sociological Review* 30 (1965), 843–61; and "The Demography of Youth," in James S. Coleman, ed., *Youth: Transition to Adulthood* (Chicago: University of Chicago Press, 1974).

11. Matilda White Riley, Marilyn Johnson, and Anne Foner, *Aging and Society*, 3 vols., *Volume Three: A Sociology of Age Stratification* (New York: Russell Sage

Foundation, 1972); Matilda White Riley *et al.*, "Socialization for the Middle and Later Years," in David A. Goslin, ed., *Handbook of Socialization Theory and Research* (Chicago: Rand-McNally, 1969).

12. That rigid schedules may be at the source of social-psychological problems is apparent from several of Bernice Neugarten's studies, which point to such consequences when individuals are forced to adhere to schedules they do not accept, or prove unable to conform to schedules they hold legitimate.

13. Paul C. Glick and Robert Parke, "New Approaches in Studying the Life Cycle of the Family," *Demography* 2 (1965), 187–202; for a still longer historical sweep, see Robert V. Wells, "Demographic Change and the Life Cycle in American Families," in Theodore K. Rabb and Robert I. Rotberg, eds., *The Family in History: Interdisciplinary Essays* (New York: Harper & Row, 1973). Also see Paul C. Glick, *American Families* (New York: John Wiley, 1957).

14. Peter Uhlenberg's alternative approach creates from demographic parameters a set of typical careers reflecting different experience, and estimates their prevalence in the population. Like the Glick approach, however, Uhlenberg's method makes nothing of the fact of *variance* in the timing of events. See Peter R. Uhlenberg, "A Study of Cohort Life Cycles: Cohorts of Native Born Massachusetts Women, 1830–1920," *Population Studies* 23 (1969), 407–20; and "Cohort Variations in Family Life Cycle Experience of United States Females," *Journal of Marriage and the Family* 36 (1974), 284–89.

15. This paradox depends on the possibility that for many persons establishing households precedes marriage.

16. For analogous inferences, well-established procedures are available, notably John Hajnal's method of estimating age at marriage directly from a single set of census data. Like Hajnal, we will make two assumptions: first, that the distribution of statuses by age has not been affected by rapid change; and, second, that in- and out-migration and mortality are not differential by the statuses we are considering. For purposes of simplicity (and since we are concerned with comparing distributions rather than determining absolute ages) we use a pair of techniques related to but distinct from Hajnal's "singulate mean age at marriage." To determine timing, we use a variant of Hajnal's "singulate median" age at marriage; and to get measures of the age-spread of the marriage transition, we use a crude "process of differencing" to estimate the number of marriages during each successive year of experience. Thus if 40 percent of 21 year olds are still single but only 30 percent of the 22 year olds are, we can estimate that 10 percent of the population in question marries between 21 and 22 years of age. See John Hajnal, "Age at Marriage and Proportions Marrying," *Population Studies* 7 (1953), 111–36. Also see, Ansley J. Coale, "Age Patterns at Marriage," *Population Studies* 25 (1971), 193–214.

17. Howard S. Becker, "Notes on the Concept of Commitment," *American Journal of Sociology* 66 (1960), 32–40.

18. United States Bureau of the Census, *Census of Population: 1970*, Subject Report 4C, "Marital Status" (1972); *Census of Population: 1970*, Subject Report 4A, "Family Composition" (1973); *Census of Population: 1970*, Subject Report 4B, "Persons by Family Characteristics" (1973); *Census of Population: 1970*, Subject Report 5A, "School Enrollment" (1973); and *Census of Population: 1970*, Subject Report 6A, "Employment Status and Work Experience" (1973).

19. The data are drawn from a far larger base collected by the Philadelphia Social History Project. Directed by Theodore Hershberg, the PSHP focuses on the impact that urbanization, industrialization, and immigration had upon social and family structure; the formation and transformation of neighborhoods; the organization, mechanization, and journey-to-work; the development of an intra-urban transportation network; the spatial differentiation of residence, commerce, and industry;

and patterns of migration and social mobility. Blacks (about 4 percent of the population) and members of households headed by persons born outside the United States, Ireland, and Germany (about 5 percent of the population) are omitted from our tabulations. The blacks introduced thorny problems of household definition we preferred to sidestep; the others omitted were for substantive reasons never a part of the Project sample. (See Appendix II.)

20. We have been able to make the most thorough comparisons for marriage and workforce participation. In the former, Philadelphia's pattern of age by marital status essentially resembles that for Boston in 1845, Rhode Island in 1875, United States cities in 1890, and all United States in 1890. Philadelphia's age-pattern of workforce participation is similar to that for Massachusetts in 1885 and the United States in 1890. Finer analysis of the Massachusetts materials reveals that age at entrance to the work force did not vary widely there by urban/rural distinctions; while data from the United States census of 1910 show minor differences in this regard. We feel entirely justified distinguishing "nineteenth-century" patterns (which Philadelphia shared) from "contemporary" ones. We include supplementary nineteenth-century material in Table 1, but for subsequent presentation of data, we rely on Philadelphia in 1880, since only for Philadelphia are our data uniform and useful for examining individual-level relationships. Data for Boston (1845) and Rhode Island (1874) are derived from censuses carried out by the two political entities. The sources of data for the other areas are indicated in the notes to Table 1.

21. The statistic is a by-product of the ECTA program for iteratively fitting different "models" to a given set of cell frequencies, and, for our purposes, are derived from the "fully saturated" model in which all the marginal frequencies are determined by the given data. See James A. Davis, "The Goodman System for Significance Tests in Multivariate Contingency Tables," unpublished paper, National Opinion Research Center, University of Chicago (April 1972); and "The Goodman Log Linear System for Assessing Effects in Multivariate Contingency Tables," unpublished paper, National Opinion Research Center, University of Chicago (June 1972).

22. Were the distribution of such careers known, we would of course know also the distribution of the component transition ages; but, equally obviously, the reverse is not the case. The connectedness of information about careers is considerably greater than that of information about a set of transitions examined singly.

23. Saveland and Glick anticipate our measure of "spread" in their discussion of marriage patterns, noting that by comparison with the American experience for the 1920–40 period, "the 'spread' of age at first marriage tended to become narrower by 1958–60." The authors draw no conclusions about trends, however, explaining the observed narrowing by the Depression. See Walt Saveland and Paul C. Glick, "First-Marriage Decrement Tables by Color and Sex for the United States in 1958–60," Demography 6 (1969), 243–55.

24. These dimensions do not exhaust all aspects of the scheduling of transitions. For the moment, we should list two more dimensions: 1. Reversibility, already discussed, and 2. Order, referring to the time-sequence of two or more transitions, summed over a population. The order of a pair of transitions may be relatively fixed or relatively variable.

25. Unfortunately, census data from the nineteenth century, lacking retrospective items, do not indicate the proportion of individuals within a given cohort who ever went to school, worked, married, left home, or set up a separate household. Since some of these statuses are "reversible" it is difficult to ascertain exact prevalence estimates from cross-sectional data. As a rough approximation, we shall measure the prevalence by the maximum proportion achieving the transition in any age group. Needless to say, this is a conservative measure of prevalence because it does not take

into account individuals who had achieved the transition by the age at which most other members of the population had "retired." Yet, it is most unlikely that these limitations do great violence to the comparisons we are drawing, since in both instances we are relying on similar types of census material.

26. In reporting these differences, we are choosing to ignore the fact that at certain points the prevalence of marriage in the past was slightly lower. We prefer to disregard minor variations, concentrating instead on gross differentials.

27. While our "modern" picture could undoubtedly be improved by working out cohort-based figures really representing the experience of a given birth cohort, once again the differences would not be so substantial as to vitiate our major point: the age-based organization of the process of transition to adulthood changed markedly over the century.

28. Carter and Glick note that "first marriages have (in the past few decades) been increasingly concentrated within a narrower range of years," and use an inter-quartile range of age at marriage as their measure. They concentrate, however, on the quantitatively less significant shift upward in the younger portion of marriages, explaining this hypothetically by "widespread expressions of disapproval of very young marriages." They ignore the more substantial foreshortening of the marriage transitions at the older end, and fail to consider the implications of the narrowing of the spread. See Hugh Carter and Paul C. Glick, *Marriage and Divorce: A Social and Economic Study*, "Vital and Health Statistics Monographs," American Public Health Association (Cambridge: Harvard University Press, 1970), 78–80.

29. Six students under the direction of Frank Furstenberg examined a variety of forms of literature from the late nineteenth century—including marriage manuals, popular fiction, journalism, and sermons—seeking information about the timing of transitional events. The literatures (which shared a middle-class bias) included almost nothing about leaving school or entering the work force. The decision to leave the family of origin was discussed occasionally, as was also headship. Marriage was a favorite topic, a fact suggesting the importance of the event for the entrance to adulthood.

30. The trend lines are simply drawn in freehand between single-year-of-age observations to suggest a sense of orderliness. Economies of space preclude printing graphs for all relationships, and a simple summary measure has eluded our imaginations.

31. Whether or not the obscuring of a once-strong pattern of integration pointed to a general lack of integration of workforce departure and family formation, or whether instead it pointed to the presence of a pair (or more) of mutually effacing patterns in the population (a "liberated pattern" opposed to a "traditional feminine" pattern) cannot be discovered with the data at hand.

32. Michael Anderson, *Family Structure in Nineteenth Century Lancashire* (Cambridge: Cambridge University Press, 1971).

33. The other side of the coin, however, was a necessarily tolerant outlook upon individual and situational variation in behavior, unusually high by our current standards. The nineteenth-century family could ill-afford to exact precise behavior, since what it needed most was emergency backing. The study of transitions, seen in this light, fits neatly into our understanding of larger themes of family behavior.

34. The data below are excerpted from a remarkably rich table presented in Carter and Glick based on 1960 census compilations. By controlling for age (men 45 to 54 years old only are included), educational background, occupational type, and race, we are enabled to document the assertion that timing has substantial consequences, though we cannot with single-observation data specify the routes. The table, at any rate, shows that age at first marriage, within a single occupational stratum, has an effect on subsequent income twenty or more years later. Very

crudely put, to marry early was about as consequential for income prospects as to marry late; and for this occupational stratum, the scheduling of marriage rightly was worth about as much as continuing on into high school, or entering college. See Carter and Glick, *Marriage and Divorce, op. cit.,* 107.

Mean Earnings in 1959 for White Men 45–54 Years Old Who Are Operatives and Kindred Workers, by Educational Level and Age at First Marriage

	Married 14–20	Married 21–26	Married 27–33	Married 34 +
0–8 years' education	$4384	$4658	$4600	$4339
Some high school	5131	5302	5283	4814
Finish high school	5407	5686	5513	5072
Some college	5394	6151	5733	5340

PART IV

GROUP EXPERIENCE

The study of group experience must carefully consider the environmental context. The comprehensive data base available at the PSHP makes it possible to sustain three distinct sets of studies. The first is concerned with the development of the urban-industrial environment: housing, manufacturing, transportation, spatial differentiation, and infra-structure.[1] The second set deals with a wide range of behavior that cut differentially across distinct subgroups within the larger population: work, migration, social and residential mobility, fertility, marriage, and mortality.[2] The third set of studies involves a broad spectrum of groups differentiated by race, ethnicity, class, and sex: blacks; Irish and German immigrants; welfare recipients, criminals, the aristocracy of labor, the manufacturing elite; teachers; and women.[3] When these crisscrossing and interdisciplinary perspectives are combined, researchers can treat *urban as process* by examining group experience within a rich behavioral and ecological setting. The history of urban blacks, to note a clear example, has been the subject of many studies, but only recently has their fate begun to be understood in an urban-industrial as well as racial-ethnic context.[4]

The arrangement of essays in this volume is to an inescapable degree arbitrary. Many of the essays that appeared in the sections *Work, Space,* and *Family* could easily have been included here. Laurie, Hershberg, and Alter's discussion of occupational profiles across the ethnic spectrum; Burstein's treatment of immigrant residence and intra-urban migration; Greenberg's study of industrial location and ethnic residential patterns; Goldin's examination of the labor force participation of secondary workers among native whites, blacks, Irish, and Germans; Laurie and Schmitz's analysis of the labor productivity of men, women, and children—each of these essays could be appropriately placed in this section. In a partial though important sense, the study of these individual groups requires the integration of the separate analyses. The study of the Irish experience, for example, would involve a "summing up" of occupational, residential, migration, and family experience across the behavioral analyses. We say "partial" because even so comprehensive a synthesis would be incomplete without consideration of such nonmaterial factors as expectations, goals, cultural values, norms, urban and rural background, prior skills, and the degree of discrimination that individual groups encountered in Philadelphia.

The first of the four essays that follow, "The Irish Countryman Urbanized," by social historians John Modell and Lynn Lees, offers a valuable comparative perspective by focusing on the experience of Irish immigrants in Philadelphia and London. Comparability is a topic to which historians have paid considerable lip-service; yet despite the fact that concern with the general rather than the unique distinguishes the "new" history from the "old," it is case studies—not comparative studies—that best characterize current historical research. This is less a contradiction than a compromise with reality. The kinds of questions being asked normally require individual-level micro-data such as that found in manuscript censuses and city directories; since the collection of such data is costly and time-consuming, it is extremely difficult for individual researchers to undertake such efforts for more than one community.

It is important to recognize that there is nothing inherent in the case study that precludes the making of accurate comparisons. Given the quantitative nature of much of the data, the almost identical information sources, and the striking similarity of the analytic questions being asked, it is definitely possible to make these efforts comparable. Yet advantage has not been taken of opportunities for exact comparability which are provided by quantitative materials and computer-assisted research. Just as nineteenth-century railroad magnates came, however grudgingly, to realize the value of common gauge track, so, too, must contemporary researchers work self-consciously and deliberately to achieve comparability; case studies must consist of interchangeable parts much like that of machinery in modern technological society. That these case studies have been and continue to be conducted largely in isolation, and in the absence of agreed-upon conventions governing the collection, manipulation, and categorization of the data (e.g., record linkage and the classification of occupations and families), tells us a great deal about how the current organization of research among professional historians affects the acquisition of knowledge.

The essay by Modell and Lees is one of the few exceptions to the general failure of historians to make their case studies comparable. Like the earlier PSHP-sponsored paper that compared occupational structure and property-holding among ethnic groups in five nineteenth-century cities, the study of Irish immigrants in Philadelphia and London was done systematically.[5] Although the larger research efforts of the authors were not begun with this set of comparisons in mind, painstaking care and PSHP support ensured comparability across a range of topics.

The authors argue that the Irish "exodus . . . should be seen as part of a long term process of rural to urban migration within a developing Atlantic economy." They would agree with Gabriel Kolko that the waves of people who left Europe as industrial capitalism spread across the continent represented the "internationalization of the Western world's labor supply."[6] To understand the character of the Irish emigration one must appreciate first why they left their homes; this, in turn, helps explain why they settled where they did. The vast outpouring from Ireland was above all else associated with the deterioration of Irish agriculture; although the Great Famine cetrainly accelerated the movement, large-scale emigration preceded it. Because Ireland had a poorly developed urban hierarchy, the worsening of agricultural conditions sent rural people not to their nation's cities (as was often the case elsewhere even prior to ultimate emigration),[7] but to urban centers in foreign lands which offered them a more balanced set of opportunities. The rural background of the transients explains their unique demography and thus a good deal of their kinship structures, life-cycle, and subsequent family experiences in their new homes. The immigrants used the urban hierarchies in America and Britain "from the top down": after initial entry in the large port cities, they sought out smaller, lower level settings. Overall, despite some differences, the Irish who settled in Philadelphia and London had a great deal in common. This was partly due to the forces which sent them from their homeland and partly a result of the similarity in the economies they found in these two great cities of the Atlantic community.

The three remaining essays in this section deal with the experience of one of the city's smallest groups. That these essays all concern black Americans reflects not only the fact that blacks were the focus of the earliest PSHP research, but that their history has a great deal to tell us about the nature of American life and the origins of many contemporary problems. The following essays deal with several major historiographic issues: social stratification and differentiation within the black community; the uniqueness of the black experience; and the impact of the urban experience and its implications for reassessing the role of slavery in black history.

The black history literature of the 1950s and 1960s had little to say about how the black community was internally differentiated. It was concerned rather with documenting that the black experience differed substantially from that of whites: blacks suffered unique injustices. This made sense; to win compensation for their historical grievances, these had first to be brought to the attention of the public.

Understanding the black experience on its own terms, however, requires more than intergroup contrasts. Treating the black community monolithically makes no more sense than writing Irish history without distinguishing between Catholics and Protestants; Italian history while ignoring the differences between the North and the South; or Jewish history without separating Spanish, German, and Russian Jews. Research into the history of black Americans in the 1970s began to break down the conception of a monolithic black experience. The consequences of being born slave or free, growing up in the Upper or Lower South, having a dark or light skin, laboring as a field hand or an artisan, working on a small farm or a plantation, living in a rural or urban setting, and the welter of situations resulting from the combination of these separate conditions—all are being examined by students of the black experience.[8]

The essays by Theodore Hershberg, "Free Blacks in Antebellum Philadelphia," and by Hershberg and Henry Williams, "Mulattoes and Blacks," deal with two of the most important stratifiers within the black urban community: free and slave birth and black and mulatto skin color. These differences played a particularly significant role in the black experience because Afro-Americans have always been less able than whites to differentiate their community along the usual stratification axes of occupation and wealth. In documenting that blacks were bypassed by industrialization, we argue not simply that they were denied access to many of the avenues for upward mobility enjoyed by the Irish and German immigrants, but that their internal system of social stratification did not experience the growth in vertical differentiation that industrialization brought to the social structure of the white immigrant communities. Throughout the period under discussion, for example, the number of occupations that accounted for most of the black workforce could be counted on the fingers of both hands, while the number for the white ethnic groups was many times greater. A similar reality characterized wealth holdings. More wealth in greater per capita amounts was held by more persons among white groups than among blacks. Thus limited in their ability to stratify internally by means of occupational and economic differentiation, blacks used factors unique to their experience such as free or slave-birth, the attainment of freedom before or after the Civil War, and intra-group color differences.

As a group, for example, ex-slaves were at least as well off and in many instances better off than freeborn Pennsylvania blacks. Their families were larger and were more often headed by two parents; their rates of affiliation with beneficial societies and of church attendance were higher; they sent a greater proportion of their children to school; they lived in the more desirable neighborhoods; they were wealthier, owned considerably more real property, and enjoyed a more diversified occupational profile.[9]

The essay on mulattoes and blacks marshals evidence to document that the lighter skinned were on average considerably better off than their darker skinned brothers. There were little or no differences between the two groups in family structure, marital status, and age and sex structures; slight but consistent differences in fertility; important and suggestive differences in migration patterns; significant differences in residential patterns, literacy, occupation, and wealth; and revealing patterns of intermarriage between blacks and mulattoes which were consistent with the socioeconomic profiles.

Perhaps the most interesting differences between blacks and mulattoes, however, come not from the census information alone, but from the joining of these data with the information describing the memberships of several thousand individuals in some fifty-six organizations in nineteenth-century Negro Philadelphia. This section of the research is significant in both its substantive findings and its methodological approach. Although mulattoes were outnumbered four to one in the entire Negro population, and two to one in the high economic strata, they enjoyed *parity* within the social elite, and, what is more, within these organizations, they held 60 percent of the highest positions of leadership and responsibilty (presidents, vice-presidents, treasurers).[10]

The design of research on blacks remains inherently comparative. The data permit us to answer the question posed at the outset of our research: "were the burdens and disabilities faced by Negroes *peculiar* to their historical experience or simply obstacles that every immigrant group entering American society had to overcome?" The black experience was *sui generis;* it was different from that of white ethnic groups in kind as well as in degree. The socioeconomic condition of blacks throughout their history in urban America, moreover, was closely tied to the ebb and flow from abroad of European immigrants: deteriorating when the Irish and Germans arrived in the mid-nineteenth century; improving in the 1870s; and declining once again as the Italians, Poles, Slavs, and Eastern European Jews arrived at the turn of the twentieth century. More recently, the job competition which historically dominated black-white immigrant relations has become even more difficult, for not only are there regionally even newer ethnic groups with whom blacks must contend (Cubans, Puerto

Ricans, Mexicans, Asians), but technological change and structural alterations in the national economy have eliminated most of the unskilled and
semiskilled jobs that once offered white immigrants and rural migrants
alike an opportunity to make a living and get ahead in the urban setting.

The interpretative framework in which our research on blacks proceeds
argues that the slave experience must be deemphasized as the root cause
of most problems. In its place should be racism and discrimination—
wherever they manifested themselves—especially in the urban environment where blacks settled in proportions so great that today they are the
most urbanized of Americans. Slavery in some instances may have been
a sufficient cause of low status and decay, but it most certainly was not a
necessary one. Philadelphia blacks were overwhelmingly freeborn; direct
contact with the slave experience cannot be invoked to explain the rather
terrible plight in which they found themselves throughout the nineteenth
century. With most blacks at this time Southern and rural, the significance
of the Philadelphia black experience derives not from the numbers of
people it represented, but in its foreshadowing by half a century the experience in many of the same particulars of millions of blacks who would
leave the "plantation" for the "ghetto." Though they sought "cities of opportunity," most found instead "cities of destruction."[11]

The essay, "The Origins of the Female-Headed Black Family: The Impact of the Urban Experience" by Frank Furstenberg, Jr., Theodore Hershberg, and John Modell, discusses how the legacy of slavery was always invoked to explain the disproportionate presence of the matrifocal family
form, and documents that it was a product of forces peculiar to blacks in
the urban environment.[12] One of the few shortcomings of Herbert Gutman's critically important recent study of the black family is its failure to
understand that the black female-headed family was a product of the city
during slavery, immediately following its abolition, and long after that institution was destroyed.[13]

Our data support Gutman in his critique of Frazier, Myrdal, and Moynihan, but we have documented that the female-headed family characterized
between one-third and one-quarter of Philadelphia's black population
throughout the nineteenth century, a proportion two and three times that
found among the city's Irish, Germans, and native whites. The factors that
explain these differences—most importantly mortality rates roughly twice
that for whites, highly imbalanced sex ratios with adult women far out-
numbering men, extremely limited remarriage markets, low wages, and
poor working and living conditions—make clear that the origins of the
female-headed family are decidedly urban and structural. Cultural factors
—the argument based on the legacy of slavery—do not explain the differences in family structure among blacks, immigrants, and native whites.

The hold of slavery on scholar and layman alike as the explanation for the low socioeconomic standing of contemporary blacks requires careful consideration. Because the institution was so morally reprehensible, brutal, and inhumane, it followed in logic but not in fact that the slave experience was consistently destructive. The half-century long battle waged by blacks and their white liberal allies to destroy racial inferiority as the reigning explanation for the poor condition of blacks in American life is a second factor. In the 1920s, the environmental argument dethroned racial inferiority as the dominant explanation for black problems. It has remained unchallenged except for the recent work of Jensen, Shockley, and others. The point is not that *an* environmental explanation is incorrect, but that slavery is the *wrong* environment to blame. As an explanation, slavery was accepted so widely because above all else it was the classic expression of the environmental position. That slavery happened a "long time ago," and is thus safe and convenient to blame, is an insight that should not escape our thinking. It is to more recent injustices—particularly the problems blacks faced in cities and structural changes in the national economy —that we must turn if the condition of contemporary black Americans is to be comprehended. In short, we must cease blaming the distant past for socioeconomic injustices rooted in the more recent present.

NOTES

1. Most PSHP studies falling into this category are cited above in "Space" section essays.

2. Michael Haines is at work on a series of studies dealing with fertility, marriage, and family. See his "Fertility and Marriage in a Nineteenth-Century Industrial City: Philadelphia, 1850–1880," paper presented at Population Association of America (Philadelphia: April 1979), in *Journal of Economic History* 40 (March 1980). The PSHP has undertaken a major study of the determinants of mortality decline and the socioeconomic, ethnic, and ecological differentials in mortality in late nineteenth-century Philadelphia. For early work focusing on the methodology used in this research, see Gretchen Condran and Jeff Seaman, "Linkages of the 1880–81 Philadelphia Death Register to the 1880 Population Manuscript Census: Procedures and Preliminary Results," paper presented at Population Association of America (Philadelphia: April 1979), to appear in *Historical Methods* (forthcoming); and Seaman and Condran, "Nominal Record Linkage by Machine and Hand: An Investigation of Linkage Techniques Using the Manuscript Census and the Death Register, Philadelphia, 1880," paper presented at American Statistical Association (Washington, D.C.: August 1979), appears in *1979 Proceedings of the Social Statistics Section of the America Association* (Washington, D.C.: American Statistical Association, 1980).

3. With a city of Philadelphia's size and a data base as rich as the PSHP's, the list of particular groups available for study is extensive. A socioeconomic, demographic, and spatial profile of any group can be generated quickly with the technology at hand, and change over the thirty-year period in the group as a whole or in the lives of specific individuals within it can be studied with relative ease. Many

doctoral dissertations using these data are now complete, and others are well underway; for a complete listing, see the PSHP bibliography.

4. See Kenneth Kusmer's fine study, *A Ghetto Takes Shape: Black Cleveland,
1870–1930* (Urbana: University of Illinois Press, 1976).

5. Theodore Hershberg, Michael Katz, Stuart Blumin, Laurence Glasco, and
Clyde Griffen, "Occupation and Ethnicity in Five Nineteenth-Century Cities: A Collaborative Inquiry," *Historical Methods Newsletter* 7 (June 1974), 174–216.

6. Gabriel Kolko, *Main Currents in Modern American History* (New York:
Harper & Row, 1976), 68, cited in Michael B. Katz, "Toward a Two-Class Model
of the Nineteenth-Century City in North America," paper presented at International
Congress of Americanists (Vancouver, B.C.: August 1979).

7. Carol Golab, *Immigrant Destinations* (Philadelphia: Temple University Press,
1978).

8. Ira Berlin discusses many of these distinctions in *Slaves Without Masters: The
Free Negro in the Antebellum South* (New York: Pantheon, 1974).

9. Hershberg expands upon the themes developed in the essay included here in
"Free-Born and Slave-Born Blacks in Antebellum Philadelphia," in Eugene Geno-
vese and Stanley Engerman, eds., *Race and Slavery in the Western Hemisphere*
(Princeton, N.J.: Princeton University Press, 1975).

10. Methodologically, the linking of an individual's socioeconomic, demographic,
and residential data found in the census to his or her associational activities at different career points, adumbrates the approach being used in the research on members
of all groups for whom such information can be found. Whether dealing with the
Irish, the Germans, the new industrial elites, or the labor aristocracy, the success
already enjoyed in implementing this approach for the study of the black experience
promises considerable gains for understanding the experience of other groups. What
kind of institutions and associations were formed by what kinds of people? Who
were their leaders? From what sections of the social structure were they drawn?
How did the membership patterns change over time, from what causes, and with
what consequences? What does this tell us about group values and the sources of
power? Such are but a few examples of the questions that this method permits us
to pose and answer. This approach, moreover, has important implications for the
study of social class, for it enables us to transcend the limitations of the economic
strata derived from isolated use of census data by touching on the life style and socioeconomic networks maintained by the individuals in question. Dale Light, Jr., used
this method with considerable success in his discussion of the associational activities and social networks developed by Philadelphia's Irish immigrants; see "The
Making of an Ethnic Community: Philadelphia's Irish, 1840–1890" (Ph.D. dissertation, History, University of Pennsylvania, 1979).

11. E. Franklin Frazier, *The Negro Family in the United States* (Chicago: University of Chicago Press, 1939).

12. The PSHP is now engaged in a more extensive examination of the female-
headed black family using new longitudinal family data and mortality data; this
research is supported by the Center for Studies of Metropolitan Problems, NIMH
(MH-33510).

13. Herbert G. Gutman, *The Black Family in Slavery and Freedom, 1750–1925*
(New York: Pantheon, 1976).

10. The Irish Countryman Urbanized:
A Comparative Perspective on the Famine Migration

JOHN MODELL   LYNN H. LEES

No episode in the nineteenth century is more dramatic than the flight of hundreds of thousands of Irish from their famine-stricken country in the late 1840s. This exodus, however, should be seen as part of a long-term process of rural to urban migration within a developing Atlantic economy. Because of Ireland's pattern of economic and political development, the Irish became an urban people unable to remain in their predominantly rural homeland. We shall show how to a remarkable extent the Irish urbanized abroad, reinforcing in Ireland an attenuated urban network. This pattern, like Irish emigration itself, long antedated the famine, which merely accelerated already existing trends. And as the Irish chose in increasing numbers to live in foreign cities, they changed their way of life to accommodate to an urban environment.

The change we propose to discuss in this essay lies in the realm of demographic behavior. At least in Dublin, London, and Philadelphia, Irish migrants by 1850 had adopted an urban family and demographic pattern. Rural to urban migration produced a change in demographic behavior, because of the nature of emigrant streams and of the urban environments and labor markets. The cataclysmic events of the late 1840s only intensified this shift and concentrated its practitioners abroad. We base our arguments on data drawn from emigration data and on highly comparable

This paper originally appeared in the *Journal of Urban History* 3 (August 1977), 391–408. Except for the updating of several footnotes, it is reprinted here without revision. Beyond the agencies acknowledged in the Prologue which support PSHP research, Lynn Lees wishes to thank the Woodrow Wilson Foundation, the Joint Center for Urban Studies of Harvard and MIT, and the American Philosophical Society.

census enumerations of the Irish-born residents of London in 1851 and Philadelphia in 1850.[1]

Rural and Urban Irish Families

During the latter eighteenth century and early nineteenth century, potato cultivation, inheritance customs, and landlord attitudes combined to permit the Irish population to expand at a rapid rate. Laborers married early and supported families on the produce of a leased potato garden. Farmers' children could remain on the land and marry because of partible inheritance. Each child could receive a share of the farm; and in the early stages of subdivision, the increased yields resulting from the substitution of the potato for a grain crop permitted a new household to survive on a smaller holding. By the 1830s, however, subdivision had produced minuscule farms and reduced more and more of the Irish to the status of day laborers.[2] As a result of growing impoverishment, strategies of family formation among the rural Irish changed. Marriages were postponed until adequate material provision could be made. Analysis of the 1841 census of Ireland shows that 44 percent of the male and 36 percent of the female population aged 26 to 35 were still single, a pattern of late marriage that became more marked over the next several generations. This pattern was complemented by increasing rates of lifetime celibacy.

Particularly for rural families, remaining in Ireland necessitated very late marriage or no marriage at all, but migration to a city brought some escape from this situation (see Table 1). In the Irish civic population in 1851 more males and females were married than in rural districts in every age group except for females between 35 and 54. Irish males could marry earlier by moving from farm to city, whether that city was at home or abroad. Females could gain somewhat earlier marriage by moving to Irish cities, but women made their greatest gains in marriage opportunities by moving to another country. Irish cities simply had so many females per male that the effect of unbalanced sex ratios offset the impact of the urban environment, where the economic opportunities for marriage were greater and constraints to marriage were diminished. As Kennedy has argued, the critical determinant of marriage age was the access of an individual to the resources he or she considered satisfactory to support a family.[3] In American and English cities, where the availability of work brought an independent income at an earlier age than in the Irish countryside, the Irish married at approximately the same age as the native population. The rural Irish restricted and delayed marriage, waiting until they had a dowry or inherited the family farm.

Table 1. Percentage Ever Married in Ireland and in Irish Households in London and Philadelphia, 1851

	Males					Females				
	Ireland		London		Phila.	Ireland		London		Phila.
Age	Rural	Civic	A.	B.	B.	Rural	Civic	A.	B.	B.
17–24	3%	8%	3%	N.A.	N.A.	9%	15%	13%	N.A.	N.A.
25–34	39%	56%	57%	50%	66%	60%	61%	73%	60%	60%
35–44	78%	83%	82%	70%	77%	70%	62%	89%	74%	76%
45–54	88%	89%	90%	78%	80%	88%	85%	90%	80%	69%

A = All Irish-born in sample.
B = Household heads and spouses only.

The net effect of migration on the Irish ability to marry is illustrated most clearly by comparing Irish marriage ages in different settings. Even in 1851, before the shift to the pattern of high celibacy and late marriage was far advanced in Ireland, migrant males in London were married on the average by age 28.3, almost three years younger than those remaining at home. Females married at age 26.2, 2.7 years earlier than rural Irish women. Migrants in London adapted their marital behavior almost immediately to that of the host population, moving quickly away from the marriage age prevalent in rural Ireland. This shift to much earlier marriage seems also to have taken place in Philadelphia, although the form of the U.S. census does not permit us to make the same calculation of Irish marriage age in 1850. Comparative rates of household formation for males and females in these two cities show that Irish migrants in Philadelphia became household heads or heads' spouses at even younger ages than in London.

Not only did the Irish marry earlier in cities, but the average fertility of rural and urban Irish couples differed. In 1851 in Ireland, rural families had an average of 5.5 persons. Urban families both at home and abroad at this time were smaller, despite the pattern of earlier marriage. In Dublin, families averaged only 4.5 persons, while Irish families in London had 5.0 members and Philadelphia Irish families averaged 5.3 persons. These comparative sizes reflect clear differences in the numbers of surviving children in these several settings. Ratios of children to women of fertile ages for each of our cities and for the rural and urban Irish populations confirm a similar hierarchy of effective fertility. Variations in death rates may account for some of the differences in these ratios, since the city that seems to have had the lowest level of mortality, Philadelphia, also had the highest child-woman ratio. Nevertheless, there also appear to have been differences in marital fertility, differences that suggest that immi-

Table 2.   Household Composition: Mean Numbers in Irish Families,*
in London and Philadelphia, 1851

Age of Head	Head & Spouse		Children		Others		Total	
	L	P	L	P	L	P	L	P
18–22	1.75	1.62	.63	.31	.62	1.76	3.00	3.69
23–27	1.71	1.79	.76	.82	1.33	1.36	3.80	3.97
28–32	1.89	1.80	1.50	1.51	1.04	1.45	4.43	4.76
33–37	1.95	1.79	2.00	2.50	1.00	1.19	4.95	5.48
38–42	1.88	1.78	2.27	2.75	1.32	1.16	5.47	5.69
43–47	1.95	1.76	2.70	3.19	1.06	1.25	5.71	6.20
48–52	1.85	1.68	2.32	2.94	1.09	1.31	5.26	5.93
53–57	1.96	1.47	2.56	2.39	.67	1.15	5.19	5.01

*Household heads only; excludes secondary families.

grants responded both to the exigencies and rationales surrounding their migration and to local conditions. Fertility levels were higher in cities where the Irish lived in less crowded housing and where the chances for survival of children were higher. And, over the long run, Irish fertility levels became similar to those of their host populations and unlike those obtaining in rural Ireland.[4]

In Philadelphia, where death rates were lower and single-family housing more readily available than in London, the Irish responded by forming relatively large urban households.[5] They took in more boarders and relatives, employed more servants, and produced more children. Table 2 charts the average household composition of Irish families in London and Philadelphia in 1850–1851 during successive stages in the family life cycle. The sizes of the Irish-American residential units grew from 3.7 persons in very young households where the heads were 18 to 22 years old to 6.2 persons at their peak of development when the head had reached his mid-40s. Irish households in London followed much the same pattern of growth, but, at every stage, they had fewer members in each category. In both cities, after heads reached their late 40s, children, lodgers, and relatives gradually moved out, although these groups of people never entirely disappeared. One child often remained with the parents until he or she was past 30. Once married, the average Irish migrant couple spent the rest of their lives in the company of one or more of their children.

Irish families in London and Philadelphia resembled each other more than they did rural Irish families. Not only did they marry earlier and more frequently, but they had fewer children. This urban Irish demographic pattern existed by 1850 among Irish migrants in Ireland, England, and America, despite the wide differences in culture, economy, ecology, and sheer size which separate the major cities in each of these countries.

A full treatment of the strength of this pattern lies beyond our resources and our data at this time, but we would like to propose an explanation of its origins. Ireland's colonial status in the rapidly expanding Atlantic economy perpetuated deficiencies in the network of Irish cities and cut down on opportunities at home, forcing the Irish to urbanize aboard. Thus, the overseas urbanization of the Irish was both an expression of and the means of perpetuating the initial imbalances which, in part, produced it. Once abroad, at least in London and in Philadelphia, Irish rural migrants filled much the same occupational roles, which set similar constraints upon their demographic and family behavior. We will first examine the setting in which the Irish, but not Ireland, were becoming urban and then look at the demographic composition of all overseas migrants and of those who had settled in London or Philadelphia by the mid-nineteenth century. The demographic characteristics of Irish emigrants set the parameters for the emergence of an urban Irish family pattern.

Migration and the Irish Urban Hierarchy

Not only was Ireland a colonial country governed from abroad, but its economic life was dominated by the needs and the development of the English market. Not only did the English Parliament remove tariff protection for Irish industries and encourage the export of raw materials rather than finished goods, but the greater productivity of English industries drove their Irish counterparts out of business. At the time that England industrialized, Ireland deindustrialized as the rural production of textiles and other goods declined in the face of English competition. The country increasingly became an exporter of food, and, with urban functions and potential urban population drawn off elsewhere, prefamine Ireland developed only a truncated system of cities (see Table 3). In 1851, Ireland had only fourteen towns of more than 10,000 people, far fewer than either England or the United States, both absolutely and on a per capita basis. This was more evident toward the lower end of the urban spectrum. The subregional capitals which played such an important role in mediating economic and cultural exchange in America and Great Britain were less dynamic and less numerous in Ireland. Moreover, the Irish urban population grew hardly at all, while that of the full partners in the Atlantic economy grew explosively.[6]

Irish urban stagnation resulted from the relative lack of urban opportunities available for both workers and middle-class Irish. With the exception of Dublin and Belfast, most Irish "cities" were small, sleepy market towns or ports. Their industries consisted mainly of simple crafts, brew-

Table 3. Comparative Urban Hierarchies, 1850–1851

Country	Towns 10,000–20,000		Towns 20,000–100,000		Towns 100,000 +		Growth of Urban Population	
	N	N/1,000,000 total pop.	N	N/1,000,000 total pop.	N	N/1,000,000 total pop.	1800–1850*	1840–1850†
Ireland	7	1.06	6	.92	1	.15	61%	7.3%
England and Wales	63	3.51	54	3.01	9	.50	316%	26.4%
U.S.A.	36	1.55	24	1.03	6	.26	1273%	92.1%

*Growth in towns, 10,000 +, except England towns 20,000 +.

†Growth in urban districts; Ireland, places 1,500 +; England, places 2,000 +; U.S.A., places 2,500 +.

eries, and flour mills, each of which employed only a few people.[7] No large increases in the urban demand for labor during the 1840s attracted people into these towns. Irish men with property or education could become urban shopkeepers or professionals, but this group was relatively small. The growth of a Catholic middle class had been retarded during the eighteenth century by the Penal Laws, which were not repealed until 1829. As a result, Catholic access to education, state and municipal office had been restricted; important administrative posts went to Anglo-Irish Protestants. Then, after the Act of Union in 1801, when the Irish Parliament was abolished, the Irish political elite traveled yearly to London rather than to Dublin. The top rungs of the urban hierarchy for ambitious Irishmen lay abroad, even before the famine. In 1841, only Dublin and Belfast among Irish cities had attracted as many as one-quarter of their residents from beyond county boundaries. Internal migration of more than a few miles was not an option exercised by the Irish during most of the nineteenth century.

The stagnation of Irish urban life precluded the Irish from making a simple adjustment to the hardships of crop failure and rural overpopulation, as could be done in America or Britain when local imbalances of population and resources occurred. If each region in Ireland had had a well-articulated and growing urban hierarchy consisting of towns and villages of varying sizes with varying labor demands all linked by transportation, marketing, and communication networks, the pressures on the rural Irish to move could have been handled by short-distance migration without forcing them to abandon their culture and their country.

Normally most internal migration is short distance, involving step-by-step movement among the towns and cities of a region. A regional system of urban options thus permits the sorting out of new urbanites. The urban hierarchy may be seen as an interlocking set of opportunities. Where urban hierarchies have been filled out, migrants regularly move from lower level to higher level urban places, where the structure of opportunity is wider and the setting more demanding of varied skills than the rural hinterland. As they become ready, a portion of urban migrants go from the smaller to larger urban units in a region, their places being filled by another wave of newcomers. In this view, the urban hierarchy expresses geographically a gradient of occupational mobility and cultural change.[8] Short-distance migrants moving within such a system had many options and could choose the appropriate setting for their combination of skills, contacts, and experience.[9] Lacking fully articulated urban hierarchies at home, Irish emigrants had a less elaborated screening process than had British and American migrants to cities, who reached the largest cities by choice and often after proving themselves in smaller, less complicated places.[10] Although there were plenty of sleepy villages within a short walk, few jobs were available. Residents of rural Munster parishes, when asked where local people were migrating in the 1830s, said America or England, not Bantry, Killarney, Macroom, or Cork.[11]

Expatriate Irish communities in England and the United States were large and dynamic. In the mid-nineteenth century, only Dublin housed more Irish than New York or London. Philadelphia was the sixth ranking Irish city in the world in 1850, when Irish-born persons constituted almost 18 percent of the city's population. The Irish inflow into both London and Philadelphia around 1850 was larger than the contemporary movement into Dublin or any other city in Ireland (See Table 4).

Irish migrants sailed away to other countries, entering their urban hierarchies at the ports. Unfortunately, nineteenth-century English and American ports were at or near the top of regional urban hierarchies. The Irish had to compete, therefore, with the most seasoned of domestic migrants who had already undergone a step-by-step process of cultural change. In a sense, Irish migrants traversed these American and English regional urban hierarchies in reverse, moving from the top down. Over time, the Irish moved from their centers of settlement in London, Liverpool, and Manchester to a variety of smaller towns in virtually every region of the country except for central Wales, Norfolk, and Suffolk. By 1861 they spread out from London into Berkshire, Buckinghamshire, Oxfordshire, and Wiltshire and became much more numerous along the Thames valley to the east and south into Kent and Surrey. A similar process can be documented for the Irish of New York state between 1845 and 1855, and for the United States as a whole between 1850 and 1860. As the American urban hierarchy spread into the hinterland, so did Irish immigrants, thus modifying their early concentration at the ports. With time, the famine Irish found their urban hierarchy abroad.[12]

Irish Migration: Patterns and Destinations

The transfer of Irish population from tiny farms and rural villages to urban settings had, by the years of the potato famine, been going on for some time. The Irish Emigration Commissioners show that the half-decade of enormous overseas migration during the famine (1846–1850) did not initiate but only enlarged by four times the mass migration of the preceding half-decade.[13] The census of England and Wales for 1841 listed 415,000 Irish-born already resident there, and estimates based on American data suggest a roughly similar number of Irish living in the United

Table 4. The Urbanization of the Irish Population at Home and Abroad, 1840–1861

	Ireland		United States		England and Wales	
	Places of over 1500 population ("Civic")	Rural	25 largest cities†	Elsewhere	Greater London, Lancashire†	Elsewhere
No. Irish persons in						
1840–41	1,215,000	6,960,000	150,000*	331,000*	181,000*	234,000*
1850–51	1,279,000	5,273,000	358,000	604,000	300,000	427,000
1860–61	1,174,000	4,625,000	551,000	1,305,000	324,000	482,000
Growth of urban Irish pop. in each country						
1841–51	5%		139%		66%	
1851–61	–8%		54%		3%	
Percentage of all urban Irish who are resident in each country						
1840–41	79%		10		12	
1850–51	66%		18		15	
1860–61	57%		27		16	

*Estimated population.

†We use the numbers of Irish residing in 25 large U.S. cities and in Greater London and Lancashire to stand for the urban Irish in America and England, respectively, because more complete figures cannot be tabulated. Thereby, we obviously understate the actual proportion of urban Irish living outside of Ireland, because our measure there is much the most comprehensive of the three.

States by that date. We conclude that more than a million persons of Irish birth were living beyond Ireland's borders in 1840 (see Table 4).

The potato famine sped the process of redistributing the Irish population. By 1851, the number of Irish living within Ireland declined to 6.5 million; 727,000 were found in Great Britain, and 962,000 could be found in the United States. Perhaps two of every eight or nine Irish lived outside Ireland in 1851. During the next decade, the population of Ireland declined to six million, while the number of Irish-born in Great Britain increased to 806,000, and the figure for the United States was more than double this. One in three Irish persons now lived outside Ireland.

The movement abroad consisted of two types of migrants—seasonal workers and permanent emigrants. Individuals no doubt shifted between these two groups. Despite the sketchy nature of port records, it is possible to examine seasonal migration into Great Britain, which was particularly heavy during the decade before the famine, owing to the need for supplementary incomes to pay high Irish rents. In the four and one-half months of the 1841 growing season, no fewer than 57,651 emigrants embarked from Ireland for England and Scotland. Most were seasonal agricultural workers.[14] The composition of this group was characteristic of short-term emigration. Almost all the emigrants were young men (about 30,000 between the ages of 16 and 35); few families made the trip. Port officials counted less than 6,000 adult women and 2,000 children under the age of 15. The size of the migratory flow of males is impressive. In the summer of 1841, fully one in 50 Irish men, ages 16 to 25, and one in 40, ages 26 to 35, made this trip. The regional incidence of seasonal migration was highest in the northwest. In counties Mayo and Roscommon, one person for every 6.5 and 8.3 households, respectively, traveled across the Irish Sea. Since not all seasonal migrants would have made the trip every year, the proportion of young men who during their lifetimes would have gone to work at least once in Great Britain was clearly very large, and the proportion of families benefiting from such journeys no doubt even larger.

This regular exodus of young males overseas contrasts markedly with the type and amount of internal migration within Ireland. Primarily it was young women who moved within Ireland, going from the countryside into the nearby towns and larger villages. Already in 1841 the movement of young adult females into the cities had produced a massive shift in urban sex ratios. In the five quinquennial age groups between 15 and 40, there were respectively 747, 755, 728, 857, and 746 males per 1,000 females in Irish civic districts. But below the age of 15 and above 40, males attained relative parity.

Female majorities among adolescents and young adults were, to be sure, typical phenomena in urban populations during the nineteenth century; similarly imbalanced sex ratios can be found in the populations of Philadelphia, other eastern cities in the United States, and London as well. In the Irish case, however, urban sex ratios confirm the existence of dual, complementary patterns of male and female migration. Irish cities had places for young women (many presumably were servants), but not many for men.

In contrast, American and English cities could give the Irish a more balanced set of opportunities. The Irish apparently perceived this fact, for movement overseas that was not identified as seasonal drew a much wider cross section of the Irish population. Age-specific sex ratios among overseas Irish migrants show that between 1831 and 1841 the movement was dominated by males. Nevertheless, this dominance was far less than among seasonal migrants. Most prefamine migrants were between the ages of 10 and 50, but the ratio of children to adult women among the emigrants was substantial, suggesting at least some movement by families. This particular pattern of migration did not continue after the famine. By the early 1850s, a massive infusion of young adult females, generally unmarried, was added to Irish overseas migration, and the family component decreased relatively. Over time, Irish emigrants came to resemble more and more the age and sex distributions of the Irish urban population. Females increasingly dominated the young adult portion of the stream. The nature of this migratory flow of people abroad was critical in determining the initial postfamine demographic characteristics of the Irish in cities both in Britain and in the United States. The age and sex distribution of immigrants moving into Philadelphia around 1850 was virtually identical to that of Irish emigrants in 1851, despite the fact that Philadelphia was somewhat off the main routes overseas for Irish migrants.[15]

Demographic Structures of Overseas Irish Communities: London and Philadelphia

The Irish who settled in London and Philadelphia shared several demographic patterns that marked them off from the rural communities they had left behind. Rural to urban migration had produced, in fact, two sorts of communities easily distinguishable in their age and sex composition. In the countryside, the numbers of males and females were approximately equal, while in the cities the proportion of females was markedly higher, at least among what we would now term adolescents and young adults. In rural Ireland in 1841, there were 989 males per 1,000 females; but in urban areas, this ratio dropped to 844. Within Irish-headed households in London there were more women than men (941 men per 1,000 females), while in Philadelphia Irish-headed households the balance was tilted in favor of males (1,025 per 1,000 females). But not all Irish immigrants lived in households of their own. If only the Irish-born population of Philadelphia is counted, the sex ratio in Philadelphia drops to 940, owing to large numbers of young Irish women working as live-in servants. Many did so, too, in London, but our data do not permit us to count them.

If the sex ratio in London and Philadelphia Irish-headed households is calculated for age groups, a complex pattern of male dominance in some age categories and female dominance in others is revealed (see Table 5). The excess of females shows up most strongly among those aged 15 to 24. At these ages, more Irish women than men lived with their parents, while their brothers were more likely to move out of the city to look for work elsewhere in agriculture or railroad and canal building, presumably to return at a later point in the life cycle. Moreover, a number of Irish-headed households employed young women in domestic tasks. The proportion of males was highest in both London and Philadelphia among residents in their 40s, after which age higher male death rates began to take effect. The pattern also resulted from the combination of two basic phenomena. First, the famine emigration contained something like this same age-specific sex imbalance. And, second, the older resident Irish, in London as in Philadelphia were more likely than younger men to be survivors of the heavily male prefamine migration. In view of the complex origins of the 1850–1851 age and sex structures, the similarities of the urban Irish pattern in London and Philadelphia are striking, indeed.

The difference between urban and rural Irish communities can be illustrated with data on age as well as sex composition. As the young left the countryside, children and old persons became an even higher proportion of the rural population. At the same time, urban Irish communities contained abnormally high proportions of younger adults; this was also true in both London and Philadelphia. But the age distributions of the Irish-born in those two cities differed in one major respect: the Philadelphia Irish community in 1850 had more residents between the ages of 15 and 30 than did sampled areas in London, while more Irish-born children under 15 and adults over 40 could be found in the English capital. This difference had concurrent bases in the timing and the distance of population movement. Since the Philadelphia Irish community had grown especially rapidly in the late 1840s, it had a higher proportion of young adults. In addition, America was more difficult and more expensive to reach than England. These constraints mattered more to families than to single adults,

Table 5. Distribution by Age and Sex, Resident Members of Irish-Headed Households in London and Philadelphia, 1850–1851

| | London | | Philadelphia | |
Age	Males	Females	Males	Females
0–2	7.3%	7.0%	8.9%	8.8%
3–7	10.1	9.9	12.9	13.3
8–12	11.6	10.7	11.2	11.2
13–17	10.4	9.6	9.2	9.3
18–22	9.2	11.6	9.5	11.8
23–27	7.8	9.2	10.6	10.4
28–32	10.7	10.0	10.5	9.8
33–37	7.8	6.9	7.4	7.2
38–42	7.4	8.6	6.8	6.0
43–47	5.5	4.4	3.7	3.2
48–52	5.6	4.9	4.6	3.5
53–57	1.7	2.1	1.4	1.8
58+	4.9	5.1	3.2	3.8

so that when crops failed and employment opportunities contracted during the 1830s and 1840s, forcing whole families to leave Ireland, many more with young children chose London instead of Philadelphia.

The Economic Constraints of the Urban Environment

Despite differences in the timing of American and British industrial growth, Philadelphia and London had quite similar labor markets around 1850.[16] The position of Philadelphia in the vanguard of U.S. economic development brought its economic structure close to that of London, a city less affected by the new textile-based industrialization than the Lancashire cities. Although differing greatly in size and in concentration of foreign immigrants, both cities were ports and major centers of small-scale industrial production. Both cities had thriving commercial and financial sectors, although London's was the larger, as one would expect in an imperial capital. Measured crudely, one-quarter of the male labor force in each provided commercial, financial, professional, or personal services. About one-third produced or sold manufactured goods, and one-tenth worked in the construction industry. There were differences, of course; more people produced textiles in Philadelphia, while a higher proportion worked in the transportation, paper, or printing industries in London. But these are minor dissimilarities (see Table 6).

The Irish took up nearly identical niches within these two urban economies. Table 6 shows the occupational distributions for the male portion of the labor forces of both cities and for the male members of Irish-headed households.[17] In both cities, the Irish occupied very low

Table 6.   Distribution of Male Occupations, London and Philadelphia, 1850–51

	London, 1851 Total pop.	Irish	Philadelphia, 1850 Total pop.	Irish	Differentials* London	Phila.
Construction	9.4%	12.8%	10.0%	5.9%	1.36	.59
Metals & Machinery	8.2	2.5	7.2	3.4	.30	.47
Gas, fuel, glass	1.6	.7	.8	.4	a	a
Textiles	3.0	.8	5.2	13.4	.27	2.58
Clothing, shoes	8.8	7.2	10.5	8.4	.82	.82
Leather	1.8	.6	1.9	1.3	.33	.68
Wood	4.7	1.1	4.8	1.3	.23	.27
Printing	2.7	.5	1.7	.8	.19	.47
Food, liquor	9.5	7.3	5.9	4.3	.77	.65
Transport	12.0	20.8	4.0	5.4	1.73	1.35
Service	4.9	1.8	3.8	3.6	.37	.95
General Labor	7.2	30.7	13.5	31.3	4.26	2.32
Administration	1.8	.3	.6	.3	a	a
Commerce, Finance	6.3	3.8	9.2	4.5	.60	.49
Professions, Art, Ed.	4.4	1.0	2.9	1.0	a	a
Other + unknown	10.8	7.3	18.0	14.8	b	b

a = too few cases to compute ratio.

b = meaningless comparison.

*Differentials: $\dfrac{\text{Irish percentage in a given industry}}{\text{percentage of total urban population in given industry}}$

rungs in the occupational hierarchy. The Philadelphia economy had to absorb proportionally far more Irish. But despite this difference in the relative sizes of the migrant populations, the Irish took up much the same lines of work in the two cities. Males were to be found primarily in general labor and in the clothing and food industries. Small numbers of Irish artisans worked in every sector of the economy, but most Irish males carried bricks, portered goods, or produced textiles and clothing.

We have constructed an index of occupational differentials, comparing Irish occupational concentrations by industrial category to overall occupational figures for all males in the laboring population in London and in Philadelphia. The index shows where differences are visible within the basic pattern of likeness. Irish males were more excluded in London than in Philadelphia from a variety of widely practiced skilled trades. In Philadelphia, perhaps because of the proportionately larger numbers of Irish, perhaps because of the presence of blacks to take up other spaces at the bottom of society, the Irish could be found somewhat more frequently in artisan trades and in middle-class occupations. More Philadelphia Irish entered metal-working trades and leather industries.

The major difference among the occupational profiles of Irish males in London and Philadelphia occurred in textile production and in construction. In Philadelphia, the threatened handloom sector of the weaving trade remained lively enough to employ over 13 percent of the Irish males in 1850; by that date this occupation had almost disappeared in London. Far more London Irishmen found jobs in construction than did migrants to Philadelphia. The construction industry was particularly vibrant in nineteenth-century London, since the English capital was the hub of an elaborate railway network and the site of the port. In addition to vast amounts of new housing, several railway termini and expanding and giant wet docks were built in the capital between 1815 and 1880.

Though the Philadelphia labor market provided a somewhat larger range of opportunities for Irish immigrants, on the whole the occupational structure of both Irish communities conformed to the contours of the local occupational structure, modified by a general exclusion from the most favored lines and a clustering in occupations that required few previously required skills. The Irish were beneficiaries of and contributors to the rapidly urbanizing and integrating Atlantic economy, while Ireland remained a third sector in this economy, exporter of labor and agricultural goods.[18] In both London and Philadelphia, the Irish were a distinctive minority, typically providing much of the heavy labor and, through the employment of young women in service, many of the household amenities which the growth of these cities required. This somewhat truncated range of opportunities helped to produce the "urban Irish" demographic pattern we have proposed, much of it abroad. It channeled the urban Irish, wherever they were located, into highly similar socioeconomic positions and encouraged the patterns of family composition, fertility, and marriage that we have noted.

Perhaps in a structural sense it made little difference that so many rural Irish urbanized abroad. Perhaps the same demographic patterns would have been produced no matter what an urban migrant's destination. Yet this conclusion stems from a quite narrow view of the process of population redistribution. We have here confined our inquiry to a brief span of time; subsequent processes may well have distinguished among the varieties of urban Irish settlements. Our perspective is also narrow in scope, neglecting the impact of the massive migration on both the sending and the receiving countries. And, while discussing the structural outcomes of demographic decisions, we have given no attention to the cultural changes which behavioral change and foreign migration produced. Life in an Irish neighborhood abroad no doubt cushioned discontinuities; so did letters from home and to home. Nevertheless, we are certain that the impact of migration upon the culture of the migrants induced some considerable shock. The annals of American and English cities alike hardly suggest that accommodation was always easy or pleasant for the Irish. And the path of change led them away from easy contact with the traditional culture of their homeland. Such distancing was felt by those who migrated, and by those who did not. That an urban Irish culture grew up beyond Ireland's borders made a difference to both.

Such discontinuities in experience are rarely chosen by those undergoing them. But neither were they uncompensated. The historian's task, however, is not to weigh costs and benefits, but rather to point out that if these are to be specified, we must know a great deal more both about migrants' patterns of adaptation to cities and the systemic context in which they made their choices.

NOTES

1. The London 1851 sample of 819 families from five parishes selected to be representative of the range of London Irish settlements is described in Lynn H. Lees, "Social Change and Social Stability among the London Irish, 1830–1870" (Ph.D. dissertation, Harvard University, 1969). The Philadelphia sample includes 1,941 Irish-headed households drawn randomly throughout the city. It was collected as part of the Philadelphia Social History Project and is described in Theodore Hershberg, "The Philadelphia Social History Project: A Methodological History" (Ph.D. dissertation, Stanford University, 1973). (Also see Appendix II.) We also use published census tabulations for the total London and Philadelphia populations and for various other English, American, and Irish populations for 1840–1841, 1850–1851, 1860–1861: Great Britain, Commissioners of the Census, *Introductory Remarks to the Census of 1841* (London, 1844); Great Britain, Census Office, *Census of Great Britain, 1851, Population Tables, II, Ages, etc.* (London, 1854); Great Britain, Census Office, *Census of England and Wales for the year 1861, Population Tables, II, Ages, etc.* (London, 1863); United States, *Statistics of the United States of America . . . at the . . . Sixth Census: 1840* (Washington, D.C., 1841); United States, Census Office, *The Seventh Census of the United States: 1850* (Washington, 1853); United States, Census Office, *Population of the United States in 1860* (Washington, 1864); *Reports of the Commissioners Appointed To Take the Census of Ireland for the Year 1841* (Dublin, 1856); *Census of Ireland for the Year 1861, Part V. General Report* (Dublin, 1864). We also use retabulations of census data published in Adna Ferrin Weber, *The Growth of Cities in the Nineteenth Century* (1899; Ithaca, 1963); B. R. Mitchell and Phyllis Deane, *Abstract of British Historical Statistics* (Cambridge, 1962); United States, Bureau of the Census, *Historical Statistics of the United States, 1789–1945* (Washington, D.C., 1949); Ireland, Commission on Emigration and other Population Problems, 1948–1954, *Reports* (Dublin, 1956).

2. T. W. Freeman, *Pre-Famine Ireland* (Manchester, 1957), 16–24; K. H. Connell, *The Population of Ireland, 1750–1845* (Oxford, 1950).

3. Robert E. Kennedy, Jr., *The Irish: Emigration, Marriage, and Fertility* (Berkeley and Los Angeles, 1973), chs. 5, 7, and throughout.

4. Robert E. Kennedy, Jr., "The Persistence of Social Norms: Marriage and Fertility Among the Overseas Irish," unpublished paper.

5. On Irish housing in Philadelphia, see Dennis Clark, *The Irish in Philadelphia* (Philadelphia, 1973), ch. 9.

6. Dov Friedlander discusses this development in England and Wales; see "The Spread of Urbanization in England and Wales, 1851–1951," *Population Studies* 24

(1970), 423–48. The more sudden American pattern is discussed in James E. Vance, Jr., *The Merchant's World: The Geography of Wholesaling* (Englewood Cliffs, N.J., 1970), ch. 5.

7. Freeman, *Pre-Famine Ireland,* 33.

8. The classic literature on urban size distribution and migration patterns is summarized in Walter Isard, *Location and Space Economy* (Cambridge, Ma., 1960), ch. 3.

9. John Modell, "The Peopling of a Working-Class Ward: Reading, Pennsylvania, 1850," *Journal of Social History* (1971), 71–95.

10. Using a cross-national survey of urban hierarchies, Berry and Horton hold that smaller countries and younger countries lack fully developed urban hierarchies; Brian J. L. Berry and Frank E. Horton, *Geographic Perspectives on Urban Systems* (Englewood Cliffs, N.J., 1970), ch. 3.

11. Poor Inquiry (Ireland), Appendix F, P.P. 1836, XXXIII.

12. Because the U.S. census before 1850 lacks counts by nativity, estimates of earlier Irish-American populations are necessary. Ours are based on the Boston and Massachusetts Censuses of 1854 and 1855, the New York State Censuses for these same years, and on the 1850 and 1860 U.S. Censuses. For information on Irish migration in Britain, see John Archer Jackson, *The Irish in Britain* (London, 1963), 8–13.

13. Extracts from the Reports of the Emigration Commissioners are printed in *Census of Ireland for the Year 1851,* Part VI, General Report, lv–lxxvii.

14. Reports of the Commissioners Appointed To Take the *Census of Ireland for the Year 1841,* 450–51.

15. The U.S. Secretary of State annually published quarterly reports from collectors of each of the American ports under variations of the title, "statement of Passengers from Foreign Countries." These reports are available among the *House Executive Documents.* The form of the documents varies somewhat from year to year and from port to port; they apply to passengers, rather than only to immigrants, and say nothing about ultimate destination. Even so, in their port and period specificity, they are a valuable source.

16. A characterization of labor markets in London and Philadelphia and of the local occupational position of the immigrant Irish can be found in Lynn H. Lees, *The Exiles of Erin: Irish Migrants in Victorian London* (Ithaca, N.Y., 1979); Bruce Laurie, Theodore Hershberg, and George Alter, "Immigrants and Industry: The Philadelphia Experience, 1850–1880," *Journal of Social History* 9 (1975), 219–48; and Theodore Hershberg, "Free Blacks in Antebellum Philadelphia: A Study of Ex-Slave, Freeborn, and Socioeconomic Decline," *Journal of Social History* 5 (1972), 183–209; the latter essays both appear in this volume.

17. The U.S. Census omitted inquiries about women's work until 1860. With considerable regret, therefore, we have limited ourselves to analyzing male occupations only.

18. For a discussion of population movements within the Atlantic economy, see Brinley Thomas, *Migration and Economic Growth* (Cambridge, 1973) especially ch. VII, X, XI, XV.

11. Free Blacks in Antebellum Philadelphia: A Study of Ex-Slaves, Freeborn, and Socioeconomic Decline

THEODORE HERSHBERG

Afro-American history in general has received a great deal of attention from historians in the past decade. The same cannot be said about the history of black Americans who were free before the Civil War. Studies published since Leon Litwack's *North of Slavery* have considered racial discrimination in the legal tradition, the relationship between race and politics, the establishment of black utopian communities, and the role of blacks in the abolitionist movement.[1] With a few exceptions notable in the earlier studies of the free Negro by Luther P. Jackson and John Hope Franklin, the literature lacks a solid empirical base, a sophisticated methodological and theoretical approach, and a focus on the black community itself.[2] There exists an important need for new studies of the family and social structure, of the development of community institutions such as the church, school and beneficial society, of migration and social mobility.[3]

Antebellum Philadelphia offers the historian an important opportunity to study each of these topics. The free-black population of the city had its roots in the eighteenth century. Its free-black population in 1860, more than 22,000, was the largest outside of the Slave South and second only to Baltimore. All-black churches, schools, and voluntary societies were numerous. The National Negro Convention Movement met for the first time in Philadelphia in 1830, and the city hosted such meetings frequently

This essay was originally read at the Annual Meeting of the Association for the Study of Negro Life and History (Philadelphia: October 1970) and was presented in a revised form at the Temple University "Conference on the History of the Peoples of Philadelphia" (Philadelphia: April 1971). It was revised once again for publication and appeared in the *Journal of Social History* 5 (Winter 1971–1972), 183–209. Except for the updating of several footnotes, it is reprinted here without revision.

thereafter. Many of the leading black abolitionists such as James Forten, Robert Purvis, and William Still were Philadelphians. Most significantly for the historian, the data describing all facets of this history are extant. The black history collections and the papers of the Pennsylvania Abolition Society at the Historical Society of Pennsylvania and the Library Company of Philadelphia are even richer for the antebellum period than the Schomburg Collection of the New York Public Library.

In many ways this essay resembles a preliminary progress report.[4] Despite the research and analysis that remain to be done, it is appropriate to discuss several important themes which emerge early in the study of nineteenth-century black Philadelphians: the socioeconomic deterioration of the antebellum black community, the condition of the ex-slaves in the population, and the value of understanding the urban experience for the study of black history.

A Context of Decline

The decision of the Pennsylvania Abolition Society in 1837 to take a census of Philadelphia's free-Negro population was made for both a specific and a general purpose. The specific purpose was to defeat the move, already underway in Harrisburg, to write into the new state constitution the complete disfranchisement of Pennsylvania blacks. The general purpose was "to repel" those who denounced "the whole of the free colored people as unworthy of any favor, asserting that they were nuisances in the community fit only to fill alms houses and jails."[5]

The strategy employed to accomplish these ends reveals a good deal about the faith which the abolitionists had in hard fact and reasoned argument. The data from the census were presented to the delegates at Harrisburg and to the public at large in the form of a forty-page pamphlet summarizing the findings.[6]

The pamphlet argued that disfranchisement should be defeated because the free-Negro population made a worthy contribution to the well-being of the entire community. Blacks paid considerable taxes and rents, owned property, were not disproportionately paupers and criminals, cared for their own underprivileged and, finally, put money as consumers into the income stream of the general economy. The facts contained in the published pamphlet, therefore, "gave great satisfaction affording the friends of the colored people strong and convincing arguments against those who were opposed to their enjoying the rights and privileges of freemen."[7]

Although unsuccessful in the specific purpose—blacks were disfranchised in Pennsylvania until 1870 when the Fifteenth Amendment was adopted—the Abolitionists and Quakers undertook further censuses in 1847 and 1856.[8] As in 1838, these later censuses were followed with printed pamphlets which duly noted the discrimination and problems facing free Negroes and counseled patience to the "magnanimous sufferers," as they referred to their Negro brethren. The general tone of the pamphlets, however, was *optimistic* and pointed to important *gains* made in past decades. The overall optimism, however, proved unfounded when the actual manuscript censuses were submitted to computer analysis.

The "friends of the colored people," unfortunately, had been carried away by their admirable purpose. It was one thing to document that free Negroes were not worthless, that they could indeed survive outside of the structured environment of slavery and even that they could create a community with their own churches, schools, and beneficial societies; but it was quite another thing to argue that the people and the institutions they created actually *prospered* in the face of overwhelming obstacles. It is not so much that the Abolitionists and Quakers were wrong, as that they went too far. And in so doing, they obscured a remarkable deterioration in the socioeconomic condition of blacks from 1830 to the Civil War.

Beginning in 1829 and continuing through the ensuing two decades, Philadelphia Negroes were the victims of half a dozen major anti-black riots and many more minor mob actions. Negro churches, schools, homes, and even an orphanage were set on fire. Some blacks were killed, many beaten, and others run out of town.[9] Contemporaries attributed the small net loss in the Negro population between 1840 and 1850 in large part to riots.[10] In the same decade, white population grew 63 percent. While it is important to maintain the perspective that the anti-black violence occurred within a larger context of anti-Catholic violence, this knowledge must have been small comfort to Philadelphia Negroes.

A victimized minority, one reasons, should organize and bring *political* pressure on local government officials. But black Philadelphians after 1838, as we have seen, were denied even this remedy. Disfranchisement of all Negroes, even those citizens who owned sufficient property to vote in all elections during the previous 23 years, was all the more tragic and ironic because, at the same time, all white males in Pennsylvania over the age of 21 were specifically given the right to vote.

In addition to the larger, less measurable forces such as race riots, population decline,[11] and disfranchisement, after 1838 black Philadelphians suffered a turn for the worse in wealth, residential segregation, family structure, and employment.

The antebellum black community was extremely poor. The total wealth —that is, the combined value of real and personal property holdings—for

Table 1.

Census: Pa. Abol. Soc. 1838 Variables	Total Households				Male-Headed Households					
								Ex-slave HH's		
								Ex-slave Heads		
	All Free-born	Ex-slave HH's	Ex-slave HH HD's	Ex-slave HH HD's Bought Selves	All Free-born	All	Free HD's	All	Manumitted	Bought Selves
Non Church Goers	17.8%	9.3%	5.4%	3.2%	18.5%	10.5%	13.5%	4.8%	7.1%	3.7%
CHURCHGOERS										
White Churches	5.5%	5.1%	5.7%	7.5%	5.2%	4.3%	4.1%	4.6%	3.8%	5.1%
Baptist	8.7%	10.3%	11.4%	12.9%	8.1%	11.0%	10.0%	12.7%	13.9%	12.8%
Methodist	70.7%	76.5%	74.1%	76.3%	71.1%	75.1%	77.7%	70.6%	70.9%	75.6%
Episc.	7.0%	4.8%	4.7%	2.2%	8.1%	4.6%	0.4%	5.1%	3.8%	2.6%
Presbyt.	7.6%	5.3%	6.7%	5.4%	7.8%	5.8%	4.7%	7.6%	7.6%	5.1%
Cath.	4.1%	1.1%	1.3%	1.1%	2.6%	1.3%	0.9%	2.0%	2.5%	1.3%
Misc.	1.9%	2.0%	1.7%	2.2%	2.3%	2.2%	2.4%	2.0%	1.3%	2.6%
SCHOOL HH Chld Attnd	27.6%	29.2%	29.0%	35.4%	29.7%	35.9%	35.3%	37.2%	36.5%	38.3%
HH Chld Not Attd	22.5%	25.4%	15.9%	22.9%	25.2%	28.3%	32.2%	20.1%	17.6%	24.7%
Chld Attnd	55.0%	67.1%	71.7%	71.2%	54.9%	61.4%	55.7%	72.7%	75.0%	70.8%
BEN HH w/ Members	56.4%	56.1%	60.8%	64.6%	52.0%	57.7%	53.8%	65.2%	62.3%	69.1%
Members	27.1%	27.0%	35.1%	32.4%	25.5%	26.2%	22.6%	34.5%	34.6%	33.0%
SOCC White Collar	4.0%	5.4%	8.2%	4.9%	4.2%	5.4%	4.4%	7.0%	7.3%	5.1%
Skilled	17.6%	16.6%	18.8%	20.7%	17.5%	15.6%	14.2%	18.4%	17.1%	20.3%
Unskilled	78.4%	78.1%	73.1%	74.4%	78.3%	79.0%	81.4%	74.6%	75.6%	74.7%

three out of every five households in both 1838 and 1847 amounted to sixty dollars or less. This fact, it can be noted in passing, precludes the use of simple economic class analysis in determining social stratification in the black community.[12] The distribution of wealth itself, moreover, was strikingly unequal within the black population. In both 1838 and 1847 the poorest half of the population owned only one-twentieth of the total wealth, while the wealthiest 10 percent of the population held 70 percent of the total wealth; at the very apex of the community, the wealthiest 1 percent accounted for fully 30 percent of the total wealth.[13]

Between 1838 and 1847, there was a 10 percent decrease in per capita value of personal property and a slight decrease in per capita total wealth among Philadelphia blacks. Although the number of households included in the 1847 census was 30 percent greater than in 1838, the number of real property holders fell from 294 to 280, and their respective percentages fell from 9 to 6 percent. There was, in other words, despite a considerable increase in the number of households, both absolute and percentage decrease in the number of real property holders.

Another way of highlighting the decline is to create roughly equal population groups, rank them by wealth and determine at what point in the rank order blacks ceased to include owners of real property. In 1838 owners of real property extended through the wealthiest 30 percent of the ranked population; in 1847 they extended less than half as far. In 1838, moreover, it required a total wealth holding of between two hundred and three hundred dollars in order to own real property; by 1847 an individual required a total wealth holding twice as high before he could purchase land or own a home.

This statistic is complemented by a measurable rise in residential segregation over the decade. Disfranchisement (perhaps as valuable to us as a symptom of contemporary feelings about Negroes as it was a cause), a decade of race riots, and a general blacklash against abolitionist activities, all contributed to the creation of a social atmosphere in which it was considerably more difficult for even the wealthiest of Negroes to acquire real property. It is tempting to conclude quite simply that rising racism meant that a far higher price had to be paid in order to induce a white man to sell land to a black man. Stating such a conclusion with complete confidence, however, requires further *comparative* research in order to determine if instead this phenomenon applied equally to all ethnic groups, i.e., a period of generally appreciating land values.

The actual measurement of residential segregation depends upon the use of a "grid unit"—an area roughly one by one and one-quarter blocks —and is a vast improvement over far larger geographical entities such

Table 2.

Census: Pa. Abol. Soc. 1838

Variables	Total Households (3,295) (12,084 Persons)				Male-Headed Households (2,361) (9,609 Persons)					
	All Free-born	Ex-slave HH's	Ex-slave HH HD's	Ex-slave HH HD's Bought Selves	All Free-born	All	Free HD's	Ex-slave HH's All	Ex-slave Heads Manu-mitted	Bought Selves
Total HH's	2489	806	314	96	1760	601	394	207	85	81
Total persons	8867	3217	1013	358	6966	2643	1852	791	312	327
Fam. size (w/o singles)	3.88	4.27	3.84	4.12	4.06	4.40	4.70	3.99	3.80	4.72
Two-par HH (%)	77.0	79.8	79.3	90.5	99% of all male-headed households with 2 or more persons were two-parent households.					
$0-20 (%)	23.9	19.6	17.5	10.4	21.8	16.3	19.0	11.1	16.5	6.2
$21-40 (%)	21.1	19.6	19.7	11.5	18.6	18.1	19.5	15.5	16.5	8.6
$41-90 (%)	17.8	15.1	14.6	11.5	16.7	14.0	14.7	12.6	12.9	11.1
$91-240 (%)	18.6	21.1	18.8	25.0	20.9	23.0	22.6	23.7	24.7	28.4
$241+ (%)	18.6	24.6	29.3	41.7	22.1	28.6	24.1	37.2	29.4	45.7
Ave. TW	$252	$268	$295	$388	$257	$317	$284	$380	$388	$409
Ave. PP* All HH's	$176	$175	$191	$223	$181	$204	$180	$249	$269	$252
Ave. RP All HH's	$76	$93	$105	$164	$69	$113	$103	$131	$119	$157
Ave. RP Owners only	$987	$730	$567	$527	$768	$770	$1017	$564	$776	$472
% RP owners	7.7	12.8	18.5	31.2	9.0	14.6	10.1	23.2	15.3	33.3
Ave. rent	$48	$50	$47	$53	$53	$55	$55	$54	$49	$56

(Left margin wealth-category labels: WEALTH CATS)

TW = Total Wealth   PP = Personal Property   RP = Real Property   HH = Household

*There is little observable difference between the ave. PP for all HH's and the ave. PP for owners only: 95%–100% of all HH's owned PP.

as districts or wards. Each Negro household was located on detailed maps and its precise grid unit recorded. All variables about each household, then, are observable and measurable in small, uniquely defined units.

Residential segregation is measured in two dimensions: 1. the *distribution* of the household population—that is, the number of grid units in which Negro households were located; and 2. the *density* of the population—that is, the number of Negro households per grid. Residential segregation was rising in the decade before 1838, and it increased steadily to 1860. Between 1838 and 1847 average density increased 13 percent in all grid units inhabited by blacks; more importantly, however, the percentage of households occupying the most dense grid units (those with more than one hundred black households) increased by almost 10 percent. Between 1850 and 1860 the average density changed very little, but the trend toward settlement in the more dense grids continued. By 1860 the number of households occupying the most dense grid units reached more than one in four, an increase of 11 percent over the previous decade and the high point between 1838 and 1880. During the Civil War decade, residential segregation fell off but rose again from 1870 to 1880 as migration from the South swelled the Negro population of Philadelphia to 31,700, an increase of 43 percent over both the 1860 and 1870 totals.

Data from the Abolitionist and Quaker censuses, the U.S. Census of 1880, and W. E. B. Du Bois's study of the seventh ward in 1896–97 indicate, in each instance, that two-parent households were characteristic of 78 percent of black families. That statistical average, however, belies a grimmer reality for the poorest blacks. There was a decline in the percentage of two-parent households for the poorest fifth of the population from 70 percent in 1838 to 63 percent ten years later; and for the poorest half of the black population the decline was from 73 percent to 68 percent. In other words, among the poorest half of the community at midcentury, roughly one family in three was headed by a female.[14]

An unequal female-male sex ratio no doubt indirectly affected family building and stability. Between 1838 and 1860 the number of black females per 1,000 black males increased from 1,326 to 1,417. For whites in 1860 the corresponding figure was 1,088. Between 1860 and 1890 the sex ratio for blacks moved in the direction of parity: 1,360 in 1870, 1,263 in 1880, and 1,127 in 1890. The age and sex distribution throughout the period 1838 to 1890 indicates that the movement away from, and after 1860 back toward, equal distribution of the sexes was due to a change in the number of young black males in the 20 to 40 age bracket. Changes in this age bracket usually result from two related factors: occupational opportunities and in- and out-migration rates. The remarkably high excess of females over males throughout the period probably reflects poor employment opportunities for black men (while the demand for black female domestics remained high) accompanied by net out-migration of young black males. The gradual improvement of industrial opportunities for young black males after 1860, accompanied by net in-migration of increasing numbers of young black men reduced the excess of black females. The sociological consequences of such an imbalance in the sex ratios are familiar: illegitimacy, delinquency, broken homes, and such. In light of these statistics, it is surprising that the percentage of two-parent households was as high as it was.

More important for our purposes, however, is another measure of the condition of the entire black population often obscured by the debate over the matrifocality of the black family, focusing as it does on narrow statistical analysis of traditional household units. How many blacks were living outside of black households? How many were inmates of public institutions? How many were forced not only to delay beginning families, but to make lives for themselves *outside* the black family unit, residing in boarding houses as transients or living in white homes as domestic servants?[15]

The data indicate that there was a slow but steady rise in the percentage of black men and women who found themselves outside the black family. Between 1850 and 1880 their numbers nearly doubled. By 1880, six thousand persons—slightly less than one-third of the adult population (inmates, transients, and servants combined) were living outside the normal family structures. One out of every five adults lived and worked in a white household as a domestic servant. That so many Negroes took positions outside their traditional family units is testimony to the strength and pervasiveness of the job discrimination that existed at large in the economy; that this occurred within a context of widening occupational opportunities for whites, a benefit of increasing industrialization and the factory system, makes it even more significant. In 1847 less than one-half of 1 percent of the black male workforce was employed in factories. And this came at a time, it should be remembered, when thousands of Irish immigrants were engaged in factory work.

Blacks were not only denied access to new jobs in the expanding factory system, but because of increasing job competition with the Irish they also lost their traditional predominance in many semiskilled and unskilled jobs. The 1847 census identified 5 percent of the black male workforce in the relatively well-paying occupations of hod carrier and stevedore. The following letter to a city newspaper written in 1849 by one "P. O." attests to the job displacement.

That there may be, and undoubtedly is, a direct competition between them (the blacks and Irish) as to labor we all know. The wharves and new buildings attest this fact, in the person of our stevedores and hod-carriers as does all places of labor; and when a few years ago we saw none but blacks, we now see nothing but Irish.[16]

"P. O." proved perceptive indeed. According to the 1850 U.S. Census the percentage of black hod carriers and stevedores in the black male workforce fell in just three years from 5 percent to 1 percent. The 1850 Census, moreover, reported occupations for the entire country and included 30 percent more black male occupations than the 1847 Census; nevertheless the absolute number of black hod carriers fell sharply from 98 to 28 and stevedores from 58 to 27.

A similar pattern of increasing discrimination affected the ranks of the skilled. Blacks complained not only that it was "difficult for them to find places for their sons as apprentices to learn mechanical trades,"[17] but also that those who had skills found it more difficult to practice them. The "Register of Trades of the Colored People," published in 1838 by the Pennsylvania Abolition Society to encourage white patronage of black artisans, noted that 23 percent of 656 skilled artisans did not practice their skills because of "prejudice against them."[18] The 1856 Census recorded considerable deterioration among the ranks of the skilled. The percentage of skilled artisans not practicing their trades rose from 23 percent in 1838 to approximately 38 percent in 1856. Skilled black craftsmen were "compelled to abandon their trades on account of the unrelenting prejudice against their color."[19]

Job discrimination, then, was complete and growing: blacks were excluded from new areas of the economy, uprooted from many of their traditional unskilled jobs, denied apprenticeships for their sons and prevented from practicing the skills they already possessed. All social indicators— race riots, population decrease, disfranchisement, residential segregation, per capita wealth, ownership of real property, family structure, and occupational opportunities—pointed toward socioeconomic deterioration within Philadelphia's antebellum black community.

Ex-slave and Freeborn

Among the 3,300 households and 12,000 persons included in the 1838 census, about one household in four contained at least one person who although free in 1838 had been born a slave. Living in these 806 households were some 1,141 ex-slaves or 9 percent of the entire population.

What was the condition of the ex-slave relative to his freeborn brother?

Were ex-slaves in any way responsible for the socioeconomic deterioration just described? Contemporaries perceived two very different effects of direct contact with slavery. "Upon feeble and common minds," according to one view, the slave experience was "withering" and induced "a listlessness and an indifference to the future." Even if the slave somehow managed to gain his freedom, "the vicious habits of slavery" remained, "worked into the very grain of his character." But for others "who resisted . . . and bought their own freedom with the hard-earned fruits of their own industry," the struggle for "liberty" resulted in "a desire for improvement" which "invigorated all their powers and gave energy and dignity to their character as freemen."[20] An analysis of the data permits us to determine whether both groups were found equally in antebellum Philadelphia or whether one was more representative of all ex-slaves than the other.

The richness of detail in the census schedules allows us to make several important distinctions in the data describing the ex-slave households. We know which of the 806 households were headed by ex-slaves themselves—314—and how these 40 percent of all ex-slave households were freed—if, for instance, they were "manumitted" or if, as they put it, they had "bought themselves."

We are dealing, then, with several ex-slave categories: 1. 493 households in which at least one ex-slave lived, but which had a freeborn household head; I shall refer to this group as free-headed, ex-slave households; 2. 314 households in which at least one ex-slave lived, but which had an ex-slave household head; I shall refer to this group as ex-slave-headed households. In this second group of ex-slave-headed households, I have selected two subgroups for analysis: a. 146 ex-slave household heads who were manumitted, and b. 96 ex-slave household heads who bought their own freedom.[21]

Cutting across all of these groups is the dimension of sex. The census identified household heads as males, females, and widows. There was a strong and direct relationship between family size, wealth, and male sex, so that the largest families had the most wealth and the greatest likelihood of being headed by a male. Because there was also a strong and direct relationship between sex and almost all other variables, with males enjoying by far the more fortunate circumstances, it is important to differentiate by sex in comparing the general condition of the ex-slave groups to that of the freeborn population. Ex-slaves differed from their freeborn neighbors in a variety of significant social indicators:

Family Size. The family size of all ex-slave households was 10 percent larger than households all of whose members were freeborn: 4.27 persons as compared to 3.88. Families of ex-slave households headed by freeborn males and those families headed by males who bought their own freedom were 20 percent larger: 4.70. The instances in which freeborn families were larger occurred only where female and, to a lesser extent, widow ex-slave households were involved. (This, by the way, is the general pattern in most variables; in other words, ex-slave females and widows more closely resembled their freeborn counterparts than ex-slave males resembled freeborn males.)

Two-Parent Household. Two-parent households were generally more common among the ex-slaves. Taken together, two-parent households were found 80 percent of the time among ex-slaves, while the figure for the freeborn was 77 percent. A significant difference, however, was found in the case of ex-slave household heads who bought their own freedom. In this group 90 percent were two-parent households.

Church. For two basic reasons the all-black church has long been recognized as the key institution of the Negro community: first, an oppressed and downtrodden people used religion for spiritual sustenance and for its promise of a better life in the next world; second, with the ability to participate in the political, social, and economic spheres of the larger white society in which they lived sharply curtailed, Negroes turned to the church for fulfillment of their secular needs.

Important in the twentieth century, the church was vital to blacks in the nineteenth. Philadelphia Negroes were so closed off from the benefits of white society that church affiliation became a fundamental prerequisite to a decent and, indeed, bearable existence.[22] For this reason, nonchurch affiliation, rather than poverty, was the distinguishing characteristic of the most disadvantaged group in the community. Nonchurchgoers must have enjoyed few of the benefits and services that accrued to those who were affiliated with a church in some manner. The socioeconomic profile of nonchurchgoers is depressing. They fared considerably less well than their churchgoing neighbors in all significant social indicators: they had smaller families, fewer two-parent households, high residential density levels, and they were disproportionately poor. Their ratios for membership in beneficial societies and for the number of school-age children in school was one-fourth and one-half, respectively, that of the larger community. Occupationally they were decidedly overrepresented among the unskilled sectors of the workforce.

In this sense, then, the percentage of households with no members attending church is a more valuable index of general social condition than any other. Eighteen percent of the freeborn households had no members attending church; for all ex-slave households the figure was *half* as great. Although ex-slave households were one in four in the community-at-large, they were less than one in ten among households with no members attending church. The ratios were even lower (one in 20) for ex-slave-headed households and lowest (one in 30) for ex-slaves who bought themselves.

About 150 households or 5 percent of the churchgoing population of the entire community attended 23 predominately white churches. These churches had only "token" integration, allowing a few Negroes to worship in pews set apart from the rest of the congregation. Ex-slaves of all groups attended white churches in approximately the same ratio as did the freeborn—one household in 20.

The churchgoing population of the entire community consisted of 2,776 households distributed among five religious denominations: Methodists (73 percent), Baptists (9 percent), Presbyterians (7 percent), Episcopalians (7 percent), and Catholics (3 percent). Methodists worshiped in eight and Baptists in four all-black congregations scattered throughout the city and districts. Together they accounted for more than eight of every ten churchgoers. The various ex-slave groups were found more frequently among Methodists and more frequently among Baptists.

In any case, Methodists and Baptists differed little from each other and to describe them is to characterize the entire community: poor and unskilled. Within each denomination, however, a single church—Union Methodist and Union Baptist—served as the social base for their respective elites. And while ex-slaves attended all of the community's all-black churches, it was in these two churches where the ex-slaves were most frequently found. The ex-slave members of these two churches shared the socioeconomic and cultural characteristics of the community's elite denominations, the Episcopalians and the Presbyterians; and it should not be surprising, therefore, to find ex-slaves of all groups underrepresented in each of these last two denominations.

Beneficial Society. Next to the church in value to the community were the all-black beneficial societies. These important institutions functioned as rudimentary insurance groups which provided their members with relief in sickness, aid during extreme poverty and burial expenses at death.

There were over 100 distinct societies in antebellum Philadelphia. They grew out of obvious need and were early manifestations of the philosophy of "self-help" which became so popular later in the nineteenth century. Almost always they were affiliated directly with one of the all-black churches. The first beneficial society, known as the "Free African Society," was founded in 1787. A dozen societies existed by 1815, fifty by 1830, and 106 by 1847.

Slightly more than 50 percent of freeborn households were members of the various societies. Making good the philosophy of "self-help," half a century before Booker T. Washington, the societies found ex-slaves more eager to join their ranks than freeborn blacks. Each group of ex-slaves had a higher percentage of members, especially ex-slave-headed households (61 percent), ex-slaves who purchased their own freedom (65 percent), and the males among the latter group (70 percent).

Membership in beneficial societies varied significantly by wealth and status. Ranking the entire household population in 30 distinct wealth categories revealed that, beginning with the poorest, the percentage of membership rose with increasing wealth until the wealthiest six categories. For this top 11 percent of the population, however, membership in beneficial societies declined from 92 to 81 percent. Among the wealthiest, and this applied equally to ex-slaves, there was less need for membership in beneficial societies.

Education. One household in four among the freeborn population sent children to school. For ex-slave households the corresponding figure was more than one in three. Ex-slave households had slightly fewer children, but sent a considerably greater percentage of their children to school. For freeborn households the percentage was 55 percent; for all ex-slave households 67 percent; and for ex-slave-headed households the figure rose to 72 percent. To the extent that education was valuable to blacks, the ex-slaves were better off.

Location and Density. Small groups of ex-slaves clustered disproportionately in the outlying districts of Kensington, Northern Liberties, and Spring Garden. Twenty-five percent of the entire black population of Philadelphia, they comprised about 35 percent of the black population in these areas. Most ex-slaves, however, lived in the same proportions and in the same blocks as did the freeborn population.

More interesting than the pattern of their distribution throughout the city, however, was the level of population density in which they lived, i.e., the number of black neighbors who lived close by. To calculate the number of black households in a grid unit of approximately one and one-fourth blocks, three density levels were used: 1–20, 21–100, and in excess of 100 households per grid unit.[23]

The less dense areas were characterized by larger families, greater presence of two-parent households, less imbalance between the sexes, and fewer families whose members were entirely nonnatives of Pennsylvania. In these areas lived a disproportionately greater number of wealthy families, and among them, a correspondingly overrepresented number of real property owners. Here white-collar and skilled workers lived in greater percentages than elsewhere in the city, and unskilled workers were decidedly few in both percentage and absolute number. The major exceptions to the distribution of wealth and skill came as the result of the necessity for shopkeepers and craftsmen to locate their homes and their businesses in the city's more densely populated sections.

Ex-slave households were more likely than freeborn households to be found in the least dense areas (one in four as compared with one in five). Conversely, ex-slave households were less likely to be found in those areas with the greatest density of black population.

Wealth. The parameters of wealth for Negroes in antebellum Philadelphia have already been described. The community was impoverished. Poverty, nevertheless, did not touch all groups equally. In terms of average total wealth, including both real and personal property, free-headed ex-slave households differed little from the freeborn population. In considering the ex-slave-headed household, however, differences emerge. Average total wealth for this group was 20 percent greater; for males in this group 53 percent greater; and for males who freed themselves, 63 percent greater.

The most significant differences in wealth by far occurred in real property holding. One household in 13 or slightly less than 8 percent among the freeborn owned real property. For all ex-slave households the corresponding ratio was one in eight; for ex-slave-headed households, one in five; for males who were in this group one in four; and most dramatically, for males who purchased their own freedom, one in three owned real property. To these ex-slaves, owning their own home or a piece of land must have provided something (perhaps a stake in society) of peculiarly personal significance. Distribution of wealth, to view the matter from a different perspective, was less unequal for ex-slave households, particularly ex-slave household heads. The poorest half of the freeborn and ex-slave-headed households owned 5 and 7 percent respectively of the total wealth; for the wealthiest quarter of each group the corresponding figure was 86 and 73 percent; for the wealthiest tenth, 67 and 56 percent; and for the wealthiest one-hundredth, 30 and 21 percent. Overall wealth distribution, in other words, while still skewed toward pronounced inequality, was more equally distributed for ex-slave household heads in the middle and upper wealth categories.

Occupation. The final area of comparison between the ex-slaves and the freeborn is occupation.[24] Analysis of the data using the same classification schema for Negroes as for white ethnic groups confirms an earlier suspicion that, although such schemata are necessary in order to compare the Negro to white ethnic groups, they are entirely unsatisfactory tools of analysis when social stratification in the Negro community is the concern. Despite the fact that the Negroes who comprised the labor force of antebellum Philadelphia described themselves as engaged in four hundred different occupations, a stark fact emerges from the analysis: there was almost no occupational differentiation!

Five occupations accounted for 70 percent of the entire male workforce: laborers (38 percent), porters (11.5 percent), waiters (11.5 percent), seamen (5 percent), and carters (4 percent); another 10 percent were employed in miscellaneous laboring capacities. Taken together, eight out of every ten working men were unskilled laborers. Another 16 percent worked as skilled artisans, but fully one-half of this fortunate group were barbers and shoemakers; the other skilled craftsmen were scattered among the building-construction (3.2 percent), home-furnishing (1.3 percent), leather goods (1.2 percent), and metal work (1.2 percent) trades. Less than one-half of one percent of Negroes, as pointed out in another context, found employment in the developing factory system. The remaining 4 percent of the labor force were engaged in white-collar professions. They were largely proprietors who sold food or second-hand clothing from vending carts, and should not be considered as "storeowners."

The occupational structure for females was even less differentiated than for males. More than eight out of every ten women were employed in day-work capacities (as opposed to those who lived and worked in white households) as domestic servants: "washers" (52 percent), "day workers" (22 percent), and miscellaneous domestics (6 percent). Fourteen percent worked as seamstresses, and they accounted for all the skilled workers among the female labor force. Finally, about 5 percent were engaged in white-collar work, which, like the males, meant vending capacities in clothing- and food-selling categories.

It should come, then, as no surprise that there were few distinctions of significance in the occupational structure of the ex-slaves and freeborn workforces. The differences in vertical occupational categories find male ex-slave household heads more likely to be in white-collar positions (7 percent as opposed to 4 percent for the freeborn), equally distributed in the skilled trades, and slightly less represented in the unskilled occupations (75 percent as opposed to 78 percent). Within the horizontal categories there were few important differences. Male ex-slave household heads were more likely than the freeborn to be employed as porters, carpenters, black-smiths, preachers, and clothes dealers.

In summary, then, we find the ex-slaves with larger families, greater likelihood of two-parent households, higher affiliation rates in church and beneficial societies, sending more of their chlidren to school, living more frequently in the least dense areas of the county, generally wealthier, owning considerably more real property, and being slightly more fortunate in occupational differentiation. By almost every socioeconomic measure the ex-slave fared better than his freeborn brother. While ex-slaves were distributed throughout the socioeconomic scale, they were more likely to be part of the community's small middle class which reached into both the lower and upper strata, characterized more by their hard-working, con-scientious, and God-fearing life style than by a concentration of wealth and power.

An Urban Perspective

On the basis of the data presented it is possible to state two conclusions, offer a working hypothesis, and argue for the necessity of an urban per-spective. First, the relatively better condition of the ex-slave, especially the ex-slave who was both a male and who bought his own freedom, con-firms the speculations of a few historians that the slave-born Negro freed before the Civil War was exceptional: a uniquely gifted individual who succeeded in internalizing the ethic of deferred gratification in the face of enormous difficulties.[25] More striking was the fact that the socioeconomic condition of the great majority of ex-slaves was not markedly inferior to that of the freeborn. That ex-slaves were generally better off than free-born blacks, however, should not suggest anything more than relative superiority; it does not imply prosperity and should not obscure the gen-erally impoverished and deteriorating condition of the black community. Second, because the remaining 91 percent of Philadelphia's antebellum black population was freeborn, the dismal and declining socioeconomic circumstances of that population cannot be attributed to direct contact with the "slave experience." Direct contact with slavery was undoubtedly a *sufficient* cause of low status and decay; it most certainly was not a *necessary* cause.[26]

In a very important sense the first conclusion has little to do with the second. The latter is not arrived at because those who had direct contact with slavery fared better in the city than those who were born free. The second conclusion is not based upon a recognition that slavery was less destructive or benign (although in some aspects it certainly could have been so), but rather that the antebellum Northern city was destructive as well. It is significant to understand that slavery and the discrimination faced by free Negroes in the urban environment were both forms of racism which pervaded the institutions and informed the values of the larger white society.

The comparison of the freeborn and the ex-slave was undertaken in an effort to learn more about the question that students of the black experience want answered: What was the effect of slavery on the slaves? In the case of antebellum Philadelphia the ex-slaves may not be representative of the slave experience. If they were, however, our insight would necessarily be limited to the effect of the mildest slavery system as it was practiced in Maryland, Delaware, and Virginia.[27]

Deemphasizing direct contact with slavery does not imply that the institution of slavery, and the debasement and prejudice it generated, did not condition the larger context. The indirect effect of slavery cannot be underestimated. The pro-slavery propaganda provided the justification not only for the institution, but for the widespread discriminatory treatment of the free Negro both before and long after emancipation.

Yet, on the other hand, one must not allow this understanding, or an often overwhelming sense of moral outrage, to lead to a monolithic interpretation of the effects of the slave experience. Stanley Elkins's treatment of slavery may be in error, but few historians doubt that his urging of scholars to end the morality debate and to employ new methods and different disciplines in the study of slavery was correct and long overdue.

There is no historically valid reason to treat the slave experience as entirely destructive or entirely benign; nor, for that matter, does historical reality necessarily fall midway between the two. It may be more useful to study the problems that blacks faced at different times and in different places in their history and make the attempt to trace their historical origins rather than to begin with slavery and assume that it represented in all instances the historical root. Some of the problems faced by blacks may more accurately be traced to the processes of urbanization, industrialization, and immigration, occurring in a setting of racial inequality, rather than to slavery.

One of the most significant contributions to black history and sociology in recent years presents data that suggest the post-slavery, possibly urban, origins of the matrifocal black family. In groundbreaking essays on the Negro family after the Civil War, Herbert Gutman has demonstrated convincingly that traditional interpretations of slavery and its effect on the black family are seriously misleading. Examining "the family patterns of those Negroes closest in time to actual chattel slavery," Gutman did not find "instability," "chaos," or "disorder." Instead, in fourteen varied Southern cities and counties between 1865 and 1880, he found viable two-parent households ranging from 70 to 90 percent.[28]

It is significant to note that of the areas studied by Gutman the four lowest percentages of two-parent households were found in cities: Natchez and Beaufort, 70 percent; Richmond, 73 percent; and Mobile, 74 percent. The urban experience was in some way responsible for the weaker family structure, and for a whole set of other negative socioeconomic consequences, all of which are found in the Philadelphia data.

Yet the city is more than a locale. Slavery itself underwent major transformations in the urban setting.[29] Sustained advances in technology, transportation, and communication made the city the context for innovation; and the innovation, in turn, generated countless opportunities for upward mobility for those who could take advantage of them. And here was the rub. Blacks, alone among city dwellers, were excluded not only from their fair share, but from almost any chance for improvement generated by the dynamics of the urban milieu. That the exclusion was not systematic, but, by and large, incidental, did not make it any less effective. The city provided an existence at once superior to and inferior to that of the countryside: for those who were free to pursue their fortunes, the city provided infinitely more opportunities and far greater rewards; for those who were denied access altogether (or for those who failed) the city provided scant advantages and comforts. There were few interstices.

The data presented in this essay point to the destructiveness of the urban experience for blacks in nineteenth-century Philadelphia.[30] To proceed, data comparing the black experience to that of other ethnic groups are necessary and they are forthcoming. Although much research remains, it is possible to offer a hypothesis. The forces that shaped modern America—urbanization, industrialization, and immigration—operated for blacks within a framework of institutional racism and structural inequality. In the antebellum context, blacks were unable to compete on equal terms with either the native-white-American worker or the thousands of newly arrived Irish and German immigrants. Philadelphia Negroes suffered in the competition with the Irish and Germans and recovered somewhat during the Civil War and Reconstruction decades, only to suffer again, in much the same circumstances, in competition with the "new" immigrant groups, this time the Italians, Jews, Poles, and Slavs who began arriving in the 1880s. Best characterized as a low-status economic group early in the century, Philadelphia's blacks found themselves a deprived and degraded caste at its close.

Students of black history have not adequately appreciated the impact of the urban experience. In part this is due to several general problems: to the larger neglect of urban history; to unequal educational opportunities which prevented many potential black scholars from study and other students from publication; to difficulties inherent in writing history "from-the-bottom-up"; and to present reward mechanisms which place a high premium on quickly publishable materials involving either no new research or shoddy and careless efforts.

There are, however, other and more important considerations, with no little sense of irony. The moral revulsion to slavery prevented development of alternative explanations of low status and decay. In the immediate post-slavery decades and throughout the twentieth century blacks and their white allies took refuge in an explanation used by many abolitionists before them, namely, that slavery and not racial inferiority was responsible for the black condition. They were, of course, not wrong; it was rather that they did not go far enough. It was, and still is, much easier to lament the sins of one's forefathers than it is to confront the injustices in more contemporary socioeconomic systems.

Although August Meier and Elliot Rudwick titled their well-known and widely used text, *From Plantation to Ghetto,* and, with the little data available to them, subtly but suggestively wove the theme of the impact of urban environment through their pages, scholars have been slow to develop it in monographic studies.

The Philadelphia data from 1838 to 1880 enable one to examine this theme in minute detail. Although 90 percent of the nation's black population in 1880 was Southern and overwhelmingly rural, the key to the twentieth century lies in understanding the consequences of the migration from the farm to the city. The experience of Philadelphia Negroes in the nineteenth century foreshadowed the fate of millions of black migrants who, seeking a better life, found different miseries in what E. Franklin Frazier called the "cities of destruction."

If we are to succeed in understanding the urban experience, we must dismiss simplistic explanations which attribute all present-day failings to "the legacy of slavery" or to "the problems of unacculturated rural migrants lacking the skills necessary to compete in an advanced technology." We must understand, instead, the social dynamics and consequences of competition and accommodation among different racial, ethnic, and religious groups, taking place in an urban context of racial discrimination and structural inequality.

NOTES

1. Leon Litwack, *North of Slavery* (Chicago, 1961); Arthur Zilversmit, *The First Emancipation* (Chicago, 1967); Eugene H. Berwanger, *The Frontier Against Slavery: Western Anti-Negro Prejudice and the Slavery Extension Controversy* (Urbana, 1967); V. Jacques Voegeli, *Free but Not Equal: The Midwest and the Negro During the Civil War* (Chicago, 1969); James A. Rawley, *Race and Politics* (Philadelphia, 1969); Eric Foner, *Free Soil, Free Labor, Free Men* (New York, 1970); William and Jane Pease, *Black Utopia* (Madison, 1963); Benjamin Quarles, *Black Abolitionists* (New York, 1969); Carleton Mabee, *Black Freedom: The Non-Violent Abolitionists, 1830 to the Civil War* (New York, 1970).

2. Luther P. Jackson, *Free Negro and Property Holding in Virginia 1830–1860* (New York, 1942), and John Hope Franklin, *The Free Negro in North Carolina, 1790–1860* (Chapel Hill, 1943); there are, of course, many other state and local studies: W. E. B. Du Bois, *The Philadelphia Negro* (Philadelphia, 1899); Edward R. Turner, *The Negro in Pennsylvania* (Washington, 1911); John Russell, *The Free Negro in Virginia, 1830—1860* (Baltimore, 1913); John Daniels, *In Freedom's Birthplace: A Study of Boston's Negroes* (Boston, 1914); James M. Wright, *The Free Negro in Maryland* (New York, 1921); Robert A. Warner, *New Haven Negroes* (New Haven, 1940); Emma Lou Thornbrough, *The Negro in Indiana* (Indianapolis, 1957). Especially valuable articles include Carter Woodson, "The Negroes of Cincinnati Prior to the Civil War," *Journal of Negro History* 1 (January 1916); Charles S. Sydnor, "The Free Negro in Mississippi before the Civil War," *American Historical Review* 32 (July 1927); E. Horace Fitchett, "The Origin and Growth of the Free Negro Population of Charleston, South Carolina," *Journal of Negro History* 26 (October 1941); J. Merton England, "The Free-Negro in Ante Bellum Tennessee," *Journal of Southern History* 9 (February 1943).

3. There are, of course, important beginnings. Among them are E. Franklin Frazier's *The Free Negro Family* (Nashville, 1932) and Carter G. Woodson's *The Education of the Negro Prior to 1861* (Washington, 1915), *History of the Negro Church* (Washington, 1921), and *Free Negro Heads of Families in the United States* (Washington, 1925). Fortunately there are studies of the free Negro currently underway and others awaiting publication which will make important contributions to the literature. I am aware of the following studies: Ira Berlin, University of Illinois, Chicago Circle, on the free Negro in the Upper South; Rhoda Freeman, Upsala College, on the free Negro in New York; Carol Ann George, Oswego State College, on the free Negro church; Laurence Glasco, University of Pittsburgh, on the free Negro in Buffalo and Pittsburgh; Floyd Miller, Hiram College, on Martin Delany and the colonization movement; Carl Oblinger, Johns Hopkins University, on free Negro communities in Southeastern Pennsylvania towns; Armisted Robinson, University of Rochester, on free Negroes in Memphis; Harry Silcox, Temple University, on free Negro education in Philadelphia and Boston; Arthur O. White, College of Education, University of Florida, on the free Negro in Boston; Marina Wikramanayake, University of Texas, El Paso, on the free Negro in Charleston.

4. For a description of the data compiled by the Philadelphia Social History Project, see Appendix II.

5. Edward Needles, *Ten Years' Progress: A Comparison of the State and Condition of the Colored People in the City and County of Philadelphia from 1838 to 1847* (Philadelphia, 1849), pp. 7–8.

6. Pennsylvania Abolition Society, *The Present State and Condition of the Free People of Color of the City of Philadelphia and Adjoining Districts* (Philadelphia, 1838).

7. Needles, *op. cit.*, pp. 7–8.

8. Society of Friends, *Statistical Inquiry into the Condition of the People of Color of the City and Districts of Philadelphia* (Philadelphia, 1849); Benjamin Bacon, *Statistics of the Colored People of Philadelphia* (Philadelphia, 1859), second ed., revised.

9. Sam Bass Warner, Jr., *The Private City* (Philadelphia, 1968), see ch. 7, "Riots and the Restoration of Order," pp. 125–57.

10. Society of Friends, *op. cit.,* p. 7.

11. There was also a net population loss for blacks of 0.17 percent between 1860 and 1870; the white population in the same decade, however, increased some 20 percent.

12. Social distinctions indispensable to the study of social stratification do exist among this 60 percent of the household population; however, they do not emerge along economic lines. Households averaging thirty dollars of total wealth are not distinctively different from households worth twenty dollars or fifty dollars. Important social distinctions can be determined by using specific noneconomic measures such as church affiliation or a more general noneconomic measure such as "life style" which, in turn, is described by a number of other variables: residence, family structure, education, occupation, etc.

13. The unequal distribution of wealth was not unique to the black population. Stuart Blumin, "Mobility and Change in Ante-Bellum Philadelphia," in Stephan Thernstrom and Richard Sennett, eds., *Nineteenth-Century Cities* (New Haven, 1969) found greater inequality among a sample of the entire Philadelphia population in the U.S. Census for 1860 than I did among all blacks in the Abolitionist and Quaker censuses in 1838 and 1847: the wealthiest 10 percent in 1860 owned 89 percent of the wealth and the wealthiest 1 percent owned 50 percent of the wealth. Data describing the universe of black, Irish, and German property-holders in the U.S. Census for Philadelphia in 1860, however, indicate that inequality was pronounced in all three groups: in each case the wealthiest 10 percent of the population owned about 88 percent of the wealth. The Lorenz measures for the blacks, Irish, and Germans were .95, .94, and .92 respectively.

14. Ninety-nine percent of all male-headed households were two-parent households as well. Female-headed households in the Abolitionist and Quaker censuses were invariably one-parent households.

15. The data necessary to answer a series of important questions concerning the black men and women who lived and worked in white households as domestic servants will soon be available. Their age structure, marital status, mobility, social status, and the possibility of their families living close by will be examined. It will be valuable to know whether "live-in" service was a short-term or long-term experience and to determine its effects on family-building, family structure, and child-rearing techniques. Perhaps the most important question, and one which relates this form of employment to the experience of other ethnic groups, is whether such employment was seen by blacks as severely limiting, demeaning, and poor-paying—engaged in only because there were no other occupational alternatives available to them—or if they embraced such work as their own domain, desirable and pleased by the standards of living it afforded them.

16. The *Daily Sun,* November 10, 1849. I am indebted to Bruce Laurie who originally came across this letter in his rigorous research on ethnic divisions within the working class of antebellum Philadelphia.

17. *Register of the Trades of the Colored People in the City of Philadelphia and Districts* (Philadelphia, 1838), pp. 1–8.

18. Appendix to the *Memorial from the People of Color to the Legislature of Pennsylvania,* reprinted in *Hazard's Register,* 1832, Vol. IX, p. 361.

19. Benjamin C. Bacon, *Statistics of the Colored People of Philadelphia* (Philadelphia, 1859), second ed., pp. 13–15.

20. Needles, *op. cit.*, p. 2.

21. The data describing the ex-slaves and the freeborn, although comprehensive, are not complete; specific age, specific place of birth, and length of residence information are not included in the census. Such data will become available for a significant number of individuals only after linkage between censuses (especially between the Quaker census of 1847 and the U.S. Census of 1850) is accomplished because the latter began in 1850 to list age and place of birth data for every individual. While no explicit data exist in any of the censuses describing the length of residence, linkage will provide approximations of this information, especially where in-migrants (those not listed in 1838 but found in ensuing censuses) are concerned.

David Gerber of Princeton University pointed out to me that the absence of such data in this essay may represent serious limitations, for "there may well be intervening variables which offer a better and very different interpretation of the data than the simple fact of free-birth and ex-slave status." No doubt other variables such as age and length of residence will affect some of my conclusions; however, I am of the opinion that when such information is analyzed the essential findings will remain intact. The most significant differences between the ex-slave and the freeborn are found among a specific group of ex-slaves: those who purchased their own freedom. This information makes it clear that we are dealing not with children who left slavery before its mark was firmly implanted on them, but with adults who must have worked long and hard in order to save up the money necessary to secure their freedom. I do not believe that knowing their exact age or length of residence in the city would affect to a great degree their peculiarly high level of achievement in Philadelphia.

22. The data describing church affiliation are derived from the Abolitionist and Quaker census categories "name of religious meeting you attend" and "number attend religious meeting." These terms and the very high percentage of positive respondents make it clear that we are not dealing here with formal, dues-paying, church membership, but rather with a loose affiliation with a church.

23. Admittedly crude at this stage of research, the population density technique of analysis nevertheless yields interesting and important information; and with refinement promises to be an invaluable tool for the study of neighborhood, and its relation to social mobility, class ecology, and community structure.

24. The construction of meaningful occupational categories has thus far proven to be the most difficult part of the research. While constructing such categories for the Irish, German, and native white American workforce (currently underway) is certainly complex, one at least has the benefit of considerable occupational differentiation which provides vertical distance, a prerequisite for the study of social mobility and social stratification. Some 13 vertical categories including white collar/skilled/unskilled, nonmanual/manual, proprietary/nonproprietary, and combinations of these schemata, and 102 horizontal categories including building-construction, food, clothing, and domestic service were constructed for the study of the black occupational structure.

25. See the discussion of the "hiring-out system," pp. 38–54, in Richard C. Wade, *Slavery in the Cities* (New York, 1964). It is highly likely that many of the ex-slave household heads who bought their freedom had, in fact, experienced the hiring-out system first-hand and migrated to Philadelphia.

26. There is some reason to believe that the total number of ex-slaves (1,141 or one out of every five persons who migrated to Pennsylvania) is understated. 1838 was not too early for free blacks to fear being sent South illegally or legally as runaway slaves. It is understandable, therefore, that despite the fact that Philadelphia blacks were asked by their clergymen to cooperate with the two census-takers (a white Abolitionist, Benjamin Bacon, and the black minister of the First African Presbyterian Church, Charles Gardner), many blacks who had in fact been born slaves reported instead that they had been born free. Although it is impossible to

determine whether those who were nonnatives of Pennsylvania had been in fact slave-born or freeborn, the likelihood that ex-slaves are underestimated is further supported by the fact that 50 percent of the black population had been born outside of Pennsylvania.

Of course, the important consideration concerns the consequences of understating the actual number of ex-slaves among the black population. If the socioeconomic condition of the ex-slaves who identified themselves as freeborn was significantly worse than the actual freeborn; and if their numbers were sufficiently large enough, the conclusions offered in this essay would to a certain extent be compromised. The problem, however, can be resolved.

Consider the following: for the same reasons that one suspects that the ex-slaves are underenumerated, it is unlikely that many blacks born free or slave in the free states migrated to Philadelphia. It is also unlikely that more than a few elderly Pennsylvania-born blacks who had once been slaves were included in the 1838 census: Pennsylvania's gradual emancipation law had been passed in 1780. When we speak of the ex-slaves, whether or not correctly identified in the census, therefore, we can be fairly certain that they were not natives of Pennsylvania, but had migrated from the Upper South. When all freeborn migrants (read as including a significant number of unidentified ex-slaves) were compared to all freeborn natives their socio-economic profile was strikingly similar to that of the identified ex-slaves. In other words, the one population cohort in which unidentified ex-slaves might be found was at least as well off as the freeborn native population and in some important respects was better off.

27. To determine the effect of slavery on the slaves as compared to blacks who were born free or who won their freedom before the Civil War, we would have to look someplace after 1865. No one has yet found any data for the post-Emancipation period that distinguishes the freed men from the freeborn (or from those freed before the Civil War). We can make the assumption that because 94 percent of the blacks in the South were slaves in 1860, a significant percentage of the migrants from the South after the Civil War were ex-slaves. But even if we discount the fact that if the migrants came from Maryland, Delaware, or the District of Columbia they were more likely to have been free before the Civil War (55 percent of all blacks in these areas were free in 1860), we are still left with the problem of representativeness. To put it another way, even if we had data that distinguished the freed men from the freeborn we would still be left with only the typical migrant, not the typical ex-slave. There is every reason to believe that Carter Woodson was correct in his observation that the migrants who came to the cities of the North before the Great Migration were not typical at all, but rather, representatives of the "Talented Tenth." The migrants who came after 1910, and especially after 1915, although not "typical" of the millions of Southern blacks who did not migrate, were nevertheless far more representative of Southern blacks than those who migrated before them. They came to the North for different reasons than did those who left the South a generation earlier, say between 1875 and 1900. The "push and pull" factors (floods, drought and the boll weevil, and the demand for industrial labor heightened by the end of immigration from Europe) which led to the Great Migration simply were not operative in the earlier period. Those who came before 1900 were probably motivated for different reasons; the problems they faced in the South and the opportunities they saw in the North, if not different in kind, were certainly different in degree.

The logic of the situation suggests that we examine a Northern city during the period of the Great Migration, which had a significantly large antebellum black community and which experienced migration from the South between 1865 and 1900, hoping to identify and study three distinct groups of blacks: natives-of-the-city, migrants arriving before 1900 (the "Talented Tenth") and migrants arriving after 1900 (the "typical" migrant). The problem with this approach is twofold: first, we would no longer be dealing with the "typical" ex-slave, but with his children; second, the data necessary to distinguish the three groups among the population are not available.

28. Herbert Gutman, "The Invisible Fact: Negro Family Structure Before and After the Civil War," paper read at the *Association for the Study of Negro Life and History* (Birmingham: October 1969) and in a revised form at the *Organization of American Historians* (Los Angeles: April 1970). Also see Gutman, *The Black Family in Slavery and Freedom, 1750–1925* (New York, 1976).

29. Richard Wade, *op cit.*, "The Transformation of Slavery in the Cities," pp. 243–82.

30. A major interest of my research is to develop and make explicit for the city the characteristics of an "urban component" which distinguishes the urban from the rural experience. There is certainly general agreement that urban conditions differ from rural ones in significant dimensions: family structure, sex ratios, mortality, fertility, housing conditions, diet, educational and occupational opportunities plus the intangibles of values and expectations. In future work, however, I hope to demonstrate that it is seriously misleading to treat these urban/rural differences monolithically. The racial discrimination and structural inequality of the city affected each ethnic group differently. The advantages of the city were never equally available for all.

12. Mulattoes and Blacks:
Intra-group Color Differences and Social Stratification
in Nineteenth-Century Philadelphia

THEODORE HERSHBERG   HENRY WILLIAMS

Introduction

The writing of Afro-American history in the 1950s and early 1960s reflected the turmoil of the times. Blacks and their white allies were fighting
to make good on the broken promises of American life. These decades were
filled with human drama associated with painful social change. The boy-
cotts, sit-ins, freedom rides, school desegregation, mass protests, and voter
registration drives of the Civil Rights crusades were followed by the stri-
dent militancy of the Black Power movement, ghetto riots, and separatism.
The flood of studies that appeared focused unmistakably on "blacks and
whites," especially on the historic injustices blacks suffered in America at
the hands of whites and on black contributions to society despite these
obstacles. The titles of the most influential studies—Charles Silberman's
Crisis in Black and White and Winthrop Jordan's *White Over Black*—
capture this concern with the two races as did the pessimistic conclusion
of the Kerner Commission that America was rapidly becoming "two societies, one black, one white, separate and unequal."[1]

The black history literature of the late 1960s and 1970s, in contrast,
began to look inward at the ways blacks had acted and reacted to the external forces of the larger white society. Enough had been written to document the discriminatory uniqueness of the black experience, and writers

We wish to thank August Meier, Bruce Laurie, and Robert Ulle for their helpful
criticisms of an earlier draft of this paper presented at the Organization of American
Historians (Denver: April 1974). Numerous statistical tables which appeared in
earlier versions were deleted from this draft due to considerations of space. These
tables are available upon request from the authors.

turned their attention to the organization of the black community. The recent literature has begun to dispel the myth that the black experience was monolithic and to make clear the complexities of the variant forms of black internal differentiation and social structure. A spate of urban biographies appeared that examined the formation of black ghettoes in northern cities. These studies built upon the community histories of earlier decades. Scholars had identified a broad range of dimensions through which black society was differentiated, but few dealt with what is our central concern in this essay: color.[2]

Historical studies of Negroes in the United States contain few sustained discussions of the influence of color in differentiating their communities and even these offer little in the way of systematic data with which to evaluate its impact. Moreover, most of the literature mentioning color treats Southern Negroes; scholars have generally neglected its potential significance for Northern cities.[3]

The picture emerging from these scarce and rather superficial examinations reveals that color played quite different roles in different geographic regions at different times, but that, overall, its importance has been in decline since the late nineteenth century. August Meier contends that class and color were closely associated in a number of Southern and border cities in the antebellum and immediate post–Civil War periods, but that this intimate relationship had clearly waned by the early years of the present century. He briefly mentions color in the North in a passing reference to Boston's Negro upper class.[4] E. Franklin Frazier's *Black Bourgeoisie,* while asserting that the significance of color remained longer in the South and placing more emphasis on color stratification in the North, also notes the declining importance of color in determining social position in the Negro community.[5]

Studies of Northern Negro communities also generally indicate that color-based social systems in the nineteenth century largely disappeared in the twentieth.[6] St. Clair Drake and Horace R. Cayton, in their classic study of Chicago's Negro population, offer the most comprehensive consideration of the impact of color in differentiating a Northern Negro community. They contend that even as late as the 1940s Chicago Negroes were quite sensitive to skin color in fashioning their social relationships, and they present evidence indicating a strong association between light-skin color and upper-class status. Nevertheless, they conclude that by the 1920s "the importance of skin-color as the measure of the man within Bronzeville" had noticeably declined since the late nineteenth century.[7]

Color played a much more critical role among Southern Negroes. Before the Civil War, light skin was closely correlated with free status throughout the entire South. Comprising only 12 percent of the South's Negroes, by 1860 mulattoes accounted for 40 percent of the free Negro population, but only 10 percent of the slave population. Within the region, skin color was more consequential in the Lower than the Upper South. Ira Berlin, in the most detailed study of free Negroes in the antebellum South, demonstrates that after the American Revolution the free Negro population of the Upper South grew darker while in the Lower South it remained light. On the eve of the Civil War, about one-third of the free Negroes in the Upper South and over three-quarters of those in the Lower South were mulattoes. Within the free Negro population, color produced a series of social and economic distinctions. These color-based differences were particularly severe in late eighteenth- and early nineteenth-century Charleston where elite mulattoes established associations which excluded the darker skinned. Yet, "most" mulattoes, even in the Deep South, as Laurence Glasco cautions us, "were [not] free," and "the color line between brown and black," as Berlin reminds us, "never rigidly followed class divisions. There were many poor mulattoes and a few wealthy blacks."[8]

After the Civil War, color stratification in the South assumed a more rigid structure. Berlin argues that the latent antebellum hostility between light-skinned free Negroes and the generally darker-skinned slaves erupted into open conflict as members of the old Negro elites struggled to maintain their social status in a society jarred by the results of Emancipation.[9] In Washington, D.C., and in Savannah, color lines quickly became inflexible.[10] In post-bellum South Carolina and in Reconstruction New Orleans, color also served as an important stratifier, but apparently did not produce the open intra-group rivalries found elsewhere.[11]

Studies of twentieth-century Southern Negro communities suggest that color distinctions were more ingrained and lasted longer than those in the North, but even here, they were becoming less consequential. In Washington, D.C., color lines remained largely intact until after World War II.[12] In one Mississippi town, even as late as the 1930s, "whiteness and its associated physical traits [were] still the most important of upper-class criteria for high status."[13] Yet even in the Lower South, color stratification was clearly on the wane by the Depression decade. Speaking of another Mississippi community, Hortense Powdermaker observed that while "there is at present a larger proportion of mulattoes in the upper class than in lower ones . . . color is by no means a reliable index of class, nor does it in itself determine class."[14] In Atlanta, the correlation between light-skin and high status declined between 1890 and 1958.[15]

Two unmistakable conclusions emerge from a survey of the literature on the subject of color. The first is that despite regional differences a consensus exists that color stratification has been on the decline in the United States since the late nineteenth century. The second, all too evident, is that recent scholarship has avoided, sometimes painfully, careful examination of color as an important stratifier. Indeed, many of the studies mentioned above fail to present sufficient evidence to document their assertions about color, and many allude to color only in passing. Other studies, especially those on Northern Negro communities, do not do so at all.[16] Why the importance of color declined will be considered in our concluding remarks. For the moment it is more germane to examine the question that springs to the fore when these two conclusions are juxtaposed: if the importance of color has declined over the last century, what was its significance earlier? What role did color play in urban Negro society of the nineteenth century?

It is our contention that the role of intra-group color differences will provide significant insights into how Afro-Americans structured their community, who their leaders were, what informed the values of this leadership class, and why certain courses of action were followed and others rejected. Where scholars have shown sensitivity to intra-community division, they have largely focused on the traditional categories of class and occupation group. There are other categories which differentiated the historical experience of Afro-Americans: servants who "lived in" white households; Negroes who lived in white neighborhoods; families who subtenanted; those who were free before the Civil War; migrants; and mulattoes. In focusing on color as a potential stratifier of Philadelphia's nineteenth-century community, we will determine the extent to which the historical experience of mulattoes differed from that of blacks and indicate particular social and economic consequences of those differences. In so doing, our capacity to understand a remarkably complex, peculiarly fascinating, and important history will be measurably strengthened.

Before turning to the empirical research, let us establish our conceptual approach and hypotheses. We offer an operational distinction between the meaning of the terms "differentiation" and "social stratification." They are not necessarily interchangeable. Dimensions of differentiation do not have to function as stratifiers in a social system. The former term connotes differences without significant social consequences, while the latter assigns these differences hierarchical values. Color may have been a source of "horizontal" differentiation within Negro society; mulattoes may have been viewed and acted simply as another subgroup within the larger Negro population. We argue a different position. In mid-to-late nineteenth-century Philadelphia, color was more than a source of differentiation; it functioned as an important stratifier of social experience. To sustain this argument, Negroes with lighter skin color must be found disproportionately among the wealthy and powerful in their community and differences between mulattoes and blacks should manifest themselves in the system of stratification that characterized their society. It is to these concerns that our paper is addressed.

Data Reliability

Let us carefully consider the reliability of the color designations "black" and "mulatto" reported by the census marshals. In 1850 the instructions to the census marshals, under the heading entitled "Color," were

> in all cases where the person is white, leave the space blank; in all cases where the person is black, insert the letter B; if mulatto, insert M. It is very desirable that these particulars be carefully regarded.

In 1870 and 1880 the instructions to the census marshals were revised:

> It must not be assumed that, where nothing is written in this column, "White" is to be understood. The column is always to be filled. Be particularly careful in reporting the class *Mulatto*. The word is here generic, and includes quadroons, octoroons, and all persons having any *perceptible* trace of African blood. Important scientific results depend upon the correct determination of this class in schedules 1 and 2.[17] (emphasis added)

Although the instructions are vague, they indicate that skin shading, not ancestry, was the census marshal's sole determinant of color. It is not known how the enumerators arrived at their conclusions; we suspect that most did not ask the respondents their color, but made their own evaluation. Moreover, it is likely in most instances that census marshals saw only one member of a household during their interviews and based their color designations for the entire household on the complexion of the individual respondent and his or her color description of other household members. The difficulties inherent in color perception thus force us to consider a set of questions concerning the validity and consistency of the reported data: did the color reported for the same individual change over time? If so, how frequently did color change occur? What was the proportion of the color change in the two possible directions, black to mulatto, and mulatto to black? Is there any correlation between the direction of the color change and socioeconomic mobility? And finally, is the assignment of color random?

To answer these questions we examined three groups of Negroes traced through successive manuscript population schedules of the U.S. Census from 1850 to 1880. The tracing process, known as "record linkage," is described elsewhere and need not be detailed here.[18] Those individuals whom we could link form the basis for the color validity analysis; only for those persons do we have color reported at two points in time. Of course, color was not used to make identifications between individuals over time so the content of change in the color designation can be studied without fear of built-in bias favoring stability.

The statistics on color change offer reason to pause. In each of the three decades between 1850 and 1880, approximately one-third of those Negroes linked from census to census were assigned a different color designation by the census marshals in the later survey. Among those who changed color, a distinct difference is found in the direction of the color change: while only 26 percent of those reported as black in 1850 were designated as mulatto in 1860, 47 percent of mulattoes in 1850 were designated as black a decade later. A far greater proportion of mulattoes than blacks, in other words, changed their color between 1850 and 1860. Proportions changed slightly for the next two decades, but the data reveal an essential imbalance in the direction of color change. A mulatto color designation was highly sensitive to a census marshal's color perceptions.

The direction of the color change, moreover, appears to be correlated with occupational change. In the black to mulatto change, only 13 percent of the men were downwardly mobile, while in the mulatto to black change, 38 percent—or three times the proportion—were downwardly mobile. It is an open question whether the visible accumulation of property by some Negroes "lightened" them in the eyes of the census marshals. The association between color change and occupational change can be interpreted in this fashion. The problem of the census marshals can be appreciated if we imagine a color spectrum along which the entire Negro population could be arrayed from darkest to lightest. The marshals appeared to characterize accurately three-fourths of the black population at one end and half of the mulattoes at the other. They apparently had their greatest difficulties making consistent color determinations for those on the color spectrum where skin color distinctions began to blur.

One way of measuring the randomness of color distribution is to apply tests of statistical significance to the "within-census year" comparisons of blacks and mulattoes across a spectrum of socioeconomic and demographic variables; these analyses comprise the core of this essay. Can the distributions which emerge in these cross-tabulations occur by chance? The chi square tests indicate that the chances of the distributions occurring randomly are well beyond the realm of one in one thousand. When one considers, moreover, that the data presented below were collected by scores of different census marshals at four different points in time over a thirty-year period, the consistency of the differences between blacks and mulattoes across so many variables of comparison is all the more remarkable.

Moreover, the overall proportion of mulattoes in Philadelphia's Negro population conforms nicely to the percentages found in Pennsylvania and elsewhere throughout the country. In 1860, for example, mulattoes comprised about one-third of the population in Pennsylvania and in the Northern and Western states, and between one-fifth and one-half of the total Negro population in Richmond, Charleston, Savannah, Mobile, and New Orleans. In Philadelphia, mulattoes constituted about one-third of the city's Negro population. The similarity of these proportions indicates that color designations may have been based on genuinely uniform national perception.[19]

Our findings are presented with the caveats clearly marked and allow readers to form their own judgments concerning the validity of the data on color. At the least, this study is one of the few to investigate empirically the effect of color on social stratification in the nineteenth-century urban Negro community, and its conclusions, as will become clear, fit into the broad range of scholarship sketched above.

Empirical Findings

The following analysis is based on a 100 percent sample of the Negro population enumerated in the federal population manuscript schedules and includes some 95,000 persons listed for 1850, 1860, 1870, and 1880 (see Appendix II).

Population Movement. Nineteenth-century Philadelphia Negroes were a geographically volatile population. For each decade between 1850 and 1880, no more than 30 percent of the Negroes residing in the city at the beginning of the decade were there at its close. Although direct comparison with other studies is tenuous because considerably different record linkage techniques were used and different subgroups were studied, these rates of persistence are less than those reported by other researchers studying white populations.[20] Significantly, too, while there may have been no *net* change in the population of Philadelphia Negroes during certain decades (that is, comparing total population figures at two points in time), there was always considerable *gross* change. Few Negroes living in Philadelphia at any census year had lived in the city for more than ten years.

As Table 1 shows, there were two decades in which occurred remark-

Table 1. Total Negro Population by Color, 1850–1880

	# Black	% Black	% Incr.	# Mulatto	% Mulatto	% Incr.	Total Pop.	% Incr.
1850	15828	81.5		3594	18.5		19422	
1860	15163	68.6	−4.2	6935	31.4	+93.0	22098	+13.8
1870	15204	74.0	−0.3	5346	26.0	−22.9	20550	−7.0
1880	25535	82.5	+67.9	5432	17.5	+1.6	30967	+50.7

In 1870 two enumerations were made in Philadelphia. Although the second lists more individuals than the first, it provides only name, age, sex and race. Therefore, we have used the first enumeration figures in our work. However, if the second enumeration totals were used in the above table, the following would be the result for 1870 and 1880.

	# Black	% Black	% Incr.	# Mulatto	% Mulatto	% Incr.	Total Pop.	% Incr.
1870	16386	74.0	+8.1	5761	26.0	−16.9	22147	+0.2
1880	25535	82.5	+55.8	5432	17.5	−5.7	30967	+39.8

ably large color-differentiated shifts in population. During the pre–Civil War decade the mulatto population almost doubled while the net black population declined slightly. In the decade from 1870 to 1880, the reverse took place: the black population increased by more than 50 percent while the net mulatto population decreased slightly. These changes in the proportions and absolute numbers of blacks and mulattoes migrating in different decades are of such orders of magnitude that they simply cannot be explained by changing perceptions of color among the census marshals.

The task of speculating about the causes of such migrations is formidable, largely because we are trying to explain changes in net population knowing full well that enormous changes in the population are taking place that are not recorded in decennial population statistics. In other words, despite the fact that the net black population changed hardly at all between 1850 and 1860, the vast majority of blacks living in Philadelphia in 1860 had migrated there in the previous ten years. While recognizing the huge increase in mulattoes in that decade (or the reverse during 1870–1880), it must be understood not only that mulattoes migrated to Philadelphia, but rather that proportionately more mulattoes than blacks migrated in numbers large enough to affect the net population figures.

In explaining the massive mulatto migration to Philadelphia between 1850 and 1860, it might be argued that since at the time in nearby slave states a high proportion of mulattoes were free and almost all blacks were slaves, mulattoes were simply more able than blacks to migrate. While this is true in logic, the argument rests on proportions and migration rests on absolute numbers. The number of free blacks in Maryland, Delaware, Washington, D.C., and Virginia, the states from which most migrants to Philadelphia came (see Table 2), in fact, constituted a pool more than

Table 2.   Place of Birth by Color, 1850–1880

(Col. %s) Place of Birth	1850 Black	1850 Mulatto	1860 Black	1860 Mulatto	1870 Black	1870 Mulatto	1880 Black	1880 Mulatto
Pennsylvania	53.3	60.5	60.2	64.1	50.8	60.6	48.0	57.1
New Jersey	5.4	5.0	5.4	4.1	5.1	4.4	4.9	4.3
New York	0.7	1.3	0.6	1.0	0.8	1.3	0.9	1.4
New England	0.4	0.6	0.3	0.6	0.4	0.6	0.6	0.9
Delaware	18.5	11.3	15.3	9.7	14.7	7.2	12.2	7.7
Maryland	12.0	8.6	9.6	7.9	13.5	7.9	16.5	9.1
Virginia	6.3	7.5	6.0	7.4	10.1	10.2	11.8	11.7
Washington, D.C.	0.5	1.0	0.5	1.0	0.7	1.0	0.9	1.2
North Carolina	0.4	0.7	0.5	0.4	0.9	1.0	1.1	1.3
South Carolina	0.6	1.8	0.5	1.8	1.0	3.0	0.9	1.6
All Others	1.7	1.7	0.7	2.0	1.8	2.8	2.2	3.6
Total	15828 (81.5)	3594 (18.5)	15163 (68.6)	6935 (31.4)	15204 (74.0)	5346 (26.0)	25535 (82.5)	5432 (17.5)

twice the size of the one from which mulattoes were drawn (see Table 3). Considering the low rate of persistence among Negroes, moreover, black migrants to Philadelphia outnumbered mulatto migrants several times over, but again, their numbers were insufficient to affect the net black population totals. It appears that among both free blacks and mulattoes in nearby slave states there were those who perceived that the decade of the 1850s was an increasingly grim one with the passage of the Fugitive Slave Laws, the Dred Scott decision, and the like, and they concluded that getting out of the Slave South would well serve their interests. If in these states, as the literature suggests, free mulattoes were disproportionately better off than free blacks, and hence in a better position to migrate, then there is a reasonable explanation for the color-differentiated migration. In considering the massive black migration to Philadelphia in the 1870s, we should bear in mind that all Negroes were free and that the numerical superiority of blacks simply asserted itself.[21]

Residential Patterns. Although both blacks and mulattoes resided largely apart from the white population of nineteenth-century Philadelphia, the two groups manifested somewhat distinct residential patterns. The areal unit used in our research is a "grid unit," a spatial rectangle 660′ by 775′.[22] In 1880, 2,000 of Philadelphia's 7,000 inhabitable grids were lived in. Of these, Philadelphia Negroes lived in 575. The Index of Segregation of Negroes to whites in 1880 Philadelphia was 70; that is, 70 percent of the Negroes would have to be moved to another grid unit in order to approximate the residential pattern of the native-white population.[23] Using an identical index to describe the different residential patterns found among blacks and mulattoes, we find that 47 percent of the mulattoes in 1880 would have to be moved to other grids in order to approximate the same residential distribution for blacks. Another context for viewing the differing black/mulatto spatial pattern would be to note that blacks and mulattoes were separated from each other to virtually the same extent as the Irish were separated from the Germans in 1880 Philadelphia.

The over-time spatial patterns are similar to other patterns we observe in the data. Mulattoes were separated from blacks in 1850 to almost the same degree as in 1880 (47); the Index fell to 29 in 1860 as the number and proportion of mulattoes in the Negro population increased sharply over the decade; rose to 38 by 1870; and in response to the huge black migration following 1870, increased sharply to 47 by 1880.

There is another way of observing the differential spatial patterns of blacks and mulattoes. If blacks and mulattoes were distributed evenly throughout the city, then one would expect to find at each census year mulattoes and blacks living in each of the Negro-inhabited grids in the same proportion as they were found in the Negro population. In fact, in all four census years, between 40 and 54 percent of the grids in which Negroes lived did not contain any mulattoes, and in these grids lived between 15 and 20 percent of the black population.

Table 3.   Color and Civil Status in States Contributing Heavily to Philadelphia's Negro Population, 1850–1860

A. State	# Free Negroes	% Black	% Mulatto
1850:			
Delaware	18,073	90.9	9.1
Maryland	74,723	81.8	19.2
Washington, D.C.	10,059	67.4	22.6
Virginia	54,333	34.7	65.3
Total	157,188	65.6	34.4
1860:			
Delaware	19,829	85.4	14.6
Maryland	83,942	80.4	19.1
Washington, D.C.	11,131	59.6	40.4
Virginia	58,042	59.5	40.5
Total	172,944	72.9	27.1

	1850				1860			
B. State	# Black	% Free	# Mulatto	% Free	# Black	% Free	# Mulatto	% Free
Delaware	18632	88.2	1731	95.2	18648	90.8	2979	97.2
Maryland	143588	42.6	21503	63.3	146218	46.4	24913	64.4
Washington, D.C.	9668	70.2	4078	80.3	8883	74.6	5433	82.8
Virginia	447086	4.2	79775	44.5	455443	7.5	93464	25.1
Total	618974	16.7	107987	50.0	629192	20.3	126789	37.0

Source: Department of Commerce, Bureau of the Census, *Negro Population: 1790–1915* (Washington, D.C.: United States Government Printing Office, 1918), 220–21.

To test our notion that mulattoes would be more likely to reside in the "better" parts of town and less likely to live in less desirable areas, we probed beneath the grid unit level to examine the color composition of selected residential blocks. Although the results are preliminary—we have not yet used this procedure to examine all blocks—the information is suggestive and confirms our expectations. Two types of blocks were sampled: those on which prominent Negroes lived and those which were characterized in the literature as among the worst socioeconomically. In 1860, mulattoes were 31 percent of the Negro population, but on these "better" blocks, mulattoes constituted 48, 70, 49, 83, and 53 percent of all Negroes. The five blocks with "bad" reputations—that is, where the newspapers reported much crime and slum conditions—on the other hand, were inhabited by low proportions of mulattoes: 16, 22, 24, 19, and 9 percent. As will become clear later, these residential differences are indicative of the general socioeconomic distinctions between the two groups.

Household and Family. The striking finding which emerges from an analysis of the age and sex ratios, household and family structures, and marital statuses is that most of the differences between blacks and mulattoes were minimal. On the other hand, there were suggestive differences between them in fertility and boarding, and important differences in intermarriage patterns.

Table 4 summarizes the age-sex composition for each census year. Three indices of dissimilarity were computed: the index of dissimilarity between the age-sex composition of the color groups, and the indices of dissimilarity for each group between the age-sex composition in the given year and that of the census year preceding it. One can see, therefore, not only the extent of the differences between the two groups in one year, but also the extent of the change in the age-sex composition of each group over time. The index of dissimilarity as applied to age-sex distributions is directly analogous to the index of dissimilarity used to determine segregation in spatial studies. In this case, it indicates the proportion of one group which would have to be in a different age-sex category in order to match the age-sex composition of the other group.

The sex ratios and indices of dissimilarity show quite clearly that there were *no* substantial differences either between blacks and mulattoes or over time within groups. Throughout the period, both groups had sharply unbalanced sex ratios favoring women, and in general, the picture presented in the age and sex compositions is one of a population moderately high in fertility and extremely high in mortality with substantial age-differentiated migration. Accordingly, those differences that do occur between

13 2321 2311 2311 2313 2313 2313 2313 2313 2313 2313 2313 2313 2313 2313 2313 2313 2313 2313 2313 2313 2313 2313 2313 2313

Table 4. Sex Ratios and Indices of Dissimilarity Between the Age-Sex Categories of the Color Groups, 1850–1880

	1850	1860	1870	1880
Blacks				
Total Males	6707	6312	6339	11279
Total Females	9112	8716	8754	14182
Mulattoes				
Total Males	1469	2731	2083	2313
Total Females	2122	4131	3204	3107
Sex Ratio (p/100 females)				
Black	73.6	72.4	72.4	79.5
Mulatto	69.2	66.1	65.0	74.4
Index of Dissimilarity * (Between age-sex categories for color groups)				
Blacks vs. Mulattoes	6.6	6.4	6.6	7.8
Black change (from previous decade)	—	3.3	7.1	5.7
Mulatto change (from previous decade)	—	3.9	6.9	5.5

*These data summarize age-specific sex ratios for blacks and mulattoes for each census year.

the distributions are due primarily to migration. Finally, although the difference is not large, mulattoes tend to have a higher proportion of children in their population, while blacks tend toward a higher proportion of aged.

The two color groups also exhibited similar patterns of household structure and composition.[24] Roughly three of every four families among both blacks and mulattoes were nuclear. The differences in expanded and extended household configurations in the remaining families were small (see Table 5). Families in both groups were typically characterized by the presence of both parents, but one family in four was headed by a female. In 1850, black families were more likely than mulatto families by a third to be headed by a female, but by 1880 the proportion of female-led families (that is, families with husbands absent) was virtually the same: one in four (see Table 6). Imbalanced sex ratios favoring women had a good deal to do with this high proportion of female-headed families (as compared, for example, to Philadelphia's Irish, German, and native-white families), for among both groups throughout the period there were fewer than 70 men per 100 women in the important 15–44 age cohort (see Table 10); but the full explanation for this high incidence of female-headed families includes differentially high male death rates and severely limited occupational opportunities for Negro men.[25]

Recorded census data on marital statuses are available only for 1880, and they show identical patterns among black and mulatto men: 55 per-

Table 5. Household Structure, 1880

(Col. %s)	With Children		Without Children		All	
Household Type	Black	Mulatto	Black	Mulatto	Black	Mulatto
Nuclear	76.0	71.4	80.7	76.8	77.5	72.8
Extended −1	11.9	14.4	—	—	8.0	10.3
Extended −2	5.2	3.7	3.4	3.1	4.6	3.5
Expanded	7.0	10.5	15.9	20.0	9.9	13.4
Total	(2459)	(486)	(1206)	(194)	(3665)	(680)

Note: For category definitions, see Frank Furstenberg, Jr., Theodore Hershberg, and John Modell, "The Origins of the Female-Headed Black Family: The Impact of the Urban Environment," *Journal of Interdisciplinary History*, 6 (September, 1975), 211–33; also in this volume.

cent were married, 40 percent were single, and 5 percent were widowers. Mulatto women were married slightly more often and widowed slightly less often than black women, but the percentage difference was quite small. And as we expected to find given the imbalanced sex ratios (see Table 10), one-third more proportionately of the men than the women were married.

One of the most interesting and significant aspects of the family analysis is the consideration of color in married couples. Most marriage was endogamous: that is, it occurred between spouses of the *same* color. Ninety-three percent of black men married black women, and 85 percent of mulatto men married mulatto women. Black women, by far, had the lowest rate of marriage outside the color group: only 2.8 percent of black women were married to mulatto men. Mulatto women, on the other hand, had the highest rate of exogamy: 31 percent married black men (see Table 7).

A striking economic pattern is observable among those who intermar-

Table 6. Family Structure by Headship and Color, 1850 and 1880
(Families with Children Only) (Col. %s)

Type	Black	Mulatto
A. 1850:		
Spouse Absent		
Female Head	24.4	18.4
Male Head	2.7	3.0
Two Parents	72.9	78.6
	(1120)	(201)
B. 1880:		
Spouse Absent		
Female Head	24.0	23.7
Male Head	2.8	1.7
Two Parents	73.2	74.6
	(1513)	(291)

Table 7. Marriage and Intermarriage, 1880

| Males | Marriage Patterns—1880 | | |
	% With Black Wives	% With Mulatto Wives	Number of Couples
Black	93.0	7.0	3064
Mulatto	15.1	84.9	551

Females	% With Black Husbands	% With Mulatto Husbands	Number of Couples
Black	97.2	2.8	3031
Mulatto	31.1	68.9	707

ried. When black men in 1880 were ranked by their occupational status, the proportion who married mulatto women rose linearly from a low of 5 percent among laborers, through 9 percent among the skilled to 11 percent among black professionals and businessmen. In other words, more than twice the proportion of black men at the top of the occupational ladder married mulatto women than at the bottom. The pattern can also be seen in marriages between mulatto men and black women: twice as many mulatto laborers married black women than did mulatto craftsmen or businessmen (one of four as opposed to one of eight—see Table 8).

Table 9 shows the economic relationship in 1850 in a different way. The four kinds of marriages are ranked by the proportion among them

Table 8. Intermarriage Patterns: 1880
(Husbands Ranked by Vertical Occupational Status)

Black Males: Occupational Status	% with Black Wives	% with Mulatto Wives	Total #
Professional, White-collar and Proprietary	88.8	11.2	134
Skilled Craftsmen	91.4	8.6	545
Specified Unskilled	92.5	7.5	1361
Laborers	95.0	5.0	1024
Total	93.0	7.0	3064

Mulatto Males: Occupational Status	% with Black Wives	% with Mulatto Wives	Total #
Professional, White-collar and Proprietary	13.6	86.4	44
Skilled Craftsmen	13.2	86.8	167
Specified Unskilled	13.2	86.8	258
Laborers	25.6	74.4	82
Total	15.1	84.9	551

Table 9.   Intermarriage Patterns, 1850
Real Property Ownership by Color*

	% with Real Property
Black males with Black wives	7.5 (1192)
Black males with Mulatto wives	11.0 (91)
Mulatto males with Mulatto wives	12.4 (233)
Mulatto males with Black wives	3.4 (29)

*Total N's in parentheses.

owning real property. If the marriage of a black woman to a mulatto man is in fact indicative of a man's "marrying down," as Emma Lou in Wallace Thurmond's novel[26] was told all through her life, then the lowest proportion of property ownership should be found in such unions. And it is: only 3.4 percent of the marriages between mulatto men and black women reported real property ownership, while black men with black wives reported twice that proportion; black men with mulatto wives three times the proportion; and mulatto men with mulatto wives approached four times the proportion.

Interesting differences between blacks and mulattoes also emerge in examining the patterns in fertility and boarding, differences which also may be significantly attributed to socioeconomic factors. Mulatto families were larger, and the difference in size is accounted for by the presence of more children. The ratio of children aged zero through four born to women aged 15 through 44 consistently favored mulatto women. Throughout the period there were four to ten more children per hundred women among mulattoes than among blacks (see Table 10). Fertility is a complex phenomenon. It

Table 10.   Sex Ratios and Fertility, 1850–1880

A. Sex Ratios (Males per 100 Females)				
	1850	1860	1870	1880
Blacks				
All	74	72	72	80
15–44	69	69	69	78
Mulattoes				
All	69	67	69	74
15–44	63	63	67	68
B. Fertility (Children Aged 0–4 per 100 Females Aged 15–44)				
	1850	1860	1870	1880
Blacks	33	28	22	28
Mulattoes	37	37	32	36

is affected by mortality, fecundity, remarriage rates, and sexual appeal. The socioeconomic data favoring mulattoes support the speculation that black men died at earlier ages than did mulatto men and that infant mortality was higher among blacks; that health conditions associated with the general standard of living were less favorable for blacks; and that blacks and mulattoes had different marriage pools.[27]

Boarding is another phenomenon suggestive of socioeconomic factors. In the 1880 data, the proportion of boarders among black males and females was one-third higher than among mulattoes. One in five black men, one in seven mulatto men, one in seven black women, and one in ten mulatto women were listed as boarders in the pages of the census manuscripts. Men of both groups boarded more frequently than did women, while women of both groups far more often responded to their room and board needs by working as "live-in" servants in white households. The larger proportion of boarders among blacks is partially explained in terms of the housing needs of large numbers of disproportionately impoverished blacks who migrated to the city in the 1870s. Their needs coincided with those of poor Negro families who may have accepted boarders as a source of supplementary income.[28]

Thus, although the age distributions, sex ratios, and household structures of black and mulatto populations were similar, their respective intermarriage, fertility, and boarding patterns were not. The data suggest that socioeconomic differences between the two groups were responsible for these distinctions. The following sections on education, occupation, wealth, and organizational membership will address these issues more directly; this evidence will make clear that more than simple skin color differentiated mulattoes from blacks. From these differences was forged an important basis for social stratification of Negro society in nineteenth-century Philadelphia.

Education and Literacy. Throughout the period a higher proportion of mulatto than black children (ages 5–14) attended school. Roughly ten percentage points separated the groups at all points in time. In 1850 males of both groups attended school more often than did females, but by 1880 the margin of five percentage points which separated the sexes had all but disappeared. The over-time trend was toward greater enrollment (although there was a temporary downturn during the Civil War decade). In 1850 between four and five of every ten black children and between five and six of every ten mulatto children attended school. By 1880, 25 percent more children in each group were enrolled: roughly 60 percent of the black and 70 percent of the mulatto children attended school at the period's close.

Virtually all school-aged children of both groups were reported as able to read and write throughout the period. Differences among blacks and mulattoes, and in over-time trends, on the other hand, were noticeable among adults. The literacy pattern, in part, closely resembled that of school attendance: that is, higher proportions of mulattoes than blacks for all years could read and write (separated by a range of 5 to 12 percentage points). But little improvement was noticeable over time: roughly 80 percent of the blacks and 90 percent of the mulattoes could read and write in both 1850 and in 1880, while in the decades between, the proportions of both groups and both sexes who were literate were somewhat lower.

Birthplace had a clear effect on the proportions of adults who could read and write. In almost every instance between 1850 and 1880, Southern-born Negroes were less likely than Northern-born Negroes to read and write. Close to nine out of ten Pennsylvania-born Negroes were literate, as opposed to only between seven and eight out of ten born in the South. Access to education was clearly greater in the North than in the South.

Place-of-birth, then, might be the intervening variable responsible for the differential proportions of literacy among blacks and mulattoes. However, when place-of-birth is controlled—that is, when the proportions of blacks and mulattoes who could read and write are examined by state—the identical differences between the groups persist. Once again, the proportions of blacks and mulattoes of both sexes who were literate differed by a margin of six to twelve percentage points and followed the same over-time trend reported above for literacy as a whole (slightly higher in 1850 and 1880 than in the intervening decades).

A further attempt was made to determine whether another variable might be intervening. Controlling for occupational level might eliminate the variation in literacy found between blacks and mulattoes. When skilled craftsmen and laborers were examined for literacy on a state-by-state basis, the range separating the two groups narrowed somewhat, but, in most instances, greater proportions of mulattoes than blacks were able to read and write. While the differentials are not always large and do not appear in every state for each census year, a general pattern of mulatto educational superiority does emerge from the data. In most states at most times, mulattoes apparently enjoyed a greater access than did blacks to education.

Occupational Structure. Before discussing the significant differences in the occupational structure of blacks and mulattoes, it is important to establish the larger context in which these differences were set. When the occupational structure of all Philadelphia's Negroes is compared to that of the white ethnic groups—Irish, Germans, and native whites—two salient features emerge. First, Negroes exhibited less occupational differentiation; that is, the number of occupations at which Negroes labored were few in number. The number and kinds of jobs at which whites of all ethnic groups earned their livelihood were greater and more varied than those of Negroes, and the margin of difference increased sharply between 1850 and 1880. The second major difference concerns the distribution of jobs along a vertical ranking scheme. The vast majority of Negro men and women—three of four throughout the period—labored in unskilled capacities at the bottom of the occupational ladder. Negroes were virtually ignored by industrialization, which over the thirty years altered the occupational structures of the white ethnic groups in significant ways.[29]

Within the Negro community, however, there were differences along the dimension of color. Mulattoes were more occupationally differentiated than were the blacks, and the differentiation increased from 1850 to 1880. While the growing occupational differentiation among mulatto men did not keep pace with that of white workers, it outdistanced black workers. In 1840, 9 and 13 jobs were required by black and mulatto males, respectively, to account for 80 percent of their workforces. By 1880, the corresponding figures were 25 and 42. The number of jobs available to black and mulatto women was so limited throughout the period that women of neither group (in the first 80 percent of their workforce) labored at more than 8 occupations (see Table 11).

The second feature of the occupational structure—the distribution of jobs in a vertical ranking scheme—shows mulattoes ranked disproportionately at the higher positions (see Table 12). Although neither mulattoes nor blacks were heavily represented in white-collar positions, mulatto men, throughout the thirty-year period, were usually twice as likely as black men to earn their living as professionals, proprietors, and skilled artisans. This differential was especially pronounced in the artisan category. The proportions of both groups in the category "specified unskilled" were equal, but black men were twice as likely as mulatto men to be common laborers (the census did not specify the nature of the unskilled work they performed). A similar pattern describes the vertical job distributions of black and mulatto women (see Table 12). One-third fewer women than men worked in professional and proprietary capacities, but mulatto women were twice as likely as black women to be found in such work. The differences between black and mulatto women in skilled work were also clear; but the margin of difference varied from three times as many in 1850 to only half as many in 1880. The bulk of black and mulatto women were found in the specified unskilled category, largely in different kinds of domestic work; and as expected, given the distributions noted above, black

Table 11. Occupations in Top 80% of Work Force, by Color and Sex, 1850–1880

MALE OCCUPATIONS				FEMALE OCCUPATIONS*			
Blacks	%	Mulattoes	%	Blacks	%	Mulattoes	%
A. 1850:							
Laborer	28.7	None	22.0				
None	20.6	Laborer	16.3				
Waiter	11.7	Waiter	14.1				
Porter	7.9	Barber	7.5				
Barber	3.5	Porter	3.9				
Seaman	2.8	Coachman	3.5				
Coachman	2.3	Shoemaker	2.5				
Carter	2.0	Seaman	2.1				
Brickmaker	1.8	Carpenter	2.0				
		Hairdresser	1.8				
		Housekeeper	1.6				
		Carter	1.4				
		Servant	1.2				
	81.5		80.2				
	(3629)		(753)				
# of occ in top 80%	9		13				
B. 1860:							
Laborer	19.8	Waiter	20.2	None	40.7	None	43.1
Waiter	15.2	None	10.4	Washer-woman	17.2	Washer-woman	12.5
None	13.2	Laborer	9.4	Domestic	12.0	Domestic	8.3
Porter	8.8	Barber	8.7	Servant	10.2	Servant	7.5
Mariner	5.7	Mariner	7.8			Seamstress	6.6
Barber	3.6	Porter	6.0			Cook	5.6
Servant	2.7	Seaman	2.7				
Coachman	2.7	Servant	2.0				
Brickmaker	1.8	Coachman	1.9				
Seaman	1.6	Carpenter	1.6				
Whitewasher	1.5	Carter	1.3				
Domestic	1.3	Domestic	1.2				
Day Laborer	1.3	Shoemaker	1.1				
Carter	1.2	Waterman	1.1				
		Tailor	1.0				
		Steward	1.0				
		Brickmaker	0.8				
		Whitewasher	0.8				
		Bartender	0.7				
		Musician	0.6				
	80.4		80.3		80.2		83.6
	(3549)		(1432)		(5213)		(2374)
# of occ in top 80%	14		20		4		6
C. 1870:							
Laborer	28.9	Laborer	16.4	Domestic Servant	24.3	Keeping House	24.9
None	9.8	Waiter	10.9	Keeping House	21.6	None	22.4
Waiter	8.5	None	10.7	None	20.6	Domestic Servant	12.0
Domestic Servant	4.8	Barber	7.6	Domestic	8.5	Domestic	8.8
Coachman	4.2	Porter	3.7	Washer-woman	3.9	Dressmaker	7.0
Barber	3.2	Hotel Waiter	3.4	Domestic Employee	3.4	Domestic	4.8
Porter	2.8	Domestic Servant	3.2			Employee Seamstress	3.0
Seaman	2.4	Coachman	3.2				
Hotel Waiter	2.4	Seaman	2.8				
Brickmaker	2.0	Shoemaker	1.5				
Hod Carrier	1.4	Private Waiter	1.1				
Whitewasher	1.1	Caterer	0.9				
Servant	1.1						

*In 1850, female occupations were not regularly recorded; hence, we have not included these data.

Table 11. Occupations in Top 80% of Work Force, by Color and Sex, 1850–1880, continued

MALE OCCUPATIONS				FEMALE OCCUPATIONS			
Blacks	%	Mulattoes	%	Blacks	%	Mulattoes	%
Huckster	0.9	Carpenter	0.8				
Farm Hand	0.9	Huckster	0.8				
Driver	0.8	Teamster	0.8				
Private Waiter	0.8	Cook	0.7				
		Brickmaker	0.7				
Domestic	0.2	Upholsterer	0.7				
Shoemaker	0.7	Bartender	0.7				
Public Waiter	0.7	House Carpenter	0.7				
Brick Yard Worker	0.6	Musician	0.7				
		Public Waiter	0.7				
Sailor	0.5						
Private Porter	0.5	Private Porter	0.7				
Hostler	0.5	Driver	0.6				
		Teacher	0.6				
		School Teacher	0.6				
		Domestic Servant	0.6				
		Restaurant Waiter	0.5				
		Domestic Employee	0.5				
		Clergyman	0.5				
		Store Porter	0.5				
		Sailor	0.5				
		Steward	0.4				
		Furniture Car. Dr.	0.4				
		Whitewasher	0.4				
	80.3 (3911)		80.1 (1247)		82.3 (5781)		82.9 (1929)
# of occ in top 80%	24		36		6		7
D. 1880:							
Laborer	26.3	Waiter	17.1	Keeping House	24.6	Keeping House	26.0
Waiter	14.3	Laborer	12.7	Servant	24.1	Servant	18.9
None	6.1	None	7.9	None	13.7	None	14.0
Servant	6.0	Barber	7.8	Cook	5.5	Dressmaker	6.2
Coachman	4.1	Coachman	4.6	Washerwoman	5.2	At Home	4.2
Barber	3.5	Servant	4.5	At Home	3.5	Washerwoman	4.1
Porter	2.9	At School	3.1	Housekeeper	3.5	Cook	3.5
Sailor	2.0	Porter	2.1			Housekeeper	3.2
Stevedore	1.8	Driver	2.1				
Driver	1.7	Caterer	1.8				
Whitewasher	1.4	Cook	1.5				
Brickmaker	1.2	Janitor	1.1				
At School	1.0	At Home	0.9				
Hod Carrier	1.0	Messenger	0.8				
Cook	0.9	Brickmaker	0.7				
Hostler	0.8	Stevedore	0.7				
Shoemaker	0.8	Whitewasher	0.7				
Caterer	0.8	Cart Driver	0.7				
Janitor	0.7	Shoemaker	0.6				
Huckster	0.5	Huckster	0.6				
Brick Yard Worker	0.5	Upholsterer	0.6				
		Sailor	0.6				
Teamster	0.5	Clerk	0.5				
At Home	0.4	Bartender	0.5				
Seaman	0.4	Store Porter	0.5				

Table 11.   Occupations in Top 80% of Work Force, by Color and Sex, 1850–1880, continued

MALE OCCUPATIONS				FEMALE OCCUPATIONS			
Blacks	%	Mulattoes	%	Blacks	%	Mulattoes	%
Wagon Driver	0.4	Hostler	0.5				
		Seaman	0.5				
		School Teacher	0.5				
		Hotel Waiter	0.4				
		Furniture Car. Dr.	0.4				
		Bricklayer	0.3				
		Plasterer	0.3				
		Musician	0.3				
		Restaurant	0.3				
		Minister	0.3				
		Wagon Driver	0.3				
		Teamster	0.3				
		Carpenter	0.3				
		Cabinet Maker	0.3				
		Private Waiter	0.3				
		Farm Hand	0.3				
	80.0		81.0		80.1		80.1
	(6835)		(1220)		(8887)		(1824)
# of occ in top 80%	25		42		7		8

women were more likely to be found in such work. The percentage point gap which separated the women narrowed somewhat over the period, so that by 1880 roughly eight black and seven mulatto women among ten earned their livings in unskilled domestic capacities.

We will now consider how the occupational structure varied with place of birth. It is important to bear in mind that in this analysis we do not know how long the individual workers lived in Philadelphia; they may have migrated to the city with their parents while still children and appear in these tables as adults, or they may be quite recent arrivals. Given the remarkably high population turnover from decade to decade, however, it is quite likely that the vast majority of the people with whom we are dealing were adult migrants who lived in Philadelphia less than ten years.

About 95 percent of both blacks and mulattoes were born in the four areas under discussion: 1. Pennsylvania; 2. "Other" North, consisting of New Jersey, New York, and New England; 3. Maryland and Delaware; and 4. Virginia and Washington, D.C. It is difficult to generalize about five occupational levels and four places of birth over a thirty-year period,

Table 12. Vertical Occupations by Color, 1850–1880 (Males and Females, 20–99)

(Col. %s)	1850		1860		1870		1880	
Males	% B	% M	% B	% M	% B	% M	% B	% M
Professional & High-White Collar	1.1	1.2	0.9	0.9	0.9	1.3	0.9	1.3
Proprietary & Low-White Collar	3.0	6.4	4.3	5.5	3.8	7.8	5.3	8.5
Artisan	14.5	28.2	12.1	23.2	12.4	23.7	12.2	21.5
Specified Unskilled	44.8	44.0	56.6	58.4	46.0	46.8	47.8	48.4
Unspecified Unskilled	36.4	20.9	25.3	11.2	33.0	18.5	28.1	14.0
Total	(3311)	(650)	(3393)	(1392)	(3908)	(1230)	(7905)	(1383)
Females								
Professional High-White Collar	—	—	—	0.1	—	0.1	—	0.2
Proprietary & Low-White Collar	1.5	3.1	1.0	1.8	1.0	2.8	1.0	2.2
Artisan	7.9	24.6	18.9	32.6	9.4	19.3	11.4	16.2
Specified Unskilled	84.5	69.2	77.6	63.7	86.9	75.1	79.6	72.5
Unspecified Unskilled	5.1	3.1	1.6	0.7	0.7	0.3	1.0	0.7
Total	(316)	(65)	(3320)	(1335)	(4854)	(1567)	(9540)	(1947)

Examples of Ranking Values				
Professional & High-White Collar	Proprietary & Low-White Collar	Artisan	Specified Unskilled	Unspecified Unskilled
Physician	Agent	Apprentice	Waiter	Laborer
Attorney	Salesman	Engineer	Servant	Worker
Banker	Teacher	Cab. Maker	Janitor	
Merchant	Huckster	Barber	Driver	
Minister	Clerk	Founder	Sweep	
Lawyer	Coach Dealer	Cook	Porter	
		Weaver		
		Carpenter		
		Shoemaker		

B = black; M = mulatto.

but the data lend themselves nicely to the task (see Table 13). "The further the migration distance, the better the occupational profile" seems to be an accurate generalization.[30] Migrants from Virginia, Washington, D.C., and South Carolina were generally better off than those from Maryland and Delaware, but only in 1850 and 1860 were they as well off as Negroes living in Pennsylvania and the North. The nature of the migrants from the South appears to have changed for the worse after the Civil War. Regardless of whence they came, the occupational distributions of Southern-born migrants were inferior to those of Pennsylvania and Northern-

Table 13. Vertical Occupation by Place of Birth, 1850–1880 (Males, 15–99)

(Col. %s)	Pennsylvania			North			Maryland & Delaware			Virginia & D.C.		
	B	M	All	B	M	All	B	M	All	B	M	All
A. 1850:	B = black; M = mulatto.											
Professional & High-White Collar	0.7	0.9	0.7	1.4	1.7	1.5	0.9	0.9	0.9	2.1	2.3	2.1
Proprietary & Low-White Collar	3.2	7.9	4.1	4.3	0.0	3.5	2.2	2.8	2.2	1.5	2.3	1.6
Artisan	20.7	31.1	22.7	9.9	13.8	10.6	11.0	25.6	12.9	17.8	31.0	20.5
Specified Unskilled	40.3	39.6	40.2	48.6	58.6	50.3	44.8	43.3	44.6	47.5	47.1	47.4
Unspecified Unskilled	34.6	18.9	31.5	35.8	25.9	37.0	40.4	26.0	38.5	29.7	16.1	26.9
Total	(1331)	(318)	(1649)	(282)	(58)	(340)	(1472)	(215)	(1687)	(337)	(87)	(424)
B. 1860:												
Professional & High-White Collar	0.4	0.5	0.4	0.3	0.0	0.3	1.1	1.0	1.1	1.0	1.9	1.3
Proprietary & Low-White Collar	4.2	4.0	4.1	3.1	2.5	5.3	2.8	3.9	2.4	5.1	5.0	5.1
Artisan	13.9	26.1	17.6	7.5	14.8	9.7	9.7	15.2	11.0	14.0	29.2	19.3
Specified Unskilled	55.5	56.0	55.6	71.2	73.0	71.7	57.6	64.0	59.1	48.3	51.3	38.1
Unspecified Unskilled	24.0	11.3	20.9	16.8	9.0	14.5	27.7	13.6	24.3	30.8	9.1	25.6
Total	(1816)	(797)	(2613)	(292)	(122)	(414)	(1221)	(381)	(1602)	(292)	(154)	(446)
C. 1870:												
Professional & High-White Collar	0.4	0.6	0.5	1.1	6.2	2.5	1.4	0.7	1.3	0.8	1.4	1.0
Proprietary & Low-White Collar	4.2	9.4	6.0	2.8	3.1	3.1	2.4	4.5	2.8	3.0	3.7	3.3
Artisan	15.3	25.9	19.4	10.9	24.7	15.5	8.6	15.3	10.1	9.6	15.7	11.5
Specified Unskilled	42.9	40.8	44.9	54.9	44.3	56.1	46.0	52.2	49.1	50.2	63.9	55.6
Unspecified Unskilled	30.8	19.0	29.2	22.9	16.5	22.8	37.2	24.6	36.7	32.5	13.0	28.7
Total	(1547)	(603)	(2150)	(263)	(92)	(355)	(1335)	(261)	(1596)	(633)	(211)	(844)
D. 1880:												
Professional & High-White Collar	0.9	0.6	0.9	0.9	0.6	0.9	0.6	4.2	1.2	0.8	0.7	0.9
Proprietary & Low-White Collar	5.0	7.3	6.0	3.7	12.6	5.3	3.0	3.1	3.2	3.6	6.6	4.4
Artisan	15.1	23.4	18.2	12.5	24.2	15.0	8.6	14.3	9.7	10.4	17.7	12.4
Specified Unskilled	44.4	43.5	48.6	52.8	46.3	54.8	47.3	54.7	51.1	52.4	56.0	57.2
Unspecified Unskilled	25.8	15.4	26.3	25.3	6.3	23.8	34.4	20.6	35.1	25.6	8.6	24.9
Total	(2625)	(556)	(3181)	(517)	(89)	(606)	(2406)	(268)	(2674)	(1252)	(219)	(1471)

born Negroes. These differences were considerably clearer in the skilled and laboring categories than in the professional and proprietary ones. The differences in the ante- and post-bellum migration from the South suggest that the pool itself from which the migrants came consisted of less skilled individuals. Prior to the Civil War the pool was composed of free Negroes, many of whom had trades, while afterwards it contained masses of newly freed slaves.

What is most striking about the occupational profiles when studied by place of birth, however, is that the superior occupational condition of mulattoes is generally observed regardless of state of origin. The differences between blacks and mulattoes were small in the professional and proprietary categories and, in several instances, the trend is reversed, but in the skilled and laboring categories the differences between men in the two groups are unmistakable: mulattoes are twice as likely as blacks to be in the skilled category and between one-third and one-half as likely to be in the laboring category.

Another limited, but nevertheless interesting, way of looking at the differences between blacks and mulattoes in the occupational universe is to examine the distribution of opportunities for learning a trade (apprenticeship), performing the trade under the guidance of a master (journeymanship), and becoming the master craftsman himself. Opportunities for Negroes in such occupational settings were severely restricted, but there were suggestive differences in the distributions by color. Of the seventy-seven such instances for 1850 to 1880, mulattoes accounted for slightly less than half though they were less than one-quarter of the workforce.

In sum, mulattoes enjoyed an occupational standing superior to blacks. The size of the differential was not sufficient to suggest that occupational success was solely determined by color, but it was large enough to indicate that color did influence occupational achievement.

Wealth Structure. In examining wealth-holding within the Negro community, regardless of how we measure the distribution of wealth—by the percentage who held property, by observing its distribution among those fortunate enough to have held it, by the value held in relation to the total value of property owned, or by the average holding on a per capita and "holders only" basis—mulattoes enjoyed a position far superior to blacks.[31]

It is once again important to place the discussion of wealth-holding within a larger perspective. When compared to the white ethnic groups, proportionately fewer Negroes owned wealth of any kind. Moreover, the value of the real and personal property they held was less than that of whites (see Table 14).

Table 14. Wealth-Holding, 1850 and 1870 (Males, 18 +)

	Negroes	Irish	German	Native White
% Holding Real Property (1850)	4.2	6.0	7.2	12.9
% Holding Real Property (1870)	5.3	15.9	19.4	14.3
% Holding Real & Personal Property (1870)	13.8	35.4	49.7	36.8
*Mean Value: Real Property (1850)	$103	$308	$411	$1236
*Mean Value: Real Property (1870)	$221	$1008	$1326	$2131
*Mean Value: Real & Personal Property (1870)	$318	$1578	$2133	$4209

*For holders and non-holders of wealth.

Of the wealth owned by Negroes, mulattoes controlled a sum vastly disproportionate to their numbers in the Negro population: 18 percent of the population in 1850, they owned 43 percent of the real property; 31 percent of the population in 1860, they owned 53 percent of the real property and 50 percent of the total wealth; 26 percent of the population in 1870, they owned 57 percent of the real property and 58 percent of the total wealth. The trend in these figures is striking: despite a decrease in the proportion of mulattoes in the population from 1860 to 1870, the proportion of the wealth owned by mulattoes increased steadily from 43 percent in 1850 to 50 percent in 1860 to 58 percent in 1870 (see Table 15).

The superiority of mulatto wealth distributions held across the sex line: mulatto women generally enjoyed the same position vis-à-vis black women as mulatto men enjoyed vis-à-vis black men. To speed our discussion, then, the following description will be presented for males only; the relevant data for women are presented in the corresponding tables.

Few mulattoes or blacks owned real property: in 1850, one black in twenty-five as compared to one mulatto in fourteen; in 1860, one black in twenty as compared to one mulatto in twelve; and in 1870, one black in twenty-one as compared again to one mulatto in twelve. Mulattoes, in other words, were roughly twice as likely as blacks to own real property. The average value of the real property owned by mulattoes on a per capita basis, moreover, was three to five times greater than that owned by blacks, and two to three times greater when the value of the property is averaged among the owners themselves (see Table 15).

Among the owners of real and personal property, mulattoes were found

Table 15. Property and Wealth, 1850–1870 (Males and Females, 20+)

		Total $	$ Owned by M	% $ Owned by M	Ind* Dis.	Per Capita of All Mulattoes and Blacks			Per Capita of Holders Only			% With		
						B	M	All	B	M	All	B	M	All
A.	Real Property													
1850	M	518782	233220	45.0	2.74	71	297	109	1854	4240	2482	3.9	7.0	4.4
	F	97000	34300	35.4	1.97	11	27	14	1844	3118	2155	0.6	0.9	0.6
1860	M	688450	354650	51.5	1.80	89	236	131	1757	2955	2220	5.1	8.0	5.9
	F	218790	121750	55.6	1.33	17	53	28	1493	2899	2045	1.2	1.8	1.4
1870	M	1386879	822099	59.3	2.49	133	620	249	2810	7275	4417	4.7	8.5	5.6
	F	408575	197500	48.3	1.97	35	101	51	3059	2992	3026	1.1	3.4	1.7
B.	Total Wealth													
1860	M	1154587	557065	48.2	1.68	155	371	220	662	1243	873	23.4	29.9	25.2
	F	370747	197242	53.2	1.27	31	85	47	479	930	646	6.5	9.2	7.3
1870	M	1963524	1170044	59.6	2.50	187	882	353	1440	4366	2397	13.0	20.2	14.7
	F	557685	280600	50.3	2.05	46	144	70	1872	2440	2120	2.5	5.9	3.3

B = black; M = mulatto.

*This index was computed as follows:

% of male/female dollars owned by mulattoes

% mulattoes are of all male/female 20-99

Table 16. Proportion of Real Property Ownership, by Age, 1850–1870*

(Row %s) Ages	1850 Black	1850 Mulatto	1860 Black	1860 Mulatto	1870 Black	1870 Mulatto
A. Males						
15–19	—	0.7	—	—	—	—
	(571)	(150)	(625)	(272)	(546)	(194)
20–29	1.3	2.6	0.9	1.3	0.8	1.1
	(1375)	(307)	(1274)	(609)	(1656)	(551)
30–39	2.9	7.7	4.1	5.1	3.6	7.8
	(1133)	(220)	(1052)	(393)	(1030)	(345)
40–49	6.1	10.0	7.6	18.0	5.0	13.4
	(815)	(130)	(725)	(289)	(733)	(224)
50–59	6.5	9.3	12.6	21.9	12.1	25.4
	(400)	(75)	(390)	(128)	(488)	(130)
60 +	9.9	18.9	10.3	14.8	16.3	22.1
	(272)	(53)	(302)	(81)	(338)	(77)
Total	(4566)	(935)	(4367)	(1772)	(4791)	(1521)
% with R.P.	3.4	4.9	4.3	6.8	4.2	7.4
% Mulatto of All R.P. Holders	23		39		36.0	
Index	1.4		1.4		1.5	
B. Females						
15–19	—	—	0.3	0.2	0.2	—
	(903)	(234)	(946)	(512)	(989)	(366)
20–29	0.2	0.2	0.3	0.4	0.2	0.4
	(2175)	(532)	(1955)	(895)	(2263)	(731)
30–39	0.4	1.2	0.5	1.6	0.7	1.4
	(1504)	(324)	(1397)	(624)	(1469)	(515)
40–49	0.7	1.4	1.6	2.2	1.4	7.1
	(1025)	(217)	(1057)	(402)	(988)	(312)
50–59	1.7	1.0	3.1	4.4	3.3	7.4
	(579)	(101)	(581)	(206)	(666)	(204)
60 +	1.4	2.0	3.2	5.3	3.1	9.1
	(503)	(99)	(556)	(189)	(618)	(187)
Total	(6689)	(1507)	(6492)	(2828)	(6993)	(2315)
% with R.P.	0.5	0.7	1.1	1.5	1.0	2.9
% Mulatto of All R.P. Holders	24.4		38.7		48.2	
Index	1.4		1.4		2.0	

*Total N's in parentheses.

disproportionately among the wealthiest. Mulattoes were two to three times more likely than blacks to be concentrated in the highest total wealth categories.

Because property ownership usually varies directly with age, it is necessary to control for age when analyzing property holding. We have already seen that the age structures of blacks and mulattoes were similar, and Table 16 shows that at every age category, mulattoes more often than blacks owned property.

When the relationship between real property ownership and place of birth is considered, the data are among the most interesting presented. In 1850, 1860, and 1870, migrants to Philadelphia from the North, Maryland, and Delaware, and Virginia and Washington, D.C., were more likely than Pennsylvania-born Negroes to own real property. Since those owning real property constituted only a small proportion of all migrants from their respective states, these data show only that among those migrating to Philadelphia, there were a select few who were well-off. It is not possible to determine the extent to which the real property owned was outside Philadelphia, but it is unlikely that the numbers involved would be significant; most people probably sold their property prior to migration.

The relationship between total wealth ownership and place of birth followed a similar pattern. In 1860 and 1870, a greater proportion of migrants than Pennsylvania-born Negroes owned property. The per capita and "holders only" value of the property owned also conformed to the patterns described above.

As in the case of occupation and place of birth, the disproportionate ownership of property by mulattoes over blacks held for males in *all* places of birth and in *all* census years. As in the larger pattern described immediately above, blacks and mulattoes who migrated to Philadelphia were more likely to own property than the Pennsylvania-born Negroes of the corresponding color. And, once again, the same patterns generally can be found when per capita and "holders only" measures are applied.

The place of birth and property data show that many of the black migrants were better off than Pennsylvania-born mulattoes. This was consistently true of blacks from Virginia and Washington, D.C., and often true of blacks from Maryland, Delaware, and the North. These data serve as a reminder that the argument being made is *not* that *all* mulattoes were better off than *all* blacks, but only that when mulattoes and blacks in similar circumstances are compared, a greater proportion of mulattoes than blacks enjoyed the superior condition.

We can now combine several of the most important variables in an attempt to explain some of the consistent variation found between blacks and mulattoes.[32] Most research on the topic has demonstrated a clear relationship between property ownership and occupation. That is, the higher the occupational level, the more the earnings, and the greater the likelihood that the individual will be able to purchase land or a home, or acquire more liquid assets.

To test whether the higher proportion of property ownership of mulattoes over blacks was a function of the greater proportion of mulattoes in the higher occupational categories, tables were constructed comparing real property ownership across the color line, but *holding the level of occupation constant*. The results of such tests show rather conclusively that occupation cannot explain *all* the variation observed between blacks and mulattoes. Tables 17 and 18 show that in all census years, among professionals, proprietors and skilled craftsmen, little of the variation is eliminated; mulattoes remain more likely than blacks to own property, and the per capita value of the property owned by mulattoes remains higher than for blacks (except for the per capita value of property owned by "professionals" in 1870). On the other hand, at the lowest occupational levels —the specified and unspecified unskilled—the variation almost disappears (although the per capita value of the property owned remains somewhat higher for mulattoes).

The meaning of such data is not contradictory. They indicate that if a Negro had a low-status occupation, being mulatto offered little advantage in acquiring property. Roughly the same, small proportion of blacks and mulattoes owned property in these unskilled occupational categories. That the variation was eliminated in these categories, but not in the highest three occupational categories, can be understood if one considers the con-

Table 17. Real Property and Total Wealth by Vertical Occupation, 1850–1870* (Males 20–99)

	1850		1860		1870	
Vertical	Black % with	Mulatto % with	Black % with	Mulatto % with	Black % with	Mulatto % with
A. *Real Property*						
Professional & High-White Collar	11.4 (35)	37.5 (8)	31.0 (29)	41.6 (12)	17.1 (35)	31.2 (16)
Proprietary & Low-White Collar	7.0 (100)	17.1 (35)	15.8 (146)	18.2 (77)	13.3 (150)	23.9 (96)
Artisan	5.4 (481)	12.0 (183)	8.8 (410)	13.6 (323)	7.0 (484)	13.1 (291)
Specified Unskilled	2.4 (1483)	2.8 (286)	2.7 (1919)	4.4 (813)	3.6 (1796)	4.0 (576)
Unspecified Unskilled	4.5 (1205)	6.6 (136)	5.0 (860)	5.1 (156)	4.0 (1290)	4.4 (228)
B. *Total Wealth*						
Professional & High-White Collar			58.6 (29)	66.7 (12)	54.3 (35)	62.5 (16)
Proprietary & Low-White Collar			34.5 (139)	42.6 (68)	30.0 (140)	44.8 (96)
Artisan			33.4 (410)	38.1 (323)	18.0 (484)	25.4 (291)
Specified Unskilled			22.1 (1919)	26.2 (813)	12.2 (1796)	15.3 (576)
Unspecified Unskilled			6.0 (728)	6.1 (132)	9.7 (1290)	11.8 (228)

*Total N's in parentheses.

text in which money was earned by members of these two different occupational groups. Regardless for whom they worked, the unskilled had only so much labor they could perform and only so much in the way of wages they could earn. The income earned by professionals, proprietors, and skilled craftsmen, on the other hand, depended in part on the superiority of the wages they commanded for their services, but in a great many instances their income was affected more directly by the size and composition of the *constituencies* they served. Mulattoes in these three categories apparently were more successful than were blacks in having access to or dealing with a white constituency, and perhaps with their Negro constituents as well. If a lighter skin was preferred in the larger society, then being mulatto would have clear economic value in the supply and demand setting of the marketplace, and the advantage would certainly be more likely to appear in this context than in the unskilled situation. Whites, mulattoes, and blacks might well have preferred mulattoes to blacks when it came time to pay for their goods or services. And judging by the proportions who held property among blacks and mulattoes within the same occupational levels, they did.

Membership Patterns of Negro Organizations

We now shift our concern from the entire population to the color patterns found among individuals who were members of a wide range of community organizations. Using a few memoirs, usually of contemporary Negro leaders, an important collection of reprinted manuscript materials, and over 700 "broadsides" describing the organizational activities of Philadelphia Negroes from 1830 to 1890, a list was compiled of roughly 2,300 mem-

Table 18. Per Capita Total Wealth of Those Having Wealth, 1860–1870* (Males, 15–99)

Vertical	1860		1870	
	Black	Mulatto	Black	Mulatto
Professional &	470	3888	2584	1147
High-White Collar	(29)	(12)	(37)	(16)
Proprietary &	344	1518	589	2970
Low-White Collar	(140)	(65)	(136)	(92)
Artisan	243	426	243	781
	(475)	(374)	(531)	(312)
Specified	101	120	103	265
Unskilled	(2152)	(929)	(1994)	(640)
Unspecified	58	75	85	108
Unskilled	(933)	(176)	(1387)	(250)

*Total N's in parentheses.

berships in 56 different organizations.[33] The organizations include groups with diverse interests cutting across the spectrum of political, social, and economic activities: abolition and civil rights, literary and debating societies, athletic clubs and social "fraternities," beneficial societies, charitable groups, and religious denominations. For each entry we recorded the individual's name, organization, position held, and year of membership. The individuals were then traced from the organizational lists to the population manuscript schedules of the U.S. Census. By joining the information from the two documents, the organizational patterns of Philadelphia Negroes can be studied.

Membership and positions of leadership held within these organizations are the result of a complex process of human preference and selection in which many individual characteristics were considered and decisions made. The socioeconomic and demographic characteristics of the aggregate membership tell us a great deal about what the community itself defined as important and desirable within the broader population pool from which members were drawn.

The wealth and occupational characteristics of the aggregate membership indicate that the organizational members constituted an "elite" group. One adult Negro male in twenty owned any real property as compared to one in five among the organizational members. There were important differences in occupation as well. Seven times the proportion of professionals, six times the proportion of white-collar and small shop owners, and three times the proportion of skilled craftsmen were found among the organizational members. Two of three adult male organizational members earned a living at these prestigious and better-paying occupations as contrasted to one among five in the population at-large. Similarly significant differences appear in almost all other socioeconomic characteristics. However the "elite" may be defined, these organizational members certainly qualify as a select group.[34]

Not all associational members, however, were part of the socioeconomic elite. Despite the clustering of individuals with property and high occupational rank in the membership of the community's organizations, most members were unpropertied and fully one-third were unskilled. In a largely impoverished and unskilled population, wealth-holding and the distribution of occupations lacked the vital element of vertical differentiation requisite to social stratification. This circumstance suggests that membership in elite community organizations serves as a more direct indicator of social standing than the socioeconomic variables of wealth and occupation reported for the entire population in the manuscript census. Indeed, the color distribution among organizational members indicates that socioeconomic rank *alone* was not enough to determine social status. If the census variables of wealth and occupation were by themselves sufficient to identify the members of the community's organizations, one would expect the color distribution of memberships to match the color distribution among the wealthy and high occupation groups. In fact, it did not.

Mulattoes were significantly overrepresented among the organizational membership of Philadelphia Negroes and were found disproportionately among the leaders of the varied organizations. Fully *half* of the organizational memberships were held by mulattoes, despite the fact that they were outnumbered two to one in the socioeconomic elite identified in the census and four to one in the population at-large. Moreover, mulattoes held six of every ten major leadership positions: presidents, vice-presidents, treasurers, and secretaries. The generally superior position of mulattoes was reflected in economic variables as well. They were usually more likely than their elite black brethren to hold real property, and the value of the real property they owned was almost always many times greater. By all four measures, then—membership, leadership, frequency and value of property ownership—mulattoes were better off (see Table 19). Clearly, skin color played a role independent of socioeconomic status in delineating the organizational elite.

While the color patterns for the aggregate membership of the fifty-six organizations are evident, no clear color patterns emerge within specific organizations or groups of organizations. No simple division among the organizations can be made. The problem is further compounded by the lack of continuous membership lists throughout the period under discussion. Change-over-time patterns, in other words, are difficult to discern.[35]

The extremes in the proportions of mulatto membership are set on the high side by the Pythian Baseball Club, 70 percent of whom were mulatto. The Pythians were elitist to be sure, but manuscript fragments from the other baseball clubs hint that at least some of the other teams might have been largely black in membership. Although we have lists of their starting "nines," we were unable to link them to the population manuscripts with the required degree of certainty. At the other extreme, mulattoes were found least often among the Odd Fellows and Grand Army of the Republic (GAR) posts which were more working class in their occupational profile. Between the extremes of the Odd Fellows/GAR groups and the Baseball Clubs ranged the other groups: those involved in abolition and civil rights activities with higher proportions of mulattoes (roughly one of two in their membership), followed by the charitable and miscellaneous organizations. Once again, however, no clear color pattern emerges.

We come, finally, to the denominational groups: the African Methodist

Table 19. Negro Organization Membership Patterns: Group Totals and Grand Totals

Group Title	# of Organizations	Tot Memberships	Tot # Color Known	% M	Ind of Dis*	% with R.P. B	% with R.P. M	$ Aver. Value R.P. B	$ Aver. Value R.P. M	Pres #	Pres %M	V-Pres #	V-Pres %M	Treas #	Treas %M	Secy #	Secy %M	Total #	Total %M
Civil Rights	9	486	317	55	2.6	27	39	1022	7686	6	33	24	58	2	100	6	50	38	55
Literary	7	379	269	50	2.4	16	15	562	1947	14	57	10	20	9	67	3	33	36	47
Baseball	8	143	91	70	2.9	15	17	241	941	1	0	—	—	—	—	3	67	4	50
GAR/Odd Fel	4	172	71	22	1.3	2	6	91	187	—	—	—	—	2	50	3	0	5	20
Early Benef	4	306	137	32	1.9	20	16	686	3520	6	33	—	—	—	—	5	80	11	55
Late Benef	5	153	99	64	3.3	6	19	292	762	7	100	10	90	7	100	9	44	33	82
Charities	2	107	33	45	1.8	—	33	—	1413	—	—	—	—	1	100	—	—	1	0
Misc	3	61	31	39	2.5	11	33	316	2917	—	—	2	50	1	0	1	0	3	33
Denom-AME	1	26	13	15	1.0	—	50	—	2500	1	0	—	—	—	—	—	0	1	33
Denom-Pres	9	332	136	50	2.8	6	7	190	263	—	—	—	—	12	50	6	17	19	42
Denom-Bapt	2	66	22	36	2.3	—	—	—	—	1	100	—	—	—	—	—	—	1	33
Denom-Episc	2	59	37	62	2.9	57	26	1664	1289	—	—	—	—	1	100	1	50	1	33
Grand Totals:	56	2290	1256	50	2.4	16	22	461	3165	36	56	46	56	35	69	39	41	155	55

B = black; M = mulatto.

*Index of Disproportion: relative to proportions in population at-large. Blacks outnumbered mulattoes by about four to one in the general population.

Episcopal (AME), African Baptist, African Presbyterian, and African Episcopal. Our data on membership are fragmentary at best for the AME and Baptist groups. On the other hand, there are enough memberships with color identified to warrant some statements about the Presbyterians and perhaps the Episcopalians as well. The extant data show an interesting pattern, all the more significant because we are examining the leaders of each denomination. The percentage of mulattoes rises as we follow an economic ranking of the denominations: AME (15), Baptist (36), Presbyterian (50), and Episcopalian (62). The leadership of the latter two denominations is disproportionately mulatto, but it is worth noting that black Episcopalians are economically better off than their mulatto brothers. In any case, it is important to close the discussion of the denominations with the reminder that the data are incomplete.

In recognizing that half the membership of Philadelphia's Negro organizations and 60 percent of their leadership were mulatto, the role of color is confirmed as a significant determinant of membership in the city's nineteenth-century organizational elite. Although much research remains in analyzing the color patterns of specific associations, it will be carried out within the larger context of an elite characterized by socioeconomic rank and color.

Conclusions

Why were mulattoes so often better off than blacks? The answer is rooted in the historic advantages from which mulattoes benefited. In general, they enjoyed a greater access than blacks to the limited spectrum of opportunities that were available during slavery. During American slavery, mulattoes were more likely to be freed, and by the Civil War, far greater proportions of mulattoes than blacks were already free.[36] The circumstances in which mulattoes found themselves made it easier for them to acquire the fundamental educational skills of reading and writing. They were urbanized sooner than were blacks,[37] and the occupational skills and experience in the ways of city life put them ahead of blacks. Many mulattoes, some of whom were children of white fathers, were directly provided with economic resources such as capital and land. They established more and closer contacts with whites, especially whites in positions of power, and this operated to their advantage in securing desired aims. When whites attributed the achievements of mulattoes to the "white blood which coursed through their veins," they were assigning a racial or genetic interpretation to conditions which, in fact, had sufficiently clear environmental explanations.[38]

A second explanation is derived from the psychology of racism and the psychological effects racism has on its victims. To an important extent, Negroes themselves internalized the hatred for the black. Contemptuous of the darker-skinned among them, many Negroes openly preferred the mulatto. This attitude is not confined solely to the distant past. Despite its decline in importance over the last century, color is not bereft of contemporary significance. It was not very long ago that some Negroes proudly belonged to "blue vein" churches, that young women were presented at some debutante balls not by age, beauty, or height, but by skin color, and that some parents advised their children to "marry lighter." Indeed, the recent slogan, "Black Is Beautiful," was aimed at Negroes as well as whites and cannot be fully understood without an adequate historical perspective on intra-group color attitudes. It is the uneasiness and controversy associated with this aspect of color, perhaps more than any other factor, that explains the reluctance of some scholars to discuss the role of color in the Afro-American past.[39] In recent years the manifestations of racism have been extensively catalogued; intra-group color discrimination must be recognized as a response to and consequence of the racism widespread in the larger white society.

A final explanation is found in the requirements of social stratification. American society, like other societies, is steeped in social distinctions. However abused and mistreated Negroes were by the society in which they lived, they inescapably shared many of its social and cultural imperatives. To stratify socially was among the most important. But because of the racist attitudes and practices of whites, Negroes were historically denied access to the two most important stratifiers: distinctions in occupation and wealth. Unable to build the critical vertical dimension which occupation and wealth gave to stratification in the larger white society, Negroes created their own system of stratification which stressed as well other means of social differentiation. Color set the Negro experience off from that of other ethnic groups who stratified along socioeconomic lines. The Negro experience was more complicated because, in addition to all the variables which differentiated and stratified other groups, Negroes had to contend with color differences *within* their own group as well as between them and other ethnic groups. Color was an obsession in the larger society, and it set the "few" off from the "many." It was an historic stratifier closely intertwined with the actual distribution of socioeconomic and political advantage well into the twentieth century.

The decline of color as a source of differentiation with social consequence was intimately associated with racism and the nature of opportunities available to Negroes within both their own community and the larger white society. The Great Migration played a fundamental role in this process. Before World War I, Negro elites were heavily, or at least disproportionately, mulatto. Allan Spear's valuable discussion of Chicago documents that the old elite was swamped by the migration, and although the new elite—the Black Bourgeoisie about whom Frazier wrote—tried to emulate the old in several ways, they by and large replaced it.[40] As the Great Migration swelled the Negro populations of many American cities, making it possible for increasing numbers of Negroes to prosper serving the needs of their own people, more blacks assumed positions of wealth, social status, and power within Negro society. In the early twentieth century, industrialization accelerated this process by differentiating the Negro occupational structure, giving it greater vertical dimension.

We should bear in mind that there probably were differences in this process when cities with older and more established Negro populations such as Philadelphia, New York, Baltimore, and Washington are compared to the newer ones such as Chicago, Cleveland, and Detroit. The elite in the older cities probably survived for two reasons: first, they were present in far larger numbers than in the newer cities; and second, their dependence upon whites was less, because many of them were already making their living serving the business needs of the large pre–Great Migration Negro populations in their respective cities. In cities like Philadelphia, then, the old elite probably accommodated the newcomers by moving over and sharing power to some extent, but it is likely that they did not relinquish control. Thus color probably influenced the system of Negro stratification for a longer period in the older urban centers.

If the elite classes of the older cities remained disproportionately mulatto, and the poor predominately black, it may help to explain *some* of the gap which separated the masses from the elite.[41] Such a view is consistent with the plight of the Negro middle and upper classes in general: set off from the masses by virtue of socioeconomic considerations and color, on the one hand, and set off from whites of similar socioeconomic standing, on the other, with color differences, this time *inter*group in nature, ironically responsible.

After World War II, the decline of racism in American society presented Negroes with a broader range of new career options that extended opportunities for advancement beyond the confines of their segregated communities. The change in racial attitudes and the introduction of federal legislation to protect Negroes from job discrimination accelerated the vertical differentiation of their social structure. As increasing numbers of blacks moved into prestigious and important positions, color ceased to be a useful descriptor of reality. As light skin lost its close correlation with high socioeconomic condition, color lost the significance that characterized it in the last century. In the sociological sense, achievement rather than ascription came increasingly to characterize Negro mobility both inside and outside their communities.

In concluding, we must remember that the great majority of nineteenth- and twentieth-century mulattoes were members of neither the socioeconomic nor the organizational elites. The proportion of mulattoes in white-collar occupational positions, for example, never exceeded 10 percent in any of the four census years between 1850 and 1880. Thus, while color did stratify the Negro community, it did not produce totally distinct and hierarchically ordered racial groupings. The transcendant implications of being a Negro in white society affected both blacks and mulattoes.

Nevertheless, no comprehensive understanding of the system of social stratification which characterized Negro society in the past is possible without systematic knowledge of the role played by color. The decline of color was intimately associated with the changing opportunity structures in which Afro-Americans found themselves at different points in their history. The linkage of color to broad structural and attitudinal changes makes it a useful barometer of the overall conditions faced by Negroes in American society.

NOTES

1. Charles Silberman, *Crisis in Black and White* (New York: Random House, 1964); Winthrop Jordan, *White Over Black: American Attitudes Toward the Negro, 1550–1812* (Chapel Hill: University of North Carolina Press, 1968); *Report of the National Advisory Commission on Civil Disorders* (Kerner Commission Report) (New York: Bantam Books, 1968), 1.

2. Throughout this essay, we use the term "Negro" (and not "black") to refer to the entire community of dark- and light-skinned blacks. "Black" indicates dark-skinned and "mulatto" the lighter-skinned individuals among all Negroes. The word "Negro" is not used for ideological reasons, but only to permit the term "black" specifically to indicate skin color as designated in the U.S. Census of Population.

3. The literature review in this essay has benefited from the work of two historians. See Laurence A. Glasco, "The Mulatto: A Neglected Dimension of Afro-American Social Structure," paper presented at the Organization of American Historians, (Denver: April 1974); and Robert F. Ulle, "Interracial Sex in the American South and the Writing of History, 1880–1945," unpublished manuscript in possession of PSHP (1972).

4. August Meier, *Negro Thought in America, 1880–1915: Racial Ideologies in the Age of Booker T. Washington* (Ann Arbor: University of Michigan Press, 1963), 150–56, 300.

5. E. Franklin Frazier, *Black Bourgeoisie* (New York: Free Press, 1965; orig. ed., 1962), 198–200. See also Frazier, *The Negro Family in the United States* (Chicago: University of Chicago Press, 1939); and *The Negro in the United States* (New York: MacMillan, 1949). Meier claims that color became less significant after

the turn of the century, while Frazier pushes the date closer to the end of World War I. Neither author, however, presents compelling empirical evidence to support his conclusions.

Laurence A. Glasco also argues that the social importance of color declined during the twentieth century. See Glasco, "The Mulatto: A Neglected Dimension," *op. cit.*, and "Black and Mulatto: Historical Bases for Afro-American Culture," *Black Line* 2 (Fall 1971), 22–23. In contrast to Meier and Frazier, however, Glasco hypothesizes that color-based "subcultures" existed in the antebellum South, a radical extension of the more moderate argument that color carried with it "social and economic significance."

Writing shortly after World War I, E. B. Reuter proposed that the group of leading American Negroes was then and always had been disproportionately mulatto. He presented a series of lists to make his point, but did not specify how he determined the skin color of his selected individuals. Clearly, too, Reuter's racist thinking affected his analysis and led him to claim mulatto superiority. See E. B. Reuter, *The Mulatto in the United States* (New York: Haskell House, 1969; orig. ed., 1918), 183–314.

6. Carl Oblinger finds that mulattoes in mid-nineteenth-century Lancaster County, Pennsylvania, were disproportionately found in skilled positions, relative to blacks. W. E. B. DuBois intimates that some "well-to-do black Philadelphians" in the late nineteenth century were "largely descendants of favorite mulatto house servants." John Daniels firmly depicts Boston's early twentieth-century Negro upper class as "generally characterized by a considerable strain of Caucasian blood and by lightness of complexion," though he does not speculate how this compares to an earlier period. Roi Ottley's and William Weatherby's study of New York asserts that "there are certain social lines among American Negroes based upon color" but does not specify change over time. Kenneth Kusmer's account of Cleveland's Negro community posits the existence of a light-skinned Negro elite that was essentially replaced by a darker-skinned upper class by 1930. Allan Spear briefly alludes to the group of "mixed stock" Negroes who dominated Chicago's Negro leadership positions before 1900 but provides little data on developments after that date. See Carl Oblinger, "In Recognition of Their Prominence: A Case Study of the Economic and Social Backgrounds of an Ante-Bellum Negro Business and Farming Class in Lancaster County [Pa.]," *Journal of the Lancaster County Historical Society* 72 (1968), 65–83; W. E. B. DuBois, *The Philadelphia Negro: A Social Study* (New York: Schocken, 1967; orig. ed., 1899), 203; John Daniels, *In Freedom's Birthplace: A Study of the Boston Negroes* (New York: Houghton Mifflin, 1914), 227, also see 163, 178–84; Roi Ottley and William J. Weatherby, eds., *The Negro in New York: An Informal Social History, 1626–1940* (New York: Praeger, 1967), 216–17; Kenneth L. Kusmer, *A Ghetto Takes Shape: Black Cleveland, 1870–1930* (Urbana: University of Illinois Press, 1976), 214, also see 100, 209; Allan H. Spear, *Black Chicago: The Making of a Negro Ghetto, 1890–1920* (Chicago: University of Chicago Press, 1967), 54–55.

7. St. Clair Drake and Horace R. Cayton, *Black Metropolis: A Study of Negro Life in a Northern City* (New York: Harper & Row, 1962; orig. ed., 1945), 495–506, 531, 535, 539, 543.

8. Ira Berlin, *Slaves Without Masters: The Free Negro in the Antebellum South* (New York: Pantheon, 1974), 49–50, 57–58, 178, 276–77, 279; Glasco, "The Mulatto: A Neglected Dimension," *op. cit.*, 19. For supporting data on the significance of color in the antebellum South, see Letitia Woods Brown, *Free Negroes in the District of Columbia, 1790–1846* (New York: Oxford University Press, 1972), 143–46; John Hope Franklin, *The Free Negro in North Carolina, 1790–1860* (New York: W. W. Norton, 1971; orig. ed., 1943), 35; Marina Wikramanayake, *A World in*

Shadow (Columbia: University of South Carolina Press, 1973), 80–89. Eugene Genovese claims that sharp social divisions did not exist between black and mulatto slaves, though he concedes the presence of a free Southern "mulatto elite . . . overwhelmingly concentrated in a few cities and rural pockets." See Eugene D. Genovese, *Roll, Jordan, Roll: The World the Slaves Made* (New York: Pantheon, 1972), 429–31.

9. Berlin, *Slaves Without Masters, op. cit.,* 386–91. Genovese places the origins of the "fateful division between lighter- and darker-skinned Negroes" in the postbellum era. See Genovese, *Roll, Jordan, Roll, op. cit.,* 429–31.

10. Constance McLaughlin Green, *The Secret City: A History of Race Relations in the Nation's Capital* (Princeton, N.J.: Princeton University Press, 1967), 65, 98–99, 121, 141–42; Robert E. Perdue, *The Negro in Savannah, 1865–1900* (New York: Exposition Press, 1973), 90–93.

11. Joel Williamson, *After Slavery: The Negro in South Carolina During Reconstruction, 1861–1877* (Chapel Hill: University of North Carolina Press, 1965), 313–17; John W. Blassingame, *Black New Orleans, 1860–1880* (Chicago: University of Chicago Press, 1973), 152–56; David C. Rankin, "The Origins of Black Leadership in New Orleans During Reconstruction," *Journal of Southern History* 40 (August 1974), 417–40.

12. Green, *The Secret City, op. cit.,* 180, 206–8, 279, 356.

13. Allison Davis, Burleigh B. Gardner, and Mary S. Gardner, *Deep South: A Social Anthropological Study of Caste and Class* (Chicago: University of Chicago Press, 1947), 235, also see 216–17, 234–36, 244–48.

14. Hortense Powdermaker, *After Freedom: A Cultural Study in the Deep South* (New York: Atheneum, 1968), 64; also see, John Dollard, *Caste and Class in a Southern Town* (Garden City, N.Y.: Doubleday, 1949; orig. ed., 1937), 391, 450–52. Both volumes examine Indianola, Mississippi.

15. August Meier and David Lewis, "History of the Negro Upper Class in Atlanta Georgia, 1890–1958," *Journal of Negro Education* 28 (1959), 128–39.

16. Seth Scheiner and Gilbert Osofsky on New York, Richard Wright on Pennsylvania, and Robin Winks on Canada do not refer to color as a stratifier. See Seth M. Scheiner, *Negro Mecca: A History of the Negro in New York City, 1865–1920* (New York: New York University Press, 1965); Gilbert Osofsky, *Harlem: The Making of a Ghetto, Negro New York, 1890–1930* (New York: Harper & Row, 1966); Richard R. Wright, *The Negro in Pennsylvania: A Study in Economic History* (Philadelphia: A.M.E. Book Concern, n.d.); Robin W. Winks, *The Blacks in Canada: A History* (New Haven, Ct.: Yale University Press, 1971). Moreover, even those authors who do consider color in the nineteenth century minimize its importance relative to other potential differentiators, such as occupation, wealth, education, and "culture." The extent to which these personal attributes are correlated with color is only implied in their studies, never empirically tested. See Kusmer, *Black Cleveland, op. cit.;* Spear, *Black Chicago, op. cit.;* DuBois, *Philadelphia Negro, op. cit.;* Wright, *Negro in Pennsylvania, op. cit.;* David M. Katzman, *Before the Ghetto: Black Detroit in the Nineteenth Century* (Urbana: University of Illinois Press, 1973).

17. See Carroll D. Wright, *The History and Growth of the United States Census* (Washington, D.C.: U.S. Government Printing Office, 1900), 131, 152, 154, 157, 171. Wright noted that at the time of his writing no copies of the census instructions for 1860 had been located.

18. Theodore Hershberg, Alan Burstein, and Robert Dockhorn, "Record Linkage," in Theodore Hershberg, guest editor, "A Special Issue: The Philadelphia Social History Project," *Historical Methods Newsletter* 9 (March–June, 1976), 137–74; the issue containing this essay is hereafter cited as "PSHP: Special Issue." Other PSHP papers on record linkage include Gretchen Condran and Jeff Seaman, "Linkages of

the 1880–81 Philadelphia Death Register to the 1880 Manuscript Census: Procedures and Preliminary Results," presented at Population Association of America (Philadelphia: April 26–28, 1979), to appear in *Historical Methods* (forthcoming). Jeff Seaman and Gretchen Condran, "Nominal Record Linkage by Machine and Hand: An Investigation of Linkage Techniques Using the Manuscript Census and the Death Register, Philadelphia, 1880," presented at the American Statistical Association (Washington, D.C.: August 13–16, 1979); appears in *1979 Proceedings of the Social Statistics Section of the American Statistical Association* (Washington, D.C.: American Statistical Association, 1980).

19. Glasco, "The Mulatto: A Neglected Dimension," *op. cit.,* 14. Much of the criticism of the census color designations rests to large extent on remarks made early in this century by Ray Stannard Baker and by the census report itself. Referring to the 1900 federal census, Baker claimed that

> the government gave up the attempt in discouragement of trying to enumerate the mulattoes at all, and counted all persons as Negroes who were so classed in the communities where they resided. The census of 1870 showed that one-eighth (roughly) of the Negro population was mulatto, that of 1890 showed that the proportion had increased to more than one-seventh, but these statistics are confessedly inaccurate; the census report itself says: "The figures are of little value. Indeed, as an indication of the extent to which the races have mingled, they are misleading."

See Ray Stannard Baker, *Following the Color Line: American Negro Citizenship in the Progressive Era* (New York: Doubleday, Page & Company, 1908), 153.

The "confessed inaccura[cy]" of the census, however, was made out of context; it referred to the attempt to subdivide the mulatto population further into "quadroons" and "octoroons," and not to the "trustworthiness" of the traditional black and mulatto breakdowns which even, as the census bureau put it, with "wholly indeterminate probable error, have shown a general agreement of results." See Reuter, *The Mulatto in the United States, op. cit.,* 119; United States Census of Population, 1890, *Population,* Vol. I, Part I, 185.

Nevertheless, the debate continues. Ira Berlin has remarked that "census figures on the color of both the free Negro and slave populations must be viewed with even more than the usual skepticism." Berlin, *Slaves Without Masters, op. cit.,* 179 (footnote 62).

20. For a summary of other research on geographic mobility, see Stephan Thernstrom, *The Other Bostonians: Poverty and Progress in the American Metropolis, 1880–1970* (Cambridge: Harvard University Press, 1973), ch. 9. For a more complete listing of social and geographic mobility studies, see Theodore Hershberg, "The New Urban History: Toward an Interdisciplinary History of the City," *Journal of Urban History* 5 (November 1978), 37–38 (footnote 32); also in this volume.

Due to differences in the Irish, German, and Negro population files, even record linkage at the PSHP has had to adopt various approaches and trace population subgroups which are not directly comparable. See Hershberg *et al.,* "Record Linkage," *op. cit.,* 137–74.

21. The argument, however, need not hinge only on the size of the pools from which the migrants were drawn, but on differential opportunities, and the perceptions thereof, available to blacks and mulattoes in the South. Whatever opportunities were available in the Reconstruction South, chances are good, given the likely superior position of mulattoes, that they were disproportionately available to mulattoes. If this were the case, then mulattoes had good reason to remain in the South and, for these very same reasons, blacks in large numbers began leaving the South for the North, where they speculated *they* would find greater opportunities. The decade

of the 1870s, then, marks the beginning of sharp increases in Philadelphia's Negro population. The Great Migration began early.

22. For a fuller discussion of spatial methodology, see Theodore Hershberg, "The Philadelphia Social History Project: A Methodological History" (Ph.D. dissertation, History, Stanford University, 1973), chs. III and V, section 3. Also see Appendix II.

23. The Index of Segregation (or dissimilarity) is more fully described in Stanley Lieberson, *Ethnic Patterns in American Cities* (New York: Free Press of Glencoe, 1963); Otis Dudley Duncan and Beverly Duncan, "Residential Distribution and Occupational Stratification," *American Journal of Sociology* 60 (1955), 493–503; "A Methodological Analysis of Segregation Indexes," *American Sociological Review* 20 (April 1955); Karl E. Taeuber and Alma F. Taeuber, *Negroes in Cities: Residential Segregation and Neighborhood Change* (Chicago: Aldine, 1965), 195–245. Also, see Alan N. Burstein, "Patterns of Segregation and the Residential Experience," in "PSHP: Special Issue," *op. cit.,* 105–13. The Index of Segregation is sensitive to the size of the areal unit used. In general, the smaller the unit, the higher the index. Using the grid as the areal unit, the index score measuring the residential separation of Negroes and whites in 1880 is 70, but it is 52 when the larger census tract units are used. See Theodore Hershberg, Alan N. Burstein, Eugene P. Ericksen, Stephanie Greenberg, and William L. Yancey, "A Tale of Three Cities: Blacks and Immigrants in Philadelphia, 1850–1880, 1930 and 1970," *The Annals* 441 (January 1979), Table 2; also in this volume.

24. Herbert Gutman has written on the resiliency of the Negro family in the face of economic hardship—that is, on the ability of the family unit to remain stable in the face of poverty. See Herbert G. Gutman, *The Black Family in Slavery and Freedom, 1750–1925* (New York: Pantheon, 1976).

25. For a fuller discussion of the comparative family structures, and specifically the reasons cited for the high degree of female-headed families among Negroes (relative to the white ethnic groups), see Frank Furstenberg, Jr., Theodore Hershberg, and John Modell, "The Origins of the Female-Headed Black Family: The Impact of the Urban Environment," *Journal of Interdisciplinary History* 6 (September 1975), 211–33; Claudia Goldin, "Family Strategies and the Family Economy in the Late Nineteenth Century: The Role of Secondary Workers"; both in this volume.

26. Wallace Thurman, *The Blacker the Berry: A Novel of Negro Life* (New York: Macauley, 1929).

27. Mulatto women likely enjoyed a wider remarriage market, being able to marry black men more frequently than black women could marry mulatto men, and perhaps even appealing to white males more frequently than could black women.

Research underway at the PSHP will determine black and mulatto mortality rates for 1880–81 and will provide more evidence on the comparative socioeconomic positions of the two groups. Although the color designation in the Philadelphia Death Register for 1880–81 indicates only whites and Negroes and not mulattoes, we will differentiate blacks from mulattoes by linking the Negroes listed in the register to Negroes enumerated in the 1880 census schedules, where color is stipulated.

28. Michael Haines's work on the boarding patterns of *whites* suggests that the practice was not typically used by low-income families to generate income. Claudia Goldin's research comparing the labor force participation of white and Negro household members, however, does indicate significant differences between the two groups, and we speculate here that Negroes may also have acted singularly in their use of boarding. See Michael Haines, "Poverty, Economic Stress, and the Family in a Nineteenth-Century American City: Philadelphia, 1880"; and Claudia Goldin, "Family Strategies and the Family Economy," *op. cit.;* both essays appear in this volume.

29. For a thorough discussion on the impact of industrialization on the working classes of Philadelphia, see Bruce Laurie, Theodore Hershberg, and George Alter,

"Immigrants and Industry: The Philadelphia Experience, 1850–1880," *Journal of Social History* 9 (December 1975), 219–48; also in this volume. This essay does not discuss Negroes, since they held so insignificant a proportion of manufacturing jobs. For a comparison of Negro and ethnic occupational experiences, see Theodore Hershberg *et al.,* "A Tale of Three Cities," *op. cit.*

30. Although migrants from South Carolina are not discussed in the above text because they were too small in number to affect the data, they were by far the best-off group. Measured by their occupational structure, property-holding, and literacy rate, this group of men and women, black and mulatto alike, were especially well situated.

31. Two kinds of wealth (not income) are reported in the population manuscripts: *real property* (land and/or buildings) and *personal property* (cash and/or other valuables). Real property holdings valued at $100 and above were recorded in 1850, 1860, and 1870; personal property above this same minimum amount was reported in 1860 and 1870. No property holdings of either kind were recorded in the 1880 manuscript census. Also see Appendix II.

32. Several years after the original version of this paper was completed, we conducted a multivariate analysis of the effects of color on patterns of wealth-holding among Philadelphia Negroes in 1860. The results confirm the conclusions presented here. We did not include these additional statistics because our basic arguments are effectively conveyed through contingency tables.

33. A special note of thanks and acknowledgment is due Robert Ulle, a graduate student in History at the University of Pennsylvania, who was employed as a PSHP research assistant. Mr. Ulle played a major role in cataloguing the extensive Black History Collection of the Historical Society of Pennsylvania and the Library Company of Philadelphia. Drawing on the experience gained as part of the cataloguing procedures, Mr. Ulle quite ably selected the "broadsides" used in this paper. To date, brief sketches of twenty-one of the organizations have been completed; these organizational descriptions are available upon request from the PSHP.

The PSHP has expanded its list of organizations and memberships to include some 200 organizations, 4,500 memberships, and 3,200 individuals. These individuals have been traced to the four federal and three Quaker and Abolitionist censuses, but the data for this expanded data set have not yet been fully analyzed (see Appendix II).

34. Hershberg, "Philadelphia Social History Project," *op. cit.,* Appendix II, 384.

35. Membership lists from Bethel A.M.E. Church (an organization on our newly expanded list), St. Thomas African Episcopal Church, and First African Presbyterian Church provide the best change-over-time patterns for single organizations, but these particular associations are probably not representative of other voluntary organizations. Preliminary analyses indicate that the proportion of mulattoes in these churches tended to rise and fall with the changes in the percentage of mulattoes in Philadelphia's Negro population. See Francine Mitlitzky, "Mulattoes and the Negro Elite," unpublished ms. in possession of PSHP (January 1979).

36. Glasco, "Black and Mulatto," *op. cit.,* 26. Berlin notes that in the burst of manumission activity following the American Revolution, the free Negro population of the Upper South "grew darker" while its counterpart in the Lower South "remained light-skinned." Nevertheless, within both regions in this period, a higher proportion of mulattoes than blacks were free. In the District of Columbia, for example, despite a "shift in the character of the free Negro caste from brown to black," the free Negro population was "still disproportionately brown." Berlin, *Slaves Without Masters, op. cit.,* 49–50.

37. Glasco, "Black and Mulatto," *op. cit.*

38. Glasco develops this argument in his essay. See *ibid.,* 25–26.

39. Indeed, when an earlier version of this paper was presented to the Organiza-

tion of American Historians in 1974, a noted Negro scholar withdrew from the session when it was learned that it dealt not simply with social stratification, but with color.

40. Spear, *Black Chicago, op. cit.;* Frazier, *Black Bourgeoisie, op. cit.*

41. In some respects, the Garvey movement of the 1920s demonstrated this division. Marcus Garvey, a dark-skinned charismatic black nationalist, heavily attacked light-skinned American Negroes and explicitly aligned himself with his darker brethren. Although his support among the black masses did not emerge solely from the consequences of black-mulatto conflict, color stratification and differentiation within the American Negro community contributed to his appeal. For background on the Garvey movement, see E. Franklin Frazier, "The Garvey Movement," *Opportunity* 4 (November 1926), 346–48; E. David Cronon, *Black Moses: The Story of Marcus Garvey and the Universal Negro Improvement Association* (Madison: University of Wisconsin Press, 1955); Theodore G. Vincent, *Black Power and the Garvey Movement* (Berkeley, Cal.: Ramparts Press, n.d.).

13.   The Origins of the Female-Headed Black Family: The Impact of the Urban Experience

FRANK F. FURSTENBERG, JR.   THEODORE HERSHBERG
JOHN MODELL

The link between family structure and social mobility has been a topic of considerable sociological speculation. For some years now, there has been a running controversy among scholars working in the area of the family as to whether certain kinship arrangements are especially conducive to success in an industrial society. Specifically, a general proposition was set forth, principally by Parsons, that the most prevalent family form in this society—the nuclear household—emerged at about the time of industrialization in response to demands of the economy for a highly flexible, mobile, emotionally bonded, small kin unit. Parsons contends that extended family forms restrict social mobility by subordinating immediate economic motives to longer range familial interests. Strong commitment to kin, according to this line of reasoning, detracts from unqualified commitment to economic achievement, for its fosters a sense of collectivity rather than individualism, an emphasis on personal qualities rather than on general performance.[1]

Although the functional explanation for the family in contemporary Western society has a plausible ring, empirical support has been conspicuously absent. Indeed, many of the studies on the relationship of the economy, family forms, and social mobility have failed to confirm even basic assumptions underlying the evolution of the contemporary Western family:

An earlier version of this paper was presented at the American Sociological Association (San Francisco: 1973). It later appeared in the *Journal of Interdisciplinary History* 6 (1975), 211–33. Except for the updating of several footnotes, it is reprinted here without revision. The authors are indebted to the critical readings of Etienne van de Walle and John Durand.

1. several historical studies have cast doubt on the proposition that the traditional family in Western society was extended and nonnuclear in form in preindustrial society; 2. cross-cultural comparisons suggest that although the form of the family is changing in many societies in response to economic conditions, various family forms can coexist with industrialized economies; 3. relations with extended kin abound in contemporary society, indicating that the family is not so nuclear or isolated as was supposed in the classic formulation; 4. extensive kinship relations may promote social mobility by providing economic resources and social support not available in a small family unit.[2]

The evidence that runs counter to the classic formulation of the functional relationship between industrialization and social mobility is still inconclusive; nevertheless, it suggests that it is a sociological problem that bears further consideration. Until further historical data are assembled, there is little basis to select among the conflicting interpretations or to develop a more integrative theory.

In recent years, however, another even more compelling reason for gathering further information on this problem has arisen. As attention shifted in the 1960s from an undifferentiated examination of the experience of the "American family" to a more detailed inspection of the subcultural variations in family form, a bitter debate erupted on one aspect of the broad question of the articulation of economy, family, and social mobility. At the locus of this disagreement was the question of whether "structural defects" in the black family accounted for the economically disadvantaged position of blacks in American society. Even before and especially since the earlier writings of Frazier, the sociological writings on the black family were heavily laced with references to the destructive legacy of slavery, the missing male, and the matrifocal character of black family life.[3] However, Frazier's observations were amplified and extended in the early 1960s in Nathan Glazer and Daniel P. Moynihan's widely acclaimed book, *Beyond the Melting Pot* (Cambridge, Mass., 1964). While acknowledging the impact of prejudice and economic discrimination, Glazer and Moynihan, following Frazier, traced the current position of blacks in America back to slavery. They contended that the black family, weakened by slavery, could not withstand the pressures of urban life.

In reviewing the Glazer/Moynihan section of the condition of the black family in the nineteenth century, it is impossible not to be impressed by the absence of supporting data. Both the propositions that slavery resulted in a permanent deterioration of the black family structure and that family structure accounts for economic disadvantage are accepted uncritically. Several years later, the Glazer/Moynihan thesis was restated in the report on the black family that Moynihan prepared for the Johnson administration. In this later document, the argument is further amplified and family structure is accorded even greater importance in accounting for the current fate of black Americans:

> Obviously, not every instance of social pathology afflicting the Negro community can be traced to the weakness of family structure. . . . Nonetheless, at the center of the tangle of pathology is the weakness of the family structure. . . . It was by destroying the Negro family under slavery that white Americans broke the will of the Negro people. Although that will has reasserted itself in our time, it is a resurgence doomed to frustration unless the viability of the Negro family is restored.[4]

Needless to say, the Moynihan report has engendered a heated discussion of a number of crucial issues: what was the impact of slavery on the family structure of Afro-Americans? How does family structure shape prospects of economic success in American society? How do the answers to these questions contribute to our understanding of the potential effect of various strategies for ameliorating economic disadvantage? In a very real sense, these questions raised by the Moynihan thesis are specifications of the general problem of how family structure is linked to economic success in American society. Are certain forms of the family more or less conducive to social mobility in an industrialized economy? Specifically, is there reason to believe that the couple-headed nuclear family is better equipped to utilize economic resources and confer special advantages on their offspring than a non–couple-headed or nonnuclear family structure?

A few contemporary studies have explored the link between family structure and social mobility with largely inconclusive results.[5] The most penetrating historical studies have so far concentrated on questioning the link between slavery and black family structure.[6] As yet, little historical information has been brought to bear on the status of the black family relative to other ethnic groups and the economic consequences of family structure for people of different ethnic backgrounds. Thus, it is not even known whether sizable variations existed in the structure of families among various ethnic groups prior to this century, much less whether such variations influenced the mobility patterns of these different populations.

This paper examines how family structure and family composition varied by ethnic group in the second half of the nineteenth century in Philadelphia, the nation's second largest city. Our analysis is based on samples drawn from the decennial Federal population manuscript schedules for 1850 through 1880. The black sample consists of all black households; the white ethnic samples are drawn systematically from the whole number of households headed by immigrants from Ireland and Germany,

Table 1.   Household Structure by Ethnicity, 1880*

	Black	Irish	German	NWA
Nuclear	75.2%	82.2%	84.5%	73.1%
Extended	17.3	10.6	10.2	17.0
Expanded	7.5	7.3	5.3	9.9
	N = 2,949	N = 1,637	N = 1,766	N = 1,730

*The figures in this and the following tables refer only to households with children. Here and throughout tables, discrepancies in total percentage are due to rounding.

and by native white Americans. None includes fewer than 2,000 households for each census year.[7]

The Structure of the Household. Although our information does not reach back into the early nineteenth century, it does lend further support to the position that complex households were less common than simple nuclear structures, at least in one major urban area.[8] When we examined the 1880 data from Philadelphia, several interesting observations came to light. First, considering only those families in which a child was present, more than three-fourths of the households in Philadelphia consisted of nuclear families, that is, families comprised of parents and children with no other relatives present in the home. Of greatest significance is our finding that only minor variations exist among the four ethnic groups (Table 1). Blacks and native whites were slightly less likely to reside in nuclear households than the Irish and German, probably in large measure because the latter groups —more recent immigrants to Philadelphia—had less time for extended kin to develop in this country.

Extended families were the second most common household arrangement. Approximately 14 percent of the sample resided in three-generation families, a figure somewhat greater than the proportion in the current census of Philadelphia. Again we find little variation among the different ethnic groups in the proportion of extended households. Blacks had the highest proportion (17.3 percent); the lowest were German immigrants, of whom 10.2 percent were residing in three-generation families. Expanded families made up only 7 percent of the households. Again, no conspicuous differences appear among ethnic groups. In particular, blacks were about as likely as other ethnic groups to be organized in complex households, and the patterns between the blacks and native white Americans are almost identical. Thus, whatever the benefits or liabilities of the nuclear family in promoting ecnomic mobility, the household structure cannot explain the differential patterns of social mobility which emerge in the latter part of the nineteenth century.

Changes in Household Structure over Time. Of course, it is possible that, by 1880, many changes had already taken place in the structure of the family, that our snapshot was taken after the action occurred. In particular, one might speculate that it was too late to detect the damage done to the black family by slavery. Even if this were the case, it would represent a finding of great worth, suggesting that the presumed effects of slavery were quickly erased and that the structure of the contemporary black family could hardly be traced in an unbroken line back to slavery. Our evidence, however, casts doubt even on this hypothesis. When the household composition of the black family in 1880 is compared with the structure of the black household in the ante-bellum period in 1850, we discover a remarkable degree of continuity. Virtually the same proportion of blacks were living in nuclear households in 1850 as in 1880. Indeed, if anything, there had been a slight decrease in nuclear households.

Other ethnic groups revealed a slight trend toward nuclearity; however, the increase in each case was only a few percentage points (Table 2). Apart from the information that these figures provide about the black family, the comparisons of household structure over time are significant in another respect. They offer little support for the proposition that household structure was changing, at least within the urban areas, as a result of increasing industrialization. This finding, again, seems to run counter to the widely held view that the American family evolved from an extended family to a nuclear family in response to changing industrial conditions. Of course, the findings here are limited, not only in time, but, more significantly, to an urban population. Quite possibly the impact of industrialization on family structure was accomplished by migration from rural America to the rapidly growing cities.

Our data do not permit a direct test of the effects of industrialization on the family. In subsequent analyses, however, we shall be able to examine the link between the occupational and family structure within the city of Philadelphia during the middle and latter part of the nineteenth century. Although not definitive, this forthcoming analysis should provide some clue to the effect of industrialization on the American family in urban areas of the country.

Ethnicity and Family Composition. Earlier we drew a distinction between household structure and family composition (referring to the membership of the family unit). Most contemporary research on the black family has been concerned, not with the issue of household structure, but with that of family membership. In particular, researchers have been preoccupied with the question of who heads the family unit. As we noted earlier, there is

Table 2. Household Structure by Ethnicity, 1850 and 1880

| | Inferred Relationships, 1850* | | | |
	Black	Irish	German	NWA
Nuclear	60.6%	60.6%	61.4%	45.6%
Extended	6.6	4.4	3.5	4.7
Expanded	32.8	35.0	35.0	49.7
	N = 1,739	N = 1,844	N = 1,564	N = 1,648

| | Inferred Relationships, 1880 | | | |
	Black	Irish	German	NWA
Nuclear	57.6%	67.1%	65.5%	52.4%
Extended	4.9	5.6	4.3	5.3
Expanded	37.6	27.2	30.2	42.3
	N = 3,206	N = 1,637	N = 1,726	N = 1,680

*The Federal population manuscript schedules of the United States Census became for the first time in 1850 an enumeration of every inhabitant of the nation, and recorded important information describing each individual within each household unit; but it was not until 1880 that the relationship of each member of the household to the household head was recorded. Researchers using the schedules for 1850, 1860, and 1870, therefore, must *infer* these relationships from the information which was included, such as surname, age, sex, position of listing in the household, etc. (Also see Appendix II.) The PSHP has developed a computer program to make these inferences; see Theodore Hershberg, "A Method for the Computerized Study of Family and Household Structure Using the Manuscript Schedules of the U.S. Census of Population, 1850-1880," *The Family in Historical Perspective, An International Newsletter* I (1973), 6-20; Buffington Clay Miller, "A Computerized Method of Determining Family Structure from Mid-Nineteenth-Century Census Data," unpub. M.S. diss. (Moore School of Electrical Engineering, University of Pennsylvania, 1972); Michael A. Strong, "Computers as Logical Decision Making Tools in Demography (with Interactive Assistance from the Human Demographer)," paper presented at the Annual Meeting of the Population Association of America (Philadelphia: April 25-28, 1979). For the analysis of the 1880 data presented in this paper, however, we have used the given relationships, as recorded in the 1880 manuscript census. In the 1850 and 1880 "inferred" tables, individual relationships which cannot be determined by the computer program (such as "Servant," "Brother-in-law") are categorized as "Others." The computer program assigns households with "Others" to the expanded category (households with relatives), thus considering all "Others" as relatives. The expanded category, therefore, is inflated by the number of households with only non-relative "Others" (boarders and servants). This can be seen by comparing Table 2 for 1880 based on "inferred" relationships with Table 1 based on "given" relationships.

reason to wonder whether this question deserves the prominence that it has received. Reserving our judgment on this issue, we shall in this section examine whether the family composition of blacks differs significantly from other ethnic groups before the turn of the century.

Households were divided into three categories: couple-headed households in which a male was head and in which his wife was listed as present in the home; male-headed households in which the wife was not listed as present in the home; female-headed households. This basic division does not take into account whether the households were nuclear or some complex unit. Furthermore, we again considered only those households in which children were present.[9]

Using this simple classification scheme, there is a noticeable relationship between family composition and ethnicity in the 1850 and 1880 census data (Table 3). German Americans are most likely to be living in couple-headed households, followed by native whites, closely in 1880 but less so in 1850. Irish households were somewhat less likely to be couple-headed, and blacks had the lowest proportion of families in which both parents were present. Thus, the contemporary pattern of a high prevalence of matrifocal households among blacks is visible before the turn of the century and before the arrival in the city of numbers of freedmen.

It is one thing to demonstrate the existence of this pattern and quite another to interpret its significance. In the first place, the magnitude of the difference can be seen in two quite separate lights. We could say that blacks are more than twice as likely as foreign and native-born white Americans to live in households headed by a female. Such a statement emphasizes the differential. Alternatively, we could point out that the great majority of all ethnic groups live in couple-headed households. Even among blacks, only one-fourth of the households were headed by a female. Moreover, among the various ethnic groups there is a difference of only 17 percentage points between the group with the lowest proportion of female-headed households—the German Americans—and that with the highest, black Americans. Obviously, this characterization tends to minimize the differences by underscoring the similarities. The only reasonable way of resolving this issue of interpretation is to delve further into the source of these differences. To us, their significance is to be found more in how they came about than in their magnitude.

Contemporary research on female-headed families has demonstrated the existence of a strong link between economic status and family composition. Male absence is far more prevalent in the lower class than in the middle class. Accordingly, differences in female-headedness between blacks and

Table 3.   Family Composition by Ethnicity, 1850 and 1880

| | Inferred Headship, 1850* | | | |
	Black	Irish	German	NWA
Female Head	22.5%	13.4%	3.3%	13.3%
Male Head	6.0	7.2	3.2	4.0
Couple Head	71.5	79.4	93.5	82.6
	N = 1,739	N = 1,844	N = 1,564	N = 1,648
	Given Headship, 1880			
	Black	Irish	German	NWA
Female Head	25.3%	12.7%	8.3%	13.6%
Male Head	5.9	7.5	5.3	6.2
Couple Head	68.8	79.8	86.5	80.2
	N = 2,949	N = 1,637	N = 1,766	N = 1,730

*Although inferring household *structure* by computer is difficult, inferring household *headship* is simple and certain. Results derived by such an inference are almost exactly those found from "given" relationships. Were we to use "inferred" figures for headship in 1880, the percentage of female heads would be 24.5, 12.6, 8.5, and 11.5 for the blacks, Irish, Germans, and native whites, respectively.

whites diminish sharply under conditions of economic parity. This finding has caused many to question the position that variations in family composition can be traced to divergent subcultural standards. In many respects the argument that the roots of the black matrifocal family are to be found in slavery represents an extension of the subcultural argument, and the same criticisms that pertain to the subcultural explanation can be applied historically.

New historical studies provide compelling reason to question the destructive impact which slavery allegedly had on the black family. One of the major conclusions reached by econometric historians Fogel and Engerman is that the slave family was considerably stronger than has been believed. Further evidence which challenges the standing interpretation comes from research conducted by Gutman, whose data are consistent with conclusions reached by Fogel and Engerman. In ground-breaking essays, Gutman examined "the family patterns of those Negroes closest in time to actual chattel slavery," and did not find "instability," "chaos," or "disorder." Instead, in fourteen varied Southern cities and counties between 1865 and 1880, Gutman found viable two-parent households ranging from 70 to 90 percent. The empirical picture presented here is staggering. Gutman's data make clear that the vast majority of black families were headed by both parents, and they convincingly contradict the view that slavery "destroyed" the black family.[10]

The data for Philadelphia, moreover, are consistent with the findings of Gutman, and Fogel and Engerman. We know from unique information on status-at-birth reported in a Quaker census of Philadelphia blacks in 1847 that only 10 percent of all of the city blacks had been born slaves. More importantly, however, these ex-slaves were *more* likely than the freeborn to have two-parent households. However unrepresentative of all slaves the ex-slaves in Philadelphia's population may have been, direct contact with slavery cannot explain the degree of matrifocality that existed at mid-century.[11] In 1880, one out of every two Philadelphia blacks had been born in the South. Although it is impossible to know with absolute certainty who among these immigrants had been freeborn or slaveborn, place of birth constitutes a plausible proxy for ex-slave status, especially when considered in conjunction with illiteracy.[12] Therefore, if the slavery argument is valid, this segment of the population should account for a disproportionate share of the female-headed households. Yet this, in fact, was *not* the case: Southern–born illiterate blacks were *less* likely than their Northern–born counterparts to have female-headed families (Table 4).

Family Composition and Economic Condition. In place of the subcultural "legacy of slavery" explanation for disorganization in the black family,

Table 4. Black Family Composition by Literacy and Place of Birth, 1880*

| | | Literate | | | Illiterate | |
| | | Other | | | Other | |
	Pa.	North	South	Pa	North	South
Female Head	25.8%	23.4%	18.3%	46.9%	47.9%	31.9%
Male Head	6.6	4.4	5.3	3.5	4.2	6.6
Couple Head	67.5	72.2	76.4	49.7	47.9	61.5
	N = 798	N = 158	N = 1,103	N = 143	N = 48	N = 636

*Literacy and place of birth refer to the household head.

we wish to argue for the primacy of urban economic and demographic factors. The vast majority of Philadelphia's blacks faced a life of abject poverty. Job discrimination was ubiquitous in the economy. Of every ten black males in the labor force, eight worked at unskilled jobs; the comparable figure for the Irish was five, and for the Germans and native whites fewer than two (see Table 5). When converted to wages and yearly income, these figures bear stark testimony to the difficulty black men faced in attempting to raise and provide for their families. Although there is some disagreement over the amount of a subsistence income for families in 1880, it is quite clear that unskilled laborers were faced with a serious shortfall.[18] In such grim economic circumstances, the conditions for the maintenance of stable family life were at best precarious.

These economic circumstances bear a direct and powerful relationship to the incidence of female-headed families. This can be seen in Table 6A, which relates wealth (real and personal property holdings) to family composition. Wealth data are not reported in the manuscript schedules for 1880, but they are for 1870. In that year, as in 1880, a greater percentage of

Table 5. Occupational Structure by Ethnicity, 1880

| | (For Males 18 Years and Older) | | | |
	Black	Irish	German	NWA
Professional High White Collar	1.1%	1.6%	1.6%	5.1%
Proprietary* Low White Collar	4.4	13.4	17.5	27.8
Skilled	13.7	31.5	59.7	45.3
Unskilled	79.2	50.1	15.3	17.2
	N = 8,700	N = 36,333	N = 25,172	N = 90,756

*Percentages do not add up to 100; the missing percentages—1.6, 3.5, 5.9, and 4.6—for the four groups, respectively, represent a category of ambiguous occupational designations such as "liquor store." Based on other characteristics of this category, we suspect that such individuals were in fact proprietors and should be added to the "proprietary" category.

Table 6. Proportion of Household Heads Female, by Ethnicity and Wealth, 1870*

Wealth $	Black	Irish	German	NWA
A. All Households with Children				
0	31.2 (1,414)	21.3 (889)	9.6 (616)	18.8 (674)
100–199	20.2 (129)	15.9 (113)	8.3 (96)	16.7 (96)
200–299	18.7 (91)	12.9 (101)	4.5 (132)	8.3 (157)
300–499	14.6 (48)	10.7 (75)	3.2 (156)	10.6 (179)
500–999	8.3 (72)	9.3 (75)	3.7 (189)	10.5 (143)
1,000+	17.0 (206)	10.6 (378)	3.5 (633)	12.8 (695)
All	27.1 (1,962)	16.9 (1,636)	5.9 (1,825)	14.3 (1,946)
B. Households with Children Headed by 30–39 Year Olds				
0	25.8 (395)	18.1 (282)	6.1 (212)	14.2 (211)
100–199	11.1 (36)	5.7 (35)	5.4 (37)	9.1 (33)
200–299	8.0 (25)	7.9 (38)	0 (54)	6.9 (58)
300–499	7.1 (14)	4.8 (21)	0 (43)	3.4 (58)
500–999	15.0 (20)	0 (22)	1.5 (65)	8.1 (62)
1,000+	6.3 (32)	2.3 (86)	3.5 (172)	10.1 (178)
All	21.8 (522)	12.5 (488)	3.8 (583)	10.3 (600)

*Wealth consists of all real and personal property holding reported in the census manuscripts. Figures shown are percentages of all households in a particular ethnic wealth category headed by women; the figures in parentheses are the Ns for these classes.

black families with children were headed by females (27.1) than for the Irish (16.9), Germans (5.9), and native whites (14.3). Female-headedness varies inversely with wealth. They were found far less often among families with property valued at more than $500 than among propertyless families: half as often for the blacks and Irish; two-thirds as often for the native whites; and one-third as often for the Germans. Table 6B focuses on a special group of household heads, those 30–39 years of age. By examining this group, we eliminate variations which arise from different age structures among the four ethnic groups—an important control because age structure is strongly related both to mortality and to the acquisition of wealth. The same inverse relationship between female-headedness and wealth is found in the 30–39 age group, but the strength of the relationship is far more pronounced.

Table 7 presents these same data in a different form, as the percent differences in female-headedness between blacks and each of the three white groups. Using different wealth categories Table 7B shows that the original variation observed between all black and Irish families with children—9.3 percent—is reduced: to 4.5 percent among holders of "any wealth" and yet further to 4.0 percent among holders of "wealth greater than $1,000." The same is true for the variation observed between blacks and Germans: the 18 percent separating them is reduced to 7.0 among holders of "any" wealth and 2.8 percent among holders of "wealth greater than $1,000." Most striking, however, is the reduction of the variation between blacks and native whites. The observed variation for all families is reduced to 1.2 percent among holders of "any" wealth, and for those owning more than $1,000 the relationship is reversed: native whites in this category were more likely than blacks to have female-headed families. Among the propertied across the entire ethnic spectrum, then, most of the variation in female-headedness is eliminated.

Although the economic data presented in Tables 6 and 7 describe the dramatic reduction of observed variation in female-headedness among holders of property, among the propertyless little or none of the variation is eliminated. There remains, in other words, a variation of 11.5 percent between blacks and native whites, and 9.3 and 18.0 percent respectively, between blacks and the Irish and Germans. There are two reasons for this residual variation. The substantial portion is accounted for by differential mortality which we discuss in detail below. The remainder is at least in part an artifact of the way property holding was reported in the federal population manuscript schedules. Census marshals were instructed not to record property holding in amounts less than $100. When we observe the category "without property," we are in fact looking at *two* groups: those with some property worth less than $100 and those without any property at all. This distinction is an important one to bear in mind. Table 8 displays data describing all black families with children in Philadelphia, collected in 1838 by the Pennsylvania Abolition Society and in 1847 by the Society of Friends.[14] Unlike the federal population manuscript schedules, these forms report property holding down to amounts of $5, and permit the study of variation in female-headedness along a rank order of wealth which includes 95 percent of all black families.

As with the 1870 federal census, female-headedness and property hold-

Table 7. Percentage Difference in Female-Headedness by Property Holdings Between Blacks and the White Ethnic Groups, 1870

	All Households	Without Any Wealth	With Any Wealth	With Wealth Greater Than $1,000
A. All Households with Children				
Black-Irish	10.2	9.9	4.8	6.4
Black-German	21.2	21.6	12.5	13.5
Black-Native White	12.8	12.4	4.7	4.2
B. Households with Children Headed by 30–39 Year Olds				
Black-Irish	9.3	7.7	4.5	4.0
Black-German	18.0	19.7	7.0	2.8
Black-Native White	11.5	11.6	1.2	− 3.8

Table 8. Proportion of Black Household Heads Female by Wealth, 1838 and 1847

Wealth Families With	1838 All Children	1847 Children 0-4	1847 Children 5-14
0-50	31.4 (570)	27.8 (298)	37.9 (610)
50-99	24.2 (241)	12.0 (150)	22.3 (350)
100-499	13.3 (420)	6.1 (181)	17.3 (567)
500. . .	8.5 (216)	16.3 (49)	10.6 (254)

Sources: 1838: Manuscript Census, Pennsylvania Abolition Society.
1847: Manuscript Census, Society of Friends.

ing are negatively related (see Table 8). Significantly, this negative relationship is visible for sums of less than $100, so that in 1838, for example, black families with $50-$99 of property were only about three-fourths as likely to be female-headed as families with less than $50. If, as we have good reason to suppose in light of the occupational distributions of the several groups, whites in the 1870 "less than $100" category clustered at its higher reaches, while blacks were far more prevalent at the bottom, then an unknown but sizable proportion of the black-white variation among the 1870 "propertyless" can be understood.

Family Composition and Mortality. Differential wealth thus accounts for the observed disparity between Philadelphia's blacks and whites in family composition. Contemporary studies of family life among the poor tend to stress illegitimacy, desertion, and divorce in understanding female headship, but in the nineteenth century a different consideration was the major link between female headship and the poverty cycle: mortality.[15] Today, family instability can be traced to the limited economic prospects that the poor recognize for themselves; in the last century sickness and death played the more important part.[16] Those most ravaged were the urban poor blacks, irregularly employed, segregated, and neglected in matters of public health.

Table 9 seeks to elucidate the contribution of widowhood to female-headedness among black families in Philadelphia in 1880 by examining the reported marital status of each female-headed household (for families with children). Though, as we have seen, females constituted a larger minority of all household heads among blacks than in other ethnic groups, Table 9 shows that for blacks as for the others, widowhood overwhelmingly predominates among female household heads. In each ethnic group, most of the remaining female heads are married women whose spouses are absent—presumably deserted in some cases, with husbands temporarily away at work in others. When we combine the separated, divorced, and single mothers, they constitute only one-fourth of all female heads. It is to widowhood, therefore, that we must attribute the excess of female-headedness among black families with children. This stands in stark contrast with today, when among blacks widowhood is overshadowed by separation and single parenthood as a source of family breakup.

Mortality, of course, increases sharply with age. Had the black population been notably older than other groups, their age distribution might account for the prevalence of widowhood. But this is not the case. Table 10 presents the composition of families by age, measuring age according to the female's age when she is present, and according to the male's age when she is not.[17] At every age, the composition of black families is different, with an increasing excess of widows. So fierce was the mortality among Philadelphia's blacks that at least a quarter of the married Negro women in families with children were widowed by their 40s.[18]

Table 10, however, goes beyond the obvious and the awful. We note, for instance, that despite the extraordinarily high incidence of widowhood among blacks, *widowerhood* is rarer among them than in the other groups. This requires explanation. The figures presented are on reported marital status as a given moment in time. Thus, the number of widows counted would (under ideal census conditions) be equal to the number of persons ever widowed, less the number who had remarried; likewise for widowers. Sex differentials in black mortality cannot account for so large a difference. One implication of these statistics is that black men could remarry with relative ease, but black women could not. Another is that a larger proportion of black men than black women who were left with children by the deaths of their spouses found it impossible or inadvisable to raise the children while unmarried, and left them with relatives or others.

Data on marital status by age strongly bear this out, and point as well to a sex ratio considerably favoring the marriage and remarriage chances of males. These imbalances can be seen in Table 11. Taking all blacks in Philadelphia as our base, and not just those living in families with children

Table 9. Reported Marital Status of Female Household Heads, Households with Children, by Ethnicity, 1880

	Black	Irish	German	NWA
Widowed	74.3%	79.5%	77.8%	75.0%
Single	5.0	1.4	3.3	2.5
Divorced	1.1	0.9	0.7	1.0
Married	19.7	18.3	18.3	21.5
	N = 747	N = 219	N = 153	N = 200

Table 10. Sex and Marital Status of Heads of Households (with Children) by Age of Head and Ethnicity, 1880*

Headed by:	Age of Head				
	Less than 30	30–39	40–49	50–59	60 +
Couples					
Black	84.5	77.2	62.0	44.8	31.0
Irish	90.7	93.5	83.5	75.5	39.5
German	93.4	90.4	82.9	71.2	45.0
NWA	93.8	92.5	84.3	73.5	44.2
Widows					
Black	4.2	11.4	20.8	29.1	35.5
Irish	1.1	3.2	8.6	10.3	16.8
German	2.0	5.4	9.9	11.4	19.3
NWA	0.6	4.4	8.8	10.7	25.1
Other Females					
Black	6.7	5.3	6.1	5.7	4.7
Irish	2.3	1.0	1.4	1.8	0.8
German	1.6	1.2	2.7	3.2	4.2
NWA	0.9	1.4	1.8	2.7	2.5
Widowers					
Black	0.1	0.8	2.7	4.6	12.5
Irish	0.4	1.3	3.0	7.3	26.6
German	0.4	1.3	1.3	7.1	15.8
NWA	0	1.4	2.8	5.3	15.0
Other Males					
Black	3.9	3.6	4.2	5.0	6.0
Irish	5.2	1.7	1.9	5.0	4.8
German	2.7	1.9	2.1	3.2	5.0
NWA	4.8	1.2	1.3	5.3	6.7
Ns					
Black	899	887	526	281	168
Irish	265	418	369	220	124
German	256	470	374	253	120
NWA	336	517	394	226	120

*Female's age for couples, widows, and other female heads; male's age for widowers and other male heads. Figures shown are percentages.

Table 11. Marital Status by Age and Sex, Blacks, 1880

	Married		All Unmarried		Widowed Only	
	Males	Females	Males	Females	Males	Females
15–19	13	143	925	1,434	1	9
20–24	426	986	1,147	1,574	8	79
25–29	929	1,206	806	947	44	158
30–34	939	937	464	577	41	207
35–39	970	839	333	549	52	288
40–44	641	513	211	486	62	293
45–49	425	325	124	397	47	285
50–54	376	257	114	453	48	338
55–59	196	144	78	251	45	207
60–64	184	74	70	275	43	229
65–69	101	45	36	174	27	147
70 +	114	43	91	397	70	340
Total	5,314	5,512	4,399	7,514	488	2,580

(for the former constitute the marriage pool), we find that by ages 35–39, more than one-fifth of all black women were living as widows. Overall in this age group, four in ten black women were, for one reason or another, not currently married; this is so for only a quarter of the men.[19] Black women generally married men older than themselves by an average of about three years; therefore, we should treat the next older age category as the most likely remarriage pool for widowed black women. By this reasoning, 35–39-year-old widows looked to remarry 40–44-year-old men. This group, however, was smaller to begin with because of differential in-migration by sex. Because they were older, because males generally suffer higher mortality, and because of the physically taxing nature of "nigger work," the pool experienced still further attrition. Very nearly half of Philadelphia's large number of widows, then, can be "explained" by their inability to find suitably aged mates.

Aggravating the situation even more is the fact that black males may have had more reason to leave the city than females when their spouses died, or to have placed their children with friends or relatives, rather than raise them alone on a scant and uncertain income. Women more easily than men could find jobs and at the same time support their children. (It is also possible that Philadelphia attracted an in-migration of widowed women. A detailed analysis of the widowed black population of Philadelphia, however, indicates that unlike native whites, black in-migrants who were widowed were, if anything, *less* likely at given ages than those born in Pennsylvania to be household heads, and among those who were household heads, less likely to have children.) Many of the female heads of families were employed as seamstresses and domestics, or were able to take in boarders, thus making it possible for them not to remarry. Unless female kin were available to serve as parent surrogates, men undoubtedly found it more difficult to remain unmarried, especially with young children. Finally, men had a further advantage in the remarriage market because they could more actively initiate a marriage contract. Women without means commanded little bargaining power and therefore were in an especially weak position to attract a mate.

We have chosen to accept as *prima facie* evidence the marital status recorded by census marshals a hundred years ago. We have not done so naively. We recognize the likelihood that at least some black female respondents may have told the census marshals what they thought they wanted to hear, explaining by "widowhood" the absence of a male household head, whatever the real reason.[20] But we can validate the plausibility of the claims of widowhood by reference to death statistics contained in other documents and to known patterns of mortality by age. Our procedure has been to construct estimates of joint survival probabilities for a hypothetical population of black couples, which will allow us to suggest, at appropriate levels of mortality, the likely, or "expected" proportion of widows among the once-married female population, assuming for the moment that remarriage is negligible.[21] Table 12 compares the "expected" proportions of widows at this level of mortality with that measured for the whole black female population of Philadelphia in 1880; we have also prepared a slightly more severe mortality schedule displayed in the same Table.

The findings are unequivocal. By far the greatest part of reported "widowhood" can readily be explained by the level of mortality among black Philadelphians. To be sure, there was some remarriage of widows, which would suggest a somewhat greater discrepancy between stated "widows" and the proportion expected by mortality alone. Table 12 shows a close fit at all ages between expected and observed widowhood, suggesting that a fraction of declared widows were not so, but rather were unmarried or deserted women hiding their actual condition from the census taker.

Variant Patterns in Family Composition. In bringing out the excess of widowed female heads among blacks, the data presented in Table 10 also reveal a persistent difference in headship by "other females," most of whom are married without spouse (Table 9). The proportion of "other female" headship for blacks is about 5 or 6 percent, unvarying with age. We have here what might be considered a variant pattern.

In our attempt to probe the source of this variant pattern, we examined marital status by age of nonwidowed female heads. Divorcées at every age represent an insignificant proportion of this group. Unmarried mothers,

Table 12. "Expected" Proportion of Widows Among Ever-Married Black Women, 1887, at Two Levels of Mortality, Compared with Proportion Recorded in the 1880 Census, by Age*

Age	"Expected" at South Level 3 Mortality	"Expected" at South Level 2 Mortality	"Measured," 1880 Census
25–29	7.2	14.8	11.5
30–34	14.1	21.6	18.1
35–39	21.3	28.7	25.4
40–44	29.1	36.5	36.1
45–49	37.5	45.6	46.6
50–54	47.0	53.4	56.5
55–59	57.8	63.5	59.0
60–64	69.9	74.6	75.3
65–69	81.8	84.3	76.2

*Figures shown are percentages.

although constituting almost a quarter of all female heads less than 30, virtually disappear at older ages. Separated women are at every age the largest proportion of nonwidowed female heads, but their numbers, too, decline with age. This decline cannot be explained by mortality alone. These patterns are identical across ethnic groups.

Had there been cultural support within the black community for female-headed families (whatever the reason), we should have found a growing number of families of this type with advancing age. Instead, they decline, doing so in the face of a remarriage market that offered them extremely limited prospects. In summary, the data provide no evidence for believing that Philadelphia's blacks valued anything distinct from what poverty and death often denied them: to raise their children in stable and continuous families.

Much of the speculation about the origins of the matrifocal black family has been uninformed by systematic historical data. In recent years, historians have begun to correct this situation. It is becoming increasingly clear with each new study that misconceptions about the past have resulted in certain erroneous interpretations of the present. The PSHP data indicate that the household structure in 1850, 1870, and 1880 was highly similar among each of the ethnic groups. Black families were just as likely to be organized in nuclear households, and, hence, were not more or less able to adapt to conditions created by industrialization than other ethnic groups. A somewhat higher proportion of black families were headed by a female than was true for other ethnic groups. However, we argue that a cultural explanation cannot account for this disparity.

In the first place, the great majority of black families were couple-headed. Second, ex-slaves were more likely to reside in couple-headed households. Third, when property holding among the different ethnic grouping was held constant, variations in family composition largely disappeared. Finally, we were able to show that economic status had a powerful effect on the structure of the black family because blacks suffered extremely high mortality and females with children faced difficulties in re-marrying. To the extent that the female-headed family appeared during this period, it emerged, not as a legacy of slavery, but as a result of the destructive conditions of Northern urban life.[22]

With a few important exceptions, students of black history have not adequately appreciated the impact of the urban experience. In part, this is because the institution of slavery has so dominated the history of Afro-Americans. Ever since the 1920s when justification for the low status of black Americans shifted from a genetic to an environmental interpretation, scholars have for the most part accepted without question the slavery hypothesis. After all, it followed logically that any institution as morally reprehensible as slavery also had to be destructive.

We do not wish to imply that the institution of slavery was *not* brutalizing and dehumanizing. Yet, one must not convert a sense of moral outrage into a monolithic interpretation of the black experience. Once we recognize that the matrifocal black family is a product of economic discrimination, poverty, and disease we cease to blame the distant past for problems that have their origins in more recent times. It was, and still is, much easier to lament the sins of one's forefathers than to confront the injustices of more contemporary socioeconomic systems.

NOTES

1. Talcott Parsons, "Age and Sex in the Structure of the United States," *American Sociological Review* 7 (1942), 604–16; Parsons and Robert.F. Bales, *Family, Socialization and the Interaction Process* (New York, 1965), ch. 1.

2. Ethel Shanas and Gordon F. Strieb (eds.), *Social Structure and the Family: Generational Relations* (Englewood Cliffs, N.J., 1965); Marvin B. Sussman, "The Isolated Nuclear Family: Fact or Fiction?" *Social Problems* 6 (1959), 333–40; Sussman and Lee Burchinal, "Kin Family Network: Unheralded Structure in Current Conceptualizations of Family Functioning," *Marriage and Family Living* 24 (1962), 221–40; Eugene Litwack, "Occupational Mobility and Extended Family Cohesion," *American Sociological Review* 25 (1960), 9–21; Elizabeth Bott, *Family and Social Network* (London, 1957); William J. Goode, *World Revolution and Family Patterns* (New York, 1963). See also Michael Gordon and Tamara K. Hareven (eds.), "New Social History of the Family," special issue of *Journal of Marriage and the Family* 35 (1973).

3. E. Franklin Frazier, *The Negro Family in the United States* (Chicago, 1939).

4. Lee Rainwater and William Yancey (eds.), *The Moynihan Report and the Politics of Controversy* (Cambridge, Mass., 1967), 76.

5. O. D. Duncan and Beverly Duncan, "Family Stability and Occupational Success," *Social Problems* 16 (1969), 273–85.

6. Herbert Gutman, "Persistent Myths about the Afro-American Family," *Journal of Interdisciplinary History* 6 (1975), 181–210. See also Theodore Hershberg, "Free Blacks in Antebellum Philadelphia: A Study of Ex-slaves, Freeborn and Socioeconomic Decline," *Journal of Social History* 5 (1971), 183–209, also in this volume; Elizabeth Pleck, "The Two-Parent Household: Black Family Structure in Late Nineteenth-Century Boston," *ibid.* 6 (1972), 3–31.

7. About 4 percent of the city's population were neither black, Irish, German, nor native white. For a detailed description of how the samples were drawn, see Theodore Hershberg, "The Philadelphia Social History Project: A Methodological History" (unpublished Ph.D. dissertation, Stanford University, 1973), ch. 2.

8. For purposes of this analysis, a detailed code of family forms was developed. Families are classified into nuclear, extended (households of three or more generations), and expanded (households with additional relatives but which do not extend generationally). These family types are further subdivided into couple-headed, male-headed, and female-headed. This distinction allows us to look at the family composition within the three different structural forms. For each of these nine types, a further breakdown is made between those families with and without children.

9. In two recent studies on black family structure (Gutman, "Persistent Myths"; Pleck, "Two-Parent Household"), the proportion of female-headed households is misrepresented because the calculations include couple-headed households *without* children. We disagree with this procedure for three reasons. First, to include childless couples but not households with a single member biases the proportion of female heads substantially downward. Second, the assumption that underlies the association of the female-headed household with a set of negative social consequences is that the absence of a father adversely affects the socialization of the young. To include childless families, therefore, introduces an irrelevant component. Third, this irrelevant component has a downward bias because childless families tend to be younger and less likely to have experienced family dissolution. A further refinement might have been to remove from consideration those families where the youngest child in the household was presumably beyond the age of childhood socialization. Among the 1880 blacks, applying age 20 as the cutoff point would have removed almost 15 percent of the families from consideration. Such a procedure, however, would have affected almost exclusively the oldest categories of families, and would leave untouched the distinctions and trends treated in this paper.

10. Robert William Fogel and Stanley L. Engerman, *Time on the Cross: The Economics of American Negro Slavery* (Boston, 1974), I, 5, 126–44; Gutman, "Persistent Myths."

11. Hershberg, "Free Blacks," 192–204.

12. See Pleck, "Two-Parent Household," 18–19; note 3, above. Although there are problems in this approach, combining the variables of place of birth and illiteracy brings us closer to identifying accurately those blacks most likely to have been slave-born. There were slightly more female illiterates among both northern-born and southern-born black Philadelphians, but this difference was not at all of a magnitude to suggest that the relationships shown in Table 4 are spurious.

13. Eudice Glassberg calculates the subsistence income for a family of five in "Work, Wages and the Cost of Living: Ethnic Differences and the Poverty Line, Philadelphia, 1880," *Pennsylvania History* 66 (January 1979), 17–58. Unskilled workers rarely made as much as $400 a year. Using Glassberg's figures, the shortfall is about 40 percent. Most families were able to compensate in a variety of ways, which included working wives and children, the pooling of income in expanded and extended families, the taking in of boarders, etc.

14. See Hershberg, "Free Blacks," 184–85; *idem,* "Free-Born and Slave-Born Blacks in Antebellum Philadelphia," in Eugene D. Genovese and Stanley L. Engerman (eds). *Race and Slavery in the Western Hemisphere: Quantitative Studies* (Princeton, 1975), 395–426.

15. For evidence of the extraordinary mortality differentials by race (esp. in infant mortality), see the 1879 life tables for Baltimore and Washington (which had more blacks than Philadelphia, but similar mortality experiences) in U.S. Census Office, *Census of 1880*, XII: *Mortality and Vital Statistics* (Washington, 1883), pt. 2, 773–77. See also W. E. B. DuBois's excellent discussion of health and mortality differentials in Philadelphia, in which he lays the blame immediately on the ignorance of hygiene among the victims and on the uneven distribution of public-health effort *(The Philadelphia Negro: A Social Study* [New York, 1967], ch. 10).

Research currently underway at the PSHP utilizes the Philadelphia Register of Deaths for 1880–81 to study urban mortality. This effort will produce age-specific death rates for both whites and blacks and will allow us to assess directly the impact of mortality on household structure. For a fuller description of the research and accompanying citations, see Appendix II.

16. See Frank F. Furstenberg, "Work Experience and Family Life," in James O'Toole (ed.), *Work and the Quality of Life* (Cambridge, Mass., 1974), 341–60; Reynolds Farley, *Growth of the Black Population* (Chicago, 1973).

17. The same finding appears when, to avoid the clumsiness of measuring "age" of the family sometimes by the woman, sometimes by the man, we measure it by the age of the oldest child, as a proxy of how long the marriage has been established.

18. When all housholds, and not just those with children, are examined, quite the same white/black pattern of differences obtains.

19. This argument rests in the fact that the effective marriage pool for blacks was other blacks. See Theodore Hershberg and Henry Williams, "Mulattoes and Blacks: Intra-Group Color Differences and Social Stratification in Nineteenth-Century Philadelphia"; in this volume.

20. We would expect that among female heads with children, the proportion of widows would increase with the age of the youngest child of the female head, since (assuming no illegitimacy) the younger the child, the fewer the elapsed years since the female head's husband surely was alive. Trends along these lines are present but quite weak and irregular; they are, however, virtually identical for each of the four ethnic groups. If we have not in this fashion gained greater confidence in the literal meaning of census "widowhood," we have discovered that its meaning seems to have been similar across ethnic lines.

21. Mortality for "colored" persons (including negligible numbers of Chinese, Japanese, and Indians) for Philadelphia in 1890 and for the six years preceding 1890 are derived from registration materials tabulated in U.S. Census Office, *Eleventh Census, 1890* (Washington, 1895), IV: *Mortality*, 662, 1046–47. John S. Billings, who supervised the 1890 vital statistics volumes, noted that, as in the other 27 cities to which he devoted a volume, registration of deaths was "based upon certificates of deaths by physicians, [collected] under a compulsory registration law." The crude colored death rate in Philadelphia, 30.1, can be compared with the rate there for whites, 23.0, and with colored death rates of 32.9 in Baltimore, 34.0 in Washington, 34.6 in New York, and 30.9 for all 28 cities studied (U.S. Census Office, *Report on Vital and Social Statistics of the United States at the Eleventh Census: 1890, Part II— Vital Statistics. Cities of 100,000 Population and Upward* [Washington, 1892], 1–5). The age-specific figures, distributing the unknown ages, and taking the average one-year level from the figures for the six-year period, were then compared with linearly interpolated estimates for 1887 of the Philadelphia black population by age and sex, based on PSHP grid-square tallies for 1880 and U.S. Census Office, *Population, 1890*, II, 127. The age-specific mortality rates were matched with model life tables in Ansley J. Coale and Paul Demeny, *Regional Model Life Tables and Stable Populations* (Princeton, 1966), and a good match was found on ages 20–50 at South Level 3, a severe mortality regime where the high rate of infant and child mortality proved closer to the observed Philadelphia black mortality than did the West series tables, more often applied to American populations. Good matches were also found between South Level 3 and the black life tables centering on 1879 for Baltimore and Washington, cited above, note 15. South Level 3 implies an expectation of life at birth of 25 years; Level 2 implies 22.5 years.

22. This interpretation finds support in the statistics offered by Gutman, "Persistent Myths," above. Of all of the urban and rural communities that he studied, those with the highest percentages of female-headed households were cities: Natchez (30 percent), Beaufort (30 percent), Richmond (27 percent), and Mobile (26 percent), although the percentages for rural areas were all below 19 percent. These percentages, moreover, if re-calculated after childless households are removed (see note 9 above), may increase as much as 8 percentage points. The cities varied widely in their size, type of economy, and rate of growth, to be sure; nonetheless, some differential process must have been operating to generate these statistics.

PART V

URBAN AS PROCESS
and
HISTORY AND POLICY

It is fitting to close with "A Tale of Three Cities: Blacks, Immigrants, and Opportunity in Philadelphia, 1850–1880, 1930, 1970." Although an attempt to tie together the findings from all the essays in this volume was considered, such an approach was rejected as premature with so much research remaining to be done. Nevertheless, the essay is broadly synthetic, integrating results from those of our studies which share a common concern with urban ecology and its consequences.

In this essay, we return to the significant theme, *urban as process,* identified in the volume's introductory chapter. There we argued that if urban history were to be more than a rubric under which could be placed all things that happened in cities, it would have to clarify its conceptual framework. Such an effort could well begin by recalling that, above all else, cities are distinct environments. The challenge to students of urban history was to learn whether a wide range of society's social processes, behaviors, and group experiences were significantly affected by the particular urban environments in which they occurred—does urban matter, for what, and how?

"A Tale of Three Cities" demonstrates that the experience of a city and its diverse peoples are inextricably bound together. Since a major concern of our overall research is the experience of different immigrant groups, especially the factors that explain their differential integration into the economic mainstream of American life, we have chosen to conceive of the city as an "opportunity structure." Aware of the massive changes that our national economy has undergone in the last century, our conceptual scheme is based on the understanding that the local structure of opportunities reflected many of these changes. Change also characterized the waves of immigrants who settled in Philadelphia: the "Old" immigrants from Northern and Western Europe who came to the "industrializing" city of the mid-nineteenth century; the "New" immigrants from Southern and Eastern Europe who came to the "industrial" city at the turn of the twentieth century; and blacks and Puerto Ricans who came to the "post-industrial" city in their largest numbers after the Second World War. Thus, in simplest terms, we are observing the interaction of "structure" and "culture": the interplay between the extant urban opportunity structure—and the experiences, skills, values, and expectations that distinct immigrant peoples brought with them to the New World, a kind of human capital argument that encompasses the differing kinds and degrees of discrimination encountered by the various groups upon arrival in Philadelphia.

The following essay summarizes our initial findings. As the structure of opportunities changed, so did the fate of the city's distinct peoples. Each wave of immigrants to Philadelphia—the Irish, Germans, and British; the Italians, Poles, and Russian Jews; and the blacks and Puerto Ricans—had a substantially different experience. Structural conditions found in Philadelphia consistently explained a good deal of what happened to white immigrant groups. Racism considered as a cultural factor explained the experience of blacks in earlier Philadelphias; structural conditions in modern Philadelphia play a greater role than race in determining the experience of contemporary blacks and Puerto Ricans. Thus "A Tale of Three Cities" develops the *urban as process* theme by elaborating the factors that linked the experience of three temporally distinct waves of immigrants to the distinct structure of opportunities that existed in Philadelphia at three points in the city's historical economic development.

"A Tale of Three Cities" is the first PSHP essay to consciously address a matter of contemporary policy significance and demonstrate how systematic historical analysis can affect the range of choices currently available to policy makers. Determining whether the black experience was unique, or similar to that of earlier white immigrant groups, is central to the debate over whether blacks should be the beneficiaries of special compensatory legislation in the present. The essay examines two explanations of the socioeconomic differentials that characterize blacks and whites today. To examine the "Bootstraps" explanation, the experience of earlier white immigrants is compared with that of their black contemporaries. To examine the "Last of the Immigrants" explanation, the conditions faced by blacks in modern Philadelphia are contrasted with those encountered by the "Old" and "New" immigrants in earlier Philadelphia.

What emerges is a message with clear implications for public policy. Supporting policy that counsels doing nothing for blacks because—as the "Last of the Immigrants"—they will experience the same process of economic assimilation that worked for earlier white immigrant groups is ill-founded. The opportunities provided by the emergence and dynamic development of urban-industrial capitalism are gone. Blacks may yet make it in American life; government programs and the private sector may ultimately offer ways for their inclusion in the benefits of corporate capitalism, but it is unlikely that blacks will make it following the same paths as their earlier white counterparts. Given the structure of the contemporary economy, this process cannot be repeated. As snakes shedding their skins, Philadelphia and older Eastern and Mid-Western cities are undergoing major transformations in their economic bases. The old urban-industrial order appears to be dying. Hindsight enables us to see clearly what life in these cities consisted of for earlier immigrants; it is far less clear what the new cities will be like and who will benefit from the changes.[1]

In *The Declining Significance of Race,* William J. Wilson argues that the history of black America "is a movement from economic racial oppression experienced by virtually all blacks to economic subordination for the black underclass." The circumstances of the black poor, in other words, are deteriorating not because of their race, but because of their vulnerability to unemployment, declining economic opportunities in central cities where so many of them reside, and structural changes in the economy.[2] This argument is very close to that advanced in "A Tale of Three Cities," although Wilson distinguishes between two groups of black Americans while, in this particular piece, all blacks are treated collectively. Nevertheless, the tests to determine the general applicability of the findings and explanations in our study are essentially comparative. If racism is in fact declining today as a fundamental cause of black impoverishment, then proof should be found in two comparisons: with other blacks living in urban areas such as the Sun Belt where opportunities are expanding and with other "Last of the Immigrant" groups such as Puerto Ricans, Vietnamese, and Mexican Americans who have recently settled in older, depressed urban economies such as Philadelphia.

With this essay we thus explicitly embrace a new goal of our research: the purposeful study of history to shed light on issues of contemporary social policy. This new direction for the PSHP is manifested most clearly in its recent move within the University of Pennsylvania from the Department of History to the School of Public and Urban Policy. The new location is the more appropriate environment for the critically needed linkage of history and policy. The shift in direction for the PSHP emerges from a growing awareness, widespread among historians and historically minded social scientists, that contemporary social science literature, which provides the intellectual and scientific context for policy making, suffers from a terribly distorting ahistorical focus.

"A Tale of Three Cities" does not attempt to explain the multitude of changes that Philadelphia has undergone since 1850. A thorough history would have to consider many other topics. At least five deserve mention here. The first would deal with the evolution of the city's economic structure from laissez-faire through industrial to monopoly capitalism. The change over time from an economy composed of small-scale, family business to one of monopoly and corporate ownership implies a great deal more than significant shifts in scale. Although corporate ownership often leads to greater economic stability, for example, it also brings absentee ownership and decision-making where the needs of the local economy are rarely considered.[3] Second is the impact of the major exogenous variables: Philadelphia's relationships to the regional, national, and—of increasing importance—the international economy. The loss of jobs which hit the city so hard in the past decade cannot be understood in terms of a domestic labor market alone. Third is the changing role of education. As the economy changed so did the educational requirements of the workforce. Whether teaching necessary skills or providing requisite credentials, formal schooling played a critical part in the larger process. Fourth is the expansion of the public sector. Its extraordinary growth since World War II dramatically affected the economy. In 1949, the public sector accounted for one-fifth of GNP ($387 million); in 1977, it accounted for anywhere from one-third to one-half of GNP ($2 trillion), with most of the growth coming from state and local governments. These fiscal changes not only affected the nature of local opportunity, but made possible (for better and worse) the elaboration of the institutional state. Finally, the larger study would have to expand the unit of analysis from Philadelphia proper to the metropolitan area. Changes in transportation, production, and communication technologies, the emergence of the trucking industry, and new Federal highway, housing, and mortgage policies greatly accelerated the deconcentration of jobs and population to the surrounding suburbs; these changes make the SMSA a far more appropriate analytic unit.

The following essay also previews some exciting conceptual and theoretical future directions. Although our conception of the city as an "opportunity structure" is an abstraction, it finds material expression in urban ecological form. It is important to reiterate that the city's spatial patterning did not play a passive role—it did more than reflect changes in the industrialization process. It had a critical impact of its own. People live in the real world, not in scholarly abstractions. A distinct ecological form characterized each phase in the development of the city's "structure of opportunities." Both the nature of the urban economy and its ecological form—despite the fact that the latter is a manifestation of the former—*independently* affected group experience. Blacks who came to Philadelphia after the Second World War, for example, settled not only in a city whose economy offered limited opportunities, but in segregated neighborhoods that no longer had an adequate number of jobs. In other words, it is crucial to consider both *when* a group arrived in the city and *where* on the urban plane it chose to or—in the case of blacks—had to settle. To understand fully the urban dimensions of the industrialization process, we must consider more than the kinds of jobs, housing, and transportation facilities that existed at given points in historical time. We must determine the actual spatial arrangements assumed by these fundamental building blocks of urban structure and how their distribution in space affected the experience of different ethnic groups.

"A Tale of Three Cities" calls into question our standing notion of the assimilation process by challenging the ecological underpinnings of a common ghetto experience through which all immigrant groups are supposed to have passed. Assimilation does not occur in a vacuum; it is not a process that operates "timelessly," independent of structural realities. The opportunity structure that greeted three waves of immigrants was itself enormously different at each moment in time. The data presented here demonstrate that "ghettoization" depended less on what immigrant groups may have desired than on the structural constraints imposed by the housing and job markets. "A Tale of Three Cities" also identifies, although implicitly and tentatively, the bases for a reformulation. Along with our sociologist collaborators William Yancey and Eugene Ericksen, both of whom are studying twentieth-century Philadelphia, we are now working toward a new theory of neighborhood stability and ethnic residential succession.

In the place of ethnic cultural stereotypes, the theory emphasizes the role of structural factors. Philadelphia's slums in 1930 emerged in areas that were heavily industrial in 1880, but which over the half century either lost their jobs or fell far behind the pace of industrial growth for the city as a whole. The slums of the 1970s emerged in similar areas and for similar reasons, although here the impact of the automobile and suburban housing was significant. The consequences of the impending energy crisis, in once again bringing people and their job sites in close geographic proximity, may make the city of the future more like the city of the past than anyone could have guessed as little as a decade ago. Thus the lessons we learn from history about how work, residence, and transportation were systematically interrelated will help us not only to understand the operation of basic historical urban processes, but also to choose wisely among the urban policy alternatives that will affect the fate of cities and their people in the critical years ahead.

NOTES

1. A new scenario for Philadelphia's future can emerge if the "energy crisis" continues. If it is understood basically in terms of increasingly high costs for oil, the energy crisis may have a rather dramatic impact on the future of Philadelphia and other older Northeastern cities. This explains the somewhat tentative tone of the above text. For some of the same reasons that Philadelphia's economy "took off" in the 1830s and 1840s, the city may enjoy a future that closely resembles its happier economic past. The high cost of oil will soon make the natural gas deposits of the Baltimore Canyon and nearby shale oil economically feasible; and Philadelphia still sits downstream from abundant anthracite coal deposits, a fuel which ceased being used because of cheaply available oil. In an era of expensive energy, transportation becomes one of the few components in which costs can be contained by locating closer to markets. Thus the city's other historic advantages make it a very attractive place for economic development: it has the nation's largest freshwater port; it is located within a 200-mile radius of one-quarter of America's population; it has a fully developed urban infra-structure, especially a regional railroad network and system of public transportation which, although in disrepair, will be far less expensive to upgrade than the cost of new construction; its labor force has large pools of highly educated, skilled, and unskilled workers; and its real estate is greatly undervalued. From this perspective, its 25,000 abandoned houses which are located close to the central city, which can be rehabilitated cheaply, and which are energy efficient row homes, begin to look like the proverbial blessing in disguise. The energy crisis, in short, may work to Philadelphia's considerable benefit.

2. William J. Wilson, *The Declining Significance of Race* (Chicago: University of Chicago Press, 1978). In neither our argument nor Wilson's do race and economics have to be considered as mutually exclusive explanations. Although we agree that the latter is considerably more important today, it is quite likely that race compounds the structural economic problems of contemporary black Americans.

3. This is the contemporary version of the historic theme of "privatism" in which the pursuit of private wealth and the public interest in Philadelphia diverged as the city's colonial economy gave way to industrial capitalism; see Sam Bass Warner, Jr., in *The Private City: Philadelphia in Three Stages of Its Growth* (Philadelphia: University of Pennsylvania Press, 1968).

14. A Tale of Three Cities: Blacks, Immigrants, and Opportunity in Philadelphia, 1850–1880, 1930, 1970

THEODORE HERSHBERG   STEPHANIE W. GREENBERG
ALAN N. BURSTEIN   WILLIAM L. YANCEY
EUGENE P. ERICKSEN

Significant differences in socioeconomic condition characterize the experience of black and white Americans. Why and how this happened, and what, if anything, should be done about it, are among the central questions of our time. Their answers have important implications for public policy. The crux of the matter can be put this way: were the burdens and disabilities faced by black Americans peculiar to their historical experience or were they simply obstacles which every immigrant group entering American society had to overcome?

Over the years we have come to see how the study of the black experience requires a broader context than gross comparisons with whites. Recent research has finally recognized that white America consists of diverse groups and that the study of their distinct experiences requires a comparative ethnic perspective. While this constitutes a major advance, what remains conspicuously absent from the literature—especially from the history of blacks in cities—is an awareness that the study of the black experience

This essay is based on the research of five authors. It originally appeared as "A Tale of Three Cities: Blacks and Immigrants in Philadelphia: 1850–1880, 1930, and 1970," in *The Annals* 441 (January 1979), 55–81. It is reprinted here with minor revisions. Beyond the grants already acknowledged that support PSHP research, we wish to thank the Center for Studies of Metropolitan Problems, NIMH, for their support of the research on twentieth-century Philadelphia (MH 25244), William L. Yancey and Eugene P. Ericksen, coprincipal investigators. A special note of thanks is due to Henry Williams and Richard Greenfield who assisted in the preparation of this paper.

necessitates an urban perspective as well.[1] Two distinct environments embrace much of Afro-American history: plantation and ghetto.[2] Once the most rural of Americans, blacks are today the most urbanized. Unfortunately, the histories that have been written treat the city in passive terms, as a kind of incidental setting for the subject at hand; in order to learn how the "city" affected blacks it is necessary to construct a history that treats the city in dynamic terms. Such a history would conceive of "urban" as a "process" linking the experience of people to aspects of the particular environment in which they lived.[3]

This essay will focus on Philadelphia's "opportunity structure." Such a term encompasses a wide variety of factors. Although much more than the hierarchy of occupations define an opportunity structure, the distribution of occupations is certainly central to the concept and may be considered its most important single attribute. For the sake of brevity, a vertical distribution of occupations will be used as a proxy measure for a group's place in the larger opportunity structure. The term "ecological structure" or the distribution in space of people, housing, jobs, transportation, and other urban elements is understood as the material expression of the opportunity structure. A city's ecological structure can thus be considered as a major determinant of differential "access"—to jobs, housing, transportation, and services. Finally, the term "structural perspective" encompasses both the opportunity structure and its ecological form and is used here to characterize our overall conceptual approach.

The experience of black and white immigrant groups, then, must be understood within a changing urban environment, recognizing the effects that such environments had upon different groups of people at different points in Philadelphia's past. The ecological "rules" that explain important elements of the white immigrant experience do not explain, for most of Philadelphia's history, what happened to blacks. Where blacks were concerned, the rules were inoperative, suspended, as it were, by the force of racism. Racism, particularly its manifestation in discriminatory hiring and housing practices, is the final dimension in our explanatory framework. The subsiding of the worst of racial discrimination in contemporary American life suggests that blacks will at last begin to be treated as other people. But the potential gains will not be realized because other offsetting changes have occurred simultaneously. Philadelphia's opportunity structure has altered radically for the worse, and the ecological manifestations of these changes leave blacks at a severe disadvantage: they find themselves in the wrong areas of the wrong city at the wrong time. Despite the lessening of racial discrimination, major changes in Philadelphia's opportunity and ecological structure prevent today's blacks from experiencing the successes enjoyed by the city's earlier immigrant groups.

Those who argue that the black experience was not unique offer two explanations for the socioeconomic differentials. The first of these can be captured in a single word from the metaphor most often used to describe it—"bootstraps." "Bootstraps" may be thought of as "opportunities." According to this point of view, blacks, like all immigrant groups, had equal access to opportunities. If they took advantage of these opportunities—that is, if they pulled long enough and hard enough on their bootstraps—they made it. The bootstraps argument claims that everybody had it tough and that the problems faced by blacks were no tougher than those encountered by other immigrant groups entering American society. The message of this view for contemporary public policy is obvious: if blacks did not have a uniquely discriminatory past, they do not deserve to be the beneficiaries of compensatory legislation in the present.

The second explanation, known as the "Last of the Immigrants," rejects the bootstraps view of the past, and concedes that blacks—in cities such as Philadelphia—were the victims of a peculiarly racist past. Such a concession, however, only documents how racist America was "back then," and suggests that time will be a sufficient remedy. As late as 1910, the well-meaning holders of this viewpoint remind us, 90 percent of black Americans were rural and 80 percent were Southern. Of all American blacks ever to live in cities, the vast majority settled in them after World War II: thus, in demographic terms, blacks can be considered as the last of the immigrants. Although this explanation differs from the notion of bootstraps in its view of the black past, its implications for public policy in the present are identical. Special legislation to ameliorate the condition of blacks need not be undertaken today because the same process of assimilation through which European immigrants were integrated into the urban American mainstream will take care of black urban immigrants. Since the process of assimilation worked for other groups, it will work for blacks: all we need to do is stand by and give it time.[4]

The Assimilation Process

Unfortunately, viewing blacks as the last of the immigrants is inaccurate and, in its false optimism, may ultimately prove to be as pernicious as the bootstraps explanation. Assimilation is not a mysterious process rooted in the individual, but a combination of factors: opportunities available at a given time; housing stock; the nature and condition of the local, regional, and national economy; the number of skilled and unskilled positions available in the labor force; the location of jobs; the transportation facilities; the fiscal circumstances of the local government; and the degree of discrimination encountered. Nor is there much validity in dealing with the assimilation process at the individual level; every immigrant group has its specially gifted members who "make it" despite the barriers erected by the host society. The concern here is with the experience of entire groups, rather than the exceptionally talented few, and the focus is on the opportunity structure which affected all people and which regulated the degree of group progress.

The experience of blacks and immigrants will be compared at three points in Philadelphia's history. Although blacks were present in the city over the entire period, the reference to three cities reflects temporally distinct waves of immigrants to Philadelphia: the "Old" immigrants—Irish, Germans, and British—who settled in the 1840s and 1850s; the "New" immigrants—Italians, Poles, and Russian Jews—who arrived in the years between 1885 and 1914; and the "newest" immigrants—blacks—who came in their greatest numbers after 1945 (see Table 1).[5]

What happened to these groups depended upon not only what they brought with them from the Old World and the South—values, language, skills, urban or rural and industrial or agricultural experience—but what awaited them upon arrival in Philadelphia. It was not only that people with different backgrounds came to the city, but that the structure of opportunities that they found in Philadelphia was different as well; each time period represented a different stage in the city's urban-industrial development. And it was these differences that shaped a wide range of subsequent experience for each immigrant group. A full treatment of these differences would require discussion of a breadth of topics. This essay will focus on the changing opportunity structure and the residential experience of the black and white immigrants who lived in the designated three cities.

According to the accepted notion of the assimilation process, upon arrival in America urban immigrants settled in densely populated ghettoes among friends and neighbors of the same ethnic background. "With the probable exception of the British in the nineteenth century," according to Milton Gordon, "all such groups . . . initially flocked together in colonies . . . and developed a form of communal life."[6] A few, the most successful among them, were able to move out of the ghetto within their own lifetime, but for most others, integration into the fabric of the larger society was the experience of their children and grandchildren. Several generations were required to complete the process. This point of view pervades our culture; we find it embedded in our literature, film, and folklore. Its most recent and popular expression is found in Irving Howe's best-selling study, *World of Our Fathers*.[7]

Settlement in dense, ethnically enclosed, urban enclaves made sense. Indeed, "to have expected otherwise was absurd." It was seen as the logical

Table 1.   Ethnic Composition of Philadelphia: 1850–1970
(As Percent of Total Population)

	1850	1880	1900	1930	1970
Blacks	4.8	3.6	4.8	11.3	33.6
Ireland*					
Born	17.6	11.9	7.6	2.7	0.4
2nd		15.1	13.6	6.8	1.9
Stock		27.0	21.2	9.4	2.3
Germany					
Born	5.6	6.6	5.5	1.9	0.6
2nd		9.6	9.6	4.8	1.4
Stock		16.2	15.1	6.7	1.9
Great Britain†					
Born		3.8	3.6	1.9	0.4
2nd			4.8	3.2	1.1
Stock			8.4	5.1	1.5
Italy					
Born		0.2	1.4	3.5	1.3
2nd			0.9	5.8	4.0
Stock			2.2	9.3	5.3
Poland					
Born		0.1	0.6	1.6	0.6
2nd			0.3	5.8	1.8
Stock			0.9	7.4	2.4
USSR‡					
Born		0.03	2.2	4.5	1.3
2nd			1.3	5.3	3.2
Stock			3.6	9.9	4.5
Total Foreign					
Born	29.0	24.2	22.8	18.9	6.5
2nd		30.4	32.1	31.7	16.6
Stock		54.6	54.9	50.6	23.1
Total Population	408,081	840,584	1,293,697	1,950,961	1,950,098

Sources: Figures for 1850 and 1880 are computed primarily from Philadelphia Social History Project compilations of the United States manuscript censuses of population. In 1880, figures for Italy, Poland, and USSR are taken from published United States Census totals. See Department of the Interior, Census Office, *Census of Population: 1880*, v.I, "Statistics of the Population of the United States at the Tenth Census" (Washington, D.C.: U.S. Government Printing Office, 1883), 540. Figures for 1900, 1930 and 1970 are computed from published United States Census totals. See Department of the Interior, United States Census Office, *Census of Population: 1900*, v.I, pt. 1, "Population" (Washington, D.C.: U.S. Census Office, 1901), 780, 866–905; U.S. Department of Commerce, Bureau of the Census, *Census of Population: 1930*, v. III, pt. 2, "Population" (Washington, D. C.: U.S. Government Printing Office, 1932), 701–8: U.S. Bureau of the Census, *Census of Population: 1970*, v.I, "Characteristics of the Population," pt. 40, Pennsylvania—Section 1 (Washington, D.C.: U.S. Government Printing Office, 1973), 356.

Note: In 1880, "2nd Generation" refers to native born with *fathers* born in specified country. Native born with native fathers and foreign-born mothers are classified as native. In 1900, 1930, and 1970, "2nd Generation" refers to native born with *fathers* born in specified country or, if father is native, with *mother* born in specified country. If parents are born in different foreign countries, birthplace of father determines parentage of native born. "Stock" includes foreign born plus 2nd generation.

*Includes Northern Ireland.

†Includes England, Scotland, Wales.

‡Includes Russia, Lithuania, Estonia, Latvia.

response of the newcomers to the hostility of the native population and to the strangeness of white Anglo-Saxon Protestant culture at the societal core. "The self-contained communal life of the immigrant colonies served, then, as a kind of decompression chamber in which newcomers could, at their own pace, make a reasonable adjustment to the new forces of a society vastly different from that which they had known in the Old World." A piece of Europe was transplanted in the streets of America.[8]

The pervasiveness of this notion, however, did not rest solely on logic or cultural trappings. With the nation absorbing twenty million immigrants in thirty years at the turn of the last century, some scholars, particularly a group of sociologists at the University of Chicago, undertook major studies of the immigrant experience.[9] Their empirical observations corroborated those of the social reformers who were dealing with the problems of the immigrants, as well as those of the writers and artists who were capturing the immigrant saga in word and on canvas.

Residential Segregation

Most sociologists accept the view "that both immigrant and Negro migrants originally settled in segregated patterns in central areas of cities . . . ," and that assimilation was accomplished in part through ". . . a decreasing residential concentration in ethnic colonies."[10] Sociologists have maintained that the degree of residential segregation is an acceptable indicator of, or a proxy for, assimilation. An ethnically enclosed residential experience insulates a group from important mechanisms of assimilation, limits cross-cultural contacts that affect the socialization of the young, and has serious implications for subsequent experiences such as intermarriage, upward job mobility, and the formation of social ties. Thus, the lower the degree of segregation the greater the likelihood that a group is experiencing assimilation. The accepted notion of the assimilation process found what appeared to be scientific confirmation in the levels of segregation observed for Northern and Midwestern cities in 1930. Expectations based on the accepted model were apparently confirmed by the data: "Old" immigrants from Ireland, Germany, and Britain, who had arrived in America in the 1840s and 1850s, were the least segregated residentially (20–30); while "New" immigrants from Italy, Poland, and Russia, who came between 1885 and 1914, were considerably more segregated (50–60).[11] Here was proof—or so it seemed—that an assimilation process was operating in American cities; with the passage of time immigrants were being integrated into the mainstream. When the logic of this argument is applied to the high levels of segregation for urban blacks (70–80) observed in 1970, one is left with a comforting conclusion. With time, these latest newcomers will assimilate, as did earlier groups. The optimistic implications of this viewpoint for public policy are obvious: no legislation need be passed when a social process operates to generate the desired results.

Unfortunately, while the segregation scores are accurate, the interpretation is not. The data on white immigrant residential segregation are cross-sectional for 1930; when cross-sectional data are used to infer historical process they can distort history and lead to an erroneous conclusion. The low scores for the Irish and German immigrants—half the level observed for the Italians, Poles, and Russian Jews—are not indicative of change over time from high to low segregation, and thus proof of an assimilation process; rather, they are the *retention* of segregation levels experienced by the Irish and German immigrants upon initial settlement (see Table 2).[12] In other words, the low segregation scores for the "Old" immigrants, the higher scores for the "New" immigrants, and the highest scores for the blacks are not evidence for the existence of an assimilation process rooted in the individual and responsive to the passage of time, but are a reflection of changing structural conditions that awaited each wave of immigrants who settled in Philadelphia at three different points in time.[13]

The Nineteenth-Century City: 1850–1880

Immigrant ghettoes did not form in the nineteenth-century manufacturing city. In simplest terms, no supply of cheap, concentrated housing existed to quarter the thousands of Irish and Germans who poured into the city seeking work in the 1840s and 1850s. As the manufacturing center of America and one of the largest in the Atlantic community, Philadelphia's job market was a magnet not only for immigrants, but for large numbers of native whites from the surrounding countryside.[14] The rapidly expanding population, which doubled between 1840 and 1860, reaching 565,000 by the latter year, far outstripped growth in the city's housing supply.

Thus newcomers found housing wherever they could. Since the large homes which faced each other on the main streets were expensive, most new settlement occurred in the smaller, cheaper houses and shanties that sprang up in sidestreets, lanes, and back alleys. Boarding with other families was quite common; one household in four took in lodgers. Population expansion in the pre–Civil War years led to sharply increased density, and growth in general was characterized by a "filling-in" process which ensured socioeconomic heterogeneity within a geographically compact city. The Irish and German immigrants, 18 and 6 percent of the 1850 population, respectively, were dispersed across the face of the city.

Table 2.   Indices of Dissimilarity from Native Whites:
1850, 1880, 1930–1970 (248 Tracts)

	1850	1880	1930	1940	1950	1960	1970
Blacks	47	52	61	68	71	77	75
Puerto Ricans							
Stock						81	82
Ireland							
Born	30	32	28	32	29		
2nd		31					
Stock		31	21			24	28
Germany							
Born	33	36	32	35	31		
2nd		33					
Stock		34	27			25	26
Great Britain							
Born			24	23	22		
Stock			22			21	22
Italy							
Born			59	60	54		
Stock			58			47	48
Poland							
Born			54	55	46		
Stock			55			32	35
USSR							
Born			56	57	54		
Stock			53			50	52
Foreign							
Born	21	26					
2nd		25					
Stock		25					
Other Foreign							
Born		27					
2nd		21					
Stock		24					

Sources: Figures for 1850 and 1880 are computed from Philadelphia Social History Project compilations of the United States manuscript censuses of population. Figures for 1930–1970 are computed from tract-level data taken from the United States censuses.

Note: See Note for Table 1. "Stock" for 1960 includes foreign born plus 2nd generation which is defined as for 1900, 1930 and 1970. "Other Foreign Born" refers to all immigrant groups except Irish and Germans.

By 1880, when data are available to identify the American-born children of the immigrants, Irish stock were 30 percent and German stock 16 percent of the city's population. With these data, the residential patterns of the immigrants and their children can be reconstructed in detail. There were five identifiable clusters of Irish stock and one of German stock. However, only one person in five of Irish background and one person in eight of German background lived in such clusters. What is more, even in these areas that represented the heaviest concentrations of Irish and German stock in the city, each group composed only half of the population in their respective clusters.[15]

In 1850, the city's rudimentary transportation system—the horse-drawn omnibus lines which operated over mud and cobblestone streets—was irregular in service and prohibitively expensive for all but the wealthiest. Almost everyone lived within walking distance of their workplaces; indeed, for many at mid-century, home and work were not yet separated. Most blue-collar workers appear to have lived within a radius of half a mile of their jobs in 1850 with a median distance of two blocks.[16]

Most jobs were concentrated within the city's historic core. Half of all manufacturing jobs, which accounted for one male worker in two, and an even greater proportion of nonmanufacturing jobs, were found within a few square blocks of Philadelphia's downtown. Industry—the location of manufacturing jobs—dominated the organization of the city's spatial arrangements. Workers' residential patterns reflected the spatial characteristics of their industries. For example, the residences of workers in concentrated, centralized industries were clustered in or adjacent to the city's core; those who labored in dispersed industries lived scattered across the city.[17]

Industry was more important than ethnicity in organizing the city's residential patterns. Workers of different ethnic groups employed in the same industry had residential characteristics—segregation, clustering, density, and centrality—more in common with each other than with members of their own ethnic group. German leather workers, to choose a representative example of an ethno-industrial type, were distributed over space more like Irish or native-white leather workers than like Germans in other industries. Under conditions of limited transportation and housing availability, workers had more in common residentially with coindustrial workers than with those of common cultural background.[18]

Another way of making this point is to examine the socioeconomic and demographic characteristics of the Irish population who lived in ethnic clusters. If ethnicity rather than industry were determining the organization of residence, the Irish in these areas should have resembled each other; the areas should have been similar pieces from a common cultural nucleus that was prevented from forming by the state of the housing market. Yet, when the areas are empirically examined, they turn out to be thoroughly distinct from each other. The characteristics of the Irish in each of the five clusters match the industrial opportunities available there; thus they differed markedly in occupational structure, unemployment rates, property-holding, age and sex structure, household and family types.[19]

The only major exception to the above generalizations were blacks. They were marginal to the rapidly industrializing urban economy of this period, and were considerably more segregated than white immigrants. They had few manufacturing jobs, even though they lived within easy access to more

Table 3.   Distribution of Ethnic Groups by Accessibility to Manufacturing Jobs: 1880 (Males 18 +)

	Blacks	Irish	Irish-2nd	German	German-2nd	Native Whites	Total
Mean Jobs within 1 mile	23,289	15,179	14,985	18,894	17,863	15,313	16,074

Source: Figures are computed from Philadelphia Social History Project compilations of the United States manuscript census of manufactures.

Note: See Table 1.

jobs of this type than any other ethnic group. Although the typical black worker lived within one mile of 23,000 manufacturing jobs—half again as many as were accessible to the typical Irish, German, or native-white worker—he was refused employment (see Table 3).[20] Racism proved more powerful than the rules that normally governed spatially conditioned job access. In the few instances when blacks did obtain manufacturing jobs, they did not live close to their white coworkers. Rather, they tended to live close to one another, regardless of industrial affiliation.[21]

It is fundamental to understand that, as the result of the new industrial order and the emergence of the factory system, all of this occurred within a context of widening occupational opportunity for whites. This is especially significant because the manufacturing sector has traditionally provided the first step up the occupational ladder to new arrivals to the city. Opportunities for upward mobility created by an expanding economy—which provided the bootstraps for the Irish and German immigrants—were so limited for blacks that they were virtually nonexistent. In 1847, for example, less than one-half of 1 percent of the adult black male workforce could find jobs in the economy's dynamic new sectors such as iron and steel and machine tools. During the antebellum years, blacks were not only excluded from the new and well-paying positions, they were uprooted as well from many of their traditional unskilled jobs, denied apprenticeships for their sons, and prevented from practicing the skills they already possessed.[22] Little changed between 1850 and 1880; although the number and proportion of skilled positions increased significantly with the economy's expansion, which benefited the immigrants and especially their American-born children, blacks experienced little or no progress (see Table 4). Thus, at least as far back as the mid-nineteenth century, the position of blacks in the city was unlike that of any other group.

Rapid growth in the years between 1850 and 1880 affected Philadelphia's ecological structure. The traditional view of immigrant residential settlement is firmly rooted in the original Park-Burgess notion of concentric zones, in which socioeconomic status of the population increases with increasing distance from the center of the city.[23] It is this model that de-

Table 4. Occupational Distribution of Males, 18 +, by Ethnicity: 1850, 1880
(As Percent of Ethnic Group)

	Blacks	Irish	German	Foreign Born‡	Native Whites†
			1850		
High White Collar and Professional	1.1	1.4	2.6	1.8	8.9
Low White Collar and Proprietary	4.2	11.2	13.6	12.0	23.2
Artisan	17.1	42.1	67.3	49.6	57.0
Specified Unskilled	44.0	11.2	3.9	9.1	6.3
Unspecified Unskilled	33.3	33.9	12.3	27.6	4.3
Totals	4245	25389	10633	36022	51930
(Row %os)	(4.5)	(27.5)	(11.5)	(39.1)	(56.3)
Dissimilarity from all Native Whites†	67	34	18	26	—

	Blacks	Irish	Irish-2nd	German	German-2nd	Foreign Born‡	Native Whites*	Native Whites†
					1880			
High White Collar and Professional	1.0	1.2	1.7	1.9	1.8	1.5	5.5	4.6
Low White Collar and Proprietary	6.6	18.3	22.4	23.6	26.0	20.5	33.7	31.2
Artisan	14.0	31.8	43.5	57.9	54.0	42.6	42.7	43.8
Specified Unskilled	52.2	19.5	18.4	10.5	13.0	15.8	12.8	13.7
Unspecified Unskilled	26.2	29.2	14.0	6.1	5.2	19.7	5.3	6.7
Totals	9043	38035	21780	26780	12690	64743	105165	139635
(Row %os)	(4.2)	(17.8)	(10.2)	(12.5)	(5.0)	(30.3)	(49.3)	(65.4)
Dissimilarity from Native Whites of Native-White Parents*	60	31	15	16	12	17	—	—
Dissimilarity from all Native Whites†	58	28	12	14	10	15	—	—

Sources: Figures are computed from Philadelphia Social History Project compilations of the United States manuscript censuses of population.

Note: See Note for Table 1.

*Excludes 2nd Generation Irish and Germans.

†Includes 2nd Generation Irish and Germans.

‡Includes Irish and Germans only.

scribes a city with a low status core and a high status periphery, and it is in the low status core that the immigrant ghettoes are to be found. It is clear, however, that such a model did not fit the preindustrial city. In the preindustrial setting, transportation was poor and did not facilitate movement within the city. Since jobs and services were relatively centralized, the most desirable residences were those close to the center of the city. Thus the preindustrial model, postulated by Sjoberg, describes a city in which the most affluent live close to the center while the impoverished live on the periphery.[24]

In 1850, the residential pattern in Philadelphia could still be partially described by the preindustrial model. But in 1854 the City of Philadelphia merged with twenty-seven other political subdivisions within Philadelphia County, and the greatly enlarged city (it grew from 2 to 130 square miles) rapidly changed; consolidation led to the professionalization of the police and fire departments and the expansion of the public school system. But more importantly for what concerns us here, governmental rationalization facilitated the implementation of critical technological innovations in transportation and building construction. That, in turn, dramatically accelerated Philadelphia's transition to the modern form. Iron track was laid in the streets of the city in 1857; when the horse-drawn cars were hauled over the rail instead of street surfaces, the decline in friction made it possible to carry three to four times more passengers than had the omnibus. The effects of this transportation breakthrough were felt after the Civil War. The war brought boom times to certain sectors of the city's economy, but it retarded building construction as it accelerated capital accumulation. By the late 1860s the building industry, spurred by the new transportation technology, exploded in a surge of construction that continued into the twentieth century. The horsecar lines, which carried some 99 million passengers in 1880, led the way to residential and commercial deconcentration, while growth in the city's railroad network led to manufacturing decentralization; though the city's population more than doubled between 1850 and 1880, reaching 841,000 by the end of the period, the rate of building growth after 1870 far surpassed population growth.[25]

Population density declined; the average dwelling by 1880 (roughly 6 persons) contained almost one person less than it had in 1850. The modal housing type shifted from the freestanding or semidetached three and four story dwelling to the two story row home. Moreover, houses that previously were erected by carpenters on demand were now built by large contractors anticipating the form of modern tract development. Some 50,000 homes—one-third of the 1880 housing stock—were built in the preceding decade. The ratio of new population to new homes was 8 to 1 in the 1840s; by the 1870s it had declined to 4 to 1.[26]

The dramatic growth during the latter period did not result in a duplication of the spatial patterns that characterized the 1850 city; the decade of the 1870s can be considered the beginning of modern urban form in Philadelphia. The shuffling of the occupational universe brought about by the process of industrialization—the creation of jobs with new skills and the dilution of others, the emergence of bureaucracy and a managerial class—coincided with the city's ability to accommodate wholly new changes in land-use specialization. Not only did industry and commerce accelerate their carving up of urban space, but social differentiation and spatial differentiation proceeded in tandem. Social differences in work—wages, status, and work environments—now began to be mirrored in increasingly homogeneous residential settings. The supervisors and clerks who left the shop floor for woodpaneled offices now sought to leave their older heterogeneous neighborhoods for new residential areas where they could live with people more like themselves. The differentiation of residential areas along class, racial-ethnic, and life-cycle lines accelerated. The more affluent Irish and German immigrants and their children started to join native whites in an exodus from the city's center to new modern neighborhoods developing at its peripheries. Over the ensuing thirty years, large residential areas of cheap concentrated housing in the old city center were vacated, making room for the next wave of immigrants and ensuring that the residential patterns of the "New" immigrants would be far more segregated than those experienced by the "Old" immigrants.

The Early Twentieth-Century City: 1900–1930

The availability of cheap, old housing concentrated in close proximity to plentiful manufacturing jobs contributed to the considerably higher levels of residential segregation of the Italians, Poles, and Russian Jews who settled in the industrial city of the early twentieth century.[27] The forces set in motion in the 1870s proceeded apace, led by the tract development of the row house, and major changes in transportation technology. The trolleys were electrified in the 1890s, the elevated train and subway were introduced in the early decades of the next century, and the automobile made its appearance shortly thereafter.

The new means of transportation made it possible to open large outlying areas of the city for residential settlement.[28] Unlike building practices in major cities, Philadelphia's landlords erected few tenements. The row house remained the modal-housing type; in 1915, roughly nine houses in ten were of this architectural form.[29] The emergence of the streetcar suburbs and the row house ensured the continued decline in residential density. Despite an increase in the city's population to almost two million by 1930, the average density per dwelling fell to 4.2 persons. Philadelphia richly deserved its nickname as "The City of Homes."

The city's economy did not change dramatically over the half century between 1880 and 1930.[30] Its most salient feature remained its diversification. Despite the entrance of some new industries, most notably in the electronics field, Philadelphia's economy was characterized by the same range of activities found in the nineteenth century: textiles, apparel, printing, publishing, and foundry and machines. Two important changes were noticeable in 1930. First, although the number of manufacturing jobs increased 60 percent over the period, it fell as a proportion of all jobs (from 48 to 31 percent) and grew far less rapidly than did the population as a whole; second, changes in transportation and production technologies began to accelerate the shift of manufacturing activity from the city's center to outlying areas. The full impact of these changes, however, would not be felt until the 1960s and 1970s.[31]

The new occupational opportunities that emerged tended to be located in the economy's white-collar sector (see Table 5). By and large, expanding jobs were found in the professional, white-collar, or service categories; faced with discrimination, language difficulties, and limited educational backgrounds, few blacks and immigrants worked in these desirable positions. As a result, "New" immigrants tended to find their occupational opportunities more limited in this period than the "Old" immigrants had encountered in the nineteenth century; improvements in the overall occupational distribution of black workers during these years were at best marginal.

The socioeconomic differentiation of the city's space that resulted from transportation innovation, the decentralization of manufacturing and greater housing availability produced an urban form well described by the Chicago School model of concentric zones. At furthest remove from the center, in the streetcar suburbs, lived white-collar and highly skilled "aristocrats of labor"; these groups were composed largely of native whites and the successful descendants of Irish, German, and British immigrants. Although the automobile suburbs would not emerge until after World War II, roughly one person in seven in Philadelphia was sufficiently well-off to commute regularly to work by auto in 1934 (this is almost the same proportion of the workforce that could afford regular use of the horse-drawn streetcars in their "journey-to-work" in 1880).[32]

In the zones surrounding the manufacturing and retailing core lived the bulk of the working classes, largely "New" immigrants and blacks, roughly one-third of whom walked to work. In general, ethnic concentrations were located near concentrations of industrial employment.[33] This was particularly true of the Italian and Polish areas. Workers living in these neighborhoods were overrepresented in industrial occupations. Once again, the rela-

Table 5. Occupational Distribution of Males and Females, 10+, by Ethnicity: 1900, 1930 (As Percent of Ethnic Group)

1900	Blacks	Ireland	Germany	Great Britain	Italy	Poland	Russia	White Foreign Born	2nd Generation Foreign Born	Native White of Native Parents
Professional	1.6	2.8	3.7	5.2	3.5	0.6	2.0	2.5	4.5	7.5
Owners & Executives	1.5	5.6	8.6	8.3	7.0	3.7	12.6	8.0	7.1	9.6
Clerks & Sales	1.0	8.9	8.6	10.4	1.6	2.3	6.9	4.2	13.6	17.4
Trade & Transportation	10.8	11.5	7.0	7.0	6.4	4.4	7.5	6.9	9.9	10.3
Manufacturing	8.2	40.2	54.3	56.2	32.6	55.5	62.8	47.3	49.2	40.4
Domestic and Personal Service	54.1	18.0	11.1	8.2	12.4	4.8	4.5	17.4	8.9	8.8
Laborers	21.6	10.7	4.0	3.2	34.8	25.9	3.0	11.0	4.6	3.4
Agriculture	0.6	1.0	1.0	0.9	1.4	1.4	0.4	1.2	0.7	1.1
Other	0.6	1.3	1.5	0.6	0.3	1.4	0.3	1.5	1.5	1.5
Dissimiarity from Native-White Parents*	64	18	17	16	35	38	25	23	10	—

1930	Blacks	White Foreign Born	Total Native White
Professional	2.4	3.9	8.5
Owners and Executives	1.5	13.6	8.6
Clerks and Sales	2.6	9.3	27.8
Trade and Transportation	17.1	7.9	9.3
Manufacturing	12.6	42.8	33.7
Domestic and Personal Service	43.4	12.4	6.0
Laborers	17.6	7.3	2.5
Agriculture	0.6	0.9	0.4
Other	2.1	2.0	3.2
Totals	118890	203692	565481
(Row %)	(13.4)	(22.9)	(63.7)
Dissimilarity from all Native Whites†	61	26	—

Sources: Figures are computed from published United States Census totals. See Department of the Interior, United States Census Office, *Census of Population: 1900*, V.II, pt. II, "Population" (Washington, D.C.: U.S. Census Office, 1902), 583, 585; U.S. Department of Commerce, Bureau of the Census, *Census of Population: 1930, v. IV*, "Population" (Washington, D.C.: U.S. Government Printing Office, 1933), 1412–15.

Note: See Note for Table 1. *Excludes 2nd Generation. †Includes 2nd Generation.

tionships between the occupational distribution of immigrant groups and the location of their jobs and residences can be seen.[34] The principal exception were Russian Jews who, after initial settlement in South Philadelphia, established neighborhoods in the nonindustrial streetcar suburbs in the west and northwestern areas of the city. Workers here were disproportionately found in wholesale and retail rather than industrial jobs.[35]

By 1930 native whites and "Old" immigrants had moved into better jobs and were able to use their greater income to ensure more housing choice; they lived in many different areas of the city characterized by greater housing value and distance from the center. As a result, they were less segregated. The relationship between occupational segregation and residential segregation was a close one. The data suggest that the segregation of "newer" immigrants was not complete because their occupational segregation was not complete; and, as in the nineteenth century, work location took precedence over the desire to live in an ethnic neighborhood in the residential location decision.[36]

Blacks again stand in sharp contrast. Although they continued to live in and near areas characterized by high industrial concentrations, blacks were excluded from industrial work. Although 80 percent of the blacks in the city lived within one mile of 5,000 industrial jobs, less than 13 percent of the black workforce found gainful employment in manufacturing. Blacks earned their livelihood as best they could, concentrating as they had in the last century in menial, domestic, and largely unskilled low-paying occupations (see Tables 5 and 6).[37]

The Modern City: 1970

Modern Philadelphia bears little resemblance to earlier periods. Technological change has continued to alter urban form and the means of crossing its increasingly inhabited spaces. Automobile suburbs have emerged in all directions, and a wide range of choice characterizes the housing market. Philadelphia's population peaked in 1950 at 2.1 million and was, in 1970, exactly as it had been in 1930: 1.95 million. Population density, however, continued its decline, reaching three persons per dwelling in 1970—almost exactly half of what it had been in 1850.

Significant changes affected the city's economy. Some 75,000 manufacturing jobs were lost between 1930 and 1970, and the appearance of new jobs in the service sectors have not made up the loss.[38] Indeed, between 1970 and 1978 Philadelphia lost an additional 130,000 jobs, over 80,000 of which were in the manufacturing sector. In this regard, Philadelphia's experience resembles that of many older industrial cities in the Northeast.

Table 6.   Location of Ethnic Populations by Distance from City Center and Access to Industrial Jobs: 1930 (Percent of Foreign Stock Living in Census Tract with the Following Characteristics)

	Within 3 Miles of City Center	Within 1 Mile of 5,000 or More Industrial Jobs	Of Those Who Are Within 3 Miles of City Hall, Percent with Access to 5,000 or More Industrial Jobs	Of Those Who Are Beyond 3 Miles of City Hall, Percent with Access to 5,000 or More Industrial Jobs
British	.305	.614	.816	.520
Irish	.411	.610	.791	.483
German	.336	.633	.838	.529
Polish	.404	.815	.943	.724
Russian	.565	.537	.778	.223
Italian	.794	.714	.801	.627
Blacks	.786	.799	.882	.489
Native Whites	.393	.593	.803	.472
Total	.469	.643	.829	.473

Source: Figures are computed from tract-level data taken from the United States Census.

Note: See Note for Table 1.

Large manufacturing employers have abandoned the city for regions with lower taxes and a workforce of nonunionized labor. The location of the remaining manufacturing activity has changed significantly. The earlier shift in production technology from coal and steam to electricity, combined with important changes in transportation technology in the post–World War II years, produced a marked decentralization of manufacturing jobs. The advent of the interstate highway system connecting with urban expressways—and the emergence of the trucking industry—has led to the suburbanization of manufacturing activity in industrial parks in the surrounding SMSA (Standard Metropolitan Statistical Area). Of every ten manufacturing jobs in the city, the three-mile ring from the city's center held nine jobs in 1880, six in 1930, and four in 1970 (see Table 7).

These changes have had important consequences for Philadelphia's blacks—the city's most recent immigrants. Their numbers increased from 221,000 in 1930 to 654,000 in 1970, and their proportion of the city's population increased from one-tenth to one-third. Today's blacks inherit the oldest stock of deteriorated housing once inhabited by two earlier waves of immigrants, but the jobs that once were located nearby and that provided previous newcomers with avenues for upward mobility are gone. Precisely at the moment in time when the worst of the racist hiring practices in industry appear to have abated, the most recent black immigrants find themselves at considerable remove from the industrial jobs that remain and thus are unable to repeat the essential experience of earlier white im-

Table 7. Percent Manufacturing Jobs at Given Distances (in Miles) from Center of Philadelphia: 1850–1970

Distance	1850*			1880†			1930‡			1970‡		
	#	%	Cum%	#	%	Cum%	#	%	Cum%	#	%	Cum%
0–0.99	30,366	60.9	60.9	78,111	47.2	47.2	52,794	18.8	18.8	32.380	15.7	15.7
1.00–1.99	15,576	31.3	92.2	44,848	27.1	74.3	62,062	22.1	40.9	26,812	13.0	28.7
2.00–2.99	1353	2.7	94.9	20,521	12.4	86.7	48,582	17.3	58.2	23,305	11.3	40.0
3.00–3.99	192	0.4	95.3	4,634	2.8	89.5	39,596	14.1	72.3	31,143	15.1	55.1
4.00–4.99	387	0.8	96.1	3,806	2.3	91.8	42,404	15.1	87.4	37,536	18.2	73.3
5.00+	1959	3.9	100.0	13,570	8.2	100.0	35,384	12.6	100.0	55,067	26.7	100.0
Total Jobs:	49,833			165,489			280,823			206,243		

Sources: Figures for 1850 and 1880 are computed from Philadelphia Social History Project compilations of the United States manuscript censuses of manufactures. Figures for 1930 and 1970 are computed from tract-level data taken from the Pennsylvania Industrial Directory.

*Center is 3rd and Market.

†Center is 7th and Market.

‡Center is 14th and Market.

migrants. When understood in light of changes in the city's economy as a whole, especially the decline of manufacturing activity and the demand for unskilled labor, it is plain to see that blacks in 1970 Philadelphia are faced with a very different set of circumstances from those that existed in the nineteenth and early twentieth centuries.[39]

The uniqueness of the black experience can be understood in yet another way. Blacks have always been the most segregated group in Philadelphia; this was true in the years 1850–1880 when blacks constituted but 4 percent of the city's population; in the years 1900–1930 when they were roughly 8 to 12 percent; and in 1970, when 33 percent of the city was black. Thus population size alone cannot explain their consistently higher levels of segregation. Indeed, despite the fact that smaller groups requiring less housing are often the most segregated, as the size and proportion of the black population increased over time, so did their segregation from native whites: 47 (1850), 52 (1880), 61 (1930), 75 (1970) (see Table 2). This development is tied to the rapid growth of new suburban housing after World War II; whites settled in these automobile suburbs, and in classic "trickle down" manner, blacks inhabited the older housing vacated by whites.[40]

What sets the contemporary black experience off from that of earlier white immigrants (and earlier black Philadelphians), however, is not simply the consistently higher level of segregation. A new measure of residential experience has been developed that asks what proportion of a typical person's census tract consisted of the same group; for example, what percentage of the population in the typical black person's census tract was black? In this measure of "dominance," the composition of the areal unit is sought.[41] On the other hand, the Index of Segregation asks what percentage of a group would have to move to another location in the city to achieve a distribution throughout each areal unit in the city equal to their proportion of the city's total population.

Using our dominance measure, the striking differences that distinguish blacks from white immigrants can be seen.[42] The typical Irish immigrant in 1880 and the typical Italian immigrant in 1930, for example, shared a similar aspect of their residential experience. When the hypothetical immigrant in each era walked through his neighborhood, what kind of people might he have met? The Irishman in 1880 lived with 15 percent other Irish immigrants, 34 percent Irish stock, 26 percent all foreign-born persons, and 58 percent all foreign stock. The typical Italian immigrant in 1930 had an almost identical experience. He lived with 14 percent other Italian immigrants, 38 percent Italian stock, 23 percent all foreign-born persons, and 57 percent all foreign stock.[43] In striking contrast, the typical black in 1970 lived in a census tract in which 74 percent of the population was black (see Table 8). What is more, the "dominance" of blacks has risen steadily since 1850 when it was 11 percent; it was not until 1950, however, that the typical black lived in a census tract with a black majority. Ghettoes are the product of the post–World War II city.

The black residential experience differs from that of white immigrants in yet another important regard. As ethnic occupational segregation decreased over time—that is, as white immigrant groups gained access to a broader range of occupations—their residential segregation decreased. Quite the opposite was true for blacks: despite the occupational desegregation produced in recent decades by the opening of new job opportunities for blacks, their residential segregation has increased over time.

As measured by the index of dissimilarity, the differences between the occupational distributions of blacks and native whites did not fall below 60 percent until 1940 when it reached 52 percent. After 1930, compari-

Table 8. Indices of Dominance: 1850, 1880, 1930–1970 (248 Tracts)

	1850	1880	1930	1940	1950	1960	1970
Blacks	11	12	35	45	56	72	74
Ireland							
Born	24	15	3	2	2		
2nd		19					
Stock		34	8			5	3
Germany							
Born	9	11	4	3	2		
2nd		14					
Stock		25	11			5	3
Great Britain							
Born			4	3	2		
Stock			12			5	3
Italy							
Born			14	13	9		
Stock			38			23	21
Poland							
Born			7	6	4		
Stock			20			9	8
USSR							
Born			14	12	9		
Stock			28			17	14
Foreign							
Born	32	26	23				
2nd		32	34				
Stock		58	57				
Native White	68	44					
Other Foreign							
Born	7	8					
2nd		7					
Stock		14					

Sources: See Sources for Table 2.

Note: See Notes for Tables 1 and 2.

Table 9. Occupational Distribution of Males and Females, 16+, by Ethnicity: 1970 (As Percent of Ethnic Group)

	Blacks		Puerto Ricans		Whites*	
	City	SMSA	City	SMSA	City	SMSA
Professional	7.7	8.1	4.4	5.3	15.1	17.2
Owners and Executives	2.5	2.5	1.4	1.9	7.0	8.8
Clerks and Sales	21.6	20.4	14.7	13.2	32.7	29.9
Trade and Transportation	5.2	5.3	4.3	3.4	3.8	3.4
Manufacturing	30.1	30.1	52.8	49.3	27.6	27.6
Domestic and Personal Service	22.7	23.1	13.8	14.2	8.0	7.8
Laborers	8.0	8.0	6.8	8.4	3.1	3.0
Agriculture	0.6	0.8	0.8	3.9	0.1	0.6
Other	1.7	1.6	0.8	0.5	2.5	1.5
Totals	232,192	279,703	6270	10,749	525,058	1,570,045
(Row %)	(30.4)	(15.8)	(0.8)	(0.6)	(68.8)	(83.6)
Dissimilarity from *All* Whites	24	25	36	37	—	—

Sources: Figures are computed from published United States Census totals. See U.S. Bureau of the Census, *Census of Population: 1970*, v.I, "Characteristics of the Population," pt. 40, Pennsylvania—Section 1 (Washington, D.C.: U.S. Government Printing Office, 1973), 395, 400, 451, 456, 499, 504.

*Includes a small number of non-black non-whites, i.e., Chinese, etc.

sons can be made only with all whites (native- and foreign-born combined); it fell to 42 percent in 1950, 29 percent in 1960, and 25 percent in 1970. The significance of the relatively sharp decline in occupational dissimilarity between blacks and whites after World War II, especially in the decade of the 1950s, however, should not be exaggerated (see Table 9). In a 1975 survey of adult males in the Philadelphia Urbanized Area, blacks reported a mean income of $3,000 below that of whites even after the effects of age, education, and occupation were controlled.[44]

Summary and Conclusions

Systematic data on levels of segregation as measured by the index of dissimilarity and our measure of ethnic dominance make clear that a "Tale of Three Cities" is a story about three distinct waves of immigrants, three distinct opportunity structures and ecological forms, and three distinct settlement patterns. In each of the three cities, immigrants interacted with the urban structure they encountered and produced markedly different residential patterns. The first city—the industrializing city of the mid-nineteenth century—was settled by large numbers of Irish, Germans, and British of the "Old" immigration. They established integrated residential patterns which have persisted throughout the twentieth century.

The second city—the industrial city of the early twentieth century—was home for even greater numbers of Italians, Poles, and Russian Jews of the "New" immigration. The residential patterns they formed were much more segregated than those of their predecessors. Yet even here the stereotypic notions of settlement and adjustment to conditions in the New World require some qualification. The experience of initial segregation in working- and lower-class ghettoes and subsequent occupational and residential mobility, as Sam Warner and Colin Burke pointed out, is a limited case in American history: limited to the "New" immigrants in the largest cities at the turn of the last century.[45] And, as our dominance data make clear, most immigrants never lived in ghettoes if they are understood as places inhabited only, or largely, by a single ethnic group.

The third city—"post-industrial" modern Philadelphia—was the destination for thousands of black migrants largely from the Southeast. Their segregation and dominance scores have increased steadily from 1850. Unlike earlier groups, today's blacks live in isolated ghettoes.[46]

Changes in the patterns of ethnic settlement, we have argued, can only be fully understood within the context of an ecological explanation that focuses upon changes in the housing market, industrial base, and transportation, production, and communication technologies. The ecological perspective makes it possible to explain the changing measures of segregation and dominance, important aspects of ethnic history, and the uniqueness of the black experience.

The many significant changes in the relationship between work and residence, which characterized Philadelphia's growth over the last century, had direct implications for the location, character, and stability of ethnic communities. Under constraints of expensive transportation and limited housing, industrial affiliation had a greater impact on the residential choice of immigrants than did their ethnicity.

To the degree that specific ethnic neighborhoods were based on their concentration in nearby industrial employment, the stability of these neighborhoods has depended upon the stability of jobs. When contemporary observers seek explanations for stable neighborhoods, for example, they find strong ethnic ties; yet their analyses all too often confuse causes with effects. The strong ethnic ties are themselves the product of stable neighborhoods; the stability of the neighborhood results from the continuing presence of industrial employment opportunities. The black slums in 1970, for example, were located primarily in areas that had no manufacturing jobs in 1930.[47]

This structural view, then, suggests that the presence of nearby industrial employment reinforces the stability of white ethnic communities, and it is the industrial concentrations of white ethnics rather than ethnic culture or historical accident that underlies resistance to black "invasion."

Previous research by Burgess and Duncan and Lieberson has suggested that historical accidents or differences in ethnic tolerance for blacks account for white ethnics' differential resistance to black settlement.[48] Our results indicate that the frequently expressed stereotypes of resistant Poles and Italians and fleeing Russian Jews are supported only when one does not consider the impact of the ecological structure of the city, the position of these groups in the occupational structure, and their location and access to industrial employment. The reason that white ethnics on Chicago's South Side were able for so many years to prevent black residential penetration has more to do with the continued presence of their job opportunities in the nearby stockyards and steel mills than with cultural factors. The lack of adjacent industrial turf explains the rapid racial turnover that characterized Harlem's transition from an upper-middle-class suburb to a lower-class slum in the early decades of the twentieth century.[49] These same factors emerge when we examine the ghettoes of blacks and Puerto Ricans in contemporary Philadelphia; unlike the earlier white ethnic villages, these racial ghettoes have not formed around abundant employment opportunities; they emerged instead in economically depressed residential areas which were abandoned by affluent whites who moved to more distant suburbs seeking greater socioeconomic homogeneity, better schools, and more spacious housing.

A decade ago the *Report of the National Advisory Commission on Civil Disorders* asked why "the Negro has been unable to escape from poverty and the ghetto like the European immigrants." Their answer stressed historical factors. They pointed out that the nature of the American economy had changed; a "mature" urban-industrial economy no longer offered the range of opportunities to blacks that it once had to white immigrants. They found "racial discrimination" as the "second major reason" why the Negro has been left behind. They noted different cultural factors arising from the slave experience, especially those affecting family life and incentive mechanisms. They argued that the "political opportunities" that enabled European immigrants to adjust and prosper "had altered dramatically." White immigrants gained considerable advantage by joining urban political machines which delivered jobs and other services. This no longer exists as a viable possibility for blacks. Even when political power is won by black voters today, as has been done in Newark, Gary, Cleveland, and other cities, it is a hollow victory indeed. The economic condition of American cities has seriously deteriorated since the time that European immigrant groups gained access to political power and its patronage. Philadelphia's physical and economic conditions are far worse today than they were when the immigrants from Western and Eastern Europe settled here. Our present circumstances should be familiar by now. Philadelphia's schools, transportation facilities, housing stock, and public services are in disrepair. With the local economy contracting rather than expanding, and with the loss of so many jobs and middle-class residents, the city's tax base has eroded to the point where it can ill-afford the cost of the required improvements.[50]

To the arguments of the Kerner Commission, three further points can be added. First, it is clear that the changing opportunity structure and the different ecological arrangements of the city provide the basic parameters within which the experience of white ethnics and blacks must be understood. To assume a constant opportunity structure and an unchanging ecological form is to seek explanations for differences in ethnic settlement and adjustment in the cultural origins of ethnic groups and thus to misdirect inquiry from the obvious. Cultural factors come into play only within the larger structure of the urban environment.[51] Second, the impact of housing and industrial location—the constraints that work and residence imposed on earlier immigrants—is significant. Western European immigrants came at the most propitious time; both the highly skilled Germans and British and the relatively unskilled Irish found ample opportunities. Even though the industrial base of the city began to decline at the turn of this century, it is clear that Eastern European immigrants, when compared with post–World War II blacks, settled in what must be considered to be "ghettoes of opportunity." Finally, the experience of blacks stands in sharp contrast to that of white ethnics. Not only has their segregation increased over the last century—contrary to the standing theory of assimilation—but it is also clear that blacks have been forced to settle in the oldest industrial and residential areas of the city—areas which have been left behind by the processes of modern urban-industrial development.

There is little to be gained by continuing a debate among advocates of structural and cultural points of view where one is posed to the exclusion of the other. Both play critical explanatory roles. Structural considerations explain well the occupational and residential experience of white immigrants who settled in mid-nineteenth and early twentieth-century Philadelphia; they do not explain the black experience. Here the explanation must be racism. If it is understood as a cultural factor, then culture explains why blacks who lived in Philadelphia at the same time fared so badly despite the twin structural advantages of abundant industrial opportunities and residential location where these opportunities were particularly plentiful. If racial discrimination had been absent in earlier Philadelphia, blacks should have done at least as well if not better than their white immigrant contemporaries. In modern Philadelphia racism has somewhat abated, but the twin structural advantages of the past have disappeared. Thus structural constraints loom large today; though different from the racial barriers that prevented advancement in the past, they function just as effectively. They retard the economic progress of all groups—blacks and whites alike—who still inhabit the depressed areas of a city with a declining opportunity structure.

Although the "Bootstraps" and the "Last of the Immigrants" explanations for the socioeconomic differential that characterize blacks and whites today are of markedly different types, they have the same implications for public policy: do nothing. Both explanations are false and based on a mistaken understanding of our history. Why these points of view persist is important to comprehend. They are accepted in large part because they justify things as they are now. And in legitimating the status quo, these two views demonstrate how what we believe about the past affects the present—not in abstract scholarly logic, but in the material daily life of real people, not only in Philadelphia, but across the nation. Since our sense of history—conscious or not—exercises a real power in the present, it should sensitize us to the dangers of ahistorical social science.[52] This essay provides an empirically grounded and interdisciplinary historical perspective so often absent in discussions of contemporary social problems and their solutions.

The "Bootstraps" explanation looks to the past, but however heroic the sound that comes from praising the courage and stamina of earlier white immigrants, it rings totally untrue when applied to the historical experience of blacks. The "Last of the Immigrants" explanation looks to the future, but the conditions that blacks face in modern Philadelphia are so different from those that earlier groups found that the analogy is thoroughly inappropriate. Unless major structural changes and perhaps some form of preferential treatment are undertaken at all levels of public and urban policy, it is doubtful that assimilation and economic progress for blacks will be possible. The approaches that blacks utilize to enter the American mainstream will certainly not be the same as those used by the white immigrants; of necessity, they have to be devised in ways yet unanticipated. As a national policy is formulated to revitalize our cities, it must be remembered that racial discrimination, though less pervasive, persists. The challenge is to recognize how our cities have changed and to use this understanding to provide real "bootstraps" for blacks so that they may indeed become the "last of the immigrants."

NOTES

1. Recent monographs on urban black communities provide an ethnic and racial perspective, but fail to adequately treat its urban context. See Gilbert Osofsky, *Harlem: The Making of a Ghetto: Negro New York, 1890–1920* (New York: Harper & Row, 1963); Allan H. Spear, *Black Chicago: The Making of a Negro Ghetto, 1890–*

1920 (Chicago: University of Chicago Press, 1967); Seth M. Scheiner, *Negro Mecca: A History of the Negro in New York 1865–1920* (New York: New York University Press, 1965); David M. Katzman, *Before the Ghetto: Black Detroit in the Nineteenth Century* (Urbana: University of Illinois Press, 1973); John W. Blassingame, *Black New Orleans, 1860–1880* (Chicago: University of Chicago Press, 1973).

An exception is Kenneth L. Kusmer, *A Ghetto Takes Shape: Black Cleveland, 1870–1930* (Urbana: University of Illinois Press, 1976). Following in the tradition of W.E.B. DuBois, *The Philadelphia Negro: A Social Study* (New York: Schocken, 1967; orig. ed., 1899); and St. Clair Drake and Horce R. Cayton, *Black Metropolis: A Study of Negro Life in a Northern City* (New York: Harper & Row, 1945), Kusmer discusses how the urban environment affected the collective experiences of blacks in late-nineteenth and early twentieth-century Cleveland.

2. For an interpretative overview of Afro-American history that develops this theme, see August Meier and Elliot Rudwick, *From Plantation to Ghetto*, 3rd ed. rev. (New York: Hill & Wang, 1976).

3. The concept "urban as process" is elaborated in Theodore Hershberg, "The New Urban History: Toward An Interdisciplinary History of the City," *Journal of Urban History* 5 (November 1978), 3–40; an expanded version appears in this volume.

4. This point of view is held by many in positions of considerable influence in our society. In discussing the impact of the Bakke case with a black clerk in a Washington, D.C., bookstore, no less than Chief Justice Warren E. Burger was quoted as saying that ". . . his grandparents had come from Europe and were illiterate and it had taken 150 years for his people to improve themselves." Miss Audrey Hair, the bookstore clerk, replied: "I asked him if he didn't think 300 years was enough time for my people?" *New York Times,* November 5, 1978, 6. The "Last of the Immigrants" explanation is cogently presented by Nathan Glazer, "Blacks and Ethnic Groups: The Difference, and the Political Difference It Makes," in Nathan I. Huggins, Martin Kilson, and Daniel M. Fox, eds., *Key Issues in the Afro-American Experience* (New York: Harcourt Brace Jovanovich, 1971), 193–211. A more popular expression can be found in Irving Kristol, "The Negro Today Is Like the Immigrant of Yesterday," *New York Times Magazine,* September 11, 1976.

No particular author is identified with the "Bootstraps" explanation; rather it is considered endemic in American culture and is associated with a racist interpretation of the black experience; that is, blacks failed because they are racially inferior.

5. Sam Bass Warner has also described "three" Philadelphias: "The Eighteenth-Century Town" of 1770–1780; "The Big City" of 1830–1860; and "The Industrial Metropolis" of 1920–1930 in *The Private City: Philadelphia in Three Periods of Its Growth* (Philadelphia: University of Pennsylvania Press, 1968); see also Warner, "If All the World Were Philadelphia: A Scaffolding for Urban History, 1774–1930," *American Historical Review* 74 (October 1968), 26–43.

A more recent study also identified "three cities": the "commercial" city of the eighteenth and early nineteenth centuries, the "industrial" city of the late nineteenth and early twentieth centuries, and the "corporate" city of the post–World War II period; see David Gordon, "Capitalist Development and the History of American Cities," in Larry Sawers and William K. Tabb, eds., *Marxism and the Metropolis: Perspective Political Economy* (New York: Oxford University Press, 1978).

The differences here reflect purpose. Warner initially wanted to demonstrate to historians that systematic data were available with which to document the major changes that occurred in the urban environment over the last two centuries. His major purpose in *The Private City,* however, had far less to do with changes in the city's opportunity and ecological structure than with the failures of urban life in a capitalist economy; he attributes urban problems to the pursuit of private profit at the expense of the public good. Where these once coincided in the colonial city, they diverged permanently with the emergence of the urban-industrial order in the nineteenth century. Gordon's purpose was to classify cities according to stages in their historical economic development, arguing that urban form and the requirements of capitalism are inextricably linked to each other. Our purpose differs; we wish to characterize the particular kind of economy and environment that awaited the settlement of three temporally distinct waves of immigrants. Thus we have designated our three cities as "The Industrializing City," "The Industrial City," and "The Post-Industrial City."

6. *Assimilation in American Life: The Role of Race, Religion, and National Origins* (New York: Oxford University Press, 1964), 105. As characteristic support of his position, Gordon cites Robert E. Park and Herbert A. Miller, *Old World Traits Transplanted* (New York: Harper and Brothers, 1921); and Oscar Handlin, *The Uprooted* (Boston: Little, Brown, 1952); and *The American People in the Twentieth Century* (Cambridge: Harvard University Press, 1954).

7. (New York: Harcourt Brace Jovanovich, 1976).

8. Gordon, *Assimilation in American Life*, 105–6.

9. See, for example, Robert E. Park, "The Urban Community as a Spatial Pattern and a Moral Order," in Ernest Burgess, ed., *The Urban Community* (Chicago: University of Chicago Press, 1926); Louis Wirth, *The Ghetto* (Chicago: University of Chicago Press, 1928); Ernest W. Burgess, "Residential Segregation in American Cities," *Annals of the American Academy of Political and Social Science* 140 (1928), 105–15; Robert E. Park, *Human Communities* (Glencoe, Ill.: Free Press, 1952).

10. Karl E. and Alma F. Taeuber, "The Negro as an Immigrant Group: Recent Trends in Racial and Ethnic Segregation in Chicago," *American Journal of Sociology* 69 (January 1964), 375. The Taeubers' "concern with diminishing residential segregation as a necessary concomitant of the assimilation process derives from Myrdal's discussion of the 'mechanical importance' of residential segregation in facilitating other forms of segregation and discrimination, and Hawley's discussion of the impact of spatial patterns on race relations." See Gunnar Myrdal, *An American Dilemma*, 2 vols. (New York: Harper and Brothers, 1944), I, 618; Amos H. Hawley, Dispersion versus Segregation: Apropos of a Solution of Race Problems," *Papers of the Michigan Academy of Science, Arts, and Letters* 30 (1944), 667–74.

11. Stanley Lieberson, *Ethnic Patterns in American Cities* (New York: Free Press of Glencoe, 1963). The Index of Segregation expresses the percentage of a group that would have to move to another location in the city to achieve a distribution throughout each areal unit equal to their proportion of the city's total population; the Index measure is often expressed as a whole number ranging from 0 (no segregation) to 100 (complete segregation). For a detailed explanation of the Index of Segregation, see also Otis Dudley Duncan and Beverly Duncan, "Residential Distribution and Occupational Stratification," *American Journal of Sociology* 60 (1955), 493–503; Otis Dudley Duncan and Beverly Duncan, "A Methodological Analysis of Segregation Indexes," *American Sociological Review* 20 (April 1955); Karl E. Taeuber and Alma F. Taeuber, *Negroes in Cities: Residential Segregation and Neighborhood Change* (Chicago: Aldine, 1965), 195–245.

12. The dissimilarity scores reported in Table 2 are calculated in the same manner as the Index of Segregation but describe the degree of difference from native whites as opposed to the remainder of the city's population. The scores reported in Tables 2 and 8, moreover, *are based on identical areal units.*

Tract level data were not collected by the nineteenth-century U.S. Census Bureau. For the 1930 and 1970 censuses, Philadelphia was divided into 404 and 365 tracts, respectively. To achieve compatible boundaries, it was necessary to collapse these into 248 tracts. The much smaller PSHP areal units for the nineteenth century— 7,100 rectangular grids, one by one and one-quarter blocks—were aggregated up to the level of the 248 census tracts. Areal compatibility was thus achieved across the entire 120-year period. For information on the construction of the PSHP grid areal unit, see Theodore Hershberg, "The Philadelphia Social History Project: A Methodological History" (Ph.D. dissertation, History, Stanford University, 1973), 150–87; and Theodore Hershberg, Alan N. Burstein, and Susan M. Drobis, "The Historical Study of Urban Space," in Theodore Hershberg, guest editor, "A Special Issue: The Philadelphia Social History Project," *Historical Methods Newsletter* 9 (March–June, 1976), 99–105; the issue containing this essay is hereafter cited as "PSHP: Special Issue."

13. Given the standing notion of the assimilation process, moreover, the decline in residential segregation over the period 1930–1970 is less than might be expected: the greatest decline was found among Polish stock (55 percent in 1930 to 35 percent in 1970), but Italian stock fell only slightly (58 percent to 48 percent) and Jewish stock did not change (53 percent to 52 percent). See Table 2.

14. Bruce Laurie and Mark Schmitz, "Manufacture and Productivity: The Making of an Industrial Base: Philadelphia, 1850–1880," in this volume.

15. Hershberg, "The PSHP: A Methodological History," 285–323; see especially Tables 21 and 23; A. Burstein, "Patterns of Segregation and the Residential Experience," in "PSHP: Special Issue," 105–13.

16. Theodore Hershberg, Harold Cox, Dale Light, Jr., and Richard Greenfield, "The 'Journey-to-Work': An Empirical Investigation of Work, Residence and Transportation in Philadelphia, 1850 and 1880"; in this volume. Although the estimated journey-to-work doubled between 1850 and 1880, reaching a radius of one mile and a median of one-half mile, the absolute distances involved remained quite short.

17. Richard Greenfield, "The Dynamics and Determinants of Manufacturing Location: A Perspective on Nineteenth-Century Philadelphia," paper presented at Social Science History Association (Columbus, Ohio: November 1978); and Stephanie Greenberg, "Industrial Location and Ethnic Residential Patterns in an Industrializing City: Philadelphia, 1880"; in this volume.

18. Greenberg, *ibid.*

19. Miriam Eisenhardt, Jeffrey Sultanik, and Alan Berman, "The Five Irish Clusters in 1880 Philadelphia," unpublished manuscript in possession of PSHP (May 1974).

20. Greenberg, "Industrial Location and Ethnic Residential Patterns"; and "Industrialization in Philadelphia: The Relationship Between Industrial Location and Residential Patterns, 1880–1930" (Ph.D. dissertation, Sociology, Temple University, 1977).

21. On the other hand, given black overrepresentation in such service occupations as waiter and porter, their residential pattern was functional: the single largest black residential concentration was located adjacent to the city's largest concentration of hotels, restaurants, and inns in the downtown area.

22. Theodore Hershberg, "Free Blacks in Antebellum Philadelphia: A Study of Ex-Slaves, Freeborn, and Socioeconomic Decline," *Journal of Social History* 5 (December 1971), 183–209, also in this volume; and "Freeborn and Slaveborn Blacks in Antebellum Philadelphia," in Eugene Genovese and Stanley Engerman, eds., *Slavery and Race in the Western Hemisphere* (Princeton, N.J.: Princeton University Press, 1975).

The characteristic difficulties that blacks faced in finding employment were described by Joshua Bailey, member of the Board of Managers of the Philadelphia Society for the Employment and Instruction of the Poor. Bailey wrote in his diary that "Employers express themselves willing to receive such an one (a young 'colored' man) into their shops, but they cannot dare to do it knowing the opposition such an act would meet with from their workmen who will not consent to work with colored persons" (10 January 1853).

The process of adjustment to conditions in the New World was a difficult one for all newcomers—black and white immigrants alike. Yet the historical record makes clear that much about the black experience was different—some times in degree, other times in kind. Blacks were the victims of frequent race riots and saw their homes, schools, and churches burned again and again. Though legally a free people and citizens, only members of the black race were denied the right to vote in the State of Pennsylvania after 1838. They occupied the worst housing in the Moyamensing slum and suffered from the greatest degree of impoverishment. Their mortality rate was roughly twice that of whites, and the death of black men early in their adult lives was the major reason that blacks were forced, far more often than whites, to raise their children in fatherless families; see F. F. Furstenberg, Jr., T. Hershberg, and J. Modell, "The Origins of the Female-Headed Black Family: The Impact of the Urban Experience," *Journal of Interdisciplinary History* 6 (September 1975), 211–33; also in this volume.

For the occupational experience of the white immigrant workforce, see B. Laurie, T. Hershberg, and G. Alter, "Immigrants and Industry: The Philadelphia Experience, 1850–1880," *Journal of Social History* 9 (December 1975), 219–48, also in this volume; and Laurie and Schmitz, "Manufacture and Productivity."

23. Robert Park, Ernest W. Burgess, and Roderick D. McKenzie, eds., *The City* (Chicago: University of Chicago Press, 1928).

24. Gideon Sjoberg, "The Preindustrial City," *American Journal of Sociology* 60 (1955), 438–45; Gideon Sjoberg, *The Preindustrial City: Past and Present* (New York: Free Press of Glencoe, 1960).

25. Hershberg *et al.,* "The 'Journey-to-Work.' "

26. *Ibid.* We do not wish to leave the impression that the decline in population densities over the period was due solely to the increased availability of housing. Declining population densities were also tied to declining fertility, a process experienced over at least the last century in Western Europe and North America.

When the city is divided into concentric rings of roughly one mile, the inner two rings lost population consistently over the period. The first ring fell from 206,000 persons in 1880 to 67,000 in 1970; and in the second ring population fell from 241,000 in 1880 to 135,000 in 1970. Although contemporary population density gradients from the center outward are not level, their smoothing over time is one of the striking changes in urban population structure.

27. For an excellent discussion of the Polish experience in Philadelphia in the first two decades of the twentieth century, and less detailed but useful information on other immigrant groups in the city at the same time, see Carol Golab, *Immigrant Destinations* (Philadelphia: Temple University Press, 1978).

28. Sam Bass Warner, Jr., has described this process for late nineteenth-century Boston, *Street Car Suburbs: The Process of Growth in Boston, 1870–1900* (Cambridge: Harvard University Press, 1962).

29. Golab, *Immigrant Destinations*, 153.

30. Stephanie W. Greenberg, "The Relationship Between Change in the Location of Industrial Work Opportunities and Neighborhood Change, Philadelphia, 1880–1930," *Journal of Urban History* (forthcoming, 1981).

31. Eugene P. Ericksen and William L. Yancey, "The Location of Manufacturing Jobs in Philadelphia: Changes in the Pattern, 1927–1972," unpublished paper, Temple University (1976).

32. Greenberg, "Industrial Work Opportunities and Neighborhood Change"; Hershberg *et al.,* "The 'Journey-to-Work.' "

33. Ericksen and Yancey, "Work and Residence in Industrial Philadelphia," *Journal of Urban History* 5 (February 1979), 147–82.

34. The relationship between work and residence was for Polish immigrants in 1915 what it had been for the Irish and German immigrants in the nineteenth century. Golab summarizes their experience in these words: "Each Polish settlement

(and there were nine such areas) directly reflected the industrial structure of the neighborhood in which it was located. It was the availability of work that determined the location of the Polish colony, for the Poles were invariably employed in the neighborhoods where they resided." *Immigrant Destinations,* 113.

A similar conclusion was reached by E. E. Pratt in his study of immigrant worker neighborhoods: *Industrial Causes of Congestion of Population in New York City* (New York: Columbia University Press, 1911).

35. Yancey and Ericksen, "The Structural Antecedents of Ethnic Communities," unpublished paper, Temple University (1976).

36. Yancey and Ericksen, "The Structural Antecedents."

37. *Ibid.;* Greenberg, "Industrial Work Opportunities and Neighborhood Change."

38. Ericksen and Yancey, "The Location of Manufacturing Jobs"; and "The Structural Antecedents."

39. Ericksen and Yancey, "Work and Residence"; and "The Structural Antecedents."

40. William Alonso, "The Historic and Structural Theories of Urban Form: Their Implications for Urban Renewal," in Charles Tilly, ed., *An Urban World* (Boston: Little, Brown, 1974), 442–46.

41. The dominance measure is an "experiential" rather than a "distribution" measure; it expresses "the proportion of the population in the mean individual's areal unit comprised by his group. . . ." The measure is calculated as a weighted arithmetic mean:

$$I_{dom} = \frac{1}{G} \sum_{i=1}^{n} \left(g_i \frac{g_i}{P_i} \right) = \frac{1}{G} \sum_{i=1}^{n} \frac{g_i^2}{P_i}$$

Where G is the total population of the group whose residential pattern is being examined; g_i is the population of that group residing in the ith areal unit; P_i is the total population of the ith areal unit; n is the total number of areal units. A. Burstein, "Patterns of Segregation and the Residential Experience," 111.

42. The "dominance" measure not only operates to homogenize the experience of the two earlier waves of white immigrants, but also calls into question too great a reliance on the Index of Segregation as a useful tool to infer social experience. To the extent that cross-cultural contacts are central to our thinking about the socialization of the young and subsequent mobility and assimilation experience, the dominance measure, in getting more directly at who lives near whom, may be a better measure than the Index of Segregation; indeed we have seen that although some groups can be twice as segregated as others—as the "New" immigrants were compared to the "Old"—they can display identical levels of dominance. Although the thrust of this essay is not methodological, we think it time that the uses of the Index of Segregation, particularly the assumptions that underlie its correlation with a wide range of social behaviors, be carefully reconsidered. We are not claiming that the Index of Segregation is without value, but rather that in many instances it may be (and has been) inappropriately applied. The socioeconomic correlates of the Index of Segregation and our new measure of dominance remain a topic for empirical investigation.

Although when compared to the black experience the differences between the "Old" and "New" immigrants appear small indeed, there were differences nonetheless. While the dominance measures for the white immigrant groups were approximately equal, this does not mean that they had the same residential *pattern.* In order for the "New" immigrants, proportionally smaller than the "Old" immigrants, to achieve so much higher measures of segregation than, and measures of dominance equal to, the "Old" immigrants, they would have had to have been considerably more clustered. Thus, relative to the entire settled area of the city, the residential pattern of the "New" immigrants must have been much more compact than that of the "Old." Accordingly, an examination of the dimensions of segregation reveals that while the very localized experiences of the "Old" and "New" immigrants may have been the same, the old immigrants had access to more diverse areas of the city. See Burstein, "Patterns of Segregation."

43. Golab's description of 1915 immigrant residential patterns corroborates the argument presented here: "No immigrant group in the city ever totally monopolized a particular neighborhood to the extent that it achieved isolation from members of other groups." Golab, *Immigrant Destinations,* 112.

44. Ericksen and Yancey, "Organizational Factors and Income Attainment: Networks, Businesses, Unions," unpublished paper, Temple University (1978). This result is consistent with those reported in many national studies.

The occupational dissimilarity scores are reported at the bottom of each occupational table. The scores can be interpreted in the same manner as the segregation scores: the percent of blacks who would have to shift to another occupational strata in order to approximate the same distribution as whites.

45. Sam Bass Warner and Colin Burke, "Cultural Change and the Ghetto," *Journal of Contemporary History* 4 (1969), 173–87.

46. Puerto Ricans, a much smaller group than blacks, are in fact the most recent immigrants to the city and are also slightly more segregated than blacks; see Table 2.

47. Gladys Palmer, *Recent Trends in Employment and Unemployment in Philadelphia* (Philadelphia: Works Project Administration, Philadelphia Labor Market Studies, 1937); Ericksen and Yancey, "The Location of Manufacturing Jobs."

48. Burgess, "Residential Segregation"; Otis Dudley Duncan and Stanley Lieberson, "Ethnic Segregation and Assimilation," *American Journal of Sociology* 64 (January 1959), 364–74.

49. Gilbert Osofsky, *Harlem: The Making of a Ghetto.* While carefully documenting the real estate boom and bust that followed the construction of the elevated lines which connected Harlem with lower Manhattan, Osofsky overlooked entirely the significance of the work-residence relationship in his explanation of the dramatic changes in Harlem's racial demography.

50. (New York: Bantam Books, 1968); see chapter 9, "Comparing the Immigrant and Black Experience," 278–82. For a convincing critique of the "Last of the Immigrants" theory that focuses on patterns of intra- and intergenerational occupational mobility and supports our argument nicely, see Stephan Thernstrom, *The Other Bostonians: Poverty and Progress in the American Metropolis* (Cambridge: Harvard University Press, 1973), ch. 10, "Blacks and Whites," 176–219. "By now . . . ," Thernstrom concluded, somewhat too optimistically in our opinion, "American Negroes may face opportunities and constraints that are fairly analogous to those experienced by the millions of European migrants who struggled to survive in the American city of the late nineteenth and early twentieth centuries. But until very recently, the problems of black men in a white society were different in kind from those of earlier newcomers. . . . The main factor that will impede black economic progress in the future will be the forces of inertia that have been called passive or structural discrimination" (218–19).

51. William Yancey, Eugene Ericksen, and Richard N. Juliani, "Emergent Ethnicity: A Review and Reformulation," *American Sociological Review* 41 (June 1976), 391–403.

52. See Stephan Thernstrom, "Further Reflections on the Yankee City Series: The Pitfalls of a Historical Social Science," *Poverty and Progress: Social Mobility in a Nineteenth-Century City* (Cambridge: Harvard University Press, 1964), 225–39; and Michael B. Katz, "Introduction," *The People of Hamilton, Canada West: Family and Class in a Mid-Nineteenth-Century City* (Cambridge: Harvard University Press, 1975), 1.

Epilogue: Sustaining Interdisciplinary Research

Despite decades of unanimous agreement that interdisciplinary historical urban research should proceed, the blunt truth is that precious little has been done. The reasons for this are manifold. A thorough discussion of this problem and the challenge it poses would consider ideological, cultural, psychological, and structural factors. Scholarship is inherently political. The tools of the social scientist are not—any more than is the technology of the engineer—neutral. The assumptions and world views of the various disciplines are the source of much conflict. Socialization has created an internalized set of values that make achievement in scholarship almost synonymous with individual effort. Our educational experiences leave all too many of us ill-prepared to undertake team research. As if these factors were not enough, personality differences are fully capable of disrupting interdisciplinary research even among those whose politics are compatible and who subscribe in principle to collaborative efforts.

It is one thing to explain why the pace of interdisciplinary historical urban research has been so slow, and quite another to effect the kind of changes that will encourage and support this valuable form of research organization. The writer's task is usually complete with the documentation of an intellectual point. We would normally be content to make the argument from a sociology of knowledge perspective that the reward structure of American colleges and universities operates to inhibit successful interdisciplinary research. However, since the nature of what we learn about the past depends on how we organize to do research in the present, we must do more than observe. We must work to change the existing system so that it will sustain rather than discourage interdisciplinary research efforts.

Though recognizing that a variety of factors inhibits the development of interdisciplinary research, our own experience has made it strikingly clear that the system of rewards that controls hiring and promotion in our institutions of higher learning plays a fundamental role in undermining it.

The remarks that follow deal with the reward structures found in the humanities and social sciences. The "hard" sciences and to a lesser extent the applied sciences, by virtue of their involvement with a real world whose workings are not compartmentalized along departmental lines, have had little choice but to bring together the requisite knowledge and expertise.

A comprehensive data base containing information central to the paradigmatic concerns of the individual disciplines, we established earlier, can attract a range of social scientists. The very existence of a data base can thus facilitate multidisciplinary research. But involving these scholars in interdisciplinary research and sustaining their participation is quite another task. The problem lies in the evaluation of the scholarly product. If the scholarship that results is collaborative and interdisciplinary, it runs head on into the existing reward structures. Since each discipline has defined what it considers "central" and "marginal" and relies openly on these "rules" in its hiring and promotion practices, neither interdisciplinary scholars nor their products are as competitive as those working within traditionally prescribed boundaries.

Collaborative interdisciplinary research is greeted with the intellectually irrelevant observation: "This isn't history!" (or economics or sociology and so on) as if the test for true knowledge were disciplinary purity. The key question posed concerns the smooth functioning of the system and often has no intellectual content: "Who is the smart author?" rather than "Has this collaboration resulted in a significant expansion of the frontiers of knowledge?" Junior faculty, in particular, know this all too well. Rather than challenge the existing system of rewards, especially in times of financial exigency which heighten the difficulty of securing tenure, and thus jeopardize their professional futures, they avoid interdisciplinary research.

The effect of the current system, then, is seriously to qualify our commitment to research. Scholars are not in a position to ask what are the pressing intellectual questions—regardless of disciplinary and institutional boundaries—and respond with the appropriate forms of research organization. Quite the contrary. The current system operates to reward research conducted in an atomized, individualistic manner. The selection of research topics is in fact not as open as we would like to think. Choices are constrained by the need to avoid a losing battle with a system that discourages collaborative interdisciplinary work. Thus the structure of both our professional disciplines and our institutions of higher learning, rather than the intrinsic merit of the questions involved, dictate the *form*—and hence much of the *content*—of all research undertaken.

The argument should not be construed as critical of disciplinary research *per se;* we are not advocating the end of disciplinary specialization. With the individual scholar unlikely to gain competence in more than one discipline, specialization must remain the basic form for initial professional training and much subsequent research. Indeed, collaborative interdisciplinary research cannot proceed without the contributions of specialists from different academic backgrounds. It is the skills of people trained in the fullest range of disciplines that we wish to bring to bear on the complexities of the urban experience. What is more, the current system has produced generations of fine scholarship. Many questions can be answered by individuals working with intellectual tools developed within a single discipline. In other words, the current system is not so much wrong as it is limited and constraining. Certain topics, the study of the city for one, require interdisciplinary models of research organization. The point is that the existing system must be made flexible enough to accommodate these new and essential research forms.

Much can be done to alter the existing system. The first thing is to recognize that change will not come about by force of reason; the history of unheeded calls for interdisciplinary research makes that much clear. The second is to acknowledge that academic departments resemble feudal fiefdoms, each with their own set of interests to be protected. Since it is clear that departments will not move beyond rhetoric in their endorsement of interdisciplinary research, we propose that the central administrations of our universities take the initiative by establishing new criteria for at least some new appointments. They already control *whether* a "slot" that opens due to retirement, death, or leaving can be filled. Neither university presidents nor deans, however, need tell a department *whom* to hire; the only condition set is that an appointment be made in interdisciplinary research. In practice, the hiring guideline might be that the interests of at least two departments or programs must be served if a position is to be filled.

The next step is to protect the future promotion possibilities of these new recruits or of older faculty who may wish to expand into interdisciplinary research. This would involve the creation of faculty committees with composition determined by expertise in and commitment to interdisciplinary research. A scholar being considered for tenure or promotion would be able to choose either departmental or interdisciplinary committee review.

These reforms, in both providing jobs for interdisciplinary scholars and a mechanism for equitably evaluating their research records for promotion, would enormously encourage interdisciplinary research. Significantly, moreover, they would also address the problem of shrinking resources faced by virtually every academic institution in the country. Faculty who can teach and contribute intellectually to more than one department will enable institutions to maintain their offerings while reducing their personnel costs.

Perhaps the most exciting possibilities for interdisciplinary research exist not within individual schools, but among many institutions cooperating on a local or regional basis. If resources can be pooled at this level, they may be sufficient to provide a major facility capable of supporting more expensive forms of research and a greater number of users. We are certainly aware of the obstacles such an approach must overcome. The narrowness of vision and self-interest at the departmental level that mitigates against cooperation within universities is exceeded only by the enormous institutional egos that stand in the way of cooperation among different institutions (especially when they do not see each other as "equals" and are proximate in location). These possibilities could be effected without external funding only if those in positions of power viewed the proposed structural changes as valuable.

It would be nice to think that our institutions of higher learning would move ahead by themselves. Given the historical record and the values of the existing system, however, it is unlikely that change will come solely from within. Therefore the role of external funding agencies, both public and private, is a critical one, for only they can provide the financial benefits that might induce universities to move toward sustaining interdisciplinary research. The suggested changes in reward- and infra-structures must be parallelled by changes in funding agencies. New programs specifically designed to support interdisciplinary research should be established, and existing disciplinary ones should allocate some portion of their total funds to support interdisciplinary research. This is especially important because many federal funding agencies are themselves extensions of the established disciplines.

Assuming this were done, national committees consisting of faculty, administrators, and funding agency representatives should specify the conditions considered necessary to exist within universities before financial support would be committed. The availability of funds earmarked for interdisciplinary research could then be used to induce our institutions of higher learning to create an environment capable of sustaining interdisciplinary research.

Once these conditions were met, a school would be eligible for external funding. In this context the economic straits in which our institutions of higher learning find themselves could be the proverbial blessing in disguise. If adequate external funds were available to support interdisciplinary research, universities might be more willing to reorganize. It is time to mobilize more societal resources in order to overcome the fragmentation of knowledge and expertise which increasingly confounds our ability to deal with the complexities of the world around us.

Appendix I: Philadelphia Social History Project

Papers Published and Unpublished

Burstein, Alan N. "Intra-Urban Migration Patterns of Irish and German Immigrants," paper presented at Social Science History Association (Philadelphia, Pa.: October 1976); appears as "Immigrants and Residential Mobility: The Irish and Germans in Philadelphia, 1850–1880"; in this volume.

————. "Patterns of Segregation and the Residential Experience," *Historical Methods Newsletter,* 9 (March–June, 1976), 105–13.

Condran, Gretchen; Cheney, Rose. "Mortality Trends in Philadelphia: Age and Cause-Specific Death Rates, 1860–1920," paper presented at Population Association of America (Denver, Co.: April 1980).

Condran, Gretchen; Seaman, Jeff. "Linkages of the 1880–81 Philadelphia Death Register to the 1880 Manuscript Census: Procedures and Preliminary Results," paper presented at Population Association of America (Philadelphia, Pa.: April 26–28, 1979), to appear in *Historical Methods* (forthcoming).

Drobis, Susan M. "Occupation and Residential Differentiation: A Historical Application of Cluster Analysis," *Historical Methods Newsletter,* 9 (March–June, 1976), 114–34.

Eisenhardt, Miriam; Sultanik, Jeffrey; and Berman, Alan. "The Five Irish Clusters in 1880 Philadelphia," unpublished manuscript in possession of PSHP (May 1974).

Ericksen, Eugene P.; Yancey, William L. "Immigrants and Their Opportunities: Philadelphia, 1850–1936," paper presented at American Academy for the Advancement of Science (Houston: January 1979).

Fishbane, Richard B. " 'The Shallow Boast of Cheapness': Public School Teaching as a Profession in Philadelphia, 1865–1890," *Pennsylvania Magazine of History and Biography,* 103 (January 1979), 66–84.

————; and Cutler, William W., III. "An Occupation in Transition: Public School Teaching in Philadelphia, 1850–1890," paper presented at the American Educational Studies Association Conference (Washington, D.C.: November 1978).

Furstenberg, Frank, Jr.; Hershberg, Theodore; and Modell, John. "The Origins of the Female-Headed Black Family: The Impact of the Urban Environment," *Journal of Interdisciplinary History,* 6 (September 1975), 211–33. Reprinted in Robert Staples, ed., *The Black Family: Essays and Studies* (Belmont, Cal., 2nd ed., 1978); and in this volume.

————; Strong, Douglas; and Crawford, Albert G. "What Happened When the Census Was Redone: An Analysis of the Recount of 1870 in Philadelphia," paper presented at the Brigham Young University Family Research Conference, "Historical Change in Marriage and the Family" (Provo, Utah: March 1978); in a special issue of *Sociology and Social Research,* 63 (April 1979), 475–505.

Gillette, Howard. "The Emergence of the Modern Metropolis: Philadelphia in the Age of its Consolidation," in Howard Gillette and William Cutler, eds., *The Divided Metropolis: Social and Spatial Dimensions of Philadelphia, 1820–1940* (Greenwich, Ct.: Greenwood Press, 1980).

Glassberg, Eudice. "Work, Wages and the Cost of Living: Ethnic Differences and the Poverty Line, Philadelphia, 1880," *Pennsylvania History,* 66 (January 1979), 17–58.

Goldin, Claudia. "The Family and Household Economy in a Late Nineteenth-Century American City: Philadelphia, 1880," paper presented at Social Science History Association (Ann Arbor, Mich., 1977).

————. "Household and Market Production of Families in a Late Nineteenth-Century American City," *Explorations in Economic History,* 16 (1979), 111–31.

————. "Family Strategies in Late Nineteenth-Century Philadelphia," paper presented at the Conference on Regional Economic History, "Economy and Society: Philadelphia and Its Hinterland" (Wilmington, Del.: October 1978); to appear as "Family Strategies and the Family Economy in the late Nineteenth-Century: The Role of Secondary Workers"; in this volume.

Greenberg, Stephanie W. "Industrial Location and Ethnic Residential Patterns in an Industrializing City: Philadelphia, 1880," paper presented at Social Science History Association (Philadelphia, Pa.: October 1976); in this volume.

————. "The Relationship Between Work and Residence in an Industrializing City: Philadelphia, 1880," in Gillette and Cutler, eds., *The Divided Metropolis.*

————. "Industrial Location and the Residential Patterns of Occupational Groups: Philadelphia 1880," paper presented at the Social Science History Association (Columbus, Ohio: November 1978).

————. "The Relationship Between Change in the Location of Industrial Work Opportunities and Neighborhood Change, Philadelphia, 1880–1930," *Journal of Urban History* (forthcoming, 1981).

Greenfield, Richard R. "Models of Spatial Access and Interaction: Ethnicity, Employment and Transportation in Philadelphia, 1850–1880" (1977).

————. "The Determinants and Dynamics of Intra-Urban Manufacturing Location: A Perspective on Nineteenth-Century Philadelphia," paper presented at Social Science History Association (Columbus, Ohio: November 1978).

Gruenstein, John. "Components of Manufacturing Location Change, 1850–

1880," paper presented at Social Science History Association (Philadelphia, Pa.: October 1976).

———. "The Use of Bid-Rent Theory to Explain the Land Use of Firms in Nineteenth-Century Philadelphia," unpublished manuscript in possession of PSHP (1979).

Haines, Michael. "Poverty, Economic Stress and the Family in a Nineteenth-Century American City: Whites in Philadelphia, 1880"; in this volume.

———. "Fertility and Marriage in a Nineteenth-Century Industrial City: Philadelphia, 1850–1880," paper presented at Population Association of America (Philadelphia, Pa.: April 26–28, 1979); appears in *Journal of Economic History* 40 (March 1980).

Hershberg, Theodore. "Free Blacks in Antebellum Philadelphia: A Study of Ex-Slaves, Freeborn, and Socioeconomic Decline," *Journal of Social History,* 5 (December 1971), 183–209. Reprinted in Mark H. Haller and Allen F. Davis, eds., *The Peoples of Philadelphia* (Philadelphia, 1973); Michael B. Katz, ed., *Education and American Social History* (New York, 1973); Eugene Genovese and Elinor Miller, eds., *Plantation, Town and County* (Urbana, Ill., 1974): the Bobbs-Merrill *Reprint Series in American History* (Indianapolis, Ind., 1973); Theodore Kornweibel, Jr., ed., *In Search of the Promised Land: Essays in Black Urban History* (forthcoming); in this volume.

———. "Free-Born and Slave-Born Blacks in Antebellum Philadelphia," in Eugene Genovese and Stanley Engerman, eds., *Race and Slavery in the Western Hemisphere* (Princeton, N.J., 1975).

———. "Toward the Historical Study of Ethnicity," *Journal of Ethnic Studies,* 1 (Spring, 1973), 1–5.

———. "A Method for the Computerized Study of Family and Household Structure Using the Manuscript Schedules of the U.S. Census of Population, 1850–1880," *The Family in Historical Perspective,* 1 (Spring, 1973), 6–20.

———; Williams, Henry. "Mulattoes and Blacks: Intra-Group Color Differences and Social Stratification in Nineteenth-Century Philadelphia," originally presented by Hershberg at Organization of American Historians (Denver, Colo.: April 1974); in this volume.

———. "The Organization of Historical Research," *AHA Newsletter,* 12 (October 1974), 5–6.

———. Cox, Harold; Light, Dale, Jr.; and Greenfield, Richard. "The 'Journey-to-Work': An Empirical Investigation of Work, Residence and Transportation, Philadelphia, 1850 and 1880," originally presented by Hershberg, Cox, and Light at American Historical Association (Chicago, Ill.: 1974); in this volume.

———. Katz, Michael; Glasco, Laurence; Blumin, Stuart; and Griffen, Clyde. "Occupation and Ethnicity in Five Nineteenth-Century Cities: A Collaborative Inquiry," *Historical Methods Newsletter,* 7 (June 1974), 174–216.

———. "The Philadelphia Social History Project: An Overview and Progress Report," *Review of Public Data Use,* 4 (January 1976), 29–36.

———. ed., *Philadelphia: Work, Space, Family, and Group Experience in the Nineteenth Century: Essays Toward an Interdisciplinary History of the City* (New York: Oxford University Press: 1981).

————. guest editor. "A Special Issue: The Philadelphia Social History Project," *Historical Methods Newsletter*, 9 (March–June, 1976). Included in this issue are "Introduction"; "The Historical Study of Urban Space"; "Occupational Classification," with Robert Dockhorn; "Record Linkage," with Alan Burstein and Robert Dockhorn.

————. "The New Urban History: An Interdisciplinary History of the City," paper presented at PSHP-sponsored conference (Philadelphia, Pa.: August 1–4, 1977); published as, "The New Urban History: Toward An Interdisciplinary History of the City," *Journal of Urban History*, 5 (November 1978), 3–40; in this volume.

————. "Interdisciplinary Research at the Philadelphia Social History Project: Analytic Goals, Data, and Data Manipulation Strategies for the Study of the Nineteenth-Century Industrial City," paper presented at International Conference, "Quantification and Methods in Social Science Research: Possibilities and Problems in the Use of Historical and Process-Produced Data" (Cologne, West Germany: August 1977); appears in Jerome M. Clubb and E. Scheuch, eds., *Historical Social Research* (Cologne, West Germany, 1980).

————; Burstein, Alan; Ericksen, Eugene; Greenberg, Stephanie; Yancey, William. "A Tale of Three Cities: Blacks, Immigrants, and Opportunity in Philadelphia, 1850–1880, 1930 and 1970," for a special issue on "Race and Residence in American Cities," *The Annals*, 441 (January 1979), 55—81; in this volume.

————. "The Future of Urban History," paper presented at University of Bradford Conference, "The Pursuit of Urban History" (Leicester: August 1980). Proceedings to be published by Edward Arnold (London).

Laurie, Bruce. *Working People of Philadelphia, 1800–1850* (Philadelphia, Pa.: Temple University Press, 1980).

————; Hershberg, Theodore; Alter, George. "Immigrants and Industry: The Philadelphia Experience, 1850–1880," *Journal of Social History*, 9 (December 1975), 219–48; paper originally presented at the Sixth International Congress on Economic History (Copenhagen, Denmark: 1974). Reprinted in Richard Ehrlich, ed., *Immigrants in Industrial America: 1850–1920* (Charlottesville, Va., 1977); in this volume.

————; and Schmitz, Mark. "Manufacture and Productivity: The Making of an Industrial Base, Philadelphia, 1850–1880"; in this volume.

————. "Beyond the Textile Paradigm: Philadelphia's Manufacturing Sector, 1850–1880," unpublished manuscript in possession of PSHP (1979).

Lees, Lynn; and Modell, John. "The Irish Countryman Urbanized: A Comparative Perspective on the Famine Migration, London and Philadelphia," *Journal of Urban History*, 3 (August 1977), 391–408; in this volume.

Licht, Walter. "The Railwaymen of Philadelphia, 1860–1880: A Socio-Demographic Portrait," paper presented at Social Science History Association (Cambridge, Mass.: November 1979).

Miller, Roger. "Household Activity Patterns in the Emerging Nineteenth-Century Suburb," paper presented at Social Science History Association (Columbus, Ohio: November 1978).

————; and Siry, Joseph. "The Emerging Suburb: West Philadelphia, 1850–

1880," unpublished manuscript in possession of PSHP (1978); appears in *Pennsylvania History*, 46 (April 1980), 99–145.

Modell, John; Furstenberg, Frank F., Jr.; Hershberg, Theodore. "Social Change and Transitions to Adulthood in Historical Perspective," *Journal of Family History*, 1 (Autumn, 1976), 7–32. Reprinted in Michael Gordon, ed., *The American Family in Social-Historical Perspective* (New York, 2nd ed., 1978), 192–219; in this volume.

———; Furstenberg, Frank F., Jr.; and Strong, Douglas. "The Timing of Marriage in the Transition to Adulthood: The Continuity of Change, 1860–1975," in John Demos and Sarane Spence Boocock, eds., *Turning Points: Historical and Sociological Essays on the Family* (Chicago, 1978, supplement to *American Journal of Sociology*, v. 84), 120–50.

———. "Suburbanization and Change in the American Family: Their Connection," *Journal of Interdisciplinary History*, 9 (Spring, 1979), 621–46.

———. "Suburbanization, Schooling, and Fertility in Philadelphia, 1880–1920: Toward an Ecology of Family Decisions," paper presented at United States Department of Housing Conference, "The Dynamics of Modern Industrial Cities" (Storrs, Ct.: September 1979).

Putman, Stephan H. "Calibrating a Disaggregated Residential Allocation Model—DRAM," in D. B. Massey and P. W. J. Batey, eds., *London Papers in Regional Science 7. Alternative Frameworks for Analysis* (London, 1977), 108–24.

———. "Calibrating a Residential Model for Nineteenth-Century Philadelphia," *Environment and Planning A*, 9 (1977), 449–60.

Roberts, Jeffrey. "The Central District," paper presented at Social Science History Association (Philadelphia, Pa.: October 1976).

———. "Railroads and the Growth of the Downtown: Philadelphia, 1830–1900," in Gillette and Cutler, eds., *The Divided Metropolis*.

Schmitz, Mark. "Alternative Estimators for the Elasticity of Substitution: Micro Evidence from Nineteenth-Century Manufacturing," unpublished manuscript in possession of PSHP (January 1979).

———. "The Elasticity of Substitution in Nineteenth-Century Manufacturing: A Comparison of Alternative Estimators," paper presented at Southern Economic Association (Atlanta, Ga.: 1979); to appear in *Explorations in Economic History* (forthcoming).

Seaman, Jeff; Condran, Gretchen. "Nominal Record Linkage By Machine and Hand: An Investigation of Linkage Techniques Using the Manuscript Census and the Death Register, Philadelphia, 1880," paper presented at American Statistical Association (Washington, D.C.: August 13–16, 1979); in *1979 Proceedings of the Social Statistics Section of the American Statistical Association* (Washington, D.C.: American Statistical Association, 1980).

Sobotowski, Christopher. "Software," *Historical Methods Newsletter*, 9 (March–June, 1976), 164–74.

Talbott, Page. "Shop and Factory: Philadelphia Furniture Makers and Manufacturers, 1850–1880," in Kenneth L. Ames, ed., *Furniture in Victorian America* (Watkins Glen, N.Y.: forthcoming, 1980).

Thomas, George. "Architectural Patronage and the Shape of the City, 1850–1925," in Gillette and Cutler, eds., *The Divided Metropolis*.

Whitney, William. "Manufacturing Location at Mid-Century," paper presented at Social Science History Association (Philadelphia, Pa.: October 1976).

Williams, Henry; Ulle, Robert. "Frankford, Philadelphia: The Development of a Nineteenth-Century Urban Black Community," *Pennsylvania Heritage* (December 1977), 2–8.

Ph.D. Dissertations Completed

Hershberg, Theodore. "The Philadelphia Social History Project: A Methodological History" (History, Stanford University, 1973).

Burstein, Alan N. "Residential Distribution and Mobility of Irish and German Immigrants in Philadelphia, 1850–1880" (Demography, University of Pennsylvania, 1975).

Greenberg, Stephanie. "Industrialization in Philadelphia: The Relationship Between Industrial Location and Residential Patterns, 1880–1930" (Sociology, Temple University, 1977).

Miller, Roger. "Time-Geographic Assessment of the Impact of Horse-Car Transportation in Philadelphia, 1850–1860" (Geography, University of California, Berkeley, 1979).

Light, Dale. "Class, Ethnicity and the Urban Ecology in a Nineteenth-Century City: Philadelphia's Irish, 1840–1890" (History, University of Pennsylvania, 1979).

Glassberg, Eudice. "Philadelphians in Need: Client Experiences with Two Philadelphia Benevolent Societies, 1830–1880" (Social Work, University of Pennsylvania, 1980).

Crum, John. "The Citizen Versus the City: Municipal Bureaucracy in Nineteenth-Century Philadelphia" (History, University of Delaware, 1980).

Gruenstein, John. "Intrametropolitan Firm Location and Land-Use Patterns in Philadelphia" (Economics, University of Pennsylvania, 1980).

Ph.D Dissertations in Progress

Ball, Wendy. "The Female-Headed Black Family: Philadelphia, 1838–1880." American Civilization. University of Pennsylvania.

Brown, Scott. "Changes in the Structure of Labor Demand and Supply in Philadelphia, 1850–1880." Population Studies Center. University of Pennsylvania.

Cheney, Rose. "Ecological Correlates of Infant and Childhood Mortality in Philadelphia, 1880." Population Studies Center. University of Pennsylvania.

Fishbane, Richard. "Teachers in Transition: The Development of Public School Teaching as a Profession in Nineteenth-Century Philadelphia." Social Foundations of Education. University of Pennsylvania.

Kawaguchi, Leslie Ann. "The Germans in Philadelphia During the Nineteenth Century." History. University of California, Los Angeles.

Roberts, Jeffrey. "The Growth of Philadelphia's Central District, 1830–1900." History. Temple University.

Steinberg, Allen. "The Criminal Courts and the Transformation of Criminal Justice in Philadelphia, 1815–1874." History. Columbia University.

Ulle, Robert. "Institutional Development and Attitudes in Nineteenth-Century Black Philadelphia." History. University of Pennsylvania.

Wallock, Leonard. "The Impact of Industrial Capitalism on the Skilled Sector of the Workforce: Philadelphia's Artisans in the Nineteenth Century." History. Columbia University.

M.S. Theses Completed

Graduate Group in Computer and Information Sciences, Moore School of Electrical Engineering, University of Pennsylvania

Miller, Buffington Clay. "A Computerized Method of Determining Family Structure from Mid-Nineteenth Century Census Data" (August 1972).

Palladinetti, Stephen J., Jr. "The Evolution of the Source Conversion Process at the Philadelphia Social History Project" (May 1974).

Stickel, Terry. "A Computerized Nominal Record Linkage System" (December 1972).

Appendix II: Data Description

HENRY WILLIAMS

Since its inception in 1969, the Philadelphia Social History Project (PSHP) has amassed a wide range of information on Philadelphia's population, economy, and urban infrastructure in the mid to late nineteenth century.[1] While the intellectual rationale for studying Philadelphia during a period of significant spatial, demographic, economic, and infrastructural expansion is sound, the availability of reliable quantifiable historical data has provided an equally powerful inducement to study the city in the period between 1850 and 1880. Most of these data have been converted to machine-readable form and represent the primary data base for the articles contained in this anthology. To avoid unnecessary repetition throughout the text, we have deleted most discussion of the PSHP data base from individual articles and have included it in this summary section.

The contents of the current PSHP data base were not part of a "master plan" that existed at the outset of research in 1969. Funding for our efforts was never available to build a data base *per se* or provide programmatic support. Funding was available only on the basis of peer review competition for federal grants to support discrete research projects. Had we known in 1969 that resources would be available to us spanning the next decade, it is quite likely that our approach would have been somewhat different. This is not to suggest that the data which currently comprise our data base were collected in a random fashion. Each data set was added to broaden the analytic framework used in the research, and the rationale for its collection was spelled out in separate grant proposals. Thus, although the data were collected for specified and limited purposes, they have also been used to answer different questions, many of which were unanticipated at the outset of a given research topic. The comprehensive nature of the extant data base, moreover, has attracted and sustained the involvement of researchers from a broad spectrum of disciplines to explore a wide range of topics relating to the development of the urban-industrial metropolis and the experience of its diverse population groups.

PSHP researchers have standardized the boundaries of the geo-political unit known as Philadelphia by gathering all data (when possible) for the area comprising Philadelphia County. Unlike the City of Philadelphia, the County has retained the same size and shape throughout the nineteenth and twentieth centuries. In 1854, the City of Philadelphia expanded from its rather modest river-to-river boundaries, containing some two square miles, to its present-day limits, encompassing about 130 square miles. The Act of Consolidation which accomplished this enlargement made the City of Philadelphia coterminous with surrounding districts of Philadelphia County. Thus, although the City expanded, the County kept its borders; it is these boundaries which operationally delineate "Philadelphia" in PSHP research.

This appendix will first describe the PSHP's principal data sources and indicate some problems encountered with their use. (A concise list and description of these sources is presented in tabular form at the conclusion of this appendix.) It will then discuss some of the ways PSHP researchers have integrated these separate data sets to gain more comprehensive perspectives on particular topics. In a final section, the appendix will consider the several spatial categories employed by the PSHP and will relate the creation of this areal system to the Project's present ecological focus. Indeed, it is precisely our ecological orientation that permits the effective linkage of our varied data on population, economy, and urban infrastructure and creates the potential for a more holistic view of the city.

Population

The primary source documents for the study of population are the United States Manuscript Censuses of Population for 1850, 1860, 1870, and 1880. Federal censuses have been taken every ten years since 1790 as required by the Constitution, but until 1850 the census generally recorded only the names of household heads with summary data describing the age and sex structure of the household. Beginning in 1850, however, census marshals enumerated each member of the household separately and recorded specific information on each person's age, sex, color, place of birth, school attendance, literacy, physical and psychological handicaps (deaf, dumb, blind, insane), and, for males, occupation. In addition, a number of other variables, such as real property (1850, 1860, 1870), personal property (1860, 1870), female occupations (1860, 1870, 1880), parents' place of birth (1870: whether foreign born; 1880: actual place of birth), relationship to head of household (1880), and street address (1880) were variously recorded.[2] Unfortunately, the manuscript schedules of the 1890 census were accidentally destroyed in a Commerce Department fire in the 1920s and are lost to scholars. The 1900 census was not opened without restrictions to researchers until 1977 and was not available during the primary data collecting stage of the Project. Post-1900 manuscript censuses remain closed to the general public.[3]

Scholarly interests and the constraints of time and resources dictated the data sets that PSHP researchers created from the census schedules. Three basic files were developed. To study individuals and groups, all blacks, all Irish and German males eighteen years and above, and a sample of native-white males eighteen years and above (one-sixth in 1850 and 1860; one-ninth in 1870 and 1880) were selected from each census. The PSHP recorded all census information pertaining to these individuals. Except for blacks, however, this data set excludes women, children, and households. Thus, to study these individuals as well as households, another data set was created consisting of 2,000 complete households of each ethnic group for each census year. Again, researchers recorded all census information reported for each member of each household. The third data set contains information on a small areal unit basis (described below) for all those enumerated in the four federal censuses but includes only data on age (categorized into five-year intervals in 1850, 1860, and 1870, and ten-year intervals in 1880), sex, and ethnicity as indicated by place of birth. The number of dwellings and households for each spatial unit was also recorded. This file permits the computation of age and sex ratios for each ethnic group for each census year and, because it is arranged by spatial unit (see later discussion), it also permits the examination of how demographic patterns differed across the face of the city at different points in time.

Once the information from the censuses was transcribed and placed on computer tape, researchers assigned a series of numeric codes to certain data categories. Places of birth and occupations received codes to permit a variety of higher level aggregations. For example, the PSHP appended a series of codes to indicate the sectoral and industrial affiliation, socioeconomic rank, and worksite of the occupational designations included in the census.[4] Household relationships were inferred for families found in the 1850, 1860, and 1870 censuses in which the relationships of individuals to the household head were not made explicit. Clearly, various interpretations can be placed on the assignment of certain of these codes, particularly the socioeconomic rank (VERT) and household relationship codes. Because researchers did not alter the original data, however, future scholars can amend these codes and/or manipulate code categories as they deem appropriate. The flexibility of the coding format allows researchers to define their analytic groupings according to their particular conceptual and theoretical orientations.

Although historians have rarely scrutinized census data as closely as they have more traditional materials, some studies have questioned the inclusiveness of the enumerations and the validity of the census data.[5] PSHP researchers have attempted to investigate these possible sources of census error by taking advantage of a unique historical occurrence: the retaking of the 1870 federal census for Philadelphia. Philadelphia's municipal leaders believed the 1870 census severely undercounted the city's population and demanded, for political and civic reasons, that the census be redone. The recount, taken six months after the initial survey, showed only an increase of 16,000 in population over the first tally (a 2.4 percent increase), but individual wards exhibited wide disparities from the first to the second enumeration, suggesting the possibility of census error. An analysis undertaken by Frank Furstenberg, Jr., Douglas Strong, and Albert Crawford indicates that about 82 percent of the households sampled from the June survey were located in the November enumeration and that within these persisting households, the household members most likely to disappear between the two surveys were not members of the immediate nuclear family.[6] Although the lowest rungs of the working-class, particularly blacks, were probably missed by the census-takers in both censuses, the relatively high persistence rate of households and of nuclear family members suggests that the failure to locate individuals and households in the second census is probably due primarily to real physical mobility and not to census underenumeration.[7] Moreover, preliminary results from the analysis of the census data itself, implemented by comparing the data on persisting households in the two censuses, indicate a close similarity between the information recorded at the two points in time. These findings have buoyed our confidence in the reliability of the census data on which much of our research relies.[8]

The Quaker and Abolitionist censuses of blacks for 1838, 1847, and 1856 constitute the other major machine-readable population resource. Initially taken in 1838 to demonstrate the stability and significance of the black community and to forestall the abrogation of black voting rights, the censuses were continued and present an invaluable view of the mid-nineteenth-century black population of Philadelphia. Although these censuses list only household heads, providing aggregate information for other household members, and exclude the substantial number of blacks living in white households, they provide data not found in the federal population schedules. When combined with the information on blacks taken from the four federal censuses, they offer researchers a richly detailed view of Philadelphia's black community spanning some forty years.

The three censuses are not of equal inclusiveness or quality, however. The 1838 and 1847 enumerations cover only the "old" City of Philadelphia (river-to-river and from Vine to South Streets) and the immediate surrounding districts (Spring Garden, Northern Liberties, Southwark, Moyamensing, Kensington—1838, West Philadelphia—1847); the 1856 survey includes blacks living throughout the newly enlarged city which, as today, conforms to the boundaries of Philadelphia County. In spite of this deficiency in areal coverage, the earlier censuses are superior historical documents. The 1838 and 1847 censuses contain data on a wide range of social and demographic variables describing the household indicating address, household size, occupation, whether members were born in Pennsylvania, status-at-birth, debts, taxes, number of children attending school, names of beneficial societies and churches (1838), property brought to Philadelphia from other states (1838), sex composition (1847), age structure (1847), literacy (1847), names of schools attended (1847), temperance (1847), number belonging to beneficial and temperance societies and to churches (1847), size of rooms and number of people per room (1847), and miscellaneous remarks (1847). While the 1856 census includes the household address and reports literacy, occupation, status-at-birth, and occasional passing remarks about individual households and their occupants, it excludes the other informational categories. Moreover, unlike the other two surveys, it lists the occupations of only higher status blacks, excluding unskilled and semiskilled designations, and records the status-at-birth of adults only. Indeed, it even fails to provide data permitting the calculation of the size and age and sex structure of households.[9]

Another important source of population data, although not made machine-readable by the PSHP, is the Philadelphia City Directory series. Analogous to the "White Pages" of today, city directories were published annually throughout the nineteenth century, are arranged alphabetically, and contain the occupations, home addresses, occasionally the business addresses, and, in the case of partners or owners, the business affiliations of those listed. Including less information than the federal censuses described above, the directories offer the obvious advantage of providing a yearly survey of the city's population.

The city directories, however, must be used with caution. Coverage in the pre-1854 city directories, as in the case of the 1838 and 1847 censuses of blacks, does not include individuals from an area much beyond the limits of the "old" city and "adjoining districts." Table 1 demonstrates that the 1850 directory contains a markedly lower proportion of Philadelphia County's population than the post-1854 volumes. Moreover, all of the directories tend to include a disproportionate number of those in the middle and upper ranks of society and exclude many of those in the working class, especially blacks and transients. In addition, most of the listings in each directory, though not all, are of male household heads and exclude most women as well as young men who did not head their own households. Nevertheless, as the following table indicates, the city directories do include a good proportion of the city's adult male population. They have proved vital in determining addresses for individuals in the 1850, 1860, and 1870 federal population manuscript censuses and for individuals found on organizational lists and have been invaluable in discovering the owners and partners of the city's major businesses.[10]

Aside from the federal censuses and city directories which provide a file of Philadelphia's entire population, the PSHP has also developed more specialized lists of individuals. For example, the Project has collected membership lists of individuals belonging to Irish, German, and black voluntary associations for the period from about 1820 to about 1900. Data includes the name, organization, position, and year of membership for each individual. The types of associations include political, literary, beneficial, recreational, business, para-military, fraternal, and church organizations.

Table 1.   Estimated Coverage of Philadelphia City Directories, 1850–1880

	Estimated Tot. Persons Listed in C.D.	% of Tot. Pop. (Total pop.)	% of Adult Pop.: 20+ (Adult pop.)	% Adult Male Pop. (Adult male pop.)
1850 (McElroy's)	51,420	12.6 (408,081)	23.1 (222,939)	48.3 (106,455)
1860 (Cohen's)	118,422	21.0 (564,587)	38.3 (309,106)	81.5 (145,231)
1870 (Gopsill's)	176,318	26.8 (656,808)	47.1 (374,342)	100.5 (175,453)
1880 (Gopsill's)	206,350	24.5 (841,399)	41.0 (503,599)	86.7 (238,118)

Sources: For full bibliographic information on city directories, see note 9. Figures on adult population of Philadelphia are derived from the manuscript schedules of the U.S. Censuses of Population for 1850, 1860, 1870, and 1880.

Note: For each of the census years, an estimate was made of the number of entries in the Philadelphia city directory of that year. It was then determined what proportion of three selected population groupings—total, adult, and adult male—these estimates represented. As indicated in the table, the 1850 city directory offers the least satisfactory coverage, but this is not surprising since directory coverage was confined to the "old" City and surrounding districts while the population totals are for the entire county. The proportions obtained for the other years are fairly regular, except for the proportion derived for the 1870 adult male population. Because the percentage of the total adult population is not far different than the figures found for 1860 and 1870, this unusually high percentage may indicate the inclusion in this directory of an uncommonly large number of women.

The file thus permits an analysis of the formal social networks that constituted the fabric of the various nineteenth-century ethnic communities. Moreover, when individuals on these lists are linked to the censuses, as has already been done for the blacks and the Irish, the foundation will be constructed for a socioeconomic and demographic analysis of these several ethnic and racial groups.[11]

The final primary population source consists of the some 20,000 individuals included in the Philadelphia Register of Deaths during the twelve-month period beginning July 1 following the mid-June 1880 federal census enumeration. Not until 1860 did the city begin systematic efforts to record all of the deaths occurring within its borders; by 1880, death registration in Philadelphia was nearly complete. The twelve-month period was selected to permit the linking of people on the register to the census population schedules and thus allow the combination of the two data sets. This strategy is intended to provide an independent check on the validity of the information found in the two sources and to analyze the household context which preceded death. The mortality register contains sufficient information (see list at end of this appendix) to study mortality differentials by disease, age, ethnicity, and residence (and through address access to ecological factors) in the period just before the sharp decline in death rates in late nineteenth-century American cities.[12]

Economy

Two basic sources exist for the study of Philadelphia's businesses and economic growth: the United States Manuscript Censuses of Manufactures for 1850, 1860, 1870, and 1880 and the Philadelphia Business Directories. The Census of Manufactures was first taken in 1810, again in 1820 and 1840, but omitted in 1830. According to Carroll Wright, however, these early "efforts were of little avail . . . and the results, although printed, have but little value."[13] Beginning in 1850, census officials made a concerted attempt to compile a set of usable industrial statistics, an effort that continued in the later enumerations gathered by the PSHP. In 1850, 1860, and 1870, the census listed firms by their geographic area within the city. In 1880, the census grouped firms of certain industry types (paper, slaughtering, meat packing, salt works, boots and shoes, leather, lumber, sawmills, brickyards, tile works, agricultural implements, flour and grist, and dairy), but most firms were listed in their geographic sequence.

Although the variables included in these censuses differ slightly from year to year, data on name and type of firm, number of employees, power, raw materials, wages, finished product, and amount of capital are found in each year. In most cases, the categories are quite compatible from census to census. The classification of power changed slightly in 1880, but it is easily reconciled with earlier definitions. In addition, the number of employees are disaggregated into males, females, and youths in 1870 and 1880 but only into males and females in 1850 and 1860. Except for the detail lost in the early years, this poses no severe problem, since youths were most likely included in the earlier enumerations and just not reported as such; hence, the total employee figures are compatible for all four years. In no year were specific addresses provided for any of the establishments. The PSHP determined these by linking individual firms to their listing in the business directories and to a variety of other sources that contained street addresses.

Potentially more serious problems involve the validity of the data recorded for each firm and the inclusiveness of the census itself. In her recent book, Diane Lindstrom claims that "Pennsylvanians" regarded the 1850 returns as "inaccurate," particularly in their underestimation of manufacturing activity. Lorin Blodget, a late nineteenth-century local booster and statistician, labeled the 1880 survey "inadequate and injurious" for its failure to demonstrate the alleged industrial growth of the city between 1870 and 1880. He conducted his own industrial enumeration two years later.[14]

While the Censuses of Manufactures do not comprise unimpeachable sources, our own analyses of the returns indicate that the data reported are, for most purposes, reliable. For example, economic theory predicts an inverse relationship among industries ordered by labor and then by capital productivity. In "Manufacture and Productivity," Laurie and Schmitz find that, for the most part, this hierarchy is obtained when selected industries in 1850 and 1880 are ranked according to these two measures.[15] This result strongly suggests that the essential data on number of workers, capital, and product, used to generate the indices, are valid.

The other potentially major problem noted by contemporaries concerns the inclusiveness of the censuses. In all four years, the censuses enumerated only firms producing an annual product exceeding $500. Thus, the smallest shops were necessarily missed. Because this cutoff is made explicit, however, these constraints pose no real obstacle to the variety of analyses undertaken. Moreover, we know that the censuses did, in fact, record a large number of small firms and that these establishments had only a peripheral impact on the course of industrialization in Philadelphia between 1850 and 1880. In each of the four census years, the proportion of firms with 5 or less employees constituted more than 57 percent of all firms in the census, but in no year did these firms employ more than 13 percent of the workforce and in no decade between 1850 and 1880 did they contribute more than 7 percent to the growth of industrial employment in the city.

Although it is a manageable problem to allow for companies that were explicitly excluded by census instructions, it is another matter to account for firms that should have been enumerated in the census but were not. The most glaring omission occurred in the 1880 census where 80 percent of the textile firms and some clothing businesses were missing from the manuscript schedules, although they were counted in the published aggregate statistics for the city. To fill this gap, the PSHP supplemented the census with Lorin Blodget's survey of the city's major industries.[16] Blodget's enumeration, although not as detailed as the federal census, serves as a good proxy, and indeed our only proxy, for the firms missing in the manuscript schedules. As Stephanie Greenberg observes, "While Blodget's count of firms and employees is often substantially higher than that of the federal census, the two data sources are well matched for textiles—55,000 jobs counted by Blodget versus 51,000 counted by the federal census."[17] Unfortunately, the Blodget survey contains fewer variables than the federal censuses, including information only on the firm's name, type of product, location, number of employees (not differentiated by sex), number of engines and horsepower, and number and type of machines. The possibility that the federal schedules missed other firms also exists, but it is a problem that potentially plagues all historical documents.

By its nature, of course, the manufacturing census excludes nonindustrial establishments. To analyze commercial, financial, and service businesses, the PSHP utilizes the Philadelphia Business Directories. Published annually throughout most of the nineteenth century, these volumes, much like today's "Yellow Pages," provide a comprehensive tabulation of all business enterprises in the city. They are arranged by type of business (product sold or service offered) and then alphabetically by firm name and include the street address of each company listed. Thus, unlike the industrial censuses, the business directories can produce a spatial distribution of all firms included in their lists. As with the city directories, however, the pre-1854 surveys limited their areal coverage to firms in the "old" City and its adjoining districts. Between 1850 and 1860, for example, the number of entries in the directories almost tripled, from 10,275 to 28,031, but the larger part of this increase was undoubtedly due to the expanded County-wide coverage in the latter year. Unfortunately, the directories contain no information about the nature of the firms themselves. Broad in its inclusion of firms, the business directories offer only a limited view of Philadelphia's business economy.[18]

As with the individuals selected from the population schedules, a series of numeric codes was appended to each firm in the manufacturing censuses and business directories. These codes indicate the business type of each company and permit aggregation into categories requisite for analytical purposes. Again, as with the population schedules, these codes have permitted researchers considerable latitude in defining business groupings.[19]

Urban Infrastructure

The most significant component of the infrastructural data is the information on the transportation networks. For the period from 1840 to 1880, PSHP researchers have located, plotted, and made machine-readable the routes of all street railways, trolleys, omnibuses, and railroads. Thus, we are now in a position to measure the relative proximity of people and business to transportation routes and to assess the impact that these transportation forms have had on the development of the city. The railroad data are particularly valuable, since they include not only the route of the main line but also the number of tracks, sidings, and spurs in a given geographic area as well as the size and potential importance of stations, depots, and junctions.[20]

The data on sewage facilities represent our initial efforts at gauging the level of public services available in the nineteenth-century city and determining the population groups that first benefited from the provision of these amenities. While the collected PSHP data cover only the post–Civil War period and thus miss the earliest periods of sewer line construction, the data offer an in-depth view of an era of major residential expansion.[21] The PSHP also has compiled maps of water lines in Philadelphia between 1800 and 1880, but has yet to computerize these data.

The PSHP file on institutions describes some 3,000 public, private, secular, and religious organizations that constitute the social infrastructure of the city. Culled largely from the appendices to the city directories for 1850, 1860, 1870, and 1880, this data set contains the name, year, type, and address of each institution, and a set of codes that permit aggregative analyses across these variables. In addition, the business directories contain lists of many other institutions such as schools and hospitals that also provided services to the Philadelphia community.[22]

Data Integration

Although the major data collection stage of the PSHP is now complete, researchers are still engaged in document linkage. This process involves the assembling of all possible information about a particular activity, individual, business, or geographic area, and the creation of an integrated data set that combines data from several sources on the given topic of interest. Two basic approaches characterize the PSHP's attempts at record linkage: a. the linking of information from the same type of document across several years; b. the linking of information across several documents but within the same year or proximate years.

The first approach is well known to students of social and geographic mobility who measure the socioeconomic and physical movement of individuals by tracing them through successive censuses and city directories. The PSHP has developed a computerized linkage program which was used to link Irish and German males and the entire black population within the three decades from 1850 to 1880.[23] The program can also be modified to perform linkages between firms in the manufacturing censuses and the business directories.

The linking of data in several documents within proximate years is also well understood by social historians. The PSHP has carried out these combinations in a variety of projects. To undertake a social and demographic analysis of the Irish and blacks who were members of nineteenth-century voluntary associations, researchers have linked individuals found in the organizational lists to the various census years. For the Irish, linkage was made only to the census closest to the date of membership, but for the blacks, tracing attempts were made to all four federal censuses of population and to the three Quaker and Abolitionist censuses.[24] Researchers interested in the social origins of the industrial elite have made linkages among the censuses of manufactures, the city directories, and the censuses of population. The industrial censuses provide the names of and data pertaining to the city's largest industrial establishments; the city directories provide the names and addresses of the owners and partners of these firms; the federal population schedules provide the social and demographic data necessary to carry out the analysis of this social group.[25] In a related venture designed to differentiate artisan employers from employees, a distinction not often made in the occupational listings in the federal censuses, the PSHP traced shoemakers and printers found in the population schedules to the city directories and then to the business directories and manufacturing censuses. The population censuses provide the initial sample of artisans; the city directories provide their exact home addresses and also offer clues as to their status within the trade; the business directories and manufacturing census offer the clearest way to distinguish between artisans who were employers, those included in these two sources, and those who were employees, those not so included.[26] Another project currently underway involves the linking of individuals found in the mortality register of

1880–1881 to the 1880 population census to investigate the social, demographic, and ecological context of death in the nineteenth-century city and to evaluate the validity of census data through comparison with an independent source.[27]

Areal Units

Perhaps the most formidable, and with hope the most consequential, attempt at linking documents within the same year involves PSHP efforts to connect activities located in close spatial proximity. For even relatively small areas of the city, we are able to describe in some detail their population, economic, and infrastructural characteristics. This ecological orientation offers the greatest potential for fusing together our disparate data sources to explore the relationship between spatial context and individual-level behavior. It relies heavily on the creation of spatial units which accurately delineate the boundaries of social and economic phenomena.

Project associates have used a number of areal units in their analyses of urban space. Street addresses, necessary to assign aggregate spatial unit locations, are found on many of the original, but not all, PSHP machine-readable documents (see list at end of this appendix). Where street addresses do not appear on the original document, as in the 1850, 1860, and 1870 manuscript population censuses and all of the manufacturing censuses, researchers determined addresses by linkage to other documents. For example, individuals in the population censuses were traced to the city directories. Those that could not be linked to the city directories received addresses approximating those of the people on the same or nearby census pages who were traced. The patterns of street addresses contained in the 1880 census document that census marshals, most of the time, followed a logical route.[28] Manufacturing firms were traced to the business directories which include exact street locations. The determination of street addresses was most difficult for the city's outlying areas where city and business directory coverage was more sporadic than in the downtown. This problem was especially acute for the 1850 population and manufacturing censuses, since the directories for those years did not include people or firms from those regions and contemporary maps had to be consulted. Even for later census years, however, the peripheral areas presented problems.

Wards, the spatial unit most often utilized by those studying the nineteenth century, are found on all the population census schedules; the 1850, 1860, and 1870 censuses of manufactures; the mortality register for 1880–1881; and on the list of sewage facilities. Although the wards' unequal sizes and shapes and the political considerations entering into the determination of their boundaries limit their usefulness for spatial analysis (especially over time analyses), wards do have value as areal units. Much Philadelphia data, both for the 1850–1880 period as well as before and after, is aggregated by ward, and to incorporate that information into our analysis requires the use of comparable areal units. In addition, ward boundaries often roughly correspond to natural community boundaries and thus can be used to investigate neighborhood development. The modification of the basic ward boundaries in the 1854 Act of Consolidation reduces their compatibility over the 1850 to 1880 period, but the changes were not extensive and the ward parameters in 1850 approximate those in the latter three census years. It is also true that new wards were created between 1855 and 1880, thus further altering the post-Consolidation pattern. After 1861, these new units, however, were formed out of the old wards, thus permitting a statistical combination of 1880 wards to duplicate the post-Consolidation distribution.[29]

The limited value of the ward as a unit for spatial analysis necessitated a search for a more flexible, less arbitrary unit. The fronting block, "a unit composed of all buildings facing each other on a single block lying between intersecting streets,"[30] was rejected as an alternative owing to the lack of precision of street addressing on a number of our most important documents, specifically the 1850, 1860, and 1870 population schedules and the 1838, 1847, and 1856 Quaker and Abolitionist censuses of blacks. The unit finally selected as the basis for the PSHP's spatial system is the grid unit. Each unit is quite small and fixed in size—660 by 775 feet or one by one and one-quarter blocks—and, unlike either the ward or fronting block, has boundaries which "neither change over time nor [are] drawn with deliberate bias, and which . . . accommodate imprecise addresses."[31] A "grid" system, adopted from F. J. Robert's 1838 "Map of the Old City of Philadelphia and the Adjoining Districts," is superimposed over the entire map of the city, creating roughly 7,000 grid units. Each location in the city is part of a grid unit; thus for each person, business, transportation route, institution, or sewage facility for which we can determine even an imprecise street location, a grid unit can be assigned (see list at end of this appendix). Some firms in the manufacturing censuses whose addresses could not be determined could not receive grid units. These firms were disproportionately located in peripheral areas of the city, a result of the deficiencies inherent in the business directories used to provide addresses. In all four years, however, a majority of firms employing an even greater majority of the industrial workforce did receive grid units (see Table 2).

The limited size and fixed boundaries of the grid unit are its two most significant qualities. Specifically, they permit the aggregation of the grid

Table 2.   Manufacturing Firms and Employees with Addresses, 1850–1880

	Total Firms	% With Addresses	Total Employees	% Employees In Firms With Addresses
1850	4542	69.8	57958	86.0
1860	6330	75.5	99993	86.6
1870	8366	86.2	134501	95.4
1880	9163	81.2	174764	96.0

into larger spatial units which are appropriate for various kinds of analyses. The 16 zones and the 363 zones used in research on industrial location and the census tract-level units used in "Industrial Location and Ethnic Residential Patterns" (404 tracts) and "A Tale of Three Cities" (248 tracts) were created by aggregating up from the grid-unit level.[32] Each of these units has its accompanying advantages: the 16 zones approximate the ward structure of the city (but are consistent through 1880, unlike the ward system), and thus can be used in conjunction with data available only at the ward level; the 363-zone system, consisting of a series of units 5 grids long by 4 grids wide, provides larger units than the grid but remain consistent in size and shape; the 404 (or 248) census tract units permit direct comparisons with twentieth-century census data which are already grouped in tract units. In sum, the grid unit constitutes an appropriate building block which can be aggregated to produce spatial units of different shapes and sizes permitting comparison with already existing spatial systems.

PSHP attempts to conduct ecological analyses of Philadelphia have generated efforts to combine data from different sources within the same year for all grid units within the city. The fashioning of a grid record represents our most ambitious attempt at document linkage and involves the collection within a central file arranged by spatial unit of all data pertaining to the population, economy, and infrastructure of the city. By aggregating from the grid unit, or from whatever unit is eventually employed, we will be able to reconstruct the texture of life in nineteenth-century Philadelphia and to assess the impact of environment on individual behavior as well as on the growth and development of the city itself.

NOTES

1. For a background history of the Philadelphia Social History Project, see Theodore Hershberg, "The Philadelphia Social History Project: A Methodological History" (Ph.D. dissertation, History, Stanford University, 1973); Theodore Hershberg, guest editor, "A Special Issue: The Philadelphia Social History Project," *Historical Methods Newsletter* 9 (March–June, 1976), hereafter cited as "PSHP: Special Issue."

2. For a complete listing of all variables for each census year, see Carroll D. Wright, *The History and Growth of the United States Census* (Washington, D.C.: U.S. Government Printing Office, 1900), 131–77. The Censuses of Population prior to 1850 did variously specify number of slaves (all years), race (1820, 1830, 1840), industrial affiliation (1820, 1840), unnaturalized foreigners (1820, 1830), physically or emotionally handicapped individuals (1830, 1840), and school attendance (1840), but this information was collected at the household level and cannot be disaggregated. Moreover, the data on age and industrial affiliation was aggregated into fairly broad categories (i.e., 10-year age groupings and fairly inclusive economic sectors) that severely limit their use for social historians.

3. The PSHP will utilize the 1900 manuscript census schedules.

4. See Buffington Clay Miller, "A Computerized Method of Determining Family Structure from Mid-Nineteenth Century Census Data" (Masters thesis, Graduate Group in Computer and Information Sciences, Moore School of Electrical Engineering, University of Pennsylvania, 1972); Theodore Hershberg, "A Method for the Computerized Study of Family and Household Structure Using the Manuscript Schedules of the U.S. Census of Population, 1850–1880," *The Family in Historical Perspective* 1 (Spring 1973), 6–20; Michael A. Strong, "Computers as Logical Decision-Making Tools in Demography (with Interactive Assistance from the Human Demographer)," paper presented at the Annual Meeting of the Population Association of America (Philadelphia: April 25–28, 1979); Frank Furstenberg, Jr., Theodore Hershberg, and John Modell, "The Origins of the Female-Headed Black Family: The Impact of the Urban Environment," *Journal of Interdisciplinary History* 6 (September 1975), 211–33; also in this volume. For a more complete discussion of the occupational and industrial codes and the process by which they were assigned, see Theodore Hershberg and Robert Dockhorn, "Occupational Classification," in "PSHP: Special Issue," *op. cit.*, 59–98.

5. Even those intimately involved in the census enumeration process recognized problems with the survey. See Francis A. Walker, "Preface," *Ninth Census of the United States, 1870* (Washington, D.C.: U.S. Government Printing Office, 1872), I, xix–xxxiv. For a twentieth-century evaluation, see John B. Sharpless and Ray M. Shortridge, "Biased Underenumeration in Census Manuscripts: Methodological Implications," *Journal of Urban History* 1 (August 1975), 409–39. In addition, contemporary social mobility literature is replete with references to the value of nineteenth-century census data. For a list of citations, see Theodore Hershberg, "The New Urban History: Toward an Interdisciplinary History of the City," *Journal of Urban History* 5 (November 1978), 37–38 (note 32); also in this volume.

6. Frank Furstenberg, Jr., Douglas Strong, and Albert G. Crawford, "What Happened When the Census Was Redone: An Analysis of the Recount of 1870 in Philadelphia," in a special issue of *Sociology and Social Research* 63 (March 1979), 475–505.

Another PSHP study also seeks to evaluate the census. It links people listed in the Philadelphia mortality register for the twelve months following the taking of the 1880 census to the population schedules of that year and will attempt to determine possible underenumeration and data misrecording. See Gretchen Condran and Jeff Seaman, "Linkages of the 1880–81 Philadelphia Death Register to the 1880 Manuscript Census: Procedures and Preliminary Results," paper presented at Population Association of America Meeting (Philadelphia: April 26–28, 1979), to appear in *Historical Methods* (forthcoming); Jeff Seaman and Gretchen Condran, "Nominal Record Linkage by Machine and Hand: An Investigation of Linkage Techniques Using the Manuscript Census and the Death Register, Philadelphia, 1880," paper presented at the American Statistical Association (Washington, D.C.: August 13–16, 1979); appears in *1979 Proceedings of the Social Statistics Section of the American*

Statistical Association (Washington, D.C.: American Statistical Association, 1980).

7. Michael Katz, in linking males from the 1851 census of Hamilton to the 1852 tax assessment rolls compiled three months later, found that 70–80 percent of the *household heads* could be traced. Katz's figures for traceables may differ from the Philadelphia study for several reasons: his effort covers a three-month span as compared to a six-month period; it attempts linkage for the entire city, not just a single enumeration district; and it includes only property-owners. In another analysis, Peter Knights used Boston City Directories to examine persistence rates for one-year intervals over the period of 1830–1860. From 1830 to 1831, 84.4 percent of his sample remained in the city; from 1840 to 1841, 91.6 percent remained; and from 1850 to 1851, 88.0 percent remained. The biases in Knights's study relative to the Philadelphia study run in contrary directions: on the one hand, Knights's period is twelve months, suggesting that persistence may be less than in a six-month period, but conversely, Knights's work focuses primarily on city directory households which may have been more established than the census households investigated by Furstenberg, Strong, and Crawford. Moreover, both Katz and Knights concentrate on an earlier era than that considered in the PSHP research. See Michael B. Katz, *The People of Hamilton, Canada West: Family and Class in a Mid-Nineteenth-Century City* (Cambridge: Harvard University Press, 1975), figures obtained through personal communication with author, March 28, 1979; Peter Knights, *The Plain People of Boston, 1830–1860: A Study in City Growth* (New York: Oxford University Press, 1971).

8. Condran's and Seaman's preliminary analysis of data for individuals located in the 1880–1881 Philadelphia Register of Deaths and the 1880 census has also produced heartening results. Linkage rates between the two documents range from 50 percent to 70 percent depending upon ethnic group, and the data found in the two sources are highly similar, depending upon the individual's age. See Condran and Seaman, "Linkages," *op. cit.*

9. The Pennsylvania Society Promoting the Abolition of Slavery, *The Present State and Condition of the Free People of Color of the City of Philadelphia* (Philadelphia: Pennsylvania Society for Promoting the Abolition of Slavery, 1838); Society of Friends, *Statistical Inquiry into the Condition of the People of Colour, of the City and Districts of Philadelphia* (Philadelphia: Kite & Walton, 1849); The Pennsylvania Society for Promoting the Abolition of Slavery, *Statistics of the Colored People of Philadelphia* (Philadelphia: Pennsylvania Society for Promoting the Abolition of Slavery, 1859).

10. *A. McElroy's Philadelphia Directory, For the Year 1850* (Philadelphia: 1850); *McElroy's Philadelphia City Directory for 1860* (Philadelphia: 1860); *Cohen's Philadelphia City Directory, 1860* (Philadelphia: 1860); *Gopsill's Philadelphia City Directory for 1870* (Philadelphia: 1870); *Gopsill's Philadelphia City Directory, 1880* (Philadelphia: 1880).

11. In his dissertation, Dale B. Light, Jr., has analyzed associational linkages in the Irish community. See "The Making of an Ethnic Community: Philadelphia's Irish, 1840–1890" (Ph.D. dissertation, History, University of Pennsylvania, 1979).

12. Coprincipal Investigators: Theodore Hershberg, Gretchen Condran, "Determinants of Urban Mortality Decline: Late Nineteenth-Century Philadelphia," funded by Center for Population Research, National Institute for Child Health and Human Development (RO 1 HD 12413); Coprincipal Investigators: Theodore Hershberg, Gretchen Condran, "Urban Mortality Differentials: Ethnic, Socioeconomic, Spatial and Household Context, Philadelphia, 1880," funded by Sociology Program, Division of Social Sciences, National Science Foundation (SOC 79 07128). Applications are available upon request from PSHP. See also, Condran and Seaman, "Linkages," *op. cit.*

13. Wright, *History of the Census,* 38.

14. Diane Lindstrom, *Economic Development in the Philadelphia Region, 1810–1850* (New York: Columbia University Press, 1978), 183–84. The Philadelphia Board of Trade complained about the census slights, but, as a local booster, this organization certainly might have exaggerated its claims. Also see Lorin Blodget, *Census of Manufactures of Philadelphia* (Philadelphia, 1883), 4. Blodget, too, promoted local interests.

15. Bruce Laurie and Mark Schmitz, "Manufacture and Productivity: The Making of an Industrial Base, Philadelphia, 1850–1880," Table 10; in this volume.

16. Blodget, *Census of Manufactures, op. cit.*

17. Stephanie Greenberg, "Industrialization in Philadelphia: The Relationship Between Industrial Location and Residential Patterns, 1880–1930" (Ph.D. dissertation, Sociology, Temple University, 1977).

18. PSHP Business Directory computerized lists include data merged from the following sources: *O'Brien's Philadelphia Wholesale Business Directory and Circular for the Year 1850* (Philadelphia: 1850); *Bywater's Philadelphia Business Directory and City Guide, For the Year 1851* (Philadelphia: 1850); *Cowell's Philadelphia Business Directory* (Philadelphia: 1860); *Cohen's Philadelphia City Business Register* (Philadelphia: 1860); *Boyd's Philadelphia City Business Directory* (Philadelphia: 1859–60); *McElroy's Philadelphia City Business Directory, 1860* (Philadelphia: 1860); *Gopsill's Philadelphia Business Directory for 1870* (Philadelphia: 1870); *Gopsill's Philadelphia Business Directory for 1880* (Philadelphia: 1880).

19. Hershberg and Dockhorn, "Occupational Classification," in "PSHP: Special Issue," *op. cit.,* 59–98.

20. See Theodore Hershberg, Harold Cox, Dale Light, Jr., and Richard Greenfield, "The 'Journey-to-Work': An Empirical Investigation of Work, Residence and Transportation, Philadelphia, 1850 and 1880," in this volume; Richard R. Greenfield, "The Determinants and Dynamics of Intra-Urban Manufacturing Location: A Perspective on Nineteenth-Century Philadelphia," paper presented at the Social Science History Association (Columbus, Ohio: November 1979). Railroad data was taken from two sets of maps: Samuel L. Smedley, *Smedley's Complete Atlas of Philadelphia* (Philadelphia: 1862); *Baist's Atlas of the City of Philadelphia* (Philadelphia: 1888).

21. John Crum, "The Citizen Versus the City: Municipal Bureaucracy in Nineteenth-Century Philadelphia" (Ph.D. dissertation, History, University of Delaware, 1980).

22. Roger Miller, "Time-Geographic Assessment of the Impact of Horse-Car Transportation in Philadelphia, 1850–1860" (Ph.D. dissertation, Geography, University of California, Berkeley, 1979).

23. Theodore Hershberg, Alan Burstein, and Robert Dockhorn, "Record Linkage," in "PSHP: Special Issue," *op. cit.,* 137–63; Terry Stickel, "A Computerized Nominal Record Linkage System" (Masters thesis, Graduate Group in Computer and Information Sciences, Moore School of Electrical Engineering, University of Pennsylvania, 1972).

24. Substantive results of these linkages appear in Light, "Making of an Ethnic Community," *op. cit.;* Theodore Hershberg and Henry Williams, "Mulattoes and Blacks: Intra-Group Color Differences and Social Stratification in Nineteenth-Century Philadelphia"; in this volume.

25. Substantive results will appear in Bruce Laurie, Theodore Hershberg, and Mark Stern, "A Profile of Philadelphia's Manufacturing Elite, 1850 and 1880," in progress.

26. Leonard Wallock, "The Impact of Industrial Capitalism on the Skilled Sector of the Workforce: Philadelphia's Artisans in the Nineteenth Century" (Ph.D. dissertation, History, Columbia University, in progress). This method played an important part in Michael B. Katz's most recent work; see Michael B. Katz, Michael

J. Doucet, and Mark J. Stern, *The Social Organization of Early Industrial Capitalism* (Harvard University Press, forthcoming); and "Toward a Two-Class Model of the Nineteenth-Century City in North America," prepared for XLIII International Congress of Americanists (Vancouver, B.C.: August 10–17, 1979).

27. See note 11.

28. For a fuller discussion of this procedure, see Theodore Hershberg, "The Historical Study of Urban Space," in "PSHP: Special Issue," *op. cit.*, 100–104.

29. Also see *Ibid.*, 100.

30. *Ibid.*

31. *Ibid.* Timothy Cook and Andrew Pollott compare the capacities of the grid unit and the fronting-block systems to describe the residential patterns of morocco workers in 1880. They conclude that although analysis undertaken at the grid unit level tends to mask some ethnic or occupational clustering, fronting-block analysis is too time-consuming to be used often. In sum, "the PSHP grid [unit] analysis provides more than adequate accuracy, with the considerable advantage of being rapidly and conveniently available." See "A Fronting Block Analysis of the Residential Patterns of Late-Nineteenth Century Philadelphians: Morocco Workers, 1880, as a Test Case," unpublished manuscript in possession of PSHP (Spring 1975).

32. Greenfield, "Intra-Urban Manufacturing Location," *op. cit.;* Stephanie W. Greenberg, "Industrial Location and Ethnic Residential Patterns in an Industrializing City: Philadelphia, 1880"; Theodore Hershberg, Alan Burstein, Eugene Ericksen, Stephanie Greenberg, William Yancey, "A Tale of Three Cities: Blacks and Immigrants in Philadelphia, 1850–1880, 1930 and 1970," *The Annals* 441 (January 1979), 55–81; both essays also appear in this volume.

Philadelphia Social History Project:
Machine-Readable Data Describing Philadelphia County

I. Areal Unit

A grid pattern, with each unit one by one-and-one quarter blocks (660′ × 775′), was imposed on the map of the entire county (130 square miles) producing ca. 7,100 total grids.

All the machine-readable information identified below has been (or will be) coded for precise grid location; therefore it is possible to create an extensive set of variables for use in ecological analyses.

II. U.S. Population Manuscript Census Schedules: 1850, 1860, 1870, 1880.

Variables for each of 500,000 individuals (differ slightly by census year): name, address, age, sex, race, color, occupation, real and personal property, place of birth, literacy, marital status, school attendance.

> *For the study of individuals and groups:* Blacks: all persons (94,000); Irish: all males 18+ (142,000); Germans: all males 18+ (84,000); native-white Americans: sample males 18+ (50,000). Longitudinal files (between-census linkages) of individual black males and females, Irish males, and German males have been created.
>
> *For the study of family structure:* 2,000 households with ca. 6 persons per household for each ethnic group (Irish, German, native-white American) in each census year. Total sample 144,000.

For the study of neighborhood: Total population: 1850—408,000; 1860—565,000; 1870—647,000; 1880—840,000. For each inhabitant of the 7,100 grid units, we record the age (8 categories), sex, and ethnicity (9 categories including 2nd generation in 1880). Data are arranged by grid unit and by ward.

III. Pennsylvania Abolition Society and Society of Friends Manuscript Census Schedules: 1838, 1847, 1856.

Data describe 11,500 households—all black households in Philadelphia County.

Variables for each household head and his household include (differ slightly by census year): name, sex, status-at-birth, occupation, wages, real and personal property, literacy, education, religion, membership in beneficial societies and temperance societies, taxes, rents, dwelling size.

IV. U.S. Manufacturing Manuscript Census Schedules: 1850, 1860, 1870, 1880.

Data describe ca. 29,000 individual firms (100 percent sample). Firms: 4,700 (1850); 8,500 (1880).

Variables: name of firm; type of product; amount of capital investment; type of power; type and number of machines; number of employees by sex; average wages paid by sex; number of months in operation each year; raw materials: kinds, quantities, values; finished products: kinds, quantities, values; and address and grid location.

V. City Business Directories: 1850, 1860, 1870, 1880.

Data describe ca. 127,000 individual firms (100 percent sample). Firms: 10,000 (1850); 28,000 (1860); 39,000 (1870); 47,000 (1880).

Variables: name of subscriber; type of product or service; and address and grid location.

VI. Transportation Network: 1840–1880.

Data describe a total of 150 routes including all forms of transportation: street railways, railroads, trolleys, omnibuses.

Variables: date of incorporation; company name; date of merger; reconstruction of block-by-block routes and conversion of precise grid coordinates to machine-readable form.

VII. Mortality Register: July 1, 1880–June 30, 1881.

Data describe ca. 20,500 individuals who died in Philadelphia during the twelve-month period following the Bureau of the Census (June 1880) enumeration of the city's population.

Variables: name, color, sex, age, marital status, date of death, cause of death, attending physician, occupation, birthplace, parents' names (if a minor), ward, address, place of burial.

VIII. Sewage Facilities: 1867–1885.

Data include the following variables: year of construction of sewer line; street; ward; dates of authorization, approval and final estimate; length; assessment; cost to city and property owners; builder; grid location.

IX. Institutions (public, private, secular, religious): 1850, 1860, 1870, 1880.

Data describe 3000 institutions.
   Variables: name, year, type, address, grid location.

X. Voluntary Associations: 1820–1900.

Data includes black, Irish, and German individuals who were members of various Philadelphia organizations. *Blacks:* 3,200 individuals, 4,500 memberships, 200 organizations. *Irish:* 3,500 individuals, 6,000 memberships, 350 organizations. *Germans:* 2,500 individuals, 5,000 memberships, 200 organizations.
   Variables: name, ethnicity, organization, position, year of membership.
   In addition to these organizational data, our files include census information for those people we have linked to the four U.S. and three Quaker and Abolitionist censuses. To date, we have completed linkages for the black associational members. Extensive lists for the Irish and Germans are in preparation; individual members will be linked to four U.S. Censuses.

Contributors

George Alter received his doctorate in History from the University of Pennsylvania in 1978. He is currently Assistant Professor of History at Indiana University.

Alan N. Burstein received his doctorate in Demography from the University of Pennsylvania in 1975. He is currently Assistant Professor of Sociology and Urban Studies at Washington University, St. Louis.

Harold E. Cox received his doctorate in History from the University of Virginia in 1958. He is currently Professor of History at Wilkes College.

Eugene P. Ericksen received his doctorate in Sociology from the University of Michigan in 1971. He is currently Associate Professor of Sociology at Temple University.

Frank F. Furstenberg, Jr., received his doctorate in Sociology from Columbia University in 1967. He is currently Associate Professor of Sociology at the University of Pennsylvania.

Claudia Goldin received her doctorate in Economics from the University of Chicago in 1971. She is currently Associate Professor of Economics at the University of Pennsylvania.

Stephanie W. Greenberg received her doctorate in Sociology from Temple University in 1977. She is currently Research Sociologist at the Center for the Study of Social Behavior at the Research Triangle Institute.

Richard R. Greenfield did graduate work in Political Science at the University of Pennsylvania. He is currently Research Coordinator at the PSHP.

Michael R. Haines received his doctorate in Economic History from the University of Pennsylvania in 1971. He is currently Associate Professor of Economics at Wayne State University.

Theodore Hershberg received his doctorate in History from Stanford University in 1973. He is currently Director of the Philadelphia Social History Project and the Center for Philadelphia Studies and is Associate Professor of History and Public Policy at the University of Pennsylvania.

Bruce Laurie received his doctorate in History from the University of Pittsburgh in 1971. He is currently Associate Professor of History at the University of Massachusetts at Amherst.

Lynn H. Lees received her doctorate in History from Harvard University in 1969. She is currently Associate Professor of History at the University of Pennsylvania.

Dale B. Light, Jr., received his doctorate in History from the University of Pennsylvania in 1979.

John Modell received his doctorate in History from Columbia University in 1969. He is currently Professor of History at the University of Minnesota.

Mark Schmitz received his doctorate in Economics from the University of North Carolina in 1974. He is currently visiting Associate Professor of Economics at Washington State University.

Henry Williams did graduate work in History at the University of Pennsylvania. He is currently Assistant Director of the PSHP.

William L. Yancey received his doctorate in Sociology from Washington University, St. Louis, in 1967. He is currently Chairman and Professor of Sociology at Temple University.